Hull Pals

This book is dedicated to the memory of all ranks of
the Hull Pals 1914-1919

92 BRIGADE
10th(Service) Battalion East Yorkshire (1st Hull Pals)
11th(Service) Battalion East Yorkshire (2nd Hull Pals)
12th(Service) Battalion East Yorkshire (3rd Hull Pals)
13th(Service) Battalion East Yorkshire (4th Hull Pals)
14th(Reserve) Battalion East Yorkshire (Hull)

92 Brigade Headquarters
92nd Machine Gun Company
92nd Light Trench Mortar Battery

* * * * *

Also available in the same series:

Accrington Pals: The 11th (Service) Battalion (Accrington)
The East Lancashire Regiment by William Turner

Barnsley Pals: The 13th & 14th (Service) Battalions (Barnsley)
The York & Lancaster Regiment by Jon Cooksey

Sheffield City: The 12th (Service) Battalion (Sheffield)
The York & Lancaster Regiment by Paul Oldfield and Ralph Gibson

Liverpool Pals: A History of the 17th, 18th, 19th & 20th Service Battalions
The King's (Liverpool Regiment) by Graham Maddocks

Leeds Pals: A History of the 15th (Service) Battalion
The Prince of Wales's Own (West Yorkshire Regiment) by Laurie Milner

Salford Pals: A History of the 15th, 16th, 19th & 20th Battalions Lancashire Fusiliers
by Michael Stedman
Manchester Pals: The 16th, 17th, 18th, 19th, 20th, 21st, 22nd & 23rd Battalions of the
Manchester Regiment by Michael Stedman

Birmingham Pals: The 14th, 15th & 16th Battalions of the Royal Warwickshire Regiment
by Terry Carter
Tyneside Irish: The 24th, 25th, 26th & 27th Battalions of the Northumberland Fusiliers
by John Sheen

Tyneside Scottish: The 20th, 21st, 22nd & 23rd Battalions of the Northumberland Fusiliers
by John Sheen & Graham Stewart

HULL PALS

10th, 11th, 12th & 13th Battalions
East Yorkshire Regiment

A HISTORY OF 92 INFANTRY BRIGADE
31st DIVISION

David Bilton

Pen & Sword
MILITARY

First published in Great Britain in 2014 by
PEN & SWORD MILITARY
an imprint of
Pen and Sword Books Ltd
47 Church Street
Barnsley
South Yorkshire S70 2AS

ISBN 978 1 78346 185 1

Printed and bound in England by
CPI Group (UK) Ltd, Croydon, CR0 4YY

Typeset in Palatino Light by CHIC GRAPHICS

Pen & Sword Books Ltd incorporates the imprints of
Pen & Sword Archaeology, Atlas, Aviation, Battleground, Discovery, Family
History, History, Maritime, Military, Naval, Politics, Railways, Select, Social
History, Transport, True Crime, and Claymore Press, Frontline Books, Leo Cooper,
Praetorian Press, Remember When, Seaforth Publishing and Wharncliffe.

For a complete list of Pen and Sword titles please contact
Pen and Sword Books Limited
47 Church Street, Barnsley, South Yorkshire, S70 2AS, England
E-mail: enquiries@pen-and-sword.co.uk
Website: www.pen-and-sword.co.uk

Contents

Acknowledgements

Special thanks are necessary to my wife and family for putting up with the upheaval to family life and for not complaining, too much, that I was never there.

The personal information on the officers and men would not have been possible without the detective work of Malcolm Mann, a veteran Local History researcher. Malcolm also helped with a number of parts of this book – many, many thanks. Hopefully it was not just a one-way process.

Without the help of the Prince Consort's Library in Aldershot I would have been unable to easily do the background reading necessary for a work like this; neither would I have had such easy access to the *London Gazette* or Army Lists.

Peter Liddle (The Liddle Collection, Leeds University) kindly allowed me to look through his collection and to use material from the memoirs of G L Goldsmith, W E Aust, A D Wilson, A F Wolfe, B L Pearson OBE DSO MC, W Dawson MM and D B Watson. Similarly, thanks to the IWM for giving me access to the papers and/or letters and to copyright holders of the papers of A Surfleet, V Jenkin, J Beeken, J Graystone, C Carter, C Traill and Captain R B Carver.

Thanks to Ian Anderson for reading and checking the manuscript and for asking so many questions; my wife for helping with checking the manuscript, Graham Stewart for suggestions and possible leads on sources; Julian Fenton for his chauffeur services and Valerie Bilton for running backwards and forwards to Hull Library.

Without the friendly help of the Keeper and Staff of the Public Record Office there would be no nominal roll and much else besides.

Especial thanks are due to Miss B Beck, Mrs A Broadbent, Mr P Calvert, Mr J Leighton, Ian Anderson, Richard Van Emden, Mrs S Turner, Mr P Smith, Mr P Boynton, Mr E Johnson, Mrs S Burr, Mrs Waite, Mr P Reed, Mr E Farrah, Mr N Walker and the Editor of *The Hull Daily Mail* for loaning me photographs, postcards and documents. Also to Roni Wilkinson for his help in the preparation of this book and for sharing his knowledge so freely.

Select Bibliography

Barnes, B	This Righteous War. Richard Netherwood Ltd. 1990
Becke, Major A F	*Order of Battle of Divisions Part SB*. HMSO. 1945
Becke, Major A F	*Order of Battle of Divisions Part 4*. HMSO. 1945
Buchan, J	*The History of the South African Forces in France.* Thomas Nelson.
Buchan, J M	*Britain and the Great War 1914 - 1918*. Edward Arnold. 1989
Carver, R B et al	*History of the 10th (Service) Battalion The East Yorkshire Regiment (Hull Commercials)*. A Brown & Sons Ltd. 1937
Coolsey, J	*Pals: the 13th & 14th battalions York & Lancaster Regiment*. Pen & Sword. Reprinted 1998
East Lancashire Regiment	War diaries of the 11th Battalion. Unpublished. Held at the Public Record Office
East Yorkshire Regiment	War diaries of the 10th, 11th, 12th and 13th Battalions. Unpublished. Held at the Public Record Office.
Easy Yorkshire Regiment	Medal rolls for the 1915 star and the British War medal Unpublished. Held at the Public Record Office
Edmonds, Brigadier-General Sir James	*Military Operations - France and Belgium 1916* Volume I. Macmillan. 1932
Edmonds, Brigadier-General Sir James	*Military Operations - France and Belgium 1918.* Volume II. HMSO. 1948
Edmonds, Brigadier-General Sir James	*Military Operations - France and Belgium 1918.* Volume II. Macmillan. 1937
Edmonds, Brigadier-General Sir James	*Military Operations - France and Belgium 1918.* Volume V HMSO. 1947
Falls, Capt. C	*Military Operations - France and Belgium 1917.* Volume I. Macmillan. 1940
Farrar, P	*Diary of Private J Tait*. Malet Lambert Local History. 1982
Gibson, R & Oldfield, P	*Sheffield City Battalion*. Pen & Sword. 1988
Gillett, E & MacMahon, A.	*A History of Hull*. Hull University Press. 1989
Gliddon, G	*The Battle of the Somme – a Topographical History.* Alan Sutton. 1998
Hull Daily Mail	Various dates

MacMunn, Lt. Gen. Sir G, & Capt. C Falls	*Military Operations – Egypt & Palestine.* Volume 1. 1928.
Maddocks, G	*Liverpool Pals.* Leo Cooper. 1991
Markham, J	*Keep the home fires burning.* Highgate Publications (Beverley) Ltd. 1988
Middlebrook, M	*The First Day on the Somme.* Allen Lane 1971.
Miles, Capt. W	*Military Operations – France and Belgium, 1916.* Volume II, MacMillan & Co. 1938
Milner, L	*Leeds Pals.* Pen & Sword. Reprinted 1998
Mitchinson, K W	*Pioneer Battalions in the Great War.* Leo Cooper. 1997
NER	*The North East Railway Magazine* – March and June 1915
Putkowski, J & Sykes, J	*Shot at Dawn.* Leo Cooper. 1993
Sheppard, T	*Kingston-Upon-Hull before, during and after the Great War.* A. Brown & Sons Ltd. 1919
Simkins, P	*Kitchener's Army. The raising of the new armies, 1914–16.* Manchester University Press. 1988
Some of them	*A Short Diary of the 11th Service Battalion, East Yorkshire Regiment. 1914–1919.* Goddard, Walker & Brown, 1921
Williams, J	*The Home Fronts 1914–1918.* Constable. 1972
Wilson, M & Kemp P	*Mediterranean Submarines.* Crecy Publishing. 1997
Wyrall, E	*The East Yorkshire Regiment in the Great War 1914–1918.* Harrison & Sons. 1928
31st Division	War diary of the 31st Division. Unpublished. Held at the Public Record Office
92 Brigade	War diary of 92 Brigade. Unpublished. Held at the Public Record Office
93 Brigade	War diary of 93 Brigade. Unpublished. Held at the Public Record Office

Foreword

As a young schoolboy I went on many church trips to the seaside with my grandparents. On the way home the people on the bus always broke into song, invariably starting with the songs of World War Two and ending with the songs of the Great War; the latter being sung with particular gusto as all the men on the bus were veterans of that conflict, many of them 'Hull Pals' – not that I knew that at the time!

It was only when I reached secondary school and suddenly acquired an interest in military history that I became aware of them. One friend gave me his great uncle's medals (a 'Hull Pals' casualty), another gave me a copy of the 10th Battalion History that had belonged to his grandfather and some photographs, while another swopped me an Iron Cross, taken by his grandfather during the fighting on November 13th 1916, for a bundle of American comics I had been told to throw out!

Out of this grew a hunger to know more about who and what the 'Hull Pals' were. Hull folk are reticent people and the 'Hull Pals' were no exception. This book tells their story, a story similar to many other 'Pals' battalions from the Great War but in this case, one that is not dulled by the frequency of its telling.

DAVID BILTON

Introduction

In 1888 Hull became one of the new county boroughs and in 1897 it became a city. For many this was Hull's golden age, an age of Majesty, Imperial splendour and Empire; that is a time before the world was changed forever. Hull had always been a poor town but the advances in technology had started to moderate, even if it was only to a small extent, the ancient squalor of the city. However, even though it was a large city, Hull was still very poor when compared to places of a comparable size like Bradford which was able to invest twenty times more on works and public amenities.

Hull's problem was its industry. Shipyards and engineering works were too prone to the rises and falls in trade experienced in Western economies and although trade, for example, between Hull and New York was six times more productive than it had been fifty years previously, this wealth had not been passed down to the workers. In 1884 it was estimated that in East Hull 1000 families were starving, people being reduced to taking food from swill-tubs for the pigs. 1885 brought no respite to the problem of poverty and the resulting premature death of many children; the corpse being carried in an improvised coffin was so common as to constitute a nuisance. Some help was provided by private individuals and some of the large companies, such as Reckitt's, but it was not enough. The Corporation responded by providing work for the unemployed in the form of the construction of East Park. Although this was good as an idea, in practice some of the workers were so weak that they collapsed and had to be replaced by labourers from the East Riding.

Prince's Dock at the turn of the century. Behind it can be seen the Dock's Office. This dock joined onto Queen's Dock, which was right in the centre of the town. Monument bridge crossed the connecting stretch of water.

Hull paddle tugs Heather Bell and Trubriton berthed in the Old Harbour. The Trubriton had two separate engines each driving one paddle wheel, hence its two Stacks. Hull Daily Mail

A close-up of the war memorial.

Albert Dock. Built between 1863 and 1869. It cost £1 million to build and opened directly onto the Humber thereby allowing larger ships to use it.

Monument Bridge crossed over the connecting point between the docks in the centre of Hull. In the centre background can be seen the City Hall were many of the 'Hull Pals' would enlist.

UNVEILING OF SOLDIERS MEMORIAL NOV 5 & P 8 04

The inauguration of the South African War Memorial in November 1904.

Conditions were even worse in the surrounding countryside, with agricultural workers moving to Hull if they could not afford to emigrate. The influx of this multi-skilled workforce resulted in even greater poverty for the local residents. The problem was further compounded by the arrival of numerous visitors and emigrants, many of whom decided to stay on in Hull. The 1891 census showed that Hull had 906 Germans resident in its boundaries, many of them pork butchers. Hull even came to possess a headquarters of the Communist International. Pogroms in Russia in 1881 greatly increased the size of the then small Jewish population.

A large part of the resident population, but especially the emigrants from the East Riding, Ireland and the Continent, lived in Hull's vilest slums. The worst conditions were to be found in Hull's dock areas, where prostitution, sodomy and incest were common. One Hull newspaper, *The Eastern Daily News*, published in 1883 a report which compared the streets of Hessle Road with the foulest slums in Constantinople, reporting that the houses had no furniture other than wooden boxes and everywhere animals and humans lived in very close proximity. Sewage flowed from outdoor privies forming pools in the streets.

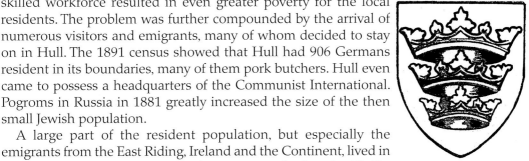

The coat of arms of the City of Kingston-upon-Hull. Hull's first Royal Charter was granted 1st April 1299 by King Edward; this turned the Borough of Hull into the King's town. The three crowns represent Royal Charters.

Hull's problems were not just of economic origin, they were also due to corruption on a grand scale. Town councillors were amongst some of the worst of the slum

Market Place, in the heart of the old town. The statue is to King William III and was unveiled on 4th December 1734. Its positioning helped increase congestion in this already crowded area.

The view of the newly built Victoria Square taken from the City Hall. On the right is the statue to William Wilberforce, the man responsible for the stopping of the slave trade. The Hull Daily Mail

East Park on Holderness Road. This was laid out towards the end of the century by the Corporation in an attempt to help unemployment in Hull. However, many of the married men it was supposed to help were so weak from hunger that they collapsed and had to be replaced by single men and workers from the East Riding.

landlords. Improvements that the council made at public expense, such as parks, resulted in enhanced property rentals as well as providing a better environment for the residents of Hull. Allegations rarely came to anything for the fear of a libel suit. Even the police force was not beyond reproach, drinking on duty was common and many police officers were frequently charged with being helpless with drink while on duty in the small hours. In 1885 the Chief Constable resigned when he was caught in circumstances that suggested that he frequented Juvenile prostitutes (children under 13 at that time). Prostitution was common in all areas of the town centre. Dog-fights took place regularly every Saturday, off Beverley Road.

However, changes were in hand. By 1891 the city had fifteen cycle dealers to support the ever growing number of weekend cyclists. The number of professional photographers grew rapidly and the number of homes lit by electricity increased. While the more affluent enjoyed recitals by Pachmann and Patti, for those less well-heeled there were German bands in the streets and concerts in the parks by the Police and Artillery bands, the latter drawing 10000 people to one concert. Racing was catered for by a new racecourse in Preston, known locally as Hedon racecourse. New swimming baths were opened in 1885, 1898 and 1905 and by 1897 the School Board had 33 schools within the city boundaries.

Coupled with these social changes were economic changes which made the city more wealthy even if there was little change for the poor. There was a rapid growth

Maple Avenue in the Garden Village. This was part of a £140,000 housing estate, built just after the turn of the century by Sir James Reckitt for his employees. It was a must for important visitors to see.

in seed-crushing mills along the River Hull paralleled by growth in the importation of timber, wheat, soya beans and food stuffs in general, with Hull providing food materials for a third of the population. Some of the larger firms, such as Reckitts, started to take a paternal interest in the well-being of their workers, providing pensions and in one case profit-sharing! The speed of the tram system allowed people to move further away from their workplace resulting in the spread of housing along the main roads into the city. The telephone system opened in 1880, was bought by the Corporation in 1906 and still survives today as Kingston Communications.

A whole new city centre was built at the turn of the century in an attempt to improve the status of the city in the eyes of visitors and in 1903 the Prince and Princess of Wales came for the Royal opening of Victoria Square, the central part of this new area. In 1904 a large memorial to the dead of the South African War was erected in Paragon Square. This same place was to be selected to honour the fallen of the next war, the Hull men who died in the Great War for civilisation.

This was the world into which the 'Pals' of 1914 were being born.

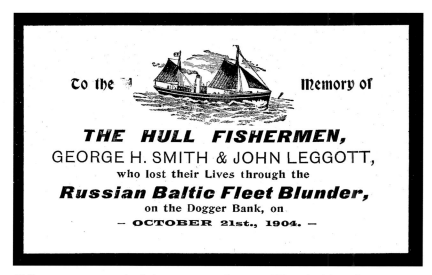

To the Memory of

THE HULL FISHERMEN,

GEORGE H. SMITH & JOHN LEGGOTT,

who lost their Lives through the

Russian Baltic Fleet Blunder,

on the Dogger Bank, on
— OCTOBER 21st., 1904. —

Hull was no stranger to death; it was an every day part of life in the fishing fleets. For example, the gales of February 1900 took sixty lives and regularly men would be washed overboard in bad weather conditions. However, not all the deaths were due to the weather. On 21st October 1904 the Russian fleet, sailing through the North Sea, on its way to fight the Japanese Navy in the Far East, fired upon the trawler Crane *which was suspected of being a Japanese torpedo-boat. The trawler* Crane *sank with two fatalities, the Skipper and the third hand.*

Chapter 1

'Tickled to death to go'

It was holiday time – July 1914. Ordinary people across Europe were basking in the most brilliant summer for years. Fashionable folk were leaving town for spas and smart resorts. Little appeared to be different to last year; Europe was at peace and had been for a long time. However, underneath the ostensibly calm exterior the reality was different.

The assassination of the Austrian Archduke Ferdinand and his consort at the end of June by a Bosnian student had deep ramifications for the intertwined alliances and rivalries that had helped keep Europe at peace. War moves, once started, spread rapidly across Europe from one country to the next, gathering speed at each juncture. Austro-Hungary, backed by Imperial Germany, presented Serbia with an ultimatum on July 23rd followed by a

Below: Opening of the new dock at Hull, Friday June 26th 1914, by King George V. Instigators of the project were the North-Eastern and Hull & Barnsley Railway companies. On the day there were 3,500 invited guests and men stood by in swim suits to rescue any who accidently fell into the dock. In his speech the King said: 'Hull will now join other great towns of the country in being able to call its chief magistrate "Lord Mayor".' Two days later Archduke Ferdinand, Crown Prince of Austria, and his wife were shot dead on the streets of Sarajevo. (above)

In that hot summer of 1914 families enjoyed their holidays little realising that those days were the last days of peace for four years. On the beach somewhere along the East Riding coast just before the war.

A German cartoon about Russian mobilisation and the lack of fighting ability likely to be shown by drunk Russian soldiers.

Russische Mobilmachung!

The Crown Prince reviewing his troops.

German troops resting during their offensive in Northern France at the start of the war.

As the Germans moved forward, those of the civilian population who could or wanted to, moved back with the Allied armies.

declaration of war on the 28th. Germany followed this with a declaration of war on Russia on 1st August and the invasion of Luxembourg on the same day. Belgium was presented with an ultimatum on 2nd August that compromised her neutrality. The next day Germany declared war on France and the deadline for the Belgian acceptance of German troops moving through Belgium expired. On the 4th Britain declared war on Germany because of its treaty obligations with Belgium. Britain, France, Belgium and Russia were now at war with Germany. The die was cast, time-tables were activated and irreversible plans put into action; armies mobilised and began to march to their war stations each believing that God was on their side.

In the early hours of 4th August the German army invaded Belgium as part of the Schlieffen Plan aiming to cut into Northern France, to the west of Paris. This thrust would by-pass the capital and encircle the French forces to the east of the country. The German timetable went smoothly but as the invading troops moved further from Germany the longer the lines of communication became, making supply more difficult; the further the troops marched the more tired they became; the deeper they got into France the more resistance they met. On the north-western axis the British and Belgian troops slowed down the advance, so that in early September the French were in a position to counter-attack. The First Battle of the Marne halted the German advance and ended the war of movement. During the remaining months of 1914 both sides settled into a static war with trenches stretching from the Belgian coast to the Swiss frontier.

The south bay at Scarborough. The withdrawal of all holiday trains due to the state of emergency resulted in a very quiet bank holiday period for the coastal towns.

Each side painted a romantic picture of the first months of the war. This German card is entitled 'The sun sank in the west'.

Like all the combatant nations the Germans believed that God was with them. The caption reads 'Your will be done'.

On Bank Holiday Monday, August 3rd, although war had not yet been declared by Britain, there were obvious signs that something was going to happen. The Bank Holiday was a time when the families from the crowded terraces of Hull took their annual trip to the seaside at Withersea, Hornsea or Bridlington (Scarborough for those who were more affluent) to breathe fresh clean air and forget their troubles. The *Hull Daily Mail* commented that it was one of the loveliest days of a beautiful season but unfortunately there were no cheap facilities to get the population to the coast, all the trains were needed for the transport of troops. The day before, the

Stories of German atrocities were used by the press to inflame public feeling. The Germans shot Franc-tireurs (armed opponents who were not in uniform).

North-Eastern Railway had announced the withdrawal of all its excursions for Sunday 2nd August, Monday 3rd August and Tuesday 4th August.

Before the declaration of war the local Territorial battalions, the 4th and 5th East Yorkshires and the Territorial Royal Field Artillery, were mobilised and reservists received their call-up papers. This sudden loss of men was expected to have a major effect on the land-owners' ability to bring in the harvest and would hit the fishing fleet and merchant navy very hard as many of its men were also called to the colours. The *Hull Daily Mail* recorded that about 100 naval reservists left Hull for the south of England on the 5.05 train for London. There were pathetic scenes as the train left. The sailors steadied their nerves and said 'Goodbye' to wives and children. Meanwhile at the shipping office, there were Royal Naval Reserve men in their uniforms responding to the call and signing on, their 'Jack Tar' garments not quite at home on their bodies. This sudden loss of men was also apparent in other walks of life. The *Hull Daily Mail* recorded that 'The Three Aeros', trapeze artistes, would be unable to appear at the Palace Theatre because they had been called up for military service.

The declaration of war on Germany was met with enthusiasm and a certainty in its short duration. A recruiting boom was under way even before the British Ultimatum had expired. *The Times* reported

Lord Kitchener of Khartoum was appointed to Secretary of State on August 5th. Two days later the papers carried his famous appeal for men – YOUR KING AND COUNTRY NEEDS YOU!

British regulars march through Le Mans in late August 1914.

that on the day of the 4th the recruiting officer at Great Scotland Yard took twenty minutes to get through the crowd outside his office and when he was able to start work he and his medical staff worked non-stop all day to process the recruits. The next day was even busier and by the 7th it was necessary to employ mounted policemen to keep control. In Hull the war was also greeted with enthusiasm.

Field Marshal Earl Kitchener was appointed as the Secretary of State for War on the 5th. The next day he sought permission from Parliament to expand the size of the army and in the early morning papers of the 7th his famous appeal for men appeared – YOUR KING & COUNTRY NEED YOU – in which he asked for men between 19 and 30, 5 foot 3 inches and over, with a chest size greater than 34 inches to volunteer for the duration of the war. These were to be the soldiers of Kitchener's New Army, modelled and numbered after the battalions of the regular army.

O.H.M.S.

Quotation from

Lord Kitchener's Speech:

" It has been well said that **in every man's life there is one supreme hour** to which all earlier experience moves and from which all future results may be reckoned. For every individual Briton, as well as for our national existence, **that solemn hour is now striking.** Let us take heed to the great opportunity it offers, and which most assuredly we must grasp now and at once, or never. Let each man of us see that we **spare nothing, shirk nothing, shrink from nothing,** if only we may lend our full weight to the impetus which shall carry to victory the cause of honour and of our freedom."

"GOD SAVE THE KING."

Poster used for recruiting in Hull.

There were gatherings and speeches at theatres in Hull and on 10th August there was a spontaneous patriotic outburst at the Alexandra Theatre of applause and

British regulars take on the advancing Germans. Here they are hoping to draw 'enemy scouts' to investigate the German casualties, in the field in front of the ditch, when they hope to ambush them.
Taylor Library

Battlefield debris in the first few days of the war. In this case Belgian troops had been surprised by the Germans.

singing culminating in the National Anthem when portraits of national figures like Admiral Jellicoe were shown to the audience. A portrait of the Kaiser was greeted by the band playing 'He'll have to get out and get under'. Even with this level of enthusiasm, by the 15th August the number of recruits in Hull had slowed to a trickle. However, the reports of the battle of Mons and the subsequent withdrawal pulled the nation to unequalled heights of patriotism. Recruiting once more increased with the result that in the first six months of the war over 20,000 men from Hull had enlisted and by the end of the war over 75,000 had served in His Majesty's Services. The national flood of volunteers was too much for the army to deal with and increasingly the task of accomodating, housing and feeding the volunteers was taken over by civilian authorities. One result of this civilian effort was the formation of locally raised battalions, specially raised by individuals, committees or local authorities and generally being composed of men from the locality, often of men sharing a common social background. Such battalions were expressions of civic pride and imbued the units with a strong local identity. These 'Pals' units, as they became known, eventually comprised a sizeable percentage of the New Army battalions and gave a distinct flavour to the divisions they served in. [Simkins quotes 215 out of the 557 Service and Reserve Battalions raised up to June 1916 as being raised initially by bodies other than the War Office.]

The national flood of volunteers was too much for the army to deal with as men responded to Kitchener's appeal.
Taylor Library

The East Yorkshire Regiment drew its recruits technically from Hull and the East Riding but volunteers were able to specify which regiment or corps that they wished to serve in. Hull was the major centre of population in this recruiting area but as it was also a major port, a large percentage of the available manpower was already spoken for by the Merchant Navy, the fishing fleet and the Royal Navy.

As well as the demands of the sea there were other units in existence which further reduced the available supply of men for the Pals. In the East Riding there was a Yeomanry regiment, two Territorial battalions, a Royal Garrison Artillery battery, a Field Ambulance of the Royal Army Medical Corps and a Field Company of the Royal Engineers. With the onset of war each of these (except the 5th Battalion) recruited, firstly up to full strength and then each recruited a second line unit to replace the first when it went on active service. The 4th Battalion actually raised a third line battalion. Competition was particularly keen

The sight of a portrait of the Kaiser during a performance at the Alexandra Theatre caused a patriotic outburst resulting in the band playing 'He'll have to get out and get under'!

to get into the cyclists, who were seen as being a rather glamorous unit to belong to. One ex-member of the 12th Battalion, A D Wilson recalled why in 1915 at the age of 17 he joined the 5th Battalion: 'they wore knee britches and had black bugle buttons' and as a consequence they were very noticeable.

By August 28th there were sufficient volunteers to form the first New Army Battalion of the East Yorkshire Regiment, the 6th, which before it sailed for active service, became a pioneer battalion. The second battalion to be raised was the 7th Hull Battalion on the 29th, later becoming the 1st Hull Battalion and finally the 10th (Service) Battalion (1st Hull). When the first had completed its recruiting the second battalion began and so on until Hull had raised four active service battalions and a local reserve battalion, the 14th, to provide replacements for the other four battalions. This latter battalion was, according to the Kingston-upon-Hull Peace Souvenir,

Lord Derby was almost certainly the first to employ the term 'Pals battalions' in a speech on the evening of 28th August 1914.

'*largely composed of men of smaller stature. These men were known as "Bantams",*

Lieutenant Colonel Richardson who took over command of the 1st Hull Battalion on 12th September 1914.

City Hall where the 2nd, 3rd and 4th Battalions were raised.

little men with big hearts. This fine battalion was also known as 'Lord Roberts'
("Bobs") Battalion'.

Considering the size of Hull, the recruiting of four 'Pals' battalions was a signal achievement un-paralleled in Britain.

One criticism laid at the feet of the recruiting authorities in Hull was that the main office in Pryme Street was inadequate and dowdy. The Lord Lieutenant, Lord Nunburnholme soon came to the conclusion that a more central recruiting office was necessary and as a result of his approaches the City Hall was provided by the Corporation free of charge. This change of venue both gave space and speeded up the process of recruitment.

Raising the Hull Pals

The credit for the raising of Pals battalions is generally given to Lord Derby who on 24th August had, after discussions with Kitchener, received the Secretary of State's consent for the raising of a battalion from among Liverpool's business houses. This battalion, the 17th King's, was raised in two hours on 21st August and on 5th September a further two battalions were raised. However, there is evidence that the original idea came from the War Office. Over lunch on the 19th, Sir Henry Rawlinson, Director of Recruiting at the War Office, asked his lunch partner, Major the Hon. Robert White, to raise, on Kitchener's behalf, a battalion of men who worked in 'The City'. Later that day White received a letter detailing how this might be achieved. On August 21st as a result of this meeting a new battalion of the Royal Fusiliers was raised, the 10th (Service) Battalion also known as 'The Stockbrokers Battalion', the precursor of the many 'Pals' battalions to follow.

This same principle of serving alongside men of the same background was later used to recruit the first of the Hull battalions. Lord Derby was almost certainly the first to employ the term 'Pals battalions'. In a speech to would be recruits on the evening of August 28th he said,

> *'I am not going to make you a speech of heroics. You have given me your answer, and I can telegraph to Lord Kitchener tonight to say that our second battalion is formed. We have got to see this through to the bitter end and dictate our terms of peace in Berlin if it takes every man and every penny in the country. This should be a battalion of Pals, a battalion in which friends from the same office will fight shoulder to shoulder for the honour of Britain and the credit of Liverpool.'*

Although nationally recruiting had picked up again the response in Hull was not as good as the authorities had hoped. The *Hull Daily Mail* published numerous letters about the problem and one, who signed themselves 'Middle Class' of Newland wrote on August 26th that many men were not enlisting because they did not like 'the idea of having to herd with all types of men now being enlisted', this was keeping 'young athletes and men of good birth and training from joining the colours'. 'Middle Class' detailed the answer to the problem:

> *'Instead of some of the larger employers of labour in Hull giving big donations of money they should use their influence to organize Corps of the middle class young men – clerks, tailors, drapers assistants, grocers assistants, warehousemen and artisans. Then we should see men living, sleeping and training in company of others of their own class.'*

On August 29th, three days after 'Middle Class' of Newland expounded his idea, Lord Nunburnholme, Lord Lieutenant of the East Riding of Yorkshire, had an audience with Kitchener in which they discussed such a matter. As a result of this discussion Lord Nunburnholme received instructions to recruit the First Service Battalion

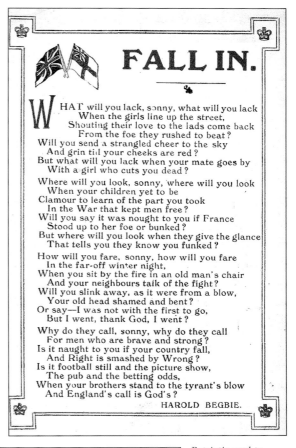

FALL IN.

WHAT will you lack, sonny, what will you lack
 When the girls line up the street,
 Shouting their love to the lads come back
 From the foe they rushed to beat?
Will you send a strangled cheer to the sky
 And grin till your cheeks are red?
But what will you lack when your mate goes by
 With a girl who cuts you dead?

Where will you look, sonny, where will you look
 When your children yet to be
Clamour to learn of the part you took
 In the War that kept men free?
Will you say it was nought to you if France
 Stood up to her foe or bunked?
But where will you look when they give the glance
 That tells you they know you funked?

How will you fare, sonny, how will you fare
 In the far-off winter night,
When you sit by the fire in an old man's chair
 And your neighbours talk of the fight?
Will you slink away, as it were from a blow,
 Your old head shamed and bent?
Or say—I was not with the first to go,
 But I went, thank God, I went?

Why do they call, sonny, why do they call
 For men who are brave and strong?
Is it naught to you if your country fall,
 And Right is smashed by Wrong?
Is it football still and the picture show,
 The pub and the betting odds,
When your brothers stand to the tyrant's blow
 And England's call is God's?

      HAROLD BEGBIE.

Patriotic card to shame men into joining the army.

HULL RECRUITS FOR KITCHENER'S ARMY.

Recruits marching to Hull Paragon Station from Wenlock Barracks on 5th September.

in Hull. On August 30th, around 7.30pm, he phoned Major W H Carver, newly recommissioned on the 29th, to discuss the matter and to ask him to take responsibility for the initial stages of the project as Commanding Officer of the new battalion. The *Hull Daily Mail* of August 31st carried a proposal from Lord Nunburnholme regarding the raising of a Hull 'Commercial Battalion' in which men would serve with their friends. Conditions of service would be the same as in other battalions of the regular army. This new battalion was to be 1000 men strong and would be known as the 7th (Hull) Battalion of the East Yorkshire Regiment. Recruiting was to begin on September 1st at 10am in Wenlock barracks on Anlaby Road, Hull. This barracks had been loaned by the East Riding Territorial Force to help improve the amount of space for recruiting. Ex-officers were asked to help with the training. Initially, recruits would be billeted at home. Headquarters of this new battalion would be at Wenlock Barracks.

O. H. M. S.

IT has been suggested to me that there are many men, such as Clerks and others, engaged in commercial business, who wish to serve their KING and COUNTRY, and would be willing to enlist in the New Army if they felt assured that they would be serving with their own friends, and not put into Battalions with unknown men as their companions.

EARL KITCHENER has sanctioned the raising of a Hull Battalion which would be composed of the classes mentioned, and in which a man could be certain that he would be among his own friends.

THE CONDITIONS OF SERVICE WILL BE THE SAME AS IN OTHER BATTALIONS IN THE REGULAR ARMY.

The New Battalion will be 1000 strong, and will be named the

7TH (HULL) BATTALION EAST YORKSHIRE REGIMENT.

Those who wish to serve in it will be enrolled, enlisted and clothed at the WENLOCK BARRACKS, HULL. Recruiting will commence from 10 a.m. on TUESDAY, 1st SEPTEMBER. For the present, Recruits joining will be billeted in their own homes.

I shall be glad to receive the names of ex-Officers who will help in the above work until the Officers have been appointed to the Battalion.

Major W. H. CARVER has been temporarily appointed Acting Adjutant for the Battalion at Wenlock Barracks.

GOD SAVE THE KING.

NUNBURNHOLME
LORD LIEUTENANT, E. YORKS.

The recruiting poster for the 1st Hull Battalion issued on 30th August 1914.

The next day posters were printed and put up all over the city. On September 1st recruiting began, The *Hull Daily Mail* commented:

> 'Today has seen the commencement of recruiting for the middle-class, clerks, and professional men, or the "black-coated battalion". It must not be thought there is a desire for class distinction but just as the docker will feel more at home amongst his every day mates, so the wielder of the pen and drawing pencil will be better as friends together.'

Recruiting was brisk and around 200 men were medically examined, measured, attested and given a service number. Just how cursory this examination could be is shown by the following passage, from the diary of J Beeken, a schoolteacher, who enlisted in the 1st Hull Battalion. One of his friends was blind in one eye and was certain to fail the eye-test:

> 'I watched him anxiously as his sight test came along. He was told to cover up one eye and read the letters on a test card. He covered up the left eye and easily read the letters. When told to cover up the other eye, he calmly covered up the left eye and so passed the sight test. He was declared physically fit.'

Another friend of Private Beeken, a teacher from the same school, had a similar sort of problem. He was told:

'by the doctor that he could not pass him on account of some foot trouble he had. Well, my friend, who stood 6 3″, was a rugby forward and a very good boxer, pleaded so hard to be passed that another doctor was called to give a second opinion. Eventually he was passed as medically fit.'

If it was this easy for a recruit to pass the medical, how much easier was it for a would-be officer?

At the start of the war one young hopeful officer was B L Pearson, whose family hailed from the West Riding. He had a sister who lived in Cottingham and was therefore familiar with Hull and was happy to pursue a temporary career in the East Yorkshire Regiment. He opted for a commission in the New Army, rather than the

Recruits came from all over Hull and the East Riding to join the Hull Brigade. Hallgate in Cottingham where a number of the recruits came from.

Beverley, the regimental depot town of the East Yorkshire Regiment also provided a number of men for the 'Hull Pals'.

Recruits even came from Scarborough to specifically join the Hull Brigade.

Regular Army or the Special Reserve of Officers, because he felt that the career prospects would be better. Unfortunately, due to a knee problem caused by falling off a tram in Hull, he was classed as unfit for service. However, his brother was a newly qualified doctor who had just been gazetted to the RAMC. In order to help his brother he:

> *'very kindly wrote the word "fit" in all the appropriate places on a medical exam-ination form which I had got hold of. I was then introduced to the officer commanding a recently raised battalion (the 12th) of the East Yorkshire Regiment who ordered me to join D Company, then training in a public park.'*

How brisk recruiting was is proven by the fact that at one point there were no more attestation forms and Major Carver illegally had the form copied locally so as not to slow down the recruiting. Private Beeken who joined on the first day was allocated number 695, over half way to a full complement on the first day. In some cases the recruits came en masse from one particular firm, like Reckitts.

One such group came from the office of the NER Dock Superintendents in Hull who, after thinking about enlistment for a couple of days, came to a conclusion. Private Ives and Metcalf wrote in the North Eastern Railway Magazine of June 1915:

> *'A little serious thought brought us to the conclusion that we really ought to go, and Monday, September 7, saw our party of eight at the recruiting station in grand spirits and fervently hoping the doctor would certify us as "fit".*
>
> *We were not disappointed and we were quickly through enlistment formalities, along with scores of other city young men in straw hats, caps and every variety of*

Wenlock Barracks where the 1st Hull Battalion was raised.

"Knutty" attire, all eagerly intent on taking a place in the great game of war our country had been "forced" into. Next morning we fell in on the barrack parade ground. We are afraid we hardly realised on that beautiful summer's day the strenuous nature of the life we had laid down our pens to embark upon, although during the first week or two we had what is familiarly known as a soft time.'

Recruits did not just come from Hull; they came from all over the East Riding – Beverley, Hornsea, Withernsea, Bridlington. They also came from north Lincolnshire and in some numbers from Goole.

Captain E F Twiss from the East Yorkshire Regiment Depot at Beverley became battalion adjutant and Sergeant Tholander became the first orderly-room sergeant.

Recruiting figures rose with the retreat from Mons. This photograph shows British Prisoners of War being held in a French church.

B.

10,000. 1/9/14 M.H.&S. 10,224.

Discharged to Commission Rank. 11-2-1917.

Army Form B. 2065.

SHORT SERVICE.
(Three years with the Colours.)
ATTESTATION OF ~~No~~ 10th (SERVICE) BN. E. York R.

No. 226 Name *Frederick D. Brown* Corps *The East York*

● Questions to be put to the Recruit before enlistment.

1. What is your name?	1. *Frederick D. Brown*
2. In or near what Parish or Town were you born?	2. In the Parish of...... in or near the Town of *Hull* in the County of *Yorkshire*
3. Are you a British Subject?	3. *Yes*
4. What is your Age?	4. *30* Years *8* Months
5. What is your Trade or calling?	5. *Leather Merchant*
6. Have you resided out of your Father's house for three years continuously in the same place or occupied a house or land of the yearly value of £10 for one year, and paid rates for the same, and, in either case, if so, state where?	6. *No*

You are hereby warned that if after enlistment it is found that you have given a wilfully false answer to any of the following seven questions, you will be liable to a punishment of two years' imprisonment with hard labour.

7. Are you, or have you been, an Apprentice? If so, where? to whom? for what period? and when did, or will, the period of your Apprenticeship expire?	7. *No*
8. Are you Married?	8. *No*
9. Have you ever been sentenced to imprisonment by the Civil Power?	9. *No*
10. Do you now belong to the Royal Navy, the Army, the Royal Marines, the Militia, the Special Reserve, the Territorial Force, the Army Reserve, the Militia Reserve, or any Naval Reserve Force? If so, to what Unit and Corps?	10. *No*
*11. Have you ever served in the Royal Navy, the Army, the Royal Marines, the Militia, the Special Reserve, the Territorial Force, the Volunteers, the Army Reserve, the Militia Reserve, the Imperial Yeomanry, the Volunteers, the Army Reserve, the Militia Reserve, or Imperial Naval Reserve Force? If so, state which unit, and cause of discharge.	11. *No*
12. Have you truly stated the whole, if any, of your previous Service?	12. *Yes*
13. Have you ever been rejected as unfit for the Military or Naval Forces of the Crown? If so, on what grounds?	13. *No*
14. Are you willing to be vaccinated or re-vaccinated?	14. *Yes*
15. Are you willing to be enlisted for General Service?	15. *Yes*
16. Did you receive a Notice, and do you understand its meaning, and who gave it to you?	16. *Yes* Name...... Corps......
17. Are you willing to serve upon the following conditions provided His Majesty should so long require your services?	17. *Yes*
(a) For a term of three years, unless War lasts longer than three years, in which case you will be retained with the Colours. If employed with Hospitals, depots of Mounted Units, and as Clerks, etc, you may be retained after the termination of hostilities until your services can be spared, but such retention shall in no case exceed six months. If, however, the War is over in less than three years, you may be discharged with all convenient speed.	

I, *Frederick D. Brown* do solemnly declare that the above answers made by me to the above questions are true, and that I am willing to fulfil the engagements made.

Frederick D. Brown, SIGNATURE OF RECRUIT.

E Whittard Signature of Witness.

OATH TO BE TAKEN BY RECRUIT ON ATTESTATION.

I, *Frederick D. Brown* do make Oath that I will be faithful and bear true Allegiance to His Majesty King George the Fifth, His Heirs, and Successors, and that I will, as in duty bound, honestly and faithfully defend His Majesty, His Heirs, and Successors, in Person, Crown, and dignity against all enemies, and will observe and obey all orders of His Majesty, His Heirs, and Successors, and of the Generals and Officers set over me. So help me God.

CERTIFICATE OF MAGISTRATE OR ATTESTING OFFICER.

The Recruit above named was cautioned by me that if he made any false answer to any of the above questions he would be liable to be punished as provided in the Army Act.

The above questions were then read to the Recruit in my presence.

I have taken care that he understands each question, and that his answer to each question has been duly entered as replied to, and the said Recruit has made and signed the declaration and taken the oath before me

at *Hull* on this *2nd* day of *Sept* 1914

Signature of the Justice *C H Milburn*

If any alteration is required on this page of the Attestation, a Justice of the Peace should be requested to make it and initial the alteration under Section 8 (6), Army Act.
The Recruit should, if he require it, receive a copy of the Declaration on Army Form B. 111A.

By Thursday, September 3rd there were enough men enlisted to start drilling in company order and by the 5th the battalion was officially at full complement. Many ex-officers, both regular and Territorial, and ex-regular NCOs volunteered to serve with the battalion and quite quickly companies and sections became formalised. Some of the early officers were well connected; Lieutenant R B Carver was the nephew of Major Carver: Lieutenant Harrison-Broadley was the son of Colonel H Harrison-Broadley, Honorary Colonel of the 4th Battalion of the East Yorkshire Regiment and Lieutenant J L Sherburn was the son of Sir J Sherburn.

Lieutenant-Colonel Carver wired Sir Herbert Plumer in York for permission to pay the battalion and on the 5th they received their first pay. Each man received the 'King's Shilling' for each day they had been in the army and also a two shilling a day billeting allowance because they were being billeted at home.

The shortage of officers and NCOs for service with the New Army battalions is described by J M Bourne:

R B Carver, the first member of the Hull Brigade.

'*The conversion of the New Army's volunteers from civilians into soldiers was also inhibited by a lack of trained instructors. 'Kitchener's men' were desperately keen and anxious to learn, but there was no one to teach them. The Regular Army's cadre of training instructors, including those on Territorial attachment, were allowed to disperse to their regiments on the outbreak of war. The exigencies of the army in the field made it impossible to get them back. Their experience was difficult to replace. Every effort was made to scrape together a nucleus of professional officers and to send at least one to each New Army unit. Former Regulars were 'dug out' of retirement. Sandhurst and Woolwich were emptied of their cadets. Officers of the Indian Army home on leave were seconded to New Army duties. It was not enough.*'

As the men were recruited they were formed into companies under the old eight company system because Lieutenant-Colonel Carver, who was a retired Militia Officer, had no experience of the newly introduced four Company system. When each company was formed it was taken charge of by retired officers assisted by pensioned NCOs. In order to provide sufficient junior NCOs each company was searched for men with any sort of military or other training. This resulted in 120 men, who had some slight acquaintance with military or other drill and discipline, becoming section and squad leaders. With such rudimentary knowledge they proceeded to teach their fellow recruits squad drill without arms as there were neither rifles or uniforms for some considerable time. So keen were they all to learn that the battalion history records that within a few weeks most members of the battalion had a copy of 'Infantry Training, 1914' in their pocket. On September 12th Lieutenant-Colonel Carver was replaced by Lieutenant-Colonel A J Richardson, a 'dug-out' (retired officer) who had commanded the 1st Battalion of

Volunteers for the 13th Battalion on Corporation Field.

The 10th Battalion drilling at Walton Street. Nearest to the camera is Fred Walton.

Roll call at Wenlock Barracks for the 1st Hull Battalion.

the East Yorkshire Regiment in 1911. His son served with the battalion and was wounded in 1918 on his way to the assembly trenches prior to an attack on 28th June 1918.

On Monday September 7th while 'The Commercials', as they were known, were parading on Walton Street fair ground the new recruiting office in City Hall opened its doors under its new director, Mr. Douglas Boyd, a Rating Supervisor with the Corporation. In view of his position he was granted the rank of Lieutenant (later becoming a Captain and then a Major, a rank that he was still using in 1935). The exterior of City Hall was bedecked with flags, buntings and posters, with the balcony being used for military band performances and patriotic speeches.

As the raising of the 1st Hull Battalion had proceeded smoothly it was decided to recruit a further battalion, the 2nd Hull. This was to be a tradesmen's battalion. Within three days the battalion was up to a strength of just over 1000. Lieutenant-Colonel J L Stanley was placed in temporary command of this new battalion, with its headquarters in the cricket pavilion on Anlaby Road, Hull. Like the 1st Hull, the officers and men were billeted in their own homes or in lodgings in Hull and the immediate neighbourhood. In order to differentiate them from the 1st Hull Battalion, the 2nd Battalion wore a blue armlet. Sergeants and Corporals had the added distinction of a red or white stripe respectively.

It was while the 2nd Hull were being raised that the 'Hull Pals' suffered their first loss. On September 9th, eight days after enlisting in the 1st Hull, Private Adams

BURIED WITH MILITARY HONOURS

Private T. Adams, of the 1st Hull Battalion E.Y. Regiment, a new recruit, who died last week, was buried on Sunday last with military honours. Photo shows the funeral procession leaving Greek-street, and his comrades in procession.

On the 9th September the 1st Hull Battalion recorded its first death. Private T Adams died of brain fever and was buried with full military honours.

The 1st Hull Battalion marching down Walton Street in September 1914.

New recruits for the 10th Battalion parading at Wenlock Barracks in September 1914.

The 1st Hull Battalion learning about the 'triangle of errors'. They have Short Lee Enfield rifles – unusual at this stage in their training.

(regimental number 10/40) died of brain fever and was buried with full military honours in Western Cemetery, Hull. Naturally The *Hull Daily Mail* carried photographs and details.

Following on immediately from the 2nd Hull Battalion came the 3rd Hull. This was to be a battalion for sportsmen and on Saturday September 12th a meeting was held at the Park Street Artillery barracks to attract sportsmen and sports enthusiasts to come forward to fill the ranks of this new battalion. The chief speaker was the Yorkshire cricketer F S Jackson. Later in the month advertisements appeared in The *Hull Daily Mail* asking for volunteers from the sports fraternity 'If you mean to play the game join at once'.

This House has sent
William Calvert
to Fight for
King and Country.

HARRY WRAY, Mayor.   J. WILLIS MILLS, Town Clerk.

The 2nd Hull Battalion learning how to shoulder arms in October 1914.

Above right: The placard displayed in every home in Beverley that had a man in the army. William Calvert had joined the 10th Battalion.

The 2nd Hull Battalion undergoing squad drill.

In an attempt to maintain the strength of the recruiting drive a route march of those men who had already enlisted into the new Hull battalions was organised for October 3rd. The march started at 3.50pm from Cannon Street and proceeded through the main areas of the city with enthusiastic crowds turning out to cheer them. No uniforms were available so the men marched in their civilian clothes and wearing an armlet to denote the battalion to which they belonged. The march succeeded in attracting more volunteers and the battalion was able to close enlistment. On October 3rd the 11th Battalion history recorded that it:

'took its first route march, a recruiting one, round Hull, amid scenes of wild enthusiasm and much emotion'.

Shortly after this it took possession of 550 rifles.

Lieutenant-Colonel H R Pease from the Regimental Depot at Beverley was appointed the first Commanding Officer. All the CSMs of the regiment were time-served ex-East Yorkshire Regiment soldiers, as were many of the NCOs. The headquarters of the battalion were at Park Street Barracks and the battalion was allowed, courtesy of the Commanding Officer of the 5th (Cyclists) Battalion to use the drill hall belonging to the Cyclists. The battalion did not reach full strength until some time in October but by the end of the year it numbered 25 officers and 1228 other ranks, including a depot company. Early drill practice was carried out in Pearson Park.

Even though the three Hull battalions were now up to full strength there were still large numbers of men coming forward. As a result Lord Nunburnholme received permission from Lord Kitchener to raise a fourth battalion and on November 12th an advertisement in The *Hull Daily Mail* appealed for volunteers for the new battalion. Recruiting began on the 16th at City Hall. By the afternoon there had been sufficient recruits to start rudimentary drill practice. Recruiting was brisk and by the end of the month the battalion was at full strength and had also been able to raise a depot company. The 4th Battalion was known locally as 'T'Others' because it took any able-bodied man, regardless of their class or trade.

As a result of the way in which the battalions had been recruited there was much snobbery between the four battalions, especially from 'The Commercials' who, the other battalions felt, thought themselves to be a cut above the others. Private Ernest Land of the 2nd Hull Battalion told one researcher that the 1st Hull was a 'nobs' battalion: 'the Commercials used to snob you a bit, they was all clerks and teachers'. Whether this was real or just imagined by the other battalions, who were from different walks of life, is another matter.

A mountain of clothing but even this was not enough to clothe the numbers coming forward. The majority of Kitchener's men had to put up with a blue uniform which made them look like they were Post Office workers. The Hull Battalions were lucky. By the end of 1914 all four battalions were in khaki.

The first Commanding Officer of the 4th Hull Battalion was Lieutenant-Colonel J L Stanley, but on November 30th he was replaced by Lieutenant-Colonel R H Dewing, a retired Indian Army officer (76th Punjabis). Captain E F Twiss from the Depot was appointed as the battalion adjutant. Unlike the other three battalions there were no permanent barracks or orderly room. Drill was carried out in the Market square or the nearest field. However, this did not hamper the battalion's progress towards being an active service battalion.

During December the designations of the four battalions were altered to that of Service Battalions. Each battalion was also numbered in sequence with the rest of the East Yorkshire Regiment which was in existence at the time. As a result of these changes the 1st Hull became the 10th (Service) Battalion (1st Hull), the 2nd Hull became the 11th (Service) Battalion (2nd Hull) and so on. The four battalions formed the 113th (Hull) Brigade of the 38th Division in the Fifth New Army. When

Postcard to convince people that they should be in khaki.

the 5th Hull Battalion was formed in 1915 from the depot companies of the 10th, 11th, 12th and 13th Battalions it became the 14th (Reserve) Battalion (Hull).

By the end of 1914 Hull could proudly boast of four 'Pals Battalions', each at full active service strength and possessing a depot company which could be used to provide replacements when the time came. These men had joined for many different reasons and came from many walks of life. But one thing they all had in common was a dangerous, uncertain future.

While the 'Pals' as a concept was an obvious success and had brought in many thousands of recruits in numerous local battalions, engendering a local esprit de corps, it had a very fatal downside that had been overlooked, and if not overlooked deliberately taken out of the equation – casualties. Heavy casualties in a Pals battalion would hit one town very hard, possibly even decimating the male population of an entire street. This will be shown in November 1916 when the Hull Pals experienced their first battle.

Chapter 2

'I'll make a man of you'

The training of the 'Hull Pals' was paralleled all over the country wherever 'Pals' battalions were trained; faltering beginnings due to a lack of accommodation; a lack of knowledge among both officers and men and a reliance on imagination as men marched and trained without weapons. All of this was done in civilian clothes that were not meant for such rigorous activity.

As each of the four battalions was formed they followed the same pattern of integration and assimilation aimed at producing a homogenous battalion with discipline and structure from a heterogenous group of civilians lacking in these basics of military life. In more simple terms, they drilled and route marched. On Hull fair ground, on the cricket pitch on Anlaby Road or wherever it was, the new recruits learned the basics of close order drill from their officers and NCOs, many of whom were as 'green' as their men.

B L Pearson recalled, as a newly commissioned officer in the 12th battalion, that on his first day:

> '*My Company was doing company drill in the park when I turned up and I was given command of number 15 platoon. No-one had uniform and our "equipment" consisted of broomsticks instead of rifles. My Company Commander (not a regular officer) was a man who threw his weight about a lot in the parade ground and since I had missed the OTC camp that summer (due to knee injury) I hardly knew what a platoon was and certainly had scarcely a rudimentary idea of the new company drill. However, with the very loyal help of a platoon sergeant who had once served in the Territorial Force, I survived.*'

A scene repeated all over the country: P.T. in civilian clothes, on any available open space.

While the Hull Battalions trained the war on the Western Front was becoming deadlocked and both sides were digging in for the duration.

The level of individual discipline in each battalion differed from man to man. In a battalion such 'The Commercials', self-regulation was the norm and while they may not have liked the rigidity of army discipline and life they generally accepted it. The 12th Battalion contained men who classed themselves as sportsmen or men who had an interest in sports. This concept cut across the class barrier and allowed some interesting characters to join up. 2/Lieutenant B L Pearson on joining the battalion found that the

> *'men were generally speaking a sound and very hardy lot, mostly recruited from the Hull Docks area and including some members of a body known as "The silver hatchet gang", which had made for itself in peacetime quite a reputation for violence in the dockland.'*

Company order drill on an available open space.

Instilling discipline into such a heterogenous group was not always easy.

Even in the basically middle class 'Commercial' battalion not everyone conformed easily to military discipline. Some even revelled in their indiscipline by giving themselves nicknames that summed them up. Two such men were Walter Aust and Walter Silverwood, neither of whom had met each other before the war; they were united in their dislike of army discipline and became life long friends, both dying at ripe old ages. Ironically, Walter Silverwood was commissioned into the East Yorkshire Regiment in January 1918; Walter Aust stayed in the ranks.

Walter Aust was training to be an agent with the Central Hull Conservative Association when he enlisted on 7th September. He immediately chummed up with Walter Silverwood who enlisted either on the same day or the next. What brought them together was their stubborn disposition, which to their dismay they found did not blend with military discipline. For the whole of the time that they served together they called each other 'Walter Mule'.

The punishment given out for infractions of drill or behaviour was 'Pack Drill' which the two Walters experienced on a number of occasions as Walter Aust recalled:

'ARF A 'MO KAISER!'

The phlegmatic approach of the British to everything is epitomised by this famous painting. The war could just wait while 'Tommy' had a smoke. This card was used to secure funds for The Weekly Dispatch cigarette and tobacco fund.

'Predictably, the muleish streak of my pal and myself quickly brought us into conflict with the forces of law and order and so it came to pass that we were to be found, with distressing frequency, in the very early morning and again in the evening in the company of our Provost Sergeant on a special patch of ground reserved for pack drill for the awkward squad. The Provost Sergeant, possessor of an untidy "Old Bill" ginger moustache set in uncharitable features, allied to a bitter and illiterate tongue, engendered revolt rather than reformation. The insulting remarks he hurled at us between constant commands of "about turn" did nothing to endear this unlovable character to us".

Initially route marches were short and were generally around the city. But soon they went further afield to local villages, like Anlaby. That they were still civilians at this stage is evidenced by the fact that during the march on September 12th, in pouring rain, one recruit produced an umbrella. The comments from the NCOs are unfortunately not recorded by the 10th Battalion history.

Being billeted at home and not having a uniform was a further problem encountered by a large number of men. B L Pearson recalled that:

'*we experienced that rather odd phenomenon of ladies handing chaps white feathers in the streets with the question "Why are you not in uniform?" – to which the truthful answer in most cases was: "because I haven't been able to get a uniform yet".*'

Training gradually took on a wider aspect with companies practising extended order drill, outpost duty, judging distances and skirmishing. Company drill and physical training also increased. As most of the new officers and men did not know what to do for physical training they had to parade at an earlier time than the men to learn the skills from those senior NCOs that did.

In the same way that officers and NCOs were supposed to know everything about drill and physical training, officers were also expected to talk to their men on a regular basis on some topic of use or interest. After

Field Marshal Roberts, VC. He was appointed Honorary Colonel of the Regiment. This was to last just four days as he died November 14th 1914.

a full day of parades and drill, the platoon commander had to give their NCOs and men a half hour lecture. 2/Lieutenant B L Pearson recalled that these lectures were:

'*on a variety of subjects, about which their knowledge, if any (and then generally derived from some pre-war Army red book) was very vague and small. For instance,*

Situated near to the 10th Battalion at Hornsea were a battery of the Royal Artillery whose job was to defend the coast against invasion.

I myself was once called upon to lecture my chaps on knotting and lashing. Coming, as I have said, largely from Hull's Dockland area, they were nevertheless, very kind and understanding about my predicament and in a very short time, with my connivance, they were showing me all kinds of things about knots and lashes that I never conceived in my 21 years of existence.'

Sports and competitions were a useful way of welding team spirit and were encouraged by all the battalions in whatever shape they could manifest themselves, throughout the war – even in the middle of the carnage of the Somme. As a young platoon officer B L Pearson recalled the setting up of a rugby team in order to both weld the men into a team but also, of course, to win their matches:

'The team was, in fact, quite a formidable lot and included four men who had played what was then called Northern Union – now Rugby League Football. One of these four was a man called Spivey, also a former member of "The Silver hatchet gang", who adopted a rather protective role towards me both on and off the field: once, when I had been bundled with rather unnecessary force into touch, he went up to the man who had tackled me and said, "If you do that again to my officer I'll mark you for life" – no idle threat from a man who was fast (a wing three-quarter), strong, weighed about 13 stone and handed off his man with a clenched fist.'

Officers and NCOs of C Company, 12th Battalion, in March 1915. The Company Commander is Captain Worthington.

16 Platoon, D Company, 10th Battalion, in February 1915.

10th Battalion Warrant Officers and NCOs taken at Ripon in July 1915.

The training routine adopted was basically the same for each of the four battalions. Route marches became progressively longer and went further afield. Drill became more complex and was held on grounds more distant from the city centre. These distant grounds being, of course, reached by marching. One company of the 10th Battalion earned the sobriquet of 'Glossop's Greyhounds' because they marched at the double to get to the more distant grounds. There were numerous inspections and the separate battalions started to undertake field exercises and manoeuvres. Eventually they were initiated into musketry training, aiming and trigger pressing, and the mysterious triangle of errors, all of course without serviceable rifles or ammunition.

On November 10th 1914 the *London Gazette* announced that Earl Roberts had been appointed Honorary Colonel of the Battalion. This was sadly curtailed by his death on November 14th 1914.

November also saw the arrival and issue of the first part of the kit. Up until this time the only identification that each soldier of each battalion had was their armlet. While many of the battalions of Kitchener's New Armies had to suffer the indignities of the blue 'Post Office' style uniform, the Hull Pals were fortunate to acquire a complete khaki uniform, making them into real soldiers.

Things come in threes and in the middle of November the 10th Battalion was moved to Hornsea, on the East Yorkshire Coast, leaving the other three battalions still training in Hull. Local men on arrival were allowed to spend the night at home and join the battalion the next morning.

The original plan was for the four battalions to go to new camps at Rolston, Dalton and Millington but the need for troops for Coast Defence altered this plan. However, the other battalions did eventually leave Hull for training in these camps.

Due to the sudden need for extra troops as a precaution against possible German invasion, the camp that 'The Commercials' arrived at was unfinished and ankle deep in mud – up to eighteen inches in places. Private Aust recalled:

'A camp was being built for us adjoining a rifle range near Howden on the East Yorkshire coast. An invasion scare caused us to move prematurely to this unfinished camp. It was a sea of mud and we were packed like sardines into the most habitable huts.'

Fortunately there were enough blankets to go around. However, the move had been so rapid that the Army Service Corps had been unable to respond and there was very little food available. When leave was granted the next evening after a busy day the battalion history records that the men made a general raid on the food shops in Hornsea. Private Aust summed up the situation:

'No food, no bedding. All we had was one bucket of water for 60 men and we had to drink that out of the pail. At the end of twenty-four hours we were let loose and a famished battalion descended on Hornsea like a swarm of locusts.'

On 16th December the German fleet bombarded Scarborough, Whitby and Hartlepool. The loss of life in Scarborough was nineteen civilians, one of whom was a boy scout killed while going to the shops to buy a newspaper; more than 80 were injured. 10th Battalion troops in Hornsea could hear the bombardment. The photo shows the remains of the Coastguard Station (old barracks then in use as a storehouse) in Scarborough. It was finally estimated that 500 shells fell on the town.

An example of damage to private property – Springfield House in Whitby was hit by a shell. The occupant of the house was a woman who was confined to her bed; she died of her injuries a few days later.

The battalion was tasked with the guarding of the coast from Mappleton to Ulrome, in all weathers and at all times of day. To the north were the Yorkshire Hussars and to the south the Norfolk Cyclists.

Acclimatisation to the trenches was provided by the constant digging of trenches and the practice of 'Standing To' each morning before going to breakfast. The battalion history records that owing to the clay based nature of the cliffs in that area the trenches constantly fell into the sea and had to be replaced.

There was little to relieve the monotony of trench digging and guard duty until December 16th. On that morning the whole battalion manned the trenches in full force owing to part of the German High Seas Fleet being missed by Naval Intelligence. The missing ships duly arrived off the east coast and proceeded to shell Scarborough, Whitby and Hartlepool. So loud was the bombardment of Scarborough that it could be heard by the troops at Hornsea.

Christmas Day was a special day in the life of the battalion at Hornsea. It was the day they got to fire their long Lee-Enfields for the first time. The battalion had a supply of ammunition, but this was specifically for use only against the enemy. This special dispensation had arisen through the persistence of Lieutenant-Colonel Richardson who, after much correspondence with the War Office about being allowed to let the men shoot live ammunition, received a telegram asking him to report on the efficiency of the battalion's rifles. The Colonel's reply, which jolted the War Office into granting permission for the rifles to be fired, was:

'Reference your telegram... Rifles will certainly go off, doubtful which end'.

In January 1915 the camp was inspected by Officer Commanding 113 Infantry Brigade, Brigadier-General Sir Henry Dixon. An interesting account of the camp at this time is contained in the March edition of the *North Eastern Railway Magazine* written by a serving 'Commercial':

A sleeper-road is laid from the entrance to the far side of the camp. On the left are the officers' huts, the office, guard room, store rooms, &c. Further along on the right are the garage and the tailor's and electrician's workshop. Then come the huts themselves. They are built at right-angles to the road in four lines or rows, two rows on each side. Each row consists of nine huts. The rows are about 30 yards apart, and the space between them is taken up by the Sergeant's quarters, baths and drying room. The situation of the camp is a splendid one, about 150 yards from the cliff top, and invigorating winds blow along our lines. The huts are fine places, and are lighted by electricity. Between the lines are washing houses and lavatories with a plentiful supply of water. The sleeping accommodation is quite good, each man being supplied with sleeping-boards raised about eight inch from the floor, with a paillasse and pillow filled with straw, and three blankets.'

The writer went on to describe food and life in the camp.

Guard duty at the Christmas Tree Hut at Atwick at the end of 1914. Note the obsolete rifle being used.

A typical rifle range of the period. The 10th Battalion first got to fire their rifles on Christmas day 1914.

'Every morning the reveille sounds at 7 am, and breakfast follows at 7.45. This consists alternately of bacon, bread and jam, and quaker oats, bread, butter and jam. The recruit class parades at 9 am. Usually, we have physical drill for two hours and, during the rest of the morning, are instructed in the handling of arms. "Cookhouse" sounds at 12.45, and the following is a typical menu: Roast beef, potatoes, rice pudding and stewed prunes. Who could complain? On some days when we are away from the hutments for a long period, bread and cheese are served out as lunch and we dine on our return – usually about 6 pm. In the afternoons, musketry and shooting practice.

'Our social welfare is well looked after. There is a Regimental Institute in which one may spend a leisurely hour in reading, or at the piano, or in playing one of the many games provided. Sometimes there are concerts on quite a grand scale, and on such occasions the Institute is gaily decorated.'

Another writer noted that:

'The latest newspapers of the day can be seen at the regimental reading room, and here, also, the men can write home to their friends and relatives, writing tables and a plentiful supply of paper being provided free of charge. At the Institute the men can also have everything they are in need of at a reasonable price, and every Wednesday night a whist drive is held and on Friday nights a concert is given.

Three months later in the same magazine the picture painted was not quite so rosy:

'We quickly realised that army life was much different from the civil life we had been accustomed to. "Reveille" blows now at 6 am, at which time the stentorian voice of the sergeant is heard calling, "Show a leg there, show a leg," accompanied by the clanging of a stick on the nearest form, and if the aforementioned limb does not make a timely appearance the sleepy member's

In order to replace battle casualties, when the battalions eventually embarked for active service, it was decided to raise a further battalion of 'Hull Pals'. These later men formed the 2nd Depot Companies of the four original battalions eventually becoming the 14th (Reserve) Battalion (Hull). This is an early 1915 recruiting poster.

Another group of 13th Battalion men outside their hut. The ground has turned to mud because of the lack of proper pathways.

The 'Hotel Cecil', one of the 13th Battalion huts on the Westwood at Beverley. The men are probably the battalion signallers.

boards are dragged from underneath him and he has no option but to tumble out. Blankets, palliasses, bed-boards and tressles are quickly arranged in regulation fashion, and, after a hasty wash, coffee and biscuits are served and a few minutes to 7 o'clock the sergeant's voice is again heard calling: "Fall in for the run! Come on let's be having you outside". A distance of two or three miles is covered, alternative running and walking for which the men turn out in light sandshoes, trousers and shirts. "Cookhouse" blows at 7.45 am and the orderlies, detailed from each section, can then be seen making their way to the various huts with food provided for breakfast... Breakfast over, each company falls in independently for collective training, and for the first hour Swedish drill and bayonet fighting are indulged in, to be followed by semaphore signalling, musketry, knotting &c. Dinner (usually roast beef potatoes and beans, with rice or bread pudding) is served at 12.45 pm and the afternoon is devoted to trench digging or company drill. One of the chief features of our training is the attacking of flagged enemies across the fields. The tea bugle blows at 4.45 pm, and after the meal of jam and marmalade, stewed fruit, butter and bread, the men are free (unless on special duties) to leave barracks until roll call at 10 pm, "Lights Out" being sounded at 10.15 pm.

Bayonet fighting has a peculiar fascination to the modern reader. However, it was also of great interest to the readers of the North Eastern Railway Magazine in June 1915. The writer continued:

'*A few words here on bayonet fighting will no doubt interest the reader, who assuredly, will have gathered from the Press that British superiority in this method of close fighting is playing a predominant part in the present campaign. In the elementary stage the recruit is taught how to handle his rifle quickly and easily without strain. He is shown how to adopt the "On guard" position, pointing and parrying in any direction and also the method of shortening arms, which is used to extract the bayonet cleanly after a point has been made. The instructor impresses upon recruits the vital importance of quickness of movement both in dealing with an opponent and at the same time guarding oneself. After thoroughly mastering the art of bayonet fighting, instruction is in using the, butt, knee, trip &C, and in order to demonstrate more clearly the reality of the business recruits are paired off, and, after donning protective gear for the head and body, fight each other with spring bayonets, under the guidance of an instructor, who points out to the class the varied faults of the combatants. Finally, practice in taking enemy trenches at the point of the bayonet are indulged in, sacks representing the enemy.*'

At the start of the new year, specialists were selected and company commanders recommended men for a commission or confirmation in their present rank – all ranks having been temporary until this point. As the 10th Battalion was raised from the middle classes there were a large number of potential officers serving in the ranks. With the high wastage of young subalterns on the Western Front there was a constant

A squad of 13th Battalion men somewhere in Hull in early 1915. Second from left, front row, is Private Haldenby.

need for replacements. In many battalions social class or money were sufficient for a potential officer to be released for training as an officer; not so in 'The Commercials'. Lieutenant-Colonel Richardson, as shown by his replies to the War Office over the use of rifles, was not afraid of the repercussions of his comments or decisions. The battalion history records that he felt that only officer material should become officers:

> *'Commissions. Qualifications:*
> *Character and determination strong enough to ensure discipline. Mental powers sufficient to assimilate the regulations and instructions that guide the army. The C.O. will recommend no one who does not give proof of possessing the above, no matter how many employers, fathers, or grandmothers try to pull strings.'*

However, before the battalion sailed for Egypt, a good number of the ranks had become officers, with more to follow throughout the war.

Even when guarding the coast the recreational side of life was not neglected, with soccer being the prevalent game. Battalion cross-country runs were also very common and only those deemed essential to the maintenance of the camp and security of the coast were excused. On April 21st 1915 a Brigade Cross-Country run was organised, with the best from the four battalions competing. The run was to start from Dalton, where the 12th Battalion was camped, and end at Victoria Barracks in Beverley, the Regimental Depot. As all four battalions were competing, the whole of the 1st Hull Battalion was given leave to see the finish of the run, which was won by Private P Sellers of D Company of the 10th Battalion; unfortunately another runner, Private J Hughes, from the 10th Battalion, was disqualified and the overall team winners were the 11th Battalion. [2nd place – Lieutenant Williams, 3rd place – Corporal Norton, 4th place – L/Corporal Kirk and 5th place – Private Langdon, all from the 11th Battalion. The battalion honours were first place – 11th Battalion (Ousethorpe Camp), 2nd place – 10th Battalion (Hornsea), 3rd place – 13th Battalion (Beverley Westwood) and 4th place – 12th Battalion (South Dalton).]

Privates Ives and Metcalf described the place of sport in their weekly timetable in an article for the *North Eastern Railway Magazine*:

> *'Tuesday afternoon is devoted to crosscountry running, Thursday afternoon is set apart for football and other outdoor games and Saturday afternoon is a half-day holiday.'*

Route marches were not forgotten and Privates Ives and Metcalf recorded:

> *'Wednesday is "battalion" day, ie, the whole battalion is taken out by the commanding officer, either for a route march of between 20 and 30 miles or training in "battle formation". Dinner on this day is served about 4 pm.'*

The 10th Battalion camp at Hornsea had railway sleepers put down to form pathways. This group of men are part of D Company. The soldier in the centre is Private D McLachlan.

A group of 10th Battalion men outside their hut at Hornsea. Many of the men in the photograph were ex-employees of the North Eastern Railway.

The 10th Battalion history records that one officer and twenty-five percent of other ranks of those on detachment and 50 percent of all pickets were left behind to deal with any enemy invasion. Not all of those left behind had ideas of fighting to the last man, as Private Aust recorded. While the battalion had been given leave to go to a cross country meeting the two Walters had been detailed to stay behind and dig on the range. They had decided to go to Hornsea regardless of the consequences and

The art of trench digging was taught to the recruits as soon as the companies had some form of basic military training and discipline.

April 1915. The start of the inter-brigade cross-country match. The race started at Dalton and finished at Victoria Barracks in Beverley.

Practising the taking of a trench at bayonet point.

Learning to approach the enemy stealthily.

On June 6th 1915 Hull experienced its first Zeppelin attack. The photo shows damage to north Church Side.

slipped off as soon as no one was watching. After an enjoyable time they returned to camp:

> 'Our luck was out. As soon as we reentered camp we were charged with being absent and would be tried at Company Orderly room the next morning. Still feeling in a rebellious mood we decided we might as well be "hung for a sheep as a lamb" and caught the next train to Hull. Fortunately both our fathers were away on the high seas and our mothers were delighted to learn that we had been granted seven days unexpected leave. So unexpected that we had drawn no ration money or pay and were completely broke. Having "touched" our respective mums we changed into civvies and proceeded to have a whale of a time. Not a care in the world.
>
> We knew we would not be posted as deserters until we had been absent a week. So on the seventh day we returned to camp.'

Fortunately for them both the Colonel and the Major were away so they were tried by their Company Commander. They felt that they had got away lightly but unfortunately they found themselves back once more in the clutches of their unlovable Provost Sergeant.

Even this experience was not enough to prevent further indiscipline from Private Aust. As a Boy Scout he was proficient in signalling with flags and as a consequence he eventually found himself in a more secure occupation as a signaller. However, he was quickly returned to his company for indiscipline.

Interior of a hut at Hornsea.

Private Clifford Carter of the 10th Battalion who was later commissioned and served in Cologne after the war.

Press Bureau, OFFICIAL MESSAGE.
"A Zeppelin visited the East Coast on Sunday night (June 6th, 1915.) "Incendiary and explosive bombs were dropped. "Number of deaths 24; Injured 40."

The Midnight ASSASSIN

A postcard issued shortly after the raid. Hull was known as an East Coast town and not by name.

Throughout the time the battalion spent at Rolston, Zeppelins made numerous raids over the East Coast and on June 6th 1915 made their first attack on Hull where a number of the battalion were at home on leave. Fortunately none of the battalion were injured. This was not the battalion's first experience of Zeppelins. Earlier in the year the battalion had been called out at 4am to deal with a reported Zeppelin. Unfortunately although they had the ammunition the only rifles available were for drill purposes and would not fire. The 10th Battalion history records that:

'The repulsion of the Zeppelin was to be by moral force only... the company "wags" were in evidence keeping up a running fire of comments which would have nonplussed the enemy more than our rifle fire.'

On the 8th Captain Watson wrote home to his mother:

'At 10-15 I was half undressed when the orderly room clerk came in white as a sheet, four Zepps over Hull. I was the senior officer in camp so I turned out the camp and telephoned to the Hall for the Major. We served out ammunition and one Zepp was seen from the camp. We heard innumerable bombs drop at Hull. The whole sky was lit up, when the fires broke out. They say only five lives lost but I know for a fact there were lots more.'

On June 6th the buzzers sounded at 11.15 to signal Zeppelins overhead. Damage was caused to buildings in Constable street, Coltman Street, Porter Street, Bright Street, High Street, Campbell Street, South Parade and Church Street. Forty people were injured, five treated for shock and nineteen killed. The raid 'all clear' signal was sounded at 2 pm.

A group of 13th Battalion soldiers outside their tent on Beverley Westwood. Private Arthur Donnelley is behind the number at the bottom. He was to be killed on 13th November 1916 aged 26.

Boxing was a popular pastime. Here the boxers square-up while their seconds watch the camera.

The officers of the 10th Battalion at Hornsea, 1915. In the front row centre is Lieutenant-Colonel Richardson.

A camp group of the 13th Battalion preparing food, potatoes, turnips and canned peas, on Beverley Westwood in the summer of 1915.

In order to increase recruiting, marches through targetted localities occurred on a regular basis. The 10th Battalion undertook one on May 4th when 250 men and officers marched through Goole; an area where a number of the Pals had come from.

As training progressed it was inevitable that the four battalions would leave the local vicinity and move to an area which allowed brigade and divisional manoeuvres. Before leaving for Ripon at the end of June, Dalton Camp, home of the 12th Battalion, held a highly successful gala on June 4th to celebrate the King's Birthday, which was reported in the *Hull Daily Mail*:

Newly commissioned officers from the 13th Battalion based on Beverley Westwood. Second Lieutenant R S Watt and Second Lieutenant C Glover (right).

'Whatever the future may have in store for them, the 12th Service Battalion East Yorkshire Regiment, or 3rd Hulls as we know them, will not soon forget the King's birthday. The day was given over to pleasure. With military-like precision regimental sports were arranged. The greatest pleasure, though, was from the visits of relatives and friends and the little family reunions which took place.

The gala day spirit was in the air, yet frivolity was not always the dominant note. Let us direct our gaze towards one corner of the encampment. There is an elderly woman talking quietly, happily and thoughtfully to her only son. Young wives with a child or two forget their anxieties in the reunion with their husbands. At the hedges by the entrance not a few men were expectantly on the look-out for a welcome visitor.'

After marching through Beverley, York and Boroughbridge the battalions arrived at Ripon to begin divisional training. Specialist training was also intensified. Although there was considerable land technically available for training, due to its agricultural use, in reality its potential during the summer was much restricted. It was not until September 18th that the 10th Battalion experienced active service conditions in the form of a two day march over the local moors.

It was during this period that all acting ranks in the 10th Battalion were confirmed and a number of other ranks and NCOs were sent off for officer training. The battalion was further depleted by men being transferred to the Divisional Cyclist Company and by the Ministry of Munitions canvassing among the men for skilled workmen to return to their trades.

By October, the three brigades of the 31st Division (renumbered in April when the original Fourth Army was broken up to provide reinforcements for the first three

A group of 10th Battalion soldiers displaying the essentials of camp life.

Soldiers of the 10th Battalion sparring on the beach near Rolston in 1915.

11th Battalion scouts at Pocklington 1915.

A platoon of the 13th Battalion just before the brigade left for Ripon.

The orderly room of the 13th Battalion in May 1915.

Soldiers of the 11th Battalion at Pocklington 1915.

The 10th Battalion marching to Ripon.

The 10th Battalion band taken at Ripon, July 1915. The officer is Lieutenant Flintoff who was later killed in action.

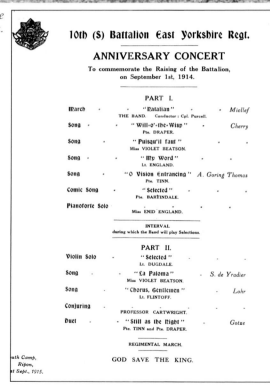

10th (S) Battalion East Yorkshire Regt.

ANNIVERSARY CONCERT

To commemorate the Raising of the Battalion,
on September 1st, 1914.

PART I.

March	-	-	"Ratalian"	-	-	Miellef
		THE BAND. Conductor : Cpl. Purcell.			
Song	-	-	"Will-o'-the-Wisp"	-	Cherry
		Pte. DRAPER.			
Song	-	-	"Puisqu'il faut"	-	-
		Miss VIOLET BEATSON.			
Song	-	-	"My Word"	-	-
		Lt. ENGLAND.			
Song	-	"O Vision Entrancing"	A. Goring Thomas
		Pte. TINN.			
Comic Song	-	"Selected"	-	-
		Pte. BARTINDALE.			
Pianoforte Solo	-	-	-
		Miss ENID ENGLAND.			

INTERVAL
during which the Band will play Selections.

PART II.

Violin Solo	-	"Selected"	-	-
		Lt. DUGDALE.			
Song	-	"La Paloma"	-	S. de Yradier
		Miss VIOLET BEATSON.			
Song	-	"Chorus, Gentlemen"	-	Lohr
		Lt. FLINTOFF.			
Conjuring	-	PROFESSOR CARTWRIGHT.
Duet	-	"Still as the Right"	-	Gotze
		Pte. TINN and Pte. DRAPER.			

REGIMENTAL MARCH.

GOD SAVE THE KING.

uth Camp,
Ripon,
st Sept., 1915.

'New Armies'), were ready for full divisional exercises and were warned on the 18th to be ready to move to Salisbury Plain. On the same day the 10th Battalion lost its CO, leaving Major Carver in temporary command. Lieutenant-Colonel Richardson was removed from post because of his impatience with higher authority. Before leaving them he addressed them, dressed in civilian clothing, just as he had on the day he arrived to command them. On each occasion he addressed them as 'gentlemen'. In his farewell speech he thanked them for being such a well behaved battalion, for their hard work and for their unfailing cheerfulness and hoped that they would fight hard. Privately, Lieutenant-Colonel Richardson recorded that:

'My fear was that their zeal would outrun itself and that they would get stale before we went across the water.'

The programme of the Anniversary Concert to commemorate the raising of the battalion.

He took his dismissal as a matter of course. When he received a letter from the War Office recommending that he be removed from command and also asking him if he had anything to say on the matter he sent back a characteristic reply:

'"...Nothing, thank you", then (I) got into a pony and trap and went for a ten days drive among the Pennine hills. Returning from the drive, I handed over my command and left, to stay at various places, and chew the cud, and no, not exactly, of remorse. And yet when it got about the battalion that I was leaving I was shown such affection that had I been able I think I might have recalled that, "Nothing, thank you".'

At the beginning of November the division left Ripon for Fovant on Salisbury Plain. A few weeks earlier Canon Waugh, who was leaving Ripon Cathedral, complimented the whole division for their exemplary conduct.

The brigade soon settled into its new quarters at Hurdcott Camp but the 10th Battalion with its new Commanding Officer (Lieutenant-Colonel Burges, an officer with considerable active service experience) moved to Larkhill. While at Salisbury the division experienced trench life, in the form of trench relief and inhabitation, and also received SMLE rifles prior to active service. This introduction to the trenches was described by Private Tait of the 10th Battalion as an interesting experience:

The Mess Hall at Ripon Camp.

The huts on Salisbury Plain.

Women munitions workers. Before the Hull Brigade went overseas a number of skilled 'Hull Pals' left the army to take up their old trades to help the war effort by producing war materials.

'*Wednesday November 24th 1915*

Trench warfare – Spent day in trenches – most interesting. I descend a sap and we build a dug out. Attack on "enemy" trenches led by bombers. My first experience as regards bombers. Spend night in trenches and act as sentry. Thanks to those at home I am remarkably warm. Secured no sleep, but plenty of sport.

Thursday November 25th 1915

Very cold morning. Still in the trenches and the 11th batt. attempts assault, but retires. Left trenches at 7am in fine spirit. Just like a nigger in appearance. A Coy a trifle worse for rum. Band accompanies us back and poor devils can hardly play, the instruments being frozen.'

It was during this time that the weeding out of the medically unfit began; their replacements coming initially from those in the Depot companies formed in 1915. Private Tait in his diary noted the:

'*arrival of 57 depot men, including Frank (his step-brother) & C Stockdale (a friend). A pleasant surprise to me!*'

At the same time a number of men were released for munitions work.

On December 2nd, the day the 10th Battalion returned to Hurdcott, the division received orders to be ready to proceed abroad at a very early date. The war diary of the 11th Battalion records that on the same day they received orders to indent for sun helmets, so it must have been obvious to all ranks that they were not destined for France. The imminence of the departure must have been obvious to all when, on December 3rd they were issued with identification discs. Although it was becoming more obvious to everyone that they would be going to Egypt, this was not the original destination of the division.

Originally the division had been scheduled for the Western Front and with that intention, 31st Divisional Headquarters had been informed on November 29th that embarkation would start on December 9th with advance parties leaving for Southampton and Folkestone on November 30th and December 1st respectively. It was not until December 2nd that the Division was warned that it would not move to France but that it would go to Egypt accompanied by the 32nd Division artillery which had been raised in April and May 1915 by Lord Derby in the Lytham and St. Anne's area (Lancashire). The divisional artillery received the designation of 2nd County Palatine.

Private McLachlan wearing the emergency 1914 pattern leather equipment with an obsolete Lee Metford rifle.

Private Carter of the 10th Battalion, later to be commissioned, recorded that on December 4th: 'equipment for France was issued'. And on the 6th he wrote:

'equipment for France withdrawn. Pith helmets and puggarees were handed out, and it was rumoured that Camel Humps would be issued! Everyone was certain that the battalion was going to India or Mesopotamia or Arabia or Egypt or somewhere else.'

The 11th Battalion history records a similar story:

'gas helmets were issued and we prepared for France. Suddenly they were withdrawn and sun helmets took their place.'

The King inspecting a New Army Division just before it sails for France. Unfortunately for the 31st Division, due to an accident while in France the King was unable to inspect the division. He sent a message to them instead.

Orders to proceed abroad and entrain at Salisbury were received by the 10th Battalion on the December 6th, by the 11th Battalion on the 7th, by the 12th Battalion around the 11th and by the 13th Battalion around the 9th. The orders directed them to the railway station at Salisbury for a train ride to Devonport (each battalion requiring three trains), in the depths of night and final embarkment aboard the appropriate ship. All the battalions of 92 Brigade appear to have left after marching to Salisbury but the majority of the 12th had to march to Wilton (five and a half miles away) in pouring rain. Apart from the 11th Battalion, which sailed short of twelve privates, all the battalions were at full strength (the 10th Battalion history records the issue of 1025 sun helmets), and in the best of health. Private Beeken recalled the day of departure:

'On the 7th December 1915, we marched in rain and with sun helmets on to Salisbury where we entrained and arrived in Devonport on the 8th December.'

The 11th Battalion history recorded that:

'after two days' intense practice at folding puggarees we marched in greatcoats and sun helmets through a snowstorm to Salisbury Station, there to stand or sit for some five hours in an open yard waiting for our train.'

Due to the short notice given prior to proceeding abroad there was no time for embarkation leave. Prior to embarkation it was the norm for the division to be inspected by the King in a march past on Salisbury Plain. However, the King had been hurt while in France and was unfit, so he sent a farewell message to the division instead.

Chapter 3

'It's a long way to Tipperary'
Egypt 1915–1916

The adventure began on December 8th 1915 with the embarkation of the 10th Battalion, a detachment of the 12th KOYLI and a brigade of RFA, aboard HMT *Minnewaska* and its departure shortly after final loading at 5.20am. On the 10th, HMT *Grampian* sailed, at 9.20am, with Division and Brigade headquarters and the 11th Battalion aboard, minus a detachment of 3 officers and 70 men, with all the horses and mules, who sailed on HMT *Nitonian*. The next to sail was the 13th Battalion aboard HMT *Minneapolis*, leaving Devonport at 1.25am on December 14th. Finally the 12th Battalion sailed on the 16th at 12.30pm aboard HMT *Ausonia*.

Only the 12th Battalion detailed who sailed on the 16th. The battalion war diary recorded the officers and their assignments as listed in the table below.

Neither the war diaries of three of the four battalions or the brigade recorded any details of the journey apart from arrival times at Malta and Port Said. The 10th Battalion being on the lead ship arrived first, at Port Said, on December 21st at 2pm. It disembarked and encamped in Number 4 Camp. The diary records that the battalion was at war strength minus one private who had been left in hospital on Malta. The 11th arrived at Valetta at 8am on the 19th and sailed at 3.30pm the same day. On December 24th at 7.45am Port Said was reached and the battalion encamped with the 10th outside the town alongside 93 Brigade. The 12th Battalion

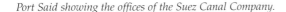

Port Said showing the offices of the Suez Canal Company.

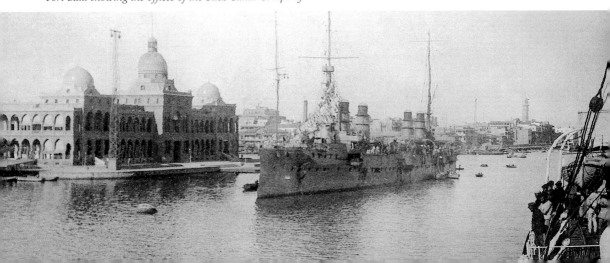

	CO	Lt. Colonel H Pease
	2i/c	Major Wellesley
	Adjutant	Captain C C H Twiss
	LT&QM	H E Claxton
	MGO	LT. T W Burch
	MO	Lt. V H Mason, RAMC
	Chaplain	Rev. J Martyn Roberts

	A Company	B Company	C Company	D Company
i/c	Capt. D Watson	Capt. H Walker	Capt. A J Webb	Major R H Tatton
2i/c	Lt. L L Rosenberg	Lt. S S Walker	Lt. E Morrison	Lt. L O Habersohn
	Lt. A C Bulmer (SO)	Lt. B H Harper	Lt. S M Crabtree	Lt. H N Marriott
	Lt. O L Frizoni	Lt. C H Jones 2/	Lt. E H Tatton	Lt. L M G Du Pre
	2/Lt. M W Dunne	2/Lt. N Constant	2/Lt. C Drewett	2/Lt. R N Taylor
	2/Lt. R G Backrath	2/Lt. L R LeBouvier	2/Lt. A Wilson (TO)	2/Lt. G W Walker

Plus RSM Charles Arnett and 990 other ranks.

The other three battalions followed the same structure but have left no record.

SO = Signals Officer   TO = Transport Officer

arrived at Port Said on December 29th at 8.30am and the 13th Battalion arrived at 9am on the 29th. Only the 12th Battalion diary writer took the time to record anything about the journey:

'Called at Malta and Alexandria. Good voyage, no incidents worth recording. 10 men left at Malta suffering from contagious disease and 1 horse died of pneumonia on the Minneapolis.*'*

A good voyage might have been disputed by the majority of those involved. Readers familiar with the other books in the *Pals* series concerning the units of the 31st Division will recognise the story about to be told.

Hull was a major port but the number of actual seafarers that joined the 'Hull Pals' was very small so for the majority of those on the five ships that carried 92 Brigade it was their first trip to sea. The journey started in December and sailed through the notorious Bay of Biscay before reaching the calm of the Mediterranean sea. Conditions on board were cramped and stuffy, the food was poor and in true army fashion each man was inoculated against cholera at the start of the journey; an inoculation that had side-effects on many men. Barnes, in *This Righteous War* quotes from Private Carter's (10th Battalion) 1915 Diary: 'For two whole days I was seasick'. The 10th Battalion history records that:

'there was much good humoured fun at the first cases of sea-sickness, but soon almost every man had disappeared below with the same complaint. Some tried to lie

down on the hard tables or narrow forms (a long thin bench for sitting on), only to roll off among their fellow-sufferers huddled together on the floor. For two days sea sickness easily overshadowed all the other discomfort.'

Private Tait confirmed the unpleasantness of the journey to start off with:

'Thursday December 9th 1915
We start at last - time 7 am. It is a terrible day, wind and rain plentiful, consequently a haze is cast over the horizon.'

Watching the destroyer escort emphasised the unpleasantness of the weather. Private Tait recorded in his diary:

'now we are on the move accompanied by destroyers that appear most formidable. See how they cut through the water! Now up - now dipping their stalwart bows in the trough of the sea, which is fairly high, and now, in the Channel many of us are sick. I am feeling 'inclined' that way, but not yet actually experienced these pleasures. Issued with lifebelts.'

10th Battalion troops aboard HMT Minnewaska, December 1915.

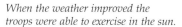
When the weather improved the troops were able to exercise in the sun.

After a couple of days or so, most of the men had started to find their sea legs especially once the boats entered the relative calm of the Spanish coastal waters. The 11th Battalion history records a similar story with unpleasantness in the Bay of Biscay but generally a relatively straightforward journey.

It was not just the men who suffered. On board the ships were horses and mules who like the men were being kept in cramped and stuffy conditions. There was little the men in charge of these transport animals could do to help and a number of them died on the journey.

The ships carrying the brigade sailed separately and without a destroyer escort; the destroyer had returned to port after escorting the boats for only a few hours. As a result everybody kept a keen eye out for anything breaking the surface and armed guards were placed around the boat specifically to watch for U-boats. A zig-zag course was maintained and no lights were shown to reduce the risks of being spotted. Everybody was issued with a life-jacket and ordered to keep it close at hand. As they made good pillows and seats, the order was generally obeyed. The HMT *Minnewaska* was an armed merchantman. The 10th Battalion history records that the gun was used on the trip but only in practice, which is just as well for the occupants of the *Minnewaska*:

> *'The ship's gunner indulged in occasional practice, his first shot causing considerable excitement as no warning was given. He would frequently throw an empty barrel overboard, wait until it had drifted well astern and then before our critical eyes he would blow it clean out of the water.'*

The arrival of the better weather meant a return to normalcy. Church parades were held, letters were written and battalion bands played to captive audiences. Being on

72

active service all letters from now on would have to be censored by platoon commanders but there would be no postage to pay.

As the Straits of Gibraltar are narrow it was an obvious place for U-boats to wait, so the troopships waited for night before proceeding into the Mediterranean and the only sights that could be seen were searchlights playing on the water. Generally, the waters of the Mediterranean were kinder than those of the Atlantic but for the 10th this was not the case. Shortly after leaving the straits, with the Atlas mountains of Morocco and the snow-capped Sierra Nevada of Spain clearly in view, the weather broke:

> 'and for three days as we sailed in sight of Africa, conditions became equally as bad as they had been in the Atlantic. A cold driving wind brought violent storms with rain and hail, and once again sea sickness became the general order. The decks were often awash and the anti-submarine guards carried out their long spells of duty wet through to the skin'.

Private Tait's diary entry for December 13th confirms this change of weather:

> 'we are now in the Mediterranean. The weather again changes, a strong wind prevailing. The ship tosses worse than ever. Seasickness is revived.'

Eventually the weather changed and HMT *Minnewaska* arrived in The Grand Harbour, Malta to anchor beside the *Empress of Britain* which was carrying the Leeds and Bradford Pals. The *Empress of Britain* was being repaired after it had collided with the French steamship *Dajurjura*. The French mailship had sunk quickly but fortunately only two seamen were killed.

Shortly after leaving Valetta the *Empress of Britain* was attacked by a submarine but was not hit, arriving safely in Port Said on December 21st. The 10th Battalion also had a submarine scare but fortunately it turned out to be a harmless piece of wreckage gently floating past.

The arrival of the troopships in Valetta harbour was greeted by the presence of numerous 'bum-boats' manned by Maltese traders who sold fresh fruit, Turkish Delight and a cheap brand of local cigarette which were not all that they should have been. The 10th Battalion history records that they:

> 'were rapidly bought, only to be quickly thrown overboard when their quality was ascertained.'

Even the native boys who dived for the coins thrown overboard by the troops did not bother to attempt to retrieve them.

Shore leave was not given to the brigade, as they each in turn arrived in Malta, because the stop was for refuelling and was only of a few hours duration, however, Private Tait commented in his diary:

'If only we could proceed ashore! The officers are there, while we do not receive such privileges.'

Private Beeken remembered arriving at Valetta:

'Soon the ship was surrounded by small boats from which boys dived for pennies which we threw to them. Men from these boats threw up to us ropes. On hauling these up we found small baskets in which we placed money and then shouted our orders for cigarettes and Turkish delight, the cigarettes were terrible.'

Upon leaving Malta, company commanders were able to tell the men that their destination was Egypt and the Suez Canal Defences and not Gallipoli, as many had suspected.

The prevailing calmer weather allowed the battalions to begin to exercise on deck and the warmer weather permitted men to sleep on the deck in clean, fresh air. Submarine alarm drills were carried out frequently because the boats were now in a real danger zone. Also frequent were the inspections of the boat carried out by the ship's Captain. Free-time on board was catered for by boxing matches, sing-songs, band concerts and learning how to wrap yards of fine muslin round the sun helmet to form a pagri.

Each boat arrived in Alexandria Harbour before proceeding, under cover of darkness for the final destination of Port Said at the head of the Suez Canal. The *Minnewaska* was fortunate in its time of arrival. Coming in to Port Said it passed a Japanese steamer, the *Macceim*, and as it berthed an oil-tanker left port. Both were torpedoed and sunk within a few miles of the Canal entrance. However, the *Minnewaska* was not to survive the war: she was sunk in Suda Bay (Crete) in November 1916 by a mine laid by UC23 (a German U-boat) commanded by Leutnant Kirchner.

Upon arrival full equipment was issued (rifles and other articles not needed on board had been placed in deep storage) and stores unloaded with the help of the local Arab workforce. Once unloaded, the troops marched off to their new camp near Port Said. Private Beeken recalled their arrival in Egypt:

'In the afternoon we received our full equipment and then cheerfully left the Minnewaska. It was good to see the horses and mules when they landed on the Quay. They reared, kicked and rolled about. The poor animals had had a bad time on the ship for their standings were so small. Many horses and mules died on the voyage.

'We were led to a stretch of sand near the native quarter and immediately set to work to put up our tents. As soon as the tents were pitched we were free and set off

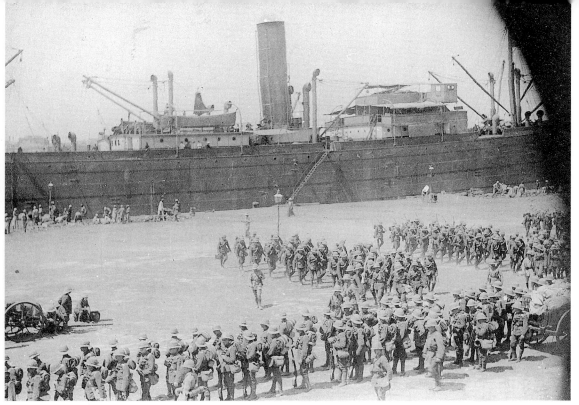

Prior to the arrival of the 31st Division Port Said had been the starting point for troops bound for Gallipoli. Here dismounted yeomanry board the ship that will take them to the Dardenelles.

for the town where we found cafes and restaurants. My friends and I were soon enjoying ham and eggs.'

Arab ways caused some amusement. Private Carter recalled seeing:

'a native strike a match on the sole of his bare foot. Evidently they are thick skinned in more ways than one.'

Guarding the Canal

The 31st Division had been sent to Egypt to counter a perceived threat to the Canal from Turkish forces and formed part of the Imperial Strategic Reserve. Two other divisions were scheduled to go to Egypt, the 14th and 46th (also part of the Imperial Strategic Reserve), both already fighting in France. The 14th never sailed and the 46th was recalled before it had fully disembarked. The reason that they were not needed in Egypt was because of the successful withdrawal of the troops at Anzac and Suvla. This would eventually result in the arrival of thousands of seasoned soldiers who would be available for defending the Canal Zone, even if they were only there temporarily.

At the start of the war, Turkey, although nominally a German ally and though she had mobilised her army, remained a neutral. However, the arrival of two German warships, which were then sold to the Turkish Navy and used by their German Commander to bombard Russian Black Sea ports compromised this neutrality. Accordingly, on 5th November 1914, Britain, France and Russia declared war on the Turkish Empire.

War with Turkey meant fighting on another front with all the logisitical and manpower problems this would bring. It also meant that access to the Black Sea would be stopped because the Turks would close the Dardanelles. There were two other possible threats that the British Government needed to take prompt action to prevent; the seizure of the Suez Canal which would make it difficult for Britain to remain in contact with her Empire and the possible loss of the Mesopotamian oil fields in which Britain had a large interest.

A typical souvenir bought in the bazaars of Port Said and Cairo. A miniature Middle Eastern rug mounted on a card to protect it during transit through the mail to England.

The recall of British regular troops from across the Empire to fight on the Western Front meant that there were few European troops to spare, especially as those Territorial Divisions which were ready for service were needed to garrison India. Initially, all that were available to garrison the Canal Zone were two Indian infantry divisions supported by three mountain artillery brigades and a cavalry brigade. Heavy artillery was to be provided by the British warships on station in the area.

If the Turkish army were to attack the Suez Canal its only way to do so would be through the Sinai Desert, for the British were able to control both the coastal route and the sea route. To counter the threat, the main land defences were on the right bank of the Canal in the Sinai desert and in order to reduce the number of troops needed, a cutting in the Canal bank was made which resulted in a large area of the desert being flooded at the northern end of the Canal.

Within just over two months of entering the war, British intelligence reports showed a large Turkish force was assembling, prior to crossing the Sinai Desert. The Turkish commander, Djemal Pasha, had as his main goal the temporary seizure and permanent closure of the Canal to ships. On the night of 2nd/3rd February 1915 the Turkish troops launched their attack but were resoundingly beaten by the Indian troops. Further attacks at dawn on the 3rd were similarly thrown back and by the 5th the Turks had left the area in full retreat, athough this latter fact was not known at the time. The allies then took the war to the Turks by attacking the Dardanelles.

When the Gallipoli campaign came to an end with the final, successful evacuation in January 1916 it freed large numbers of Turkish troops who could then be used against the Allies in Egypt or Mesopotamia. Egypt was the prime concern and consequently it would need reinforcing. Lt. General Sir George MacMunn in the *Official History of Military Operations – Egypt and Palestine* wrote that there was to be:

'*little delay in the reinforcement of Egypt, for Lord Kitchener was deeply impressed by the danger in store for the country when the hands of the Turks were freed*'

and that Sir J. Maxwell (GOC - Egypt Force) was to:

'*receive 250 machine guns, a welcome reinforcement, since he was particularly weak in this respect; and 2,000 rifles a week for the Australian troops, now arriving without arms. In the 8th Australian Brigade, for example, which landed in the first week of December, only ten per cent of the men had rifles. The ration strength of the Force in Egypt had by the 7th December risen, in round figures, to 100,000 men and 50,000 animals, but these still represented mainly drafts, transport and administrative services.*'

The problem was still a shortage of trained and armed troops to combat the supposed Turkish threat. Although technically, there were a large number of men in Egypt, MacMunn records that:

'*on the Canal at this date there were twelve battalions only*'.

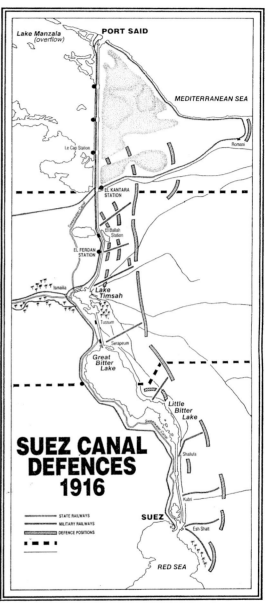

The Suez defences at the start of 1916. The Hull Brigade were stationed in Sections 3 (top) and 2 (middle).

In other words three brigades or nearly a division. This is when the 31st Division came in.

No more troops would be retained in Egypt than was necessary once the

B Company of the 11th Battalion. An alarm post at Point 140 in January 1916.

Two views of the 11th Battalion camp at Point 140, January 1916.

situation stabilised. In the meantime, in order to create an effective strategic reserve, it was necessary to reorganise the depleted and tired divisions from Gallipoli. The CIGS promised that everything needed to bring these divisions back up to war establishment would be sent from Britain as soon as possible. The army would provide the material while the good weather and some hard physical work and training would improve the morale and physique of the Gallipoli veterans. As part of the Imperial Reserve, the 31st Division would bolster the defences of Egypt, be the only British division completely up to strength and fully armed and be ready to move if the situation needed it, to some other theatre of operations. The majority of these divisions were to be sent to France when they were at war establishment. Included in this reserve were:

11th Division	(to France June 28th 1916)
29th Division	(to France March 15th 1916)
31st Division	(to France February 28th 1916)
46th Division	(to France February 4th 1916)
1st Australian Division	(to France March 22nd 1916)
2nd Australian Division	(to France March 16th 1916)
4th Australian Division	(to France June 3rd 1916)
5th Australian Division	(to France June 18th 1916)
New Zealand Division	(to France April 6th 1916)
42nd Division	(remained in Egypt)
52nd Division	(remained in Egypt and then to France in 1918)
53rd Division	(remained in Egypt)
54th Division	(remained in Egypt)
13th Division	(to Mesopotamia February 15th 1916)

The canal was divided into three sections, called sectors in military terms:

Number 1 Section (Southern) was responsible for Suez to Kalbrit and consisted of IX Corps commanded by Lt. General the Hon. Sir J G Byng. With headquarters at Suez it consisted of the 29th and 46th British Divisions and the 10th Indian Division.

The 10th Battalion canteen at Point 140, January 1916.

Number 2 Section (Central) was responsible for Kabrit to Ferdan and consisted of the Anzac Corps commanded by Lt. General Sir W R Birdwood. Its headquarters were at Ismailia and it consisted of the 1st and 2nd Australian Divisions and the New Zealand and Australian Division.

Number 3 Section (Northern) was responsible for Ferdan to Port Said and consisted of XV Corps commanded by Lt. General H S Horne. With headquarters at Port Said and advanced headquarters at Qantara it consisted of the 11th, 13th and 31st British Divisions.

Before commencing their first duty on active service the troops were given a few days to acclimatise during which they, like the other troops in the division, went sight-seeing and bought souvenirs for themselves and their friends and relatives back home. The strange sights and sounds took some time to get used to. However, there was always guard duty to do.

One priority, as was usual with soldiers, was food. When 92 Brigade arrived in Egypt the day's rations consisted of a tin of bully-beef and three sour Army biscuits. Even trading with the natives did not get them fresh vegetables and the meat that could be procured was inedible. The 10th Battalion history records that very soon after they settled in a native canteen appeared:

> 'conducted by Jim Irish, a very fat old Arab who dispensed his curious assortment of native sweetmeats whilst squatting in the midst of them, and who was reputed to have countless wives. This same wily Arab secured the catering for the officers' mess, which was a sort of Heath-Robinson hut with rush sides. At first he extorted an exorbitant figure per head for the poor food he provided, until a much-improved fare was secured by the simple expedient of refusing to pay him at all and then offering him less money, which he gladly accepted.'

Another view of the canteen at Point 140.

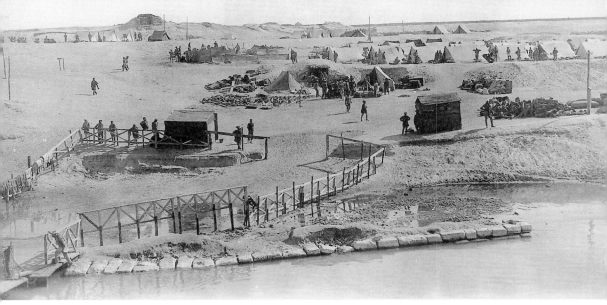

A view of the Indian camp on the side of the Suez as seen from a passing boat.

The Christmas of 1915 was certainly different from Christmas 1914; it was warmer and there was considerably less to eat. It was also a long way from home and it was hard for the troops of the brigade to dispel thoughts of home and the family get together for Christmas dinner; although this hardship was not so new to the 10th, who had spent last Christmas on the rifle range at Hornsea. According to the 10th Battalion history it was the day that the authorities unleashed a new type of biscuit on the unsuspecting troops:

> *'it was almost as big as a plate and nearly as hard, so much so that one bright spirit gummed a label to his specimen and sent it home through the post as a permanent souvenir.'*

On a more positive note all ranks of the brigade received a small brass box containing tobacco, cigarettes, a pencil and a small christmas card from HRH Princess Mary. The 10th Battalion had an English Christmas dinner arranged for them by the Rev. R M Kedward with music provided by the Leeds Pals. As the Leeds and Bradford Pals bands were also providing a concert at the Casino Palace it is likely that this is what is being referred to. However, not everyone could share in the festivities in the same way; there were still tasks that needed to be done. Private Tait wrote in his entry for Christmas Day:

> *'we had a jolly time among ourselves in the tent, being on duty we are not allowed into Port Said. Not one of us will forget this quaint Xmas of the year 1915.'*

The Christmas dinner had been provided in the European quarter which consisted

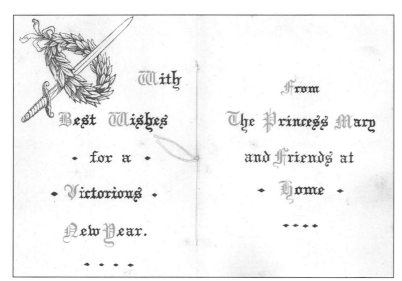

The Christmas card contained in the brass box from Princess Mary that all members of the brigade received. All members of the armed forces on the Western Front received these at Christmas 1914. There is no box dated 1915.

The delights of the Army Biscuit are illustrated by this cartoon.

Making 'Gooseberries' at Point 140, January 1916.

of fine spacious streets in direct contrast to the native quarter's dirty and unpaved streets. Because it was so different to anything that the troops of the 31st Division had experienced it had a special pull. However, it was put out of bounds to European troops because of the potential dangers. While there are no recorded instances of the 'Hull Pals' causing any trouble in the area or being attacked, there were instances of other units of the Division having problems. Milner in the *Leeds Pals* cites trouble in the Arab quarter on Christmas Day which is corroborated by the 10th Battalion history. A picquet composed of men from A and B Companies of the Leeds Pals were sent in to clear the area of troops. Private A V Pearson recalled:

> *'We were fallen in at the double and marched into Arabtown, 'belt and bayonet' as a company to clear the 'low dives' of Arabtown of all troops. A British soldier had been fished out of the Canal with his eyes gouged out. He had been set upon by Arabs in some back alley in the Kasbah.'*

After this brief and relatively uneventful period work started for the brigade. On 27th December at 7.30am B Company of the 10th Battalion left for a two week detachment to take over the defence of the Salt Works from the 39th Garwhal Rifles. This was a redoubt between the sea and the canal entrance on the east side. It was a series of outposts around the Salt Works that controlled the coastal approach to Port Said. The Salt Works consisted of a flat plain that was deliberately covered in sea water and then allowed to evaporate to leave behind the salt crystals. At the same time B Company also provided a strong guard for the petrol and oil depots in the area. Private Tait wrote of this change of scene:

> *December 27th 1915*
> *'B Coy leaves camp at 7.30 am and encamps at some salt works, 4 or 5 miles from Port Said. Means of conveyance – tug boats. No 6 platoon moves to an advanced position two miles away and is guarding the coast. The redoubt is built with sandbags and we are again under canvas, while on our front is barbed wire. We are away from anywhere but greatly enjoying it, as the sea is only a few yards away, presenting splendid bathing facilities. The only people we now see are three Indian Lancers, whose duty it is to patrol. Our food and water supplies are brought up by six camels, which were captured from the Turks in their last raid here. But life is plenteous whilst millions of beautiful shells are strewn on the sands.'*

Only a few days later Private Tait was complaining of the work and its effect on the men and the petty regulations and the inconsistencies of the officers:

> *January 7th*
> *'Reinforced by a platoon of R.E.s. Just what we need too! In the past we have been strengthening the redoubt during the day, besides being on guard four nights out of*

The 11th Battalion machine gun section at Point 140, January 1916.

five, which seems to be telling on our physical strength. Another inspection by the Generals, & Medical during the afternoon.'

January 11th
'Rations again very poor.'

January 14th
'On guard. The Batt (sic) are now training as keen as ever but we have the unwelcome task of cleaning buttons and equipment. What an absurd idea for active service! Why, the battn. did not do this, even in England! Our officers are very erratic and everything will have to alter before we are under fire.'

Private Tait further complained about his officers on January 29th:

'Complaint has been made by the officers that we are writing too many letters. It has been hinted by them that we are allowed too much free time. Are we a navvy's Batt. or a commercial? A most unnecessary complaint surely, could never have been harboured. We are entitled to our own time at night and as literature is very scanty what have we to occupy our time with? What delights us more than communicating as much as possible, with the old land?'

And on February 26th they were forbidden to send pictorial postcards.

For the few months that the brigade was in Egypt life was both monotonous and at times very hard and taking the entries in the war diaries of the four battalions into account, of very little consequence. There were no Turks to fight or accidental killings or deaths to record as in the other battalions of the division, just the continual movement of one battalion from one place in the desert to somewhere else in the desert to relieve either one of the Hull battalions or a battalion in another brigade. The brigade diary further highlights the monotony of this period:

Jan 1st to 8th
'Brigade doing mostly physical drill and route marches over the sand.
Weather cold, sandstorms prevailing.

Jan 9th
Warmer.

Jan 10th
12 noon. Return of detachments at Saltworks and Redoubt found by 10th, relieved by 12 Y &L.

Jan 19th
8.25am 10th left for Ballah by train finding following detachments –
one Company (A) to El Kab - one Company (C) at the Spit – half Company (D) at Swing bridge – half Company (D) at Point 50.8 (south of Kantara) – One Company (B) at Ballah.
12.50 pm 11th Battalion left for Ballah – one Company at Bir-Abu-Raidhar (three and a half miles east of Ballah). Both Battalions relieving 93 Infantry brigade.

Jan 21st
10th Battalion headquarters to Swing bridge; baggage transported on camels of CTC [Camel Transport Corps.] *359 L/cpl. Spikins M,D Company invalided to England.*

Jan 22nd
8.05 am 13th moved to Ballah; 12th moved to Ballah. Brigade supply ASC joined HQ.

Jan 24th
9.15 1 Company 11th left for Point 140 about 80 miles east of Ballah to commence work on first line defences. This Company picked up the Company at Bir-Abu-Raidhar. 50 NZRE [New Zealand Royal Engineers] *joined this detachment.*

Jan 30th
9am 12th moved to Sweetwater Canal to complete function of same with Suez Canal.
10am 1 Company 11th to Point 140.

Jan 31st
10am 1 Company of 11th and brigade HQ to Point 140.

Feb 2nd
2pm 1 Company 13th to Railhead due east of Ballah.

Feb 7th
11am HQ and 1 Company 13th to Railhead and 1 Company 12th returned to Ballah from SW Canal.

Feb 9th
2pm 13th to Artillery Hill via Railhead. 12th returned to Bullah from SW Canal.

Feb 12th
3pm Headquarters and 1 Company 12th returned to Ballah from SW Canal. One Company of 10th relieved at Spit post by DLI and proceeded to Kantara.

Feb 14th
10am Two Companies 13th to first line trenches between Point 66 and Point 102.
2pm Headquarters and two Companies of the 12th to railhead to replace the 13th.

Feb 16th
1.30 Headquarters 92 Brigade moved to Railhead.

Feb 19th
1 Company 10th moved from El Kab to Kantara.

Feb 26th
Headquarters and 1 Company of the 10th back to Kantara.
Feb 27th

The Indian camp on the bank of the Suez.

Rations arriving at Point 140.

Orders received for Brigade to move to France.

Feb 28th
Brigade Headquarters, 11th and 13th and two companies 12th returned to Ballah.

Feb 29th
7.25 am Brigade Headquarters and 10th (HQ and three Companies from
Kantara) to Port Said by train.
9.35am 12th left for Port Said by train.
11.40 am 11th left for Port Said by train.
2pm Four officers, 323 other ranks of 11th Battalion and four officers and 271 men
of the 13th sailed on HT City of Edinburgh.
2.30pm 13th left for Port Said by train.
4pm 26 officers and 694 other ranks of the 13th on HT Simla.

March 1st to 3rd
Sea calm – nothing to report.

March 4th
7.30am touched at Malta; received orders to proceed on voyage.

March 7th
1pm Marseilles Brigade Headquarters and 10th East Yorks and 2 and 1/2
Companies of the 11th disembarked.
10.30pm entrained for Pont Remy.'

In more human terms the 10th Battalion history is a little more forthcoming.
Initially the battalion was involved in a programme of general smartening-up, with

drill being plentifully interspersed with short route marches wearing only light battle order and no tunic. The battalion also provided guard details around Port Said and on neutral ships passing through the Canal to make sure that they did not drop mines.

Life in Egypt produced new problems. Cold wet winds blew sand into food, face and equipment. Dysentry reduced the brigade's efficiency with several men having to be treated in hospital and finally, the bane of the soldier's life in the Great War – the louse – finally caught up with the men from Hull:

> 'Many a packet of cigarettes was used up to give them a fiery exit, but all in vain: a permanent task was now added to the soldier's daily routine.'

While initially rations had been a problem the 10th Battalion history records that after the visit of General Sir Archibald Murray there was a distinct improvement in their rations:

Two different views of the Suez defences.

'It seems that GHQ had seen fit to place all troops arriving in Egypt on peace-time rations, but this was now rectified and we found ourselves on full field service rations, with jam, cheese and bacon.'

That this was a problem experienced by all in the division is shown by Laurie Milner in the *Leeds Pals* who quotes Private Yeadon:

'1 January 1916 – relieved from Guard 9.30am. Smashed a tooth with eating Army Biscuit... Rotten grub – Only Biscuits and Bully. Had this since leaving Port Said.'

Private Tait of the 10th Battalion, wrote in his diary on January 1st:

'Early morning – on guard
Afternoon off – bathing twice during the day. The rations are considerably short just now.
Menu: – Breakfast – Cheese & Jam
Dinner – Stew
Tea – Cheese & Jam.
We are allowed four biscuits per day and tea minus milk.'

And Private Bell of the *Leeds Pals*:

'For tea we drew lots for bread as some was mouldy. One slice per man was rations.'
All of this was in spite of the changed European soldiers' rations specified by the army from January 1st 1916:

Meat	1lb	Vegetables	1/2lb	Salt	1/2oz
Bread	1lb	Potatoes	1/4lb	Pepper	1/36oz
Tea	5/8oz	Sugar	1/4lb	Mustard	1/50oz
Bacon	4oz	Cheese	3oz	Jam	1/4lb

As the supply service could not guarantee these rations, alternatives were cited. Instead of fresh meat an equivalent weight of preserved meat could be substituted, that is Bully beef; 1lb of bread could be 1lb of biscuit or 3/4lb of flour; condensed milk at the rate of 1 tin for 16 men in lieu of the cheese ration.

As well as food, water was also a problem, as one would expect in a desert area. Each man had to exist on a:

'daily ration of one water-bottle for drinking and washing purposes and two for cooking!'

All the water that was used had to be transported along the canal from Port Said in small water-tank boats and then transferred to large tins which were carried on the

Ballah Station from the east, January 1916.

sides of camels to the forward troops. This was not just because water was scarce but also because the water in the Sweetwater Canal was not fit for human consumption because of the bacteria and parasites it contained.

93 Brigade issued an order regarding the use of horse trough water that shows how desperate the situation must have been at times for men to risk these diseases:

> *'drinking water from horse troughs is strictly against orders and officers commanding units will in future deal with these cases very severely. All men are to be informed that drinking this water will produce Red Water Fever, which is in most cases fatal.'*

The water may not have been drinkable but it came in handy for cooling the men down. Barnes mentions that the favourite pastime of Private Land, of the 11th Battalion, was standing in the Canal:

> *'Wearing only his helmet, he would stand up to his neck in water and enjoy a cigarette while watching Dutch ships sail by.'*

The 11th Battalion history records the taste of the water that was classed as fit for drinking:

'the most lasting impression that we got was the gritty feeling produced by over-chlorinated water, since the doctor, with true Scotch caution, put a double dose in the water tanks to make sure of killing all possible germs.'

Problems were not always of such importance as water or just confined to other ranks. No orders from 92 Brigade have survived from this period but the problems experienced appear to have been common across the division. Dressing 'in mufti' appeared to be a problem with some officers; as in the Second World War officers in the desert dressed in what was comfortable, not necessarily in what was regulation. 93 Brigade orders pointed out the corrrect apparel to miscreant officers:

'drab flannel collars of sealed pattern, drab flannel shirts, and a drab tie, fastened in a sailor's knot will always be worn with the service dress. Pins of any description are prohibited.'

And on the important issue of belts and coloured socks:

'GOC directs that belts should always be worn by officers when out of doors in Cairo, Alexandria and other towns. The wearing of coloured socks, and hunting stocks, and the carrying of hunting crops and fly whisks, is prohibited.'

The battalion diaries confirm the monotony of the existence but add a little more detail with the occasional personal reference that, in this case, shows the commercial origins of the 10th:

'Jan 2nd
9.05am 10/73 Pte. G Blenkin (signaller), C Company to Ismailia for duty as shorthand writer and typist with GHQ (Intelligence Branch), MEF.
10/745 Sgt. C Tennyson (MG section) C Company to Ismailia for duty as Instructor at MG School of Instruction established there.

Jan 23rd
2pm 16 Regimental Transport Drivers attached to 217 Company ASC. Conduct and work while attached formally commended in letter received from OC 31st Division transport.'

The 10th Battalion War Diary clearly highlights the differences between officers and men in its entry for February 28th. It is very unlikely that an other ranker would have been given the following freedom:

'Major W Glossop granted leave of absence for business reasons proceeded to England'.

He later joined the 14th (Reserve) Battalion.

The arrival of mail was a welcome break from the drudgery of serving in the Egyptian desert. Not only did it bring news from home but it often brought home comforts and food. Submarine activity was high in the Mediterranean and as a consequence a large number of ships were sunk and sometimes it was a ship carrying mail from England. Mail for the MEF was lost when the P&O liner, SS *Persia* (8000 tons) was sunk in December 1915 with the loss of 300 lives, including two Americans (America was still neutral at this time). As a result of this the Hull Pals did not receive mail until well into January.

92 Brigade did not even have the satisfaction of being out there, possibly facing any Turkish attacks. As the other brigades of the 31st Division moved further towards Palestine, the 'Hull Pals' merely followed in their wake, taking up the posts that they had vacated. These outposts consisted of shallow trenches surrounded by barbed wire entanglements which in theory were a formidable barrier to Turkish penetration.

A cartoon done by Private C Hirst for The Hull Daily Mail.

That this was not so was shown by the wandering of an escaped camel which managed to get through them with no difficulty. Trenches in shifting sand were very difficult to maintain and required constant repair. The 10th Battalion history records that as well as a constant eye being kept on the state of the trenches and for the appearance of Turkish troops at 'Stand To', an especially careful eye had to be kept out for unannounced visiting generals:

> *'The usual camp fatigues and an occasional quarter-guard were all the daytime duties we were called upon to perform on account of the mid-day heat, though a flying visit by Major-General Wanless O'Gowan, in his smart pinnace and attended by a fine bodyguard of Mysore Lancers, would suddenly cause an outpost to spring to life. In fact, inspecting generals were so common that almost as careful a watch had to be kept for them as for the enemy.'*

Even the capture of spies, who usually turned out to be Arab refugees, did little to relieve the boredom.

However, this move into the 'blue' did put the brigade near some marsh lands with abundant bird life which produced a welcome change in diet for some, especially the officers. The marshes contained many fish and these also supplemented the diet of those who mastered the art of casting nets.

Some Turkish activity was detected towards the end of January when the weather brought heavy rain and hail which blew down the tents and covered everything in sand. The Turks advanced their positions a little but there was no immediate prospect of battle. Even so, further defensive precautions were taken including the sending of further troops to the area, including the 6th East Yorkshires, pioneers to the 11th Division and recently returned from Gallipoli. Also stationed in Cairo were the East Riding Yeomanry.

Private Beeken recorded in his diary a strange nightly ritual in the desert:

'I was very interested in the operation of sweeping the desert. Every evening a large beam of wood was pulled, broadside on, by camels from one post to another post. In this way a broad smooth track was left on the sand, stretching the whole length of the east bank of the canal. At dawn patrols went out to see if any footprints were left in the smooth sand by any intruder. Nothing ever happened. No footprints were found.'

After the fall of Kut rumours abounded about a move to Mesopotamia which eventually came true. Orders were received which directed the 31st Division to proceed to that part of the world, but they were quickly withdrawn and the 13th Division went instead. Perhaps it had been numerical juxtaposition in the first place? At the end of February the division received orders to proceed to France and on the 28th, troops of the 31st Division handed over their posts and animals to the 52nd Division.

The brigade diary records the times of departure very exactly:

'February 29th
7.25 am Brigade HQ and 10th (Hq and three Companies from Kantara) to Port Said.
9.35 am 12th left for Port Said by train.
11.40 11th left for Port Said by train.
2.30pm 13th left for Port Said by train.
Four officers 323 other ranks 11th Battalion; 4 officers and 271 other ranks 13th Battalion sailed HT City of Edinburgh.
26 officers and 694 other ranks of 13th Battalion on HT Simla.'

The battalion diaries show the same sort of exactness and disinterest:

'Feb 29th - 11th Battalion
A B and half C Company and Battalion Headquarters on H T Tunisian i/c Lt.
Colonel Ford. Sailed at 6pm. D and half C and 6 horses on HT City of Edinburgh
i/c Major Wilberforce. Sailed at 8pm.'

The destination was supposed to be secret but the 11th Battalion knew where it was going:

'The fact that our helmets were changed for caps at Port Said left us in no doubt as to our destination.'

The Battalions leaving Egypt, although nominally the same as those that arrived in Egypt, were not the same. They had experienced active service, experienced hardships together and strengthened their bonds with the others in their units, be they fellow rankers or officers, they were fitter and wiser and in some small way they had contributed to the final drive into Palestine later in the war.

Not all of those who had arrived in Egypt were sailing to France. Some had already been returned to England and some stayed on in Egypt because they were hospitalised. The 10th recorded that it sailed with 33 officers, 6 Warrant Officers and

The 11th Battalion crossing the canal at Ballah en route for France, February 1916.

94

920 men (including Private Fisher of the 11th Battalion, who was the Chaplain's batman), leaving behind eight men in hospital and seven on attachment to the Bikanir Camel Corps and various other parts of the MEF. Private Collingwood, who was one of those left behind in hospital, caught up with the battalion on 18th March. Another soldier to rejoin the battalion later was Private Blenkin, who had been attached to the Intelligence branch of GHQ MEF; he arrived on 13th March.

Upon the departure of the 31st Division the GOC XV Corps, Lieutenant-General H S Horne, sent a message of thanks and congratulations:

> *'The Corps Commander, in wishing the 31st Division farewell and good luck, expresses his gratitude to all ranks for the good work they have done for him. It has been a great pleasure to him to be associated with such a capable body of officers and men. They have borne the brunt of the work in the XV Army Corps sector and have done wonders, and there exists a very fine spirit in the Division. He wishes all ranks the best of luck and hopes soon to have the pleasure of being associated with them again. He is confident that they will fight as well as they have worked.'*

The holiday was over. Real active service was about to begin.

Chapter 4

'Hush! Here comes a Whizzbang'
France 1916

According to the brigade diary, the journey to France was uneventful. The 10th Battalion history recorded that the weather was good for most of the journey and certainly on board HMT *Tunisian* there was more space and better food than on the outward journey. The horses had been left behind in Egypt and as a result conditions below deck were much improved. Private Tait in his diary felt otherwise:

> *'Part of the battn. are sleeping in bunks. No 6 Platoon being unlucky, we on the second lower deck, where sleeping accomodation is worse than experienced on the "Minnewaska". We have been issued with hammocks but there are only three hooks to a table of 14 men! There is nothing worth calling a canteen on board.'*

After passing Malta the weather changed. The sea became rougher and the temperature dropped, however, sea sickness was not the problem that it had been before because the ships were much bigger and less prone to roll and pitch. For some reason neither the 92 Brigade Diary or the 11th Battalion Diary recorded the death

British front line trench on the Western Front. Taylor Library

Port Said, February 1916. The 10th Battalion embarking aboard HMT Tunisian.

Left: Captain Ivor Jackson playing Shuffle-board on the officers' deck.

and burial at sea of Private Walter Edwards on March 6th (the first death on active service).

The men passed their time reading or playing cards with the occasional lifeboat drill. On March 3rd, Private Tait again recorded the distance he felt there was between the officers and the men. During the evening the troops were enjoying a singsong when it was abruptly stopped, with no reason given:

> *'Singing on board during the evening until stopped by the officers. Perhaps it is because it is disturbing them and their excellent repast!'*

As the boats approached France the weather improved and in the early hours of 7th March HMT Tunisian entered Marseilles harbour to a most impressive view:

> *'A glorious panorama unfolded itself early the following morning (after a farewell concert at sea by the combined bands of the 10th and 11th Battalions) as the Tunisian, passing the famous Chateau d'If entered Marseilles harbour. Ahead lay the port, in a gap between the gleaming white cliffs and backed by hills, surmounted here and there by the ruins of some old castle. In the distance the snowcapped Alpes Maritimes sparkled with a bluish tint in the glorious morning sun.'*

The first view of the port of Marseille-Chateau d'Ilf and the Frioul Islands.

To Lily with best love
Joe
March 10th 1916
Somewhere in France

A view of the docks where the Hull Brigade landed taken from the hills that surround Marseille.

Postcard notifying arrival in France.

After docking, the troops on board disembarked at 1pm and proceeded to the harbour station of the Paris-Lyons-Mediterranean Railway where at 10.30pm they entrained for Pont Remy. On the way they encountered their first German troops. Private Tait managed to get a short walk before boarding the train during which time he saw:

'a batch of German prisoners, working under an armed guard. They all appear ugly square-faced chaps, but possess splendid physique. An officer is among them but hangs aloof. What an expression he has - so miserable, feeling so idle! but as we look at him, he seems to snarl with rage.'

The next day, the remainder of the 11th Battalion disembarked and on the 9th both the 12th and 13th Battalions arrived and disembarked. As the 12th and 13th were entraining for Pont Remy, Brigade HQ and the 10th and two and one half companies of the 11th were already at their destination, Longpré-les-Corps-Saints, after a route march from Pont Remy. Unfortunately for the early arrivers there were no billets to be had so they had to wait in the snow until the Mayor woke up. On the morning of 12th March both the 12th and 13th Battalions caught up with the rest of the Brigade and proceeded to their billets in Airaines.

The journey to the Western Front took around three days, the trains moving so slowly at times that it was possible for a man to be left behind at one halt and catch the train up at the next. Unlike most troops travelling in France the men of HMT *Tunisian* were privileged to travel in third class carriages with compartments for eight men; 1600 men in total. It was a very long train, which moved very slowly and according to Private Tait: 'the train literally shakes one's life out'. What the men following travelled in is not recorded.

The train travelled along the Rhone valley, past Aries and Avignon; through Lyons and Dijon, past Versailles and on to St. Germain and Amiens before reaching Pont Remy. During the journey Private Tait recorded that:

'one is impressed by the politeness of the French. We are received with cheers everywhere. Girls throwing kisses, and the gentlemen raising their hats to us.'

The main street of Longpre-les-Corps-Saints in March 1916. The first destination of the Hull Brigade.

When the Hull Brigade arrived on the Western Front much of France was covered in snow and when the first troops detrained it was into a blizzard. Taylor Library

As well as the marked contrast between the scenery, there was also a marked contrast in the weather. Much of France was covered in snow and when the first troops detrained it was into a blizzard.

The whole division needed time to acclimatise and for the first two weeks or so this was achieved in the time honoured way of intensive training (in bitter cold). Although they had been trained only a few months before, there was a lot to learn about warfare on the Western Front: trench warfare, gas attacks, mining and bombing were some of the subjects that needed to be mastered before the brigade was fit for trench service. It is interesting to note that the arrival in France caused a rush of men to apply for commissions. In B Company of the 10th Battalion there were 56 applicants!

On arrival at their billets the men were able to receive their mail. Some of the news that arrived was not good. Private Graystone recalled the news of an air raid on Hull (5/6 March) and its effects on one soldier for whom the news was especially bad:

> '*his three sisters and father had been blown to pieces by a bomb. The lad is roaming about the village half distracted.*'

The raid caused damage to nine streets and killed 16 and wounded 52 people.

One problem that had to be beaten was soft feet. After a spell of duty in Egypt and a long journey, the brigade diary confided that after marching around 23 kilometres to billets in Vignacourt (10th Battalion were in Flesselles) the men's feet were: 'soft owing to recent voyage'.

Corroborating this, the 10th Battalion history records that the battalion medical officer, Lieutenant Fletcher, RAMC, held:

'a record sick parade as a result of the march, there being more than a hundred cases of blistered feet which had to be repaired before the next day's move.'

Private Tait noted in his diary entry for March 13th:

'First route march in France - 4 hours of damned torture! We march at a terrific pace - many drop out and much straggling is the result. Never the less the battn stick it well, but arrive back in an exhausted state. The band plays well, and helps us a great deal in keeping up. Many parade sick with bad feet.'

However, on the 26th, after another march to another set of billets, the brigade diarist was able to report that: 'all men stood the march much better'.

It was at this time that the brigade first experienced the rum ration. The 10th Battalion history records how one platoon commander lectured his men on the reason for the issue and how important it was for each man to receive only his exact ration. Upon declaring that any surplus would have to be poured away he spurred a number of men on to committing an offence. The battalion historian wrote that he:

A typical French town as the Hull Brigade would have experienced it; rather a contrast to Egypt and the journey from Marseille.

'hoped that he (the platoon commander) never knew how certain of his men, anxious to prevent this waste, paraded before him three times, first in tunics, then without, and finally in greatcoats.'

In the same vein, Private Tait records the first pay day in France:

'Paid in the afternoon 28/- (35frs) [£1.40]. Noisy scenes in the billets - many cases of drunkardness.'

Behaviour like this could result in disciplinary proceedings and for more serious cases a Field General Courts Martial. It was shortly after the Brigade's first spell of duty in the front line that there is a mention of such disciplinary proceedings occuring in 92 Brigade. The 10th Battalion War Diary entry of 8th April records that Captain Carrol was appointed a member of a FGCM which was to be convened at the Headquarters of the 11th Battalion on April 10th. Unfortunately it does not record why [see appendices for details of soldiers sentenced for desertion].

As well as being fit they also had to be properly attired. Some of the brigade had arrived on the Western Front wearing sun helmets which had become so wet that they resembled, according to the 10th Battalion history; 'corrugated iron'.

Private Tait recorded a route march on March 24th: 'Snowing nearly all day. - cold intense. Short route march through snowstorm, in sun helmets!'

Equipment was overhauled, replaced or dumped: 'at last we receive the trench caps, after the march'. At least there was no problem about food. Private Tait recorded that:

'the rations are very good - plenty of tinned butter, jam, army and navy rations, beef, etc. A liberal supply of bread'.

The Trenches
Before going into the trenches for the first time it was necessary for some members of each battalion to gain some form of trench experience. On 21st March ten officers and 40 men from each battalion went into the trenches for a 72 hour tour of duty with the 36th (Ulster) Division, commanded by Major-General Nugent, who had been the General Officer Commanding the Humber Garrison when the 'Hull Pals' had been in training. Captain Carver was one of the first officers to go into the trenches. He recorded in his diary that on the:

'afternoon of 22nd I was warned to go up to the line next day for instruction along with nine officers and 40 NCOs. Rather a curious feeling of mixed curiosity and "wind up", impossible to describe.'

British trenches in France.

On 27th March the 10th and 11th Battalions began the march towards their first tour of duty; marching to Engelbelmer to take over the reserve billets of 108 Brigade while the Brigade Major and Staff Captain of 92 Brigade took over the headquarters occupied by 108 Brigade. This was also the first time that the troops of the 10th and 11th had worn steel helmets, having been issued the previous day; they may have been issued to save lives but at what price? The 10th Battalion history records that:

> *'the unaccustomed weight made it impossible to wear them long without a headache and on no part of one's equipment would they ride comfortably.'*

A few days earlier the men had been issued with gas helmets for the first time. Private Tait wrote in his diary:

> *'First demonstration with gas helmets. What an ordeal! Just as though one is going through the first stages of chloroform.'*

The next day the two battalions moved into the trenches to relieve the 11th and 12th Battalions of the Royal Irish Rifles. A, C and D Companies of the 10th Battalion marched to Auchonvillers and entered the trenches to hold the sector in front of Beaumont Hamel with the 11th Battalion to their left and the 15th West Yorkshires on their right. In front of the 10th Battalion was Y-Ravine (this was to be an obective

The new steel helmets and PH gas masks took some getting used to. The helmets were heavy and caused headaches while the gas masks were claustrophobic and restricted the wearer's vision.

The German trenches were generally much better constructed and were designed to withstand considerable punishment. Note the grave and its close proximity to the cooking stove.

for 29th Division at the onset of the Battle of the Sorame, 1st July 1916. It was a deep ravine containing numerous German dugouts which could safely withstand the heaviest of bombardments).

Trench names in the area had a distinctly Essex flavour, with names such as Pompadour and Essex. Not that they were aware of it, but the area they were moving into was to become a very active front in less than four months' time – an area that would be engraved on British Military History for a long time to come – The Somme.

With half the brigade in the trenches, the remainder, the 12th and 13th East Yorks, remained behind the front in billets at Beauquesne. On the 28th, the 13th Battalion moved to Engelbelmer where 92 Brigade HQ was situated and the 12th Battalion marched to Acheux for billeting. On the same day 92 Brigade officially took over the sector from 108 Brigade and the war really started for the men from Hull.

There was a lot to learn about trench warfare but fortunately for these inexperienced battalions this was a quiet sector with only minimal interference from the Germans in the form of sniping and machine gun fire. However, trench mortar (Minenwerfer) activity seems to have been quite brisk at the am and pm 'Stand To'. As a result of this, both battalions suffered fatalities. On the 29th the 11th Battalion lost two other ranks, both killed by a trench mortar bomb (see appendices). The severity of the bombing resulted in five other ranks being admitted to a divisional Field Ambulance for shell shock. On the same day the 10th Battalion suffered its first casualty, Private Stanley Horsfield, of C Company, killed at dusk, by a trench mortar bomb explosion. This introduction to trench life and the first fatality were recalled by Private Aust of the 10th Battalion:

'Each dawn and dusk there was what was known as a "Stand To" when every man was stood at his "alarm post" ready for instant action. There was then a sharp artillery bombardment (known as a "strafe") of the trenches by both sides for some 10/15 minutes which then died down to normal. At each "strafe" Gerry sent over 3 "minnies" [Trench mortar shell]. At that time these were like five gallon oil drums filled with high explosive and shrapnel and you could see them turning over and over as they catapulted towards you - a very unnerving sight. Our first fatal casualty was caused by one of these. It was our battalion goalkeeper and a cynic is reported to have remarked, "he has stopped one at last".'

The battalion diary recorded the incident exactly:

'6.16 pm during Stand To - enemy fired three Minenwerfers - into trenches Q.10.9 killing one man. One failed to explode. Weather very cold.'

Shortly after this first tour in the line the division formed its own Stokes mortar batteries with the personnel coming from each of the four battalions. On 15th April the 10th Battalion transferred Captain Worsley and eleven men to 92/1 Light Trench Mortar Battery.

As darkness fell activity increased; rations would be brought up and parties sent out to mend or add to the wire and to reconnoitre in No Man's Land. In the 10th Battalion area there was a Royal Engineer Tunneling Company which was driving a sap under No Man's Land in preparation for a large mine which was to be blown just before the big offensive planned for the end of June. The reserve company of the battalion which was in the trenches came up each night to assist both the battalion working parties and the Royal Engineers. Lying out in front of the working parties was a protective screen of bombers.

Life in the trenches was very tiring but few were able to sleep properly. As a result, even during stressful times, it was easy to find oneself drifting off. Private Aust recalled just such an experience during this first spell in the front line:

'as a member of a Mills bomb team I had my first experience here of lying out in no-man's land as part of a protective screen for a wiring party. Gerry's trenches were about 100 yards from ours and we laid out in an arc some 2 to 3 yards apart. I remember I was about "10 o'clock" in the arc and at first thought about all the horrible possibilities. Amazingly after a few minutes lying there I found myself nodding off to sleep and when I felt the NCO's hand press on my back (the signal to withdraw) I nearly jumped out of my skin.'

Private Aust was a trained signaller but had been returned to his platoon for indiscipline and so he had volunteered to be a bomber while in England. After landing in France he found out how hazardous it was and returned to being an infantryman. (Bomb teams were known as the 'Suicide Squads'.)

Working in the tunnels was dangerous work; tunnels were countermined, they collapsed, were often invaded from an adjacent enemy tunnel and the air in them quickly became stale. Private Beeken recalled the hazardous work:

> *'I was in a party to help a Tunneling Company to drive a Sap under No Man's Land to the German trenches, to place a mine which was to be exploded on the opening of the Somme Offensive. Sappers made the tunnel and we had to drag the soil, etc in sand bags to the exit. This was very hard work for the tunnel was so low and narrow. The lighting was by candles held in place on the sides. We were each given a section of the tunnel and the bags were dragged in relays from one section to another and so to the mouth of the tunnel. Here the bags were emptied at night, the soil being thrown out of the trench.*
>
> *'One day we had great difficulty in breathing and the candles often went out. The following day a pump was placed in the trench and air was pumped to the far end of the tunnel.'*

One constant aspect of trench life was improving the trenches. In an area that had been fought over before, digging deeper was not always the most pleasant of prospects, as Private Graystone discovered when they had reached the original bottom of the trench:

Much of Tommy's rest time was spent doing working parties.

Sketches
of Tommy's life
Up the line → N° 2

The first trench I ever saw was an old communication trench where we were taken one night on fatigue. We did more star shells gazing than trench repairing that night !

Private Stanley Horsfield

Mr and Mrs Horsfield, of 12, Curzon-street, Newington, Hull, have received intimation that their son, Private Stanley Horsfield, of the Hull " Commercial" Battalion, has been killed in action.

The Rev. R. M. Kedward, the chaplain to the battalion, in a letter to the bereaved parents says;-

I write to express my deepest sympathy with you in your sad bereavement. Your son Stanley has given his life fighting for his country.

He died in the trenches on the evening of Wednesday, March 29th. He suffered no pain, as death was instantaneous. He is buried in a little cemetery just to the back of the lines. I will give you the name of the place as soon as the military regulations permit. He was a brave lad, and the first of our battalion to make the "great sacrifice " for Britain.

My heart goes out to you in your loneliness and sorrow. May the God of all comfort sustain you in this hour of trial. Again expressing the sympathy of all the officers and men;-

Yours faithfully, "R. M. Kedward, C.F."

Private Stanley Horsfield, who was 24 years of age, was prior to enlistment a painter and decorator in the employ of Mr J.H. Fenwick, Analby-road, and was highly esteemed by all who knew him. A lover of football, he played for the North Newington Church club as goalkeeper, and was chosen for the local Church League.

Mr and Mrs Horsfield have also another son with the colours in the Royal Engineers.

Hull News 5th April 1916.

Private Horsfield was the first 'Hull Pal' to be killed in action.

'we wish we had left the trench as it was, safe or not, for the stench coming out of the soil is horrible. It is discoloured with decomposed blood - enough to give anyone the fever.'

Along with various pieces of uniform and equipment (of the three nationalities that had fought over the area) bits of body and grave markers turned up. In this trench one soldier found a wooden cross that had previously marked the grave of 40 German soldiers. Further digging was not a pleasant thought as Private Graystone recorded:

'I hope we do not stumble across their bodies. I have seen one already and it was a ghastly enough sight for me.'

This was a quiet part of the front, where the troops practised a system of 'live and let live', where opposing troops held an unofficial truce. This is corroborated by Private Tait's Diary entry of April 2nd: Sketches of Tommy's life up this line:

> 'This battle front can be described as quiet. Engelbelmer is the headquarters of Right: Private Horsfield was the first 'Hull Pal' to be killed in action the Brigade and is not shelled or bombed, as there is a mutual agreement with the enemy that we shall not shell their headquarters and they shall not shell ours. It is a kind of a tit for tat business. If we send a bomb into their trenches they send half a dozen into ours. If we wish to remain quiet the enemy will do the same, hence we seem to have the upper hand. Certainly we have the advantage with artillery fire, for every six we send they can only reply with one. The only shell we really dread is their 'whizz-bang', which gives us no warning of its approach. It simply whizzes on the parapet, and the next second bangs into the trench. The enemy use their machine guns a great deal, especially for sniping. At night they practise sweeping afoot above our parapet with the above, and anyone with their head above, "goes west".'

On April 17th one such casualty was Private Hyde who was shot by a rifle bullet while in a forward sap.

Further evidence of the *laissez-faire* attitude of the Germans in this sector is provided by Private Graystone's experiences on 12th May when he was detailed to mend the wire at Post No. 7. As they would be visible to the Germans everyone was

The forward saps were very exposed places. Here a German officer poses in front of mobile barbed wire entanglements.

naturally nervous but they knew that the job had to be done because this particular post was a weak spot in the defences. Night work was generally done as quietly as possible to avoid detection but that night the group were particularly noisy because they wanted to get the job done. Even though they were making a noise there was no response from the Germans who had both seen and heard them. The answer was obvious:

> 'They had a party out among their own wires. They laughed and talked as they worked, so we followed suit. It was a case of tit for tat and the confidence of both parties - less than 50 yards apart - was surprising.'

When the Germans finished they returned to their trenches and a silence set in. Private Graystone's party knew it was time to go but they continued with their work waiting for the Germans to open up. They were very fortunate, for instead of putting down a barrage the Germans sportingly dropped flares where they were working to let them know that it was time to return to their own trenches. They took the hint and there were no casualties.

The darkness made things come to life or change their appearance and the temptation to move when flares went up had to be resisted. The 10th Battalion history recorded just this experience:

> 'on wiring parties or on patrol in "No Man's Land" at night the temptation to lie flat when German Very Lights went up had to be resisted, and we learned to remain motionless in whatever position we were caught, until the flare died away. We learned, too, not to lose our heads when a harmless group of tree stumps gradually assumed the appearance of an enemy patrol or a big rat creeping up to the trench would seem to be a man's head, and all the time a watch was kept for the mysterious "three green lights", there being a persistent rumour at the time that these were to be the signal for peace, which was supposed to be imminent.'

Private Surfleet experienced the work party in No Man's Land and the desire to drop to the ground when suddenly illuminated:

> 'Very lights were trying, it is so natural to want to duck as these terrors of the working party streak upwards, but our platoon sergeant told us to remain motionless. And what a sight it was over the top in the sickly glare of those lights. Everything seemed to stand out: the barbed wire, the posts, the shell-holes - all bare and desolate, a spectacle of utter devastation.'

On 18th April the 11th Battalion suffered their first officer fatality, 2/Lieutenant H Muir, who is listed as Killed in Officers Died in the Great War. His death in No Man's

Land resulted in a court of enquiry being convened on the 19th in the headquarters of A Company by Lieutenant-Colonel St. Clair-Ford. The first witness was Sergeant Gardham of the 11th Battalion, who stated:

> 'I was in charge temporary (sic) of a party of one NCO and four men who were going out to repair the wire in the evening of the 18th April 1916 about 9pm. We heard someone in the trench about six or seven yards in the rear of us. The noise was a kind of splash. We saw a dull outline in the corner of the trench. We waited a short time while I ordered three men to fall back thinking it might be a bomb thrower from the enemy. I challenged the man and received no reply. I challenged again, still no answer - not being quite sure that he was a German I ordered Pte. Wilkinson to fire above the man. The figure or man was stationary as if he was listening. I told Pte. Wilkinson to challenge again which he did, and again received no answer. Pte Wilkinson then fired. The man dropped down. Then a black shadow seemed to appear and we both shot again. Another man then appeared behind the man who was down. We challenged him and it turned out to be Lt. C.J Oake 11th East Yorkshire Regt. Lieut Oake halted behind the body and asked us what was the matter. I then told him what I had seen and done. Lieut Oake then looked at the body and recognised Lieut Muir and then sent for the stretcher bearers.'

Four pals of the 13th Battalion shortly after their arrival in France.

In his statement Private Wilkinson agreed with Sergeant Gardham but added that after they shot at the figure the first time:

> 'the man walked boldly towards us. He advanced about two yards, and I fired again... Lieut Oake then went up to it, and recognised Lieut Muir and said "Good God it is Harry".'

The relief sentry in No 5 Post heard both of the challenges but each time heard no reply. He stated:

> 'I then heard a shot go, I then heard a commotion as men talking in an exciting way (sic). Then I heard another shot, and then as if a bomb had been thrown. Then an order came down to extend along the trench, which we did and we then waited. The

stretcher bearers were called for and Lieut. Willmots patrol came in - and we then got to know what had really happened.'

Sergeant Norton on trench duty in the sector of the incident heard the first challenge of Halt! Who are you? and like the other witnesses heard no reply:

'No reply was made to the challenge, although it was given louder than it should have been. The challenge was again repeated, no answer the next thing I heard was a shot, and then another challenge, no reply, and a second shot was fired. I then heard a groan - after that two more shots were fired.'

Lieutenant Oake had been accompanying 2/Lieutenant Muir but had stopped to speak to some soldiers. On hearing the shots he took immediate action:

I concluded some Germans had got in, I rushed towards the spot, collecting some men as I went, we had Mills grenades with us, and then I heard another shot. I stopped my party and went around a traverse where I was challenged. I gave the countersign and I saw a man kneeling with his rifle pointed at me... I proceeded about two yards towards him when I saw a figure on the ground in the trench, between myself and Pte. Wilkinson. The figure was in a crouching position, suspicious of him, I ordered Pte. Wilkinson to cover him with his rifle, and advanced to it when I recognised Lieut Muir... Pte. Wilkinson had not the slightest knowledge or suspicion that the man on the ground was one of his own officers.'

A cartoon from a 1916 issue of Punch *magazine.*

THE INCORRIGIBLES AGAIN.

"BIT OF LUCK WE WEREN'T SENT TO EGYPT. HEAR IT'S A ROTTEN PLACE—ALL DUST AN' HEAT AND SNAKES AND THINGS."

Night time artillery flashes.

Lieutenant Irvine, the battalion doctor, carried out an examination when the stretcher bearers brought the body to him. He stated that on arrival he found:

> *'life to be extinct. The bullet had entered obliquely through the right lung, and had emerged at the lower part of the spine. The bullet was found lying underneath the clothing. The lower part of the spinal column was badly shattered and death must have been almost instantaneous.'*

The final witness called held the vital piece of evidence. Private Charles Bogg stated that previous to the shooting of Lieutenant Muir:

> *'Lt. Muir had passed me, who was on sentry No 2 post. I challenged him twice, and he was almost on the point of my bayonet, before he mumbled the countersign.'*

The court of Inquiry concluded that:

> *'he was unfortunately shot thus failing to answer when challenged.'*

Accidental death at the hands of one's own comrades was not uncommon. Private Surfleet recorded a similar incident in the 13th Battalion:

> *'One of our sergeants went out on patrol just in front of our line. They had done their job and were coming in when, owing to a misunderstanding over the password, our company Lewis gunners opened fire, killing the sergeant and two men. They had got no reply to their challenge; raids by the enemy were very frequent then so, fearing an attack, they thought to do their duty by opening fire on the supposed raiders.'*

Such tragedies cast long shadows over the participants.

On the 30th the brigade diary recorded a quiet day with just four other ranks casualties; Private George Wells, of the 10th was killed by a sniper, three other soldiers were hospitalised, two of them (in the 11th Battalion) suffering from shell shock, one with the 10th being hit by a shell splinter.

B Company of the 10th Battalion had been left in reserve and was called up to the front line as a working detail. Private Tait recorded that:

> 'being our first time under fire many of us are in no joking mood. Directly we enter trenches we see Wells of C Company being carried out dead (our second casualty). This upsets us a great deal, as he is a terrible sight.'

During this tour in the front line the battalion was visited by their Brigade Commander, Brigadier-General Parker, and Brigadier-General King of the relieving brigade.

During the night of the 31st March/1st April the 13th Battalion relieved the 11th Battalion and four Officers and 25 NCOs of the 12th Battalion went into the trenches with the 10th Battalion. Prior to this relief the trenches of the 11th had been heavily shelled during the 'evening hate' (a regular time when the Germans would strafe the British trenches). This shelling rapidly took its toll on officers and men. The 10th Battalion War Diary recorded:

> 'May 11th
> 1 other rank suffering shellshock
>
> May 12th
> 1 other rank suffering shellshock
>
> May 13th
> 10 wounded (shellshock), 2 other ranks wounded - shrapnel 1 other rank wounded (accidental).'

The relief of a battalion was a complicated procedure and resulted in both brigade and battalion orders detailing the exact procedure to be followed and the passwords to be used when the relief was complete. 92 Brigade Order 7 of 31/3/16 among many instructions included:

> '3. The cookers of the 11th Battalion will be handed over to the 13th Battalion and vice versa.
> 4. The 11th Battalion will provide 1 guide per platoon to be at HQ of 13th Battalion at 6.30pm to lead Company as detailed; also guides for battalion HQ and reserve platoon on night of 1/2nd and guides for cooks on both nights.
> 7. The 11th Battalion will arrange to hand over steel helmets to 13th Battalion on arrival in trenches.'

Examples of the passwords used are contained in the 13th Battalion War Diary for November 1917. On November 25th when they were to be relieved by the 11th Battalion the battalion orders indicated that:

'Completion of relief will be notified by wiring the following code phrases:
  A coy   Already forwarded
  B coy   Will send the same
  C coy   Sent this morning
  D coy   Do not require any.'

Almost immediately after relieving the 11th Battalion, the 13th Battalion had its first fatality, Private George Watts. Work on the tunnel continued while the 13th were in occupancy and the only other notable experience of their first tour in the front line happened to the tunnel. At 2pm on the 3rd a trench mortar bomb exploded in the entrance to the tunnel sealing it off. Inside were 21 men (six Royal Engineers and 15 other ranks of the battalion) who were buried alive. Fortunately, there were no fatalities and all were rescued safely.

On 6th April the 12th Battalion was called up in support during a particularly heavy enemy bombardment of the front line trenches but no attack followed so the battalion returned to its billets. After a further six days in reserve the battalion occupied the front line trenches for the first time on the 12th. On relief after only four days the battalion had suffered eleven dead, some dying of wounds many days later (Soldiers Died in the Great War only lists ten), and twelve wounded.

Tours in the trenches were a steady drain on the numbers of men. In early May the 12th Battalion lost 6 killed and 8 wounded and between the 21st and 29th, after particularly heavy bombardments of the trenches, 2/Lieutenant R N Taylor and 21 other ranks were killed with 2/Lieutenant J Hirst being wounded along with 54 other ranks. Similarly, during two spells in the line during April and May, the 13th Battalion recorded Private George Major being killed in action by a German rifle grenade on April 14th and the deaths of four other ranks (Privates Johnson, Langford, Preston and Rose) on May 25th and a further death from wounds the next day (Private Allatt). On April 16th the 11th Battalion had one sergeant killed (Sergeant Heseltine) and two privates wounded by shellfire. The next day Private Tennison was accidentally killed, while on the following day Lieutenant Muir was killed and a private wounded accidentally.

Sniping was a constant, slow drain on the manpower of both sides. Private Graystone of the 10th Battalion recorded in his diary how it affected his daily life:

'Several Germans had come out undercover of darkness, planted themselves in shell holes and behind tree stumps and were promising themselves a good day's work. One of them had crept up to no 6 Post and thrown bombs which made a considerable

miserable mess. Another tried to do the same thing with our post, but we heard him creeping through the wires and emptied our magazines into the place where we thought he was and he never bothered us again.'

Examining the wire was dangerous, even at night, for snipers of both sides were always on the look out for an easy target. Private Graystone had a lucky escape one night which he found out about from a patrol of the 11th Battalion:

'I was within an ace of being shot down last night without knowing it. When I climbed over the parapet at midnight to examine the wire, a 2nd Hull sniper spotted me and thinking I was a German, brought his rifle up to shoot. Just as he was pulling the trigger, his corporal who had seen me leave our lines knocked the rifle aside. And I was blissfully unconscious of it, and congratulating myself on how safe I was.'

An advert for a collapsible pocket periscope.

The periscope was the only safe way of seeing what the enemy was up to during the day. On 12th May Private Graystone recorded what he saw through the periscope that morning: 'according to the German flag post (which was flying a different brigade flag), we have been relieved during the night'. According to the Germans they had been replaced by a battalion from another brigade in the division. Generally the information given was correct – but on this occasion it was not.

The Germans also had a notice board that they used to send messages on a daily basis to the opposing troops. The message for 12th May, written in perfect legible English was: 'Peace in three weeks'. The day before it had been:

'"France is beaten, Russia is beaten, England is beaten and Germany is beaten. Let's throw up the sponge!" All their messages show how utterly fed up they are with the war. And what is more, they know that we are too!'

Sometimes the message would be humorous:

'We have more bombs in this trench than you have in the whole of England.'

Troop losses were not only the result of enemy action. There were constant transfers to other battalions of the regiment who were short of men; small numbers of men were transfered to the Trench Mortar batteries as they were formed and to other units in the Division and Corps; men were sent back to England because of their value to munitions production and as the casualty lists grew, more and more under age troops were sent home from the four battalions. Their return was usually prompted by their parents; as no birth certificate had been needed to enlist there were a considerable number of underage soldiers – all the parents had to do was to prove that their son was underage. The 12th Battalion recorded losing the following underage soldiers:

'August 1916 - 7 other ranks to base
September 1916 - 5 other ranks to base
December 1916 - 2 other ranks to base.'

One such underage soldier was Private James C Tait who had joined the Depot Training Camp of the 10th Battalion on April 19th 1915 at the age of fifteen and a half along with his step-brother, Frank Cocker. As no birth certificate was required and he was of the required stature and looked old enough he had no trouble joining up. After training with the depot he joined the battalion at Ripon prior to moving to Salisbury Plain and then Egypt. After three months' service in France he was discharged as underage, probably because his parents had requested his return. He recorded the events in a diary that he kept at the time:

'Monday June 19th Trenches cancelled.
Expects to go in on Wednesday. See Col. re my discharge. 4pm leave Acheux by train - destination 31st Div Base Etaples. I leave old Battalion with regret but nevertheless I am Happy to think I am going home. Home! - What luxury that word implies. I am very sorry for Frank, as we have always been keen pals together. 10pm - arrival at Abbeville where we wait in station.'

'Tuesday June 20th
Still in station. Plenty of eatables obtainable but funds low. There is a splendid Expeditionary Force Canteen here. We are not permitted to go into town. Leave Abbeville at 2.30pm and arrive at Etaples 4.45pm. It is a huge camp in very pretty surroundings. There are numerous YMCAs, Regt. Institutes, clubs, etc. The whole place is simply packed with soldiers, mostly Australians & Scotchmen (sic). I spend the night in a decent Bell tent.'

I WONDER WHEN THE BLINKIN' TIDE GOES OUT TED.

For many months of the year the trenches were either full of mud or literally knee deep in water.

PREVENTION OF "FROST-BITE" OR "CHILLED FEET."

1. All Officers and Non-commissioned Officers should make themselves acquainted with the following facts, in order that an effective system for the prevention of this serious ailment may be established and understood by all units which have to occupy trenches in cold or wet weather. It has been shown that when troops newly exposed to these conditions have not followed the precautions observed by more experienced and seasoned units, disastrous consequences have followed. It is, therefore, necessary to explain what has been the result of the best experience so far.

Main Principles.

2. The main principles to be observed are :—

(*a*) To put as few men as possible in trenches that are wet.

(*b*) To keep them there for only short periods without relief (not exceeding 12 hours, if practicable).

(*c*) To give them special treatment both before and after their tour of duty.

(*d*) To keep boots always well oiled or greased, and to avoid tight boots or putties which interfere with free circulation of the blood.

(B 3425) Wt. w. 11735—1550 1,500M 2/15 H & S P.15/63

Wet feet could lead to all sorts of problems. This is a 1915 leaflet designed to help. Men who were detailed for prolonged duty in wet trenches were supposed to be stripped below the waist and (under strict supervision of an officer or NCO) were to thoroughly smear and rub their feet, legs and, if necessary, their bodies with animal fat such as whale oil.

Friday June 23rd
Leave Etaples by 3.43pm train. Arrived at Boulogne late - dash for boat and just manage it. Across the Channel within an hour and a half - Arrival at Folkestone. Leave Folkestone 8.15pm. Arrive Victoria 11pm. Departure from Kings Cross 11.45pm. 4am -Arrival at York. Wait for 6.35am train to Beverley. Arrive at Beverley at 8am and proceed to the Victoria Barracks [Regimental HQ in Beverley] where I secure a good breakfast. Immediately after breakfast I enjoy a delightful bath and change into civilian clothes. I am put into A Coy for the time being. All I am waiting for are my papers.

Friday June 30th
In civilian life - once more!'

A similar slow drain on manpower is also shown by the figures for officer training; men who would be sorely missed by the battalion. This is shown by the figures in the 12th Battalion War Diary:

'July 1917 - 1 other rank to Officer training
August 1917 - 1 other rank to Officer training

September 1917 - 1 other rank to Officer training and 1 to 8th EYR for commission
October 1917 - 3 other rank to Officer training
November 1917 - 5 other rank to Officer training
December 1917 - 5 other rank to Officer training.'

Food was a very important part of the soldiers' life and its production also proved a drain on the trained soldiers of the 12th Battalion. In November 1917 the battalion sent four other ranks to England because they were skilled ploughmen. The 10th Battalion recorded the loss of five men on 2nd May because they had been sent to Etaples for dental treatment. This was followed on the 20th by fourteen more.

Sickness and the conditions the men existed in also took their toll, even when every precaution was taken for this not to happen. April was a very wet month. The 11th Battalion Diary recording on the 17th:

'situation normal - heavy rain and trenches waterlogged.'

And on the 18th:

'Continuous rain (heavy).'

The situation was just as bad in the trenches held by the 10th Battalion. Their war diary records that:

'Mark trench fell in in parts during day owing to heavy rain causing subsidence and it was impossible to clear and prevent further subsidence. A coys trenches at night completely waterlogged. Working parties could not work owing to state of trenches. Three officer patrols out at night exploring No Man's Land and wire.'

On the 22nd Captain Watson wrote home to his parents telling them that it had:

'not stopped raining for more than a couple of hours for over a week and the trenches in places are waist deep in water.'

The situation had not really improved much by May. The bad weather and the attentions of the Germans made life very unpleasant in the trenches but there was worse – duty in Post No. 7, to which Private Graystone recalled:

'It was from this post that the 3rd Hull stampeded a fortnight ago when my cousin was killed and eleven injured.'
'When we arrived at this spot we found it was even worse than expected. It was quite isolated and the Germans were shelling it quite relentlessly.'

The only warmth was provided by the rum ration. After the attack on the Ancre on November 13th, Private Surfleet of the 13th Battalion described another reason why it was necessary:

'That rum, too: many folks at home might think it unnecessary or even improper, but anyone who has to endure the hardships, the devastation and the horrors... is only too glad of it... of something to produce oblivion, to blot out the misery of the very recent past so that his mind can rest, until the next time.'

Conditions in the trenches were so wet that the men's feet suffered very badly. The 10th Battalion history records that whale oil was used to no avail:

'we conscientiously rubbed our feet with whale oil, but this did not stop the occurrence of "trench feet", a number of the more serious cases being sent out of the line to hospital.'

For those of the brigade who were unable to return to civilian life, the remainder of the war was to follow a constant pattern of time in the trenches, followed by either a period in reserve for the brigade or periods

Albert was the closest town of any size to the area where the Hull Brigade first went into the trenches. The Golden Virgin on top of the church in Albert is an icon of the Great war. This is how it looked when the 'Hull Pals' arrived.

of 'rest' out of the line with the whole brigade and occasionally with the complete division out of the line for a prolonged rest.

Rest is perhaps the wrong word to use for a period of prolonged physical activity in which troops would go back to the line carrying materials required at the front or help in laying wire or digging trenches or making roads; a rest which might have been only marginally better than being in the trenches. The 10th Battalion history records their first experience of such activities while in 'Rest':

'we were now to have our first big experience of supplying working parties to the trenches by night. Strong parties spent their time nightly under the REs, either in pushing trolleys laden with coils of barbed wire, "corkscrews", "concertinas", "gooseberries", and "sump boards" down the light railway from Euston Dump to the support lines, or else they filled in the dark hours with the eternal digging, stumbling

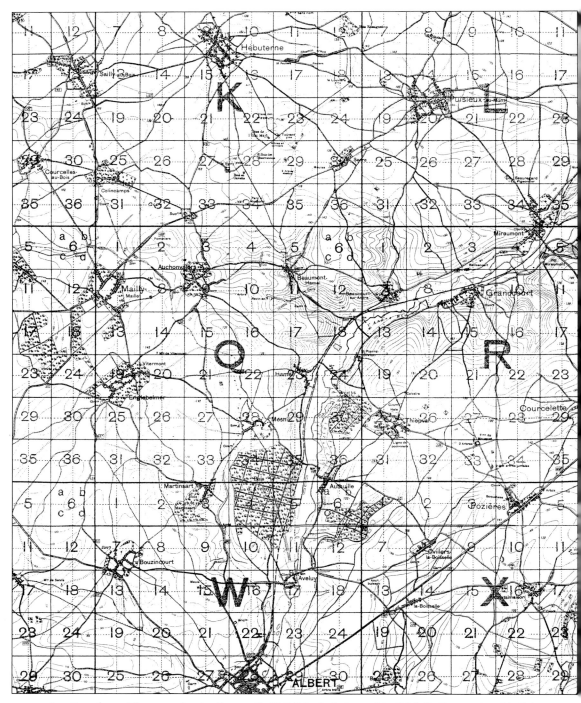

A section of an artillery map showing the area the Hull Brigade first served in: Q 10. On the morning of 1st July 1916, first day of the 'Big Push', the brigade was in reserve at K 27b /28a for the attack on the German fortified village of Serre.

back with picks and shovels to their cosy barns miles away in Courcelles at dawn. Almost did it seem better to be holding the line.'

[Sump boards – slatted planks for the bottom of the trench; Concertinas - wire used for entanglements, when touched it coiled about the intruder – usually barbed; Corkscrews – metal stake for supporting barbed wire which screwed into the ground – little noise during fixing; Gooseberries – reels of barbed wire used as an entanglement.]

However, by May 2nd with work details in the day, Private Tait was able to write:

'on permanent day working party to continue for 15 days. Back early and spend evening rambling through some woods. How could one imagine a war existing when everything appears so peaceful?'

During periods like this little further training was possible; it was during the resting of the brigade that tidying, cleaning, drilling and training time were made available. Rests like this, at the least, gave the men time to go to the brigade baths and to have their clothes and blankets temporarily deloused. On 28th April the battalion received 1000 blankets back from the visiting Foden disinfection truck which paid them a visit.

Having only suffered three fatal casualties by the beginning of June, the 10th Battalion had started to get a reputation for being lucky, especially as they always seemed to experience the heaviest bombardments and managed to come through safe and still smiling. Private Graystone recalled one particular tea-time strafe:

The remains of a British trench after a short German bombardment.

'They smashed up half our front with whizz-bangs, and gave us the biggest shaking up it has ever been our fortune to receive. I quite expected at any moment to see our parapet come flying down - with us underneath. A lot of the shells brought us to our knees and some flat on our stomachs, but almighty God spared us... we are earning the name of the "Lucky Tenth".'

Daily strafes were a constant drain on manpower and on the men's nerves; the death and destruction were indiscriminate, affecting both the experienced and inexperienced. A strafe by one side brought about a return strafe. Private Graystone recorded the results of such a strafe on his battalion on 1st June. The German retaliation destroyed three bays and resulted in a number of casualties, two of which were fatal; these were brought to Basin Wood and left there for later burial. One of those killed had only just arrived in the trenches, while the other was a sergeant temporarily attached to the battalion, who had been at the front since August 1914. He had died from a head wound caused by a grenade while the man who had been standing next to him had his steel helmet on, according to orders, and had survived with a wound. What made the incident even more tragic was that the sergeant had only two weeks of his pre-war engagement to serve and then he would have been entitled to go home.

Death in the trench created problems for those left alive. What do you do with a corpse when it is daylight and you are unable to leave the trench to bury it? The answer was to leave it lying around in the trench, which could be very distressing for those around, as Private Graystone recorded in his diary:

'The two bodies (killed earlier in the morning) have been lying beside us all day in a pool of blood. It is a pity that they cannot be buried at once for the sight of them is a severe trial to the nerves of the strongest. They lie there - an awful lesson of war. May God send us peace!'

The remains of the sucrerie near Colincamps. It was here that a cemetery was set up to bury the men killed in the fighting in front of Serre.

And on May 31st Private Graystone experienced the death of a friend [Private Gait]:

'It has been rather dismal looking today, for we have had the dead body of an old pal lying alongside of us all day - awaiting burial at dusk. It is hard to look on the dead face of one with whom we used to laugh and talk during those happy times at Hornsea and Ripon'.

While the general message of the area seemed to be one of live and let live there were bursts of the 'an eye for an eye' mentality. After the death of the two soldiers on June 1st, the 10th Battalion demanded retribution, which they got. The retribution was carefully planned and timed for the afternoon and required large quantities of ordnance in the shape of Stokes mortars, ammunition, bombs and 'footballs' to be carried to the front line – everything that was needed to give the Germans a 'warm time'. Private Graystone described the scene:

'Machine guns were trained on all the enemy's communication trenches to stop them running from the front line when the strafe began. Punctually at 2pm the first "football" was fired, so we craned our heads over the parapet to watch the fun. I have never seen the German trenches fly up in the air so much as they did today. It was a great sight and we were all exultant at getting a bit of our own back.'

The resulting gaps in the German parapet were carefully noted by the machine gunners. German working parties that night would be targeted as they toiled to repair the damage.

Living in a tit for tat environment meant retaliation of an unknown quantity:

'Our little effort over, the Germans commenced their bit. It was a "bit" too, consisting of a few coal-boxes, for they are palpably short of ammunition.'

Such action resulted in casualties; the lucky wounded received a 'blighty' ticket:

'One man came walking out of the line with a big gash in his cheek and a broken jaw but he was still smiling.'

Flying earth covered men and inflicted mental wounds:

'There were several cases of shell-shock caused by the explosion of a coal-box which buried half a dozen men.'

In this particular incident they were lucky, their comrades were able to dig them out without any of them suffering physical injury.

British burial party with padre conducting a brief service.

The dead were buried behind the lines and troops marching back to the trenches after a period in reserve often had to pass the cemetery in which their comrades were buried. Going back into the line during June, Private Graystone recorded the scene experienced by the battalion as they marched past Sucrerie Cemetery one crisp June morning:

> *"There were dozens more white crosses erected, and several parties of pioneers were still opening new graves. Nearby lay the bodies of several poor lads awaiting interment.'*

Death in the trenches was random, as evidenced by Private Graystone's experience of a German barrage which resulted in a large number of casualties in the battalion on the flank of the 10th Battalion – the Leeds Pals. Throughout this barrage his section was working on the parapet of their trench and did not incur a single casualty.

The 31st Division appears to have practised an offensive war from the very beginning. The diaries of the four battalions of the brigade contain numerous entries regarding successful and not so successful trench raids. Trench raids were designed to bring the war to the Germans, to provide intelligence about positions and equipment, to provide identification of the troops facing the division and also maintain the offensive spirit in allied troops. These raids could also result in large numbers of casualties, sometimes with nothing to show for all the effort.

On 27th June at 10.30pm, as part of the build-up for the Somme Offensive, a raiding party from the 11th Battalion, consisting of Captain Stevenson, Lieutenant Saville, 2/Lieutenants Caley, Hall, Haworth, Hutchinson and Oake, plus 97 other ranks from D Company, attempted to raid the German trenches. The battalion war diary recorded that they were unable to get through the German wire and when they were spotted:

> *'a sharp bombing encounter took place which lasted about five minutes which seemed to have been successful. Second Lieutenant Hall showed conspicuous gallantry.'*

Casualties on the German side are unknown but for the 11th Battalion consisted of 2/Lieutenants Hall, Hutchinson and Oake being wounded and sent to the Field Ambulance, while 2/Lieutenant Caley was wounded but was able to stay on duty. Sergeant Cox and Private Sawden were killed, one other rank was missing and one sergeant, two lance-corporals and two privates were wounded.

Similar results were achieved on the next two nights by the 12th Battalion which sent out a raiding party with Lieutenant Crabtree in charge of a party of 80. The intention of the raid was actually to enter the enemy trenches, but the party was spotted and heavy fire resulted in the raiders retiring to their trenches. This was repeated on the next night with dire consequences. The party was stopped by the enemy wire and again heavy fire caused their premature return. Lieutenant Crabtree was killed, 2/Lieutenant Drewett was listed as missing, believed killed, 2/Lieutenants Moncrieff and Morgan were wounded, Privates Archbutt and Roo died of wounds, two other ranks were posted as missing and 15 were wounded.

A typical British cemetery just behind the front-line. This one was at the Menin Road, Ypres.

Trench raids could also bring down retribution from the enemy even if the raid had been carried out by another battalion. On 3rd June the 11th East Lancashires from 94 Brigade sent out a raiding party with the two-fold intention of capturing a prisoner and wreaking as much damage as possible in the short time they would be in the German trenches. It was anticipated that the enemy would retaliate and that, owing to the poor condition of the trenches in the sector, casualties to A and C Companies would be heavy. Permission was requested for the troops in the front line to be pulled back to the new assembly trenches just behind the front line for a few hours to reduce casualties. Permission was denied, with catastrophic results.

After six days in the first line they were given twenty-four hours more to cover a raid by 94 Brigade, who were practising for the coming offensive. At dusk a strong party of dark-faced raiders appeared in the 10th Battalion trenches armed with revolvers, Mills bombs and domestic axes. Exactly on midnight the British barrage opened on the enemy front line. When the barrage advanced at 12.30, the raiders, already in No Man's Land would also advance. According to the 10th Battalion history:

Sergeant Thomas Huntington of the 10th Battalion died of wounds sustained during the bombardment.

Trench raiders often carried coshes as well as rifles and revolvers.

'hostile retaliation was prompt and heavy, and continued until 1-40, some twenty minutes after our guns had ceased, and every available German gun seemed to be firing on the short sector held by A and C Companies. The front line trenches were blown in almost beyond recognition, scarcely a fire-bay remaining intact. As expected, casualties came rapidly, but the men stood up heroically to a rain of shells to which they could not reply.'

One survivor was Private Aust who recorded that the barrage of 3rd/4th June was his first experience of a really heavy barrage:

'after about three minutes the German counter barrage came down and Bill Busby (my aptly named co-sentry and a fine soldier) and I spent most of our time being blown off the firestep and climbing up again.'

Private Tait, underaged and a few days short of discharge from the army, also experienced the barrage:

'We were warned beforehand of the bombardment and we all are compelled to Stand To. No one who has not been through such a "hell" can possibly conceive any idea of its devastation. It was a very hell upon earth. The shells screech overhead creating a weird sensation. B Coy was in the second line and we had many narrow escapes. You hear an approaching shell screeching through the air. It comes overhead and then one calls up one's utmost nerve power to withstand the shock. There is a flash across the eyes, then a deafening report, followed by part of the parapet tumbling on top of one. I think several times that it is the last time I shall see daylight. The strafing was appalling. This lasted for an hour and then immediately afterwards we rushed down to the front line to dig the poor fellows out.

What a sight! Dead and wounded are strewn everywhere. The front line is blown to hell. Soon wounded were being carried out; - some on stretchers, others struggling along with the help of a comrade. Very few stretchers were available. The dead are thrown aside until the wounded are all away. It was a veritable nightmare!

'Casualties - 26 killed and about 60 wounded.

'We are relieved at 6 pm but parties remain behind to bury our dead. The burial ground is under a typical French Avenue just behind the third line...

'Everyone presents a sad aspect and how keenly we all feel the loss of our comrades!'

An unknown survivor of the barrage recorded his experiences in the front line:

'It is difficult after twenty years to remember all the names, but I know I was in a bay with six men. Within a few minutes of the opening of the bombardment, a shell fell immediately behind the trench and two men were hit. One, Tich West, who was next *to me, was struck high up in the back. Lifting him, I placed him across my knee and was endeavouring to rip his tunic to fix his field dressing when another shell blew in the parados, burying us all. Fortunately, the trench had been banked up with a lot of new sandbags, so that for a few minutes at any rate, some air came through the crevices, which would not have been the case if the parados had been of earth alone. I was buried in a kneeling position, grasping a man I then knew to be dead. One forgets time in such circumstances, and how long I was so fixed I do not know. However, Sam Conyers came from the next bay to pull away the bags and was killed in the act. The platoon sergeant then made an attempt, but was badly wounded, and finally I believe my rescue was completed by Joe Allen, who got my head free, which was all that could then be done. I believe the rest of the men in the bay were all killed. By this time the front of the trench had gone altogether, and I was in the open, pinnioned from the shoulders downwards and unable to move until the shelling ceased, when someone freed my arms and gave me an entrenching tool to dig the rest of myself out. I suppose that I must have been somewhat lightheaded, for I remember singing and telling my leg I could not possibly go without it, until a young newly-joined officer who was doing heroic work digging others out, bid me shut up for fear the Germans heard me and came across.'*

The bombardment killed Lieutenant Palmer (the most popular officer in the battalion who was buried and suffocated to death), and 2/Lieutenant Spink (who was blown to pieces); his brother who was serving in the ranks of the 10th Battalion was with him when it happened. Twenty other ranks were also killed. Forty-seven men and two officers were wounded and eight men later died of the wounds they received during the bombardment. One of the men killed was Jack Small, a friend of Private Graystone. (Private Small had been wounded in seven places.)

Private Beeken who experienced this bombardment and a number of others during the month recalled that:

'the men were standing up to these bombardments very well indeed. One man stood on the parapet reciting Shakespeare until we brought him down. We all had a good laugh over this.'

Life on the edge bred a special kind of camaraderie. Private Aust, who was still in the front line the next morning, recalled just such a relationship:

'as dawn broke one of the raiders could be seen lying directly outside our post but just outside our wire. We thought he was dead but kept him under observation through our periscope and saw slight movement. Another member of the raiding party then entered our bay searching for a pal who had failed to return. Looking through our 'scope he said "that's him and I am going out for him." Our corporal refused to allow

this. The man turned and left our bay and the next minute had entered the adjoining bay, clambered out of the trench and was picking his way through the wire to his pal. Two of our stretcher bearers were quickly on the scene and after a struggle got the wounded man in. It seemed an eternity. All this was being done in full view of the enemy trenches (100 yards away) and we were amazed there was no immediate reaction. As the party regained our trench and the last man jumped down a sniper fired a single shot over our bay in apparent admiration and salute for a very brave though foolhardy exploit.'

Lieutenant D W O Palmer, the most popular officer in the 10th Battalion, was buried alive and suffocated to death on 4th June during the bombardment.

The Somme Offensive

Fortunately for the 'Hull Pals' their brigade was to be in reserve for the coming offensive which had as an objective the removal of pressure on the French by diverting the Germans from their attacks on Verdun. However, when the date of the offensive was changed it resulted in the 10th Battalion having to stay in the front line longer than was usual. As a result of this the battalion was given the option of being pulled out of the line and replaced by one of the other Hull battalions or staying in place until the offensive, and then going into reserve. Being pulled out of the line was rejected because the strain of the previous days had rendered the battalion incapable of offensive action.

They were particularly fortunate because Serre was one of the strongest of the German positions to be attacked – it being covered by defence works consisting of thick barbed wire entanglements, protected gun emplacements and elaborate deep dugouts which were not affected by the British bombardment. 92 Brigade would hold the divisional frontage and the 10th Battalion would hold the front line from June 24th until 'Z' hour on the 29th, the original date for the start of the Somme offensive. This date was a result of French pressure and was not as early as the French had wanted. Haig had wanted 1st July.

The coming offensive was designed to push the British Fourth Army forward on a front from Serre in the north to the Somme river in the south; the French attack would coincide with this and start at the junction of the British army and the French army at the Somme. Rawlinson, the Fourth Army Commander, believed in the strength of the bombardment as a battle winner. Middlebrook wrote:

12/1212 Private Norris Alexander Hudson who was shot by a sniper 12th June 1916. He is buried in Sucrerie Cemetery near Colincamps. On his last leave his son was born. The Military Police came to escort him back as he had overstayed his leave for the birth. He held his son once. Nine months later he was killed leaving a widow with two young children.

'Rawlinson had been impressed with the successful German opening attacks at Verdun. A heavy artillery preparation had completely

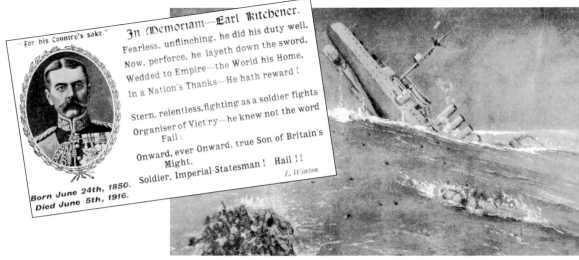

In Memoriam—Earl Kitchener.

"For his Country's sake."

Fearless, unflinching, he did his duty well,
Now, perforce, he layeth down the sword,
Wedded to Empire—the World his Home,
In a Nation's Thanks—He hath reward !

Stern, relentless, fighting as a soldier fights
Organiser of Vict'ry—he knew not the word
Fail :
Onward, ever Onward, true Son of Britain's
Might,
Soldier, Imperial-Statesman ! Hail !!

L. Winton

Born June 24th, 1850.
Died June 5th, 1916.

Britain suffered a blow when the raiser of the New Army, Lord Kitchener, was lost at sea when HMS Hampshire struck a mine off the Orkneys on 6th June 1916.

destroyed the French front-line trenches which had then been occupied by the German infantry. This process had been repeated several times and Rawlinson planned to employ it on the Somme. He had great faith in his own artillery and proposed to use the heaviest and longest bombardment of the war to destroy the German line. Every available gun was to be used for five days and nights before the infantry attacked. The infantry themselves were relegated to the role of mopping up and occupying defences that had already been destroyed for them by the artillery... So confident was he in the power of the artillery that he was convinced there would be little resistance from the Germans when his infantry attacked. Rawlinson, therefore, ordered an infantry attack plan which provided for a slow, rigid, methodical advance over No Man's Land, in place of the standard assault tactics.'

The fortified village of Serre in German hands. This was to be the main objective of the 31st Division in the big attack. The photograph was taken in 1915 and, in the coming months, the village would be totally destroyed.

The 31st Divison was at the northernmost point of the Somme Offensive (there was, however, a diversionary attack on the Gommecourt Salient, which was further north, by the 46th and 56th Divisions) and was to provide flank cover for the attacks of the 4th Division, due south, attacking, along with the 29th Division, the village of Seaumont Hamel (the Hull Brigade had started their trench experience in this area). Directly to the north of the 31st Division sector there was to be no infantry attack. In theory the attack on Serre should have been easy if the artillery had achieved what Rawlinson had hoped. Unfortunately, the Germans were well dug in and although their trenches were damaged and many casualties occured, they were too deeply dug-in to be destroyed. When the attack came they were ready and waiting.

As the ferocity of the British bombardment increased so did the German retaliation. German shells obliterated the front line and communication trenches, making movement by day extremely difficult. Buried gas cylinders were damaged, resulting in the death of Lieutenant Flintoff. Ironically Lieutenant Flintoff was the battalion gas officer and according to the 10th Battalion history he had always taken the greatest care to protect his men from gas. During this period in the trenches eight other ranks were killed by shell fire – Privates Neill, North, Buck, Cheney, Watson and Brunyee – all original members of the battalion. Total losses for the battalion were around 100 officers and men killed or wounded.

In order to provide a nucleus around which to build a new battalion in case of heavy casualties, ten percent of the officers and men of the 10th Battalion were sent to a position in front of Colincamps on June 30th. The remainder were to assist in the preparations that same night. The battalion history recorded that these preparations involved:

'providing parties to cut "lanes" through our own wire to give our attacking troops a quick means of egress into No Man's Land.'

Some of the German defenders of the Serre sector waiting for Typhus inoculations.

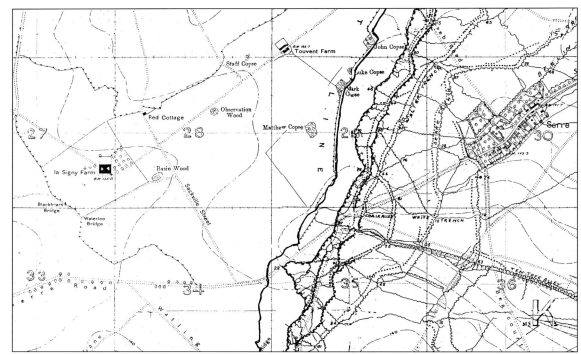

Trench map showing the German positions in front of the village of Serre. The British trenches were omitted for security reasons.

After this the battalion pulled back to allow the attacking troops to come forward. D Company was left in the front line to hold the whole divisional front and to collect stragglers as well!

On the day, being in reserve meant that the brigade was near the front line, packed into assembly trenches waiting to be used if and where necessary. Standing all day in these trenches undergoing German bombardment or assisting with the transport of boxes for the front resulted in some casualties although these were in no way comparable to those of the attacking battalions of the division. The 12th Battalion,

Many of the streets in Hull had a shrine-roll of honour which commemorated not only the dead but those who were serving in any arm of the forces. This particular one was at Woodcock Street.

waiting in Sackville Street, had one officer and two other ranks wounded; the 10th in Palestine Street suffered two fatalities on the 1st (Sergeant Jones and Private Dalton) with a further two other ranks dying of wounds the next day; the same pattern was repeated in the 11th Battalion (Lance Corporal Mason and Privates Dixon and Marchant killed – Private Harrison died of wounds on the 2nd). Only the 13th Battalion suffered no fatalities during this period, even so the battalion returns for July 1st showed 16 other ranks wounded and this from a battalion in reserve for the reserve brigade!

Private Surfleet was in a village behind the line with the 13th Battalion and on 30th June the whole Battalion were given a lecture on the coming attack and the use of the bayonet:

'his talk about bayonet work sounded rather gruesome, particularly as all our bayonets have just been specially sharpened on the village grindstone by our pioneers.'

At 7.30am the attack on Serre commenced and 93 and 94 Brigades left their trenches. When the British bombardment of the German front line moved on, the German defenders set up their machine guns. (The British barrage had finished earlier than expected giving the Germans time to collect themselves and man their trenches ready for the attack.) As the troops advanced they were met with a German counter barrage and machine gun fire. The Public Record Office contains a typewritten document produced by 93 Brigade, shortly after 1st July, which summarises their part in the offensive:

'July 1st 6-25 to 7-10 a.m.
  Casualties to 6-0 a.m. approximately 2 officers and 11 O.R.
  Bombardment of enemy 1st Line Trenches by 18prs., 4-5 Howitzer Batteries and 2 T.M. Batteries.
  Enemy replying on our front line and on our assembly trenches with shrapnel.
  7-21 a.m. 15th West Y.R.

The 10th Battalion Front on 1st July 1916. Bess Street to John Copse.

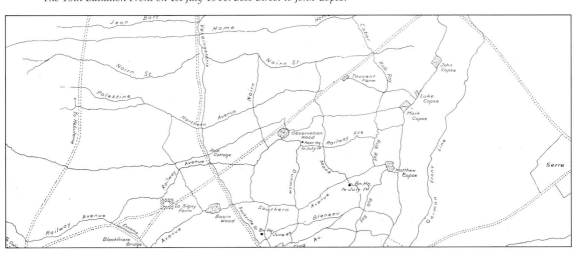

WELL DONE, THE NEW ARMY!

2/Lieutenant Read, 11th Battalion, resting in his tent somewhere behind the lines during the late summer of 1916. He later transferred to 1st King's African Rifles and died in December 1918 in East Africa.

A rather optimistic view of the July offensive is shown here by Punch Magazine.

11th Battalion pay parade.

Leading platoons of 15th West Yorks advanced over parapet and lined tape on either side of Sap 'A.' Hostile machine gun fire commenced about this time and enemy was observed firing from his front line trenches - in groups apparently in the bays in his trenches.

A good proportion of the first wave succeeded in getting to the tape and lying down. They were there subjected to heavy machine gunfire.

Only a few isolated men of the 2nd wave succeeded in reaching the tape and this and succeeding waves suffered heavy casualties immediately after leaving their front line trench - mainly from machine gunfire.

The Officer Commanding 15th West Yorks Regt (Major Neill) was wounded in the first few minutes and the Adjutant, Captain Neil, killed a few minutes later.

The 15th West Yks. R. lost practically all its officers - having 11 killed and 11 wounded.

The enemy artillery put a heavy barrage of fire (H.E. & Shrapnel) on our front line and some 20 yards in front as well as on our assembly trenches and communicators.

Of the men of the 15th West Yks R. who assembled in the front line, no man has returned to the battalion who got further than to K.35.a.70.90 on the right and K.29.d. 10.70. to K.29.d. 15.55 on the left - approximately 100 yards in front of our wire.

Of those who assembled in LEEDS TRENCH none are reported to have got further than 30 yards outside our own parapet. The story was the same for the other attacking battalions:

'7-35 a.m. 16th W Yks. R & "D" Coy 18th Durham L.I.

Leading platoons of the 16th W Yorks R. and 18th D.L.I, left MONK TRENCH and BRADFORD TRENCH respectively and advanced to LEEDS TRENCH where they laid down behind the trench. They came under machine gunfire immediately they got into the open and suffered many casualties before reaching LEEDS TRENCH.

8-35 a.m.

The Officer Commanding 16th West Yks Regt (Major Guyon) and most of the officers reported killed, and the advance checked.

12-30 p.m. to 1-0 p.m.

Events are difficult to follow but at 1-0 p.m. the front line was held by Lts. Cross, Peace and Whittaker of the 18th West Yks with some 200 men of all battalions.

2-11 p.m.

3 Coys, of the 18th Durham L.I. and 60 men of the 18th West Yorks R. held DUNMOW and MAITLAND and were reinforced by 1 Company of the 11th E. Yorks Regt.'

At the end of the report the writer summarised the reasons for the attack being held up:

(1) Enemy's artillery barrage
(2) Enemy's machine gunfire
(3) Enemy's rifle fire.

To the north the 48th Division was attacking and to the south the 4th Division attacked. The 10th Battalion had a ring side seat as it was spread out over the whole 31st Division frontage. Private Aust, who had experienced the humanity shown by the German troops when the East Lancashire soldier was rescuing his friend in No Man's Land wrote:

> *'It was difficult to hate in the face of such happenings as these – yet exactly 28 days later and within 200 yards of the foregoing incident I was stood on the firestep screaming "Bastards, Bastards, Bastards" as I saw a machine gun annihilate the remnants of a Scottish battalion as they tried to regain our lines during the abortive attack of July 1st.'*

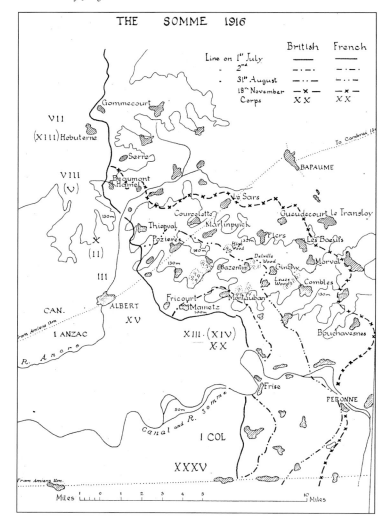

A map of the Somme Offensive from July to November. The 31st Division was opposite Serre at the top left.

Chapter 5

'Pack up your troubles'
Pastures New 1916

All four Hull battalions were very lucky indeed to have escaped the first day and even luckier to have their attack cancelled. At 9pm that night 92 Brigade received orders for a night attack against the enemy trenches that 93 and 94 Brigades had failed to take. At 11pm the order was received to withdraw from the trenches and return to Bus-les-Artois. The brigade pulled back into Corps reserve. After nine days in the line the battalions were exhausted and pleased to be moving to a more peaceful area.

As they left the area the new CO (Lieutenant-Colonel Pearson) of the 10th Battalion called the officers and NCOs together for a general talk about the battle which he prophetically concluded with:

'we shall be in it again before long, never fear, and we shall suffer casualties. But the Battalion will still go on. You may not be there, but there will be, at the end of it all, a 10th East Yorkshire Battalion to march proudly down King Edward Street.' [One of Hull's main streets.]

The 10th Battalion going into the trenches on the Somme. In reality they are looking so pleased because they are leaving the battle for a much quieter part of the front. The men are from D Company and the picture was taken near Louvencourt. 1. Private Aust (Hull), 2. Private C Hewison, 3. Private G Tether (Cottingham), 4. Private J Hughes, 5. Private E Hayes, 6. Sgt W Leech, 7. Sgt 'Nobby' Clarke (Hull), 8. Private A. Hall (Withernsea), 9. Private Walker (Goole), 10. Private Wilde (Hull), 11. Private Cooper (Goole), 12. Cpl Moody (Hull), 13. Private Shipley (Goole), 14. Private Reuben (Hull), 15. Private Veal (Hull), 16. L/Cpl Ruston (Hull), 17. Private Reedham (Hull).

The Lewis gun section of the 10th Battalion near Doullens.

The 10th Battalion leaving the battle zone.

Bus-les-Artois; the quiet front the Hull Brigade was sent to after July 1st.

10th Battalion transport on the march, near Doullens.

It was during the immediate aftermath of the first day on the Somme that the famous photograph of the 10th Battalion was taken. After relaxing in huts in Bus-les-Artois with a backlog of mail they were given the order 'Battle Order in ten minutes'. After leaving camp they were asked by the CO to smile for the photographer who was just along the road. Whether the men were impressed can be gauged by the photo and by the following from the 10th Battalion history:

> 'sure enough, there he was, with his movie camera by the roadside, merrily turning his handle as the Battalion marched past. What a pity it was before the time of sound pictures! The remarks would have given the true Somme atmosphere.'
>
> 'The battalion was moving out of the area and was glad to be going but the photo was published with the caption "Gallant East Yorkshire smiling as they go into action".'

As the division left for pastures new on July 5th they were addressed by Lieutenant-General Sir A G Hunter-Weston, who expressed his regret that the Division was leaving his command.

The division moved north to Bethune for a week's rest, training and refitting. During this period Lieutenant-General R C B Haking addressed the Brigade Officers and expressed his pleasure at having a Yorkshire Brigade under him (Hacking was a Yorkshireman).

When the brigade eventually returned to the trenches they found themselves in a quiet area. However, the inadequately protected trenches resulted in considerable numbers of casualties. Captain Watson wrote home:

> 'the trenches we are in here have been the scene of one of last year's greatest battles. The weather is hot. The ground is absolutely flat and abounds in loathsomely smelling ditches and flies are a curse.'

Although it was supposed to be a quiet area, the war diaries show that the quiet was comparative. On 19th July, the 12th Battalion were in the front line with the 13th on the right and the 2/6th Warwicks on the left. The 12th Battalion were active onlookers and as a result of enemy fire lost Captain Walker and Privates Dearlove and Bourner killed with Private North dying the next day from his wounds. Two officers and an unknown number of other ranks were wounded. The 12th Battalion War Diary recorded the action:

> '11am Artillery bombardment commenced. 13 EYR on right and 2/6th Warwicks on left.
> 6pm. The division on the left attacked, the 2/6 Warwicks occupying the German trenches, but afterwards falling back. Several of the enemy emerged from the trenches

opposite our left and apparently threw bombs back into their own trenches which had been captured. They were practically annihilated by our rifle and Lewis Gun fire. A telegram was received the next day from the GOC 61 DIV thanking the Lewis Gun detachment of 12 EYR for the valuable assistance they had rendered.'

Later the same day the 11th Battalion was also undergoing its baptism on the new front with a trench raid consisting of four officers and 70 other ranks. Like so many raiding parties this one failed – it got caught on German wire inside the outer wire defences. As a result of this no prisoner was taken and no identification made while the attacking troops had two other ranks killed (Privates Chapman and Grantham) and four others slightly wounded. The men on the raid were all volunteers. Private Chapman was shot in the head during the raid. In a letter after the raid to his parents his officer wrote:

'He could not have felt any pain. We carried him back to our trenches, where he breathed his last.'

Similarly, a raid by the 12th Battalion the next day also failed to penetrate the German wire.

The 13th Battalion had more luck with its first raid on the 20th. Two raids were attempted, one by Lieutenant Mabane and 2/Lieutenant Herring of B Company, the other by Captain Ransom and 2/Lieutenant Puddicombe of D Company. The latter party entered the German line and killed about 20 Germans and took two prisoners. Both officers were severely wounded. 2/Lieutenant Herring was slightly wounded.

August and September passed with alternate spells in and out of the trenches. Each trench duty was marked by further raids and yet more casualties and occasionally the awarding of a medal for bravery.

On August 15th a patrol under Lieutenant Beckh:

'left the lines to inspect the Ferme Cour Lavoué. Finding it strongly held and being fired on they retired but again struck the German lines. A machine gun opened fire on them and Lt. Beckh and one other rank [Private Sugarman] was (sic) killed. Later Corporal Tuton was wounded but Private L Shapero 10/1371 remained with him and eventually reached our line at 4 pm the next day.'

Private Shapero was awarded the Military Medal on August 19th 1916.

Although this was a quiet area the casualties mounted. In August/September 1916 the 13th Battalion suffered two captains wounded, one officer died of wounds (2/Lieutenant Burbidge), 13 other ranks fatalities and 84 other ranks wounded.

The psychological wear and tear on the ordinary soldier is not documented in the war diaries but self-inflicted wounds must be some indication of the strain being felt;

unfortunately most casualty returns for the brigade no longer exist, however, the casualty returns for the 13th Battalion during July show that on the 18th, Private G H Brewitt was hospitalised for a self-inflicted wound and that on 27th July Private S J Dry was reported as accidentally self-inflicting a wound.

The strain of the war was also shown by the officers. This is shown by entries in the 13th Battalion War Diary:

'July 22nd 2/Lt. Cullen Shellshock
July 23rd Captain Stevenson and 2/Lt.
Swan to 95 Field Ambulance with shell-shock.'

In the same month Captain Watson of the 12th Battalion wrote home to his parents:

'I am enjoying this rest as we all are – the nervous strain of the last month has been absolutely awful – I really think some of us have been a wee bit "touched" in the head once or twice.'

A month later he was to write:

Corporal George Dent who was killed in action on 21st August.

'how long do most people give the war now - must we have another winter? Can these politicians come to no terms?'

Finally, putting the situation into context he added:

'the garden must be topping now.'

The situation that the troops found themselves in was basically a stalemate. On the 16th August Captain Watson wrote home again expounding his understanding of the situation:

'I'm finally convinced fighting can't and won't (end it) – it's a case of you're here and I'm here – and whoever attacks loses enormously and cannot move far – while the constant wastage that goes on with this sitting opposite each other game, is the more terrible because it doesn't get either side any "forrader".'

This constant waste was not just caused by the enemy. On September 9th, B Company of the 10th Battalion was bombarded by *Minenwerfers* and aerial torpedoes which caused much damage but only one slight casualty. This was the last day of a tour in the front line and the war diary recorded its casualties:

> *'total casualties this time in - three officers wounded (one at duty) – five other ranks wounded. Of these total casualties four were caused by our artillery due to defective ammunition.'*

Before moving back to the Somme, the brigade delivered three further trench raids, one on the night of the 7th September by the 13th Battalion (three DCMs were awarded for this raid – Sergeant Jenkins, L/Corporal Fairfield and Private Foster), one on the night of 18/19th September by the 10th Battalion and another on the night of October 3rd by the 11th. The first two raids were successful but the latter was a failure when the Bangalore torpedoes (2" diameter metal tubes filled with explosives) failed to explode.

The raid on the 18/19th was to be unorthodox. For a week prior to the raid the division had practised a non-offensive policy with the intention of duping the enemy into thinking that they had a peace-loving division opposite them. Lieutenant-Colonel Stapledon, in the face of opposition from his superiors, insisted that there should be no artillery prior to the attack; stealth would be used to position the troops and Bangalore torpedoes used at the last minute to open up the German wire. One officer and twenty five men from each company would take part under the command of Captain Lambert. In the report written after the raid the aims of the raid were stated as:

> *'to enter enemy's trenches, capture and kill any of the enemy, bomb his dugouts and do as much damage as possible.'*

This was to be achieved by entering the enemy's trenches at:

> *'four separate points as silently as possible, with 4 parties, each party not to be more than 36 strong, enemy's wire being cut by a bangalore torpedo at each point of entry, the moment before entry.'*

The four raiding parties waited in No Man's Land until midnight when the Bangalore torpedoes went off and the raid started. Unfortunately, D Company's torpedo did not explode and being unable to cut through the wire they retired. At the point chosen for A Company's raiding party to cut the wire with their torpedo there was a small party of Germans working on the wire which meant that they had to wait until the Germans had gone before they could position themselves for the attack. After inspecting the wire and discovering that it was too thick to get through in the time allocated the party withdrew.

Fortunately the B and C Company torpedoes went off and the raid started. The B Company party entered the enemy trench and immediately split into two flank parties which bombed their way down the trench to the left and right. This surprise attack caused the Germans to run out of their trenches with little resistance, a number of them being shot while they attempted to escape. Two men from the left flank party captured a machine gun and the corporal in charge of it. At 12.15 the party withdrew leaving behind an estimated twenty German casualties and two bombed dugouts. Six prisoners were taken. Lieutenant Clark, the officer in charge of this party, was seen to shoot five of the enemy and also captured four prisoners from a dugout. B Company casualties were one officer and five other ranks slightly wounded and one missing.

C Company was in position at 11.57 and at midnight when the torpedo exploded rushed into the trench under the cover of the smoke. The party entered a bay occupied by four sentries, three of whom were killed and the other taken prisoner. Flank parties bombed their way down the trench while a third party bombed another trench (KAMPE STRASSE) causing the Germans to run down the trench and out into the open at the back of the trenches. At 12.10 the raiding party left the trenches leaving behind an estimated ten dead Germans with an unknown number wounded. C Company casualties were light, with one officer and three men slightly wounded. There was no enemy retaliation of any sort after the raid.

When the loss of Sergeant Tindale was noted strong parties were sent out to look for him. The search was continued until just before daybreak with no success. According to the 10th Battalion history his loss was felt by everybody because he was one of their most respected NCOs.

The raid was a great success and congratulations were received from all quarters. Battalion orders for the 20th gave details of the compliments:

'NO 264.
    Battalion Orders by Major C.C. Stapledon,
    Commanding H.X.R.
    Trenches 20th September 1916.
    1. COMPLIMENTARY - The following letter from the First Army Commander has been received from the Division to-day.
    G.O.C. XIth Corps
    I should be glad if you will ask the G.O.C. 31st Division to convey to Brig. Gen. Williams, Commanding the 92nd Infantry Brigade, my congratulations to all ranks of the 10th East Yorkshire Regiment, under Major C.C. Stapledon, who took part in the successful raid carried out last night.
    The casualties inflicted on the enemy and the capture of prisoners and a machine gun, proved that the raid was not only prepared in the most careful manner, but that

it was carried out with fine energy, determination, and gallantry by the officers and men of the East Yorkshire.

The capture of the prisoners has enabled us to establish some identifications which are of the utmost importance at the present time to the whole of the allied armies.
(signed) R. Haking, General
Cmdg First Army.'

The same battalion order also contained compliments from the Divisonal and Brigade Commanders.

The next day the 1st Army Intelligence Summary – No. 617 – carried details of the identifications made from the prisoners:

'Distribution of the Enemy's Forces

XIX (Saxon) Corps - In the course of our successful raids SE of Richebourg L'Avoue last night 9 prisoners of the 104th Reg, 40th Division and of the I Pioneer Battalion No 22 and No 310 Searchlight detachment were captured. This confirms definitely the presence of the 40th Division on our front.'

Although the raid had been a great success it hadn't been easy for Private Beeken, who had been temporarily blinded during the action:

'On the evening of the 18th September we set off to the assembly trench and on the way I was told that my role had to be changed. I had to take a bucketful of bombs and, when the raid started, I had to go about 20 yards to the right, where there was a communication trench leading to the German front line. On arrival at my post I had to prevent any enemy reinforcements going to the help of their comrades.

'We went out of the trench and lay down in No Man's Land. Everything was very quickly done for we wanted it to be a surprise raid.

'The torpedo exploded and we dashed to the gaps in the wire. As I went through I thought "What a strange thing I am doing! Dashing to hurl grenades at people".

'Just then, my foot caught in some wire and down I went into a shell hole and as I landed a hand grenade exploded in front of my face. Then I heard the word "Impshi" (our code word for "prisoner captured") was shouted. This meant that the raiders had to retire.

'I stood up but I couldn't see and didn't know which way to move, somebody saw me and seeing I was in difficulty, took me by the hand and promptly got me attached to the barbed wire. He pulled me free and we set off for our line. Somehow or other we became separated so I carried on away from the noise and eventually I fell into a ditch. I knew this ditch for I had often crossed it when on patrol. It ran in front of our barbed wire. I lay there and rested. Somebody approached and asked "Is somebody there?" It was Private Parish, a member of my platoon. He was searching No Man's Land for

Casualty return for Lieutenant Hewson of the 10th Battalion, who at this time was attached to the 48th Company of the MGC in the 16th (Irish) Division – Lieutenant Hewson was Irish.

any stragglers. Soon I was in our line. A bandage was put over my eyes and I was taken by J. Graystone, a Hull teacher, to the forward dressing station. Here my eyes were cleaned. I was so pleased that I could see. There were two small scratches on my face.'

Raids like this could have long term psychological effects on the participants. After the raid there was considerable talk about it amongst those who had taken part. One of Private Beeken's friends who was on the raid was troubled for some considerable time as a result of his part in the raid:

'I was surprised at what one man, Sunny Cook, said to me. He was in my section and we were great friends. Now he was very keen to go on this raid, but he was shaken after it. He told me, "I heard voices coming from a shelter so I lobbed in a grenade. There was an explosion and I heard cries of pain and I thought, "It is some poor mother's son". I know it worried him for a long time.'

In his congratulatory speech to the raiders, the Divisional Commander hinted that

A RFC photograph of the Boar's Head near Richebourg. A, B, C and D are the points of entry into the German trenches. X is the point of exit from the British Line.

they might be returning to the Somme. On 8th October the division moved off by train to Candas and a five and a half hour march, at night, through to the Vauchelles area in preparation for the coming offensive.

Return to the Somme

In Egypt Private Tait had complained about the officers wanting to reduce the amount that they wrote. Writing too much may have cost one of the 13th Battalion's subalterns his life. As well as censoring the men's letters, the officers had an obligation not to write too much. In a letter home, dated the week before The Battle of the Ancre, Captain Watson, replying to his parents' requests for more information, described what happened to a fellow officer:

> *'One is trusted to censor one's own letters and one has to try and keep within the limits laid down - also - one of our subalterns exceeded the limit and the letter happened to be opened by the base censor and his leave was stopped for six months and before the six months was up he was killed.'*

In Vauchelles the battalions trained and practised for the forthcoming attack, which they became aware of through rumours not long after they arrived. Having missed out on July 1st, 92 Brigade was the brigade chosen for the attack on November 13th;

146

this was to take place opposite Serre where 93 and 94 Brigades had lost so heavily on July 1st.

The decision to go ahead with the attack was not taken until the morning of the 11th, when the weather had become cold and there had been no rain for three days. When the decision was taken it was decided to go for a night start and Zero hour was fixed at 5.45am. This was to be a limited operation aimed at reducing the German Salient between the Albert-Bapaume road and Serre. The main attack was to be delivered by V Corps (consisting of 2nd, 3rd, 51st and 63rd Divisions) against the German defences north of the Ancre that had been attacked on July 1st. At the same time II Corps (consisting of 18th, 19th, 39th and 4th [Canadian] Divisions) was to attack south of the Ancre. The northern part of the attack was to be covered by 92 Brigade of XIII Corps.

In the forthcoming assault 3rd Division was to attack Serre with two brigades; 92 Brigade would provide a flank cover on the left of this attack on a frontage of 500 yards. The objective on the right of the brigade front was the reserve line of the German trenches while on the left it was the support line. By the end of the offensive no ground had been gained in the 31st Division sector.

The night before the attack the 11th Battalion were unfortunate to lose their Quartermaster, Lieutenant J B Reynolds. He was killed by a stray shell in Hebuterne as he was returning from the line after ascertaining that the battalion had everything that it needed.

Merville where the 10th Battalion went after their successful raid on the Boar's Head.

The whole brigade knew that its turn would come before too long, especially when training was stepped up.

Hebuterne Church as it was in 1915 and in the process of being reduced to a pile of rubble.

The amount of leave given to the troops was always a contentious issue.

Private Surfleet was one of the details who would not be involved in the attack. He described the day before the attack in his diary written up on the 16th:

'November 12th was the most thoroughly miserable day I ever remember. The morning broke dull, foggy and wet; everything was in a hopeless hubbub and bustle; even the mud seemed stickier and thicker. We had the usual fatigue parties, rolling the blankets

in those bundles often, cleaning up camp as far as possible...and so on. Then Sgt. Raine came along and told Bell and me that one of us had to be left at a place called Rossignol Farm until called for duty. It was a quiet moment, but without further talk, the Sgt. said he would toss for it; poor Bell lost and Sgt. Raine told him he was "for it."...to which Bell said "San fairy ann.".... "It doesn't matter", ...and now poor old Bell is dead! God, it seems awful...

'With sad hearts we watched the main part of the battalion move off to the line. There was an artifical air of jollity about; a joke here, a coarse remark there, a wave of the hand to a pal... "lucky devil staying behind."... "all the best, old man."... "get those bloody rations up early."... "We're going back for a rest after this..."... "who the hell says we aren't a scrapping division."... "Send you a postcard."...all these, and many more remarks, but it is the thinnest of veneers, a very feeble covering over the sense of grim reality which I feel the whole battalion was feeling. We stood there whilst the boys, in column of route, marched forward, slid down the hill, turned right and were gradually swallowed up in the mist and the mud and the confusion. Their sounds died out; only a rumble of guns and the creaking of heavily laden limbers remained in a scene so desolate and miserable that one could not help feeling depressed and sad...'

The attack was to begin at 5.45 am with the 12th and 13th Battalions following up behind the artillery barrage which was to land on the front line German trenches.

Hebuterne cemetery where four Hull Brigade soldiers are buried or commemorated.

How the attacking battalions might have felt prior to the battle. A Punch *magazine cartoon.*

Tommy (ready to go 'over the top'). "I suppose we shall be making history in a few minutes, Sergeant?"
Sergeant, "History be blowed! What you've got to make is geography."

The 10th Battalion were in brigade reserve in Vercingetorix trench and were to provide trench police and carrying parties, while the bombers and Lewis gunners were made ready to assist either of the two attacking battalions. At Zero Hour four carrying parties were in Caber Trench under the command of 2/Lieutenant Anderson. Three of the parties got across No Man's Land without any problems and delivered their bombs, the fourth party got caught in the German barrage and could not get through. The Lewis gunners and bombers were not needed because both of the attacking battalions had been forced to evacuate the German lines due to the failure of the 3rd Division to take its objectives.

The details spent the night in the relative comfort of three-tiered wire-netting beds at Rossignol farm, with only the rats for company. The news about the attack had started to arrive upon waking:

'Woke early on the morning of November 13th and heard the boys went over at 5.45 in thick fog and took the German first and second lines in this Serre sector fairly easily, surprising the Germans in their dugouts. Breakfast was an awful meal; news of losses, of wounded, of killed, kept coming through. Each time a man or an officer came up to

the dressing station, the news of all he could tell spread like wildfire. Everything seemed jumbled up; no one had a clear idea of what was going on, but it seemed certain that there had been a big counterattack and that our losses have been terrible. So, too, have those of the other battalions who went over with our lads. Every moment we expect to be called upon to go up and reinforce them. During the morning, a draft of thirty new men arrived from England. Poor devils!...'

Eventually the news of the failure of the 3rd Division attack came through. The situation was deteriorating and there was a need for assistance:

'It was five o'clock in the evening when Lt. John, who was in charge of us, dashed in and told us to get our fighting equipment on; we were to go up the line to help, though no one seemed to know what the job was to be. My fingers trembled as I buckled my belt: a mixture of excitement and nervousness, but we were pretty well resigned to anything...'

A map showing the battalion and divisional frontages during the forthcoming battle.

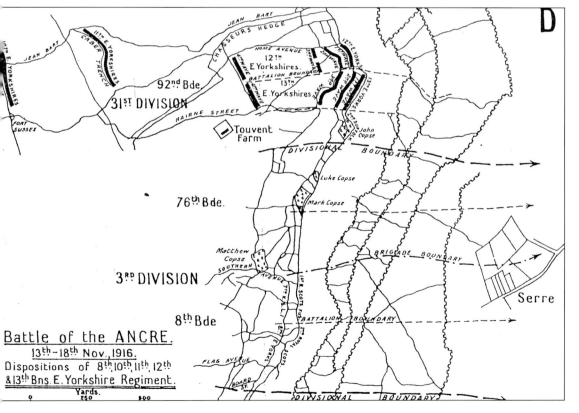

The women and children they left behind. An assembly around a Street Shrine/Roll of Honour somewhere in Hull. (Probably on Hessle Road.)

The party moved forward in the dark, heading by the most direct route to the front line. Travelling along the roads was difficult and they found themselves:

> *'hardly able to move for guns and ammunition and ambulances and limbers. The roads were packed with traffic: a stream of living going forward while the wounded and dying or dead came back.'*

Pulling off the road onto a track led them through their own gun positions:

> *'Sometimes we were so near a gun its flash nearly blinded us and the noise was appalling; some of the lads grumbled at being taken that way and some fell out, wounded by shrapnel which increased as we went on... We came in for some very heavy retaliation as the German batteries tried to cut off our reinforcements and three of our party were killed and several others wounded by shrapnel and pieces of high explosive which fell around us. It was particularly bad just as we reached the C.T. (communication trench) and our stretcher-bearers came along and attended to the wounded. The dead were lifted out of the crowded trench and placed on the parapet. We halted at the start of the trench and Lt. John went along to get instruction. It was a very nerve-racking wait and one or two of our party... thank God there were not many... took advantage of the noise and disturbance and slipped quietly down a side trench and stayed there until, all the work done, we were returning. Then the miserable devils slipped back into the file, no one of any importance being any the wiser. There are some things one can understand: I must never sneer at a man who is afraid, for I have been more frightened out here than it is necessary for me to record. That is one*

thing; scrounging to the detriment of your pals is another and we who saw those rotters have not forgotten; I don't suppose we ever shall.'

Expecting the worst they reported to the Battalion Aid Post and were told to collect the dead and wounded:

'We were told to go into Caber Trench, the "proper" front-line and get in all the bodies we could find and put them in a side trench and, after that, report back to the Aid Post to carry wounded back to the dressing station in Hebuterne. Caber was no longer a trench it was a bloody ditch. From early morning until night, it had been battered and disrupted; a pale, sickly moon came out to show us how horrible and terrifying that trench really was. The mud, churned and re-churned during the day, was indescribably sticky and we had great difficulty in moving several bodies to side-trenches where they were less liable to total disintegration and had, from there, at least some chance of a decent burial.'

After successfully transporting their first casualty through the mud, Private Surfleet arrived at the dressing station at the far end of Hebuterne:

'the sight in that Medical Post was something we shall not forget. The M.O., tunic off and sleeves rolled above the elbows, looked about finished. The place was literally jammed with bleeding men; the doctor's hands moved mechanically from one wound to another. On one side were lots of stretcher cases; on all sides there were blood-stained bandages and that sickly, penetrating odour of iodoform and iodine. That, and the look on the faces of some of those lads down there, made me hurry out into the fresh air; it was something not unlike the scene and smell of a slaughter-house.'

Dealing with the wounded.

A large shell landed on some of the new arrivals, killing them outright. Private Surfleet was round the bay and was unscathed. Lieutenant John then asked for volunteers which were not forthcoming until some personal persuasion was applied. The party set off to bring in wounded from the front line with orders to ignore anyone who could make it in by themselves. Eventually they stumbled upon a soldier from another East Yorkshire battalion who lay in a shell hole:

'The chap we picked up had both legs broken and his elbow was shattered... looked like shrapnel wounds. He had been roughly bandaged by the Battalion stretcher-bearers and the M.O.'

The MO (Captain Yorke) was awarded the MC for his work on November 13th.

The enemy as seen by a French artist. The sender of the card wrote that he had seen 400 of these yesterday under the guard of French soldiers and that they were uglier than this example by a long chalk!

Immediately that they got out of the shell hole they realised that they were lost. Private Surfleet continued:

'god only knows how we got back. It took two and a half hours of the most awful, desperate struggle against dreadful odds in such circumstances as I have never known before...

'After stumbling blindly, right down the centre of No Man's Land for three-quarters of an hour, I spotted La Signy Farm. That, I knew was in the sector on our right. With this knowledge, we moved off to the right, trusting to reach our trenches at some point. After falling into shell-hole after shell-hole...some of them horribly new...tripping over barbed wire, telephone lines, dead bodies, discarded equipment, rifles and the like, we were challenged by an outpost of the York. & Lanes. Regiment and I can honestly say I never felt so safe and secure before!'

After forcing the RAMC soldiers they found in a dugout to take the wounded man to the dressing station, they returned to the Aid Post only to be told that the battalion had been relieved and that they could return to Rossignol Farm:

'we came back to Rossignol Farm: dog-tired, foot-sore with skin off both heels, blood-stained, utterly muddy, ready to fall in our tracks. Our Lieutenant (and very able) Quarter-master was waiting with the cooks to receive us and he kept on waiting until the last man struggled home. Hot tea, soup, bread and, last but not least, a heavy tot of rum. This we gladly drank, thanking God we were able to do so, and almost before I had climbed to my place in that human hen-house and put my haversack down on the wire-netting for a pillow, a most pleasant drowsiness came over me and I fell asleep.'

154

"Ow! Gee! Bill, I've got one in the leg!"

"Well, what are you fussing abaht? Ain't you never been hit before?"

"Yes; but this is the first this winter."

"Well, did you wish a wish?"

A Punch cartoon published five days before the attack.

After dusk 2/Lieutenant Anderson and a number of the carrying party men arrived after spending the day in shell holes pinned down by snipers and artillery. Like the 11th, they were relieved by the 13th Yorks and Lancs but left the bombing parties and their MO and stretcher bearers to collect the wounded. Attached to the 12th Battalion had been two Lewis gun teams, under the command of Corporal Edlington (the son of a Methodist minister), which had been on the extreme left of the battalion throughout the attack. These guns had successfully repelled several bombing attacks and some small parties who had worked round them through No Man's Land. According to the war diary they accounted for over 60 Germans while their casualties amounted to 3 killed, 5 wounded and 1 wounded and missing. Corporal Edlington was awarded the DCM for his work. Sergeant Best and Corporal Nunns, of the carrying parties, were awarded the Military Medal for bravery on the 13th.

The 11th Battalion was in close support to the attacking battalions but not actually in the attack. Initially they were to

Private William Calvert of the 10th Battalion was wounded by the German bombardment of the support trenches. After his recovery he was transferred to the 6th Battalion (Pioneers) with which he spent the rest of the war.

wait in Caber trench near the front but the German retaliatory bombardment was too heavy and they had to be moved to Nairne Street, a lengthy communication trench. After waiting all day they were relieved by the 13th Yorks and Lancs and moved to the front line to relieve the 13th Battalion.

At 5.45am the 12th Battalion left its trenches following the barrage. Considering the importance of the day the battalion war diary recorded the situation very briefly:

> '*All objectives were captured in under twenty minutes with four casualties the barrage being excellent. Over 300 prisoners were captured, and sent back, less than 50% reaching our lines.*
>
> '*The 3rd Division having failed on our right the position was a very difficult one; the trenches had been so blown about that it was impossible to make them really defensive. The germans (sic) counterattacked in force twice during the day from the left, but were annihilated by our Lewis guns. The whole day was spent fighting small parties, bombers and snipers. In the evening as there was a danger of being surrounded it was decided to withdraw, the last party retiring about 8.45pm.*'

Of the 16 officers who had been involved only two had returned unwounded. The severity of the fighting can be seen by the officer losses for the 12th.

A Company	**B Company**
Capt. Watson (W)	Capt. Marriott (K)
Lt. Wright (W)	Lt. Williams (W)
2/Lt. Morgan (K)	2/Lt. Estridge (K)
C Company	**D Company**
Lt. Frizoni (K)	Capt. Habersohn (K)
2/Lt. Heathcote (DoW)	2/Lt. Faker (K)
2/Lt. Moncrieff (DoW)	2/Lt. Livesey (K)
	2/Lt. Elford (K)

The battalion tally for the day was estimated at more than a thousand German casualties. 2/Lieutenant Le Bouvier had a lucky escape; on November 11th he had been sent to Salonika to work as an interpreter.

It was in these conditions that Private John Cunningham was awarded the Victoria Cross. (See appendices.) Thirteen other officers and men received awards for their bravery. Captain Mason, Lieutenant Burch, 2/Lieutenant Dann and CSM Balmford received the MC. Sergeants Freeman, Dewson, Walters and Aket, and Private Spafford were awarded the DCM, while Sergeants Chapman and Chester and Privates Cotton and Kerry received the MM.

At the end of the day from the relative comfort of the 11th Advanced Dressing Station, Captain Watson who had led A Company into the battle was able to write home:

'My Dear Mother,
I have news - I have a nice clean bullet wound in my right thigh and shall be in
England in a day or two. Will write you at the earliest opportunity when I get to
England. Won't it be nice being home for Xmas.
Yours, Donald.'

Like the 12th Battalion, the 13th experienced little initial difficulty in taking their
objectives. The battalion war diary recorded the action briefly:

'The 1st wave, under command of Capt Laverack, had no difficulty in taking the
German 1st line. The 2nd & 3rd waves went through without difficulty, but by the
time the 2nd wave had got to the German 2nd line, the Battalion on our right had got
into difficulties, owing to the state of the ground and machine gun fire. The 3rd wave
took the German 3rd line but what happened after this is not certain, but about 50
men and probably one officer, are known to have been taken prisoner. The Battalion
on our right (2nd Suffolk Rgt) were back in their own front line by 7am. This left the
right flank of the Battalion completely exposed and the Germans made at least 3
counter attacks. On our right there (sic) counter-attacks were only partially successful,

Secret map to show the British trenches just before the attack.

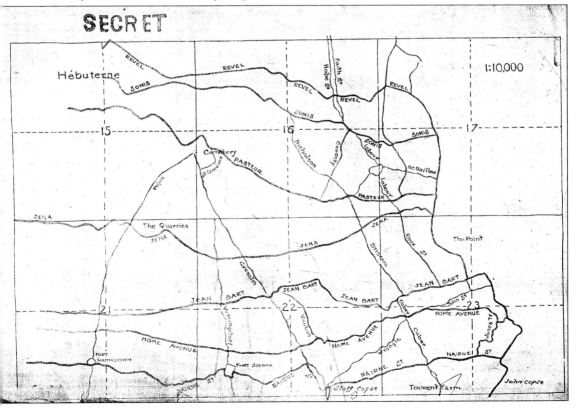

as certain parties were able to hold the German 2nd line until 2 pm. After this these parties retired, to the German 1st line. The last men left the German 1st line at 8-45pm. From 9-45 am to 6pm the Germans barraged all our lines and in particular Caber Trench, where Battn HQ were situated. Owing to this barrage it was impossible to get either supplies or reinforcements over, though several attempts were made. The Battn took over 200 prisoners, but a number of these escaped. In addition to the German Artillery barrage, they employed machine guns and snipers in sweeping our trenches and "no mans" land.'

13/75 Private Arthur Donnelly was KiA 13th November 1916. (He was originally posted as wounded and missing.) He is buried in Euston Road Cemetery. His brother, who had joined up with him, had been transferred to the 6th Battalion and so missed the attack. He was to die in the German offensive in 1918 whilst serving with the 4th Battalion.

Not all the casualties were caused by the Germans. Captain Woolley recorded in his official report of the action that:

'One of our shells fell in the middle of Coy. H.Q. and knocked out or disabled some eight men or so.'

The severity of the hand to hand fighting is clearly shown by the number of officer casualties suffered.

Captain Wooley (PoW)	Captain Laverack (W)
Lt. Lewis (K)	2/Lt. Pattison (PoW)
Lt. Mabane (W)	2/Lt. Dorman (K)
2/Lt. Glover (PoW)	2/Lt. Davey (W)
2/Lt. Bell (K)	2/Lt. Brindley (PoW)
2/Lt. Casson (W)	2/Lt. Beechey (DoW)
2/Lt. Hutchinson (K)	2/Lt. Watt (DoW)
2/Lt. Peters (K)	2/Lt. Binning (K)
Captain Yorke RAMC (W)	2/Lt. Wood (K)

Much bravery went unrewarded. Like many of those who died in the battle 2/Lieutenant Wood's bravery was seen but not acknowledged by authority. This report was written by his Commanding Officer. No reward was forthcoming:

'Recommendation for Honours 13.11.16
Lieutenant Wood 13/E. YORK Regt. was especially mentioned by all who saw him including 2/Lt. Brindley, 13th E. YORK Regt. for his great bravery and devotion to duty in an attack on Serre on the above date.
'Absolutely fearless and self forgotten he kneeled on the edge of a shell hole fully exposed to bombs and heavy machine guns and shouting for bombs for his men - bombed a German M.G. and crew who were flanking our men with fire (our men in difficulties in the mud).

'Thus, effectively bombing the gun team, he was killed by a bomb. He set a very noble example to all near him and caused, and helped them to cause, great loss to the enemy. He led his men well at all times.
R M Woolley OC D Coy.'

Relatively few awards for bravery were made to the 13th Battalion for their work on the 13th. CSM Sandilands and Lance-Corporal Fletcher were awarded the DCM and Military Medals were awarded to Corporal Annable, Lance-Corporals Levitt, Howlett, and Fisher, and Privates Beacock, Chatterton, Mumby, Neylon and Smith.

Captain Woolley was himself taken prisoner later in the day due to a dirty trick being played by the Germans. His party had held off numerous attacks when suddenly the Germans marched some captured Suffolk Regiment troops in front of them:

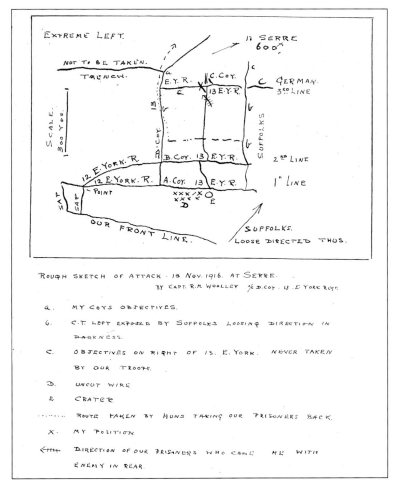

Rough sketch map drawn by Captain R M Wooley to show his position when he was taken prisoner. PRO

159

'I got round to see and found thirty or more Suffolk men prisoners (unarmed) coming straight over us - I caught one to try and get out of him some information, but Huns followed behind these fellows and were beginning to shoot them down because we were there armed, either these fellows, prisoners had to be murdered or we had to give in. While considering for a second what to do the Huns had us.'

The Official History (1916 Vol II) described the assault:

'The two assaulting battalions 13th and 12/East Yorkshire, completed their assembly by midnight, and pushed forward snipers and Lewis guns into No Man's Land to provide close support when the advance began. At 5.45 A.M. the Yorkshiremen went forward steadily through the mist behind a good barrage, and reports soon showed that the German front line had been carried. It was, indeed, entered without difficulty through the remains of the wire, and the dug-outs were then bombed to good effect, the prisoners taken being of the 66th Regiment...

Private Wilfred Farmery, regimental number 12/1258. Killed in action on 13th November 1916 aged 33.

'In the remains of his support trench the enemy resisted stoutly with rifle and bomb, but was overcome by sheer hard fighting. On the right some of the 13/East Yorkshire kept up with the barrage and reached the reserve line, where they held on in the vain hope of being reinforced. Only a few returned later in the day; the rest were overwhelmed. Bombing counterattacks up the communication trenches leading back to Star Wood developed about 8 A.M., but the Yorkshiremen in possession of the German support line stood to it grimly all morning, although bombs ran short and heavy losses were sustained.

'German shell-fire was now so heavy on No Man's Land and the British front line that communication with the forward troops became well nigh impossible. Two companies of the 11 /East Yorkshire, moving forward to reinforce, were held up, and carrying parties failed to get through. About 9.30 A.M. a German counter-attack in some force was made south-westward from Star Wood, but the machine-gun group on the left flank opened effective fire and the enemy melted away. This was the only attempt made to advance over the open.'

Corporal Robinson of B Company, 13th Battalion. Posted as missing after the battle, he was later listed as killed in action.

By 8am it was obvious that the left flank of the 3rd Division was not able to take its objectives. This left 92 Brigade troops in a salient which was constantly being shelled and counter-attacked by German bombers and unless the 3rd Division could advance, the situation was untenable. At 5.25pm V Corps decided not to renew the 3rd Division attack and as a result Fifth Army allowed 92 Brigade to withdraw.

The Official History described the slow withdrawal made by the attacking battalions:

> 'Heavy losses had compelled the dogged Yorkshiremen to give up their footing in the enemy's support line about 3 PM and retire to his front trench. Here they were making a fresh stand whilst all the wounded who could be collected were passed back to the British line. After dark the final withdrawal began, the last two parties coming in about 9.30 PM. Between them, the two battalions lost nearly 800 officers and men; but they had inflicted heavy loss on the Germans and taken over 130 prisoners.'

After the attack the battalions involved received messages of congratulation from the Army Commander, the Corps Commander, the Brigade Commander and from the 11th Battalion which had been in reserve. The back slapping continued with the King congratulating Haig, who in turn congratulated Gough.

> 'The Army Commander wishes to thank the Officers and men of the 31st Division for the gallant way in which they held their positions in the German lines throughout today. No troops could have done more to ensure success.'

From the Brigade Commander to the 13th Battalion:

> 'I am writing to offer my sincerest sympathy for the very heavy losses your battalion has suffered. The more one hears about the attack yesterday, the more one realises the magnificent behaviour of your men.'

And from the 11th Battalion to the 13th Battalion:

> 'Please accept the admiration and congratulations of all ranks of this Battn. on your splendid achievement in taking and holding the German Line throughout the day of the 13th inst.'

It had been a painful battle for 92 Brigade but one of little consequence in the course of the whole Somme campaign. This is confirmed by Haig's despatch published in the London Gazette Supplement of December 29th 1916. In this he wrote at some length about the success at St. Pierre Divion with its large numbers of prisoners for very few casualties but dismissed the high casualty rate at the northern end of the battle in two sentences:

> 'still further north - opposite Serre - the ground was so heavy that it became necessary to abandon the attack at an early stage; although, despite all difficulties, our troops

Pte. John Cunningham, V.C., East York Regt. (portrait left) in a communi-cation-trench beyond a captured line went forward alone, and meeting ten of the enemy killed them with bombs and cleared the trench up to the next line.

War Office, 13th January, 1917.
His Majesty the King has been graciously pleased to confer the Victoria Cross on the undermentioned man :–
No. 12/21 PTE. JOHN CUNNINGHAM, E.Y.R.
For most conspicuous bravery and resource during operations.

A postcard produced in Hull to celebrate Private Cunningham winning the Victoria Cross.

had in places reached the enemy's trenches in the course of their assault.'

Haig wrote in his despatch that the ground was so heavy that it was necessary to abandon the attack, laying the failure of the attack squarely on the conditions. The breaking point for the attack had been the failure of the 3rd Division to take its objectives. However, the ground conditions were bad enough to preclude the use of Tanks.

In his report on the attack at Serre, Captain Woolley, Senior Officer in the attacking force of the 13th Battalion wrote:

'No single spot of ground seemed free from shell holes and churned mud and water and we sank below the knee in places...
  'The ground was so churned up and light nil that you could not see the trenches till you crossed them.'

And in a further report written in 1919 to explain the situation he also mentioned the mud:

'Men sank in above their hips and their officers were endeavouring to get them out and forward.'

Captain Woolley blamed the failure of the attack on three factors:

'(1) Fearful mud, slush and boa into which the men sank (one or two captured men were eventually dug out the next day by Germans) - the ground was like a rough sea set in mud with water lying in the hollows.

(2) Suffolks losing direction on the right and failing to take C.T. on our right, left a gap by which enemy could reinforce and work along with strong bombing parties and get flanking machine gunfire on our exposed men.

(3) Pitch darkness at time of attack which made it very difficult to pick a track in the mud going in the right direction, and also made it impossible on such fearfully rough ground for connecting files to again gain touch between the platoons which had to go left and right of the wire (uncut).'

Even the Official History mentioned the mud:

'The ground, sodden with rain and broken up everywhere by innumerable shell-holes, can only be described as a morass, almost bottomless in places: between the lines and for many thousands of yards behind them it is almost - and in some localities, quite - impassable...

Hébuterne December 1916, when the Hull Pals were there.

'Some officers speaking from experience of both offensives, are of the opinion that the conditions on the Somme in the late autumn of 1916 were as bad as, if not worse than, those at Passchendaele a year later of which the public were to hear so much more. Certain it is that the troops of all arms were tried almost to the limit of their endurance, and bore the ordeal with admirable patience and courage.'

This terrible mud was the cause of many casualties because once caught it was difficult to get out and men stopping to help were themselves easy targets. C Company suffered considerable casualties because they were:

'being caught by German machine gun fire whilst trying to get men out of the mud.'

The mud also made the removal of casualties very difficult, as Private Surfleet discovered after being told to take a casualty back to Hébuterne:

Private Haldenby, later Sergeant (13th Battalion), outside Scruton Cottage in Cottingham. He was killed in action on November 13th.

'There was a regular bombardment taking place at the juncture of the C.T. and the front-line: this was the spot where B Company had such a hellish time during our previous tour in this sector and the trench was knee-deep in the thickest and most glutinous mud I have ever seen. We had to pass this danger point with our stretcher and were fully aware of the "windy" places as we set off not too worried about "buckshee" shells sent over at random in the hope of catching some party or other, but very concerned indeed about the steady drumfire on one or two particular places. We ploughed on, resting frequently to save our strength for the effort we knew had to come. Gradually, we approached that danger zone near the C.T. The mud got thicker; the lad on the stretcher, alarmed at our slow progress, tried to get off and walk but we persuaded him to stay where he was. The halts became more frequent; we could only go about eight paces at a time, now. Each pace meant that your boot sank slowly into the churned up mud until, the knees almost submerged, an effort had to be made to drag that leg out. This, of course, necessitated putting all your weight on the other leg, which promptly sank in the quagmire. Each pace took us nearer those rendering crashes as the shell burst and before we had gone far, the continuous dragging of our legs and the suction on our boots tore the skin off our heels. The stretcher, naturally, lurched and swayed precariously all the time; our "burden" got windier with every step. The drumfire....a shell every half-minute..continued; each shell landed with terrifying regularity almost in the same spot, right in the trench. A cold sort of sweat mingled with the perspiration of our efforts; my lips tasted salty, my mouth was parched. We were very near; we crouched as a shell swooped to earth. God only knows

Left: 11th Battalion officers - Lieutenant Jenkins, Lloyd, Andrews, Suthrien and Andrews. A dugout around Christmas 1916.

Below: 11th Battalion B Company officers at Warnimont Wood during December 1916. Lieutenant Chapman, Lieutenant J Harrison, Captain Cattley and Lieutenant Cowling.

Above: 11th Battalion HQ Mess, Hébuterne Sector during December 1916.

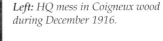

Left: HQ mess in Coigneux wood during December 1916.

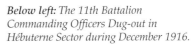

Below left: The 11th Battalion Commanding Officers Dug-out in Hébuterne Sector during December 1916.

Below: 11th Battalion Centre Company HQ in Woman Street in Hébuterne Sector during December 1916. Captain Reeve is in the right top of the picture.

how we got past that point. If I had not cursed and sworn...perhaps I cursed and prayed alternately...I should have cried out in agony at the utter hopelessness of the job. We drew nearer, waited for the shriek, the crash, ducked so low that the stinking mud touched our faces; took another pace or two, ducked again, and again, sweating and tearing our legs frantically out of that dreadful mud. The horror of that passage remains indelibly stamped on my mind.'

Upon getting to the relative firmness and safety of Warnimont Woods the stretcher case was allowed to walk, aided by two of the bearers, to the dressing station.

The casualty figures for the brigade, recorded at the time, during this operation were:

	Killed/DoW	Wounded	Missing
10th Bn			
Officers	0	0	0
Other ranks	6	34	1*
11th Bn			
Officers	0	2	0
Other ranks	12	41	0
12th Bn			
Officers	10	4	2
Other ranks	13	195	161
13th Bn			
Officers	8	4	4**
Other ranks	Total for all categories around 400		

(For more exact figures see appendices)

* Later known to be killed in action.
** Later found to have been taken prisoner.

The Battle of the Ancre was the last battle of the great Somme offensive, which officially finished on November 18th. The rest of the month was quiet for the brigade; quiet being comparative, and meaning to the army, training and working parties of one type or another. One highpoint in the post attack period was the visit by Lord Nunburnholme and party on the 18th. If the losses to the battalion were not already high enough, on the 14th an under age soldier was sent to base, nine other ranks were transferred to the 92nd Machine Gun Company and another officer died (2/Lieutenant Hoult from pneumonia). Similarly the 10th Battalion lost Sergeant

Goldthorpe to GHQ Cadet School and, due to the shortage of officers, the same battalion found it necessary to promote four NCOs to temporary 2/Lieutenants (Sergeant Shelton, Sergeant Tennison, Corporal Penn and Lance Corporal Petty).

December was also to be a quiet spell for the brigade which spent periods in the Hébuterne defences and periods around Bayencourt. Only the 11th Battalion was involved in any offensive work during the month. On the 23rd, a quiet day in which the rain continued to fall, Lieutenant Layton's enterprise party attempted to raid the German lines in two places. The war diary records that:

> '*Arrangements were made with the artillery for them to fire the usual three bursts which they had been doing during the last month. Between the 2nd and 3rd bursts of fire, the raiding party assembled in No Man's Land. Zero hour was 11pm. The 3rd burst of fire was at 11pm which was the signal for the raiding party to enter the German trenches. Both parties on arriving at the saps in the German wire which*

Privates Wharam, Sellers, Spencer and Oakes. B Company, 11th Battalion officers servants, Warnimont Wood, November 1916.

Officers mess orderlies in Warnimont Wood during November 1916.

Private Stark of the 11th Battalion in the line near Hébuterne during December 1916.

11th Battalion HQ Transport Section. Lieutenant Cowling and Sergeant Dunn at Sailly Dell during December 1916.

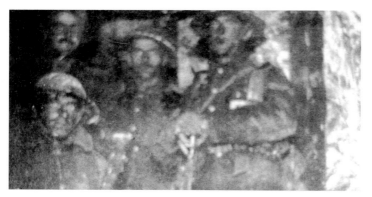

Number 3 Post dugout of the Right Company (11th Battalion) in the Hebuterne Sector during December 1916.

Lieutenant J B Mc Reynolds (ex RSM), of the 11th Battalion was killed by a stray shell on November 12th 1916 while coming back from checking that the troops had all that they needed.

Lieutenant Andrews who took some of the photographs of 11th Battalion officers and men.

Lieutenant Walshaw at the Reserve HQ in Hebuterne during December 1916.

the artillery had cut, found knife rests [portable entanglement of barbed wire stretched in cross-shaped frames] placed in the third row of wire about 10 yards from the parapet. The parties remained out for 1¼ hours trying to remove the obstacles without any results. The parties returned to our lines at 12.30am, having suffered one casualty, Pte. Gohl, who was killed by a rifle bullet.'

Even on Christmas Day the 11th Battalion was not prepared to let the Germans have any peace. Divisional artillery bombarded the German trenches from 4am to 6am with further bursts at 8am, 12pm, 3pm and 5pm. The enemy response was very muted. Lieutenant Layton took out a strong patrol to try and enter the German trenches. The patrol left the British lines at 6pm and proceeded to the German wire. The war diary recorded that:

Lieutenant N V Lewis of the 13th Battalion was killed in action on November 13th 1916 in the German lines.

> '*On arriving at the selected point the patrol found concertinas and loose wire placed across the gap in the second row of wire, with knife rests behind this obstacle. The patrol were unable to remove this obstacle and returned to our lines at 9.30pm, having suffered no casualties.*'

Reinforcements arrived constantly. One of these was Private Goldsmith who had previously served with the Army Cyclist Corps but had been transferred to the infantry as a signaller (later to transfer to the RE Signal Service). After remustering as an East Yorkshireman he was sent off to the front:

Captain Habersohn of the 12th Battalion was killed in action on November 13th.

> '*On a day in December 1916 we travelled overnight to Folkestone. When it was getting light our first sight was the cemetery at Shorncliffe!*
> '*We joined our unit, the 11th East Yorks, in due time and had our first taste of the trenches over Christmas.*'

The trenches were muddy and Private Goldsmith got stuck and was unable to extricate himself. His friend Private Johnson of Dartford reported this to their Company Commander who replied: 'What he wants is a bayonet in him.'

Private Johnson continued the story of their first days in the trenches:

> '*In the early morning some very intensive shelling was taking place and I was in a dugout on my signalling duties. Amidst all the noise of the shelling Goldsmith shouted, "Johnson, have you got a bachelor button?". Can you imagine that anyone should ask about such a thing at such a time? To Private Goldsmith it was quite an important question as his trousers kept falling down!*'

Only the 12th Battalion managed to celebrate Christmas. However, this was spread over two days, the 28th and 29th and was obviously not a particularly special one. The battalion war diary merely recorded: 'Men's Christmas dinners with concerts in YMCA hut.'

1916 finished on a different note to 1915. Then the battalions had been 'Pals' but now, with the constant flow of replacements, the battalions were quickly becoming diluted. The losses had been too great for the replacement battalion to cover and apart from the returning few originals, replacements were coming more and more from the East Yorkshire Regiment general pool of reserves and, failing that as a source, from any regiment. As early as October 12th Captain Watson wrote to his parents to tell them that: I got a draft from the Norfolk Regiment the other day'.

Fortunately, the majority of the replacements were still from Hull and the East Riding so the essential flavour of the brigade was retained for the forseeable future. However, at the rate of loss experienced since their arrival in France, it would not be long before there very few originals in the brigade.

The Iron Cross captured on November 13th 1916.

Chapter 6

'For you but not for me'
(The bells of Hell go ting-a-ling-a-ling)

France and Belgium 1917:
The German withdrawal

Unlike New Year 1916 in Port Said and any New Year in Hull, there were no boat hooters to sound in the New Year. Instead, the New Year saw the 10th and 13th Battalions in the trenches with the other two battalions in support. Still recovering from 13th November, the battalions were fortunate that January was a very quiet month both in and out of the trenches. From the battalion war diaries it seems that the month was spent in training, battalions practising battalion attacks, battalions practising brigade attacks, mending roads and playing football. The highlight of the month for the 11th Battalion was Christmas dinner on January 17th with entertainment by 'The Stunts', the battalion concert party, in the Music Hall during the early evening. The battalion band also performed.

February was also a comparatively slow month to start off with. All four battalions were out of the line and continued with their platoon, company, battalion and

Road leading into the village of Serre. In 1917 the Germans withdrew to the prepared fortifications of the Hindenburg Line and the British were able to walk into Serre unhindered.

brigade attack training as well as the obligatory working parties. There was also considerable specialist training in sniping, bombing, observing and the Lewis gun.

On the lighter side, there were a number of brigade and divisional competitions during the month. On February 10th, the 11th Battalion tug-of-war team won the brigade competition and went forward to represent the brigade in the divisional competition, beating the RE by 2 - 0 but losing 2 - 0, in the final, to the 16th West Yorks. The 11th Battalion bombing section won the brigade bombing competition on the 12th but the next day only managed to come 3rd in the Division. The highlight of the 14th was Corps Commanders Platoon Competition. Again this was won by the 11th Battalion. D16 platoon under Lieutenant Hutchinson, represented the battalion and scored 1920 out of 2080 points. The competition consisted of a five mile route march in full marching order and then each man had to fire 20 rounds rapid in under two minutes. Marks were awarded for march discipline and for the best turned out platoon. D16 Platoon were the best turned out and second in march discipline. On the 18th, the platoon competed against the rest of the Division and came first.

Captain C C Irvine MC, the 11th Battalion Doctor.

By the middle of the month the training had turned to open warfare attacks and on the 16th the Divisional Commander watched the 11th Battalion carry out a practice attack on three lines of trenches. In the afternoon was the Divisional Horseshow in which

Captain E W Reeve MC of the 11th Battalion.

both the 11th and 12th Battalions took prizes. The 11th won the final of the wrestling on horseback competition, beating the Northumberland Hussars in the final. Greater glory was achieved by the 12th which took five prizes for their animals:

1st prize (open) best pair HD [heavy draft horses] horses and vehicle
1st prize (Inf) for best turn-out of
    a) HD pair and vehicle
    b) Mules pair and vehicle
    c) Pack animal
2nd prize (Inf) officer's charger.

With the competitions over, the 11th and 12th Battalions returned to the trenches.

The German Withdrawal

The weather was very cold; so cold that the band's musical instruments froze while they were being played. But even the bitter cold did not stop small offensive operations around Serre from taking place. On February 24th information that the Germans had evacuated Serre reached the division and patrols were sent out to probe the German defences. A patrol by the 12th Battalion on the 25th met with considerable opposition resulting in two other ranks being killed, (L/Corporal Milner and Private Duggan) four wounded and 1 missing. The patrols sent out by the 11th Battalion had more luck.

At 6am two strong patrols went out into No Man's Land. The Northern patrol, commanded by 2/Lieutenant Thackray (A Company) was the leading patrol; the Southern patrol (B Company) was commanded by 2/Lieutenant Harrison. The war diary recorded:

'At 7.50 am a message from Harrison was received, stating that he had captured the German front line. At 9am another message was received from him that he had reached the German 3rd line, and that one prisoner had been taken. No news of the Northern patrol was received until 10am, when a message was received from Thackray saying that he had reached the 3rd German line at 8.50 am. A message from the Battalion on the right that they had failed and their patrol was back in our own line. At 9am a message was received that the brigade on our left had failed and had been ordered to withdraw. In the meantime the patrol under Harrison had pushed on and reached the German 4th line, but had withdrawn to the German 3rd

Company HQ of the 11th Battalion in Yankee Street in the Hebuterne Sector. On the top bunk is Lieutenant Woolcot underneath is Lieutenant Scotcher. On the right is Captain Willis.

Two heavy draught horses and vehicle, similar to those in the Divisional Horseshow competition.

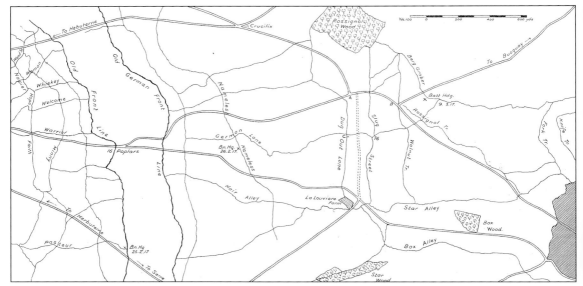

Map of the German Withdrawal from the Somme Front, February – March 1917 showing the area into which the 10th Battalion moved.

line owing to the bad condition of the 4th line. At 9.40 am Brigadier General O de L Williams ordered our patrols to withdraw, as the Battalion on our right and left had failed and not knowing how strong the Germans were holding their lines, our patrols might be cut off. At 9am Hutchinson took 16 platoon across with 60 boxes of bombs to reinforce Harrison. The Germans had now put a barrage on his old front-line and was shelling our front line. Our heavy artillery were called up to bombard all the known German batteries to quieten them while our patrols withdrew.

'The effect was excellent, both A & B Coys withdrew without suffering any casualties. Total casualties during the operation were 2 other ranks killed, 3 wounded, 1 missing believed killed [Privates Cruddas, Clare and Robinson]. All casualties with Northern patrol. German machine gun captured by Northern patrol.'

For their work that day 2/Lieutenants Harrison, Hutchinson and Thackray were awarded the MC. Private S Browne received the MM.

Shortly afterwards the two companies left the front line on being relieved by C Company with D Company in reserve.

While the 11th Battalion had been investigating the German withdrawal, the 10th Battalion had been ordered up to the front to help continue any advance. At 5.30pm A and C Companies crossed over No Man's Land to occupy the German 3rd line trenches and patrols were sent out to establish touch with the enemy.

The next day Battalion Headquarters and B and D Companies joined the other two companies in the new front line. At 1pm the battalion was ordered to advance towards Slug Street and if possible occupy it from Point 76 to La Louviere Farm. C Company occupied the farm but A Company, in clinging mud and in an unknown trench system, met with considerable resistance and had to withdraw. The battalion was then instructed to occupy the sunken road and take Berg Graben trench, if possible before dark. This attack by A Company was also unsuccessful, as was the attack in the darkness of the next morning. This series of abortive attacks had resulted in the loss of 2/Lieutenant Flicker and eight men killed, with two dying of wounds the next day. (The German account of these attacks estimated 200 British killed with 80 taken prisoner. British other rank deaths were Sergeant W Harrison, Corporal W Oxford and Privates W Warn, J Jackson, H Brown, E Smart, J Bradley and J Batchelor.) One officer and 31 other ranks were wounded and one officer, Captain Jones (later found to be a PoW), and two men were missing. Private Aust, who was present for this action, later recalled:

Major Shaw, 11th Battalion.

'It was at the outset of the German withdrawal. The division on our right reported suspected enemy withdrawal from his front trenches. Arrangements were made for our front line company to attack without bombardment at midnight and I was in a party assembled in a sunken road which was to follow over as a carrying party. At zero hour and five minutes we picked our way to the German second line of trenches, deposited our loads and returned to our lines. Imagine our surprise to find zero hour had been put back and the attacking Company were still in our own trenches.'

Major Wilberforce, 11th Battalion.

Private Beeken, who was also involved in this following up action recorded that:

'at 5.30pm we left the trench to go to the front line. From here we went over "the top" to take an evacuated German trench. As we silently walked through Hebuterne, the Germans shelled the place heavily. Our luck was in, for we suffered no casualties. The night was very dark. The guides lost their way. We prowled about. Some became entangled in barbed wire. At last dawn broke and it seemed that we had been walking in circles for we were not far from our starting point. Anyhow we arrived at the evacuated trench which was not far from our front line. On arriving at the trench we jumped in. We sank in mud, some almost to their waists. Finding I was sinking I fought hard and managed to get out of the mud and cling to the side of the trench. Not all the men were as fortunate as I had been. It took us two hours to free one man. Those who went to his assistance became stuck themselves and in turn had to be freed.

'Our Coy Hq's were in a German dugout. I was amazed at what I found when I explored it. The Germans evidently liked comfort. There were three flights of steps

Haucourt after the German withdrawal.

down. At the end of each flight was a spacious gallery. Here wire beds had been rigged up and there were stoves with chimneys. The trenches had been evacuated in a hurry for we found plenty of tobacco and coffee.'

After establishing strong points the battalion was forced to retire by the failure of the flanking battalions to hold their gains. The battalion then took up new positions in Dugout Lane and German Lane. In the afternoon contact had been made with 93 Brigade and 19th Division. Shortly afterwards the battalion was relieved by the 12th Battalion and marched to huts in Couin. The battalion war diary records that the next day:

Reverend R T Newcombe MC, the 11th Battalion Padre in Warnimont Wood.

'The Divisional Commander visited the Battalion in billets and asked the Commanding Officer to inform all ranks that he was very pleased with what the Battalion had done and that the Army Commander considered the Battalion had behaved splendidly.'

The 13th Battalion also went 'over the top' on the 27th to take over the evacuated trenches. Like the other battalions, they also found the trenches to be full of mud and difficult to navigate and although the Germans had withdrawn they found the trenches were still deadly. Private Surfleet, who had just navigated No Man's Land and was in a German trench recalled the experience:

'Lt. Col. Moore, our CO., was standing near me (like the rest of us, with one leg on each side of the trench to avoid sinking in the sludge) and he had just told one of the other Battalion to get down when the poor lad dropped flat in the mire with a bullet through his head. It was a horrible sight, yet, looking back at the incident, I am amazed how little notice we took, other than to feel sorry for the poor kid who was just being relieved. Shows how damned hard-hearted we are getting.'

March – 'In like a lion and out like a lamb'; this was certainly true for the 13th Battalion, which at 2am on the 1st, with two companies and one platoon, attacked Slug Street. By 5am the attack had failed because of thick barbed wire entanglements. The troops retired to their starting positions with the loss of two men, Privates W Dent and T Ward. A week later D Company attacked the German positions and failed to get into the trenches, this time with greater casualties; 2/Lieutenant Brown (KiA) and 16 men were missing and four wounded (seven KiA Privates R Livesey, W McNulty, J Gowans, H Kirman, F Watson, J Owen and A Barrett; Privates W Lingard and J Taylor died of their wounds the same day). A number of those missing were taken prisoner. For their part in the attack Lieutenant Herring was awarded a bar to

Officers of D Company, 11th Battalion, outside their dugout.

Bullecourt after the German withdrawal.

his MC, 2/Lieutenant Hamm was awarded the MC and Sergeants Starkey and Petrie, and L/Corporal Ward were awarded the MM.

D Company of the 10th Battalion was scheduled to attack Bucquoy on March 10th. However due to the mud, insufficient ammunition could be got to the artillery, therefore the attack was cancelled.

The only other battalion to be involved in combat during the month was the 11th Battalion. After relieving the 6th Wiltshire Regiment the battalion was ordered to advance its line into Star Wood (the old German 3rd line) which it did without opposition. On pushing further 2/Lieutenant Hutchinson was spotted and had to withdraw in the face of overwhelming fire. The next night in order to continue the slow movement forward 2/Lieutenant Cowling took out a patrol in order to capture Point 33 and then consolidate the gain. They were stopped by wire and fired upon but managed to withdraw, without loss, to Point 97. A Stokes mortar team under

Lieutenant Suthrien of the 11th Battalion, who was taken PoW in the March offensive in 1918.

Lieutenant Oakes went forward and bombarded Point 33 without success. The patrol and the Stokes mortar team withdrew but left the Lewis gunners a short way down the trench to see what might happen.

A strong German working party came down the trench and set to work. After a few minutes of watching the working party the Lewis gunners opened up and scattered them.

For the first half of the month the brigade spent a relatively quiet time in and out of the trenches providing working parties, holding inspections or being inoculated with T.A.B. [Typhoid-paratyphoid A and B vaccine]. The weather was bad and the trenches were very wet and muddy. On the 12th the 31st Division was squeezed out of the sector by the removal of the salient and on the 19th left for Robecq. After their arrival there on the 25th the brigade spent two weeks involved in light training exercises, football and resting.

On April 8th the brigade left for trenches near Vimy Ridge which fell to the Canadians on April 9th. In the following three weeks the brigade continued its programme of company training moving slowly towards its next major battle.

Their final destination was trenches near Oppy Wood. However, before arriving there, the brigade came under the orders of 2nd Division, relieving 99 Brigade. On the night of April 29th/30th, during this relief, the 13th Battalion were heavily shelled from midnight to 7am by high explosive, lachramotory and two kinds of gas shells. This made the relief very difficult, because each man had to wear box respirators all the time, but only one man was gassed. This shelling was the prelude to a German attack by bombers and rifle grenadiers. Fortunately, the attack was quickly repulsed and the attackers driven off, according to the war diary with: 'slight losses'.

Soldiers Died in the Great War shows that the attack resulted in the deaths of five soldiers on the 29th and a further six on the 1st; these were Privates H Green, G

Bell, F Murphy, C Gambles and J H Brock on the 29th; Privates R J Whaley, L Burgess, J F Fortman, J M McGlynn, J W Davison and J Bebbington on 1st May.

On 2nd May the 13th Battalion was relieved with the loss of a further six men – Sergeant R S Temple MM, and Privates G Savage, W Baker, A Schofield, A Greenwood, C A Sharp and W Ellerby.

Oppy Wood

Preparations for the forthcoming attack began on 1st May with Officers and NCOs of the 10th and 13th Battalions going forward to see the assembly positions, returning the next morning to begin issuing the material that had to be taken into the attack. At 11.00pm the 11th and 12th Battalions started to move to their assembly positions, with the 10th Battalion moving at 11.30pm. Start time for the attack was 3.45am with the 10th on the right flank next to 93 Brigade, the 11th in the centre and the 12th on the left flank next to a brigade of the 2nd Division.

The attack was designed to keep the enemy occupied and no great results were expected from what was to become the battle for which 'The Hull Pals' are best remembered. Oppy Wood was part of the Battle of Arras and the 31st Division formed part of XIII Corps' plan of attack on a two division front from the southern outskirts of Gavrelle to the southern corner of the wood south of Fresnoy. The 31st Division was fresh from reserve and was ordered to take over a considerable frontage from the exhausted 2nd Division. The Official History adds the comment that:

The battlefield near Hendecourt after the German withdrawal.

'The operation to be carried out was complicated by the fact that for about 750 yards the enemy still held the Oppy line west of Oppy Wood.'

On the 28th/29th April on the same battleground the Battle of Arleux was fought and the debris of that battle littered the ground. The assembly trenches were according to the 10th Battalion history:

'a map reference rather than an actuality, for the taping party of May 1st had found it to be merely an isolated untraversed length of trench barely four feet deep, with no communication to the rear, nor any means of contact to left or right.'

It was in this position that the 13th Battalion had incurred its casualties a couple of nights earlier.

As the battalions moved to the assembly trenches, guided by 13th Battalion troops, the moon, which was low in the sky, silhouetted the movement of the troops, while, during the assembly period, a German aircraft flew over. The assembly trench was only about 250 yards from the German trenches and Very Lights fell amongst the battalion whilst it was waiting. Finally, around midnight, a German patrol was spotted. At 12.30am the Germans commenced a twenty minute bombardment of the assembly area. After a short lull the bombardment re-started at 1.30; this time it was more fierce and continued until zero hour. Fortunately, casualties were few but confusion reigned.

The Battle of Gavrelle (part of the 3rd Battle of the Scarpe) was due to start at 3.45am, when the British barrage started. In response to this British barrage the Germans increased the intensity of their bombardment. The troops set off in four waves, in the dark, through the mist and fumes into a murderous machine gun fire. On the front being attacked by the 10th Battalion the wire had not been cut in many places and troops

2/Lieutenant Flick joined C Company, 11th Battalion, as a replacement, after the battle for Oppy Wood.

had to funnel through those areas that had been cut. All four company commanders were wounded and the smoke and dust made it impossible to see where the troops were going. While the troops were struggling forward, the barrage moved on quicker than the troops, allowing the Germans to become active with machine gun fire. The war diary admitted that it was impossible to give an accurate account of what happened but surmised that:

'A considerable number of men undoubtedly crossed the German line and got some way forward and possibly in places reached the first objective.'

After the war it was discovered that most of the 10th Battalion prisoners were actually taken in Oppy Village. In the battalion history there is an anonymous account written by a soldier who was taken near the village:

Sergeant Charles Walker of B Company, 13th Battalion, from Hull.

'*Still walking forward (at this time by himself) in the growing light, I became aware of a small party from A Company, under Lieutenant Akester. Under his order, we took up a position in an old trench, with Oppy village sixty or seventy yards away on our left front. We appeared to be isolated, and the sound of firing and bombing from a considerable distance to the rear seemed to indicate that the enemy's front line had not been taken.*

'*The officer left us to endeavour to make contact with some other party which might have also broken through, and, as our position had now been discovered, we engaged in a machine-gun duel with an enemy party about 150 yards ahead. I was with the gun on the extreme right of and somewhat detached from, our party, and so was not aware of all that took place. When a group of the enemy left their cover and advanced towards us, I prepared to open fire on what appeared to be the best target yet presented. A yell, "Cease fire," however, caused me to pause, and learned that some sign of surrender had been made further to the left. And so an action which would have been dubbed 'base treachery' was narrowly averted.*'

The battalion history also records the heroism of Private Green who went forward with the first wave of A Company and found himself alone and approaching a German machine gun with a crew of twelve. The story is better told in his own words:

'*They had stopped firing for a moment and I threw a Mills bomb which wrecked the gun, killed four men and wounded one, and the others then threw up their hands. Just then, Captain J. C. Addy jumped into the trench and when he saw the prisoners he said, "You'd better take them back, Green, you seem to have done your bit for today".*'

Captain Addy was killed shortly afterwards. Private Green was awarded the DCM for this act of bravery.

For those lying out in No Man's Land a long and harrowing day was ahead of them, unable to move because of artillery, machine gun fire and snipers in the wood, they had to lie there until dark. With the arrival of darkness the survivors were able

Lieutenant E J Andrew, 11th Battalion.

to leave their shell holes and make their way back to the assembly trenches where they were relieved by the 11th East Lanes, the war diary concluded that:

'The whole Bn although heavily tried by the German barrages attacked with the greatest dash and vigour and could not possibly have done better under the circumstances.'

10th Battalion casualties were estimated at the time as being:

	Killed	Wounded	Missing
Officers	1	7	6
Other ranks	7	103	107

These were later amended to four officers killed and seven wounded with two dying of wounds and three missing. The other ranks casualties were 68 killed in action, 46 missing and an unknown number who died of wounds (for the rest of the year there were fewer soldiers who were killed in action than died of their wounds, a large percentage of these were as a result of the fighting at Oppy Wood).

Private Beeken described the build up to the attack in his memoirs:

'The artillery on both sides, was active all night and at dawn it was intensified. The German heavies dropped just in front of us. An enemy aeroplane was brought down with the first shot from an "Archie" or anti-aircraft gun.

'It turned out to be a really lovely day. I read A Dominie's Log which I thought was a great book. In the evening we moved forward in "battle order" during which we had enemy shells dropping round us. At last we arrived at support trenches near Bailleuil.

'I slept in what we called a "funk" hole – a hole dug in the side of the trench. It gave some cover. We were not allowed to walk about on the "top" yet working parties carrying bombs, lights & rockets were walking in the open all the afternoon. There were no trenches for them to use for a fortnight previously an attack had been made by English troops with the aid of tanks, and the German artillery had been very severe in this area.

'There was an intense bombardment on our part and the Germans replied with a few shells. At night pack mules carrying 18 pounder shells made their way to our guns.

'In the evening we were busy receiving instructions for the attack.'

After the instructions came the move to the front and the wait for zero hour:

'We moved off at 9.25pm and arrived at our assembly places in front of Oppy Wood at midnight. The enemy guns were very busy but luckily we were not caught by them.

'My home now was a little shell hole which I shared with Bob Smith. We took off all our equipment for we badly needed a rest for we were worn out with carrying shovels, telephone and more besides other odds and ends e.g. more ammunition and bombs.

Robecq, a relatively undamaged village where the 10th Battalion spent some time during March and early April.

'At 12.30am May 3rd an intense German barrage fell on the almost nonexistent assembly trench. Bob and I set about making our shell hole deeper when the shelling stopped. Then at 1.30am an intense "strafe" was put on us. It lasted for about 20 minutes.'

As zero hour approached the Germans intensified their activities:

'Barrages were put on us at 2.30 am and at 3.30 am. We were having a hectic time. While this was going on our bombardment opened out and the Germans immediately intensified theirs.'

Zero hour and the Battalion moved forwards:

'We advanced to the attack. It was hell. Our shells were shrieking over us and bursting just in front. It was a creeping barrage advancing as we moved forward. The German shells were shrieking over us and bursting behind. Machine gun fire swept the whole front. Different coloured Very lights and rockets went up over the German lines.
    'As we moved forward Bill Smith said to me "Isn't it a pretty sight!". I replied with "Yes it is, but isn't it a lot of stuff missing us?".'

Unknown 11th Battalion officer outside a dugout somewhere on the Vimy front.

By 1917 the original members of the battalion were used to such minor irritations as shelling.

'Everything looked so weird in the fumes from the shells.

'Although we were only about 100 yards from Oppy Wood I couldn't see it, for a mist had descended. The fumes almost choked us and I had a splitting headache. As we walked on we saw a number of dead lying about. Eventually we met the sergeant major and his party who were lost. I was not surprised for we couldn't see where we were going. All we could do was to walk towards the lights. We then met men who were falling back. Our forward movement was checked at 5 a.m. We lay down and fired at groups of Germans who appeared out of the mist. They withdrew. We sat in a shell hole to decide on what we should do. It was decided that we should go back. Out went the men but a machine gun opened out and of course there were casualties. I was left alone. Looking out from the shell hole I saw a machine gun & crew directly in front and only about 30 yds away. I fired at the man behind the gun and then fired at the one who was on his left as he bent over his fallen comrade. Immediately I left the shell hole and was able to look round for any of the wounded men but I couldn't find them. Voices were calling me to go to them. I eventually found some of our party in a shell hole. Later we learned that three of our wounded men were with a party in a shell hole not far from us and that they had been bandaged. They were Smith, Summers and Clark. They were with a machine gun crew. We couldn't get back to our trenches for the German barrage cut us off. When at last it ceased it was too light for us to move about so we decided to wait until it became dark.'

Lying in a shell for the day in broad daylight was a dangerous proposition as Private Beeken found out:

'There was always the possibility of the Germans coming forward so we kept a sharp look out. We had plenty of excitement during the day for a sniper would persist in firing into our shell hole. He must have been in a tree but we couldn't see him. It turned out to be a very fine day but it was very hot. Aeroplanes of both sides flew over us and of course the guns blazed away at them. At 5pm after having had something to eat I was hit in the shoulder by a piece of shrapnel from the German guns firing at one of our aeroplanes.'

When the cover of darkness fell the men trapped in No Man's Land were able to try to get back to their lines. One of those trying was Private Beeken:

'At 9pm the machine gun crew informed us that they were going out. We asked them about the three wounded men who had dropped into their shell hole and were informed that one of them had died but that Summers and Smith were going with them. I told them that we were going back and I would send stretcher bearers to them, but they told me the wounded men were going back with them. We set off and eventually reached the scarcely recognisable trench of our company and then started to dig in. News was passed down the line to me that Summers had passed through our lines. Many wounded men came to our trench and all the time Fritz kept up his shelling.'

Lieutenant Traill also experienced problems during the attack. On his way across he was blown up by a shell just in front of the German line and when he regained consciousness he had lost his sense of direction entirely and wandered about in the semi-dark unable to recognise any landmark or to find his men. Once it became light he managed to round up a group of stragglers, but instead of retreating to safety he took his men forward into the thick of the fighting on the right of the battalion sector. Lieutenant Traill had suffered a shell splinter in the face on May 2nd and on the 3rd

The road to Arras from Mont St. Eloi showing the reserve positions. The 10th Battalion were stationed in the reserve trenches in Mont St. Eloi before the battle for Oppy Wood on 3rd May.

suffered from shell concussion. He was awarded the MC for his work on 3rd May.

Private Aust was fortunate to be left out of the attack:

> 'As we were waiting for nightfall before moving into our assault positions our
> sergeant came up and said he had instructions to keep 10 percent of our company
> out of the attack and that my pal and I were to be part of this.
>
> 'Two days later we realised our luck when the scanty remnants of our company
> rejoined and the roll call took place. Our Battalion's (sic) memorial at Oppy Wood
> on Vimy Ridge is a memorial to our good fortune as well as to the misfortune of all
> who died there. That was how you survived. Just being in the right place at the right
> time. You only had to be in the wrong place once.'

Shortly after Oppy Wood Private Aust joined the Company Signal team from
which he had previously been thrown out for indiscipline:

> 'instead of guns on the front-line fire-step or in shell holes I was now in the support
> trench perhaps 100 yards further to the rear and usually under some sort of
> protection.'

Another spectator was Private Surfleet, who recalled the effect of the
bombardment on the beautiful trees in the wood:

> 'they really looked beautiful and with its chateau peeping through the branches, it
> was a picture of serenity to be admired. But on the 4th day in, the wood was reduced
> by a barrage of heavies, under our very eyes, to a mere tangled mass of stumps.
> Whilst the chateau (a treacherous machine gun nest, we heard), was blown brick
> from brick. It was a wonderfully fearful sight to see the daylight gradually appear
> through the thickness of flying trees, all the more so as we could not hear the guns
> firing...When it all stopped we stood on the newly made fire-steps and were able to
> look right through the smouldering debris into part of Oppy Village: a remarkable
> sight.'

The 11th Battalion also suffered from the same starting problems:

> 'To get to the assembly positions Coys had to go over the top of a rise within 1000
> yds of the Bosch (sic) with a moon low in the sky behind them.'

The initial German bombardment did not affect them, but when it started at 1.40
am the battalion was forming up for the attack and as a consequence A and D
Companies did not form into their waves. This bombardment did not let up for the
whole of the day.

Their first objective was a line which ran east along the Arleux - Gavrelle road which runs between Oppy village and wood. The final objective was Oppy Support trench, which was 400 yards east of the village. Facing the battalion were the 1st and 2nd Guards Reserve Divisions, which the East Yorkshire Regimental history describes as: 'some of the bravest of the enemy's troops'.

At 3.45am, zero hour, the battalion had been lying out in the open under a heavy barrage for two hours and five minutes. The war diary succinctly describes the action:

> *'our barrage started at 3.45am advancing at a rate of 100 yds in four minutes and the Battalion followed 50 yds in the rear of the barrage. It was dark, the smoke and dust caused by our barrage, and the hostile barrage, also the fact that we were advancing on a dark wood made it impossible to see when our barrage lifted off the German trench. Consequently the Hun had time to get his machine guns up. Machine guns were firing from within the wood from trees, as well as from the front trench, nevertheless the men went forward, attacked and were repulsed. Officers and NCOs reformed their men in No Man's Land under terrific fire and attacked again, and again were repulsed. Some even attacked a third time, some isolated parties got through the wood to OPPY VILLAGE and were reported there by aeroplanes at 6am. These men must have been cut off and surrounded later. The Battalion was so scattered and casualties had been so heavy that it was decided to consolidate the only assembly trench we had when the battle started.'*

The Hull Brigade positions and objectives for the Battle of Oppy Wood.

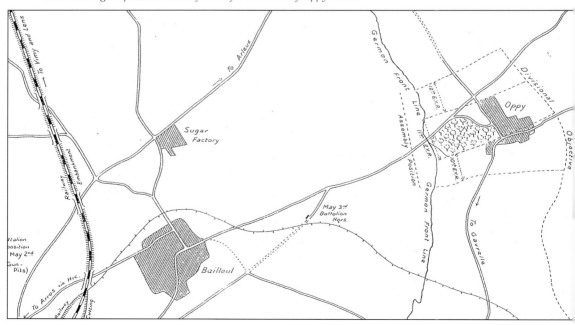

188

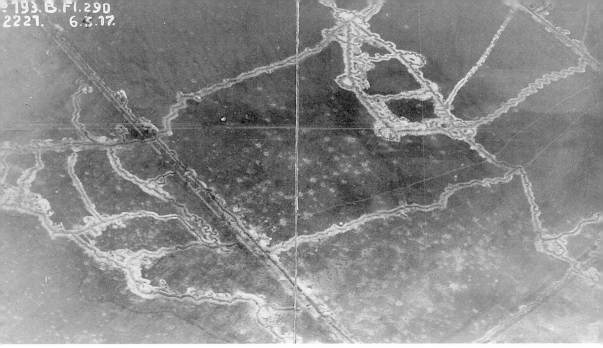

An aerial photograph to show trench layout and how much shelling was wide of the mark. The photograph was taken on 6th April 1917.

[Captain Reeve and 2/Lieutenant Harrison missing believed killed; Lieutenants Staveley and Reeves, 2/Lieutenant Ekins, Woolcott, Purll and Hutchinson missing; Captain Barber and 2/Lieutenant Burton, Davie and Galloway wounded; nine other ranks killed, 150 wounded and 98 missing – war diary casualty estimates.]

It was during this attack that 2/Lt. Harrison won the Victoria Cross (see appendices). *Soldiers Died in the Great War* shows 56 other ranks were killed in action on 3rd May, with a further seven dying of wounds the next day.

At 10pm the battalion was relieved by the 11th East Lancs and proceeded back to camp for a short rest.

As the battalions were being relieved men from the 13th Battalion were out on the battlefield collecting in the dead and wounded. One of these was Private Surfleet, who recorded his thoughts in his diary a few days later:

'*We went out at night on a stretcher-bearing party; quite the most efficient and well organised affair I have been on. We first of all got in all the wounded we could find and scoured the whole area. I think it is creditable that every wounded man was brought in: a different tale to that of previous attacks on this seemingly impregnable wood, and far easier than that of that unforgettable November 13th, when mud and shelling made the task almost impossible. There were dozens of dead bodies about; we collected all we could and stacked them in piles ready for removal to a decent burial further back. I am still amazed at the casual way we piled those bodies like so many huge logs, without any sense of horror at such a gruesome task.*'

But not all the wounded had been accounted for. Two days later Private Surfleet was in the trenches when they noticed someone waving at them from No Man's Land:

'Whilst we were gazing at this peaceful scene we noticed a chap stretched out in the strip of road, the Bailleul-Oppy road, which ran by the end of the bit of trench we were in. He waved an arm in our direction: Whole, Hirtse, Bridge and I took a stretcher from the pile outside the M.O's place and ambled along the road to him. Only until we got right up to him did we realise he must have been in full view of the enemy...we put him on a stretcher and brought him back to our Aid Post. He had been out there two days and nights with his leg shattered and had been trying to get back to our lines, using an old rifle as a crutch.'

Sergeant Henry Walter Utton who was killed in action on 3rd May. Before the war he was a wood-turning machinist. He enlisted on 10th May 1915 in the 4th Battalion, one week before his daughter (who he never knew) was born. In February 1917 he was drafted to France where he joined the 12th Battalion just before the attack. During the attack he got into the German front line where he was wounded twice. He was left behind during a German counter-attack and later reported missing. His remains were found in May 1927 and he was interred in Orchard Dump Cemetery.

On 1st May the 12th Battalion had moved from the German trenches to Railway Cutting trenches, suffering three casualties. The next day the battalion lost another soldier wounded and one to hospital sick. On the 3rd the battalion was to report casualties of two officers (Captain Carroll and 2/Lieutenant A Duguid) and seven other ranks killed, six officers (2/Lieutenant Carrall, Cooper, Fenwick, Hall, Hignett and Jennings) and 150 other ranks missing and one officer (2/Lieutenant Glaves) and 127 other ranks wounded plus one officer dying of wounds (2/Lieutenant Moore). *Soldiers Died in the Great War* lists 81 other ranks killed in action on the 3rd with the 12th Battalion.

Like their sister battalions they were seen moving up to their assembly trench and were heavily bombarded. The war diary recorded the whole day very briefly:

'The assembling took place in brilliant moonlight over quite unknown country and with four guides. The enemy evidently saw the troops assembling and put up an intensive barrage followed by another one later. This considerably distinguished things and at zero hour, the blackest part of the night, the troops moved forward to the attack. They failed to obtain their objectives and were compelled to withdraw to the assembly trench, where they remained all day under heavy shellfire.'

The 11th East Lancs relieved the battalion at 10pm and the 12th Battalion moved out of the line.

190

Considering the losses, the bravery shown by the three battalions and the confused situation in which the battle was fought, the honours awarded were not exactly generous. In the 10th Battalion Sergeant Sendall and Private Green were awarded the DCM, Captain Traill was awarded the MC, Corporal Crooks was Mentioned in Dispatches and an unknown number of soldiers received the MM. The 11th Battalion received nine awards; CSM Woodall and Sergeant Clayton were awarded the DCM, Corporal Kitching, L/Corporal Anson and Privates Dobbs and Nix received the MM and Lieutenant Bradley, RQMS Smith and Sergeant Kelly were Mentioned in Dispatches. Only five MMs were awarded to the 12th Battalion (Sergeant Norman, Corporal Robinson and Privates Early, Harrison and Sutcliffe). Although the 13th Battalion had not been directly involved in the action during May Captain Morgan, Lieutenant Roper and 2/Lieutenant Kallend were Mentioned in Dispatches and Corporal Redfern and Privates Barkworth, Challons, Refern and Redhead were awarded the MM.

Lance-Corporal John Busby, regiment number 12/551 was killed in action on 3rd May.

The losses suffered by the 12th Battalion resulted in it being reorganised into two composite companies from A and C, and B and D, with the former being attached to the 10th Battalion and the latter being attached to the 11th Battalion. After a week the Battalion was reformed, only to be loaned to 93 Brigade for two days.

On the 13th it relieved the 15th West Yorks near Gavrelle. After three days in the front line the battalion left the line for a four day rest, returning on the 20th to relieve the Hood Battalion. During this six day tour of duty the battalion constructed a strongpoint in the Red defence line east of Willerval. Upon relief the battalion

Private Walter Busby, elder brother of John Busby was killed at Oppy Wood on 28th June. Neither of the two brothers' bodies were found and they are commemorated on the Arras Memorial.

The battlefield behind Oppy Wood after its capture later in the year.

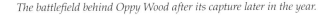

Long range heavy artillery was used to destroy Oppy Wood before the battle. Here a heavy gun is being man-handled into position.

moved to billets. During this rest period the battalion was involved in work on the roads in the Roclincourt area. In this 'rest' period it suffered a further six deaths in action and one death from wounds, five soldiers were hospitalised with sickness, 2/Lieutenant Officer died from wounds and over 50 other ranks were wounded but only 38 soldiers reported as replacements.

After the failed attack, the 13th Battalion did a spell of duty in the trenches near Gavrelle Windmill. The weather was hot and the battalion had suffered some fatal casualties and there were unburied bodies in No Man's Land. Private Surfleet had to navigate the trenches and later recorded what he experienced:

Lieutenant John Harrison MC, of the 11th Battalion, was posthumously awarded the Victoria Cross for his bravery in attacking a German machine gun position on 3rd May. He has no known grave and is commemorated on the Arras Memorial.

> *'What a bloody trench! It was blown in in several places and splashed with blood (and God knows what else) all over the place. I remembered a similar smell in a slaughterhouse when I was a boy, but I doubt if I shall forget the sight of those dismembered, torn, shell-racked bodies which, pushed up on to the parapet and parados out of the way until they could be buried, were covered with great, big, bloody awful blue-bottles. I felt physically sick. The sun was blazing down on this gruesome collection of flesh; over the top other decomposing bodies, fly infested and stinking, stewed in the heat.'*

With the division becoming the Corps reserve on the 20th, life quietened down considerably.

At the beginning of June trench activity restarted. Out of the trenches there was a considerable increase in company and battalion training, occasionally watched by senior officers such as Lieutenant General Congreve, XIII Corps Commander. During this period specific platoons were picked out for training as 'Storming Troops'. Once again there was a Brigade Horseshow and on the 16th there was a swimming sports competition. The 17th was marked by the distribution of medal ribbons by the Divisional Commander, to all those in the 11th Battalion who had won decorations that year. Finally, there was the Divisional Horseshow in which the 11th Battalion came second to the Field Ambulance team in the wrestling on horse back competition.

June 28th had been set as the date for the next attack on Oppy Wood. XIII Corps Commander was hoping to advance his line by two to five hundred yards over a frontage of just over 2000 yards. Originally scheduled for July it was brought forward because of the need to transfer some of the XIII Corps heavy artillery to Flanders for the forthcoming offensive there – the Battle of Ypres, 1917. As it had to be brought forward, the attack that was to be made in conjunction with it (on the area around the Souchez River) had to be reduced in scope. This attack was designed to focus German attention on the British front and was part of a feint towards Lens and Lille over the period June 26th to 30th carried out by the 1st, XIIIth and Canadian Corps.

German trenches like those in Oppy Wood.

Oppy Wood with a shell exploding close to the wood's edge and near the road. Taylor Library

This time Oppy was to be attacked by 94 Brigade with 92 Brigade assisting. The 10th Battalion formed the Brigade reserve, the 11th was to hold the front line with two companies while the 13th was to provide carrying parties.

On the 19th, 92 Brigade relieved 94 Brigade in the Oppy-Gavrelle sector. In order to gain information for the forthcoming attack a brigade raiding party was planned for the night of the 22nd. Each battalion was to provide two officers and fifty men for a raid on Cadorna Trench. Its object was, as detailed in Operational Order No. 1:

'to kill Germans, secure identifications, and bring back M.G.s also to reconnoitre the enemy's defences and note hostile M.G. Emplacements.'

In order to disguise the attack, at Zero hour the whole of 93 Brigade front would open fire with rifles, Lewis guns and machine guns. They would also fire white rockets, German ones if they were available, to confuse the enemy. On 92 Brigade front there would be no artillery until Zero hour when a barrage would open up fifty yards from Cadorna Trench. At Zero plus 1 the barrage was to lift to Cadorna trench and at Zero plus 3, in order to allow the raiding party to enter the trench, the barrage was to advance a further 100 yards. At Zero plus 4 the barrage was to lift to Windmill trench and after this the barrage was to continue for about forty minutes and then gradually die down. In order to confuse the enemy, the divisions on both sides of the attack would also put down an artillery barrage.

Zero hour was fixed for 10.20 pm. As the raiders advanced across No Man's Land there was slight hostile machine gun fire from Oppy Wood and before they could enter Cadorna Trench small parties of the enemy were encountered by all the battalion parties except the 13th. These parties were eliminated and prisoners taken. An account written by Lieutenant Colonel Ferrand, Officer Commanding 92 Brigade 'Enterprise', detailed what happened when they got to Cadorna trench:

'CADORNA TRENCH was found to be obliterated and the front line advanced over it and beyond without knowing it. The right Battalions found CADORNA TRENCH to be a series of shell holes connected by shallow trenches; and in rear of this were several empty M. G. emplacements.

'Several hostile posts were found in the rear of CADORNA TRENCH and these men ran away as we approached. Our men followed them up almost to WINDMILL TRENCH where the Germans ran into our barrage. A few prisoners were taken on the E side of CADORNA TRENCH and several casualties were inflicted on the Germans.

'The raiders having gone close to our barrage on Windmill Trench were then ordered to withdraw and during the withdrawal a hostile machine gun was found 30 yards East of the Gavrelle-Oppy road about c.19.a.00.30 chained and pegged to the ground.

'A great effort was made to bring it in but it was impossible to move it, so it was damaged with knobkerries [wooden truncheon with spikes].'

The dreaded telegram. Captain Leech died on 10th May in Number 1 Red Cross Hospital at Le Touquet. He had been wounded on 3rd May by a bullet in his left thigh (PRO).

195

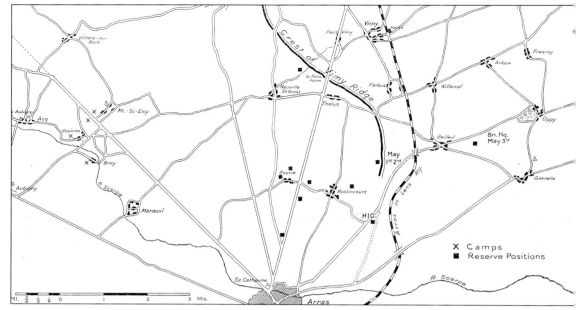

Bray was the rest area for the 10th Battalion after the battle. As with most villages in the area it was badly damaged by shelling.

The ruined church at St Vaast.

'During the raid the Germans from Wood Alley tried to get round our left flank but the flank guard which consisted of 1 Lewis Gun Section and ten men drove them off and inflicted severe casualties on them.

'The raid was most successful, a considerable number of casualties were inflicted on the enemy and 7 unwounded prisoners were brought in.

'Our casualties were: 1 O.R. Killed 1 Offr. and 31 O.R's Wounded (mostly slight) 11 O.R. Missing.'

[The four killed were Privates W Homan and P Martindale (10th Battalion); Privates A Cook and A Bull (12th Battalion) with a small number dying of wounds in the days following.]

After the raid officers reported to Raiding Party HQ, prisoners were escorted to Divisional HQ and the men returned to Railway Trench for the issue of tea and a ration of rum.

On the 26th the 11th Battalion was shelled by the enemy but fortunately they had moved back and so suffered no casualties. That night the battalion was relieved by the 12th Yorks and Lancs. The next night, prior to the attack, A Company of the 11th Battalion took over the Windmill defences from the 14th Yorks and Lancs. The brigade took no direct part in the taking of Oppy Wood, but at 5pm on the 27th carrying parties from the 13th Battalion left for duty with the attacking battalions of 94 Brigade. At 12 noon on the 28th C Company moved from the railway cutting to its assembly trenches and at 2.30 pm Battalion HQ was set up in Marine Trench. At 5pm the enemy put down a barrage on the British front and support lines causing many casualties to C Company, including six deaths, among them some original Pals (Privates Brough, Bushby, Johnson, Morley, Woollons. Also killed was Private Bussell an East Yorkshire Regiment Kitchener volunteer).

At 7.10pm 94 Brigade attacked Cadorna Trench, Wood Alley and Windmill Trench, successfully taking all its objectives; 56 prisoners were taken and one machine gun captured. The Official History (Volume 2 1917) recorded that:

'The Germans were expecting attack, and at 5.30pm, when the jumping-off trenches were full of troops, laid a barrage on them for ten minutes.'

Despite 200 casualties the assault was not affected in any way. The history continued:

'So rapid was the advance that when the barrage fell on No Man's Land, three minutes after the start, it was already clear of troops. In the actual assault, few casualties were incurred, and besides 200 hundred prisoners taken, 280 German dead were counted in the captured area.'

At 6am on the 29th the 11th Battalion moved back to billets at Aubrey Camp, leaving 94 Brigade to reorganise in depth.

Lance-Corporal George Albert Maltby of the 13th Battalion on his wedding day, 23rd June 1917. He had joined up in 1914 when he was just 18. He worked for the Post Office as a messenger boy.

This photograph of Lance-Corporal George Maltby's wife was found on the battlefield after he was wounded in the face by a bullet. The finder returned the photograph to the address on the back (his wife's parents).

The 10th Battalion, in reserve, reported that there was little retaliation on the Red line but a great deal on Bailleul Post and that they had suffered three men wounded. It was a quiet night.

That manpower was short is shown by one entry on the 10th Battalion War Diary concerning effective strength. At the end of June it was 34 officers and 623 other ranks compared with the 33 Officers, 6 Warrant Officers and 920 men with which the battalion had left Egypt.

Vimy

The division left the Gavrelle area at the beginning of July and headed for the Mericourt area to relieve the Canadians. During a period in the trenches in July, 92 Brigade found themselves in the trenches near Vimy Ridge side by side with a Canadian Division. It was during this tour that Private Aust of the 10th Battalion met his unknown cousin in the front line. The battalion were on the firestep when a Canadian patrol appeared. Private Aust was in his dugout when he was aroused by his Sergeant who said:

> '"The Canadian patrol has just come in and one of them is asking for you". I replied "Canadians? I don't know any Canadians; there must be some mistake". The Sergeant replied "He says his name is Aust - the same as yours - so you can sort it out. He says you are his cousin."'

It was indeed his cousin. Private Aust's father had a brother who emigrated to Canada and disappeared from family consciousness. While on leave in London the Canadian Private Aust had tracked down an aunt, who only two days previously had been traced by the English Private Aust's parents. They had left her with their son's army address, which the Canadian had seen, and recognised as the division that was next to them. On his first night back the Canadian had been sent out on patrol and they had been ordered to make contact with the 31st Division next to them (there being no direct trench link between the adjacent divisions) and by a strange coincidence Private Aust of the 10th Battalion just happened to be in the last platoon on the left of the battalion front.

Private Surfleet recalled the reserve trenches around Roclincourt, a destroyed village:

> 'Billeted in trenches, and such trenches! Many French and German (and a few British) buried here and the whole area is a veritable rabbit warren of trenches and old dug-outs in which we live when not on working parties up the line. The top step of our particular stink-hole consisted of a kind of soft bagging which, when wet with rain, exuded a red fluid which trickled down the steps. We found it better to ignore it, for conjectures are not pleasant when you come across more than one poor soul

buried in sand-bagging and forming part of the trench side, as we did in that area. To dig around was most unpleasant.'

The front at Vimy had a No Man's Land that was very wide and had to be constantly patrolled. Private Wilson, who joined the 12th Battalion during this period, recalled that:

'there was a tendency with the higher command to demand from us a more aggressive attitude, and not the live and let live which most of us adopted. Majors with red tabs would come and give pep talks on hating Germans. It didn't work; we laughed at them.'

In order to make sure that the men did bring back prisoners, the Commanding Officer of the 12th Battalion, Lieutenant Colonel Gurney, made them an offer they could not refuse. Private Wilson recalled that:

'we did occasional raids on the German trenches for identification purposes. Our Colonel made the raiding party an offer. It was "one barrel of beer per Bosche". They got their beer.'

Thought to be Company Sergeant-Major W Brain of the 13th Battalion.

The East Yorkshire Regiment in the Great War by E Wyrall mentions the frequency of the patrols and the infrequency of the shelling; it also mentions the great distances between the two front lines in places. Although the shelling might not have been as frequent as on their previous front it could be just as deadly. The war diary of the 11th recorded for July 27th:

'Quiet on our front. VIMY VILLAGE was heavily shelled in the evening by 8" guns.'

And on the 28th:

'Quiet on our front. Our battery positions in VIMY VILLAGE were heavily shelled throughout the day. An ammunition dump in VIMY VILLAGE was "put up" during the morning. The night was quiet.'

Sergeant William Whitby, of B Company 13th Battalion (from Hull), was wounded in 1917 and discharged because of the severity of his wounds.

That this sector was quieter is indicated by an order issued on August 5th which told the troops that: 'all inhabited dugouts must be cleaned and disinfected.'

A further order, which suggests that the enemy might not have been too close, or alternatively, that the division was not being as aggressive as it could have been, was also issued at the same time:

'Officers and men are encouraged to use their rifles daily.'

Private Aust recalled an unusual incident while manning the trenches during this period:

'on Vimy Ridge one summer's evening in 1917 we were amazed to see thousands of balloons coming from our rear and floating over the German trenches, the German air force was quickly on the scene trying to shoot them down but with negligible success. Each balloon had a number of leaflets attached by a cord which in turn had a fuse attached... there were facsimilies of letters of German POW to their families and aerial photos of the mole at Zeebrugge.'

Why the harbour defences at Zeebrugge should be so prominent is a mystery for they were not attacked until April 1918!

Losses during the period from the middle of July to September 7th (just over seven weeks) were also relatively small, indicating that it was a quiet area (32 other ranks were killed in action or died of wounds in this period). Private Goldsmith was one of the casualties:

'I was wounded at Mericourt, near Vimy Ridge, in July 1917. I remember the doctor at Rouen telling me I had got a "Blighty" one, but I was feeling pretty awful when he said this - I could not have cared less. We travelled back to England down the Seine. As I was carried on a stretcher to the train at Southampton a young lady came along with chocolates; I was very surprised to learn they were on the house!'

What was to have been a highpoint for the 10th Battalion turned out to be anything other than enjoyable. On 10th July, the battalion, as well as other troops, were to be viewed by the King while he drove to his next destination. However, the day was dull and

Private McLachlan of the 10th Battalion taken in late 1917. By now he had been in the army for three years and on the Western Front for about 20 months.

chilly and the troops, who had supposedly just fallen out for a ten minutes rest, were kept waiting for some considerable time. By the time the King eventually appeared the waiting troops could muster up very little enthusiasm or surprise, with the result that the cheering lacked spontaniety and was rather cardboard like.

Moving back to a more active zone meant that death or wounding could occur at any time, from all sorts of sources. This is shown by the following entry from the war diary of the 11th Battalion:

'Relieved 13th Battalion. Two Other Ranks of C Coy were wounded half an hour after the relief was complete by a shell which struck a tree behind the trench.'

Further north the battles for Ypres raged but for 92 Brigade August was a very quiet month, with trench duty interrupted by working parties when on rest and company training in platoon attacks. On 5th August, five officers and 120 other ranks from each battalion of 92 Brigade travelled in lorries and buses to 1st Army HQ at Ranchicourt, for a special church parade to commemorate the fourth anniversary of the start of the war. Lieutenant Colonel Ferrand was the officer commanding the 31st Division contingent. Representatives from the 1st, 2nd, 13th and

2/Lieutenant Frank Walker of the 11th Battalion who won the MC for his part in the Fresnoy raid. He had enlisted at the start of the war into the 4th Battalion and been commissioned in 1916.

Canadian Corps were present for the service which commenced at 11am. There were also French and Portugese representatives present. General H S Home, 1st Army Commanding Officer, opened the service with a short address. After the service he decorated several officers with Belgian medals. The parade ended with a march past the Army Commander.

Arleux

September saw a return to the Arleux sector where on the 7th, the 31st Division relieved the 5th Division. The next few months were static, with the battalions serving their tour in the line and then moving back and eventually the whole brigade moving into rest. Working parties were the norm, as were patrols and as the nights drew in the patrols went out by day and night.

Patrolling was continuous, with many days being spent trying to find some particularly annoying machine gun or trench mortar. The 11th Battalion reported patrols on the 14th, 15th, 16th and 17th designed to locate a machine gun and a trench mortar; neither of which were found. One night patrol on October 27th resulted in the loss of Lieutenant Lawes and two other ranks. All three were taken prisoner.

Out of the line, training continued with companies doing night wiring, company training and marching in box respirators. Light relief consisted of Divine Service with a bath in the afternoon and for officers and NCOs visits to aerodromes to see the different types of aeroplanes and bombs or visits to a tankadrome at Whalley Park for a demonstration by tanks or a demonstration of the 6 inch Newton Mortar. On October 8th the 11th Battalion were visited by journalists from Yorkshire papers who interviewed several NCOs and men who had gained honours in recent months.

The arrival of numbers of American troops in France meant that their officers had to be trained in trench warfare before they could take their men into the trenches. On October 28th Lieutenant Howe of the United States Army joined the 11th Battalion for instruction.

Two raids of importance took place between September and December, although all battalions participated in small raids throughout this period. The first important raid occured on September 12th and was carried out by the 10th Battalion and one on November 8th by the 11th Battalion.

The raid on 12th September, on a trench west of Fresnoy Road, was a relatively small affair with 40 other ranks and three officers (2/Lieutenants Piper, McDermott and Southern). Its purpose, as usual, was to kill the enemy and gain information and identifications. In this it was sucessful, returning with one live prisoner of the 15th RIR (11th Reserve Division). Its success was marred by the death of 2/Lieutenant Southern. The Corps Commander awarded the bar to the MM to Cpl. W Noble and the MM to Privates Rogers and Seacombe for gallantry and initiative during this raid.

The second important raid of this period occured on 8th November. However, preparations for this raid had started some time before this date. During the previous month officers and men from each of the four companies had been formed into special parties which had undergone special training on the 'Bullet, Bayonet, Bullet' course. Intensive training was carried out which was watched by the Brigade and Divisional Commanders.

On the night of 31st October/1st November a special party of three officers and 75 other ranks made a reconnaissance of the proposed raid area. This was followed by a further reconnaissance on the night of the 2nd/3rd with a dress rehearsal the next day. To make it easier to leave the trench, and for ease of crossing No Man's Land, the regimental history recorded that Major Shaw, the Second in Command, had, for six nights before the raid:

'one officer and four other ranks from each company making steps out of the assembly trenches for each of the 28 sections, marking the flanks of each section in the assembly trench, cutting two gaps in the wire for each company to go out by, laying camouflage tapes from the assembly trenches where there was a chance of seeing the raiders

assembling (the raid taking place in daylight), and providing and training guides to lead each raiding party through the gaps in the wire.'

At 2pm on 7th November the special raiding party of 13 officers and 406 other ranks under Lieutenant-Colonel Ferrand left the prepared training ground at Mont St. Eloi and marched to Ecoivres where the Divisional Commander addressed them. At 3pm the party entrained for the railhead and from there they marched to Long Wood for the night. The party consisted of three officers and 75 men from each company:

A Company - Captain C A Saville
B Company - Captain W H Chapman
C Company - Lieutenant F Walker
D Company - Captain C Oake.

Each company had four Royal Engineers and a small Lewis gun section attached. In reserve was a platoon of the 13th Battalion under Lieutenant Agerskow. Zero hour was 12 noon. To assist the raid the 13th Battalion put up a smoke screen which drew down considerable enemy artillery.

Two officers of the 10th Battalion. The officer on the left was commissioned into a Territorial Battalion.

The story of the raid was told by Lt. Colonel Ferrand in his report:

'On Y/Z night, the raiding party, strength 13 officers, and 406 other ranks rested at Long Wood. At 8 a.m. Z day Companies began to move up Tired Alley at ten minutes interval. The whole party was in position in the Assembly trench, 1 hour and ten minutes before ZERO hour. The whole time we were assembled hostile aeroplanes were flying up and down the trenches, about 2,000 - 3,000 feet high, but all ranks had been warned to keep absolutely still and not look up.

'At ZERO -15 a FEW (sic) 4.2"s (sic) fell in the wire in front of the Assembly Trench. At ZERO hour each section left the trench by its own steps and ladders. They went through our wire in small columns and extended when E(ast) of our wire.

'Every wave of the Companies got in touch throughout, before our barrage lifted off the German front line.

'Very few casualties were found in TORTOISE, what there were, were found, where TULIP and TOBACCO join TORTOISE. The first wave stopped in TORTOISE TR. the remainder passing on to FRESNOY TR.

'When the barrage lifted off FRESNOY TR. the trench was rushed, and very little

The entry of the United States into the war on the Allied side meant that there would be millions of extra troops available for use on the Western front. The picture shows the arrival of General Pershing at Boulogne.

opposition was encountered. A good many Germans ran away from FRESNOY TR. when our barrage lifted off it, and rapid Lewis gun and rifle fire was opened on them, inflicting many casualties. The remainder ran into our barrage, most of the Germans in FRESNOY TR. were in their dugouts with their gas masks on. [Dummy gas had been projected over the German lines]. Very few Germans would come out of their Dugouts (sic) so the R.E.s blew up all the dugouts and their occupants, with 20 lb charges.

'The withdrawal commenced about ZERO plus 20, when all the Dugouts (sic) had been blown up and the trench cleaned up.'

During the raid German reinforcements, estimated at two companies, were sent towards Fresnoy trench but were driven back by Lewis gun fire. After the raid the raiders returned to Mont St. Eloy by train.

Lieutenant-Colonel Ferrand estimated that the raiders had done the following damage:

No. of enemy Dugouts blown up by Mobile Charges	*15.*
No. of Enemy (sic) dugouts blown up by Bombs.	*1.*
No. of enemy Trench Mortars blown up by Mobile Charges	*1.*
No. of Trench Mortars blown up by Artillery	*1.*
No. of enemy Machine Guns (sic) blown up	*1.*

No. of enemy machine guns blown up by Bombs.	*2.*
No. of enemy machine guns captured	*1.*
No. of enemy trench mortars (sic) captured.	*Nil.*
No. of Prisoners Taken (sic).	*21.*
No. of Germans thought to have been killed in Dugouts at least.	*150.*
No. of Germans actually killed by our own men in enemy trenches	*54.*

'It is estimated that another 40 Germans running away from Fresnoy Trench were killed or wounded by our rapid fire, Lewis gunfire, and artillery barrage.'

The German artillery also caused casualties among its own men. A Company Commander and his staff were captured, but were killed in No Man's Land by German shells.

British casualties were Captain Saville, Lieutenant Wright and 2/Lieutenants Clift and Oliver killed and 16 other ranks killed or dying of wounds on the 8th with a further four dying within the next few days (a total of 52 other ranks were killed or wounded). Sergeant Maritt won the DCM but was killed in the raid.

The raid was a great success and on the 14th the Corps Commander inspected the raiding party and congratulated them.

Raiding was not peculiar to the British. On November 30th the Germans raided an outpost manned by the 12th Battalion. This was stoutly resisted by the defenders and the enemy raiders failed to enter the British trenches. After the encounter, which lasted 15 minutes, 2/Lieutenant Local who was commanding the post, reorganised his men for a counterattack which resulted in the enemy retiring in haste, leaving behind one wounded soldier (6th Company, 2nd Battalion, 459 Infantry Regiment, 236 Division) who died before he could be interrogated.

Shortly after this raid the platoons in each battalion were re-organised to reflect the roles played by the infantry in trench warfare; each platoon now contained a section of riflemen, rifle grenadiers, bombers and Lewis gunners. Special classes were also started for snipers. Field training for every eventuality was intensive. On November 15th a platoon from B Company of the 10th Battalion represented the Division

The 1917 Christmas card from Craiglockhart War Hospital for officers suffering from Neurasthenia (mental or physical weariness and an inability to cope with anything but the simplest tasks). 2/Lieutenant Stanley Howarth of the 11th Battalion entered the hospital on March 19th 1917. The Medical register recorded that he was aged 29, that he had served in the army for one year and eight months of which five weeks had been spent on active service in France. He was a Baptist. On 26th June he was returned to duty.

in the XIII Corps Platoon Competition. The officers of the two finalist platoons were given, on a map, the position and limits of a strongpoint they had to capture. The attack was to take place over the old battlefields near Ecurie. The 10th Battalion went first, scoring 88.6 percent with the rival platoon scoring 54 percent.

As usual when the brigade was out of the line, the battalions were busy digging. The fortifications they were building around Roclincourt would prove of great use during the forthcoming German Offensive.

December was a quiet month for the whole brigade with only two fatal casualties (Corporals Stout and Lumley). A highpoint for the 11th Battalion was on the 10th when the Divisional Commander presented medal ribbons to officers, NCOs and men which had been awarded them for their part in the raid on November 8th. The battalion paraded at 11am with the recipients formed up in front of it. After the presentation the battalion marched past the Divisional Commander and the the recipients of the medals. On the 12th, probably for the want of something else to do, 300 soldiers of the same battalion attended a talk on War Savings.

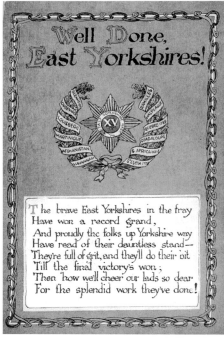

A postcard singing the praises of the East Yorkshire Regiment.

In the 10th Battalion history it is recorded that the Brigade was out of the line for Christmas and that the promised back pay materialised:

> 'The Battalion was out of the line for a month's rest, 93rd Brigade taking over the line for this period as promised by G. O. C. Division. Secondly, and equally important, was the unexpected dispersal to the Battalion of all back pay since the "dependents" allowance was paid in full by the War Office from the previous September, and the Battalion was not slow in taking full advantage of this fortuitous combination of circumstances.'

The war diary merely records: 'No training'.

The war diaries of the 12th and 13th Battalions do not even bother to record Christmas. However, Private Surfleet of the 13th Battalion recalled a pre-Christmas treat for the whole Battalion, courtesy of the Battalion Medical Officer:

> 'Delicacy in private matters, (those as a personal thing one usually does with the bolt on the door) went by the board ages ago; only yesterday we all lined up before

(5049) Wt.W11188/M152   100.000 12/16 J. P. & Co., Ltd: Forms A. 45a 14   Army Form A. 45A

Confidential.

To be used in cases of wounds or injuries received in action.

(For instructions for preparing this report see back of form.)

PROCEEDINGS OF A MEDICAL BOARD assembled by order of_____

The G. O. C-in-C., Southern Command,

for the purpose of examining and reporting on the present state of a wound or injury sustained

by _Lieut. R. C. Hewson, 10th East Yorkshire Regt._

at (Place of injury) _OPPY WOOD, France_ on the (Date of injury) _7. 5. 17_

The Board find _he received a Shell wound in left buttock wound of entrance just behind great trochanter, wound of exit just below upper third of Pouparts ligament. Wounds are now healed, and there is no disability._

The opinion of the Board upon the questions below is as follows:—

	Replies		
	As to first wound	As to second wound (if any)	As to third wound (if any)
1.—Has the officer lost an eye or a limb; or has he permanently lost the use of an eye or a limb; or is the injury equivalent to the loss of a limb, and permanent, or likely to be permanent? (Articles 639 to 644 of the Royal Warrant for Pay, &c.)	No.		
2.—If the case does not come under the category 1:— (a) Was the injury, in the first instance, very severe in character? (b) Are its effects still very severe?	No.		
3.—If the case is classified under category 2, are the effects of the injury permanent, or likely to be permanent? (Article 646.)			
4.—Injuries that do not come under the above categories should be classified here, making use of the following terms:—severe or slight and permanent or not permanent, as the case may be.	Severe, not permanent		
5.—For what period, calculated from the date of the wound or injury, is it probable that the officer will be incapacitated for military duty by such wound or injury?	3 months		

Signatures   J Duncan. Major R.A.M.C. T. Pre

Walter C. Swayne M.S. Br

Jf M. Lannahan Capt. R.

Station 2nd Southern Gen.Hospital,

Date 19/6/17.   Bristol.   [P.7

Report from a Medical Board on the future Commanding Officer of the 10th Battalion after he was wounded at Oppy Wood.

the Medical Officer for what the troops call a 'short arm inspection'. It could only have been for one purpose which, years ago, would have made a young man flush with shame. But, today, it does not seem degrading and I must confess, as we lined up facing each other with only our shirts on, the thought flashed through my mind that it was better for us all to show, however crudely, the absence or presence of that horrible disease the doctor was looking for.'

We must let the 11th Battalion war diary set the scene for Christmas 1917:

'Divine Service 11am Ottawa Camp Theatre. Xmas dinner served at 1.30 pm. Battalion sat down in 3 huts and marquee. Each man provided with a plate and basin and the menu was as follows: Soup, fish cakes, turkey, potatoes and carrots, Xmas pudding, rum sauce, apples, oranges, nuts and beer. Each man was also given a packet of cigarettes. A concert was also given in the theatre at 6pm and supper consisting of roast beef, fruit and custard and coffee was served at 8pm. The officers and sergeants of the Battalion did the carving and waiting at the dinner. Officers had their Xmas dinner in the HQ Mess, at 7.30pm, which was tastefully decorated. A very jolly evening was spent.'

Boxing Day consisted of a morning route march followed by recreation in the snow. The war diary recorded that:

'officers indulged in tobogganing. Sergeants held their Xmas dinner in Sergeants Mess in the evening.'

New Year 1918 was the last one in which the four battalions were to be together. Changes were in the wind that would reduce the brigade to two Hull Battalions and one from 94 Brigade. Somewhat ironically the 11th Battalion War Diary recorded the passing of the year:

'Pleasant evening spent and at the incoming of the New Year, "Success to the Brigade" was one of the toasts given.'

Chapter 7

'Where are the lads of the village tonight'

The Western Front 1918

January was a quiet month for the brigade. Initially the weather was unusually cold. Private Wilson remembered:

'1917 was a cold winter and there was snow on the ground for weeks. Even in the hutments where we lived our morning tea would be frozen over by midday if we left any in our mugs.'

However, on the 6th the thaw set in, making the trenches very muddy. The division was in the Arleux sector and 92 Brigade was alternating periods in the line with 93 Brigade. As the huts they were living in were some distance from the front, that is at Ecoivres and Bray, the battalions had the pleasure of travelling backwards and forwards on the light railway system in the area.

Two dead British soldiers, neither of whom has boots on; these were quickly removed by the Germans who preferred them to their own boots.

In order to improve the lot of his men, the Brigadier set up a sock factory which Private Wilson recalled:

'In the transport lines we had a sock factory. It was an idea our brigadier had. Every man in our brigade was provided wih a dry clean pair of socks when he was in the trenches. Each day the dirty socks were collected and brought to the factory and washed. They were then sent to French women who repaired them and so a continuous cycle of socks was on the move.'

One soldier who rejoined the 10th Battalion in January was Private Aust. He had been in England recovering from exposure to Mustard Gas back in September 1917. On his return he noticed just how few of the originals there were left:

'Surviving originals were scarce and becoming something in the nature of Sacred Cows.'

Two things happened during this quiet spell. Towards the end of the month there was an increase in German trench raids to collect information for the forthcoming offensive and on January 10th the War Office issued orders for a reduction in

Lieutenant-Colonel S H Ferrand, Commanding Officer of the 11th Battalion.

brigade strength from four to three battalions, in an attempt to alleviate manpower shortages on the Western Front. This was to affect the Hull Pals dramatically; the 12th and 13th Battalions were to disappear completely from the Order of Battle and be replaced in the brigade by the 11th East Lancs, the only battalion from 94 Brigade to survive. In order to keep the division up to a three brigade level 94 Brigade, which would cease to exist, was to be replaced by 4 Guards Brigade.

Although the war diaries make no mention of any feelings about the disbandments, Private Surfleet reflected the views of his comrades when he wrote in his diary:

'I understand we are going into the line again tomorrow. How long we shall exist as a battalion, no one knows; not for long, by the sound of it. Everyone is absolutely livid about it; it is a bit of a devil when chaps who have been together so long and who have come to understand each other must be pushed off to any old crowd; the expressions of disgust which I have heard on every hand today make me feel all the more depressed about the idea and if I get safely out of the line this next trip, I have made up my mind to apply for a commission in the Royal Flying Corps.'

Casualties occured behind the lines as well as in the line. Private Surfleet recalled an unusual duty on January 18th while he was at Ecurie:

'*Sgt. Bunn dashed into the hut and asked for volunteers to go with him and get some fellows out of a well in the middle of those stumps which was a wood. We all thought he was pulling our leg, but he looked serious about it, George Hirste, Charlie Gold and I got up and I followed him out of the hut. When we got to the well, we found two RFC blokes had been pretty smart and had rigged up a lot of tackle with ropes, pulleys and a "3 legs" arrangement over the opening and the RFC Sergeant Major was just being lowered down the well. I looked over the edge; it was horribly deep and at the bottom, I could see three huddled figures, partly on top of each other round the jagged stump of an iron pipe which rose from the centre.*'

Eventually the three lads were pulled up. Each had suffered multiple injuries – broken arms, legs and ribs. They were taken off to the hospital where two of them died of their injuries.

TO ALL AT HOME.

Punch *magazine's message for everyone at home. Little did they know how true it would be!*

On 27th January the 13th Battalion entered the trenches for the last time, relieving the 15th West Yorks, losing two men during the relief (Sergeant Redfern MM and Private Clater). German night time activity was becoming intense and on the 29th at 8pm, 30 of the enemy attempted to enter the 13th Battalion's trenches, but were repulsed without causing any casualties. At 10pm on the 31st the battalion was due to be relieved by the 11th Battalion but before the relief was complete three parties of about 12 Germans tried to enter the trenches. The raiders were repulsed without difficulty and four unwounded prisoners were taken, one of whom was an NCO. (The prisoners were from the 470 IR of the 240th Division.) No casualties were inflicted by the Germans. The 12th Battalion finished its front line existence in brigade support.

When not in the line the usual training occurred with the 11th Battalion carrying out a new counter attack scheme on the 26th. More restfully the battalion enjoyed a band concert on the afternoon of the 20th and on the 21st 9 Platoon of C Company represented the brigade in the Divisional Platoon Competition, coming second. The 24th saw the 13th Battalion rugby team beat the 11th Battalion by 7 points to 0.

The changes to the structure of the brigade took place at the beginning of February with the 12th and 13th Battalions out of the line at Ecoivres and Ecurie, respectively. February 8th was the chosen date for the changes. However, right up to the last minute the standard cross battalion transfers continued with, for example, the 12th Battalion recording the transfer of its Quartermaster to the 11th Battalion in return for theirs. The 13th left no record of the events but fortunately the 12th Battalion did. On the 5th the war diary recorded two other ranks joined for duty but on the same day two men were accidentally wounded. On the 6th, another soldier joined the battalion and then on the 8th transfers began:

> '*Transfers 10 officers and 198 ORanks to 10th East Yorks R*
> *T/CAPT. L.C. HUTCHINSON, T/CAPT S.C.LE BLANQ, T/CAPT G.E. LLOYD-JONES, M.C.*
> *T/LT. A/CAPT. O. SLATER, T/LIEUT J. SEVER, T/LIEUT W.H. HALL, T/LT M. SPENCER, T/LT C.H. BABER, T/2 LT F.HALL, T/2 LT E. BEST.*
> *10 Officers and 198 ORanks to 11th EAST YORKS. R*
> *T/CAPT. E. MORISON, T/LIEUT H.F. DANN, M.C., T/LT D.S. TOMEY, T/LIEUT F.W. COWLEY, M.C., 2/LIEUT R.F. PITZ, T/2 LT B. DIMOND, T/2 LT E. WRIGHT, T/2LT F.J. PICKERING, T/2 LT. C GREENHALGH.*
> *7 Officers and 150 ORanks to 6th East Yorks R.T/MAJOR R.H. TATTON, T/LIEUT S.D. HOLBROOK, T/LT A C BOX, T/2LT J LOCAL, M.C., T/ LT A.E. BURLEIGH, T/2 LT W.G. LEGG.'*

The transfers continued on the 11th with two other ranks joining the 10th Battalion. On the 12th one other rank left for officer training, Lieutenant Wilson, MC and 34 men were attached to 92 Infantry Brigade and six officers, Capt Hirst MC, Lieutenant Hills, 2/Lieutenant Robson, 2/Lieutenant Todd, 2/Lieutenant Groves and 2/Lieutenant Spink were transferred along with 187 men to the 7th East Yorks. 24 other ranks were transferred to the 2/4th West Riding Regiment on the 14th and one man to the 11th Battalion. The remaining troops moved to billets in Marest to await their fate. On the 22nd one man was transferred to the 31st Division Machine Gun Battalion. The remainder were transferred to an entrenching battalion or to the Infantry Base Depot or Corps Personnel Camp.

When the battalions were reduced it left two Lieutenant-Colonels without commands. Private Wilson worked in the signal section during this period. He recalled:

> '*When the Brigades were reduced... we had a spare Colonel living in the transport lines waiting for a command. I remember waking him early one morning to give him a signal I had received appointing him to 11 East Yorks.'*

The 11th Battalion spent a busy time in the trenches towards the end of February. As the German offensive drew nearer raiding parties increased in frequency. On the 19th the Germans put down a heavy barrage on the divisional front while they raided the battalion to the right of the 11th Battalion. The raid failed, leaving behind four wounded prisoners and seven dead in the hands of the 4th Grenadier Guards. The 11th, although not in the attack, suffered three killed and 17 wounded. While this raid was in progress the battalion were out in force wiring, which resulted in a further four men being wounded.

The 21st was again an active night. At 2.30 am a patrol of twelve other ranks commanded by 2/Lieutenant Wright left the 11th Battalion trenches to lie up and wait for an enemy patrol in order to get identification. As they left the British wire they immediately bumped into a German patrol which was about 20 strong and lying about 30 yards from our wire. The German patrol threw several stick bombs at the 11th Battalion patrol and starting firing with their rifles. 2/Lieutenant Wright, Corporal Wilde MM, L/Corporal Foster, Private Bridges and Private Cowen of the Battalion Scout party immediately replied with bombs and rifle fire, causing the Germans to run away. A search was made for identification but nothing was found.

In order to identify the raiding party from the previous night, at 6.30am Sergeant Rust and Private Greenwood left the British lines in daylight to search for some identification. They found a dead German in No Man's Land about 50 yards from the British wire. While attempting to bring him in they were heavily sniped and had to leave the body. When they eventually returned to their own trenches they had

The German HQ at Spa where much of the initial planning for 'Operation Michael' was done.

Inset: *Planning the offensive with von Hindenburg (on the Kaiser's right) and Ludendorff.*

brought in with them three rifles, two pairs of gloves and one button, a shoulder strap and cap from the dead German. This identified the raiders as being from the 51st RIR. Later that night the battalion was relieved by the 11th East Lancs.

On 1st March, 92 Brigade marched back to an area north of St. Pol for three weeks' rest and training. The 10th Battalion were billeted in Monchy-Breton, while the 11th were in La Thieuloye. As a result of this move the brigade was fortunate not to be involved in the first onslaught of the German offensive on March 21st.

Der Kaiserschlacht

The German March Offensive was Germany's final attempt at a decisive victory in the west. American troops arriving in large numbers, food shortages at home and the Allied economic blockade meant that time was running out for Germany. After the ending of the war on the Eastern Front, hundreds of thousands of seasoned troops were available for service on the Western Front. The German General Staff initially wanted to use these troops to attack the French on either side of Verdun but this was rejected because the British would not be involved. In the end Ludendorff decided upon an attack at the junction of the British and French armies opposite St. Quentin – *Operation Michael*. This would drive the German army forward, capturing Peronne and, rolling west and northwards, would take Albert and push on to Arras, splitting the British and French armies and capturing the vital railhead at Amiens.

A lot has been written about the lack of fully prepared defences in certain areas and how, as a result, it was difficult to stop the Germans. In his brief memoirs of this period Private Wilson of the 11th Battalion recalled how poor some of the defences were when they were out of the line, just before the German offensive:

> '*the battalion moved to a village called Latheloi* (La Thieuloye), *where we were in reserve. A lot of barbed wire was strung about here, but was rather thin and didn't impress us much.*'

While out of the trenches life had consisted of various types of training and inspections. On the 20th the 11th Battalion prophetically had their armourers inspect every rifle and the Divisional Gas NCO inspected all of the battalion SBRs (Single Box Respirator). The next day the German attack commenced but life for the 11th Battalion was not to be interrupted by such a trivial thing. In the morning everyone in the battalion was inspected by the Medical Officer and in the afternoon the inter-company football competition final was played, with the HQ team beating A Company. The next day the battalion began digging in the army line at Hamelincourt, moving on the 23rd to reserve at Ervillers, where more trench digging took place.

The 10th Battalion heard long-range enemy gun fire at regular five minute intervals. The target was the important railway junction of St. Pol. Like the 11th

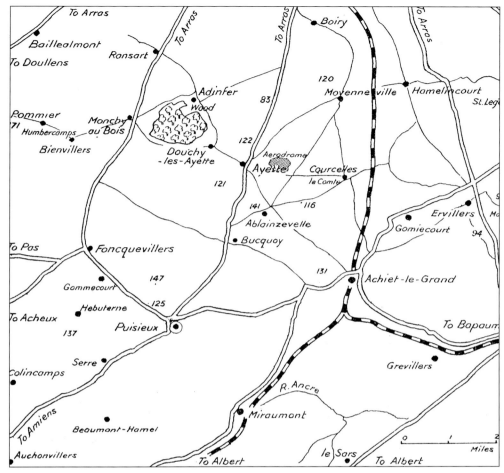

A map detailing the area where the 10th and 11th Battalions fought between 23rd and 31st March 1918.

Battalion they did not let this worry them; they continued with their work and in the afternoon watched D Company beat the Transport Section at football, five goals to three. However, the urgency of the situation came home to them when at midnight they were warned for a 4.30am 'Reveille'. At 7.30am they marched off through St. Pol, Frevent and Doullens to Bailleulmont where upon arrival they were paid. As the battalion settled down into what looked like a cushy billet, orders came round to be ready at twenty minutes notice. At the same time a percentage of each company were detailed off to stay at the Quartermaster's stores as a reinforcement – a sure sign that the battalion was going into battle.

At 8.30pm the battalion fell in but stood waiting till midnight. During this three and a half hour wait the men stood shivering and inactive, while overhead an enemy plane was dropping its bombs near the village. The sound of heavy gun fire could be heard up the line. The march from Bailleulmont to Boisleux-au-Mont in moonlight, took six hours. However, the moonlight only served to show what had been going on. The 10th Battalion history described the chaos:

> 'It was moonlight, but that only served to show up the severity of the bombardment which the villages along the road had suffered. Progress was hindered by houses which had collapsed across the road, while recent shell-holes had to be skirted, and to men unutterably weary after standing fully laden for three and a half hours, and only half able to guide their feet through lack of sleep, the march developed into a sheer test of will-power to "stick it", as hour after hour they blundered on. The men soon marched in a half-conscious state and had to be rudely shaken to awaken them after the regulation halts. To add to the horror, some building miles ahead was burning fiercely. This, in time, turned out to be an Expeditionary Force Canteen, and that it was being burned to prevent it falling into the enemy's hands showed the seriousness of the situation.'

2/Lieutenant Houghton of the 10th Battalion who died of his wounds on March 31st 1918.

On arriving at their destination the battalion were not put into the line but kept back as the reserve battalion of the brigade which was in divisional reserve. While 92 Brigade was again having a cushy time, the rest of the division was involved in fighting off two enemy divisions near St. Leger. Private Wilson, now serving with the 11th Battalion, recalled the confused situation and the effect of the shelling:

> 'Many wounded passed us as we lay there and they all had armfuls of cigarettes taken from an abandoned YMCA. As soon as it was dark we dug in, our only excitement that night being a light bombing from a German plane, two men were killed. The following evening we were shelled out of our trenches and had to lie out in front of them till the shelling died down. We had a case of shell shock. Those who are likely to get shell shock generally show signs of what is coming for some time before, that is apart from those who get blown up by a shell that burst near, and perhaps buried them. I was cutting a slice of bread as we lay out in front of our trenches, when the chap who later got shell shock said "Put that knife away, put it away". He shouted, "The moon's shining on it and the Germans will see it and shell us again". The German line was two kilometres away.'

After breakfast the 10th Battalion started work on improving the trenches they occupied and in bringing up boxes of bombs and ammunition. Later in the day, along with the rest of the brigade the battalion moved to trenches near Ervillers (south of Arras). Here the brigade took over a front of about 2500 yards running

A group of 11th Battalion officers taken in early 1918. The officer on the right is Lieutenant Walker MC, a schoolteacher who later became principal of the Technical College in Hull. Other identified officers are Captain Watts (centre) and Lieutenant Scotcher (second from left).

Lieutenants Longthorp (left) and Walker of the 11th Battalion.

north-west from the village. The 11th Battalion held the left flank with the 11th East Lancs on the right. In reserve was the 10th Battalion situated just west of Ervillers. Trenches in the area were only half finished and work was soon commenced to improve them but the enemy spotted the activity and shelled the reserve area for about half an hour, around 5pm. When Private Beeken was moving forward with the 10th Battalion he was surprised to capture some prisoners:

'We moved forward the next day and rested on a sunken road. As we marched, we met guns being withdrawn. Eventually my Company ('B' Coy) arrived near Gomiecourt. It was now dark and the Company moved forward leaving the Headquarter platoon behind awaiting orders. A few of us were standing in the road when we saw a party of Germans approaching. How had they got here through all the men in front of us?

'We challenged them and fired. Up went their hands and we took them prisoners.'

The ruins of Combles which fell early in the German offensive.

Life had a further surprise to play the next day. After escorting the prisoners and returning they had to quickly dig in:

> 'we hurriedly dug-in in front of the village using our entrenching tools for we found ourselves under machine gun and rifle fire.
>
> 'At dawn things became very quiet and I went for a walk round the village. I came across one of our field dressing stations which had been abandoned. Finding some bottles of beer I took them with me and reported to the platoon officer.
>
> 'It was a lovely day and nothing happened except that a German aeroplane passed very low over us. We didn't manage to shoot it down. We had not received any rations as we should have done. That night was strangely quiet. It worried us a little.
>
> 'Then in the morning, as we had not received any rations, the officer sent J.Bailey and myself to the Battalion Hqrs for news. As we walked through the village, rifle shots were fired at us. We were rather puzzled but carried on to the Battalion Hqrs which we found to be very silent and we found nobody there. We then set off for the Brigade Hqrs. On the way we heard the rifle and machine gun fire from the village we had just left and then saw about 50 yds away Germans advancing. We dashed off hoping to arrive at the railway embankment about one hundred yards away. It was tough going over ploughed land and despite a few shots fired at us, we reached the embankment. On the other side much to our surprise we fell into the hands of the Durhams. They were astonished at our appearance for they were fighting a rear guard action and had been assured that all our troops had been withdrawn during the night. No message had been received by us. The Germans had claimed that the village had been taken at dawn.'

During the morning of the 24th the Brigadier made a tour of inspection and expressed his satisfaction with the work done. In the afternoon and evening all positions east of the village were subjected to a heavy hostile bombardment. The 11th Battalion war diary recorded:

'about 8.30pm it was evident that a hostile attack was in progress. Much confusion was caused by the disorganised retirement of troops from the forward system of trenches, but our men were very steady. About midnight a hostile patrol succeeded in entering the village & establishing themselves in some ruins near to Bn H.Q. only to be captured intact by Bn H.Q. staff. (One Officer, one unter officer, twelve men with one machine gun in all were taken and judging from their demeanour they were quite pleased to give in).'

German infantry during the 'Michael' offensive.

Above: As the Germans advanced they brought their field guns forward. A field gun in a forward area firing on the British lines.

Left: British front line trenches, were in some areas, quickly overcome. British dead lie where they fell. Note the German hand grenades on the trench side on the right.

Below: British Prisoners of War leaving the combat zone in March.

Orderly Room Sergeant Thompson was awarded the DCM for his part in the defence of Ervillers. The Germans were pretending to be British troops retreating in order to get into the village. This resulted in British troops shooting at genuine British stragglers. Lieutenant-Colonel Gurney wrote in his official report of the Ervillers action:

'Before my Company Commanders left me, the bombardment became intensive and it appeared that an attack was in progress. About 8.30pm a body of troops about 100 strong rushed towards 'C' Company's sector from approximately 'B' Company's front shouting "DON'T FIRE. ETC". Earlier in the evening a similar incident occured in connection with an enemy patrol, and as it was impossible to distinguish whether these troops were hostile or not, fire was opened as it was thought this was another enemy ruse. Almost immediately afterwards these troops were recognised to be British and the order to cease fire was given'.

There was much German patrol activity on the right flank of the brigade and two companies of the 10th Battalion had to be rushed forward to reinforce the 11th Battalion who were fighting the Germans in the street. One company of the 10th under Captain Pearce dealt with the patrols capturing one officer and ten men and a light machine gun. The situation was becoming difficult. Lieutenant-Colonel Gurney formed a defensive line across the Mory-Ervillers road, with troops from various units, which connected with 11th Battalion's B Company to stop German infiltration from that flank. However, some of these troops retired without orders leaving a gap of 50 yards which weakened the road defences and resulted in the withdrawal of a platoon on the right of the battalion. To stop this happening again, Lieutenant-Colonel Gurney issued an order that any man attempting to leave the trench at the road was to be shot. This had the desired effect noted the battalion diary:

'after one or two isolated cases of attempted retirement had been dealt with this dribbling to the rear was effectually stopped'.

That night the Germans massed for the attack which eventually fell upon the 11th Battalion at around 1pm on the 25th. However, by that time, the 11th had been reinforced by the 10th Manchesters and the combined fire of the two battalions was sufficient to stop the German advance. Private Wilson later recalled the end of the day:

'by the next night we were down to two officers. We took a few prisoners who were very nervous and one comic individual made one of them run before him with his hands above his head. They all had coffee in their water bottles which we drank. They were sent to the rear, carrying stretcher cases'.

On the nearby Guards Brigade front the British artillery was so effective at destroying German preparations that the Official History records a complaint from them to the effect that the 'infantry was not given a fair chance with the rifle'.

At 9.30pm orders were received to evacuate the village and the British troops moved back to a line in front of Courcelles to await further German attacks. Each Company covered its own withdrawal and few casualties were incurred. During the battle, arrangements for the removal of the wounded had broken down, so that there were a considerable number of troops who would become prisoners of war when the battalion withdrew. In his report of April 3rd Lieutenant-Colonel Gurney explained the situation:

> 'The arrangements for the evacuation of wounded having broken down we were forced to use all available Headquarters staff for this purpose and with their help evacuated all wounded in the face of the enemy, although this necessitated loss of signalling and other material, as my personnel all had to be employed on this work. I considered that the evacuation of our wounded which was over 28, was the work of first importance. For this reason I was unable to salve much material which had therefore to be left behind'.

Private Beeken was wounded in the withdrawal:

> 'In the morning of 27th March orders came to withdraw to the Purple Line. So over the top we went and going through machine gun fire I was hit in the foot. Jim helped me along and at cross roads (sic) a Staff Captain was directing men to their units. I

Estaires after it fell to the Germans on April 10th. The remaining two Hull Battalions were rushed north to reinforce the defences around Hazebrouck.

was told to go forward and arrived at a dressing station where there was a considerable number of wounded. Here we were told that all who could walk should go to a dressing station in the rear. Well I decided to walk but on the way I was taken into a van and arrived at the dressing station where my wound was attended to'.

During the night German troops had found gaps through the line and as a result both the 31st and 42nd Divisions had to retire. This retirement caught the 10th Battalion having breakfast in the front line they had occupied that night; they should already have evacuated but for some reason the orders had not got through. 2/Lieutenant Pretty took out a scouting patrol but failed to return. Accordingly, the battalion withdrew to a deserted aerodrome on the Ablainzeville-Moyenneville road where they dug in, only to be shelled by the Royal Field Artillery firing short. The 11th Battalion reported a quiet day apart from a hostile attack at 4pm that they completely repulsed. Lieutenant-Colonel Gurney of the 11th Battalion took over temporary

Private Beeken served with the 10th Battalion throughout the war.

command of 93 Brigade, on the 27th, when its Commanding Officer became sick. He was replaced by Major Hewson of the 10th Battalion.

During the night of the 26th/27th the town of Albert fell to the enemy. About 11am on the same day the Germans launched a powerful attack on the front from Bucquoy to Hamelincourt which was followed by counter-attacks and further attacks and counter-attacks until about 4.30pm when the battalion withdrew to the Purple Line. Major Hewson recorded what happened in his official report written on April 3rd:

'At about 11.20 a.m. the enemy barrage opened and at 12 noon the first S.O.S. went up from the Front Line and contact with the enemy commenced. From that time for several hours there was a general battle for the possession of the crest in which at least four times the crest was lost and re-taken. The fight swayed to and fro from 11.20a.m. to 4.25 p.m., the enemy attacking in large forces but yielded in every instance to the rifle and bayonet upon which my men principally relied. As it was found that although in Mass there (sic) weight of men prevailed, the resistance of any post they occupied was feeble against Counter-attack'.

As both flanks were in the air it was decided at a Brigade Conference to pull back to the Ayette line. Although this withdrawal was made in good order some of the battalion got lost and ended up in the 2nd Irish Guards lines behind Ayette, just in front of the Purple Line. They soon returned to the battalion.

The 10th Battalion also retired to the partly-dug Purple Line but to cover the retreat the battalion left behind a small rearguard consisting of 2/Lieutenant Rutherford (an American), a Corporal and five men from Headquarters Company. (Privates Bourne, Haines, Hobbs, Naylor and Porter.) The seven men stayed for an hour, covering not just the retreat of the battalion but of the whole brigade. In an attempt to show that the position was still held in some strength they blazed away blindly every time a German head appeared above the 800 yard distant skyline. At the end of the hour they separately slid off into the sunken road behind the trench and made their way back slowly, firing periodically, to the battalion positions in the Purple Line. All seven men returned safely. The severity of the fighting in this three day period is shown by the casualty figures of the 10th Battalion. From March 24th to 27th the battalion losses were four officers and 207 men. The 10th Battalion was mentioned by Haig for: 'exceptional gallantry on March 27th'.

During the night, which passed quietly, Lieutenant-Colonel Headlam arrived with a composite battalion of troops from the Quartermasters' details of the three battalions to take up position in front of the Purple Line. Upon

An unknown soldier of the 11th Battalion taken in Hull around this time.

arrival they assisted the RFA in retrieving 18-pounder ammunition which was behind the enemy lines. The ammuniton was successfully retrieved and used against the enemy the next day.

The 28th was a quieter day. The 11th Battalion took over some trenches started by the 210th Field Company, RE and continued to dig for the day. Lieutenant-Colonel Gurney returned to the battalion and Major Hewson returned to the 10th Battalion. Nearby the Germans renewed their attacks on Arras, with the 4th Guards Brigade at Ayette being heavily engaged. The British line held and for two more days the Brigade was able to consolidate its positions and begin wiring. On the 30th, D Company of the 11th Battalion, was sent to reinforce the 18th DLI of 93 Brigade, which was in the front line next to the Guards Division, which was attacked twice during the day.

At 9.30 am on the 31st, the 10th Battalion were relieved by the 15th HLI of the 32nd Division. The 11th Battalion were relieved by the 10th A&SH of the same division. Private Wilson of the 11th Battalion recalled this period and in particularly the relief:

'We did a rapid retreat up a long slope into incomplete fresh trenches. We ran up chalk hills which made it difficult to hide. We stayed there for three days. Dead horses lay in front of the line and in the early dawn the stench was nauseating but as the day wore on the smell was less noticeable. A Scotch battalion then came to relieve us and we congratulated them on the dresses they wore as likely to be short enough to keep them clear of the mud'.

The brigade marched back to billets in the Pommier area with a hot meal being provided on the way. The men were extremely tired as Private Wilson recalled:

'we were all in an utterly exhausted condition, extremely tired from lack of sleep. As we walked we often fell asleep, and dropped to the ground in a semi-conscious state but the knowledge of ultimate rest kept us going and some relieving officers helped us along'.

After a day's rest the brigade moved back to the Monchy Breton area where they had been billeted before the start of the German offensive.

The next few days were spent with cleaning up and reorganising and receiving new drafts to replace the losses of the last few days. The 10th Battalion received 326 reinforcements while the 11th Battalion received around 500 A4 soldiers; these were trained soldiers but under the age of 19 – some of whom could have had a number of years fighting experience, but had been found to be underage and sent back to depots in France or to Young Soldiers Battalions in the UK. Private Wilson recalled what they thought of these young soldiers:

'we 20 year olds who were old soldiers in our eyes regarded them as babes for the slaughter or so we said, and thought'.

For the period March 21st to April 5th the 31st Division had suffered 2350 casualties (all ranks).

Storm troops were specially trained to take the lead in the German offensive.

On the 6th the GOC 31st Division, Major-General Bridgeford, inspected the brigade. In the afternoon the 11th Battalion Band played in a contest at XIII Corps HQ and the Corps Commander invited all officers of the brigade to tea in the grounds of his HQ at Chateau Bryas. The welfare of the other ranks was catered for by the opening of the village schoolroom as a reading and writing room.

The 11th Battalion held a ceremonial drill on the 10th and the CO inspected the latest draft of reinforcements (380 A4 boys). The 10th Battalion, which should have provided a large working detail, went for a route march instead. Soon after dinner battalion runners arrived with orders to prepare to move in battle order. Later that afternoon the brigade 'fell in' and marched to the waiting buses which took them to Vieux Berquin. At 3am the next morning the 11th Battalion found itself on outpost duty at Trois Fermes. During the day the battalion dug in. At 3pm Lieutenant-Colonel Gurney handed over command of the battalion to Major Shaw while he formed a composite battalion from the brigade details.

This move was in response to the latest German offensive north of La Bassée Canal aimed at Hazebrouck and Bailleul. The German offensive broke upon the 9th, 19th, 25th, 34th, 40th, 55th and 2nd Portugese Divisions. As a result of this new attack the Portugese Division broke, leaving a large gap in the line between the 40th and 55th Divisions. On the 10th, Armentieres, Estaires, Steewerck and Ploegsteert fell but Bethune in the south held out. Private Wilson recalled being sent off to fill this gap:

> 'the Portugese gave way and the 11th EYR were sent in London Buses to help. On the side of each bus was painted '1d all the way'.

While the 11th Battalion held the outposts, the 10th Battalion were to push forward to make contact with the enemy in the vicinity of Estaires and to form a defensive line which retiring troops could pass through to safety. 10th Battalion patrols soon discovered that there were no British troops in front of them, only Germans. On the same day that Field Marshal Haig issued his 'backs to the wall' order the 10th Battalion was able to record an advance:

> 'we succeeded in advancing the Battalion left front to the crossroads at Pont Wemeau, almost due north of Doulieu. This move was made in conjunction with the 18th Durham Light Infantry, who captured La Becque and La Rose Farms'.

The next day the German High Command threw in its reserves in an attempt to take the road and rail junction of Hazebrouck. By 7am that morning the 40th Division had withdrawn through the 31st Division's positions leaving them to face the enemy. Shortly afterwards hostile aircraft attacked the 10th Battalion positions and German infantry advanced along the road from Doulieu. The road was being held by B Company outposts which were shelled by a field gun the Germans had brought up. Casualties were high (all officers except one and a large number of other ranks were killed and wounded) and resulted in contact with the neighbouring battalion being broken (2nd Royal Fusiliers). On the left flank 93 Brigade was forced to retire leaving 92 Brigade with no option but to retire as well.

Withdrawal to the proposed new defensive position was made very difficult by the retirement of the neighbouring division's troops along the road meant to be used by 92 Brigade. The intended withdrawal through deep dykes and hedges hindered the retirement and resulted in troops becoming detached from their parent unit; it also resulted in a number of men drowning as they attempted to cross the dykes. The hedges that hindered withdrawal considerably aided the movements of the German troops, allowing them to move forward without being seen.

Upon reaching the Becque the 10th Battalion made a stand with the companies fighting almost hand-to-hand with the Germans. Without the support of the 11th Battalion the left flank was 'in the air' and it was

Left: Field Marshall Haig who praised the 31st Division and the 10th Battalion for their heroic stands in response to his famous 'Backs to the wall' order.

decided to cross the Becque which was, fortunately, less than waist high. There were no bridges so the men had no option but to wade across to the other side and set up a new defensive line on a railway embankment 500 yards west of Meteren Becque.

By 2am that day the 11th Battalion had relieved the troops of 119 and 120 Brigades and immediately become involved in heavy fighting. At 10am the troops on the battalions right withdrew and 93 Brigade on the left flank reported that it was heavily engaged. As both of the 11th Battalion's flanks were exposed orders were received to withdraw. They were pursued rapidly by the Germans, who succeeded in isolating one or two parties, forcing them to link up with troops from other units. In the meantime the Composite Battalion had taken up position west of Merris. It was to this position that the 11th Battalion eventually withdrew. Private Wilson took part in the withdrawal:

'a runner from the BHQ came in with an order to retreat. I was given the order to carry to the Company who were extended to the left of Company HQ. The majority of this Company were all new, just out from blighty, so when I had given the order I waited to see it carried out, and then returned to Company HQ. They were no longer there. They had retired and so I decided to retreat on my own. I doubled across

a road, put a farmhouse in my rear and began to run towards a second farmhouse, when I came up against a broad and deep ditch. There was no way across so I plunged in holding my rifle above my head as the water was waist deep. I scrambled out the other side and found I was in a potato field. I chose a double furrow and ran down it. Bullets whistled past and their closeness made me look back. Half a dozen Germans were kneeling down in the rear and taking shots at me as I ran, using me for target practice, in fact. I threw myself on my face and lay still, pretending to be hit. After a pause I wriggled forward but a bullet in my haversack which was on my back, stopped me. I lay still and waited. Looking up carefully I saw two young German boys approaching me from my front. They had not seen me but soon would and if I moved suddenly might shoot. I saw there was no chance to escape so I stood up without my rifle. They kept me covered till I had shed my equipment and then took me prisoner. They were very nice about it being about the same age as myself. I joined other prisoners and helped to carry a wounded German officer to hospital. On the way we passed many terribly wounded men, one with both legs and both arms broken, we hoped he would die soon'.

Private Wilson was taken across the battlefields of a few days before:

The Chateau de la Motte in Hazebrouck, April 1918 – 92 Brigade HQ.

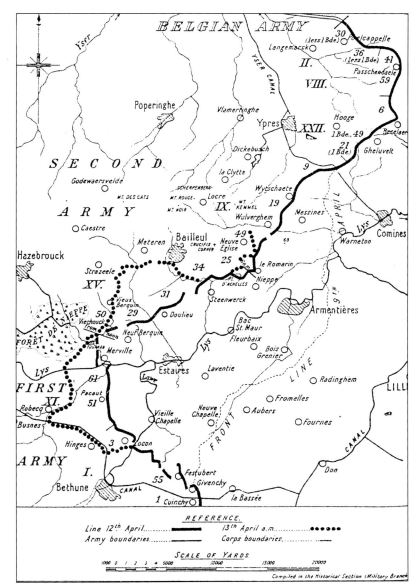

Map of the battle of The Lys, April 1918.

'We saw many tragic and ghastly sights on this journey for we were moving over the battlefield of just a few days before. The dead lay everywhere both British and German but mostly British as the German were buried first. They lay in the fields, sometimes singly, sometimes in groups. They all had their tunics and boots taken off, boots in particular being much in demand. I came across one young soldier lying dead, a half finished letter beside him. "Dear Mother (it began) I have been wounded and the stretcher bearers will soon come to pick me up..." There was little more, a piece of shrapnel had killed him as he wrote.'

Not all of the prisoners of war were sent back to the rear; many were kept to work on the roads or help the German war effort in more tangible ways. Private Wilson was kept behind the front line for a short while to help tidy up the battlefield:

'Burial parties made up of prisoners spent their days collecting the dead by means of handcarts, and so the battlefield was cleared and very soon few of the slain remained unburied'.

Another 11th Battalion soldier who was trying to escape that day was Private Wolfe who was separated from the rest of his platoon and found himself running down a dyke. He felt a sharp pain in his leg and thought that he had been shot but quickly realised that it was his entrenching tool handle digging into his leg. When he had been ordered to retire he had picked up some extra bandoliers of ammunition and as he was running back he came across some soldiers who wanted his ammunition which he gladly gave them:

'They were facing the enemy advancing almost in step with their rifles across their chests as though they were on parade'.

Shortly after this experience of last ditch heroism Private Wolfe was wounded and his war finished:

'Clang, a bullet had hit my tin hat, made a hole at the side, spun round inside the hat and taking a piece of my skull out in the process'.

Private Wolfe was lucky to be picked up by his own side and sent to England to recover.

Contact with the 11th Battalion had been lost earlier in the day and should have been renewed when the 10th Battalion reached Metern Becque, the new defensive position. A patrol which was sent out to locate them got as far as the outskirts of Merris without finding them; they had withdrawn further than anticipated and had set up defensive positions on the Outtersteene-Vieux Berquin road to the rear of the 10th Battalion.

The gap on the left flank made it difficult to retire but the battalion found much needed help from the 29th Division. The 10th Battalion history records that:

'three gunners of the 29th Divisional M.G.C. lent us invaluable assistance in holding off the enemy by supporting their machine gun barrels against the tree trunks and firing from the shoulder in standing positions'.

On reaching the embankment the battalion were ordered to extend their position along the line to the east in order to link up with Lieutenant-Colonel Gurney's

Brigade Composite Battalion. This was stopped by the arrival of the advancing Germans, who, appearing in unstoppable numbers, caused the battalion to withdraw, on orders, to the railway line about 1000 yards south-west of Merris where they linked up with the East Lancashires and the Composite Battalion. Here the men dug in and waited.

The 11th Battalion history recorded some details of this composite battalion:

> 'The composite battalion was found to consist of twenty-two different battalions and five different divisions, not to mention a representative of our allies, the Portugese and a B1 Australian private, who had been in charge of a sock-laundry at Outtersteene and had become so attached to us that he proposed to exchange his uniform for ordinary Service Dress, and adopt the name of one of our casualties. The C.O., though touched by this tribute to the battalion, had to decline the offer, though he made amends by recommending the applicant for the Military Medal for his excellent work salvaging and repairing Lewis guns. Other arms were also represented, mostly gunners and Machine Gun Corps.'

An early morning fog initially hid the German attack the next day. Vieux Berquin fell and the 11th East Lancashires were heavily attacked but did not yield, being given assistance by the machine guns of the right hand company of the 10th Battalion. One company of the 10th Battalion was attacked by about 200 Germans during the afternoon but quickly drove them off and no full scale attack materialised.

Behind the lines the 1st Australian Division had been detraining at Hazebrouck and was now holding a defensive line behind the 31st Division. The 11th Battalion war diary recorded:

British dead around their fortified strongpoint.

'In the early hours of the 13th inst. troops from the 1st AUSTRALIAN DIV and from the 33rd DIV on our left, came into support of our line which now consisted of about 1200 all ranks from at least 7 different divisions who had lost direction or straggled in the operations of the day previous'.

At about 10.45am the enemy renewed its attacks in the 11th Battalion area causing the outposts to retire. Not only infantry were attacking but cavalry as well. The battalion of the Queen's Regiment on the left flank pulled back slightly but this did not affect the defence put up by the battalion, which was recorded in the war diary:

'considerable execution was done by our M.G. & L.G. fire. Throughout the day hostile shelling was heavy but erratic, causing very few casualties'.

The 11th Battalion history has rather more to say about the day:

Map showing the places mentioned in the story of the withdrawal of the 10th Battalion to the railway cutting near Outtensteene.

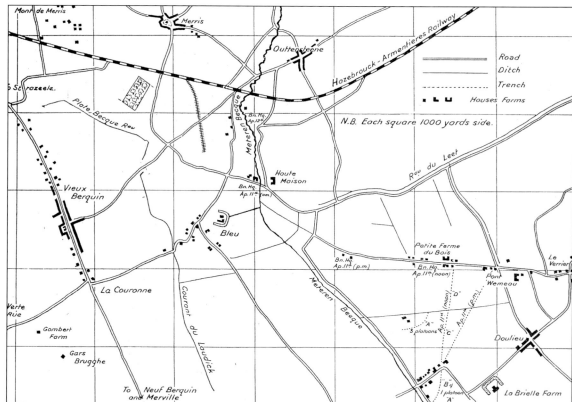

'Although, technically, this was one of the most critical days of the whole war, the British Tommy's entire inability or disinclination to appreciate the military situation properly and his desire to beautify his home, however precarious his tenancy might be, were both apparent. Such incongruous articles as a pair of china vases, a somewhat time-expired, but still vigorous, alarm clock and a mirror made their appearance on the parapet of a none too secure trench line.

'The 13th April was spent repelling a continuous succession of enemy attacks. The line held firm, and our casualties were consequently slight, while the enemy's losses were enormous. The task of devoting our full attention to the enemy was hindered at times by the misplaced exuberance of large numbers of stray horses, cattle and pigs, which bounded about from post to post, giving away our position and generally asking for trouble. In the evening they all proceeded to congregate near battalion headquarters and to draw the attention of the enemy's artillery to the spot, forcing that august body to make several rapid and undignified dashes to the shelter of some neighbouring trenches. Frantic efforts were made to drive them off, preferably in the direction of the Quartermaster's stores, but except for two pigs who were enticed into a ration limber – a noisy proceeding which could not on that acount be repeated – no success attended these efforts. Had it been known beforehand that pork is only issued to Transport and Quartermaster personnel, our efforts might have been less energetic.

'Both Battalions eventually received the order to retire at 4am on the 14th, although they should have received it by 1.30am. This lateness was due to the breakdown of telephone communications caused by the heavy shelling breaking the telephone lines. Even though the order was immediately sent out to the Companies it was daylight before the evacuation could begin. Fortunately a morning mist obscured all movement and the withdrawal went unobserved with both Battalions pulling back through the Australian lines and moving off to billets...'

Later in the day the Germans attacked the worn-out remnants of the 31st Division, only to find themselves facing fresh Australian and British troops. The attack failed. Hazebrouck was safe.

This action resulted in the 10th Battalion recording casualties of 13 killed, 141 wounded and 214 missing; the 11th Battalion did not leave a record in its war diary (*Soldiers Died in the Great War* lists 57 other ranks' deaths between April 12th and 14th). However, these events were recorded by Field Marshal Haig as:

'No more brilliant exploit has taken place since the opening of the enemy's offensive, though gallant actions have been without number'.

The Times of April 24th 1918 carried Field Marshal Haig's despatch of the 23rd:

'On April 13th the 31 DIVISION was holding a front of some 9000 yards East of the FÔRET DE NIEPPE. The Division was already greatly reduced in strength as a *result of previous fighting and the enemy was still pressing his advance. The troops were informed that their Line had to be held to the last to cover the detraining of reinforcements, and all ranks responded with the most magnificent courage and devotion to the appeal made of them. Throughout a long day of incessant fighting they beat off a succession of determined attacks. In the evening the enemy made a last great effort, and by sheer weight of numbers overran certain portions of our Line, the defenders of which died fighting, but would not give ground. Those of the enemy who had broken through at these points were however, met and driven back beyond our Line by the reinforcing troops, who by this time had completed their detrainment'.*

The grass is always greener on the other side, especially on the other side of the Channel! Many in the 11th Battalion during this period must have been wishing for a blighty one like 2/Lieutenant Richardson had received back in September 1917 after only being with the battalion a few weeks. Richardson, an ex-ranker, pre-war

Map detailing the movements of the 10th and 11th Battalions between 12th and 15th April.

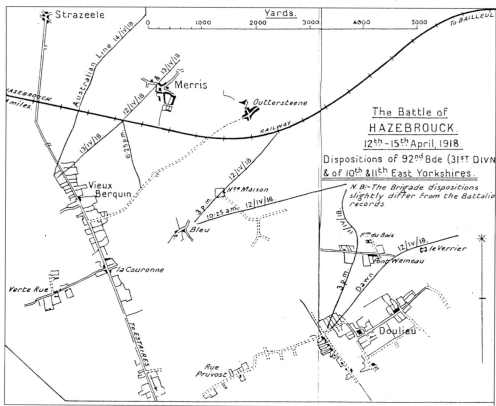

regular, turned officer, had returned to the UK for convalescence after a gun shot wound and when fit had been posted to the 3rd Battalion East Yorkshire Regiment in Withernsea.

On April 14th he had been granted twenty-four hours' leave which he had spent with his wife, whom he had married in February of the year before. His Commanding Officer reported him missing on the 30th when he had not returned from this overnight leave. Unbeknown to his Commanding Officer he had been transferred to Perham Down Camp near Andover where he joined the Southern Command Depot for what should have been a pleasant spell of duty, safe from the firing line. However, after only a few days with the unit he decided to have a ride in an aeroplane. The Commandant of the Depot reported:

'On the 25th April 2nd Lieutenant Richardson and another Officer were offered a ride in an aeroplane which was accepted. Unfortunately the wings of the aeroplane collapsed and the machine crashed to the ground. 2/Lieutenant Richardson and the others were killed instantaneously'.

So much for cushy jobs!

After a brief rest and re-organisation the battalions returned to work with new drafts of reinforcements to fill the ranks. However, as there was still a threat to Hazebrouck, a 92nd Composite Battalion was formed from two companies each from the 10th and 11th East Yorkshires. This was an emergency formation which went into the Hazebrouck defences on the 16th to relieve two companies of the 12th Australian Infantry Battalion. On the 18th this battalion ceased to exist and the 10th and 11th Battalions were reformed. Later that day the 10th Battalion returned to the front line at Grand Sec Bois while the 11th went in to the trenches the next day near Le Paradis.

Life in the trenches was the same as before the German offensive with digging, salvage work and wiring. There was considerable aerial activity during the day and gas shelling at night. One unusual activity pursued by the 11th Battalion during this stint in the trenches was the rounding up of cattle which had escaped during the recent fighting. Although this must have been an amusing interlude for the men, the officer writing the war diary did not think much of it:

'the arrangements for the collecting of cattle etc, in the forward areas, were, as usual, left to the initiative of the Infantry Commanders, & though we could ill afford the men for the work, several head were rounded up & with considerable difficulty driven to back areas. One couldn't help but think that the A.P.M.'s mounted personnel would have ben more suitable for this work but there ——'(sic).

The night of the 23rd was a bright moonlight night and as a result there were numerous enemy bombers out which caused consternation in the 11th Battalion

A shell exploding in the distance. In the foreground is a village destroyed during the German offensive.

transport lines. Raiding resumed and on the 26th a patrol of 20 men led by 2/Lieutenant Greenhalgh went out under a protective barrage to obtain identification. Even though the preparation had been good the barrage was poor and the information on the German dispositions was vague. As a result no information was gained. The same day the battalion received note that 19 men from the battalion had been awarded the MM for good work during the recent operations.

On April 26th the 10th Battalion relieved the 11th East Lancashires in the front line at Seclin, to the right of the 11th East Yorkshires. The next morning, at 3.30 am, a raiding party under Captain Pearce, with three other officers and 125 other ranks set off to raid the German trenches around La Becque Farm; these had been previously reconnoitred the night before by the Officer Commanding the raid, four officers and eight sergeants. Before Zero hour the raiding party assembled in front of the battalion's trenches and moved forward along a ditch. When the barrage started the party moved forward in sections, in single file, with twenty paces between each section. When they got to within 50 yards of the barrage they knelt down and waited. In his report of the 29th, Major Anderson (temporary battalion commander) wrote:

'At zero plus 7 the southern portion of the barrage lifted and the party detailed immediately engaged enemy in enclosure round farm at E 23 c 4.1.

'At zero plus 8 the remainder of the barrage lifted 150 yards and sections advanced up to road running through E 23 c in order to check direction and close up under the barrage again. The enemy was first encountered W of the road in E 23 c in shell holes and slits. These (evidently listening posts) were at once cleared and advance was not delayed. E(ast) of the road the enemy were met with in strength in small camouflaged trenches holding three or four men each and disposed in depth. The enemy put up some resistance here but it was overcome by the determination and dash shown by all ranks. The advance was continued to a point E 23 c 8.1. to E 23 c 5.7. All enemy encountered were either killed or captured, but many Germans ran back and were caught by our barrage. Owing to the time taken in clearing this ground the pre-arranged time for withdrawal was reached before the enclosure round LA BECQUE could be dealt with. The withdrawal was therefore ordered and carried out in good order'.

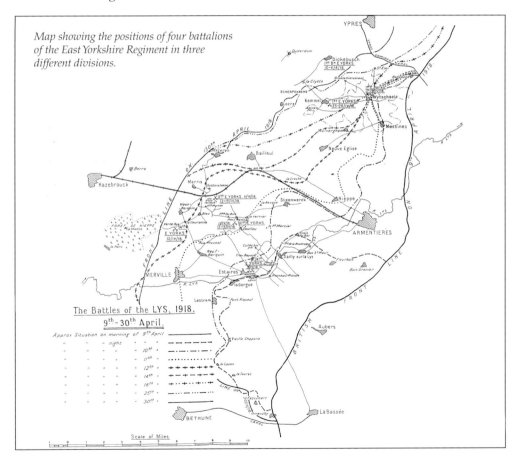

Map showing the positions of four battalions of the East Yorkshire Regiment in three different divisions.

Sergeant John Richardson of the 12th Battalion. He had been badly wounded at Oppy Wood and taken prisoner. His wounds were so bad that he was exchanged for a badly wounded German prisoner in May 1918.

Corporal Peter McNally of the 11th Battalion was transferred to the 4th Battalion and taken prisoner in May 1918. He was of Irish descent and lived in an area of Hull then known as 'The West End' (James Place, Colonial Street), an area favoured by immigrant Irish.

2/Lieutenant Williams, Lewis Gun officer, 11th Battalion.

The battalion history recorded that:

> 'the raid was a great success, as twenty-four Germans and a machine gun were brought back, while the raiders reported that they had killed 'about sixty of the enemy'.'

The report indicates that at least 75 were killed or wounded; many of the raiders' bayonets showed traces of their use and 20 Mills bombs were used by NCOs against parties of enemy who would not readily leave their slits.

Battalion casualties were six other ranks killed, 11 were wounded (one dying of his wounds that day) and three taken prisoner. Congratulations were received from both the Corps and Army Commanders. Later that day they were relieved by the 2nd Leinsters of the 29th Division.

The 11th Battalion moved back to billets for rest and training on the 27th. On the 28th three officers reported for duty along with eight other ranks. On the 30th, as a reward for good work during the recent operations, 41 other ranks were promoted. *The Hull Daily Mail* of May 3rd carried the following passage from Sir Douglas Haig:

> 'The magnificent performance in holding up the enemy advance at a critical stage of the Lys Battle has already been publicly acknowledged. I wish to add my personal tribute to the fine fighting qualities displayed by this Division.'

He was of course referring to the 31st Division. (31st Division total casualties for all ranks for the period April 9th to 30th was 4641 – fourth highest total for divisions engaged during this period.)

Neither battalion returned to the trenches until May 9th when they relieved Australian battalions. The 10th relieved the 3rd AIF Battalion in reserve in the Fletre area, while the 11th Battalion relieved the 6th AIF Battalion in the trenches near Meteren. The preceeding days had been used for training and improving the Hazebrouck defences. On May 5th Captain Pearce DCM and 2/Lieutenant Wood of the 10th Battalion were awarded the MC for their work during the German offensive in April and on the 6th, Lieutenant-Colonel Gurney was awarded a bar to his DSO, Captains Chapman, Southern and Smith were awarded the MC. In the 10th Battalion Corporal Collinson and CSM Graham were awarded the DCM while in the 11th Battalion, Private Fortes, Private Harris and Sergeant Thompson were also awarded the DCM with L/Corporal Hackitt receiving a bar to his DCM.

When the 11th Battalion returned to the front on the 15th it was in a pivotal position, with the 168th French Division on the left and 3 Australian Brigade on the right. As a result of this an International Post was established with very good liaison between the French and the British. Around this time the battalion suffered a slight epidemic of spotted fever in C Company and 40 men were kept in isolation.

There was much aerial activity each night and considerable enemy artillery activity over the rear areas. On May 17th alone between 2000 and 3000 shells fell around Caestre Mill.

Patrolling was carried out on a regular basis, generally very successfully. But not always. On the 16th while out on patrol, Captain Wallis was wounded and died within a few hours.

Brigade relief was scheduled for the night of 21st/22nd May. Just before the 13th York and Lancs relieved the 11th East Yorks, a deserter from the 12th RIR (11th Reserve Division) came over from the enemy lines to the International Post and asked to be taken prisoner by the British. Also during this tour the battalion captured a number of Germans unexpectedly. The 11th Battalion history records that while they were here:

'an unsuspecting party of the enemy walked in fours along the road from Vieux Berquin, and were suitably welcomed, though the premature discharge of a rifle prevented the bag being as large as it might have been'.

May 24th saw the brigade move by bus to Lumbres, south-west of St. Omer. Here the battalions spent considerable time in specialist training, range practice and ceremonial drill in preparation for a brigade parade which was to be inspected by the Divisional Commander and during which medal ribbons would be presented. Leave was granted to visit St. Omer and other recreational pursuits included rifle and revolver competitions, with the 11th Battalion team gaining first prize and

Lieutenant-Colonel Gurney gaining first prize in the revolver section, with Captain Smith coming second. A divisional knock-out rugby competition took place which the 10th Battalion won. The officers of the 10th beat the officers of the 11th Battalion 1 - 0 at soccer.

It was during this rest that the 11th Battalion encountered the American Army en masse:

Private John Cunningham VC was badly wounded at some point in 1918. This photograph was taken while he was recuperating. He was discharged because of his wounds.

'While we were firing a full course on the range we made our first acquaintance with the U.S.A. Army in bulk – individual members of it had been met before. Such an opportunity for liaison was not to be missed and, led by the C.O., we endeavoured to cultivate friendly relations and 'swap' souvenirs with our newly arrived allies. The vexed question of fluctuating currency values did not concern us, and the rate of exchange was based on the fact that a British jack knife was equal in value to one Yankee safety razor. Friendly relations with the Supply Branch and the Civil Power were also cultivated by the C.O., and a polo match and some races were held in a local field near the village. The Maire and various other local officials were invited, as also was the whole population of the village. Tea was provided free for them, and the band played throughout.'

La Becque

Early June saw the battalions undergoing further training in defence and retirement. The quiet period ended when the division moved to the Wallon – Cappel area where the division was to relieve the 29th Division. The division spent much time practising for the offensive. On the 23rd D Company of the 11th Battalion carried out an exhibition of the attack, while on the 25th, Company Commanders, in camouflage suits, reconnoitered assembly positions near Bois d'Aval with a view to the forthcoming attack on German trenches from La Becque Farm to Le Cornet Perdu. This attack was designed to push the enemy back from the Fôret de Nieppe which was constantly shelled with gas.

During this quiet before the storm, some light relief was provided by fishing. The 10th Battalion history recalled these expeditions:

'We were relieved on June 25th after a very quiet period (forever notable if only for the fishing expeditions with Mills bombs, organised by headquarters' details, in the canal – the signallers' ninety-four roach with the first bomb being the best catch recorded – immediately after which the 'professional' bombers drew a complete blank despite several casts).'

A further practice attack by the 10th Battalion during the 26th was interrupted by enemy shelling. On the 27th the scheme of attack was explained to all ranks using maps and aerial photos which were shown around. Stores were issued and at 7.30 the 10th Battalion moved off to assembly positions followed at 8pm by the 11th Battalion. The attack (known as Operation Borderland), on the 28th, was to be on a two brigade front with the 5th Division attacking further south. 93 Brigade were on the left flank with their objective being La Becque Farm. On the right flank was 92 Brigade with Le Cornet Perdu (a farm), as its objective. All three battalions of 92 Brigade were to attack; the 11th East Yorkshires on the left, the 10th on the right flank with the 11th East Lancashires in the centre. (The date was chosen because the year previously on that date the 5th and 31st Divisions had carried out a particularly successful operation at Oppy Wood.)

2/Lieutenant Moody, 11th Battalion, behind the lines during June 1918.

At 6am the barrage started and the battalions moved forward through the British wire along prepared lanes, through tall corn, without any difficulty. The attacking troops were able to move so quickly that they were up to the barrage by zero plus 2. Some troops moved too far forward and as a result were caught in their own barrage. On the right flank, where the 10th Battalion abutted the 12th Gloucesters of the 5th Division, a few of the 18 pounders were firing short before the lift of the first barrage, resulting in a number of casualties including the Company Commander, Major Traill, who was killed in the first five minutes of the attack. One of the soldiers wounded in this battle was Private Beeston, who recalled the troops being too far forward for their own safety that day:

'I joined up at 17 ½ in February 1917 and went to France in March 1918. I was wounded in June 1918, arrived in Leeds where I remained until December 1918 and was discharged with a small disability pension... I was unable to trace any of my comrades and assumed they were all lost in our offensive in June. I believe they were caught in our own barrage which they should have waited to lift'.

Artillery rounds falling short was a problem encountered earlier in the day by the 10th Battalion during the assembly period, prior to the attack. One 18 pounder gun

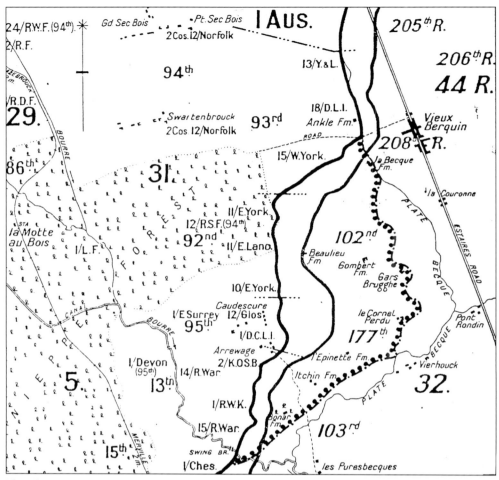

The tide was turning. A map of the successful attack on La Becque on 28th June in which the line was advanced for a small number of British casualties. Over 400 prisoners were taken, the majority of them by 92 Brigade.

which, although reported several times, continued to fire short with most of the shells falling around Battalion HQ and just behind the assembled troops, causing some casualties before the attack started. Lieutenant-Colonel Rigg's report, written on July 3rd, describes the situation:

> 'The resistance shown by the enemy was very slight. In most cases they attempted to run away after the barrage had passed and were either captured or killed by our men or else ran into our barrage in front of them. A number of prisoners were taken who had had no time to man their tranches (sic) before they were captured. At certain points there was some slight resistance and at GARS BRUGGHE the Left of the attack was held up for a short time by M.G. fire but on the flank of this farm being turned by the Company on the right, the resistance was speedily overcome'.

'Enemy retaliation was generally weak although the bombardment of the British front line was very heavy for about 30 minutes around 14 minutes after zero hour. Fortunately by this time there were very few troops about and consequently casualties were very light.'

The final objectives were reached at 7.20am and connections with flanking units were maintained throughout the operation. Consolidating the gains proved to be difficult at first due to long range machine gun fire. A very successful attack was marred by the number of casualties suffered, most of which resulted from British artillery shells falling short. All the officers of C Company were casualties and Capt. Wright from Battalion HQ had to go forward to take command.

Private Aust was present for this action and in later life recalled that the Battalion:

'attacked through waist-high corn from the trenches covering Hazebrouck where we had brought the Germans to a halt in April. Our artillery barrage was now terrific and the Germans were demoralised. I went over with the 4th wave and as we advanced through an orchard, limbs and parts of German bodies festooned the trees and blood was dripping on us as we advanced to the Plat Becq, a distance of about a mile. 300 prisoners were taken and our casualties about half that figure, many from our own barrage'.

GREETINGS

Don't worry ¡ We're winning

Although it must have been hard to believe it at the time, the fact that the Germans were no longer winning meant that the Allies must be winning.

For this action Captain Hall, Lieutenants Hall and Anderton and 2/Lieutenants Hadrill and Wallace, MM were awarded the MC. The 11th Battalion had orders to attack and consolidate the enemy trench system round Verte Rue and to the north. Like the 10th Battalion the attack went smoothly and all objectives were taken by 7.25am. Enemy resistance was generally not great but some machine gun posts fought to the end and in many cases could only be stopped by outflanking movements. Unlike the barrage received by the 10th Battalion front line, the German barrage on 11th Battalion positions was, according to the official report written by Lieutenant-Colonel Gurney: 'rather feeble and ragged'.

Their first prisoners arrived back at Battalion HQ at 6.50am. These were from the 102 RIR of the 32 Reserve Division.

When the objectives had been taken, the report continued:

'Companies sent out Patrols to PLAT BECQUE. None of the enemy were to be found WEST of the stream. It would appear that the enemy had blown up the majority of the bridges over the Becque during his retirement.

'From noon onwards a heavy enemy Barrage was put down on the front position inflicting heavy casualties'.

The 11th Battalion captured one field gun, two light machine guns, two machine gun beds, 2 light trench mortars, two heavy trench mortars and three heavy machine guns which they blew up.

There was little retaliation and no counter-attacks were attempted on the 11th Battalion front. However, on the 10th Battalion front parties of the enemy were observed in the fields near La Becque massing for a counter-attack. The battalion sent up an SOS and a barrage came down which scattered the enemy and stopped the attack. In the afternoon the Germans randomly shelled the 10th Battalion front line and intervening ground, causing casualties to the support troops and working parties.

Private Walter Sutherland of the 11th Battalion. Private Sutherland survived the war.

The attack had resulted in advance of around a thousand yards on 92 Brigade front. Although the number of wounded was quite high the motor ambulances were able to get quite close to the front line so that they were quickly removed from the area. So good was this removal, aided by the German prisoners, that the Official History recorded that: 'the advanced dressing stations specialized in hot soup and nourishment rather than surgery'. Casualties for the 10th Battalion as recorded in the war diary were one officer and 24 other ranks killed, five officers and 137 men wounded, two men wounded believed killed and two men missing.

The total number of prisoners taken by the 5th and 31st Divisions were seven officers and 432 other ranks. Materiel captured included 4 field guns, a quantity of mustard gas shells, which were fired against the Germans the next day, 14 trench mortars (light and heavy) and 77 machine guns. 92 Brigade alone buried 135 Germans. The 10th Battalion history records that:

'the prisoners were Saxons of the 32nd Division and Prussians of the 44th Division, and from both came confirmation of the rumour that influenza was rife in the German Army and that it had recently helped to hold up their advance.'

This worldwide plague, which became known as Spanish Influenza, would eventually kill more than the Great War itself.

The ease of the victory also showed that the Germans were not intending any offensives in this area. This information was one of the main reasons for the attack.

Death was ever present; even at demonstrations. Captain Oake, of 92 TMB (originally of the 11th Battalion) died of his wounds on June 26th during a trench mortar demonstration which also killed Sergeant Hill MM, Corporal Woodall (both original 'Hull Pals'), Sergeant F Russell (2/4th O & B L I), and Private Booth (East Yorkshire Regiment) and wounded two officers and two men (Lieutenant Cowley and 2/Lieutenant Wilkins and L/Corporals Baker MM and Skavington MM). What should have been a simple display, arranged by experts in the field, turned into a tragedy. The court of enquiry into the accident established that after a lecture on anti-aircraft firing, Sergeant Russell carefully prepared demonstration fuses of sufficient quality and timing for the forthcoming demonstration. Upon firing the first projectile an insufficiently crimped fuse came loose and exploded while the shell was in the barrel, killing those in the immediate vicinity. The verdict was accidental death.

On 30th June the brigade was relieved by the newly formed 94 (Yeomanry) Brigade. The 4th Guards Brigade had left the division on May 20th to be replaced by troops returning from Palestine. This new brigade consisted of the 12th Norfolks, the 12th Royal Scots Fusiliers and the 24th Royal Welsh Fusiliers. The three battalions had been formed from dismounted yeomanry regiments and had originally been in the 74th Division. They had arrived in France, from Palestine, in May and after a short period of acclimatisation they had joined the 31st Division on June 21st at Blaringhem.

The first few days of July were spent in reorganising the companies, musketry and respirator training; and the following days in the line were quiet. Army rations were supplemented from the fields between the front line and the support line; here there were crops of potatoes and peas. During this period, Lieutenant-Colonel Rigg went on leave to Paris, a new Medical Officer (Captain J C Dunn DSO, MC,

Even before the start of the 'Advance to Victory', XI Corps (of which the 31st Division were part for a short while at the end of June) managed to find time to hold a horse show. This is the winning mule team. The horse at the front was called Tommy.

DCM) arrived to join the 10th Battalion and much needed reinforcements, both of officers and men, began to arrive.

Patrolling was frequent on both sides. On the night of the 11th/12th the 11th Battalion secured identification from a German patrol that had got lost (213 RIR). The next night the 11th Battalion carried out a very successful operation in conjunction with the Australians. As a result of this the British line was advanced and a number of prisoners were taken.

This operation was unusual in that it was arranged in a matter of hours and that it arose from a conversation between Lieutenant-Colonel Gurney and the Commanding Officer of the 1st AIF Battalion at midday on the 12th. Lieutenant-Colonel Gurney was explaining how he wanted to capture Tern Farm the next day when the Australian Commander informed him that one of his daylight patrols had captured 28 prisoners with practically no opposition. He was anxious to exploit this success and advance his line.

No artillery barrage was to be called for. The method of attack was for small patrols to push forward preceded by two scouts who would hopefully find the Germans hiding in their foxholes in the waist high corn. As the crawling troops would not be seen until it was too late, the enemy would be unable to bring their machine guns to bear.

The Australians would attack at the same time as the 11th Battalion, who would be assisted by Cyclist Corps troops attached for instruction, with zero hour being set for 2.30pm. However, the Australians left their trenches at 2.15pm so the advance was brought forward to 2.25pm. The advance proceeded without any serious opposition and it was found that the forward German line was held by posts with machine guns. In his official report Lieutenant-Colonel Gurney continued:

> 'The strongpoint at point B offered no resistance and its garrison were taken prisoners. At point C opposition was encountered owing to an excess of zeal of a N.C.O. attached, who fired upon the Post when they were perfectly willing and ready to surrender, but were fired upon by this N.C.O. which action brought about a stubborn resistance. The Post was surrounded from the flanks and they then gave in without further trouble.'

Remaining strongpoints were quickly subdued by flanking movements which brought the British troops up behind the enemy. After being surrounded the posts were quick to surrender.

Unfortunately the Australians were unable to advance as easily – strongpoint A had held up their advance. Even with assistance from the 11th Battalion no further advance was possible and the Australian positions were consolidated. This lack of success meant that the line of the 11th Battalion was not tenable and the outposts were pulled back in order to maintain contact with the Australians.

The Germans did not counter-attack but that evening put down an accurate barrage on the old front and support lines and on all the tracks and roads leading to the area. Lieutenant-Colonel Gurney concluded in his report that although it was a fairly heavy barrage it was not sufficient to stop reinforcements arriving if the need had arisen. The report continued:

'As a result of this operation one officer, sixty prisoners and four Machine Guns were captured and some 50 of the enemy were killed, whilst our casualties were two killed, three missing, and thirteen wounded.'

Much is made of the falling quality and interest of the German troops towards the end of the war. The report of this advance contains a very pertinent comment about future events:

'The general morale of the enemy was nil and they seemed willing, if not anxious, to be made prisoners. One prisoner captured – a batman of the Company Commander – informed us that he could not understand why his master was not a prisoner as he saw him coming towards us in order to join the majority of his Company when they were prisoners in our hands.'

The report also emphasised the importance of allowing the officer on the ground to have total responsibility for the attack:

'the Company Commander must be given the greatest possible latitude and should be fettered only by the general line or lines to which it is proposed to advance. Throughout arrangements must be left entirely to him and he must be encouraged to seize opportunities and to exploit success in a manner found best in the course of the operations'.

German troops rest in a ditch containing a destroyed French tank sometime in July 1918.

A photograph taken outside a Public House in Hull. Essential workers, men too young, old or unfit for service and discharged soldiers make up the group.

The success of this rather cheeky operation is even more startling when the age of the troops, and therefore their experience, is considered. In a short story written much later Lieutenant-Colonel Gurney makes comment about the age of his troops during this operation and of the opinion the Australians had of the battalion until then:

> 'owing to the extreme youth of the battalion, due to hurried replacement of our terrible losses of March and April, 1918, (so far as I can remember our average age was 19) the irreverent Aussies had nicknamed us the "Crêche" with many impertinent enquiries as to where they had been grown, and after the show congratulations were showered on the plucky little "beggars" in Crêche (sic)'.

Congratulations were also forthcoming from the 2nd Army Commander, General Plumer. Operations like this secured 223 prisoners in two days.

Later that day the 10th Battalion arrived to relieve the 11th Battalion and took over the new positions. On the 14th a patrol located an enemy machine gun post west of the Vieux Berquin road. The machine gunner opened fire when he saw the patrol. Undaunted, the patrol continued towards the machine gun, at which point the machine gun team ran away, leaving the 10th Battalion patrol to capture and return with their gun.

94 Brigade relieved 92 Brigade on July 16th and the brigade returned to billets. Over the next few days the battalions rested, bathed, trained in Lewis gun operations and bayonet fighting and were inspected by the MO. Because of the startling success of the operation of the 12th, where the battalion had advanced around 300 yards on a 500 yard front, the 'Top Brass' wanted to know more about it and as a result considerable time was invested in rehearsing for and actually reliving the advance for the General Staff of the Brigade, Division and Corps.

On 26th July the 10th Battalion relieved the 11th Battalion. Even though the 11th had moved into support, it still carried out a trench raid in the sector held by the 10th Battalion. At 11.30pm on the 28th a raiding party of one officer and 29 other ranks left the trenches under a creeping barrage. (An artillery barrage that moves forward a fixed distance every so many minutes.)

After moving around for some time no trace of the enemy was found and the party returned unharmed. A patrol from C Company operating in No Man's Land also failed to find any Germans. However, on the same night, D Company of the 10th Battalion reconnoitred an enemy post only to find it strongly occupied; they too retired unscathed. During July 29th the Germans fired a considerable number of gas shells at the 10th Battalion positions.

A Punch cartoon on the problems of capturing higher ranking officers.

Private Sloggins (to German officer who has demanded an escort of equal rank). "THAT'S WOT WE'VE 'ALTED FOR. DUGGY 'AIG'S COMIN' OVER SPECIAL. I SEED 'IM MYSELF THIS MORNIN' AN' ARRANGED IT."

The officers of the 11th Battalion in July 1918.

Patrolling and raiding were becoming the order of the day. Tricks were also used to see what response the Germans would give. On the night of August 2nd the 11th Battalion fired green and red rockets in the style of enemy rockets but no response was made by the enemy – this should have resulted in a German barrage over the attacked area. The next night the 10th Battalion sent out a raiding party under Lieutenant Krog and 2/Lieutenant Hatfield with 20 other ranks at 12.15am. This was a fighting patrol and was tasked with bringing back information from the German outposts in the shellholes east of Gars Brugghe. Under the cover of a barrage the party attacked and returned with two prisoners from the 187th RIR. Only one man from the raiding party was wounded. Lieutenant Krog was awarded the MC for this raid.

The situation was changing. With the enemy slowly moving back, fighting patrols pushed forward during the day and at night patrols were necessary to keep in touch with the enemy. British artillery was very active resulting in many fires in the German back areas. During the night German artillery was active and increased in response to split green rockets. The war diary of the 11th Battalion recorded that:

> *'the enemy seems 'uneasy' – our active patrolling continues both day and night. Enemy planes are active at dusk and dawn but throughout the day our own aerial activity keeps them at a distance'.*

The Hundred Days

Active patrolling led to considerable casualties among both officers and men. A minor operation by B Company of the 11th Battalion, on the 15th, in conjunction with the 10th Battalion and a platoon of the 15th KOYLI (40th Division) led to disaster. Patrols under 2/Lieutenant Wright and 2/Lieutenant Coates crawled forward and took up position but were spotted by enemy machine gun troops. Heavy machine gun fire held up both parties. The two officers were killed and all the NCOs of 2/Lieutenant Wright's party wounded. Private Pottage took command of this party and consolidated his position in the face of hostile fire. Captain Williams and 2/Lieutenant Jenkin went out to take over the two parties at 4.30 pm and touch was established between all parties and flanks. 2/Lieutenant Jenkin was relieved by 2/Lieutenant Larter who attempted to outflank the enemy post but, owing to the open nature of the ground, no progress was made. Both parties then consolidated their positions. During the night the enemy attempted to drive the parties back but were driven off with Lewis gun and rifle fire.

The next day the 11th Battalion continued its advance using Stokes mortars and rifle grenades. After gaining 200 yards, enemy machine gun and sniper fire checked the advance. However, the units on the left, working in conjunction with the 11th East Lancashires, destroyed two enemy posts, killing five Germans and capturing two. Two light machine guns were captured.

On the 17th the battalion fell back to allow the artillery to pound the German trenches. The battalion then attempted to advance but made little progress due to machine gun fire.

Mention has previously been made of the extreme youth of the replacements. Manpower demands were so high that many men of less than perfect health were being sent to the front line. In some cases they were sent to France as Garrison Troops (B.1 Category) to relieve fighting troops but very quickly their Garrison title and role were removed and older men or men in less than first class health, often with little adequate training, found themselves in the front line. The 10th Battalion history mentions just such men:

> 'On the 13th we were unexpectedly relieved by the 15th KOYLI so that we could move to the left to replace some B.1. men of the 8th Royal Irish Regiment (40th Division) at Swartenbrouck Farm. They had only done four days trench duty altogether, while their signallers had had but six weeks training, and the whole battalion had but six weeks training, and the whole battalion seemed amazed to find themselves actually in the fighting area.'

The area that the battalion took over was very ill-defined because the 8th Royal Irish Regiment had been advancing along the lines of the least opposition. At 7.30am the 10th Battalion sent out fighting patrols to establish a new line which unfortunately was not viable because the battalion on the left initially failed to take its objective. Later in the day, when the 12th RSF had taken its objectives, the 10th Battalion was able to move forward. Vieux Berquin was now in allied hands. On the 14th the 10th Battalion once again took its objectives and took a prisoner at a cost

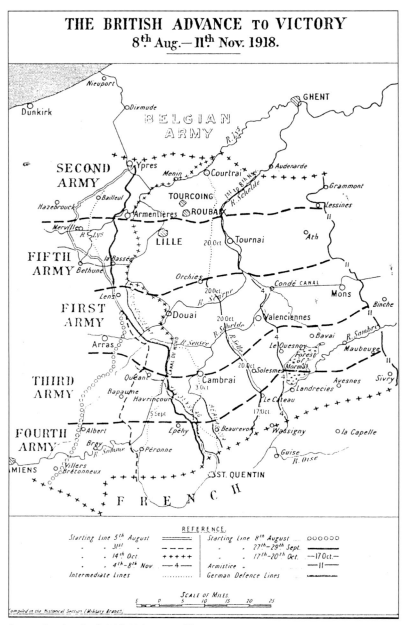

THE BRITISH ADVANCE TO VICTORY
8th Aug. — 11th Nov. 1918.

A map showing the British 'Advance to Victory'.

of nine other ranks killed with a further seven the next day – the opposition was stiffening. That night they were pulled back into brigade reserve, where the men were able to rest and bathe in the canal running past La Motte Chateau.

Returning to the trenches on the night of the 17th, the battalion found that they had posts which encircled the La Couronne cross-roads. However, the next day,

252

when fighting patrols tried to advance, they encountered heavy opposition from just this area and consequently were unable to make any progress. On the 19th, with help from the 11th Battalion on the left, fighting patrols successfully crossed the Vieux Berquin road and eliminated the pockets of resistance at the cross-roads. Attacks on these two days by the 9th, 29th and 31st Divisions cleared Outtersteene village and ridge and resulted in around 900 prisoners being taken.

Although this policy of peaceful penetration generally worked, there were occasions when the enemy resisted stubbornly. After successfully moving forward in the Vieux Berquin area on the 20th, the next day the 11th Battalion ran into serious opposition. The early morning advance had met no problems but suddenly, at around 4.30pm, the enemy artillery opened up with gas shells and machine gunners joined in, resulting in the death of one officer (2/Lieutenant Bocking) and three other ranks. The gas shelling wounded 22 soldiers.

On the 23rd the battalion left the line for rest and a clean-up, joining the 10th Battalion which had also left the line that night. As usual when the brigade were out of the line there were battalion sports, grenade demonstrations, training and divisional horseshows. When the 11th Battalion returned to the trenches on the 28th, the 10th Battalion was engaged on salvage work which, according to Private Surfleet, was something of a craze with everyone having to constantly collect discarded material. The 10th Battalion returned to the trenches on the 3rd and the 11th Battalion came out to do salvage work. Officer losses in the 10th Battalion had been high during August. Second Lieutenant Buttery was killed on the 20th, 2/Lieutenant Marshall had been taken PoW, 2/Lieutenant Taylor and 2/Lieutenant Humphries had been wounded and 2/Lieutenant Hatfield gassed.

The relief of the 10th KOSB on the 3rd was marred by a very unfortunate incident. Lieutenant Earle and his platoon were taken through Nieppe village, which had been heavily shelled during the day. As the platoon made its way through the ruined village it received a direct hit killing Lieutenant Earle and ten men, wounding a further six.

September saw no let up in the pursuit of the retreating Germans. Orders were received for a general advance by patrols on a frontage of 2000 yards to a depth of a minimum of 1500 yards. On September 4th, at 8am, the 29th Division advanced behind an artillery barrage in an attempt to take Hill 63. The enemy response was to put down a barrage on the 10th Battalion, who were waiting in concealed positions in the Nieppe trenches. Zero hour for the 10th was 8.35am. The battalion advanced against well prepared and strong German positions, without the benefit of an artillery barrage. Enemy machine guns found their targets with ease, for there was no cover and the ground was flat. In three hours C Company managed to advance about 1000 yards, D Company 500 yards while B Company had made no headway and had retired to their assembly area. Orders later in the day wanted the attack resumed if it were possible without heavy loss. In response to this order a further attempt was made at 3pm but made no progress due to the enemy opposition. Casualties were high. 2/Lieutenant Cheesborough was killed and Captain Wallace, Lieutenant Oakden and 2/Lieutenant Raynor were wounded. There were 10 other ranks killed and 59 wounded.

On the 5th the battalion left Prompt Farm for a field near Steenwerck station. During this relief a regrettable incident occured. A man picked up a dud shell and threw it away causing it to explode. This resulted in the death of Private Joseph Britton and the wounding of six more men. The man who threw the shell was only slightly wounded. Initially it was thought to be a German booby trap. Strangely enough, after leaving the trenches and this incident behind, the brigade had the 3rd Canadian Tunneling Company attached to it to test booby traps!

On the night of the 5th/6th the 11th Battalion had relieved the 11th East Lancashires after their attack earlier that day. The East Lancs had advanced and as a result there was no solid trench system for the 11th East Yorkshires to occupy.

The attack on the 6th was aimed at the road running south from Ploegsteert across to the Warnave River. When the attack was launched at 3am, C Company met with considerable opposition from strong parties of the enemy in Soyer Farm. B Company managed to reach the Warnave river but in doing so lost touch with the rest of the battalion. D Company met with considerable opposition from Poncteau Farm while A Company reached the river and the road and managed to join up with C Company. Artillery assistance was called for against the German positions and

A staged and sanitized attack for the folks back home. This card was sold to raise money for the MGC Prisoners of War fund.

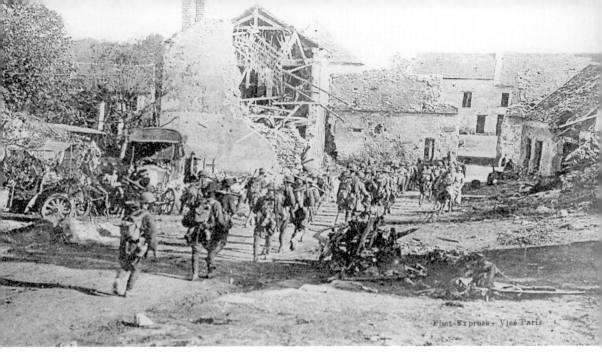

American troops passing through Latilly during the 2nd Battle of the Marne in July 1918.

minor attacks were made against the posts, but the enemy garrison proved too strong to overcome.

Brigade HQ summoned Lieutenant-Colonel Rigg, on the 6th, for a conference on the next attack to be delivered by the 10th Battalion. The final objective of this attack would be the River Lys. However, this time it would be behind a protective barrage. After this conference, Lieutenant-Colonel Rigg returned to Steenwerck, collected his company commanders and took them back to Brigade HQ to discuss details and the artillery barrage. There would be no time to reconnoitre the assembly positions, so the task of selecting them was given to 2/Lieutenant Hall, the 11th Battalion Intelligence Officer, the battalion the 10th would be passing through.

2/Lieutenant Hall had selected his positions carefully. The battalion war diary recorded that: 'at dawn the battalion was satisfactorily concealed from view'.

This was fortunate for the attacking troops because, as the battalion war diary continued:

'the Bosche was evidently nervous & his guns fired a certain amount of counter preparation. The line of his barrage was noticed to be about 500 yards in front of our assembly positions'.

A novel feature of this attack was the smokescreen that was to be put down. Unfortunately it did not blanket the troops for the first two minutes, allowing the

Germans to see what was happening. A second failure was the barrage which had been arranged to fall 500 yards in front of the assembly positions; this distance left the enemy machine gunners untouched and as a result they were able to open fire on the advancing 10th Battalion when they were at their most vulnerable – when they came to the uncut wire.

The attack started at 10am on the 7th and by 11am the attacking troops had advanced about 1200 yards, to the light railway near Harrisburg junction but still about 1200 yards short of their objective, the River Lys. Severe opposition came from the garrison in Soyer Farm which was surrounded by a moat as well as being very heavily wired. The Germans shelled the whole area all afternoon and the position was still very uncertain when the relief, by the 11th East Lancashires, took place at around 2am. Casualties were very heavy. Lieutenant Krog and 2/Lieutenant Bradbury were killed and 2/Lieutenants Gordon and Myhall were wounded. 30 other ranks were killed with a number dying of wounds over the next few days.

The attack was continued the next day by the 11th Battalion. After making good progress, their left flank was turned and the attack broke down. D Company again suffered particularly heavy casualties. (Of the 11th Battalion officers involved in these attacks the only one to escape unharmed was Captain T Southern MC of B Company).

On September 8th, the 10th Battalion relieved the 11th East Lancashires east of Nieppe. The weather was wet and the ground was becoming difficult. Poncteau Farm was found to be empty the next morning so the battalion adjusted its line accordingly, meeting with only slight opposition. Soyer Farm had still not been taken and a sniper from the garrison was responsible for the death of Lieutenant Hutchinson, the Battalion Intelligence Officer. No further offensive action was taken by the battalion and they were relieved that night by the 11th East Lancs.

By the 12th the battalion was back in Ballieul from where it went on to Hazebrouck. There they counted the casualties for the first half of September – 25 other ranks killed, 72 wounded, 1 gassed, 44 missing and 13 wounded and missing. Six officers were wounded, one was missing and one was wounded and missing.

The whole brigade was given ten days' rest to clean-up, receive drafts of officers and men and to train. The emphasis was most certainly on rest, and rest in a comparatively civilised area – Staple and Hondeghem near Hazebrouck. An almost idyllic picture of this period of rest is painted by the 10th Battalion history:

'the Sergeants established a very comfortable Battalion Mess at the Estam-inet da la Couronne; Headquarters beat 'A' Company by 5 goals to nil; the Battalion XI lost to a team of giants from the M.T. (A.S.C.) attached to the R.E. Pontoon Park, while the Rugger XV played two very close games with the 11th Battalion, losing 9-0 at Staple, and 14-9 on their ground at Hondeghem; we visited the quaint old hill-top town of Cassel; French classes were started as part of our Educational Scheme; the 'Nissen Nuts' gave several open-air shows in the village for our entertainment; most

German debris in a hastily dug trench.

of us went over to Hondeghem to see 'The Tonics' in their new black and white costumes, while our holiday ended with a Brigade Church Parade service at Hondeghem'.

On September 23rd the brigade moved back to the front line, marching to Hazebrouck and then travelling by train to Bailleul where they detrained and marched to basically the same trenches that they had left on September 10th/11th. The 10th Battalion went into the front line while the 11th was in support. This short tour of duty for the 10th Battalion was very quiet and they were relieved by a battalion from 119 Brigade on the 25th. In his diary Private Beeken recorded a prophetic conversation with his Company Commander:

'One evening I found myself in a ditch with the Company Captain who was one of the original 10th EYR. In our conversation he said "You know, we've had a lot of fighting since we came to France. So much so, that we cannot expect to survive it". I replied "Yes we've had a long and hard time in France but we've come out of it all right, so far. Our luck can hold out". On the 28th, we made an attack on Ploegsteert Wood and the Captain was killed when he burst into a clearing directly in front of a German machine gun.'

As the 10th Battalion left the trenches, the 11th Battalion went in and attempted to advance the line by peaceful penetration in the dark. Considerable opposition was

From a distance what looks like an ordinary tree. In close up, a German observation tower and/or snipers nest.

experienced and only two posts managed to move forward. The next night the battalion attempted a minor operation to gain identification but the numerous machine guns in the farm resulted in several casualties and no identification. During the same night A Company attempted to advance a number of its posts but met with too much opposition. The next night, while the 11th were preparing to leave the trenches (being relieved by the 18th DLI on the night of September 27th/28th), the 10th Battalion were coming in prior to the attack the next day.

While D and HQ Companies spent the night in an intricate system of tunnels in the chalk hillside near Hyde Park Corner the other three companies were waiting in the assembly positions previously reconnoitred by Captain Hall. The attack was initially scheduled for breakfast time but due to the rain storms in the morning the attack was postponed until 3pm. The Battalion War Diary recorded the attack:

'Battalion attacked under cover of a creeping barrage with a view to working along the NE edge of Ploegsteert Wood, thus protecting the right flank of the 11th East Lancashire Regt who were attacking on our left. They were then to turn to the right & work Southwards through the wood finally taking up a position outside the S.E.

edge. Owing however to the very effective barrage which the enemy put up as soon as ours opened & also the very heavy machine gun fire from the wood the two right companies of the battalion were unable to advance beyond the road running from Hyde Park Corner in a NE direction. The left Coy. were able to push forward, keeping in touch with the 11th East Lancs. Regt. thus affording cover for their right flank.

'In the first few minutes of the attack all three company commanders became casualties & the battalion lost heavily being reduced from 25 officers & 520 men to 14 officers & 384 men.

'Early in the evening D Coy under CAPT LE BLANQ were ordered up to reinforce & reorganise the battalion front. This was satisfactorily done, the line held running from U19b5.5 in touch with the 18th D.L.I. to U15c4.9 in touch with the 11th E. Lancs. at PROWSE POST.

'During the evening the enemy attempted a local counterattack against the left coy. but were driven off with loss'.

Even though the 11th Battalion were in support they also suffered some fatalities due to enemy shelling.

The general retirement of the German forces along the whole of the British front meant that the 10th Battalion had to move forward in order to keep in contact with them. Consequently on the morning of the 29th, the war diary recorded:

'Patrols were pushed forward along the battn. front & meeting with no opposition went through PLOEGSTEERT WOOD. The battalion following up reached a line running along Border Avenue where they met considerable fire from M.G. & snipers. The battalion was reorganised on this line holding it from U26c7.4 to U27c4.8'.

Enemy machine gun posts in the wood were extremely well concealed and those made of concrete were very well constructed. So well indeed, that they were not easily destroyed by British artillery, with disastrous results for many of the soldiers. The 10th Battalion war diary recorded:

German dead are given close attention by the photographer during the Allied advance.

'It was noticed in going through the wood that the majority of the enemy's m.g. posts, in some cases, pillboxes were absolutely untouched by our artillery fire, this no doubt accounts for the difficulty of assembling on the slopes N of HYDE PARK CORNER & the crossfire from which the battalion suffered as soon as it started to advance'.

Early the next morning B Company on the left flank were relieved by a company of the 18th DLI and moved to the right flank to relieve another company of the 18th DLI in readiness for a further advance. At 6.15am the battalion received orders to move forward to the Warnave River in conjunction with troops from the 40th Division on the right and the 18th DLI on the left. This further adjustment of the line met with very little opposition.

The next day the battalion was able to advance the line a little further. On October 1st Lieutenant-Colonel Rigg recorded in the war diary:

'In going round the line early in the morning it was noticed that whereas on the previous day M.G. & snipers fire had been heavy today there was little or none at all. Consequently at 12.0 noon a general advance was ordered & the line of the road from C7b5.1 to C4a4.7 was the objective. (The line of the road running parallel

Ripon 1918 – soldiers of the East Yorkshire Regiment, some with wound stripes. The soldier on the front row, second from the right is Corporal Maltby who had by that time recovered from his wounds (a bullet through the face). Note the soldiers wearing service chevrons on the bottom right sleeve. The soldier standing on the right has two wound stripes and is also wearing a mourning button.

with and on the south side of the Warnave River but half a mile beyond it). *The two right coys. reached this without trouble but the left coy. met considerable artillery and m.g. fire & were unable to advance beyond the GRID LINE running E and W between squares U27 & C3'.*

On the right, D Company went forward but the 18th DLI could not advance so they were forced to return to their starting point at Desperrier Farm; fortunately casualties were light. That night the battalion was relieved by the 11th East Yorks and marched off to Aldershot lines. Although this was a period when resistance was lessening and most of the advances were supposed to have been achieved using 'peaceful penetration' wherever it was possible, the month of September had been very costly, particularly over the period September 28th to October 1st. Going into the attack the battalion's strength had been 25 officers and 520 men. Coming out on the night of October 1st/2nd its strength was 12 officers and 394 other ranks. 36 other ranks were killed or died of their wounds and a further 88 were wounded. Officer casualties were Captain Dugdale (a very popular original member of the battalion who had entertained the troops with his violin playing), 2/Lieutenants Pygott, Dobson and Rendle also killed, Captains Dunn, Wright, Le Blancq and Pearce, Lieutenants Eycott and Yorke and 2/Lieutenants Heath and Copley wounded. 2/Lieutenant Banham was missing.

The battalion rested in Neuve Eglise (Aldershot lines) until October 6th when it moved to a canvas camp near Bailleul, moving again on the 8th to the remains of Bailleul asylum. Before returning to the same area it had left on October 1st, the battalion spent the time in training. On the 12th it took up positions along the River Lys. Crossing the river was the next hurdle.

On October 1st the 11th Battalion had taken over the line from the 10th East Yorks and the 18th DLI. The positions around Pont Rouge were difficult to deal with because they were very spread out and only held by small outposts. However, on the night of the 2nd/3rd and on the day of the 3rd the battalion was able to advance the whole battalion line to the River Lys using 'peaceful penetration'. That night they were relieved by the 11th East Lancs and moved off to Hill 63, where they took up positions for the day before being relieved that night. When the 13th York & Lancs arrived to relieve them they went into reserve. Here they spent time in cleaning up, reorganising and platoon training. On the 12th they returned to Hill 63 to relieve the 12th RSF.

Around midnight on October 14th a patrol from A Company crossed the river on a raft. They met with little opposition and captured two prisoners. According to Private Beeken, who was there, the two Germans did not need capturing:

'In October we moved to posts on the River Lys. One night an officer and a man crossed the river in a boat and found on the bank, two Germans with their hands up'.

One of the prisoners was of French extraction (from Alscace-Lorraine) and was able to provide much valuable information.

At 3am a platoon from the same company crossed the river to attack Uncut Trench which was found to be empty. It then established posts on the east bank. Under a barrage at 3pm the remainder of the company crossed the river and established further posts, this time along the defended Duelemont to Warneton road, where the enemy were driven back. At 5.30pm a further company crossed the river and moved east of Duelemont. With a new line firmly established, the 11th Battalion were able to pass through the 10th Battalion lines during the night to continue the advance, allowing the 10th Battalion to retire to the west bank. The next day the 11th Battalion continued to

Bosch (suddenly appearing over the top). "Kamerad, Kamerad!"
Briton. "Lor', my son, you did give me a tune. I thought you was an enemy."

advance with one company advancing through the other throughout the day. This process was continued until midday on October 17th, when the battalion line ran from north and east of Lincelles and south through Fort Debout.

A completely new phase of the war was being entered. The retirement had been so quick and had gone so far that the advancing troops began to meet civilians still living in the towns and villages that they were passing through. On the 17th the war diary recorded that:

> 'It was in and around La Vigne that the Battalion first found civilians – roughly 100 in number – the men received a great welcome as their deliverers from the German invader'.

The liberated villagers couldn't do enough for the troops. Billets for the first time in a long while were in farms and houses that were still occupied, rather than the usual deserted ruins.

Following behind the 11th Battalion were the 10th who came upon their first French inhabitants in a village near Tourcoing. Private Beeken recorded the experience in his diary:

> 'The Coy crossed on the following day on a raft or bridge made by the REs of sump boards and empty petrol tins lashed together. It was very tricky crossing but we did it without any accident. The advance continued towards Tourcoing. We entered one

village. There was dead silence – no sign of any life. We marched on. Suddenly we heard a cry "Les anglais". Doors opened and people rushed out to us. Oh dear! They couldn't do enough for us.'

While the enemy infantry and artillery were retiring, the German engineers were leaving behind a trail of destruction. The 11th Battalion history recorded not only the welcome it received in Tourcoing but the damage done before they arrived:

'The day following the battalion marched through Tourcoing, the first fairly large town that we had passed through in our advance. Everywhere were signs of the measures the enemy had taken to cover his retirement and hinder our advance. The railway had been blown up at intervals of about 100 yards, and the gasworks had been destroyed. Tourcoing was in pageant, flags were flying everywhere, and the streets were lined with the townspeople, whose delight at their deliverance knew no bounds. Their joy took at times most embarrassing forms, and the C.O., after evading successfully several attempts to embrace him by enthusiastic female admirers, finally had to post a signaller on either side of him as a flank guard, to the great amusement of the leading files. Bottles of Vin Blanc, cakes and ribbons were forced upon all and sundry, war began to assume a more pleasing aspect, and morale ran very high'.

	Killed			Wounded			Missing		
92 Brigade casualty returns for August, September and October 1918									
Month	8/18	9/18	10/18	8/18	9/18	10/18	8/18	9/18	10/18
10th EYR	11	78	6	62	261	25	20	67	0
11th EYR	18	45	1	71	208	9	2	42	0
11th ELR	11	45	5	93	264	67	3	29	0
92 TMB	0	0	0	5	6	0	0	1	0
Bde HQ	0	0	1	0	1	1	0	0	0

While the 11th rested for the day, the 10th Battalion took up the advance in company columns covered by screens of Cyclist Corps troops, a maneouvre last carried out sometime in 1915. The advance was halted along the Roncq to Bondues road (the main Lille to Menin road) and in the morning the 11th East Lancs passed through the battalion to continue the advance in the direction of Tourcoing. The 10th Battalion then moved off to Wattrelos, a suburb of Roubaix, for a week long rest in the arms of villagers who had been living under German occupation since the start of the war. What happened to the men is described in the 10th Battalion history:

'The frenzied throngs of people in the beflagged streets almost exactly fulfilled our 1914 dreams of how King Edward Street would look when we came home again. Ordered marching was impossible, women pressed flags and flowers upon us and when we were free to fraternise we found every house open to us. Food and drink of every kind were pressed upon men who, even when they realised what sacrifices were involved, found it very difficult to recompense their delighted hosts; and to crown it all, we slept in their best feather beds!

'Indeed they could not do enough for us to show their delight and gratitude at their deliverance from the Germans, who had occupied Wattrelos since the begining of the war. The band came into its own again here and gave nightly performances, much to the enjoyment of the inhabitants'.

When the 10th Battalion went out of the line on the 18th the 11th Battalion moved forward through Fort Debout, Croix Blanche, Ferme de Forest, Beau Sejour and Tourcoing to Martinore. Everywhere they went they were met by an excited population. The reception is described in the war diary:

'The inhabitants showed the greatest enthusiasm along the whole route, which through Tourcoing itself was lined by cheering civilians. In places the crowds were so large that it was only with great difficulty that the ranks were not broken. Flags, garlands, favours were everywhere – the whole town joined in general rejoicing to welcome the first unit to march through as a battalion'.

Private Billy Gafton, originally served with B Company of the 13th Battalion before being transferred to the 11th Battalio in 1918.

That night they were billeted with the inhabitants who did everything they could possibly do for the comfort of all the troops.

After a restful night the battalion continued its advance at 5.30am on October 19th. During the day it kept in constant touch with the retreating Germans, inflicting many casualties on them. On the 20th the 11th Battalion continued to advance until it was cut out by the advance of the 14th Division on the left and the Canal de Roubaix on the right. As there was now no room for the battalion it was withdrawn to Wattrelos for a rest, clean up and for further training. Of this period, Wyrall quotes an unknown East Yorkshire Regiment officer:

'training broke out again in all its fury, shaving soap, khaki blanco, 'soldiers' friend', and such-like abominations were brought forward by the transport, and we became once again a smartly turned-out body of men'.

On the 27th the battalion was employed in salvage work.

"GADGETS."

As the war entered a very fluid stage new skills had to be learned or old ones relearned. This Punch cartoon shows what equipment and skill was needed the most.

It was back to work again for the 10th Battalion on the 25th when they marched north to Cuerne. On the 26th they went by lorry to Belgiek where they marched to Ooteghem to relieve a Scottish unit in the front line. The next day the whole area was heavily bombarded by the Germans, particularly the Ootegham to Kleinronsse road. Several of the men were gassed.

While they were leaving Cuerne, Private Beeken saw a most unusual occurence. After a night's rest they:

'*set off to go to the railway station. To our surprise we found a man taking the tiles from his neighbour's house and putting them on his own. We didn't see any other person in the village*'.

The line was advanced to Biest Farm on the 28th in conjunction with troops from the 11th East Lancashire and the 35th Division. During the night of the 29th the battalion advanced the line by establishing posts east of Ooteghem and south of Ingoyghem before being relieved by the 24th RWF and marching back to billets between Harlebeke and Deerlyck. The 10th Battalion history described two recent captures from this period:

'the cooks were particularly proud of their captured German field kitchen, with its gleaming copper boiler (which was eventually brought back to Hull when the "cadre" came home). Here also was an abandoned German field gun in good condition, just outside the headquarters farm. One of the day's diversions was to fire this gun – using mangold wurzels as ammunition!'

While the battalion were out of the line the Commanding Officer, Lieutenant-Colonel Rigg, left for a six month posting in England. Major Hewson assumed command. October 31st saw the whole brigade in support for an attack by 94 Brigade, the 34th Division and the French. The attack was a great success, achieving all its objectives and capturing 18 field guns and over 500 prisoners. Due to its success the reserve brigade was not needed. Staying in reserve, the battalions spent the morning collecting German war material. Part of this salvage was a large number of Belgian hares which the hurriedly retreating Germans had left behind. No time was lost in turning them into pies!

With the granting of an armistice to the Ottoman and Hapsburg Empires on November 1st the end of the war was getting very close. The Germans were retreating rapidly and resistance was crumbling.

Around this time Private Aust had a further lucky escape. The Germans were laying booby traps and one night one of them nearly claimed a large number of the 10th Battalion:

The war was drawing to a close and this is how the people in Hull read of the final moves for peace in The Hull Daily Mail.

'A few days before the armistice we entered a barn at the end of our day's advance to pass the night when someone noticed that the earth floor had been disturbed. We were ordered to sleep in the paddock. During the night the barn went up. More luck!'

3rd November saw the brigade marching to Halluin, where they were billeted for four days of training. On the 7th the brigade moved to the River Lys to practise crossing the river using collapsible boats (planks covered by tarpaulin). This was in preparation for the forthcoming attack across the River L'Escaut by the 31st Division. All blankets and heavy kit were dumped at Marcke on the 8th and the brigade marched to billets in Ooteghem. It was on this day that the 11th Battalion recorded the first big hints of an armistice:

'The next day as we were marching towards Courtrai we got our first news of the approaching Armistice, and the newsboys were quickly sold out.

'Keen discussion took place during the rest of the march regarding the truth of the information and the advisability of such a policy.'

In the afternoon, news of a German withdrawal was brought in by a French civilian who had swum the river. The 11th East Lancashires crossed the L'Escaut without experiencing any opposition and on 9th November the 11th Battalion was informed that the enemy had evacuated the west bank of the Scheldt. It was their turn to chase the Hun!

The battalion was informed, reads the entry in the war diary, that it:

'was to cross at 12 noon by means of the infantry bridge SE of Rugge, pass through 11 E Lancs & then act as advanced guard to the Division'.

Moving forward with the 11th Battalion were a battery of the RFA, a company of the MMGC (Motor Machine Gun Corps), a company of the 31st Battalion MGC and two platoons of the XIX Corps Cyclist Company. The river was crossed at 1.10pm with A and B Companies in front, each company having an 18 pounder field gun attached to it. In front of the infantry were the cyclists. A Company followed the road through Orroir – Croisong – Labroye – De Kleype – Renaix, with B Company running parallel through woods and over high ground. Following in the rear of A Company were C, D and HQ Companies. The war diary proudly recorded:

'Renaix entered at 6.45 and posts established on the Nukerke – Renaix Road. Definite touch with the enemy was obtained throughout the day and we were close on his heels. This day the Bn marched 23000 yards in full marching order carrying Lewis guns and magazines.'

At 5pm the 10th Battalion crossed the river and marched through Amougies to Reussignies to cheering crowds of liberated civilians. That night the padre, Captain

Braithwaite, suggested to his fellow officers, that the war was over. However, the next morning the war was still on, and the 10th Battalion, following close behind the 11th Battalion, marched through Renaix where one French civilian marched the whole length of the town backwards, playing the National Anthem on the violin! The town was congested with traffic trying to move eastwards and progress through the town was slow for the marching infantry. That the battalion was close to the enemy was evidenced by the stray shells and the sound of rifles and machine guns. At 5.30pm the battalion reached the Haisette area where it was to spend the night.

Out in front of them, the 11th Battalion had advanced along the Renaix to Brussels road. C Company was out in front, making initial contact with the enemy who provided a certain amount of opposition, particularly with machine guns. German deserters, who had been hidden in the cellars of the town of Renaix, gave themselves up to the 11th Battalion on the morning of the 10th. The day's advance finished near the Bois-Puvinage road. The war diary recorded an:

'advance of 12000 yards in a straight line. In front of Flobecq resistance stiffened and a number of casualties were incurred. Lieutenant Whittington-Ince was mortally wounded by machine gun fire and a number of men were wounded.'

November 11th

News of the armistice, with its 11am cease fire, reached the 10th Battalion at 2am on November 11th. The battalion history records that:

'Battalion Runners carried the news to the Companies at 6a.m., when such a heavy bombardment was in progress so very near at hand that most of our men turned over, for that last hour in bed, well nigh incredulous! Later, when the men began to stir and to discuss the momentous news, there was a surprising lack of enthusiasm. The war had continued so long that we had come to know army life pretty well – civilian life would mean taking a fresh plunge – besides breaking up what seemed lifelong friendships.'

Private Aust recalled the end of the war:

'The night before the armistice (of which we had no inkling) we were sleeping in a cowshed with the top half of the door open. In the early morning the sentry called in "Eh lads the war's over". The only response was from someone who crashed a heavy object against the closed half of the door and everyone slept again.'

Being further forward the news did not reach the 11th Battalion until 2.30am. The battalion was to stay were it was and the 11th East Lancs would advance through them in order to establish a line as far east as possible before 11am. By the time that

As 2nd Army advanced large numbers of prisoners and material fell into its hands. The photograph shows heavy guns captured in late 1918.

the cease fire started the East Lancs had advanced as far as the River Dendre. It is interesting to note that both battalions knew so early when the armistice itself was not signed until 5.05am that day. At 6.50am Advanced GHQ sent out the following message to all British Armies:

> 'Hostilities will cease at 11.00 hours to-day, November 11th. Troops will stand fast on the line reached at that hour, which will be reported by wire to Advanced G.H.Q. Defensive precautions will be maintained. There will be no intercourse of any description with the enemy until the receipt of instructions from G.H.Q. Further instructions will follow.'

This message was sent out and received by the five armies between 7.05 and 7.30 am. The Official History records that:

> 'The less than four hours' interval gave barely time for the information to reach the front-line troops, and hostilities, both on ground and in the air, were continued until the last moment.'

There was some shelling that morning but at 11am all went quiet. The battalion history records the final minutes of the war:

> 'then as 11a.m. approached, little groups gathered in that very drab village [Ellezelles] street, under a grey sky, standing almost breathless, watches in hand, until it was all over, and we had come through!'

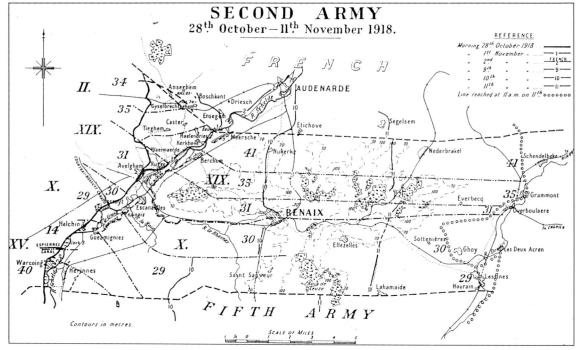

Map shows the the path of the British 2nd Army advance from October 28th to November 11th 1918.

This was good news for the 11th Battalion who had been scheduled to advance that day.

However, earlier in the morning it looked as if the battle would continue because Corps was unable to provide any concrete information about the armistice. Divisional HQ consulted Corps as to what to do. The divisional diarist cooly noted that:

'*Corps confirmed the advance*'.

This was to start at 9am but, fortunately for the 10th Battalion, at 08.45am information was received about the cessation of hostilities and orders were given for the division to set up a line of pickets as far east as possible before 11am. The divisional diarist recorded:

'*pickets eventually established without opposition. Cyclists pushed to the river bank & found it clear.*
'*The civilian population of Renaix and the neighbourhood received both the Division & the news of the armistice with the greatest enthusiasm*'.

At 11am the battalion paraded and at 11.30 marched to Everbecq to take over the line vacated by the Germans that morning; the march being led by HQ Company then B, D, C, A Companies followed by the band with the transport following up behind. A grey day turned into a wet day as the battalion marched past gaunt cheering cottagers. In the distance could be heard church bells. Arriving in Everbecq the battalion took over billets and settled down to peace. Private Aust was involved in this final march:

'The following morning we had seven miles to advance to our armistice position. This consisted of a village, the main street of which consistituted the armistice line. As we marched up this street to our position, at the junction of each side street on the German side stood a mounted Uhlan lancer in resplendent regalia.'

When the division stopped moving forward 'The Final Advance' was complete. XV Corps, of which the 31st Division had been a part during 'The Advance In Flanders', had fought its way forward across 50 miles of Flanders in 86 days.

The 10th Battalion history described the scene in Everbecq:

'It was a strange experience to take over billets which had been occupied by Germans in the morning, and even to see the villagers removing the fixed seats round the

Letter to the mother of Lieutenant Whittington-Ince informing her of his death. PRO

M.S.3.Cas./518A.   21st November, 1918.

          The Military Secretary presents his compliments to Mrs.Whittington-Ince, and begs to inform her that a report has just been received at the War Office which states that her son Lieutenant Ralph Piggott Whittington-Ince, M.C., East Yorkshire Regiment, attached 11th Battalion, died of wounds at No.36 Casualty Clearing Station, France, on November 11th.

          The Military Secretary is desired by the Secretary of State for War to express his deepest sympathy with Mrs. Whittington-Ince in the loss of her gallant son.

Mrs.Whittington-Ince,
   14, Princes Street,
     Bayswater.

estaminet walls to get out the bicycles which had been hidden there since the Germans had commandered all rubber, brass and copper. There were some French troops in Everbecq whose dancing in the estaminets to the music of the automatic pianos added to the gaiety of Armistice night, though our road had been so hilly and so badly in need of repair that we were all exceedingly weary.'

This quiet end to the war was the norm. The Official History records that:

'When 11 a.m. came the troops took the occasion in their usual matter of fact way: there was no outburst of cheering, no wild scene of rejoicing. Those who could lay down to sleep. The others went quietly about their duty with the strange feeling that all danger was absent.'

OUR MAN.

WITH MR. PUNCH'S GRATEFUL COMPLIMENTS TO FIELD-MARSHAL SIR DOUGLAS HAIG.

However, after dark:

'all gave way to rejoicing, searchlights wobbled in the sky, coloured lights of every description and S.O.S. signals illuminated the front lines, rockets went whizzing into the air, and field batteries fired their star shells. Some adventurous spirits lit bonfires, exploded small ammunition dumps and laid trails of guncotton and explosives which ran spluttering over the countryside like huge fiery serpents'.

Behind the lines the situation was different, the rejoicing began immediately. Private Beeken, who was in St Omer when the war ended, recorded the celebrations there:

'In St. Omer church bells rang, fireworks exploded and there was great excitement.'

Back home there was also much celebration. One wounded 10th Battalion soldier, Private Beeston, recovering in hospital in England, recalled that momentous day: '11/11/18 was the first time I tasted beer'.

The Great War for Civilisation had ended. All the troops had to do now was wait to go home.

Chapter 8

'Take me back to dear old Blighty'

N ovember the 12th was spent on cleaning up after the order 'There will be no move today' was received from 92 Brigade HQ. Life had suddenly become boring. The divisional diary recorded: 'Nothing to report', even though the division learned that it had been transferred to the Fifth Army and as a result would not be going to Germany as part of the Army of Occupation. As a consequence of this, it started to move west, retracing its footsteps of the recent past through Renaix, across the Schelde and back to Marcke, which was reached on the 16th. Here the brigade was rested for eight days.

When the division started to leave the area three things of interest are recorded in the Divisional War Diary. On the 13th:

'During the morning explosions heard across the river Dendre but cause unknown'.

This was heard by Private Aust:

'Two days after the armistice we were relieved and withdrew towards Ypres. After being on the march for a short time heavy artillery fire broke out just north of us

A street party in Hull to celebrate the end of the war.

where a French unit was situated. We feared the worst but after a few minutes the tumult died down and we continued our march to the rear.'

With the armistice, many Prisoners of War liberated themselves and set off to meet the advancing troops. The diary entry for the 14th mentions the PoWs and a mysterious convoy:

'A German motor car bearing the white flag and carrying three officers passed through Renaix this morning, but its destination is not known. Repatriated British prisoners continue to arrive in our area. They are badly short of food, badly clothed, and many are wearing sabots and are without socks.'

Life was changing. On 21st November censorship restrictions were lifted and the men were able to write home about whatever they wanted without anyone reading it.

The 22nd was spent practising for a Brigade Ceremonial parade the next day and playing a half-company football competition. On the morning of the 23rd the brigade was inspected by Major-General Campbell, the Divisional Commander, who handed out medal ribbons to those who had received awards for bravery since 7th June. The afternoon was passed with football matches and a cross country competition.

On 25th November the brigade moved further back, spending the night in Menin. The next day the battalion marched along the Menin road, which the 10th

The ruins of the famous Cloth Hall in 1918. The Hull battalions passed through this devastation on the way home.

1st December 1918 on the German border. British cavalry move into Germany as the occupying power.

Battalion history describes as ghostly, past Hell-Fire Corner to Ypres and on to Poperinghe and Terdeghem. On the 28th the brigade marched through Cassel to Le Nieppe and Ebblinghem, arriving on the 29th in St. Omer where it was billeted in and around the Caserne de la Barre, a French army cavalry barracks.

The beginning of December was spent in cleaning up, drill, physical training and Church Parades on Sunday. The 8th was spent in sporting activities with a mounted paperchase in the morning and football in the afternoon. In order to fit men for their return to civilian life, elementary education classes in motor mechanics and book-keeping were started on the 10th. The next day the demobilisation of the coalminers in the division began. Essential workers were to be demobilised first to boost falling output, particularly coal, now that winter had arrived.

In order to keep the men busy battalion work gangs were organised which helped to repair the roads around St. Omer or filling in disused trenches.

On December 17th French troops took over the Caserne and the British troops moved out of the barracks into Nissen huts. The camp used by the 11th Battalion became known as the 'Hull Camp' and consisted of Nissen huts which the battalion had to assemble themselves. The 11th Battalion history recorded:

> *'For a fortnight we struggled with that particular form of jig-saw puzzle known as a Nissen hut, but at last the camp was completed and occupied.'*

In St. Martin-au-Laert, where most of the 10th Battalion were billeted, the local dance hall was converted into a school in which education classes ran most mornings.

With no trench duty or other matters to occupy them the battalions were able to celebrate Christmas properly for the first time since the start of the war. On the 24th, at a Brigade Ceremonial Parade held in the Grand Place in St. Omer,

Christmas 1918. The last 31st Division card of the war.

Brigadier-General Williams presented the French Croix de Guerre to members of the brigade. The recipients in the 10th Battalion were: Lieutenant Colonel Hewson, L/Corporals Singleton and Robinson; 11th Battalion: Lieutenant Jenkin, Sergeants Hall and Deary.

Christmas Day started with a parade and service in the Munro Institute. After that the time was available for celebrating Christmas. The 10th Battalion held its dinner in the local gymnasium and it was an occasion to be remembered as the battalion history recounted:

> *'Turkeys, and plenty of them, with vegetables; also Christmas pudding flavoured with rum sauce, which was the genuine article. The canteen funds provided four barrels of beer, all of which was served to the men by the W.O.s and sergeants on real plates and in good mugs – the nearest approach to home life for three years.'*

A large canteen hut and a store hut were lent to the 11th Battalion by the 93rd Field Ambulance to form a large dining hall which when it was suitably decorated provided an excellent venue for their Christmas dinner. The 11th Battalion War Diary recorded that the: 'day was thoroughly enjoyed by all'.

The topic on everyone's lips was demobilisation, as the 11th Battalion history records:

> *'As Christmas approached we began to be occupied with filling in various forms that came under the heading Army Form Z, and discussing demobilization'.*

Boxing day activities included a short route march. The rest of the month was spent on working parties, education classes and in the afternoon of the 30th, riding classes.

Demobilisation slowly gathered speed, with officers and men from pivotal industries being sent home every day. Men going home on leave were also released if they had a promise of a job when they got home. But demobilisation was not proceeding fast enough for some. The 11th Battalion history noted that,

The cavalry barracks in St. Omer where the Hull Battalions were first billeted.

'*As time wore on demobilization became more and more the chief topic of discussion, and there was a good deal of grousing over the inevitable delays. Long and earnest post-mortems were held on every successful application for early release, but everyone's turn came in the end, and our numbers decreased steadily.*'

In January the battalions spent time working on trenches, shooting at the camp range, going to Church Parades and to education classes or working on the roads. There was to be little variation from this routine over the coming months for those not lucky enough to be in the priority de-mob groups. The only highlight of the period, from Christmas until the battalions were welcomed home in May, happened on 29th January.

In the early hours of the 29th the various battalions received orders to proceed to Calais where trouble was expected from returned leave men and workers at the arsenal where there was unrest about the slowness of demobilisation. The 10th Battalion entrained for Calais at 7am with the 11th Battalion leaving an hour later. The battalions detrained in the early hours of the 30th and spent the night under canvas, even though there was snow on the ground, at Number Three Camp, Beaumaris. The whole of the 31st and 35th Divisions were assembled ready to deal with possible riots. On the 30th, 105 Brigade picketed Calais to prevent the disorder spreading beyond the docks and storehouses which elements of the Royal Army Ordnance Corps had seized. The 10th Battalion history recorded that:

'*Next day, at 11a.m., we paraded in fighting order and moved off to take up a position in support to the 35th Division, but General Sir W. R. Birdwood, G.C.M.G., met the men's representatives, and by 1 p.m. we were back in camp.*'

With the return to work by the RAOC there was no need for the troops to remain so at around 6pm the two battalions returned to St. Omer.

During February demobilisation continued apace with the first eight days of February seeing 18 officers and 893 men demobilised from the brigade. Due to the reduction in the number of men it became necessary in the 11th Battalion to join

Loading transport for England.

A and D Companies to form a new A Company. On the 4th the brigade was visited by the Corps Commander in order for him to inspect billets and education classes. While the 11th Battalion worked on the disused trenches southwest of St. Omer, the 10th Battalion had their King's Colour consecrated by the battalion padre, Captain Tyndall (Chaplain to the Forces). This was followed the next day by the 11th Battalion presentation on the Union Sportive ground on the Rue de Longueville. In each case the Colour was presented by the Brigadier.

By the 7th it was necessary to amalgamate B and C Companies of 11th Battalion. Demobilisation hit the 10th quicker than the 11th Battalion; by the 14th they found it necessary to amalgamate all four company remnants into one full company.

As well as officers and men being demobbed, those who remained started to be transferred to other units during the closing days of February. On 25th February, 58 other ranks were temporarily transferred to the Labour Commandant at Steenvorde. As well as men leaving the battalion there were also new men coming in. The 11th Battalion War Diary recorded:

> *'During the month demobilisation proceeded apace, leaving the total strength of the battalion – men actually with the unit – approximately 12 officers and 200 o/r. Towards the end of February more recruits from the Post Bellum army were forthcoming. Our total now being about 40.'*

These were soldiers who had finished training and now at the age of 19 were sent abroad to replace time-served troops.

With Battalions now down to such sizes it was not viable for them to run their own education classes and this function was taken over by the brigade. On the 17th a Brigade Central School was opened. However, by 26th March there were so few men left in the brigade that this had to be closed down. The following day the brigade lost the 11th East Lancs to the 61st Division.

On 3rd March the 10th Battalion had sent one officer and 42 men to the 9th Northumberland Fusiliers stationed at Dieppe, while the 11th Battalion sent three officers and 111 men. Between 4th March and 27th March the battalion consisted of the cadre (essential men around which to reform the battalion in case of an emergency), and a few releasable (time-served soldiers awaiting demob) men actually at the camp in St. Omer, with a further 200 or so men of the battalion, all of whom were non-releasable (men staying on in the army and new arrivals), who were employed away from the camp on a permanent basis, on various duties from Conderque (near Dunkerque), to Ypres, Poperinghe, Bailleul, Busseboom, Cassel, Waton, Guderwaersuelde, Hazebrouck and Merris.

The Battalion War Diary noted that:

'During the following days demobilisation proceeded apace until by the 27th all available men had been demobbed About the 25th detached men ordered to rejoin the unit.'

Amongst those being discharged in March was Private Aust, who had served from the beginning of the war. He was discharged with a 20 per cent disability pension of 8/- (40p).

Later in the month, on the 28th, the 11th Battalion sent a further 25 other ranks and an officer to the 9th NF, while the next day it sent three officers and 80 men to the 242 PoW Company at Flumbaix. On the same day the diary recorded: 'all remaining non-releasable men detached from unit were transferred to 9NF'.

By the beginning of April both battalions had been reduced to cadre strength or as the 11th Battalion War Diary put it:

'During the month all remaining releasable non-cadre men were demobilised and all non-releasables remaining on the strength of the unit on 1-4-19 were transferred to 9th Bn NF at Dieppe. Thus by the end of the month the BN consisted of 'cadre' alone of

Where most of the soldiers wished they were.

WE'RE JUST WAITING TO HEAR THE SCRAPING OF YOUR FEET UPON THE MAT.

The cadres of the 10th and 11th Battalions near Paragon Station on May 26th 1919.

strength 5 officers and 40 other ranks in all, more or less patiently awaiting the order to move to England.'

As the brigade had ceased to exist there was no need for it to have a Brigadier-General in office. Consequently at the end of the month Brigadier-General Williams CMG, DSO (2nd RWF) relinquished his command and proceeded to the Rhine to take up command of the 52nd Battalion South Wales Borderers.

There are no further entries for the 11th Battalion. The 10th Battalion War Diary for April mentions fatigues and Church Parade and more fatigues. It was not until May that the order came for the cadre to return to England. On 22nd May the 10th Battalion landed in Southampton and set off by train to Hillsborough Barracks in Sheffield where they arrived at 10pm that day. They waited there over the weekend and at 8am on Monday 26th May the remainder of the battalion were demobilised. When the process had been completed the cadre left Sheffield on an official journey to Hull with the battalion colours. The 11th Battalion cadre left France on the 22nd, arriving at Catterick on the 23rd. Since these cadres and also that of the 146th Heavy Battery, RGA (3rd Hull Heavy Battery) would be demobilised at roughly the same time, it was decided to have a joint reception for all three units.

In anticipation of the arrival of the three cadres, the *Hull Daily Mail* issued a souvenir postcard which detailed the route and the proceedings. It asked all citizens to display flags and bunting and told its readers to: 'listen for the buzzers and turn out to give the Hull lads a rousing welcome'.

The cadre of the 10th Battalion was led by Lieutenant-Colonel Hewson with Captain W Hall, and Lt/QM Moore and 37 men, with the Battalion Colour being carried by 2/Lieutenant W Leech escorted by Sergeant 'Bob' Lee and Sergeant Simpson. Following behind was the German cooker the battalion had been using since October 1918. The 11th Battalion party was led by Lieutenant Colonel Ferrand with Captain T Hall, Captain/QM W Miller with 32 NCOs and men. The Battalion Colour was carried by 2/Lieutenant R Buffey.

The cadres were met at Paragon Station by a host of dignitaries which included the Lord Mayor of Hull (Councillor Peter Gaskell), along with the Lord Lieutenant of the East Riding (Lord Nunburnholme) Major-General Sir Stanley von Donop, Brigadier Williams, Colonel Pease, and Lieutenant-Colonel Savory. When the cadres had all detrained, they marched out into the square outside the station, where a large number of discharged and demobilised men from the four battalions were waiting, in a military manner, under the control of Major Carver. Also present were representatives from the Discharged and Demobilised Soldiers and Sailors Federation and the Comrades of the Great War. The cadres were inspected by Lord Nunburnholme who then welcomed and thanked them and reviewed their achievements. Major-General von Donop, Officer Commanding the Humber Garrison, added a few words of welcome, addressed particularly to the artillerymen.

After the welcome the officers and men of the three cadres and all those

The cadre marching through Hull.

Although promised a land fit for heroes, many soldiers upon demobilization were reduced to selling cards such as this.

Certificate of Demobilisation issued to William Calvert 20th March 1919.

assembled on the square marched along Jameson Street, King Edward Street and through Alfred Gelder Street to the Guildhall to the tunes 'The Yorkshire Lass' and 'Home, Sweet Home' played by the Police and other bands. After taking the salute, the Lord Mayor, standing on the Guildhall balcony, addressed the parade, which was now gathered in Lowgate. He invited them to refreshments in the Guildhall Banqueting Chamber before their dispersal. Later, the officers were given lunch. The whole town celebrated and school children and shipyard workers were given the afternoon off to welcome the soldiers back.

Eventually the cadres dispersed and the 'Hull Pals' were officially demobilised. At this time only one officer was still serving in the 10th Battalion who had joined the battalion in September 1914. The other four officers still serving had all been in the ranks at the time. There were about 120 original other ranks still serving with the Battalion.

The words used by the Lord Mayor when he addressed the cadres on 26th May 1919 were as apposite to the conclusion of the 10th Battalion history written 60 years ago as they are to this history of the four battalions of the 'Hull Brigade':

'You have fought a fight, you have gained a victory, you have won a peace.'

Appendices

Appendix 1

Officers serving with the Hull Pals
(Rank on joining battalion)

10th Battalion

Lieutenant-Colonel
D Burges
W B Pearson
A J Richardson
E H Rigg

Major
D D Anderson
W H Carver
T A Headlam
C P B Riall
C C Stapledon
D Wilson

Captain
J E M Carroll
W Glossup
W H Hall
J R Hosking
L C Huchinson
J C Lamprey
S C Le Blancq
G E Lloyd-Jones
J W A Park
T Ridsell-Smith
W L Ruthven
R Smith
E F Twiss
C C Wallace MM

Lieutenant
?? Akester
C H Baber
W Bromby
H G Eycott
J J T Ferens
E B Goatsworth
W H Hall
J Harrison-Broadley
R Holden
W P Horsley
I Jackson
S E Jones
J Kendall
E J Krog
G F Lambert

J H Lawes
D Palmer
A Plimpton
J Sever
J C Sherburn
O Slater
M Spencer
W E Upton
J A Wright
J L Yorke

Second-Lieutenant
J C Addy
R Addy
T E Anderson
W H Anderton
E J Andrew
E Banham
R W Bennetts
E Best MM
J F Blyth
W Bradbury
C Brooks
E J Butler
L M Butt
W S Butter
W Buttery
R Carlisle
R B Carver
C W Chamberlain
H Cheesbrough
C W Clark
S G W Clark
W S Clark
G Q Comper
F Copley
R C Cowl
G Cowpe
O M Davis
F R Dobson
D Dugdale
C Earle
W A Eastwood
J Ellis
G W S England
F M Field
R A Flintoff

M W Flower
W Frankish
R Frayne
A G Fricker
J Gleave
K M Gordon
C L Hadrill
F Hall
N S Harrison
F Heath
R N Heathcote
T C Herring
R C Hewson
R Hey
T R Holden
HJ P Hopkinson
A W Houghton
W Humphries
L G Hutchinson
W S Hutton
H Jackson
A G Jones
H Jones
H H Jones
A Johnston
D T Lange
N B Leech
D W Lindley
G Lockwood
E Lovell
J B Lister
B W Mapstone
A F Marshall
J W Marshall
A H Mayo
E M McDermott
H G P McIlroy
W M Meredith
W Mitchell
F C Moorhouse
R J Myhill
W E W Naylor
A W Neville
J P Norfolk
J A Oliver
J P Owens
C R Oxtoby

D W O Palmer
E M Pearce DCM
C L Penn
J D Petty
L D Pierson
B W Pickering
C H Piper
J G Power
C W Pretty
F Pyggott
H Rayner
N W Reed
G Rendle
G F Renwick
A V Rhodes
B N Rice
C C Richards
J A St. C Richardson
W L Robinson
F Rose
E H Russell
W Rutherford
H K Sanger
T R Scott
H Senior
J S Shaw
T J Shelton
A V Silvester
T R Slack
H H Smith
M Southern
C C Spink
H Stewart
R Stewart
D Stringer
H Stubbs
W C Taylor
C Tennison
C B Traill
G G Traviss
E C Vickers
E A Wadsworth
C C Wallace
R N Watkins
D Watson
G C Webster
J H Wellington

E C Williams
F Willis, DCM
A Wilson
G H Wilson
P E Wilson
R Winter
B Wood
G A Wright
B A Y Wynne-Yorke
R Wynter
?? Young

11th Battalion
Lieutenant-Colonel
S H Ferrand
B St. C Ford
C H Gurney
F Hardman
J L Stanley

Major
D D Anderson
F Fitzwilliam-Hardman
J C R King
C W Waite
F H G Wallis

Captain
H C Bilton
A Butterfield
E Cargill
R Dibb
H A C Fitzpatrick
J A Foster
A B Hall
R A Holland
E Morison
H R Pease
K Philip
A A Plimpton
C P B Riall
E B Robinson
A Schottlander
J Shaw
J S Shaw
H Smith
S S Smith
J B O Trimble
T H C G Truman
W H Wilberforce
H F Williams
S Williams

Lieutenant
C A Arnett

C D'A Caldecott
R D Caley
L A Cattley
W H Chapman
F W Cowley
H F Dann
W Duncan
R A Fraser
C Gough
A B Hall
M Hartley
E F Helmsing
W B Holiday
R A Holland
M Hurdley
R James
T B Lynch
J B McReynolds
W J Miller
K Philip
E W Reeve
C A Saville
R F Simnett
C C Smith
H S Staveley
D S Tomey
F Walker
F H G Wallis
H F Williams
D Wilson

Second-Lieutenant
E Affleck
E J Andrew
D Barber
B A S Bennett
H Berry
K W Best
G W Bladen
W L Bland
B Bocking
G Bradley
G W Burch
T Burton
J D Caley
E Cargill
D A Carpenter
C H Chapman
W H Chapman
W S Clark
T H Clarke
M H Clift
E Collinson
C A Cooper
J H Copeland

H W Cowling
J T Craddock
L S Cullen
F Davie
R W J Davis
J T R Dawson
B Dimond
W E Dobson
V Dreschfield
E A Dutton
W R Ekins
K S Evers
J Forester
E R Forward
A W Foster
E V Galloway
A V Gentry
C Greenhalgh
G F Hall
W H Hall
A Harris
J Harrison V C
R Harrison
W R Hignett
J Hirst
W J Hopkins
S Howarth
H Howdle
B Hutchinson
W Jackson
V H Jenkin
W Joy
E L Kidd
G W Koplik
A S Larter
J H Lawes
D H Layton
F Lingard
R Lloyd
W V Longthorp
R W McIntyre
B Mitchell
H Mitchell
F B Moody
H Muir
F G Nicholls
C J Oake
D Oake
A H Oliver
H Oughtred
F J Pickering
R F Pitz
W A G Purll
S T Read
F A Richardson

W Richardson
W A Roscow
J E Rudd
J A Rumsey
C A Saville
J G Scotcher
H J Sevain
J Sever
W P Skevington
N L Sissons
H Smith
T W Southern
H S Staveley
G M Stevenson
G Suthrien
H J Swain
A J Thackray
C R Thomas
G G Traviss
R Walshaw
R Whittington-Ince
A Wigginton
E L Williams
F W Willmott
J J Wilson
E W Wolfe-Keane
R Woolcott
E Wright
H I Wright

12th Battalion
Lieutenant-Colonel
C H Gurney
H R Pease

Major
C G Wellesley
Captain
D D Anderson
C W Cattley
L C Hutchinson
D W Moore
J W Springhall
C R H Tatton
C C H Twiss
S Walker
W Worthington
C H W Wright

Lieutenant
C A Arnett
E Barclay
J H Bramwell
W K Burwell
H E Claxton

285

L S Cullen
W H Dyson
A D Elford
H A C Fitzpatrick
H O Habersohn
W H Hall
W P Heaney
S H Hills
J Hirst
S Le Blancq
McCoy-Hill
W J Miller
A R Preddle
M Spencer
H Walker
D Watson
C H W Wright
A J Webb
G P Wilkinson
E R Williams
L O Williamson
G H Wilson

Second-Lieutenant
C Abbey
C H Baber
R G Backrath
R H Beckh
E Best MM
A C Box
A L Bulmer
F W Burch
A E Burleigh
G S Burton
W F A Buxton
J G Campbell
J E Carrall
W Carroll
N Constant
C A Cooke
E P Cooper
F W Cowley
R A Coxon
S M Crabtree
L S Cullen
H F Dann
F C Day
B Dimond
C Drewett
A R Duguid
H F Dunne
M W Dunne
L M D G Du Pré
A T Edwards
A D Elford

J Evans MM
E W Estridge
F L Faker
G St. C Feilden
C Fenwick
C Fitzpatrick
E R Forward
A Foster
O L Frizoni
A R Glaves
C Gough
C Greenhalgh
R Greenhalgh
E Groves
F Hall
J S Hall
B H Harper
W P Heaney
R N Heathcote
W R Hignett
B O Hildyard
S H Hills
J Hirst
L A Hirst
S D Holbrook
A Hoult
W R A Hudson
L C Hutchinson
H C Jenning
C H Jones
N J Kerr
P J Lambert
S Le Blancq
L R A Le Bouvier
W G Legg
N V Lewis
T C Lightowler
E C Livsey
G E Lloyd-Jones
J Local
H N Marriott
R G Marsh
J McCoy-Hill
W J Miller
B J Millward
G W Mitchell
C G C Montcrieff
P Moore
R G Morgan
E Morison
S Oakes
A V Officer
T S Pattison
B L Pearson
F J Pickering

R F Pitz
H W F Reid
J L Robertson
L L Rosenberg
S Robson
J Sever
O Slater
K B Spink
C E Stovin
F E Sutton
E H Tatton
R N Taylor
B D Todd
B W Todd
D S Tomey
G W Walker
S S Walker
E R Williams
A Wilson
G H Wilson
W Worthington
C Wrigglesworth
E W Wright
J Yates

13th Battalion
Lieutenant-Colonel
R H Dewing
J L Stanley
C C H Twiss

Major
B G Baker
A K M C W Savory

Captain
J C R King
H S Laverack
P G Stockley
G E Turner
E F Twiss
G H Welsford
R M Wooley

Lieutenant
G S Borton
G E Jenkins
E Kallend
E W Latham
E Maxwell-Stuart
A J Stather
T H F G Truman
J T Underhill
C W Waite
G W Walker
H Walker

Second-Lieutenant
O R W Agerskow
R M Alexander
P T Allen
E J Andrew
F C R Beechey
H Bell
R W Bennetts
C M Billington
A H Binning
G H Bradshaw
E G Brindley
C Brooke
A W Brooks
E C Brown
F B Brown
G H Brown
J W Brown
H C Burbidge
W K Burwell
E Buttle
J W Casson
L Challis
H Collins
E Cheveston-Brown
O Coope
C A Cooper
J T Craddock
E J Curtis
N H Davey
A R Dixon
A G Dorman
J G T Eccles
F A Ellis
W E Farmer
S Fearnley
A R Fenton
A Foster
H L Gardner
C Glover
G Grant
R Greenhalgh
W G Hamm
C E R Harris
W G Harrison
T C Herring
J R Hocking
W R Holdsworth
J C Horn
S W Howard
J R Hoyle
H S Hughes
R M Hughes
P G H Hunt
T M Hutchinson

G E Jenkins	S L Mainprize	J Ramsden	G H Storry
J E Johnson	A M W Mason	R E C Ranson	T D Taylor
C G Johnston-Stuart	H G C Mead	W F R Reynolds	L Thorns
E Kallend	J F Mogan	W H Roper	W H Walker
C C King	W O Montgomery	E O Rutherford	J Ward
N J Kerr	D Morley	L A Rutterford	R S Watt
P J Lambert	J P Owens	J A Sampson	C G Watts
F W Lawe	G W A Park	R J Sand	R V Wheatley
N V Lewis	T C Parker	A T Sawdon	H Whelpton
F Lingard	T D Parkes	G W Silk	A H Wild
W Linsley	T S Pattison	G W Smith	B J Wilkins
G E Lloyd-Jones	T W Pearson	H Stewart	A T Woodcock
W Mabane	A Peters	R Stewart	J Wood
G C G Macauley	D R Puddicombe	H Storch	

Appendix 2

Nominal Rolls of the
10th, 11th, 12th and 13th Battalions

10th Battalion Nominal Roll

3	Pte. George Guest (Z)
6	Pte. Robert Edward Gordon Lucas (Z)
7	Pte. G E Ledraw MM (Z)
11	Pte. Cyril Fletcher Waterhouse (Dis)
13	Pte. Robert Tall (Z)
14	Cpl. Thomas Ernest Saunderson DCM (Z)
15	Pte. Harry Stout (Z)
16	Pte. E Keene
17	L/Cpl. A W Taylor
18	Pte. E Russell
20	Pte. W Horsfall
21	Pte. Albert Edwin Holding (Dis)
23	Pte. William James Hall (Z)
25	Pte. H Gale
29	Pte. Arthur Crane (Z)
31	Pte. J Comins
34	Pte. Rowland Bryant *
35	Pte. P Bourner
36	Pte. Frederick Barraclough (Dis)
37	Sgt. Seymour Custon Watson (Z)
38	Pte. Henry Morris Wacholder (Z)
39	Pte. J S Watson
40	Pte. T Adams
41	Pte. Frederick William Wardill *
43	Sgt. W E Harrison
44	Pte. Charles Walter Tune*

45	Sgt. A Tindale
47	CSM Clifford Street DCM (Z)
48	Pte. Harold Sneetson Richardson (Dis)
49	Pte. Laurence Read (Z)
51	Pte. Sydney James Pybus (Z)
52	Pte. C Riley
53	Pte. Claude Leslie Penn*
54	Pte. Cecil Wright Mason (Dis)
56	Pte. W R Raney
58	Pte. John Good*
59	Pte. Richard Cowl*
63	Pte. Horace Stanley Johnson (Z)
64	Pte. Alfred Armistead Kennedy*
65	Pte. R Linsley
66	Pte. Frederick Cecil Watson Niven (Z)
67	Pte. P Russell
68	Pte. Walter Sheppard (Dis)
70	Pte. Harry Watson*
73	Pte. G Blenkin
74	Pte. John Bailey (Z)
75	Pte. George W Butler (Z)
76	Pte. Charles Reginald Finding (Dis)
77	Pte. W Lazenby
78	Sgt. F E Newbert
79	Pte. S Marr
80	Pte. James Smith (Z)
81	Pte. James Arthur Faihurst (Z)

82	Pte. Ernest Earnshaw Jackson (Z)
84	Pte. A E Wilson (Z)
85	Pte. George Edward Bell (Z)
88	CQMS Thomas Davison (Medaille d' Honneur) (Z)
89	Pte. H Storr
91	Pte. Edmund John Britnell (Z)
92	Sgt. E W Dawson
93	Pte. Lawrence Dalgleish (Z)
94	Pte. Robert Dewson (Z)
95	Cpl. A Turner
97	Pte. David Boddy (Z)
98	Pte. Sidney Birkbeck (Z)
99	Cpl. E C Dunn
100	Pte. A Barker
102	Cpl. F Baker MM (Z)
103	Pte. F Walton
104	Pte. Robert Wright (Z)
105	Pte. Stanley Wright (Z)
107	Pte. Thomas Norwood Prince (Z)
108	Pte. Herbert Riches (Dis)
109	Pte. Arthur Sugden (Z)
111	Pte. William Percy Skevington*
113	Pte. Donald McLachlan (Z)
114	Pte. F Stone
115	Cpl. Edwin Arthur Nunns MM (Dis)
118	Pte. H Kirman
120	Pte. G Lacey
121	Pte. Harold Reed Lidgley (Z)
123	Pte. J B Atkinson
127	Pte. George Thomas Lotherington*
128	Pte. O Leighton
131	Pte. Llewelyn O Owens (Z)
132	Pte. George Leslie Naylor (Z)
135	Cpl. Ralph Terry MM (Z)
136	Pte. P Lockey
137	Pte. Charles Randolph Stevenson (Dis)
138	Pte. Terence Stringer MM (Z)
139	Pte. Harry Smith (Z)
140	Pte. Harry Reveler MID (Z)
141	Pte. Harry Smith*
142	Pte. John William Shaw*
143	Sgt. Leonard Martin Wrigglesworth MID (Z)
145	Pte. Maurice Watson (Z)
146	Pte. Frederick C Wilson*
147	Pte. Charles Woodcock (Z)~
148	Pte. G W West
150	Pte. George W Taylor (Z)
151	Pte. William Taylor*
152	CSM Dudley Stringer*
154	Pte. James Louis Stephenson (Z)
155	Pte. Frederick John Smith (Dis)
156	Pte. Alfred Smith*
157	Pte. George Frederick Stephenson*
159	Cpl. Edgar Mooton MID (Z)
160	Pte. E. Keene

161	Pte. Philip Sydney Kendall (Z)
162	Pte. Clarence George Kay (Z)
165	Pte. George Augustus Hughes*
166	Pte. J Hodgson
167	Sgt. Charles S Henson (Z)
168	Pte. Charles H Horberry (Dis)
169	Pte. Ellis Hobson (Z)
170	Pte. Wilson Holmes (Z)
171	Pte. George Albert Haines (Dis)
175	Pte. Arthur Godfrey (Z)
176	Pte. Harry Godfrey (Z)
177	Pte. Ernest Belton Gooch (Z)
179	C/Sgt. Herbert Edwin Gibson*
180	Pte. J Galt
181	Pte. William Harold Footit (Z)
183	Pte. Jesse Fenton (Dis)
184	Pte. Richard Emslie (Z)
185	Pte. Harold Dixey (Z)
186	Sgt. John Douglas Cowl*
188	Cpl. Charles Clarke* MM
190	Pte. Carl Edgar Chatterton*
194	Pte. George F Brittain (Z)
197	Pte. Frank Atkinson (Z)
198	Pte. William Norman Langley Barr (Z)
200	Pte. Frederick Charles Robins (Z)
205	Sgt. J N Stather MM
206	Pte. Kenneth Bertram Spink*
208	Pte. Kenneth George Shackles*
209	Sgt. Edgar Thrale*
210	Pte. George Walter Waddington^^*
214	Pte. Alfred Carr Warne*
216	L/Cpl Walsh (Z)
218	Pte. Norman Walker (Z)
221	Pte. Alfred James Pratt (Z)
222	Pte. Harry Oughton (Z)
224	Pte. Percy Naylor Murray (Z)
225	Pte. M W Moran
226	Pte. Vincent West Maw (Dis)
229	Pte. Richard Loynes (Dis)
230	Pte. Arthur Allison Lamb (Z)
232	Pte. R L Kidd
233	Pte. Austin Hutchinson*
235	Pte. Leonard Maxwell Holmes*
238	Pte. Cyril Kenneth Hindson*
239	Pte. Harold Kennington Havercroft (Dis)
240	Pte. Lewis William Gregory*
243	Sgt. John Ellis MM (Dis)
246	Cpl. John Dixon* MM
247	Pte. Harry Dixon*
248	Pte. Harry Day (Z)
251	Cpl. C Collinson DCM (Z)
253	Pte. Frederick D Brown*
256	L/Cpl. Charles W Backwell*
259	Pte. Frank Hope (Z)
260	Pte. Harry Hodgson (Z)

261	Pte. B Ireland
262	Pte. Victor Ingamells (Z)
263	Pte. Leslie William Green*
264	Pte. Sydney Gray (Z)
266	Pte. Alfred Moss
267	Pte. J H Monday
268	Sgt. G W May (Z)
269	Pte. Frederick McManus (Z)
272	Pte. H F West (Z)
273	Pte. G Watt (Z)
274	Pte. Eric Samuel Willis*
276	Pte. A Yates (Z)
277	Pte. W Ascough
278	Pte. William Anderson*
279	Pte. S Arnott (Z)
280	Cpl. George Herbert Burton*
281	L/Cpl. G H Burton (Z)
282	Pte. Frank Bernard Bradley (Z)
283	Pte. A Batty (Z)
284	Pte. Frank Butler (Z)
285	Cpl. Harry Brown*
286	Cpl. W Bailey MID
287	Cpl. Frank Leslie Corlett (Z)
289	Pte. George Wilson Clark*
290	Pte. Herbert Dover MM
292	Pte. William Catron (Dis)
294	Pte. Harold Clark MID (Z)
295	Pte. S Latus
296	Cpl. Frank Davie* MM
297	Pte. Harold Leslie Cooper*
298	Pte. Clifford Carter*
299	Pte. John Dale (Z)
300	Pte. C T England (Z)
301	Pte. H R Fullerton (Z)
303	Pte. Basil Fallowfield (Z)
304	Pte. George Hodge*
305	Pte. F Holmes
306	Pte. Francis William Harrison (Z)
307	Cpl. Harold Holdsworth (Z)
308	Pte. Albert James Hancock (Z)
309	Pte. Henry Thomas Frederick Hall (Z)
310	Pte. H Gyngell (Z)
311	Pte. Horace Gill*
313	Pte. C F Tennison
314	Pte. B Tether
315	Pte. L Surfleet*
316	Pte. P Saunders (Z)
317	Sgt. Harold Edward Sendall DCM (Z)
318	L/Cpl. J R Mayor
319	Pte. ?? Mallison (Z)
320	Pte. Robert Ormston (Z)
321	Pte. Edward Kingsley Parrish*
322	Pte. Fred Portergill (Z)
323	Pte. Walter Ramsay (Z)
325	Pte. Arthur Riley (Dis)

331	Pte. John Henry Forward (Z)
332	Pte. Stephen Harvey Hall (Z)
333	Pte. Wilfred Brown (Z)
334	Cpl. Richard Bertram Bulmer (Z)
335	Pte. Frank Bird (Z)
336	Pte. Ernest Booth (Z)
338	Pte. J W Collingwood
339	Pte. Edward Dalby (Z)
340	Pte. William Irvine Cattley
341	Pte. W H Dalton
342	Sgt. William Archbutt Thompson MM (Z)
344	Pte. James William Taylor (Z)
345	Pte. Thomas Wordsworth (Z)
346	Pte. Leonard Webster
347	Pte. Harold Woolhouse (Z)
348	Pte. Frederick Wilkinson (Z)
349	Pte. Frank Young (Z)
350	Pte. L Young
351	Pte. John Armstrong (Z)
353	Pte. Charles William Bourne (Z)
354	Pte. Alan Porter (Z)
355	Pte. Charles Ernest Pattison (Z)
358	Pte. John Rishworth*
359	L/Cpl. M Spikins
360	Pte. Watson Smith (Z)
361	Pte. John E Simpson (Z)
362	Pte. John Alfred Skipsey (Z)
363	Pte. E Booth (Z)
364	Pte. Frederick Thomas Moss (Z)
365	Pte. Frederick McWilliam (Z)
366	Pte. A H North
367	Pte. William Henry Newton (Z)
369	Pte. Harold Robert Gibbons (Z)
371	Pte. Richard Ingamells (Z)
372	Pte. E T Jackson
374	Pte. Robert Taylor I'Anson (Z)
375	Pte. William Reginald Jones (Z)
376	Cpl. Llewellyn Hill Jones (Z)
377	Pte. Arthur Kirk*
378	Cpl. Lewis Koplick (Z)
379	Sgt. Charles Kenneth Lonsdale (Z)
381	Pte. Eric Lear (Z)
383	Pte. Albert Henry Martin (Dis)
384	Pte. T P Millard
385	Pte. Ernest Mainprize (Z)
386	Pte. Jack Peck (Z)
387	Pte. Charles Turnbull (Z)
388	Pte. A Leeming
389	Pte. Arthur Stanley Wright*
390	Pte. Charles William Searle (Z)
391	Pte. Herbert Smales (Z)
396	Pte. A Sykes
397	Pte. Fred Taylor (Dis)
399	Pte. John Percy Tuxworth (Z)
400	Pte. Harold Turner (Z)

401	Pte. W H Warn	485	Pte. James Stennett Watson*
403	Pte. Albert Edward Wheelband (Dis)	489	Pte. John Spring (Z)
406	Sgt. Walter Watson*	490	Sgt. James Regan (Z)
407	Pte. A Webster	491	Sgt. Frederick Edwin Railton (Z)
408	Pte. Harold Reuben Watson (Z)	492	Pte. Arthur Thomas Jackson*
411	Pte. Walter Charles Waddington*	493	Sgt. R Miller
412	Pte. Samuel Arthur Wigby (Z)	495	Pte. Ernest Madsen (Z)
415	Pte. Alfred Taylor (Z)	496	Pte. George Stanley Mansfield*
416	Pte. Harry Parker (Dis)	497	Pte. George Frederick Knowles (Z)
417	Pte. Sydney Clayton Pacey (Z)	498	Pte. Paul Kershaw (Z)
418	Pte. Wilfred Poulson (Z)	501	Pte. S E Harwood
419	CSM Roy Pinchon MID (Z)	503	Pte. Wilfred Mark Harrison (Z)
420	Pte. William Kitching (Z)	505	Pte. H Garton
422	Pte. L F Jeffery	507	Pte. J A Dobbs MM
423	Pte. Allan Kenneth Ingram (Z)	508	Pte. Thomas Hamblion Clarke*
424	Cpl. Reginald Peace Hudson*	509	Cpl. Gerald Duncan Butters (Z)
427	Pte. James Norris Houldsworth*	510	Sgt. Uriah Ellis Butters*
428	Pte. Henry Ernest Hodge (Z)	511	Cpl. Wilfred Lessey Brown*
429	Pte. Carl Hermann* MM	515	Pte. James J Allen (Z)
430	Sgt. W E Harrison	519	Pte. F H Johnson
431	Cpl. C G Hall	520	Pte. C W Riley
434	Pte. James Hudson*	521	Pte. Rupert George Smedley (Dis)
435	Pte. Frank Hall *	525	Pte. W E Adamson
437	Cpl. Joseph Goodman MM	526	Pte. Hugh Frank Blakemore (Z)
439	Pte. Joseph Gibson (Z)	527	Pte. A Blakemore
440	Pte. Basil Montague Gibbs (Z)	528	Cpl. R E Browne
442	Pte. Thomas Geraghty*	530	CQMS Alfred Holmes Grindelle (Z)
447	Pte. Ernest Fewster (Z)	532	Pte. H Johnson
448	Pte. Hugh Parker Freeborough*	533	Pte. Harry Ramsay (Z)
449	Pte. Percy Fox (Z)	534	Pte. H Powell (Z)
451	Pte. William Eastwood (Z)	535	Sgt. John C Stocks (Dis)
452	Pte. Douglas Duncan (Z)	536	Pte. John Cundall Stocks (Dis)
453	Pte. Robert Douglas Dunham (Dis)	537	Sgt. James Iveson (Z)
454	Pte. Edwin Stanley Duffield	538	QM/Sgt. Herbert Ireland*
455	Sgt. H Fisher MM	541	Pte. William Murdock (Dis)
456	Pte. Philip Morris Davidson*	543	Pte. E Pattern
458	Pte. John Noton Cooper (Z)	544	L/Cpl. H Harold Redmore
459	Pte. H S Corden	545	Pte. Harry Woodmansey (Z)
460	Pte. Wilfred Toft Corlass (Z)	549	Sgt. Albert Edward Frank (Z)
461	WOII Herbert Cowling (Z)	550	Pte. Edward Hirst (Z)
462	Pte. William Jarvis Clark (Z)	553	Cpl. D A Pudsey MSM (Z)
463	Pte. Farnill Clayton (Z)	554	Pte.Thomas Joseph Willis (Z)
464	L/Cpl. Fred Clipson MM (Z)	555	Pte. Robert Henry Stutt (Z)
465	Pte. Robert Thomas Buttimer (Dis)	556	Pte. Wilfred Newlove (Z)
466	Pte. J Brunyee	557	Pte. W V Miller
467	Pte. A Brealey	558	L/Cpl. J W Fearnley (Z)
468	Pte. Herbert Brown (Z)	559	Pte. Allan Hastings Dale (Z)
469	Pte. George Edward Boyd (Z)	560	Pte. W R Raney
470	Pte. Bryan George Bowen*	561	Pte. S Coop
472	Pte. G Birks	563	Pte. Peter McRorie (Z)
474	Pte. George Bartlett (Z)	564	Pte. Percy Atherton (Dis)
478	Pte. J W Allen C-de-G (B)	565	Pte. William Brown (Z)
479	Pte. W H Alexander	570	Pte. Samuel Windle (Z)
481	Cpl. Oscar Randall Waldemar Agerskow*	571	Pte. Sidney Smith (Z)
483	Pte. H Abba	572	Pte. T A Nasby

573 Pte. Charles H Newton (Z)	657 Pte. George Winter Anson (Z)
574 Pte. T A Powell	658 Pte. Harry Cressy Abercrombie (Dis)
576 Pte. John Henry Deyes (Z)	659 Sgt. Cecil Fritz Wikner (Z)
583 Pte. Cecil Simpkins MM (Z)	660 Sgt. Herbert Swift MSM (Z)
584 Pte. Robert Frank Scaife (Z)	661 Pte. Horatio Swift (Z)
586 L/Cpl. William Robinson MM C-de-G (F) (Z)	662 Pte. Frederick Charles Seller (Z)
588 Pte. Solomon Shapero MM (Z)	663 L/Cpl. George Austin Smith MM
589 Sgt. Harold Youngson (Z)	664 L/Cpl. Solomon Schottlander MM (Z)
590 Pte. Frank Westerby (Dis)	666 Pte. Ernest Stevens (Z)
591 Pte. Harold Wray (Dis)	667 Pte. H. Summers
593 Pte. Reginald Warren White (Z)	668 Pte. Charles Cleveland Reynolds* MM
597 RSM Christian Wilkie Thirsk*	669 Pte. Herbert Sutton (Z)
598 Pte. F Thompson (Z)	670 Pte. Stanley Victor Oliver (Z)
599 Pte. James William Pront (Z)	671 Pte. Lawrence William Newlove (Z)
600 Pte. William Andrew Pickering (Z)	672 Pte. P Martindale
601 Pte. Harold Parrish (Z)	673 Pte. Harold Lancaster (Z)
603 Sgt. Fred Graham Page MM & bar (Z)	674 Pte. Herbert Ansley Lambert* (Z)
604 Pte. F K Page	676 Pte. R Keal
606 Pte. Ernest Henry Mills (Dis)	677 Pte. Thomas Brinton Johnson (Z)
607 RQMS John Percy Milns MID (Z)	678 Cpl. Arthur Ernest Huzzard (Z)
612 Pte. George Albert Mankel (Z)	680 Pte. Francis Izon Hirst (Dis)
615 Pte. Thomas Headley Kirby (Z)	681 L/Cpl. H Hicks
616 Pte. Richard Henry King (Dis)	682 Pte. Alfred Lowther Harrison (Z)
617 Pte. Edward Kilvington (Z)	684 Pte. Charles Edward Fox (Z)
618 Pte. E L Kidd*	685 Sgt. Frank Alfred Ellis*
620 Pte. Norman Loftus Kelsey (Dis)	686 Pte. Harry Eckles*
621 Sgt. R P Jones	687 Pte. Edmond E Draper (Z)
622 Sgt. J A Johnson (Z)	688 Pte. Samuel John Cook (Dis)
623 Pte. Will Jenkins (Z)	689 Pte. Hugh Collinson*
625 Pte. Philip James (Z) ^^	691 L/Cpl. Bernard Brumby MM (Dis)
626 Pte. W J Jackson	692 Pte. Arthur Gordon Brown (Z)
627 L/Cpl. F Jackson	693 Sgt. W Bone
628 Pte. Noel Westgarth Holmes (Z)	694 Pte. J Biddlecombe
629 Pte. George Hodgson*	695 Pte. John Beeken (Z)
630 Pte. Robert Hayes (Z)	696 Pte. James Alfred Bailey (Z)
632 Sgt. James Guest (Dis)~	697 Sgt. Archibald Clifford Abba* DCM, MM
633 Pte. Herbert Graystone MM	699 Sgt. Walter Barnett*
634 Pte. James William Graystone (Z)	701 Pte. Sydney Meeton (Z)
635 Pte. William Gray	702 L/Cpl. J Metcalfe
636 Pte. John Edgar Garton (Dis)	704 Pte. Walter Linsley*
637 Sgt. John Matthews Fenwick MSM (Z)	705 Pte. George Moss (Z)
639 Pte. A V Emery	706 Pte. Douglas McAndrew (Z)
640 Pte. Alfred Eastaugh (Z)	707 Pte. Frederick Maud (Z)
641 Pte. W Dennison	708 Pte. G Jessup
643 Pte. William Henry Dickinson*	709 Pte. William Ellis Johnson*
644 Pte. Wilfred Davis MSM	710 Pte. Arthur Harris*
645 Pte. Thomas Curtis (Z)	711 Pte. Harold Hunter (dis)
646 Pte. David McGavin Cowell (Z)	712 Pte. Cyril Hirst (Z)
647 Pte. Albert Edward Collett (Z)	714 Pte. H Gamble (Z)
648 C/Sgt. Harry Colquhoun (Dis)	715 Pte. Clarence Graham (Z)
650 Pte. David Frank Chapman (Z)	716 Pte. S Horsfield
652 Pte. Stanley W M Brown (Dis)	717 Sgt. T Huntington
653 Pte. J F Brocklehurst	718 Pte. Thomas Hunter (Z)
655 Pte. P Boyd	720 Pte. Walter Fussey (Z)
656 Sgt. Arthur Baldwin MM (Z)	721 Cpl. Sidney Edlington DCM*

723	Sgt. B A Clubley	805	Pte. James Edwin Brown (Dis)
724	Pte. Walter Victor Carey (Z)	806	Cpl. T Buck
725	Pte. Sydney John Cornwall (Z)	807	L/Cpl. W B Billany (Z)
727	Cpl. Robert Granville Bennett*	809	Pte. William John Linaker Downes (Z)
728	Pte. Frank Taylor Armitage (Dis)	811	Pte. Leonard Caley (Z)
729	Pte. Walter Barr (Dis)	812	Pte. Wilfred Arthur Fletcher (Z)
730	Pte. Thomas Joseph Boag (Z)	813	Pte. J R Farnill
731	Sgt. S Bailey (Z)	815	Pte. H Farnley (Z)
733	Cpl. Harold Burgoyne*	816	Pte. Francis Geraghty*
734	Pte. P Broom	817	Pte. William Adrian Goodwill (Z)
735	Sgt. Walter Reinsford Boag MM (Z)	818	Pte. Fred Johnson (Z)
736	Sgt. J W Brown (Z)	819	Pte. C S Joys
737	Pte. William Atkinson (Z)	820	Cpl. H Johnson (Z)
738	Pte. G A Wells	822	Pte. Fred Kirby (Z)
739	Pte. Walter Herbert Wreghitt (Z)	823	Pte. Rupert Reese Lewis (Z)
740	Pte. Hugh Graham Wheeler*	824	Sgt. B Littlewood (Z)
741	Pte. David Wilkinson (Dis)	825	Pte. Thomas Lidgard (Z)
742	Pte. Charles Henry Vollans DCM (Dis)	827	L/Cpl. W A MacPherson
743	Pte. George Edward Wade (Dis)	828	Pte. ?? Mason (Z)
744	Pte. F K Woodcock	829	Pte. H Walsh (Z)
745	Sgt. Charley Tennison*	830	Pte. William George Andrew MID (Z)
746	Sgt. Thomas James Shelton*	831	Pte. Charles Henry Selkirk (Dis)
747	Pte. Frederick James Simpson (Z)	832	Pte. Wilfred Elsworth Sykes*
748	Pte. J Smelt	833	Pte. Alexander Smith (Z)
749	Pte. Leonard Stubbs (Z)	834	Pte. Reginald Noel S Sinderson (Z)
751	Pte. D A Roberts	835	Pte. B F Smith (Z)
753	Sgt. George Clifford Sugden*	836	L/Cpl. G L Spring
755	Pte. Tom Sherburn (Dis)	838	Pte. J Smith
757	Pte. George Frederick Sleight (Z)	839	Pte. Frederick Arthur Smith (Z)
759	Pte. George Herbert Nicholson (Z)	840	Pte. George Maurice Sheppard*
761	L/Sgt. Arthur Jackson* C-de-G (B)	841	L/Cpl. E Perkins
762	Pte. Frederick Edward Purcell (Z)	842	Pte. Alfred Ernest Nicholson*
764	Pte. G W Gill	843	Pte. M Malon (Z)
765	Sgt. Frederick Willis * DCM	845	Pte. GH Johnson
766	Pte. Robert Sewell (Z)	846	Pte. Frederick William Harrison (Z)
768	Cpl. J G Pippett MM (Z)	847	RSM Walter Hall MM C-de-G (B) (Z)
770	Pte. W Lazenby	849	Pte. Douglas William Garrett (Z)
771	Cpl. Reginald Sydney Newman (Z)	850	Pte. C J Finch (Z)
772	Pte. Walter Arnold Wilby (Z)	851	Pte. A Ellmer (Z)
773	Pte. G Wilcockson	853	Pte. G Blackmore (Z)
774	Pte. Wilson Webb (Z)	854	Pte. Harold Bentley (Z)
776	Pte. Eric Linnell*	855	Pte. G W Bray
777	Pte. Edward Kell (Z)	856	Pte. A H Wright
778	Pte. Robert Henry Key (Z)	857	Pte. Ernest Wilkinson (Z)
782	Pte. Henry Burn Hewitt*	859	Pte. H R Todd
783	Pte. Arthur Reginald Hasnip (Dis)	860	Pte. R E Saunby
784	Pte. George Frederick Arnold Floyd (Dis)	861	Pte. Herbert Spink (Z)
786	Pte. Cyril Arthur Credland (Dis)	862	Pte. Walter Storr (Z)
787	Pte. S Conyers	864	Pte. Aaron Peterson*
793	Pte. M Wilson	865	Pte. Eric Pentith*
795	Pte. John Spence (Dis)	866	Pte. Arthur H Oliver*
797	L/Cpl. L Jeynes	867	Pte. R C Neill
801	Pte. Alan Pearson Adamson (Z)	868	Pte. Lawrence Nowell DCM (Z)
802	Pte. Thomas Weldon Bailey (Z)	870	Pte. Henry Seymour Ryley (Z)
804	Pte. Christopher Pentith*	871	Pte. Fred Walker (Z)

872	Cpl. Cyril Travis (Z)	955	Pte. H Winter
874	Pte. James Frederick Wiles (Z)	957	Pte. A Cundy (Z)
875	Pte. W S Everigham	958	Pte. W J Cleary
876	Pte. Alfred Kersh (Z)	959	Pte. H Dougherty
877	Pte. Harold Jackson (Z)	961	Pte. Charles Hewison (Z)
878	Pte. Ernest Jenkins (Z)	962	Pte. Ernest Hayes (Dis)
879	Pte. H Illingworth	963	Pte. Oswald Anthony Haller*
881	Sgt. T Gregory*	964	Pte. Albert Hall (Z)
882	Pte. F Kirby (Z)	965	Pte. William Garton (Dis)
884	Pte. Thomas Brayton Bell (Z)	966	Pte. Joseph Hilary Hobbs (Z)
886	Pte. P C Hall	968	Pte. W Homan
887	Pte. Frederick Thomas Sleight (Z)	969	Pte. Ernest Hancock (Z)
888	Pte. Rupert Cameron Hall (Z)	970	RSM Fred Stanley Ives C-de-G (B)
890	Pte. H Storr	971	Cpl. R W Johnson
891	Pte. Robert Broxham (Z)	973	Pte. Ernest Jobling (Dis)
892	L/Cpl. K S Evers (Z)	974	Pte. Hubert Kettle*
894	Pte. H Fitton	975	Pte. William Edward Lambert (Z)
895	Pte. F Fell (Z)	982	Pte. Charles King Palmer (Z)
896	Pte. John Forrester*	985	Pte. Robert Yallop (Z)
898	Pte. George William Warriner (Z)	986	Sgt. Ernest Best* MM
899	Cpl. Stanley Booth Wilson*	987	Sgt. Sidney James Clark (Z)
900	Pte. Reginald Verity (Dis)	990	Cpl. E C Dunn
902	L/Cpl. F Stevenson (Z)	992	Cpl. James Henry Crooks MM MID (Z)
904	Pte. Herbert William Monkman (Z)	993	Pte. T A Goodwill (Z)
905	Pte. Dennis Faulkner Jordan (Dis)	994	CSM John Melton Bateman*
907	Pte. Walter Henry Kirk (Z)	995	Pte. Gilbert Popple (Z)
908	Pte. Bertie Chambers (Dis)	996	Pte. J W Fisher Bronze Medal For Bravery (I)
910	Pte. John William Dunn (Z)	998	Pte. C Kingdom
911	Pte. William Bromby*	999	Pte. Thomas Elmer Stephenson (Z)
912	Pte. Albert H Brooks (Z)	1000	Sgt. Robert Lee (Z)
913	Sgt. Frank Bold MM (Z)	1005	Pte. Leonard Dale (Z)
914	Pte. William Robert Witty (Z)	1008	Pte. S Taylor
915	Pte. Frederick Charles Wilson MID (Z)	1009	Cpl. Robert Sydney Lamming (Z)
921	Pte. Walter Edward Aust (Z)	1010	Pte. E Robinson
922	Pte. Ezra William Busby (Z)	1012	Pte. John William Chapman (Dis)
923	Pte. C Bilbe	1013	Pte. William Taylor Coleman (Z)
924	Sgt. John Law Barton*	1014	Pte. William Dawson MM
927	Sgt. Sydney Henry Moses MID (Dis)	1015	Pte. Arnold Reid (Z)
929	Pte. Baron Barnett Moss (Z)	1016	Pte. James Hughes (Dis)
930	Sgt. Arthur Moody (Z)	1017	Pte. John Todd (Z)
931	Pte. J McBride	1018	Pte. Henry Cooper (Z)
932	Sgt. A H Nash	1019	Pte. Fred Fellowes (Z)
934	Pte. Dick Norton (Z)	1020	Pte. Herbert Dearing (Z)
939	Cpl. A Potts	1023	Pte. Reginald William Everingham (Dis)
941	Pte. Harold Patrick (Z)	1026	Pte. Henry Allan Houldsworth (Z)
942	Pte. William Albert Phillips (Z)	1027	Pte. William Stanley Bartindale (Z)
946	Pte. Walter Silverwood*	1028	Pte. E Hyde
947	Pte. John Edmond Sherwood (Z)	1029	Sgt. E F Hermann MM
948	Cpl. Stanley Scarr*	1031	Pte. Arthur Francis Goldthorpe*
949	Pte. Herbert Cecil Thompson (Z)	1032	Pte. Norman Larard (Dis)
950	Pte. A Turner	1035	Pte. John Peacock Day (Z)
951	Pte. G W Tether	1038	Pte. J H Wilkinson MM
952	Pte. Wilfred Trowill (Z)	1039	Pte. G A B West (Z)
953	Pte. Herbert Tinn (Z)	1042	Pte. Arthur Milton Woods (Z)
954	Sgt. Gerald Ashley Wright*	1043	Pte. Tom Dalby (Z)

1044	Pte. Harold Stainton (Z)	1125	Pte. Harold Flintoft (Z)
1045	Pte. I Reuben	1126	Pte. Samuel Downs (Z)
1049	Pte. James Willey (Z)	1127	Pte. Walter Samuel Leech (Z)
1050	Pte. Eric Crowston (Z)	1130	Pte. F Kendrew
1051	Pte. O Bolmeer (Z)	1131	Pte. S Caley
1052	Pte. Harold Scruton (Z)	1133	Pte. W S Langdale
1054	Pte. E W Sellers	1134	Pte. William Singleton DCM, MM, C-de-G (F)(Z)
1055	Pte. Stanley Sharp (Z)	1135	Pte. Edward Owen Rutherford*
1057	Sgt. Aythan Powell (Dis)	1136	Pte. Herbert William Charity (Z)
1059	Pte. A H Dixon	1137	Sgt. Thomas Mitchell*
1060	Pte. Charles Henry Shallcross*	1138	Pte. J Laurie
1061	Pte. Harry Fanthorpe	1139	Pte. Harry Bland Cooper (Z)
1062	Pte. Eric Friis Smith*	1140	Pte. F Stone
1063	Pte. Claude Marsh Hornstedt (Dis)	1141	Pte. Percy Walker (Z)
1064	Pte. Arthur Charles Vaughan Smith*	1142	Pte. Charles William Philpott (Z)
1067	Pte. James Watson Fowler (Dis)	1143	Cpl. Alfred Masters (Z)^^
1068	Pte. C P Townsend	1144	Pte. A E West
1069	Pte. William Henry Atkin (Z)	1145	Pte. Bertram Rider (Z)
1070	Pte. Ralph Snowdon*	1147	Pte. Thomas B Lowson (Z)
1072	Sgt. F Chalmers	1148	Pte. Archie Stewart (Z)
1073	Pte. Harold Raymond Harper*	1149	Pte. A Topham (Z)
1075	Pte. Fred Russell*	1150	Pte. Alfred Clayton (Z)
1077	Pte. Fred Hall*	1152	Pte. George William B Dainton (Z)
1078	Pte. Henry Bird (Z)	1154	Pte. Fred Downs (Z)
1079	Pte. Edward Bird (Z)	1155	L/Cpl. L E Peek
1080	Pte. Walter Mallison Barlow*	1156	Pte. James Louis Page (Z)
1083	Pte. Harry Pickard (Z)	1157	Pte. W Good (Z)
1084	Pte. Harry Pickard (Dis)	1158	Pte. Edgar Oswald Clegg*
1085	Sgt. Wilfred Parker (Dis)	1159	Pte. John Lumley (Z)
1086	CQMS Sydney Cressey MID (Z)	1160	Pte. Asia Predgen (Z)
1087	Pte. Cyril Sharp (Z)	1161	Pte. John Ernest Hailstone (Z)
1088	Pte. Thomas Langley Frazer (Z)	1162	Pte. R Hyde (Z)
1089	Sgt. Arthur Bell (Z)	1163	Pte. Goodworth (Z)
1090	Pte. Arthur Cleminshaw (Z)	1164	Pte. John Newborn (Z)
1091	Pte. Fred Moore (Z)	1165	Pte. Charles Edward Campbell (Z)
1092	Pte. Leonard Donkin (Z)	1168	Pte. J L Abbott (Z)
1095	Pte. J F Edson	1170	Pte. Ernest Carter Bell (Z)
1096	Pte. Leonard Bolderson (Z)	1171	Pte. C G Walker (Z)
1097	Pte. Harold Farnaby Strachan (Z)	1172	Pte. R Stead
1099	L/Cpl. John Darneley Petty* MM	1173	Pte. M J Dakin
1101	Pte. W Robinson	1175	Pte. Alexander Hodgson Martin (Dis)
1102	Pte. Harold Charles Needham (Z)	1178	Pte. John Reginald Martin (Z)
1104	Pte. Lawrence Joseph Chapman*	1180	Pte. Reginald Hardey Pearson (Z)
1105	Pte. Harry Booth (Z)	1181	Pte. William Lindridge (Z)
1106	Cpl. E B Stevens	1182	Pte. Percy Haynes (Z)
1109	Sgt. Alfred Kemp (Dis)	1184	Pte. Fred Longhorn (Z)
1112	Pte. Horace Charles Marris (Z)	1185	L/Cpl. Edward Mowforth MM (Z)
1113	Pte. William Park Deas (Dis)	1186	Pte. G W Winter
1114	Pte. Joseph Henry George Boyes (Z)	1188	Pte. Bernard Rowland Middlewood (Z)
1115	Pte. Thomas Percival Bennett (Z)	1191	L/Cpl. Leonard Jarvis MM & bar (Z)
1116	Pte. Frank Bernard Barnby (Z)	1192	Pte. Job Petch (Z)
1118	Pte. Philip Moore (Z)	1194	Pte. Cecil Ratcliffe (Dis)
1120	Pte. L E Watt (Z)	1195	Pte. ?? Hanby (Z)
1123	Pte. H Dempsey	1196	Pte. William Robert Lancaster (Z)
1124	Pte. Tom Crayton (Dis)	1201	Sgt. Alexander Charlesworth MM

1204 Pte. Edwin Percy Close (Z)	1285 Pte. A B North
1207 L/Cpl. G E Bowen	1286 Pte. J W Clark
1208 Cpl. W Thomas	1287 Pte. V W Corlyon
1210 Pte. F Johnson	1288 Pte. W D Dymock
1212 Pte. Joseph Alban Doran (Z)	1289 Pte. C A Mainprize (Z)
1214 Pte. James Harold Markham (Dis)	1290 Pte. J H W Gleadow (Z)
1215 Pte. W High	1291 Pte. W E Fowler
1218 Pte. W H Briggs	1293 Pte. John R Kendrew (Dis)
1219 Pte. Cecil Charles Burrows (Dis)	1297 Pte. G W Buck
1220 Pte. Joseph E Wilson (Z)	1299 Pte. J G Wardle
1221 Pte. J Cheney	1300 Pte. Robert Edward Clappison (Z)
1223 L/Cpl. G F Langthorpe	1301 Pte. Leonard Stork (Z)
1226 Pte. Edwin Stephenson (Z)	1302 Pte. Arthur William Lucas (Z)
1227 Pte. Harold Atherton*	1306 Sgt. John Lewis MM C-de-G (B) (Z)
1229 L/Cpl. F O'Dell	1308 Sgt. A Walsh MM, MM (F) (Z)
1230 Pte. J B Atkinson	1310 Sgt. Benjamin C Nicholls*
1231 L/Cpl. R H Smith	1314 Pte. Edward E Boynton (Dis)
1232 Pte. William Graham Hill*	1315 Pte. William Herbert Anderton*
1233 Pte. A E Messenger	1316 Pte. George William Mitchell (Z)
1239 Pte. Samuel K Elliott (Z)	1317 Pte. Arthur D Gladwin*
1240 Pte. Hector Smith (Z)	1322 Sgt. Clarrie Alcock (Z)
1241 Pte. Alfred E Knowland (Z)	1324 Pte. F Tindale
1242 Pte. R Hurd (Z)	1325 Pte. C Tomlinson
1244 Pte. John Rotherham Hayward (Dis)	1327 Pte. Cyril Pope (Z)
1246 Pte. S Bryan (Z)	1328 Pte. F Linsley
1247 Pte. G K Deighton	1329 Sgt. G H Dimmock
1248 Pte. F E Harding	1330 Pte. Albert Jordan
1249 Pte. J E Newton	1331 Pte. S Sugarman
1250 Pte. James Clark (Z)	1332 Pte. James William Branford*
1251 Pte. H Smith	1333 Pte. William James Smith (Z)
1252 Pte. William Fox (Z)	1335 L/Cpl. J Ward MM
1254 Pte. H Hope (Z)	1336 Pte. W B Rockingham
1255 Pte. F D Boast	1338 Pte. William Ward (Z)
1256 Pte. John Fergusson (Z)	1339 Sgt. Charles H Thompson (Z)
1257 Pte. Albert Edward Denton (Z)	1341 Cpl. Henry Johnson (Z)
1258 Pte. Thomas Danby (Z)	1344 Pte. W J Whyte
1259 Sgt. William F Williams (Z)	1346 Pte. Robert Fish (Z)
1260 Pte. W Bowes	1347 Pte. H Stonehouse
1261 Cpl. Robert Ranson (Z)	1348 Pte. Charles W Richardson (Dis)
1262 Sgt. W H V Winter MM C-de-G (B)	1349 Pte. G W Taylor
1263 Pte. Percy Brown (Dis)	1351 Pte. H Jipson
1264 Pte. Thomas Jackson (Z)	1352 Pte. S Milner (Z)
1267 Pte. G Goodill	1354 Pte. Samuel Lyons (Dis)
1268 Pte. Walter Thomas (Z)	1355 Pte. J H Corby
1270 Pte. H Cross	1356 Cpl. W Dixon
1272 Pte. Harold Smith (Z)	1357 Pte. Edward N Bland (Dis)
1274 Pte. Alfred W Clark (Dis)	1359 Cpl. Leslie Scarr (Z)
1275 Pte. Leonard Lynch (Z)	1361 L/Cpl. Harold Rawling MM (Z)
1276 Pte. Percy Allen Haines (Z)	1364 L/Cpl. J Masters
1278 Pte. Horace Mabbott (Z)	1365 Pte. E F Field
1279 Pte. Frank Cocker (Z)	1366 Pte. R E Clappison (Z)
1281 Pte. James Tait (Dis)	1368 Pte. Edward Hirst (Dis)
1282 Pte. George Ernest Bethel Robinson (Z)	1369 Pte. Edward Towse (Z)
1283 Pte. Albert Higgins (Z)	1370 Pte. S E Wright
1284 Pte. A A Kennedy (Z)	1371 Pte. Louis Shapero MM (Z)

1372	Pte. Joseph B Slide (Dis)
1375	Pte. A Campbell
1377	L/Cpl. C Guisse
1378	Pte. Charles Harrison (Dis)
1379	Pte. John Thomas Rodham MID (Z)
1380	Pte. J H Morley
1381	Pte. William Storey (Z)
1383	Pte. John Whitehead (Z)
1392	Pte. G Archer
1393	Pte. Richard A Gray (Z)
1395	Pte. W Holmes
1397	Pte. J H Bartram
1398	Pte. Alfred Stanley Sutton (Z)
1399	Pte. Thomas Edwin Croudson (Z)
1402	L/Cpl. Harold Tindale MID
1403	Pte. M H Holmes
1406	Pte. Thomas W Marshall (Z)
1408	Pte. Alfred Conman (Z)
1413	Pte. H A Pawson
1415	Pte. Matthias Cobb (Dis)
1416	Pte. Harry Warkup (Z)
1417	Pte. Wilfred Thompson (Z)
1418	Pte. William B Storey (Z)
1419	Pte. Jim Blankin (Z)
1420	Pte. Harry Brabben (Z)
1424	Pte. Roland Percy Haselhurst (Z)
1425	Pte. Thomas William Burgess (Z)
1426	Pte. S Tonkinson
1430	Pte. W Middleton MID (Z)
1432	Pte. H H Jordan
1436	Pte. Albert Bricklebank (Z)
1437	Pte. George Miller
1441	Pte. J H Archbutt
1443	Pte. H Bush
1444	Pte. P Wilson
1445	Pte. William Calvert (Z)
1446	Pte. F Ellis
1447	Pte. A Cruddas
1448	Pte. Martin V Jude (Dis)~
1449	Cpl. Jess Heyhoe (Z)
1451	Pte. A J Sutton
1452	Pte. Frederick Richard English (Dis)
1454	Pte. George Storr (Dis)~
???	CSM S Cash (Z)
???	RQMS Kendall (Z)
???	Pte. F Riley (Z)
???	Pte. E Robinson (Z)
???	Pte. J B Fay
???	P Sellers
???	A T Barrett
???	T Edmondson
???	J R McAllister
???	F W Wilde
???	J V Smith

| ??? | G W Walker |
| ??? | N T Metcalf |

11th Battalion Nominal Roll

3	Cpl. P. Kirk
4	Pte. Robert Speck (Dis)
5	Pte. Harold Richard Hilton (Dis)
7	Pte. William Henry Larman (Z)
9	Cpl. John Henry Pyne (Dis)
10	Pte. Frank Holliday (Z)
11	Pte. William Knaggs (Z)
12	Pte. Thomas Wilson (Z)
13	Pte. Arthur Green (Z)
14	Sgt. H Baxter
15	Cpl. Walter Shepherdson (Z)
18	Pte. E Bearfield
20	Pte. George Stanley Lovedale (Dis)
22	Pte. Harold Lee (Z)
24	Pte. Miles Coverdale (Z)
25	L/Cpl. W H Edson
26	Pte. Herbert Bates MM
30	Pte. P Kirk
33	L/Cpl. H McLane
36	Pte. George Leonard E Dudding
37	Pte. Andrew Valentine Stow (Z)
38	Pte. Thomas Harold Silabon (Dis)
39	Pte. Herbert Brignall (Z)
40	Pte. Charles Slater Lee (Dis)
41	Pte. Frederick Kirk (Z)
42	Pte. George Henry McCollin (Z)
43	Pte. George Bromby (Z)
44	Pte. Alfred Roberts (Dis)
45	Pte. William Taylor (Dis)
46	Pte. John Thomas Landen (Dis)
48	Pte. Gilbert Howard (Dis)
49	Sgt. F Cox
50	L/Cpl. W Ling
51	Pte. J W Kirk
52	Pte. Frank Sumpton (Z)
53	Pte. Albert Joseph Parker (Z)
54	Pte. Horace Kirk (Z)
55	Pte. T Coulson
56	Pte. Charles Walter Toogood MM
57	Pte. Arthur McManus (Z)
58	Pte. Alfred Dobson (Z)
60	Pte. Tom Markham (Z)
61	Sgt. William Pickerill MSM (Z)
62	Pte. Thomas Pick (Z)
63	L/Cpl. G E Hogg
65	Pte. Louis Charles Bull (Z)
67	Pte. C Clayton
69	L/Cpl. E A Lockwood
71	Pte. H Baines
73	Pte. Herbert Vernon (Z)
75	Pte. George Henry Carter (Z)

76	Pte. Samuel Binks (Z)	172	Sgt. H Hall
77	Pte. Arthur Mark Ryley (Z)	174	Pte. Peter Harrison (Z)
78	Pte. A Pearson	176	Pte. Walter Waddingham*
81	Pte. C F McColl	177	Sgt. Harry Berry*
82	Pte. John Rowe (Z)	182	Pte. Harold L Cook (Z)
85	Sgt. George Pashley (Z)	185	Pte. William Claxton (Z)
87	Pte. R Rutledge	186	Cpl. John Palmer (Z)
88	Pte. James Atkinson (Z)	190	Pte. Stanley Simpson (Z)
92	Pte. William Wray (Z)	193	Cpl. Albert Gardham (Z)
93	Pte. Walter William Mills (Z)	198	Pte. Ernest Sharpe (Z)
94	Pte. R J Hill (Z)	199	Pte. Robert William Marshall (Z)
97	Pte. Thomas Loufborough (Z)	200	Pte. George Harold Hutchinson (Dis)
98	Pte. Arthur Kingsley Thomas (Z)	201	Pte. Robert Large (Z)
99	Pte. Joseph Stennett (Z)	204	Pte. Ernest Latus (Z)
103	Pte. H Richardson	205	Pte. Arnold Smith
104	Pte. George Hirst (Z)	207	Pte. J W Morley
105	Pte. H Chapman MM	208	Pte. Joseph Harrison McDonald (Z)
107	Pte. John F Cawthorn (Z)	210	Pte. Albert Jackson (Z)
114	Pte. Herbert Needham (Z)	212	Pte. Ernest Ridge (Z)
115	Pte. Horace Crawforth (Z)	213	Pte. Henry Wood Craven (Z)
116	Pte. J W Marshall	218	Pte. William O'Donnell
117	Pte. Robert Bateman (Dis)	220	Pte. Arthur Oliver (Dis)
118	Pte. R Kirby	222	Pte. Thomas Cooper (Z)
120	Pte. H Moor	223	Pte. William Whitelock (Z)
122	Pte. Charles Leaming Barnes (Z)	224	Pte. Frederick Sizer MM (Z)
124	Pte. Ernest Ounsworth (Z)	225	CSM Harold Offen (Z)
125	Pte. W Wells	226	Cpl. J Lumley
126	Pte. Frederick Atkinson Taylor (Z)	228	Pte. W Smith
127	Pte. A R Thurnell	229	Pte. R Lowther
128	Pte. Charles William Windas (Dis)	231	Pte. Frederick James Gothard (Z)
129	Cpl. George Dawson (Dis)	232	Pte. Thomas Henry Knight ^^
130	Pte. Frederick William Hawkins (Z)	234	Pte. Henry Barratt Reynolds (Z)
131	Pte. Reginald Thomas (Z)	236	Pte. Charles Albert Wand (Z)
132	Pte. G E Warnes	237	Pte. E E Kingston
135	Pte. G Brown	238	Pte. Charles Herbert Piper (Z)
136	L/Cpl. G A Jeffery MM	240	Pte. William Ernest Hayes (Z)
139	Cpl. C Collingworth	241	Cpl. W E Usher
141	Pte. W J Pritchett (Z)	244	Pte. H Allen
143	Pte. Joseph Ernest Ashley (Z)	246	L/Cpl. F Caborn MM (Z)
145	Pte. Douglas Black (Z)	247	Cpl. Arthur C Boynton (Z)
146	Pte. John Lawton Elston MM (Z)	248	Cpl. C F J Stout
147	Pte. Abraham Harrison Garnett (Dis)	249	Sgt. Frank Kelly MM MID (Z)
148	Pte. Stephen Allen (Z)	251	Pte. Hugh Norfolk MM
149	Sgt. A Simpson	253	Pte. Sidney Wood (Z)
150	Pte. W H Carter	254	Pte. Walter Richardson (Dis)
151	Pte. Gerald Blanchard (Z)	258	Pte. Walter Creaser (Z)
152	CQMS Thomas Wilfred Giles*	259	Pte. George Arnold Richardson (Z)
153	Pte. Lawrance Smith (Z)	262	Pte. T Harman
154	Sgt. Charles William Wilkinson MM	263	Pte. A C Butler
155	Pte. Arthur Pinder (Z)	264	Pte. H Taylor
160	Pte. Frank Bainbridge Hampson (Z)	267	Pte. Geoffrey William Dinsdale (Z)
161	Pte. Sidney Frank Dagwell (Z)	271	Pte. G H Heslop
165	Pte. Ernest Crane (Dis)	272	Pte. W B Wilson
167	Cpl. John Bottomley (Z)	274	Pte. H Capes
169	Pte. T Glenton	275	Pte. George Ellington (D)

280	Pte. George Wilfred Rowntree (Dis)
281	Pte. Thomas Burton Osram Burkes (Z)
282	Pte. W Edwards
283	Pte. B Varley
285	Pte. Horace Stephenson Timpson (Z)
291	Pte. Frank Gibson (Dis)
292	Pte. William Gray Jewitt (Z)
293	Sgt. John William Clayton DCM (Z)
294	Pte. Alonzo Watkinson (Z)
295	Pte. Sidney Chambers (Z)
296	Pte. Harry Warhurst (Z)
298	Pte. John Arthur Hogg*
299	CQMS Harry Armstrong MSM (Z)
300	Pte. Christopher Stockton (Dis)
302	Pte. John Cooper (Dis)
305	L/Cpl. J Todd
306	Pte. George Bentley (Z)
308	Pte. Alfred Benjamin Roberts (Z)
309	Pte. George Bentley (Z)
311	Pte. Edmund Coates (Z)
312	Pte. George Henry Wright (Z)
313	Pte. George Steward (dis)
314	Pte. S Gibson
316	Pte. Albert Whittaker (Z)
317	Pte. Sydney Foster (Z)
318	Pte. John Harold Wilkinson (Z)
322	Pte. Lewis Hinch (Z)
323	Pte. Albert Huteson Binning*
324	Pte. George Sylvester Clarkson (Z)
326	Pte. Tom S Good (Z)
327	Pte. Bewley James Weaver (Z)
328	Pte. Stephen Giles Freeman (Z)
329	Pte. Sid Dry (Z)
330	Pte. Joseph Jacklin Hollingworth (Z)
333	Pte. Fergus Porte (Dis)
334	Pte. James Cunningham (Dis)
335	Pte. John William Good (Dis)
337	Pte. Denis Joseph Sharples (Z)
338	Pte. Charles Scott (Dis)
339	Pte. T E Teece
341	Pte. Lewis Osborne (Z)
342	Pte. Cecil William Whitelam (Dis)
343	Cpl. James Marth (Z)
344	Cpl. W R Gardner
347	Pte. George Harold Dawson (Z)
349	Pte. A Pollard
351	Pte. Robert Wilson Humble (Z)
352	Pte. Ernest GG Dixon (Z)
353	Pte. S H Dell
355	Pte. Francis Roland Pashley (Z)
356	Pte. John Wilson (Z)
357	Sgt. Robert Cressey MM (Dis)
359	Pte. Stanley Simpson
360	Sgt. George Payne
362	Pte. William Thirsk Short (Z)

363	Pte. J W Brough
364	Sgt. J H Smith
365	Pte. Thomas William Robson (Z)
366	Pte. Charles Halliday (Z)
367	Pte. George Henry Gardham (Z)
368	Pte. Archer England (Z)
369	Pte. B Arnold
370	Pte. Wilfred Alfed Davis (Z)
371	Pte. John Alfred Shepherd (Z)
372	Pte. G Robinson
373	Pte. J J Murray
375	Sgt. H Hill MM
378	L/Cpl. M Power
379	Pte. James Henry Joseph Whitehead *
380	Sgt. John Ernest Rudd*
383	Cpl. John Wilson Windle (Dis)
384	Pte. Edward Francis Glass (Z)
385	Pte. Joseph Clipson (Z)
386	Pte. Harold Chatfield (Z)
387	Pte. G Wride
389	Pte. J Thirsk
392	Pte. G E Grantham
393	Pte. F L Sharpe MM
394	Sgt. Henry Snaith*
395	Pte. J McNally
396	Pte. James Robert Rales (Z)
398	Pte. W Peeps
399	Cpl. John Ernest Taylor (Z)
401	Pte. William Loftus Wilde (Z)
402	Sgt. Walter Richard Wray (Dis)
403	Pte. J T Clare
405	Sgt. F Clark
406	Pte. L W Miller
407	Pte. Arthur Robinson (Dis)
408	Pte. Arthur Chilman (Z)
413	Pte. Frank Richard Mitchell (Z)
415	Pte. George B Stephenson (Z)
416	Pte. Fred Walker (Z)
419	Pte. J W Jackson
422	Sgt. George Percival Rust MM & bar
423	Pte. John Henry Coultas (Z)
426	Pte. Charles Preston Bainton (Z)
428	Pte. F Ward
429	Pte. G Wemyss
430	Pte. John Nelson Girtchen (Z)
435	Pte. A W Marshall
439	Pte. Walter Lucas (Dis)
440	Pte. John Smith (Z)
441	Pte. J E Dixon C-de-G (F)
443	Pte. Charles Henry Sellers (Z)
444	Pte. William A Tuton (Z)
446	Pte. James Gunnill (Dis)
448	Pte. W Sawdon
449	Pte. Henry Russell (Z)
451	Pte. J B Megahy

456	Pte. Albert Edward Scott Hudson (Z)	538	Pte. Lewis Bailey MM (Z)
457	Pte. Frederick William Craggy (Z)	539	Pte. John William Linford (Dis)
458	Cpl. J Cox	540	Pte. John W Linford (Dis)
462	Pte. James Barnes (Z)	541	Pte. F G Greasley
463	Cpl. F Harrison MM	544	Pte. W J Cantley
464	Pte. A B Naylor	545	Pte. F Cudbertson
465	Pte. Harold Ford (Z)	546	Pte. Walter Vickerscroft Whitehead (Z)
466	Pte. Albert Francis Holt ^^	548	Pte. Charles Smith (Z)
467	Pte. Tom Gibson (Z)	550	Pte. T Coulson
471	Pte. Gerald Sharp (Dis)	551	Pte. George Sharpe (Z)
472	Pte. A B Cook	552	Pte. Harold Stephenson (Z)
473	L/Cpl. F Scottow	553	Pte. William Henry Clarke (Z)
474	L/Cpl. F Raspin	554	Pte. PE Robson
476	Pte. James Eleker Woodward (Z)	555	Pte. Walter Peacock (Z)
477	Pte. T W Iveson	556	Pte. Sidney Robert Callard (Dis)
480	Pte. Herbert Joules (Dis)	557	Pte. John Proctor (Z)
481	Pte. John Thompson (Dis)	560	Pte. Harold Cockshaw (Z)
482	Pte. George William Cook (Z)	561	Pte. Henry Bennett (Z)
483	Pte. E Brown	562	Sgt. John William Anson MM & C-de-G (B)
484	Pte. Jesse Tye (Z)	563	Pte. William Clark (Dis)
485	Pte. Edward Stainforth (Z)	565	Pte. Arthur Fisher (Z)
487	Pte. Edward Webber (Z)	566	Pte. John Thomas Timblin (Dis)
489	Pte. E Gohl	567	Pte. Arthur Welsh (Z)
490	Pte. J H Chance	569	Cpl. William Lambert (Z)
491	L/Cpl. E Dodds MM (Z)	571	Pte. J E Spetch
493	Pte. W H Noble MM & bar	575	Pte. S Carrington
494	Pte. Charles Griffin (Z)	578	Pte. Samuel Walton (Z)
495	Cpl. Charles Richard Silburn (Z)	579	Pte. Stanley Tottle (Z)
496	Pte. James Henry Forsyth (Z)	580	Pte. Herbert Peter Spencer (Z)
497	L/Cpl. James Morrod DCM (Z)	582	Pte. Sydney Thompson (Z)
498	Pte. Thomas Conboy (Z)	583	Pte. A Watson
499	Pte. Robert Henry Rhodes (Z)	589	RQMS R Smith MID (D)
500	Pte. T G Woolons	591	Pte. Walter Leonard Johnson (Z)
503	Pte. George Samuel Stephenson Stead (Z)	592	Pte. Hubert Berwell Brown (Z)
504	Pte. Ernest Searby (Z)	595	Pte. John W Hacker (Z)
505	CSM William Marshall Silvester (Z)	596	Pte. F Proctor
506	Pte. Wilfred Reed (Z)	597	Sgt. William Pool MM (Dis)
509	Pte. George William Burnes (Dis)	598	Pte. George Frederick Dunn (Z)
510	Sgt. Edward G Oliver ^^	600	Pte. J A Callaghan
511	Cpl. George James Smith (Z)	602	Pte. W Blanchard
512	Cpl. C Barker	605	Cpl. Alfred Mills (Z)
517	Pte. G Kirby	607	CSM James Camplin* MID
518	Pte. Wilfred Lawson Edwards (Z)	608	Pte. Alexandra McCard (Dis)
519	Pte. W Lewis	609	Pte. Arthur Adams (Dis)
520	Pte. Harry Kirby (Z)	611	Pte. William Hall (Z)
522	Pte. Gilder Sawdon (Z)	612	Pte. T Swinden
525	Pte. John William Hobson (Z)	613	Pte. C A Green
526	Pte. George Ernest Briggs (Z)	615	Sgt. David Fox*
527	Pte. William Henry Rudd (Z)	619	Pte. Ernest Lord (Z)
528	Pte. E A Holmes	622	L/Cpl. G H Brown
529	Pte. J W Judge	623	Pte. H Temple
530	Pte. Ernest Wharam(Dis)	624	Sgt. Arthur Leonard Marriott (Z)
532	Pte. E Coupland	627	Pte. E Kennedy
533	Pte. Charles Butterworth (Dis)	635	Pte. Benjamin Garner (Z)
535	Pte. Frank Marshall (Z)	636	Pte. C Bogg

637	Pte. Alfred Ernest Belsher (Z)	732	Pte. Alfred Martin (Z)
638	Pte. Frederick Atkinson (Z)	733	Pte. Walter Evington (Z)
639	Pte. J E Wass	734	Pte. Thomas Blackbourn (Z)
641	Sgt. A C Waudby	737	Pte. J W Longhorn
642	Pte. George Arthur Wilkinson (Z)	738	Cpl. Fred Hallgarth (Z)
645	Pte. Arthur Colley (Z)	739	Pte. Martin Holmes (Dis)
646	Pte. Harold Andrew Munro (Dis)	741	Pte. Edwin Parkinson (Z)
647	Pte. James Lee (Z)	743	L/Cpl. Bernard Trowell MM
648	Pte. Ernest Land (Z)	744	Pte. Robert Bell
651	L/Cpl. C Green	746	Pte. P Brewster
654	Cpl. F Anderton (D)	748	Pte. David Gardner (Z)
657	Pte. Charles Robert Dove (Z)	751	Pte. George Huntley (Z)
658	Cpl. Edward Jordan (Z)	753	Pte. Joseph Harold Barnaby (Z)
659	Pte. M Emmerson	754	Pte. T A Beadle
664	Cpl. Frank Bearpark Boynton (Dis)	755	Pte. Samuel Wormald (Dis)
665	Pte. William Wells (Z)	757	Pte. Frank Marsall (Z)
666	Pte. Ernest Fisher (Z)	758	Pte. John William Roche (Z)
667	Sgt. H Snaith*	759	Pte. William Henry Essington Penfold (Z)
669	Pte. Tom Hall (Z)	760	Pte. P Cooper
670	Pte. W Clayton	765	Pte. Ernest Ross (Z)
673	Sgt. Charles John Nix MM	768	Pte. John Morley (Z)
674	Pte. William Simon Ashbridge (Z)	770	Pte. John Stanley Appleby (Z)
676	Pte. Seth Beckett (Z)	772	Sgt. H Sellers MM
678	Pte. James Padley (Z)	777	Pte. R J G Grimmer
679	Pte. Arthur William Ellyard (Z)	778	Cpl. Henage Cyril Ward*
681	Pte. H Hodgson	779	Pte. Edward Byrne
682	Pte. Robert Harris Weasenham (Dis)	780	Pte. E Shepperson
683	Pte. William Howe (Dis)	781	Cpl. D S McIntosh MID
684	Pte. James Levesley (Z)	782	Cpl. Albert Charles Mondon (Z)
690	Cpl. J H Kay	784	Cpl. Charles Henry Thacker MM (Z)
691	L/Cpl. R Ollett	785	Sgt. E Marritt DCM
694	Sgt. John Samuel Dunn (Z)	786	Pte. Thomas Parker (Z)
697	Pte. George Humphreys (Dis)	787	L/Cpl. T Overton
699	Pte. Thomas Percy Sangwin (Z)	788	Pte. Robert Derving (Z)
702	Pte. John Leng Moses	790	Sgt. Archibald George Fielder (Dis)
704	Sgt. R E Hart	791	Pte. J T Huteson
706	Pte. Charlie Grimwood (Z)	792	Sgt. James William Downie MM (Z)
707	CSM William Glentworth Woodall DCM (Z)	793	Pte. Walter Sutherland (Dis)
708	Pte. Harry Wodall (Z)	795	Pte. William Roberts
709	L/Cpl. J W Mason	796	Pte. Alfred E Cook (Z)
711	Pte. Robert Ellis Roper (Z)	798	Sgt. Victor Warwick*
712	Pte. J Newlove	799	Pte. J W Mason
713	Pte. Frederick Albert Roberts (Dis)	800	Pte. Kenneth Morton (Z)
715	Pte. G Downs MM	802	Pte. J E Allison MM
716	Pte. William Carey (Dis)	803	Pte. Alan Stamford MM
717	Pte. Samuel Witchell (Dis)	805	Cpl. Charles L Dearing MM & C-de-G (B)
718	Pte. James Shooter (Z)	809	Pte. J Walton (Z); also CQMS John Hadwin (D)
720	Sgt. Thomas Fisher Lamb MM & bar (Z)	810	Sgt. Edward Matthew Thompson (Z)
721	Pte. Wakter Wardle (Dis)	812	CQMS Edward Matthew Thompson DCM
723	Pte. James Edward Oliver (Z)	819	Pte. Ernest Cyril Strickland (Dis)
724	Pte. John William Myers (Z)	820	Pte. Samuel Winn (Z)
726	Pte. Harold George Butler (Z)	822	Pte. A Tennison
727	Pte. C Baldwin	823	Pte. B Varey
728	Pte. Frederick Wilfred Farnill (Z)	825	Pte. Ernest Tutty (Z)
730	L/Cpl. George William Willerton MM & bar	826	Cpl. F Featherstone

827	Pte. Arthur Hopkin (Z)	921	Sgt. Robert Nicholson*
829	Pte. George Nettleton (Z)	923	Pte. W A Edwards MM
831	Pte. M Black	924	Pte. John Basil Berry (Z)
832	Sgt. Jack Aarons MM	925	Pte. Harold Lawrence Garton (Dis)
833	Pte. John Samuel Huteson	926	CQMS C W Miller MID
837	Pte. Robert Smith	927	Pte. George Henry Winterbottom (Z)
840	Pte. David Carmichael (Z)	928	Pte. William Marsh MM (Z)
842	Pte. Richard Read (Z)	930	Sgt. Robert Stamford (Z)
843	Pte. F Woods	933	Cpl. Arnold Harry Watts (Z)
845	Pte. James Ernest Wilson (Z)	934	Pte. R Field
847	Pte. Charles William Stockdale (Z)	936	Pte. A Ward
848	Sgt. George Panton*	937	Sgt. James Arthur Pomfrey*
851	Sgt. Wilfrid Morrisey (Z)	938	Pte. George Frederick Wright (Z)
852	Pte. E Izod	940	Pte. Ernest Magner (Z)
855	Sgt. Thomas Bowden*	942	Pte. Samuel George Barnaby (Z)
856	Cpl. Edward Henry Wright (Dis)	943	Pte. Joseph Arthur Smith (Z)
857	Pte. William Ernest Penton (Z)	945	Pte. Albert Murray (Dis)
860	Pte. Samuel Herbert Holmes	947	Cpl. James A Deary MM & C-de-G (F) (Z)
861	Pte. Henry Johnson (Z)	948	Sgt. W Townsend
862	Pte. Harry Sowerby (Dis)	949	Pte. Daniel Sutton (Dis)
863	Pte. O Johnson	951	Pte. Thomas William Andrews (Z)
864	Pte. William Fisher Gardam (Z)	952	Pte. E C Pickering
865	Pte. Frederick Charles Richards (Z)	954	Pte. W Gaunt
869	Pte. George Robert Grantham (Z)	956	Pte. W Palmer
870	Pte. Percy Kennedy (Z)	958	Pte. F Dook
872	Pte. J A Paterson	964	Pte. Charles Hewson (Z)
874	Pte. G Oakes MM	965	Pte. George Edward King (D)~
876	Pte. Albert Edward Jenions (Dis)	967	Pte. J Brand
877	Pte. Harry Walker (Z)	971	Pte. J Goulding
879	Pte. A J McKay (Z)	973	Pte. George Gray (Z)
880	Pte. Rupert Johnson (Z)	974	Pte. Walter Hildred (Dis)
882	Sgt. Fred Smith (Z)	975	Pte. Edward Topham (Z)
883	Sgt. J L Hesletine	976	Pte. Alfred Larkman (Dis)
884	Pte. John Morritt (Dis)	978	Pte. H F Houghton
885	RSM William Fillis MID (Z)	979	Pte. Albert Watson (Z)
886	Pte. Fred Dixon Marsden (Z)	980	Cpl. H Andrews
887	Sgt. Cyril Ephraim R Harris*	984	Pte. Harry Arthur Thompson (Z)
891	Sgt. John Dunn MM (Z)	985	Pte. George Dunling (Z)
892	Pte. John Alsopp Edwards (Z)	986	Sgt. W W Needler
893	Pte. A L Hayhurst	987	Cpl. Henry Mennell (Z)
895	Pte. M Everson	989	CSM Thomas Farey DCM (Z)
896	Pte. S W Lowe	990	Pte. William Fenton Binns (Z)
897	Pte. George Kirk (Z)	992	Pte. J W Matthews
898	C/Sgt. William Frankish*	994	Sgt. L Fussey MM
899	Pte. Clarence Arthur Aspinall (Dis)	996	Pte. Alfred Ernest Baker (Z)
900	Pte. Edward Dixon (Dis)	999	Sgt. Herbert Peter Norton (Dis)
902	Pte. F Herbert	1000	Pte. Thomas Baker (Z)
903	Pte. William Wilson (Z)	1001	Pte. J Boyes
904	Pte. Ernest Gibson (Z)	1004	Pte. Joseph Lancaster (Z)
908	Pte. John Dook (Z)	1005	Pte. Edward Stather (Z)
910	Pte. George Henry Bell (Z)	1006	Pte. Richard Fay (Dis)
911	Pte. Robert Frederick Lawrence (Z)	1009	Pte. Charles Needham (Z)
912	Pte. Thomas Brogden (Z)	1013	Pte. Harry Hammond (Z)
913	Sgt. K Hodgson	1015	Sgt. J F Watson
914	Pte. Cecil Hodgson (Z)	1016	Pte. G H Bell

1019	Pte. Richard Wilson (Z)	1125	Pte. S Pick
1021	Sgt. Arthur Wood (Dis)	1126	Pte. Alfred Jackson (Z)
1025	Pte. Thomas Harold Dinsdale (Dis)	1127	Pte. T Smart
1026	Pte. Alfred Barker (Z)	1128	Pte. F Carrington
1030	Pte. Frank Groves (Z)	1129	Pte. George Edward Hayes (Z)
1031	Pte. C A Herring	1133	Pte. William Henry Adams (Z)
1033	Pte. Edgar Heweth (Z)	1134	Pte. Harold Anderson (Z)
1034	Cpl. Frederick Winter (Dis)	1136	Pte. J W Bolder
1036	Pte. Gilbert Ahern (Z)	1137	Pte. T Beels
1037	Pte. James H Wheatcroft (Dis)	1138	Pte. Albert Bentley (Dis)
1038	Sgt. E Deyes	1141	Pte. H Bentley
1039	Pte. Robert Fletcher (Z)	1142	Pte. Harry June Bibby (Dis)
1041	Cpl. Norman Jules Marsh*	1146	Pte. Frederick John Carr (Dis)
1043	Pte. Clarence Leonard (Z)	1147	Pte. Thomas Patrick Clarke (Z)
1045	Pte. M Maroney	1148	Pte. Edward Daddy (Z)
1046	Pte. John Scarborough Clark (Z)	1154	Pte. J Eddison
1053	Pte. G T Barker	1157	Pte. Charles Henry Fisher (D)
1054	Pte. Alfred Watson MM (Z)	1159	Pte. Alfred Fieldsend (Z)
1057	Pte. Joseph Smith Rooke (Z)	1161	Pte. Joseph Fountain (Z)
1058	Pte. Fred Oakley (Z)	1164	Pte. E Gould MM
1062	Pte. Robert James Hill (Z)	1165	Pte. George Grassby (Dis)
1063	Pte. W Pool	1166	Pte. Herbert Harper (Z)
1064	Pte. Charles Edward Thompson (Z)	1167	Pte. Harry Harrison (Z)
1065	Pte. Clifford William Nurse (Z)	1170	Pte. William Henry Hopkinson (Z)
1066	Pte. Thomas Austwick (Z)	1171	Pte. Thomas Nart (Z)
1068	Pte. Cyril Green (Z)	1174	Pte. John Jennison (Z)
1073	Pte. Robert Cook (Dis)	1176	Pte. E W Johnson
1074	Sgt. Frank Lord (Dis)	1179	Pte. Oswald Kershaw (Z)
1075	Pte. T C Plaskitt	1180	Pte. R Kirby
1076	Pte. Gerard Walter Cuttill (Dis)	1181	Pte. Charles Lee (Dis)
1078	Pte. C W Stuart	1183	Pte. T Loft
1081	Sgt. Thomas Spencer (Z)	1184	Pte. Percy Longman (Z)
1082	Pte. Bertram Gilbert Horner (Z)	1186	Pte. J Marchant
1087	Sgt. Peter McNally (Z)	1187	L/Cpl. E E Blanchard
1088	Pte. S Laughton	1188	Pte. A T Marshall
1089	Pte. F Shaw	1190	Pte. Thomas Ernest Meara (Z)
1091	CSM Reginald Arthur Routley*	1193	Pte. John W Morrill (Z)
1092	Pte. John James Harrison (Z)	1196	Pte. William Joseph Neylon (Z)
1097	Pte. Herbert Hardwick (Z)	1197	Cpl. George Frederick Nicholson (Z)
1098	Pte. Robert Ernest Windle (Z)	1198	Pte. Hugh O'Neill (Dis)
1100	Pte. Harold Harrison (Dis)	1200	Pte. W de P Parker
1103	Pte. Robert Short (Z)	1203	Pte. F Raby
1105	Pte. Cyril Gray (Z)	1205	Pte. Thomas Richardson (Z)
1106	Pte. Peter Jackson (Dis)	1206	Pte. Robert Boynton Richman (Z)
1107	Pte. John Harrison (Z)	1207	Cpl. Thomas Saywers DCM
1111	Pte. J W Johnson	1208	Pte. Frederick Smith (Z)
1112	Pte. G E Goodson	1211	Pte. Joseph William Sykes (Z)
1114	CQMS. John Hill*	1212	Pte. Clarence William Taylor (Z)
1115	Pte. Ernest Charles Stubbs (Z)	1214	Pte. Richard Sempers (Z)
1116	Pte. Robert Samuel Robinson	1215	Pte. William Henry Wainman (Z)
1120	L/Cpl. George Broughton^^	1216	Pte. M H Ward
1121	Pte. Walter Brodie (Z)	1217	Pte. Tom Kemp Watkinson (Z)
1122	Pte. William F Bayliss (Z)	1218	Pte. George Andrew White (Z)
1123	Pte. Harold Gladstone (Z)	1219	Pte. A Willcox
1124	Pte. George Marshall (Z)	1220	Pte. G W Willcox

1221	Pte. David Sidney Willerton MM	
1222	Pte. G W Willey	
1224	Pte. John William Wilkinson (Z)	
1226	Pte. Joseph J Wise (Z)	
1227	Pte. Robert Wise (Z)	
1228	Pte. Joseph Edward Wray (Z)	
1229	Pte. Arthur Blakey MM	
1230	Pte. Edward Cottrell (Dis)	
1231	Pte. Charles Edward Craven (Z)	
1232	Pte. Henry Davies (Z)	
1233	Pte. William Stephens Elgar (Dis)	
1234	Pte. W Holdstock	
1235	Pte. Frank William Major (Dis)	
1237	Pte. Charles Proctor (Z)	
1240	Pte. John Edward Stephenson (Z)	
1242	Pte. Joseph Vickers (Dis)	
1244	Pte. G E Lowen MM	
1245	Pte. James William Atkins (Z)	
1248	Pte. Peter Burns (Z)	
1249	Pte. H Cain	
1254	Pte. Fred Broadbent (Z)	
1255	Pte. F Hamilton	
1256	Pte. H Johnson	
1259	Pte. John William Kirby (Z)	
1260	Pte. Dickinson Matthews (Z)	
1262	Pte. John Thomas Middleton (Z)	
1263	Pte. Percy Moore (Z)	
1264	Pte. Jonathan Newman (Z)	
1266	Pte. Clarence Soames (Z)	
1268	Pte. H Thompson	
1269	Pte. Percy Thornton (Z)	
1270	Pte. A R Thurnell	
1271	Pte. R Timlin (Z)	
1272	Pte. Henry Robert Baldam (Z)	
1276	Pte. Leonard Cook (Z)	
1278	Pte. Harold Norfolk (Z)	
1279	Pte. H Theakston	
1281	Pte. L H Stark	
1285	Pte. Arthur Lister (Z)	
1288	Pte. Harry Gibson (Z)	
1289	Sgt. C W Bonas MM & bar	
1290	Pte. Rawson Hanry Dunham (Z)	
1291	Pte. Henry Pearson (Z)	
1292	L/Cpl. Richard Wilson Peck MM	
1294	Pte. Thomas J Bowler (Z)	
1296	Pte. George William Sweeting (Z)~	
1298	Pte. Arthur William Curtis (Dis)	
1299	Pte. Arthur Harrison MM (Z)	
1300	Pte. Alfred Hayes (Dis)	
1302	Pte. James Cawkwell (Z)	
1309	Pte. W P Busby	
1310	Pte. Tom John Lewis Downs (Dis)	
1311	Pte. Albert Dorley (Z)	
1312	Pte. A Cade	
1313	Pte. Richard Simpkin Jackson (Z)	
1314	Pte. Charles Henry Lancaster (Z)	
1319	Pte. A B Tasker	
1320	Pte. G E Warnes	
1325	Pte. James Humphrey MM	
1327	Pte. T W Eastwood	
1328	Pte. S Edmond	
1329	Pte. George Stanley Dixon (Z)	
1331	Pte. Kenneth Brotherton (Dis)	
1334	Pte. Thomas McDonald (Dis)	
1336	Pte. C Clarke	
1339	Pte. Frank Boland (Z)	
1340	Pte. Thomas Cawkwell (Dis)	
1341	Pte. Frank Collinson (Z)	
1342	Pte. A E Elston	
1343	Pte. Arthur Ernest Fletcher (Z)	
1344	Pte. J Foston	
1345	Pte. E Harrison	
1348	Cpl. J W Keeble MM	
1350	Pte. George William Lowthorpe (Z)	
1351	Pte. A Mallender	
1352	Pte. Herbert McLean (Z)	
1354	Pte. Thomas Henry Mitchell (Dis)	
1355	Pte. George William Andrews (Z)	
1357	Pte. Alfred Rudkin (Z)	
1358	Pte. Walter Rutledge MM (Dis)	
1360	Pte. Walter Tunnard Wales (Z)	
1361	Pte. Henry Wallis (Z)	
1365	Pte. George Hawkins (Z)	
1367	Pte. James Richard Shepherd (Dis)	
1369	Pte. Walter Wright (Z)	
1371	Pte. William H Freeman (Dis)	
1373	Pte. Ernest Herbert Baldam (Z)	
1374	Pte. Thomas R Cracroft (Z)	
1375	Pte. Charlie Shirbon (Z)	
1376	Pte. Francis William Watson (Z)	
1377	Pte. James Charles Millington (Z)	
1379	Cpl. P Stothard	
1383	Pte. Albert E Derrick (Dis)	
1385	Pte. Francis Cyril Loftus (Z)	
1386	Pte. William Morgan (Z)	
1388	Pte. Joseph William Jackson (Z)	
1389	Pte. Thomas Frederick Turner (Z)	
1391	Pte. Gerald G Shields (Z)	
1392	Pte. William Thomas Smith (Z)	
1393	Pte. W Wells	
1395	Pte. J Maddra	
1396	Pte. Edmund Stephenson (Z)	
1397	Pte. A Cook	
1398	Pte. Leonard Winship (Z)	
1399	Pte. Walter George Newton (Dis)	
1400	Pte. James Henry Robertson (Z)	
1402	Pte. John Clarkson MM (Dis)	
1405	Pte. J W Dodds	
1406	Pte. Walter Atkinson (Z)	
1407	Pte. W Long	

1408	Pte. John Frankland (Z)
1409	Pte. Joseph Elliott (Z)
1411	Pte. Richard Henry Landen Medaille d'Honneur avec glaves (en argent) (Z)
1412	Pte. William Henry Gudgeon (Z)
1413	Pte. George Green (Z)
1414	Pte. John William Brown (Dis)
1415	Pte. Bartholomew Hartnell (Dis)
1416	Pte. Frederick Philips (Dis)
1417	Pte. John Henry Cox (Z)
1419	Pte. Daniel Davies (Z)
1421	Pte. William Bethel Page (Dis)
1424	Pte. Albert Victor Charles Baker
1426	Pte. Harry Reginald Porter (Z)
1428	WOII George E Sonley MM (Z)
1429	Pte. J H Turner
1430	Pte. John Watkin (Z)
1432	Pte. T Dixon
1434	Pte. Thomas Ridoutt Burfoot (Z)
1435	Pte. R Bentley
1441	Pte. Thomas Potter (Z)
1442	Pte. C W Redfearn
1443	Pte. John Spark (Z)
1445	Pte. George Wild (Dis)
1446	Pte. Gilbert Harrison (Z)
1447	Pte. Alfred Turner (Z)
1448	Pte. Thomas H Hearne (Z)
1451	Pte. Alf Hunt (Z)
1452	Pte. J Taylor
1454	Pte. Leonard Charlton (Z)
1455	Pte. Johan E Johnson (Z)
1456	L/Cpl. John Hackitt DCM & Bar & MM (Z)
1459	Pte. G C W Smith
1461	Pte. Alfred Taylor (Z)
1463	Pte. James Wakerley ^^
1465	Pte. Thomas Taylor Ibbetson (Z)
1466	Pte. Clifford Dibb (Z)
1470	Pte. Thompson Cross (Z)
1471	Pte. Walter Edward Cooper (Z)
???	CQMS John Hadwin
???	B Bland
???	C Turner
???	W Cautley
???	F W Moore
???	H Brown
???	T Cheetham
???	J Hogarth
???	D Robertson
???	Cpl. Norton
???	Pte. Langfard
???	J W Goforth
???	J Levesley

12th Battalion Nominal Roll

2	Pte. William Walter Harding
3	Pte. Wilson Holyroyd (Z)
4	Pte. George Silver (Z)
5	Pte. G H Humphrey
7	L/Cpl. S Chapman
8	Sgt. Henry Rose (Z)
9	Sgt. J W Bibby
11	Pte. R Jarvis
12	RQMS Harold Herbert Granger MID (Z)
13	Pte. Percy Smith (Dis)
14	Pte. F Beckett
17	CSM Frank Crabtree* MID
18	Pte. Arthur Dixon (Z)
19	Pte. Arthur Richard Thomas (Z)
20	Pte. Benjamin Wainman (Z)
21	Pte. John Cunningham VC (Dis)
22	Pte. C Hicks
25	Pte. R Brown
26	Pte. David Reed (Dis)
28	Sgt. Percy Freeman DCM
30	Pte. Frederick Wilkinson (Z)
33	Pte. James Stephenson (Dis)
35	Sgt. Bruce Sherwood (Z)
36	Sgt. Claude Sherwood (Dis)
37	Sgt. Frank Wardell (Dis)
40	Sgt. S W Wilkinson MID
41	Pte. Thomas Milner (Dis)
42	Pte. H Hull
43	Pte. L Knowles
44	Cpl. Edward Kent Waite*
48	Sgt. Percy Weatherhogg Bronze Medal for Military Valour (I) (Z)
49	Pte. P Jones
50	Pte. Edward Archer (Z)
51	Pte. C Challans
52	Pte. Harold Tweedy (Z)
53	Sgt. C Morley
56	Pte. A W Davies
57	Pte. F B Brown
61	Sgt. C Whitely
63	Pte. Harold A Carr (Z)
64	Pte. H Higginson
65	Pte. A E Hunt
66	Pte. Harold Hunt (Z)
67	Cpl. Claude Duval Leach (Z)
70	Pte. S Chapman
71	Pte. William Clark (Z)
72	Pte. W H Stathers
74	CSM Robert Richard Horsley Whitlam (Dis)
75	Pte. William Trow Partridge (Dis)
76	Pte. S Blackbourn
77	Cpl. T E Smith
78	Pte. W Clark
79	Pte. Gilliard Summer Palmer Gale (Dis)
82	Pte. Ernest Humphrey (Z)
83	Pte. Ernest Frank Hunt (Z)

85	Sgt. Harold Albert Smith (Dis)
86	Pte. Ernest Woolass (Dis)
88	Pte. Arthur James Coleman (Z)
89	Cpl. Alfred Applegard (Dis)
90	Sgt. J W Bibby C-de-G (B) (Z)
91	Pte. A E Cooper
92	Pte. Henry Wood Penith (Z)
93	Pte. E McManus
95	Sgt. Francis Robson Warren*
96	CSM T Chapman
98	C/Sgt. James Smail Speirs*
99	Pte. John Marwood (Z)
100	Pte. G Spink
101	Sgt. William Sydney Carratt*
105	Pte. George Bridges (Z)
106	Pte. Stanley Lancaster (Z)
107	Sgt. Harold Chandos Micklethwaite*
110	Pte. C O Robinson
111	Pte. Clifford Lee (Z)
112	Pte. H Wogden
115	L/Cpl. Arthur Jesse Tandy*
116	Pte. William Loran Bland*
117	Cpl. John Edward Ounsworth (Z)
121	Pte. George Henry Farr (Z)
126	Pte. G Harrison
127	Pte. F Ness
129	Pte. L White
130	Pte. Thomas Reginald Hilton (Dis)
132	Pte. H Binge
133	Pte. H L Bond
136	Pte. George Henry Edmond (Z)
137	Pte. Albert Bushman (Z)
139	Sgt. Ernest Lovell* MID
140	Pte. Charles Houghton (Z)
142	L/Cpl. J Tonnecliffe
147	CSM Herbert Temple (Z)
148	Pte. E V Robinson
151	Pte. Hubert William Castle (Z)
154	Pte. Thomas Cosgrave (Z)
156	Pte. Alexander Kellaway (Z)
157	Cpl. Robert Burwell (Dis)
158	Pte. Harold Hobson (Z)
159	Pte. John Henry Dunn (Z)
160	Pte. Fred Hunt (Dis)
161	Pte. F H Dobbs
163	Sgt. Cecil Claridge*
164	Pte. Charles Fred Smith (Z)
165	Pte. George Wilby (Z)
166	Pte. Walter Davidson (Dis)
169	Pte. E Cliff
170	Pte. George Harland (Z)
171	Pte. W Green
172	Pte. A Holland
175	Pte. Ernest Hunter (Z)
176	Pte. Arthur Charles Stable (Z)

179	Pte. J Hall
180	Pte. John Richardson (Dis)
184	Pte. W Irving
185	Pte. Walter George Richardson (Z)
186	Pte. E Pearson
189	L/Cpl. W Wilson
190	Pte. Edwin Talbot Billany (Z)
192	Sgt. Walter Lumb (Z)
194	Pte. Arthur Blakestone (Dis)
196	Pte. Henry Alfred Peacock (Z)
198	Pte. Arthur Rawling (Z)
200	Pte. C W Dukes
204	Pte. Harry Cook (Z)
205	Pte. Rdgar Keene Hustler (Z)
207	Pte. Benjamin Brooks (Dis)
209	Pte. Frank Wright (Z)
211	Sgt. A McDonald
212	Pte. Haold Alexander McGrath*
214	Pte. Arthur Borill (Z)
215	Pte. George Sergent (Z)
216	L/Cpl. G Burnham
218	Pte. John Henry Brown (Dis)~
222	RQMS William John Rodway (Z)
224	Pte. Harold Billany (Dis)
225	C/Sgt. Arthur Henry Empson Wingate (Z)
227	Pte. Sydney John Oliver (Z)
229	Pte. Harold Barmforth (Z)
230	Pte. George William Marson (Dis)
231	Pte. A Moulds
233	Pte. Hubert H Anderson (Z)
234	Cpl. John Arthur Smith MM
236	Pte. J W Burdon
237	Pte. Joseph C Goodson (Dis)
238	Pte. A N Woodall
241	Pte. Leonard Frank Burns (Z)
245	Pte. Arthur Jennison (Dis)
247	Pte. Frank Taylor (Dis)
250	L/Cpl. G H Lun
254	Pte. Daniel Murray (Z)
257	Sgt. Albert Walters DCM
259	Cpl. C W Henson
262	Sgt. Walter John Walker*
263	Pte. Edward Emslie (Z)
264	Pte. John Douglas Burrows (Dis)
266	Pte. Charles Robert Rushton (Dis)
267	Cpl. W A Rushton
268	Pte. Harold Fields (Dis)
269	Pte. Charles Bailey (Z)
270	Pte. Thomas Metcalfe Gibben (Z)
271	Pte. Benjamin Johnson (Z)
275	Pte. Charles Edward Bilton (Z)
277	Pte. Sidney Bricklebank (Dis)
278	Cpl. George William Holmes (Z)
279	Pte. George Herbert Lovatt (Z)
282	Pte. A Barnes

284	Pte. Edgar Blashill Harrison MM (Z)
285	Pte. George Hoyes (Dis)
288	Sgt. Herbert Dewson DCM
290	Pte. Harry Callaghan (Dis)
296	Pte. E Hadlow
297	Sgt. E W Woods
299	Sgt. Edward Spafford DCM (Z)
300	Pte. John W F Smith (Dis)
302	L/Cpl. W Milner
303	Pte. J Dimmack
304	Pte. Uriah Spencer (Z)
305	Pte. James William Kerry MM (Z)
309	Pte. Joseph Leonard Hudson (Z)
310	Pte. Lewis Anderson (Z)
311	Sgt. W W Neal
312	Pte. William Alfred Earle (Z)
316	Sgt. R Easingwold
318	Sgt. Alfred Edmund Coman MID (Dis)
319	Pte. Henry Atkin (Z)
320	Pte. Albert John Venton (Dis)
321	Pte. Charles Frederick Holiday (Dis)
323	Pte. T Pullinger
325	Pte. Frederick George Fuller (Z)
328	Pte. John Henry Brown
329	Pte. Charles William Craggy
330	Pte. W E Cox
332	Pte. Herbert Parker (Z)
334	Pte. C Dixon
335	Pte. W G Jessop
336	Sgt. S Johnson
337	L/Cpl. F Savage
342	Sgt. Henry A Curtis (Z)
344	Pte. Wilfred Taylor (Z)
345	Pte. George William Johnson (Dis)
346	Cpl. Thomas Stanley Cunningham (Z)
347	Pte. W C Jackson
349	Pte. Richard Henry Penrose (Z)
350	Pte. J A Cook
351	Sgt. Harold S Osborne (Z)
353	Pte. Fred Robinson (Z)
354	Pte. Ernest Batton (Dis)
361	Pte. Albert Edward Leadbetter (Z)
362	Pte. John William Chapman (Z)
363	Pte. George Parkinson (Z)
364	Pte. James Richardson (Z)
365	Pte. George Edward Marshall (Dis)
367	Pte. Robert Castle (Dis)
369	Pte. James William Goring (Z)
370	Pte. John William Gleeson (Dis)
372	Sgt. George Witham*
375	Pte. Thomas Hodgson (Z)
377	Pte. H Hawcroft
378	Pte. J A Hodgson
382	Pte. J A Barker
384	Pte. H Edmond
385	Pte. V Kimm (Z)
387	Pte. Matk Leetham (Z)
388	Pte. Thomas Tookey (Z)
391	Cpl. F R Marlow
392	Pte. A Benn
394	Pte. Harry Orwin (Z)
396	Pte. S Whitehead
401	Pte. T Allen
405	Pte. John William Blakestone (Z)
406	Pte. Whitfield
407	Sgt. J T Holmes
408	Pte. William Thomas Aiken (Dis)
410	Pte. T E Pearson
412	Pte. W Campion
415	Pte. Charles A Wood (Z)
417	Pte. S Rowbottom
420	Sgt. D Taylor
422	Sgt. Thomas Jackson Allen*
424	Pte. John Henry Atkin (Dis)
426	Pte. W Embley
431	Pte. Ernest Arthur Lahey (Z)
433	Pte. C Richardson
437	Pte. Robert Wilde (Z)
439	Pte. John William Silvery (Z)
440	Pte. George Edward Yarker (Dis)
441	Pte. Thomas Bromby (Z)
442	Pte. G E Binning
444	Pte. Edward Lowe (Z)
445	Pte. Thomas H Livingston (Z)
446	Pte. Robert Clayton Shaw (Z)
451	Pte. W Jameson
453	Sgt. Arthur Chester MM MID (Dis)
455	Sgt. Charles William Hailes (Dis)
456	Pte. H Oxendale
457	Pte. T Egan
458	Pte. Thomas Denton (Z)
459	Pte. Arthur Barkworth (Dis)
462	Pte. William Henry Bodecott (dis)
464	Pte. Arthur Douglas Clark (Z)
467	Pte. Mattehw Frazer (Z)
472	Pte. Arthur Heath (Dis)
473	Cpl. Arthur Kirlew (Z)
475	Pte. Thomas Albert Kerman (Z)
476	Pte. Ernest Richard Kidby (Z)
477	Pte. Frederick Kent (Z)
481	Pte. W Riches
482	Sgt. H Richardson
483	Sgt. George William Spence MID (Z)
485	Pte. Cyril Skinner (Z)
487	Pte. Herbert Steels (Dis)
488	Cpl. Arthur Lewis Tuton
489	Pte. J H Tuton
490	Pte. John William Warkup (Z)
491	Pte. George Witty (Z)
493	Pte. H Wilson

494	Pte. A Young	597	Pte. William Henry Todd (Dis)
497	Pte. Charles William Brant (Dis)	601	Pte. Charles Ernest Welburn (Z)
500	Pte. Ernest Day (Z)	602	Pte. John H Wharram (Dis)
505	Pte. Charles Brooks (Z)	604	Pte. J Beasy
508	Sgt. A Bayston	605	Pte. S Blakeston
509	Pte. John Everitt (Z)	606	Pte. Tom Blazier (Z)
510	Sgt. George Albert Aket (Z)	608	Cpl. John Haran MM (Z)
511	Sgt. C Scott	610	Pte. William Herbert Johnson (Z) ^^
512	CSM David Claude Blandford MC (Z)	616	Pte. George Livingstone (Dis)
513	Pte. W H West	627	Pte. Richard Lawson (Z)
514	Sgt. Ernest Richard Curry (Dis)	633	Pte. Edward Johnson (Z)
516	Pte. T P Edmunds	634	Pte. Tom Andrew (Z)
517	Pte. Samuel Grabine (Z)	635	Cpl. S Barker
518	Pte. H Hall	637	Sgt. Charles Cottis (Z)
522	Cpl. Charles Harry Sharp (dis)	642	Pte. W Hobson
523	Pte. John Albert Blazier (Dis)	643	Cpl. E Robinson MM
526	Cpl. George Fowler Grayston (dis)	647	Pte. William Dodsworth
534	Pte. Thomas Charles Hallgarth (Z)	650	Pte. Charles Henry Kitching MM
535	Pte. Sidney Jarvis (Z)	652	Pte. Harold Sidney Walker (Z)
536	Pte. Fred Jewitt (Dis)	653	Pte. Albert Dixon (Dis)
541	Pte. Dalton Rimmington (Z)	655	Pte. Fred Lee (Z)
543	Pte. F Searby	656	Pte. Thomas Arthur Walton (Z)
545	Pte. Fred Welch*	657	Pte. Robert Fox (Z)
546	Pte. James Welburn (Z)	658	Pte. Walter Shaw (Z)
547	Pte. Joseph Ernest Woolas (Dis)	660	Pte. Thomas Young (Z)
548	Pte. Charles Harry Ansell (Z)	663	Pte. Wiliam Snow (Z)
549	Pte. Harry Brown (Z)	665	Pte. J H Tomlinson
550	Pte. Horace Brown (Z)	666	Pte. Joseph Munday Kemp (Dis)
551	L/Cpl. J Busby	668	Pte. D Booth
554	Pte. C E Dalton	670	Pte. Henry East (Z)
555	Pte. John Richard Dick (Z)	678	Pte. Francis Wilson (Z)
556	Pte. William Donaldson (Dis)	679	Pte. James Williams (Z)
559	Pte. Leonard Farrow Green (Z)	680	Pte. Charles Thomas Kennington (Z)
560	Pte. Valentine Haines (Z)	681	Pte. Alfred Torling (Z)
561	Sgt. Alfred Hodges (Z)	683	Cpl. Daniel Mulholland (Z)
562	Pte. William Edward Hutton (Z)	684	Pte. H Leake
563	Pte. Joseph Lanch (Z)	687	Pte. J R Alcock
564	Pte. John Thomas Marshall (Dis)	691	Cpl. Thomas Vinton James ^^
565	Pte. Arthur Parker (Dis)	692	Pte. William Johnson (Dis)
566	Pte. Frank Richmond (Z)	693	Pte. Charles Peter Mayhew (Dis)
568	Pte. W S Wales (Z)	697	Pte. Sam Stephenson (Dis)
570	Pte. Frederick Charles Markham (Z)	698	L/Cpl. H Whisker MM
573	Pte. George Mee (Z)~	699	Pte. Cyril Young (Z)
574	Sgt. G Arnell	700	Pte. Christopher Allan (Z)
575	Pte. James William Bloomfield (Z)	704	Pte. Walter Brown (Dis)
578	Pte. A Brown	705	Pte. John T Hainsworth (Z)
579	Pte. John Brownlee (Z)	706	Pte. T Wiles
584	Pte. David Dickson (Dis)	709	Pte. E Pratley
585	Cpl. F Fenton	710	Pte. William Popplewell (Z)
587	Pte. R P Franks	711	Pte. G W Martin
589	Pte. W Harrison	714	Pte. John Herbert Jones (Z)
591	Pte. George Henry Jacques (dis)	717	Pte. H Heath
594	Cpl. Charles Robinson*	718	Pte. Charles Frederick Haldenby (Z)
595	Pte. Ambrose Fisher Stevens (Dis)	721	Sgt. Thomas Frederick Guest MM
596	Pte. Jack Thornburn (Z)	722	Pte. C Blackburn

723	Pte. Richard Andrews (Dis)	847	Pte. George William Dean (Dis)
724	Pte. C R Woyen	851	Pte. J E Fenton
727	Pte. Anthony Kingston (Z)	853	Pte. Christopher Turpin (Z)
729	Pte. Harry Easton (Z)	854	Pte. Arthur Moore (Z)
730	Pte. George Henry Galloway (Z)	856	Sgt. Walter Clark (Dis)
733	Pte. E Kirkwood	858	Cpl. Harry Retberg*
735	Pte. J W Steels	861	Cpl. Peter Livingston (Z)
737	Pte. Percy Starkey (Dis)	862	Pte. T Gill
745	Pte. W King	865	Sgt. A Braithwaite
747	Pte. A Hall	966	Pte. S Binnington
748	Pte. Harold Douglas (Z)	868	Sgt. James H Gosling MID (Z)
750	Pte. Edwin Staveley Noble (Z)	869	Pte. A Roo
754	Cpl. Edward Kershaw MID (Z)	871	Pte. Joseph Des Forges (Z)
755	Pte. John William Hardbottle (Z)	873	Pte. E Cowlan
760	Pte. S Blackburn	876	Pte. Charles Arthur Roberts (Z)
761	Pte. F Rudd	877	L/Cpl. A Collinson
763	Pte. R Stoker	878	Pte. Francis Joseph Clancey (Dis)
765	Pte. J H Brigham	879	Pte. E Eley
767	Cpl. George William Capper (Z)	881	Pte. H S Lowther
772	Pte. A P Waters	884	Pte. Cyril Warcup (Z)
775	Pte. Arthur Thompson (Dis)	886	Pte. Charles Bennett (Z)
776	Pte. Charles William Cobb (Dis)	887	Pte. D Boothby
779	Pte. Alfred Willaim Brooksbank (Z)	888	Sgt. William Arthur Bone DCM & MM
780	Pte. William Jackson Clark (Z)	889	L/Cpl. W R Chapman
781	Pte. Herbert Holmes (Z)	891	Pte. D Cain (Dis)
783	Pte. T H Larvin	892	Pte. F Anderson
784	Pte. Frank O'Kane (Dis)	894	Pte. H W Taylor (D)~
785	Pte. William Williams (Dis)	897	Pte. Albert Edward Wood (Dis)
788	Pte. Leonard Atkinson Scott (Z)	900	Pte. Thomas Pollock (Z)
791	Pte. H Hebden	903	Pte. G W Tarling
792	Pte. A H Cocking	904	Pte. J Blain
793	Pte. George Robert Grinsdale (Z)	905	Pte. Alfred Clubley (Dis)
797	Pte. Edward Stanley (Dis)	908	Pte. John Kennedy (Dis)
800	Pte. J McDonald	910	Pte. Harold Cyril Brown (Z)
802	Pte. H Henderson	914	Pte. John Dyson (Z)
804	Pte. Charles Kirby Harrison (Z)	915	Pte. John Bernard Cyril Cook (Z)
808	Pte. James Edward Kemp (Z)	917	Pte. William Henry Broadbent (Z)
809	Pte. G A Shea	918	Pte. George Albert Barker (Dis)
816	Pte. Frederick Anderson (Dis)	919	Pte. John Spencer (Dis)
818	Pte. A Broderick	920	Pte. William Mills Wilson (Z)
823	Pte. Frederick Joseph Murray (Dis)	921	Cpl. Hermann Alexander Wessels*
824	Cpl. William Pindar (Z)	922	Pte. Clarence Wells (Z)
826	Pte. Alfred Windle (Z)	929	Pte. G Morfitt
827	Pte. David Harrison (Z)	930	Pte. E McManus
828	Pte. D McGowan	931	Pte. Thomas Manwood Lister (Z)
830	Pte. Edgar Collinson MM (Z)	932	Pte. Philip Lenney (Z)
831	Pte. Arthur Wattam (Z)	933	Pte. Alfred Kirk (Z)
836	Pte. Frederick Harvey Wilmot (Dis)	934	L/Cpl. J Jordan
838	Pte. H Johnson	938	Pte. E Green
839	Pte. John William Moran (Dis)	939	Pte. J W Fletcher
841	Pte. H Spencer	940	Pte. A Jackson
842	Pte. G Neall	946	Pte. W H Spencer
843	Pte. William Shaw (Dis)	947	Pte. Arthur Milner (Dis)
844	Pte. Thomas Henry Tindall (Z)	948	Pte. Arthur Mallory (Z)
845	Pte. Feneley Blackburn (Dis)	949	Pte. Frank Lee (Z)

952	Pte. W Hatch		1067	Pte. Thomas Brown (Z)
955	Pte. Joseph Cooper (Z)		1070	Pte. William Brown
959	Pte. J W Shields MM		1071	Sgt. Albert Victor Bell DCM
960	Pte. George Osgerby (Z)		1072	Cpl. Thomas Henry Ryall (Dis)
961	Pte. John Wood (Dis)		1073	Pte. John MacWhirter (Z)
963	Pte. J W Mills		1075	Pte. Thomas Bowman Eastwood (Z)
967	Pte. Herbert William James (Dis)		1076	Pte. James Hall (Dis)
968	Pte. William Hopkinson (Z)		1080	Pte. George Leonard Pickering (Z)
970	Pte. George Pattison (Z)		1081	Pte. Arthur Henry Acey (Z)
971	Pte. F Motherby		1083	Pte. Arthur Stanley Akester (Dis)
974	Pte. Claude Schultz (Z)		1085	Pte. T W Charlton
978	Pte. W Stainforth		1086	Pte. Thomas Ward (Z)
981	Pte. Harold Smith (Z)		1088	Pte. Thomas Henry Cone (Z)
983	Pte. William Spencer (Z)		1091	Pte. William Proctor (Dis)
987	Pte. Robert Brown Wilson (Z)		1092	Pte. Leonard Winship (Z)
990	Pte. Edmund McKee (Dis)		1094	Pte. E Lane
991	L/Cpl. G McKee		1097	Pte. D Mc Kenzie
994	Pte. Jack Marshall (Z)		1100	Pte. Joseph Robert Jackson (Z)
999	Pte. J Hobson		1101	Pte. James Arthur Cullum (Z)
1001	Pte. Lewis Edwin Grant (Z)		1103	Pte. A D Woomble
1002	Pte. Richard Galbraith (Z)		1104	Pte. W Smith
1003	Pte. G Dearlove		1106	Pte. Henry Lawson Hewitt (Z)
1005	Pte. Henry W Nash (Z)		1111	Pte. William Bell (Z)
1006	L/Cpl. C Johnson		1112	Pte. C H Bell
1008	Pte. Robert Jackson (Z)		1113	Pte. F Fulcher
1011	Pte. William Henry Brooks (Z)		1115	Pte. W Garfitt
1012	Pte. A Hawkins		1117	Sgt. Henry H Woods (Z)
1013	Pte. John Henry Baker (Dis)		1119	Pte. Frederick Rogers (Z)
1015	Pte. Alfred Jonathan Foster (Z)		1120	Pte. Harry Batty (Dis)
1016	Sgt. Wilson Longfield*		1121	Pte. Charles Henry Leek (Dis)
1020	Pte. Fred Branson (Z)		1123	Pte. Charles Ward (Z)
1021	Pte. William Brigham (Z)		1124	Pte. Arthur Johnson
1023	Pte Charles Ward (dis)		1126	Pte. Frank Campion (Dis)
1024	Pte. Arthur Bacon MM (Z)		1127	Pte. George Marson (Z)
1025	Pte. Charles Allman (Z)		1128	Pte. G T Burnett
1027	Cpl. S Bolton		1129	Sgt. H H Vasey
1030	Pte. George Gaskin (Dis)		1130	Pte. George Robert Bailes (Z)
1034	Pte. Walter Taylor (Z)		1138	Pte. Tom Steels (Z)
1035	Pte. E W Taylor		1139	Pte. H Crawford
1042	Pte. Arthur Edward Robinson (Z)		1141	Pte. J W Andrews
1043	Pte. Gibson Robinson (Dis)		1143	Pte. Henry Wellborn (Z)
1044	Pte. F Sowerby		1144	Pte. Herbert Husband (Z)
1047	Pte. Albert Roberts (Z)		1145	Pte. Thomas Henry Puckering (Z)
1049	Pte. Thomas Edwin Cox (Z)		1146	Pte. T Newson
1051	Pte. Herbert Lewis (Z)		1148	Pte. R Hunt
1053	Pte. Harry Gawthorpe (Dis)		1149	Pte. William Coper (Z)
1054	Pte. A Doughty (D)		1152	Pte. H Horberry
1055	Pte. Herbert Dickinson (Dis)		1153	Pte. George Potts (Dis)
1056	Pte. Robert Clipson (Dis)		1155	Pte. G Anderson
1058	Pte. W Lewis		1156	Pte. T Anderson
1059	Pte. H Daddy		1157	Pte. George Boreland (Z)
1060	Pte. Leonard Dibb (Dis)		1158	Pte. J Boyd
1061	Pte. Thomas Dunn (Z)		1160	Pte. James Brown Livingston (Z)
1062	Pte. Patrick Michael Flanagan (Dis)		1161	Pte. Thomas Langdon Martin (Dis)
1064	Pte. Henry Edward Patterson (Dis)		1164	Cpl. Walter Butler*

1167	Pte. J Croft
1168	Pte. William Henry Day (Dis)
1169	Pte. William Driver (Z)
1171	Pte. William Ellison Giles (Z)
1172	Pte. J Harland
1174	Pte. James McLoram (Z)
1177	Cpl. E Park
1181	Pte. R H Warnes
1186	Pte. J W Arnold
1187	Pte. George Cattle (Z)
1188	Pte. John Edward Fleming (Z)
1189	Pte. W Foster
1190	Pte. George Garvin (Dis)
1191	Pte. A G Houghton
1195	Pte. Arthur Thompson (Z)
1196	Pte. T Wilkinson
1197	Pte. James William Harrison (Dis)
1198	Pte. T Holmes
1201	Pte. Henry Acey (Z)
1202	Pte. Sydney Allman (Z)
1203	Pte. Cyril Cammidge (Z)
1205	Pte. Charles Eyre (Dis)
1208	Pte. John Cox (Z)
1211	Pte. Oswald Gibson (Dis)
1212	Pte. N A Hudson
1213	Pte. George Henry Motherby (Z)
1215	Pte. T Wright
1216	Pte. J Baines
1218	Pte. J F Brown
1220	L/Cpl. J W Cordock
1221	Pte. Harry Fleming (Z)
1224	Pte. George Newcombe Hodson (Z)
1225	Pte. E Hotchkin
1226	Pte. F Hotchkin
1232	Pte. George William Patterson(Z)
1233	Pte. Albert George Peck (Z)
1235	Pte. G Smith
1237	Pte. Ernest Arthur Stephenson (Z)
1238	Pte. Percy Tomlinson (Z)
1239	Pte. Joe Whisker (Z)
1240	Pte. Reuben Henry Baker (Z)
1241	Pte. H Bourner
1244	Pte. John Thomas Paxton (Dis)
1245	Pte. Stanley Randerson (Z)
1248	Pte. Thomas Smith Brown (Z)
1249	Pte. George Straighton Christison (Z)
1250	Pte. Robert Sharp (Z)
1251	Pte. S Brown
1252	Pte. F Gilliatt
1255	Pte. Anthony George Lovell Akam (Z)
1258	Pte. W W Farmery
1259	Pte. J A Jackson
1260	Pte. George Robinson (Z)
1261	Pte. Owen Standerline (Dis)
1262	Pte. Richard Albert Brattan (Z)

1263	Pte. Ernest Herbert Cooper (Dis)
1264	Pte. Alfred Atkinson Cotton MM (Z)
1267	Pte. J Walsh
1272	Pte. T E Walker
1273	Pte. Leonard Rainton (Z)
1274	Pte. Thomas Edward Beacock (Z)
1275	Pte. F Cockerill
1277	Pte. Will Denton (Z)
1279	Pte. Wilfred Dutton (Z)
1286	Pte. Thomas Edward Warn (Dis)
1293	Pte. Arthur Lingwood (Z)
1295	Pte. F Wright
1297	L/Cpl. G W Barratt
1298	Pte. Paul Stanley Burnitt (Z)
1300	Pte. B Ellis
1304	Pte. Vincent Havercroft (Dis)
1305	Pte. Arthur Hodson (Z)
1306	Pte. Francis Murphy (Z)
1307	Pte. Joseph Price (Z)
1311	Pte. James Wray (Z)
1312	Pte. Arhur Wilson (Z)
1316	Pte. Walter Reed (Dis)
1321	Pte. Walter William Clarkson (Z)
1322	Pte. Richard H W Deighton (Z)
1323	Pte. W Harris
1324	Pte. John William Johnson (Dis)
1325	Pte. J W Lawson
1326	Pte. Amos Snarr (Z)
1327	Pte. John Chapman Shephard MM (Z)
1328	Pte. R A Smith
1330	Pte. Harold Leslie Bond (Z)
1331	Pte. H C Boxall
1333	Pte. W H Hodgson
1334	Pte. Stanley King (Z)~
1335	Pte. Fred Fairbank Akam (Z)
1336	Pte. James Brown (Z)
1337	Pte. Walter Douglas (Dis)
1338	Pte. Francis Freeman (Z)
1340	Pte. Charles Goodfellow (Z)
1341	Pte. H F Goodfellow
1347	CSM Walter Clarke*
1348	Pte. Albert Ernest Harding (Z)
1352	Pte. Albert Morrell Swain (Z)
1353	Sgt. J W Wallace
1359	Pte. Tom Clarkes (Dis)
1360	Pte. H Fell
1362	Pte. David Hustie (Dis)
1364	Pte. Frank Harold Holmes
1366	Cpl. W Jackson
1370	Pte. Thomas Petrie (Z)
1372	Pte. W R Rider
1374	Pte. Joseph William Spokes (Z)
1375	Cpl. Richard George Usher MM (Z)
1377	Pte. Clarence Magson Hilton (Z)
1378	Pte. William Ernest Cooper (Dis)

1380   Cpl. John Gerrard (Z)
1381   Pte. Ernest J Hunt (Dis)
1384   Pte. J S North
1385   Pte. G F Selle
1386   Pte. C W Tacey
1387   Pte. William Henry Tozer (Z)
1389   Pte. C S Edwards
1390   Pte. F Pickering
1391   Pte. Wilfrid Powell (Z)
1398   Pte. Thomas Connon (Z)
1399   Pte. Walter Ellis (Z)
1403   Pte. John William Cade (Z)
1404   Pte. Thomas William Creswell (Z)
1405   Pte. Arthur Curtis (Dis)
1406   Pte. E Heenan
1410   Pte. Benjamin Sands (Z)
1412   S/Major Charles Arthur Arnett*
1413   Pte. Edward Todd (Z) ^^
1416   Pte. James Blenkinsop (Z)
1417   Pte. Albert Carter (Z)
1420   Pte. J Baslington
1421   Sgt. H Faulkner
1422   Pte. John William Hartley (Dis)
1423   Pte. William Locke (Z)
1424   Pte. Albert Swaby (Z)
1425   Pte. George Anderton (Z)
1429   Pte. Joseph William Rogers
1430   Pte. John Edward Wilkinson (Z)
1431   CSM Charles Brooks*
1433   Pte. Claude Wilson (Z)
1434   Pte. Charles Morley (Dis)
1437   Pte. J W Higgins
1438   Pte. Lawrence Young (Dis)
1443   Pte. John Leonard Revell (Z)
1445   Pte. C Smith
1448   Pte. Frederick Joseph Wilson (Z)
1451   Pte. J S Lee
1454   Pte. George William Kemp (Z)
1455   Pte. Oliver Wells Wright (Dis)
1456   Pte. B W Hutchinson
1457   Pte. Albert Wade (Z)
1459   Pte. William Stephenson (Z)
1462   Pte. William Potter (Dis)
1463   Pte. Cyril Hutchinson (Dis)
1465   Pte. Percy Moore (Z)
1467   Pte. Herbert Clayton (Z)
1468   Pte. J W Fenwick
1470   Pte. A Blagg
1471   Pte. Richard Borrill (Z)
1481   Pte. Frank Johnson (Z)
1483   Pte. Frederick Fryer (Z)
1484   Pte. C H Coulson
1485   Cpl. J Banks MM (Z)
1486   Pte. James Albert Dannatt (Z)
1487   L/Cpl. F K G Vowles

1492   Pte. George William Sizer (Z)
1493   Pte. Clarence Boscowitch (Z)
1494   Pte. W Brett
1495   Pte. J W Norman
1496   Pte. Thomas Palmer Jones (Dis)
1497   Pte. H Shores
1498   Pte. William Henry Schultz (Z)
1499   Pte. S M Plews
1501   Pte. H W Tock
1504   Pte. Edward Roberts (Z)
1506   Pte. Thomas Wyn (Dis)
1508   Pte. Ernest Simpkin (Z)
1509   Pte. Charles Goulden (Z)
1510   Pte. James William Cope (Dis)
1511   Pte. Ernest Robson (Z)
1512   Pte. R Sergeant
1513   Pte. J Harrison
1514   Pte. A T Boothman
1516   Pte. W Wooler
1518   Pte. H Skelton
1519   Pte. P W Huntley
1522   Pte. F Paget
1526   Pte. G H Wollas MM
1527   Pte. Arthur H Atkinson (Dis)
1530   Pte. William John Stoladay (Dis)
1534   Pte. C Blake (Z)
1535   Pte. H Farrow
1536   Pte. William Megson (Dis)

????   RSM Dixon
????   Cpl. Evers
????   RQMS Marriott
????   Sgt. Nicholls
????   Pte. H Brattan
????   Pte. G Campbell
????   Pte. E Kirkwood
????   Pte. W Boynton
????   Pte. W Sollitt

13th Battalion Nominal Roll
1   Pte. Samuel Allison (Z)
2   Pte. G Allman
4   Cpl. Herbert Andrews (Z)
5   C/Sgt. H Andrews
8   Cpl. J Annal (Z)
9   Pte. M Armstrong
10   Pte. E Atkinson (Z)
11   Pte. M H Atkinson (Z)
12   Sgt. Albert Allen (Z)
13   Pte. Arthur Aingworth
14   Sgt. F Atkin
15   Pte. W Bailey DCM (Z)
17   Cpl. P Bailey
19   Pte. J H Bettison
20   Pte. George Booth (Z)

21	Pte. Charles Benstead (Z)
23	Pte. Alfred Leonard Bugg (Z)
24	Cpl. Sydney Bolderson*
25	Pte. Athur James Barron (Z)
27	Sgt. E Baily
28	Pte. Arthur Bartlett (Z)
29	Pte. Ernest Nelson Cooper (Z)
31	Sgt. John Witham Casson*
32	RSM Herbert Clifford Crookes MID
33	Pte. Harold Richard Calvert (Z)
34	Pte. H S Barrett
35	Pte. M Barnaby
36	Pte. Henry Baker (Z)
37	Pte. John William Beaumont (Z)
38	Cpl. Henry Beanland
39	Pte. Sydney Berridge (Dis)
40	Pte. Albert Blenkinsop
43	Pte. R Brough (Z)
44	Pte. Adrian Brown (Z)
45	Pte. Robert Bosworth (Z)
46	Pte. J H Brock
47	Pte. Albert Bowden (Z)
48	Sgt. Thomas HBroadhead MM & bar (Z)
49	Pte. John Burns (Z)
50	Pte. F B Challons (Z)
51	Pte. John Hubert Clarkson*
52	Pte. George Campion (Z)
53	Pte. Robert Carrison (Z)
54	Sgt. W C Cannell
55	Pte. Walter Thomas Cawkwell
56	Pte. George Clark (Z)
57	Sgt. Reginald James Chester
59	Pte. Ernest Cooper
60	Pte. Arthur Cook
62	Pte. George Alfred Cornthwaite
63	Pte. Thomas William Conkerton (Z)
65	Cpl. J Cross
66	Pte. Martin Cowton
67	Pte. Edward Cowton (Dis)
70	Pte. Thomas Henry Cooper (Dis)
71	Cpl. J Dale
73	Pte. Leonard Dearing (Z)
74	Pte. Harry Arthur Dixon (Z)
75	Cpl. Arthur Donnelly
76	Pte. J C Donnelly
77	Pte. J W Doran
79	Pte. William Doughty (Z)
80	Pte. A F Dobson (Z)
81	Pte. Thomas Dunn (Dis)
84	Pte. Alfred Dunn (Dis)
85	Pte. Herbert Dry (Z)
86	Pte. William Edwards (Z)
88	Pte. Ernest East (Z)
89	Sgt. Harold Emmitt (Z)
90	Pte. Charles Ellis (Z)
91	Sgt. J H Elston
92	Pte. Frank Eldon (Z)
94	Pte. H Falk
98	Pte. Robert French (Z)
101	Pte. William Fox (Dis)
102	Pte. Harry Foster (Z)
104	Pte. Walter Gladstone (Dis)
105	Pte. William Gamble (Dis)
107	Pte. George Henry Garton (Dis)
110	Pte. Bertie Gilliard (Dis)
111	Pte. Frederick Gilkes
114	Pte. H Goulding
116	Pte. Stanley Hamilton (Z)
117	Cpl. Stanley Hamilton (Z)
118	Pte. George Hardy
122	Pte. James Richard Hackett
123	Pte. Herbert Harman (Dis)
125	Pte. J W Hall (Z)
126	C/Sgt. Frank Hearson (Dis)
128	Pte. Charles Philip Hilton (Z)
129	Pte. A R Hodgson (Z)
131	Pte. Leonard Holdsworth (Z)
136	Pte. James Hutchinson (Z)
137	Pte. Thomas Hutchinson (Z)
138	Pte. A Jacques (Z)
139	Pte. A E Jackson
140	Pte. H H S Jennings (Z)
143	Pte. Charles Henry Jibson (Z)
146	Pte. G S Johnson
147	Pte. C Kay
148	Pte. Harry Kellett (Z)
151	Pte. L Kirby (Z)
152	Pte. J R King (Z)
153	Pte. L Langford
154	Sgt. L Langrich
155	Pte. James Lewis (Sydney Lewis in SDGW)
156	Pte. Harry Lewis (Z)
157	L/Cpl. Walter Levitt MM
160	Pte. John William Limbach (Z)
161	Pte. T Lyon (Z)
162	Pte. Frederick Longbone (Z)
164	Pte. J Lowe (Z)
168	Pte. Frank Longhorn (Z)
171	Pte. J T Marshall (Z)
172	Pte. William Sturton Maltby (Z)
177	Pte. T J Morton
178	Pte. Raymond Lancaster Mawer (Z)
179	Pte. T W Mail (Z)
180	Pte. Clifford Medforth (Z)
181	Pte. W McKernan
182	Pte. F Midforth
183	Pte. G Milner
187	Pte. John Nelson
188	Pte. Arthur Newton (Z)
189	Pte. J Neylon

191	Pte. Reginald Selwyn Nicholson (Z)
194	Pte. John North (Dis)
195	Pte. B Peak (Z)
196	Pte. W Pearson (Z)
197	Pte. Hector Louis Proby (Z)
198	Pte. R E Pullen
200	Pte. Wilfred Richardson (Z)
201	Pte. E Richardson
203	Sgt. Ernest Rotherforth (Z)
206	Sgt. Fred Robinson (Z)
207	Pte. Walter Robinson (Dis)
209	Pte. E Roberts
210	L/Cpl. J A Robbie
211	Pte. George Rogers (Z)
212	Pte. J W Rogers
213	Sgt. S Robson (Z)
216	L/Cpl. S Shakespeare
217	Pte. Thomas Sidney Stanford (Z)
218	Pte. C A Snowley
219	Pte. John Hall Stephenson (Z)
227	Pte. Benjamin A Thickett (Z)
229	Pte. J L Smith
230	Pte. C W Smith (Z)
231	Pte. T A Smith
232	Pte. James Lewis Smith (Dis)
233	Pte. Thomas Henry Smith (Z)
235	Cpl. H E C Stirk
236	Pte. Harry Wright Smith* MM
237	Pte. Frederick William Smith (Z)
238	Pte. H Smith (Z)
239	Pte. Joseph Smith (Dis)
240	Pte. Edward Albert Vincent Stones (Z)
243	Pte. Thomas Sowden (Z)
244	Pte. W R Stout (Z)
245	Pte. Leonard Bennett Scott (Z)
246	Pte. T Sugden
247	Pte. Robert Allison Taylor (Z)
248	Pte. Alexander Young Taylor*
250	Pte. Edward Tayles (Z)
251	Pte. George Tether (Z)
256	Pte. H Tomlinson
261	Pte. Thomas Alfred Townsley (Z)
264	Pte. George Will Turner (Z)
265	Pte. W Tuton (Z)
266	Pte. Albert Underwood (Z)
267	L/Cpl. Charles Verity MM (Z)
269	Pte. Joseph Henry Warrens (Dis)
270	Pte. A M Ward (Z)
271	Pte. Fredrick Waud (Z)
275	Pte. William Arthur Westerman (Dis)
276	L/Cpl. John Arthur Bassett (Z)
277	Pte. John Robert Wilson (Dis)
278	Cpl. Wilson (Z)
280	Pte. G W Williams
284	Pte. Joesph Whitehead (Dis)
286	Sgt. H M Wilkinson
288	Pte. Thomas David Williams (Dis)
289	Pte. James W P Wilson (Z)
290	Pte. Wilfred Leonard Wilkinson (Dis)
291	Pte. John William Wilson (Dis)
292	Pte. William Wilkinson (Z)
293	Pte. Eric Bywater Wright (Z)
295	Cpl. W H Woodall
296	Sgt. Robert Henry Yates MSM (Z)
297	CSM John Bennett Wilson* DCM MC MM (Z)
298	L/Cpl. J Howlett MM (Z)
303	Pte. Ernest Pickering (Z)
304	Pte. Herbert Pointin (Z)
306	Cpl. Joseph Annable* MM
308	Pte. J W Arskey
309	Pte. Harry Atkin*
310	Cpl. W Aspinall DCM
311	Pte. G Atkinson (Z)
313	Pte. J B Baron
314	Pte. William Bailey (Z)
315	Pte. Tom Johnson Beadle (Dis)
318	Pte. Robert Harold Burkwood (Z)
319	Pte. George Butler (Z)
320	Pte. W E Clark (Z)
322	C/Sgt. Arthur Leslie Chatterton*
323	Pte. Albert Campbell (Dis)
324	Cpl. Collins
325	Pte. R J Cooper
326	Pte. Percival Collins (Z)
329	Pte. Joseph Dean (Dis)
331	Pte. Alfred Doughty (Z)
333	Pte. D Duncan
335	Pte. Sydney Joseph Everatt (Z)
336	Pte. A Espiner
337	Pte. J W Eddom
338	Pte. John Matthew Fulstow (Z)
340	Pte. Martin Feeney (Z)
341	Pte. William Ernest Finch (Dis)
343	Pte. B Galbraith
344	Pte. C Gamble
347	Pte. J A Hamshaw
348	Pte. G H Hargrave
349	Pte. Richard Hairsine (Z)
350	Pte. H P Hydes (Z)
352	Pte. R H Huzzard
355	Pte. B Neylon MM (Z)
356	Pte. Joseph Ketley (Z)
359	Pte. John Leach (Z)
362	Pte. Andrew McDougall (Z)
366	Pte. W Morrison
368	Pte. Charles Padget (Z)(D)
371	Sgt. William Plum (Z)
373	Pte. J Ryan
374	Pte. James Arthur Reed (Z)
375	Pte. R W Robinson

377	Cpl. A Robinson	472	Pte. Charles Arthur Staveley (Z)
379	L/Cpl. A Rutledge	474	Pte. George Alfred Smith
380	Sgt. Samuel Russell DCM G-de-G (B) (Z)	481	Pte. Henry Wray (Z)
382	Pte. Harold Fraser Sharpe (Z)	484	Pte. George Wilson (Z)
384	Pte. Harold Morriss Spencer (Dis)	486	Pte. J Wright
386	Pte. H Stephens	487	Pte. J W Wright
387	Pte. Harry Charles Slinn (Z)	489	Pte. F Woollas (Z)
391	Pte. Fred Simpson (Z)	491	Pte. Aram (Z)
392	Sgt. Henry Thresh (Z)	492	Pte. John Anderson (Z)
395	Pte. F Turner	493	C/Sgt. Wilfred George Arbon*
397	Pte. Viner (Z)	498	Pte. Charles Benstead MM (Z)
398	L/Cpl. F W Watkin	500	L/Cpl. S R Brocklesby
399	Pte. J E Walsh	501	Cpl. John William Brown
404	Pte. W Winterbottom (Z)	502	Pte. Percy Buxton (Z)
405	Pte. Thomas William Witty (Dis)	505	Pte. G Diglin
406	Pte. William Ernest Whitley*	507	Pte. Thomas Elleston (Dis)
408	Pte. Gilbert Allison (Z)	509	Pte. Sydney Gardham (Z)
409	Pte. Henry Baines (Z)	512	Pte. Albert Victor Griffon (Z)
410	Pte. Fred Blaney (Z)	513	Pte. Bertie Handley (Z)
411	Pte. Henry Blackburn (Z)	514	Pte. Charles Holland (Z)
413	Pte. A Bellemie (Z)	518	Sgt. C McCarthy
414	Pte. C Bridges	522	Pte. C S Newby
416	Pte. Ernest Brough (Z)	523	L/Cpl. C W Noble (Z)
418	Pte. John William Tomlinson (Dis)	524	Pte. Alfred Osborne (Dis)
419	Pte. Thomas Weatherill Carmichael (Dis)	525	Pte. George Liss Parker (Z)
420	Pte. Charles Carver (Dis)	527	Pte. Peck (Z)
421	Pte. John William Carver (Dis)	528	Pte. Sidney Petty (Dis)
422	Pte. Robert William Collins (Dis)	529	Cpl. Ernest Gilchrist Pickering*
423	Pte. Charles Curtis	530	Sgt. Frederick James Pickering*
427	Cpl. G Dent	532	Cpl. John Will Rudd (Z)
428	Pte. Thomas Henry Eccles (Z)	533	Pte. A Speed (Z)
431	Pte. D W Farnill	534	Pte. W Simpson
433	Pte. Fred Rawlings Gale*	537	Pte. Philip Camm Scott*
434	Pte. E Gill (Z)	539	CSM Henry Stubbins MC (Z)
435	Pte. Athur Gorbert (Z)	541	L/Cpl. R S Temple
436	Sgt. Clifford Chawner Hasnip (Dis)	545	Pte. Alfred Ernest Alexander Yates (Dis)
439	Pte. Arthur Howard (Z)	546	Pte. C J P Allatt
444	Pte. William P Jackson (Z)	547	Pte. Frank K Atkinson (Dis)
445	Pte. Albert Jefferson (Z)	548	Pte. Alfred Bateman (Z)
446	Pte. A Johnson	549	Pte. Edward Beautyman (Z)
447	Pte. Michael Kaney (Z)	551	Pte. G H Bolsover
451	Pte. W V Kershaw	555	Pte. Thomas Dinsdale (Dis)
452	Pte. A E Kileen	556	Pte. A Dixon
453	Pte. Ernest Earnshaw Kirkup (Dis)	557	Sgt. G C Duffill (Z)
455	Pte. T J McNally	558	Pte. B Dunham (Z)
456	Pte. A McNally	559	Pte. George Ellis (Z)
457	Pte. Christopher James Marris (Z)	562	Pte. Henry Foster DCM
459	Pte. Stephen Monaghan (Z)	564	Pte. C D Harrison
461	Cpl. Walter John Orvis MSM (Z)	567	Pte. Frederick Johnson (Z)
464	Sgt. C Highton C-de-G (B)	568	Pte. James Lambert (Z)
465	Pte. Edwin Rawlings (Dis)	569	Pte. Thomas William Lawrence (Z)
466	Pte. Frank Robinson (Z)	570	Pte. John Lever (Z)
468	Cpl. A Robinson	571	Pte. Sydney Lilley
469	Pte. F Rusling	573	Pte. Charles Jennison Mouer (Z)
471	Pte. W H Stamp (Z)	574	Pte. Albert Randerson (Z)

575	Pte. Henry Edward Rawson (Z)	677	Pte. A E Bodfield
576	Pte. Edward Richardson	680	Pte. James R Budd (Z)
577	Pte. Edward Sharp	682	Cpl. H Clark MM (Z)
579	L/Cpl. Isaac Shingleton MM (Z)	683	Pte. Daniel Mulholland (Z)
580	Pte. George William Slingsby (Dis)	684	Pte. George William Cressey (Z)
582	Pte. Sydney Thorley (Dis)	689	Pte. Arthur Edward Collinson (Z)
585	Pte. George Stanley Welborn (Z)	690	Cpl. George Cotton DCM (Z)
589	L/Cpl. E A Ashley	692	Pte. William H Cudbertson (Z)
590	Pte. Sydney Collingwood Ainsworth (Z)	693	Pte. R Driver
591	Pte. J E Akrill	694	Pte. Joseph Everitt (Dis)
592	Pte. G W Amos (Z)	696	Pte. C Espin
594	Pte. John Thomas Barrett (Z)	698	Pte. George Fletcher (Z)
595	Pte. Albert James Barber (Dis)	699	Pte. John Fletcher (Dis)
598	Pte. W Betts	700	Pte. Charles Henry Frow (Dis)
599	Pte. Walter Bennett (Z)	703	Pte. Harry Jackson (Dis)
601	Pte. G W Brown (Z)	704	Pte. Thomas Henry Jackson (Z)
602	Sgt. J W Brown	705	Pte. A B Janney
603	Pte. Brown (Z)	706	Pte. F Jacques (Z)
604	Pte. Charles Frederick Broughton (Z)	714	Pte. M Lydon MM
606	Pte. Wilfred Arthur Buxton (Dis)	715	Pte. T Lyons (Z)
607	Pte. Walter Harold Chambers (Z)	717	Sgt. William Patterson McConnell (Z)
609	Pte. Herbert Colby (Z)	719	Pte. Donald McKinley (Z)
611	Pte. G Dawson	720	Pte. George Albert Maltby (Z)
614	Cpl. Francis Fendley (Z)	722	Pte. G Major
619	Sgt. Martin Gilroy (Z)	723	Pte. Douglas Mumby * MM
622	Sgt. Henry Thomas Holmes (Z)	726	L/Cpl. W Parker
624	Pte. William Robert Hope (Z)	727	Sgt. Harry Petrie* MM & MID
626	Pte. Cecil Hunter (Dis)	730	Pte. George Henry Ramster (Dis)
627	Pte. David Humphrey (Z)	731	Pte. Wiliam Ryan (Dis)
628	Pte. Albert Jewitt (Z)	735	Pte. John Thomas Ruttleton (Z)
634	Pte. John Longley (Z)	736	Pte. Joseph Seddon (Z)
636	Pte. George Richard Marsh (Z)	739	Pte. E Sproxton
638	Pte. Walter Morley (Z)	740	Pte. G R Taylor
641	Pte. Thomas Nixon (Z)	741	Pte. John William Taylor (Z)
642	Pte. J W Platts	745	Cpl. F Turley
643	Pte. H Pougher	748	Pte. N Nowell
644	Sgt. A Robinson	749	Pte. William Thomas Wass (Z)
646	Cpl. Charles H Robinson (Z)	752	Pte. Charles Edward Whitton (Z)
650	Pte. Robert Staples (Z)	753	Pte. M A Wilson
651	Pte. Charles Samuel Johnson Smith (Dis)	754	Pte. G Wright
652	Pte. H Smith	756	CSM William Arthur Brain*
653	Pte. Albert Spiring (Dis)	757	Pte. Charles Herbert Bateman (Z)
654	Pte. Ernest Bilton Shucksmith (Z)	758	Pte. P Bonnello (Z)
655	Pte. George Sutherland (Dis)	761	Pte. F T Burkinshaw (Z)
657	Cpl. A Taylor	763	Pte. Walter Leonard Charlton (Z)
660	Pte. W Rose	764	Pte. F Carr (Z)
661	Pte. Richard Wass (Dis)	765	Pte. A Chilton
663	Pte. Henry West (Z)	766	Pte. G W Clinton
664	Cpl. A Willaims	767	Pte. John Henry Copley (Z)
665	Pte. G R Wilson MM (Z)	772	Cpl. E H English MM (Z)
666	Pte. Harold Windass (Z)	774	Pte. G W Gray
667	Pte. William Henry Wright (Z)	775	Pte. J Grayburn
670	Pte. Albert Barker (Dis)	776	Pte. C Greenwood
671	Pte. T W Barton	777	Pte. Arthur Gibson (Z)
676	Pte. G Bristow (Z)	779	Pte. David Gowans (Z)

781	Pte. A Harrison	892	Pte. Ernest Alfred Watkinson
782	Pte. F Hesletine	895	Pte. G Roberts
784	Pte. W N Howell	896	Pte. Sgt. R Attwood
785	Cpl. C Huddlestone	897	Pte. C Baker
786	Pte. Sidney Lowery (Z)	898	Pte. Frederick Joseph Bateman (Z)
787	Pte. George William Marshall (Z)	900	Pte. Thomas Henry Batty*
790	Sgt. T E Norman MM (Z)	902	Cpl. Walter Brown (Z)
792	Pte. John Robert Say (Z)	903	Pte. Albert J Candy (Dis)
793	Pte. G Smith (Z)	904	Pte. A Carrick
795	Pte. R W Summerland	907	Pte. William Henry Cook (Z)
796	Pte. J Syph	909	Pte. John Cusick (Z)
797	Pte. John Hall Temperton	912	Pte. Herbert Fletcher (Z)
800	Pte. Wallis Walker (Dis)	914	Pte. V V Gill
804	Pte. C E Barker	915	Pte. William Arthur Gillgrass (Z)
805	Pte. John William Barker (Z)	916	Pte. William Henry Gotton (Dis)
806	Pte. Thomas Bradley (Z)	917	Pte. Irvin Haylock (Z)
807	Pte. W Carmichael (Z)	918	Pte. George Johnson (Z)
813	Pte. Charles Victor Harrop (Dis)	919	Pte. G F Johnson
814	Pte. J W Hester	923	Pte. J R Preston
815	Sgt. George Hodge* MM	924	Pte. Charles Quest (Z)
816	Pte. Frederick Locking (Dis)	925	Pte. T Ralph
818	Pte. Charles Morley (Z)	926	Pte. T W Smith (Z)
819	Pte. Alfred Rushforth (Z)	931	L/Cpl. C A Shaw (Z)
820	Pte. G M Stead	932	Pte. T W Smith
821	Pte. A C Voakes	933	Pte. Herbert Tate (Dis)
826	Cpl. A Dean	936	L/Cpl. T Toalster
828	Pte. Richard Dent (Z)	937	Cpl. Arthur Townend (Z)
830	Pte. L Fozard (Z)	939	Pte. Thomas George Wescott (Z)
831	Pte. J Gunnell (Z)	940	Pte. Harold Rothwell Winship (Z)
832	Sgt. E Good (Z)	941	Pte. Sam Wright (Z)
836	Pte. Fred Mathers (Z)	942	Pte. W Allen
837	Pte. Maurice Risdon Moore (Z)	943	Pte. A Arskey (Z)
839	Pte. Ernest Mortimer (Z)	947	Pte. F H Bostock
841	Pte. V Rice (Z)	948	Pte. R Bottger (Z)
845	Pte. Goerge Henry Bateman (Z)	949	Pte. Charles Henry Brooks (Dis)~
847	Pte. Tom Cooper	950	Pte. Horace Chatterton MM
849	Pte. Harry Ellis (Dis)	951	Pte. Albert Collinson (Z)
850	Cpl. Thomas F Futty (Z)	952	Pte. W Allan (Z)
852	Sgt. Ernest Good (Dis)	953	Pte. W Conn (Z)
854	Pte. Thomas Hull	954	Cpl. J W Daddy
859	Pte. C V Nelson	956	Pte. J W Fisher MM (Z)
861	Pte. T P Pennock	957	Pte. G Foster MM (Z)
862	Pte. Will Ernest Read (Dis)	958	Pte. Reginald Hardaker (Dis)
867	Pte. Frederick Weldon (Z)	959	Sgt. Donald Harrison*
868	Pte. Charles Wilson (Z)	960	Pte. Harold Howgill (Z)
870	Pte. C E Banks	962	Cpl. F W Johnson
874	Pte. George Ernest Dyson (Z)	963	Pte. Ernest Edward Kay (Z)
876	Pte. E Ellington	964	Pte. E W Knaggs (Z)
877	Pte. J R Farrah	965	Pte. William Cook Knappy (Dis)
880	Pte. G Johnson	969	Pte. William James Longhorn (Z)
881	Cpl. C W Kelland (Z)	970	Pte. John William Mann (Z)
882	Pte. John Thomas Kershaw (Z)	975	Pte. Harold Ramsey (Dis)
887	L/Cpl. C Smith MM	977	Pte. Charles Henry Sanders (Dis)
889	Pte. T Stork	978	Pte. W Stainforth
891	Pte. George Henry Townend (Z)	979	Pte. Arthur John Spencer (Z)

979	Pte. Arthur John Spencer (Z)		1074	Pte. Charles Mankel (Z)
983	Pte. Frederick Walker (Dis)		1076	Pte. John William Merrills (Z)
985	Pte. Thomas Henry Wright*		1077	Pte. William C Nielson
986	Pte. Jack Wood (Z)		1081	Pte. W L Thorpe
988	Pte. John Edward Barkworth MM (Z)		1084	Sgt. John T Allinson*
994	Pte. John Brocklesbank (Z)		1085	CSM Douglas Sandilands DCM MC (Z)
996	Pte. Charles Arthur Fenwick (Z)		1091	CSM William R Hignett*
997	L/Cpl. William Fletcher* DCM		1092	Sgt. J Hallam MM(Z)
998	Pte. Lancelot Hall (Z)		1094	Pte. James Christopher Boswell (Z)
999	Pte. Thomas William Hicks (Dis)		1097	Pte. Laurence Collingwood (Z)
1000	Pte. C Hunter (Z)		1098	Sgt. J Hallam (Z)
1001	Pte. Fred Knott (Z)		1099	Pte. A Morrell
1002	Pte. G L Lenard		1102	Pte. J W Underwood
1003	Sgt. George Thomas Myers (Dis)		1104	Pte. John W Chadwick (Dis)
1005	Pte. C Rose		1105	Pte. R E Heselwood
1006	Pte. Arthur Leslie Shaw (Z)		1106	Pte. T Hudson (Z)
1012	Cpl. Charles Wilson (Z)		1107	Pte. J Parnaby (Z)
1013	Pte. Walter Wilson (Z)		1108	Cpl. Herbert Clyde Rands (Z)
1014	Pte. Walter Brookes (Z)		1110	Pte. F Kay
1016	Sgt. Benjamin Dalton MM (Dis)		1113	QMS Thomas Taylor*
1017	L/Cpl. S Dossor		1115	Sgt. G Harrison MID
1018	Pte. G B Hardy		1116	Sgt. John Robert Hoyle*
1019	Pte. R W Leach (Z)		1119	Pte. David Robson (Z)
1021	Sgt. John Austin Nichol (Dis)		1125	Pte. G W Dixon (Z)
1022	Pte. James H Pearson (Z)		1126	Pte. D Groundrill
1023	Cpl. Sydney Rudeforth (Dis)		1127	Pte. L/Cpl. G H Messenger
1025	Pte. Frank Wray (Z)		1128	Pte. Reuben George Stark (Z)
1027	Pte. Alexander Widdas (Dis)		1129	Pte. Frank Welch (Z)
1031	Pte. William Hanry Black (Dis)		1130	Sgt. George C Badger ^^
1033	Pte. G T Banks		1134	Sgt. F Mennell
1034	Pte. Will Curtis (Z)		1137	Pte. George Arthur Gosling (Dis)
1035	Pte. Harry Gledhill (Z)		1139	Sgt. Frederick S Brint (Z)
1036	Pte. A E Holding (Z)		1140	Sgt. J R Haldenby
1038	Pte. Clarence Mills (Z)		1141	Sgt. Walter Simpson (Z)
1043	Pte. G H Austin		1142	Pte. Ernest Barker (Dis)
1044	Pte. D Barley		1143	Pte. Albert Henry Jennings (Dis)
1046	Sgt. Ebor Benson (Z)		1144	Pte. Joseph Carroll (Z)
1047	Pte. J Betts		1147	Sgt. Sam Kilburn (Z)
1048	Pte. Fred Burns*		1148	Pte. J Mann
1049	Pte. A Clark (Z)		1150	Sgt. R Maughan
1051	Pte. Walter Evers (Z)		1153	Pte. John William Ashton (Z)
1052	Pte. J Inglis		1154	Pte. George William Cressy (Z)
1054	Sgt. George Henry Mansell (Dis)		1156	Pte. James Hillan (Z)
1055	Pte. Fred Mower (Z)		1157	Pte. E Jennison
1057	Pte. Joseph Nicholls (Z)		1158	Pte. John Mason Jones (Z)
1058	Cpl. Arthur Hind Pease (Z)		1159	Pte. Harry Smith (Z)
1059	Pte. G T Scott		1162	Pte. Frederick Grubb (Z)
1061	Pte. G Boast		1164	Sgt. Charles Highton (Z)
1063	Sgt. John Richard Brown MM		1167	Pte. M Kay
1064	Pte. J Buxton		1171	Pte. John Gill (Dis)
1066	Pte. Frederick Delaney (Dis)		1173	Pte. Thomas William Morton (Dis)
1067	Pte. Thomas Duncan (Dis)		1174	Pte. J W O'Neal
1068	Pte. Henry Herbert Green (Z)		1175	Pte. A J Towle (Z)
1070	Pte. Harold Jenneson (Z)		1176	Pte. Herbert Coates (Z)
1073	Pte. Reginald McCarthy (Dis)		1177	Pte. William Finlayson*

1178 Pte. Ernest Henry Bolmeer*	1269 L/Cpl. Arthur Fisher MM
1179 Pte. Herbert Andrews (Dis)	1270 Pte. Joseph Tyler (Dis)
1180 Pte. Neill McCarter (Z)	1271 Pte. T Draper (Z)
1181 Sgt. G E Atkinson	1272 Sgt. Percy Dodds (Z)
1183 Pte. Wilfred Wright (Z)	1273 Pte. W Allon
1184 Pte. J J Collingwood	1274 Pte. J W Darby
1185 Pte. William Henry Chard (Z)	1275 Pte. Horace Gordon Hutchings MM
1186 Sgt. Percy H Knight*	1278 Pte. W Thompson
1188 Pte. W J Rogers (Z)	1279 Pte. W Collinson
1192 Pte. George Binns (Dis)	1281 Pte. William Willis Sherwood (Dis)
1193 Pte. E W Booth	1282 Pte. Joseph Roe (Z)
1194 Pte. G Burns (Z)	1285 Pte. T A Scott (Z)
1195 Pte. J T Clater	1286 Pte. H Smedley (Z)
1197 Pte. M H Driver	1287 Sgt. Charles W Mail (Z)
1198 Pte. John George Butt*	1288 Pte. J S Newman
1199 Sgt/M. Wilberforce Dufill (Z)	1289 Pte. J W Pallister
1200 Pte. Arthur Joseph Mazzini Evans (Dis)	1290 Pte. William Wilfred Holmes (Z)
1201 Pte. Henry Bolton (Z)	1292 Cpl. H Green
1202 Pte. Herbert Baggaley (Z)	1294 Pte. R Cooper
1204 Pte. F Hebblewhite	1297 Pte. R Walker (D)
1205 Pte. Arthur Horn (Z)	1298 Pte. Joseph Codd (Z)
1206 Pte. Harry Horsley (Z)	1299 L/Cpl. G Pearcy (Z)
1208 Pte. A Joyce	1300 Cpl. H Smith
1211 Pte. Frederick Laughton (Dis)	1301 Pte. J E Walsley
1212 L/Cpl. H Bows	1304 Pte. C Waudby (Z)
1215 Pte. J W Peakes (Z)	1305 Pte. G White
1217 Pte. A Storr	1307 L/Cpl. Herbert Tripp MM (Z)
1220 Pte. Harry Whiteley (Dis)	1308 Pte. William Beacock (Dis)
1221 WOII G Bulleyment	1310 Pte. Frederick William Gouldson (Dis)
1224 Pte. George Laughton (Z)	1312 Pte. J H Swift
1226 Pte. J Miles	1313 Pte. James Wray (Z)
1227 L/Cpl. J H Pearcy	1315 Pte. Joseph Culeth (Z)
1228 Pte. F Sharp	1316 Pte. G Cudbertson (Z)
1229 Pte. Harold Slaney (Dis)	1318 Pte. T Shearsmith
1231 Pte. N W Smith (Z)	1320 Pte. Sydney Barkill (Dis)
1232 Sgt. S Sissons	1321 Pte. H Dearlove (Z)
1233 Cpl. G F Waller	1323 Pte. Edward Vincent Jordan (Dis)
1235 L/Cpl. J Sample	1324 Pte. George William Bell (Dis)
1237 Pte. Ernest West (Z)	1325 Pte. Harry Oakley (Dis)
1240 Pte. Thomas Henshaw (Dis)	1327 Pte. John Rose (Z)
1242 Pte. Edward Speechey (Z)	1329 Pte. Herbert Busby (Z)
1244 Pte. Alfred Wilson (Z)	1331 Pte. G T Douglas
1245 Pte. Ernest Allison (Dis)	1332 Pte. Arthur Stevenson (Z)
1247 Pte. Harold Postill (Z)	1333 Pte. J Brown
1249 Pte. Fred Fisher (Dis)	1340 Pte. Philip Marr (Dis)
1252 Pte. Alfred Smart (Dis)	1341 Pte. Herbert Turner (Dis)
1253 Pte. Robert Brown Walgate (Dis)	1342 Pte. Arthur Douglas (Dis)
1254 Pte S J Dry (Z)	1343 Pte. Albert Edward England (Dis)
1256 Pte. J F Fortnam	1344 Pte. G B Fenwick
1257 Pte. G Hartley	1347 Pte. A Swales
1258 Pte. A Koplic	1348 Pte. George Ernest Wilson (Z)
1259 Pte. Alfred Smith (Z)	1349 Pte. Eric J Soulsby (Z)
1261 Pte. W H Wilkinson	1350 Pte. Albert Edward Wright (Dis)
1262 Pte. Harold Lonsdale (Z)	1353 Pte. H Edwards
1268 Pte. A Riby (Z)	1356 Pte. H Tomlinson

1357	Pte. G E Reed
1359	Pte. Robert Samuel Peak (Z)
1360	Pte. John Bend (Z)
1361	Pte. H Clark
1363	Pte. H Drewery
1367	Pte. George Warrener (Dis)
1370	Pte. Albert Edward Brankley (Dis)
1373	Pte. Walter Beacroft (Dis)
1374	Pte. John Sanderson (Dis)
1375	Pte. Thomas Flannagan MID (Z)
1376	Pte. George Edward Myers (Z)
1377	Pte. George A Atkinson (Z)
1378	Pte. James Arthur Barratt (Z)
1379	L/Cpl. H Barnby
1380	L/Cpl. A E Buffey
1381	Cpl. H Bulman
1383	Pte. George Cooper
1384	Pte. George Crowley (Dis)
1385	Pte. Albert Cubbison (Z)
1386	Pte. J Dodds
1387	Pte. Robert Edward (Z)
1388	Pte. J Igo (Z)
1389	Pte. John Harrison (Z)
1391	Pte. Alf Lonsdale (Z)
1393	Pte. Harry Perrin (Dis)
1394	Pte. Frederick George Poole (Dis)
1396	Pte. C Watts
1397	Pte. R Walker
1398	Pte. John W Cubbison (Z)
1399	Pte. Percy Newlove (Z)
1400	Pte. John Fowler (Z)
1401	Pte. John Fowler (Z)
1403	Pte. Arthur Staniforth (Dis)
1404	Pte. Thomas Moss (Z)
1405	Pte. A Thurlow
1407	Pte. J Blackmore
1408	L/Cpl. Benjamin Fairfield DCM (Z)
1412	Pte. J R Farrah (Z)
1414	Pte. H Tasker
1415	Cpl. George W Wilson (Z)
1416	Sgt. John W Wilson MM (Z)
1417	Pte. James Daddy (Z)
1418	Pte. D Partis
1419	Cpl. E Biglin
1420	Pte. Robert Cunningham (Z)
1421	Pte. T Davis
1424	Pte. Albert Sydney Rich (Dis)
1430	Pte. C B Curtis
1431	L/Cpl. A Gibson
1432	Pte. William Suddaby (Z)
1433	Pte. G H Brewitt (Z)
1434	Pte. Thomas Bilton (Z)
1437	Pte. Thomas Siddle (Z)
1439	Pte. J Coupland
1440	Pte. Douglas McManus (Z)

1441	Cpl. George H Codd (Z)
1442	Pte. A Cass
1444	Pte. William Crowther (Z)
1446	Cpl. J W Wilkinson
1448	Pte. A Brown
1449	Pte. A H Earle
1453	Pte. Charles Wilson*
1456	Cpl. Fred H Piper (Z)
1457	Pte. William Walter Chance (Z)
1458	Sgt. William E Ansell (Z)
1461	Pte. Frank Bransom (Z)
1466	Pte. William H Taylor (Dis)
1467	Pte. W Tolchard
1468	Pte. A Merrylees
1473	Pte. Allan Garnett (Z)
1475	Pte. J H Payne
1477	Pte. R Lockey (Z)
1480	Sgt. Sidney Bradley (Z)
1481	Sgt. L Scott
1483	Pte. Charles William Richardson (Dis)
1484	L/Cpl. H Shepherdson
1485	Pte. John Tong (Z)
1491	Pte. T W C Jefferson
1492	Pte. R Kirby
1493	Pte. Miles Whitaker (Z)
1494	Pte. E Winter
1495	Pte. J P Bradley
1497	Pte. Harry McDonald (Z)
1499	Pte. George Edward Bolder (Z)
1502	Pte. Tom C Barker (Dis)
1503	Pte. W N Brady
1504	Pte. Walter Young (Z)
1506	Pte. John Ernest Murrey (Z)
1527	Pte. Albert Cantillon (Z)
1530	Pte. Harold Brown (Z)
????	J W Hewson
????	W Brown

14th Battalion Nominal Roll

1	Pte. Fred Jefferson (Z)
3	Pte. A Brown (Z)
4	Cpl. Walter Daniel (Z)
5	Pte. R G Alderton
6	Sgt. William E Munson (Z)
7	Pte. W Porter
13	Pte. O A Jarrett
14	Pte. Harold Arnott (Dis)
15	Pte. John A Smith (Z)
16	Pte. Charles Brown (Dis)
17	Pte. M Atkinson
18	Pte. Tom Eyre (Z)
20	Pte. George F Woolons (Dis)
22	Pte. R Cooper
23	Pte. Sol Harris (Dis)
24	Pte. Marcus Cutner (Z)
28	Pte. P Gallagher

33	Pte. Alfred Markham (Dis)	155	Pte. H Catteral
36	Pte. J Cooper	156	Pte. J Herron
37	Pte. William H Bindoff (Z)	157	Pte. William O Trevor (Z)
38	Pte. Cyrus Johnson (Z)	159	Pte. Frank Bryan (Z)
39	Pte. A H Smith	162	Pte. Thomas A Hay (Z)
42	Pte. R Jackson	163	Pte. Frank R White (Dis)
44	Pte. Frederick Farmer (Z)	164	Sgt. A Waudby
46	Pte. J Shores	165	Pte. C H Collett
52	Pte. J Johnson	166	Pte. Thomas Wilkinson (Z)
53	Pte. Sidney Ward (Z)	168	Pte. John F Smart (Z)
54	Pte. John E Jefferson (Z)	169	Pte. Herbert Kennedy (Z)
56	Pte. Charles H Taylor (Z)	170	Pte. R O Freear
58	L/Cpl. J W Hill	171	Pte. G E Betts
59	Pte. T Mills	172	Pte. G Williamson
60	Pte. G Charlton	173	Pte. J H Hill
61	Pte. F Wood	176	Pte. George H Rountree (Dis)
66	Pte. H Mower	178	Pte. James W Wrench (Z)
74	Pte. Albert Higgins (Z)	179	Pte. Henry W Duck (Dis)
76	Pte. William Denman (Z)	182	Pte. A Dawson
79	L/Cpl. F Barrett	184	Pte. Clarence F Dodds (Z)
81	Pte. H N Foster	185	Pte. H Burnham
82	Pte. T W Jervis	186	Pte. William Ridley (Dis)
83	Pte. S Rogers	187	Pte. C Ingham
84	Pte. W H Harper	188	Pte. Albert Leaper (Z)
86	Cpl. H Spilman	190	Pte. Stanley Osborne (Dis)
87	Pte. H Potter	194	Cpl. Charles S Thompson (Z)
89	Sgt. Harold Milner (Z)	195	Pte. G H Sanders
90	Sgt. Jack Richardson (Z)	196	Pte. Cyril S Megson (Z)
91	Cpl. William Graney (Z)	197	Pte. T Woodmansey
94	Sgt. Stanley Hattaon (Z)	198	Pte. John Driffill (Dis)
97	Cpl. Sidney Ball (Z)	199	Pte. W Turnbull
98	Cpl. Harry Henson *	202	Pte. Frank Cartledge (Z)
99	Pte. Arthur Cook (Z)	203	L/Cpl. E W Johnson
102	Pte. James Dinsdale (Z)	204	Pte. Clifford Richardson (Z)
104	Pte. William Turgoose (Z)	206	Pte. Albert Whitlow (transferred to the RFC)
105	Pte. G H Saunders	208	Pte. H Hodds
109	Pte. T Parr	209	Pte. J J Driscoll
123	Pte. N Arthur	210	Pte. J E Sands
125	Pte. C Canty	211	Pte. J W Andrew
126	Pte. Leonard Ridsdale (Z)	213	Pte. C Bell
127	Pte. J H Woodcock	214	Pte. Harry Bell (Dis)
128	Pte. C H Franks	215	Cpl. L Whitelam
132	Pte. Frank Chilman*	216	Pte. G W Butler
133	Pte. J F Robson	217	Pte. S Pinder
136	Pte. Jack Atkinson (Z)	220	Pte. George E Everett (Z)
138	Cpl. Ernest Morley (Z)	221	Pte. Samuel Seagal (Dis)
139	Pte. Harold Travis (Z)	222	Pte. Frank Osgerby (Z)
140	Pte. F Callaghan	223	Pte. Sidney Hall (Z)
142	Sgt. Clifford Robinson (Z)	224	Pte. F Mather
143	C/Sgt. Frank Clark (Z)	225	Pte. F Skinner
146	Pte. Arthur Chine (Dis)	229	Pte. John Elshout (Z)
148	Pte. C Booth	238	Pte. Stanley W Fielding (Z)
149	Pte. Alexander Aitchison (Z)	240	Pte. Henry C Gibson
153	Pte. F R Hicks	241	Pte. Tom Hall (Z)
154	Pte. Ralph Hess (Z)	244	Pte. F Mather

Hull Battalion unknown

(Killed in action with the 11th East Lancashires
having previously served with the 31st Division Army
Cyclists Corps and the Hull Pals)

122	Pte. Arthur Moor
134	Pte. William Short
583	Pte. Walter Sunley
621	Pte. W S Dunn

KEY

^^	Stayed in the army
*	Commissioned (see following section)
(Z)	Transferred to the reserve at the end of of the war
(Z)~	Transferred to the reserve but later died
(Dis)	Discharged during the war
(Dis)~	Discharged as unfit and later died
(D)	Died but not in SDGW; Regiment not yet ascertained (but generally EYR)
DCM	Distinguished Conduct Medal
MID	Mentioned in Dispatches
MM	Military Medal
C-de-G	Croix de Guerre
(B)	Belgium
(F)	France
(I)	Italy
SDGW	Soldiers Died in the Great War Part 20

Ranks given are from the 1915 star medal roll, from the 1914 -19 War Medal roll, from *Soldiers Died in the Great War* or from the Honours section of the regimental history. Full names are given only where they do not appear in other parts of the appendices, that is, in the honours or fatalities sections, or where some names are not yet traced. Names with initals and no information at the end of the name died during the war.

Appendix 3

British Awards for Bravery

THE VICTORIA CROSS

Private JOHN CUNNINGHAM, 12th Battalion
Regimental number 12/21.
Born 28th June, 1897, Scunthorpe, Lincolnshire.
Died 21st February, 1942, Kingston-upon-Hull, Yorkshire.
Awarded for bravery on the 13th November, 1916, opposite Hebuteme sector, France.

For most conspicuous bravery and resource during operations.

After the enemy's front line had been captured, Private Cunningham proceeded with a bombing section up a communication trench. Much opposition was encountered and the rest of the section became casualties. Collecting all the bombs from the casualties, this gallant soldier went on alone. Having exploded all his bombs, he returned for a fresh supply and again proceeded to the communication trench, where he met a party of ten of the enemy. These he killed and cleared the trench up to the enemy line. "His conduct throughout the day was magnificent."

London Gazette, 13th January, 1917

2/Lieutenant JOHN HARRISON, MC 11th Battalion
Born 2nd November, 1890, Drypool, Sculcoates, Kingston-upon-Hull, Yorkshire.
Killed in action 3rd May, 1917, near Oppy, France. Awarded for bravery on 3rd May, 1917, at Oppy, France.

For conspicuous bravery and self-sacrifice in an attack.

Owing to darkness and to smoke from the enemy barrage, and from our own, and to the fact that our objective was in a dark wood, it was impossible to see when our barrage had lifted off the enemy front line. Nevertheless, Second Lieutenant Harrison led his company against the enemy trench under heavy rifle and machine-gun fire, but was repulsed. Reorganising his command as best he could in No Man's Land, he again attacked in darkness under terrific fire, but with no success. Then, turning round, this gallant officer single-handed made a dash at the machine gun, hoping to knock out the gun and so save the lives of many of his company. "His self-sacrifice and absolute disregard of danger was an inspiring example to all. (He is reported missing, believed killed.)"

London Gazette, 14th June, 1917. He is commemorated on the Arras memorial.

DISTINGUISHED SERVICE ORDER

10TH BATTALION
Second Bar to DSO (LG 1/2/19)
Major (A/Lieutenant-Colonel) Edward Harrison Rigg, DSO, *1st Battalion Yorkshire Light Infantry, attached 10th Battalion East Yorkshire Regiment.*
For conspicuous gallantry and able leadership on 29th and 30th September, 1918. When the attack south through Ploegsteert wood was held up, he reconnoitred the front under heavy machine-gun and shell fire, and located the positions of the posts. It was due to his fine work that the wood was cleared of the enemy and the line advanced to the Warnave River. All his Company Commanders were casualties, and the battalion had suffered heavy casualties, but he showed absolute disregard of danger, personally leading his patrols forward. DSO gazetted June 3rd 1916
1st Bar gazetted June 3rd 1918

Captain G.W.A. Park (LG 16/9/18)
For conspicuous gallantry and devotion to duty. This officer was in charge of the left forward flank of the line, where he displayed the greatest ability in reorganising the details and stragglers from other divisions, which were being absorbed as they came along, by the composite battalion which he was serving. Under most difficult circumstances, his tireless energy and cheerful courage were an invaluable example to all ranks of his command, exhausted as they were with prolonged fighting. At a critical moment, though twice wounded, he rallied his men, and led them forward to restore the front after a personal reconnaissance under heavy shell fire, and he remained directing his command until relieved on the following morning. His courage and resource under most trying circumstances were admirable.

11TH BATTALION
DSO and Bar
Lieutenant-Colonel C.H. Gurney (LG 24/1/16 & 28/7/18)

When his right flank was exposed owing to the troops on that flank giving way, he restored the situation, capturing several prisoners, he successfully carried out a very difficult withdrawal by night, and throughout the fighting personally superintended and visited all 194 parts of the firing line, encouraging the defence by his splendid example.

DSO
M.C., Ordre de Leopold
Lieutenant-Colonel S.H. Ferrand, Croix de Guerre, (LG 3/6/19)

Lieutenant Henry Smith (LG 15/10/18)
For conspicuous gallantry and devotion to duty. He advanced his company in daylight, and without artillery preparation, some 500 yards, capturing a new line and taking prisoner two officers, sixty other ranks and four machine guns. He assisted in the capture of strong points and sent back, under heavy shell and machine gunfire, most accurate information which enabled close liaison to be obtained with the flanks. Through his resolution and ability the operation was completely successful, with unusually few casualties.

Lieutenant-Colonel J.B.O. Trimble (LG 1/1/18)

12TH BATTALION
Lieutenant-Colonel C.C.H. Twiss (LG 1/1/18)

13TH BATTALION
Lieutenant-Colonel A.K.M.C.W. SAVORY (LG 1/1/17)
Major C.W. Waite

MILITARY CROSS
MC and second bar
T/2Lt. (A/Capt.) Will Oscar Montgomery, MC, att. 92 TMB

For conspicuous gallantry and devotion to duty, this officer was in charge of a section of trench mortars which had been reduced by casualties to three men, and was eventually cut off from the remainder of the battery. However, he took up a good position, and opening an accurate fire on the enemy's main body delayed their advance and with only one NCO left out of the whole section, they both broke through the enemy and regained out lines. He set a fine example of coolness and courage to his men under adverse circumstances, and held up the enemy's advance at a critical time. In the Armentieres section on 9th September, 1918 this officer did a very

daring daylight patrol. He went out voluntarily and penetrated the enemy lines to a considerable depth, locating enemy posts and strength and defences at a time when the sector was very obscure. At one post he encountered two of the enemy and shot one with his revolver, the other escaping. He did fine work.
MC gazetted September 16th 1916
Bar gazetted February 1st 1919

10th BATTALION
MC and Bar
2/Lieutenant E. McDermott, MC (LG 7/3/18)
For conspicuous gallantry and devotion to duty during a raid. He killed at least one of the enemy himself, and though wounded remained with his men, and brought them out of action. In preparing for the raid he patrolled both by day and night with great daring.

MC
Captain James Carlton Addy (LG 3/4/17)
2/Lieutenant William Herbert Anderton (LG 15/10/18)
Lieutenant George Wilson Clark (LG 3/6/19)
Captain John Nissen Deacon (RAMC) (LG 18/7/17)
For conspicuous gallantry and devotion to duty. He showed exceptional bravery and resource on several occasions in attending to the wounded under very heavy shell fire, with complete disregard to his own personal safety.
2/Lieutenant Thomas Geraghty (LG 13/5/18)
2/Lieutenant Cedric Ivor Hadrill (LG 15/10/18)
2/Lieutenant W.S. Hutton
Lieutenant William Henry Hall (LG 15/10/18)
Captain Reginald Charles Hewson (LG 1/1/18)
Lieutenant Eustace John Krog (LG 15/10/18)
Captain Guy Fitzroy Lambert (LG 1/1/17)
2/Lieutenant Edward Mc Dermott (LG 18/10/17)
Captain William Edward Walter Naylor (LG 1/1/19)
Captain Ernest Marks Pearce, DCM (LG 26/7/18)
2/Lieutenant Cyril Herbert Piper (LG 3/6/18)
2/Lieutenant John Sacriston Shaw (LG 16/9/18)
2/Lieutenant R. Stewart (LG 14/11/16)
For conspicuous gallantry. He led a patrol across "No Man's Land", and, entering the enemy's trench, shot five of them, captured four, and assisted in capturing two others.
Lieutenant Philip Shaw (LG 16/9/18)
Captain Colin Balfour Traill (LG 18/7/17)
For conspicuous gallantry and devotion to duty during and after an attack. Although wounded in the head, and later blown into the air by a shell, he refused to retire, displaying the greatest courage and resource, and it was only when the critical period was over he went to the dressing station.

2/Lieutenant Charles Claude Wallace, MM (LG 16/10/18)
Captain Gerald Ashley Wright (LG 15/10/18)

11th BATTALION
MC and Bar
Lieutenant Frank Wheatley Cowley, MC (LG 17/9/17 & 15/10/18)
Captain Charles Clouston Irvine, MC (RAMC) (LG 18/7/17)
For conspicuous gallantry and devotion to duty. He took his stretcher-bearers out under heavy barrage fire and brought the wounded back safely, carrying one man back on his shoulders. His complete disregard for his own personal safety was most marked.
MC 2/Lieutenant George Wilkinson Bladen, MM (LG 15/10/18)
2/Lieutenant Bernard Bocking (LG 15/10/18)
Major Leonard Arthur Cattley (LG 1/1/18)
Captain Walwyn Henry Chapman (LG 26/7/18)
2/Lieutenant John Henry Copeland (LG 15/10/18)
Lieutenant H.W. Cowling (LG 18/7/17)
For conspicuous gallantry and devotion to duty. Having led his company forward to attack an enemy trench, he found it was strongly held, and was driven back. He re-organised his company in the dark and led them again to the attack. Previous to the first attack he had kept his company together under a very heavy enemy barrage lasting two hours; the example he set to his men was splendid.
2/Lieutenant Bernard Dimond (LG 15/10/18)
2/Lieutenant John Harrison (LG 17/4/17)
For conspicuous gallantry and devotion to duty. He handled his platoon with great courage and skill, reached his objective under the most trying conditions, and captured a prisoner. He set a splendid example throughout.
2/Lieutenant Benjamin Hutchinson (LG 17/4/17)
For conspicuous gallantry and devotion to duty. He, with his platoon, took sixty boxes of bombs across "No Man's Land" to a patrol which was carrying out a reconnaissance of the enemy's line. Later, he laid a guiding tape under the most trying conditions.
2/Lieutenant Vivian Henry Jenkin (LG 18/1/18)
For conspicuous gallantry and devotion to duty. He led his platoon to the second objective 300 yards inside the enemy's lines during a daylight raid. He here supervised the blowing up of two dugouts, one Trench Mortar and a concrete machine gun emplacement, besides taking several prisoners. During the withdrawal he was the last to leave and brought all his men back safely.
Captain Cyril Joseph (LG 18/1/18)
2/Lieutenant Arthur Sydney Larter (LG 15/10/18) (Yorkshire Regiment)
Captain Reginald Thomas Newcombe, C.F. (LG 15/10/18)

2/Lieutenant Ernest Carroll Nicholson (LG 15/10/18)
Captain Douglas Oake (attached 92nd TMB) (LG 1/1/17)
Captain Ernest William Reeve (LG 4/6/17)
2/Lieutenant Horace Shakesby (LG 15/10/18)
Captain Sydney Streeton Smith (LG 15/10/18)
Captain Thomas William Southern (LG 27/6/18)
13/539 CSM Henry Stubbings (LG 3/6/18)
2/Lieutenant Alfred James Thackray (LG 17/4/17)
For conspicuous gallantry and devotion to duty. He led his platoon with great courage and determination, captured his objective, together with an enemy machine-gun. He set a splendid example throughout.
Lieutenant Percival Chatterton Thompson (LG 8/3/19)
Lieutenant Frank Walker (LG 18/1/18)
For conspicuous gallantry and devotion to duty during a daylight raid. He led his party across a long open stretch of ground to the enemy second line. After clearing the enemy trenches and taking prisoners he successfully effected a difficult withdrawal under fire.
Lieutenant Ralph Piggott Whittington-Ince (LG 18/1/18)
For conspicuous gallantry and devotion to duty during a daylight raid. He led his platoon close behind the barrage and penetrated 350 yards into the enemy's support line. He brought rapid fire to bear on the fleeing enemy, driving them into our artillery barrage, and when the remainder refused to come out of their dugouts, he had them all blown up. He handled his platoon with great skill both during the advance and the withdrawal.
Captain Herbert Farrar Williams (attached 92nd Brigade Staff) (LG 1/1/19)

12th BATTALION
MC
12/512 CSM David Claude Balmford (LG 1/10/17)
For conspicuous gallantry in action. He assumed command of his Company, organizing the consolidation of the position, posting snipers, and sending out bombing parties. He set a splendid example throughout.
Captain Frederick Whitmore Burch (LG 10/1/17)
For conspicuous gallantry in action. He visited all the strong-points established in the enemy lines and assisted in their consolidation. Later, he assumed command and carried out his work with great courage and determination.
Captain William Carroll, C F (LG 26/3/18)
Captain W. Cattley
2/Lieutenant Frank Wheatley Cowley (LG 17/9/17)
For conspicuous gallantry and devotion to duty during a raid. His party having gone too far, he withdrew them and a large party of others, and led them back to the front line under very heavy hostile barrage and machine gunfire. He shot two of the enemy himself as he entered the enemy's

trench, where he also obtained valuable information, and afterwards returned to collect any stragglers that might have lost their way, displaying total disregard of his own safety and great coolness throughout.

Lieutenant Harold Frederick Dann (LG 10/1/17)
For conspicuous gallantry in action. He assumed command of and handled his company with great courage and skill, setting a splendid example throughout.

Captain Joseph Hirst (attached TMB) (LG 1/1/17)
Captain G.E. Lloyd-Jones
Lieutenant Alexander Wilson (LG 4/6/17)

13th BATTALION

MC and Bar

Lieutenant Thomas C. Herring (LG 26/4/17)
For conspicuous gallantry and devotion to duty. He rallied his men and led them forward at a critical time. On another occasion he displayed great courage and initiative when in command of his company. He has at all times set a splendid example. (MC gazetted 25/8/16)

Captain E.D. Tyndall

MC 2/Lieutenant L. Challis (LG 17/9/17)
For conspicuous gallantry and devotion to duty during a raid. He led his men with great courage and judgement, killing a sniper with his revolver and capturing a party of the enemy on his way to their trenches. Subsequently, by his promptness in stopping them he prevented his men from running into our own barrage and on into the enemy's trenches. He displayed very great coolness and fine leadership throughout.

Lieutenant W.G. Hamm
Lieutenant S.W. Howard

2/Lieutenant P.J. Lambert (LG 1/10/17)
For conspicuous gallantry in action. He rallied men of all companies and some of another unit, and formed a strongpoint on the right flank, thereby saving a critical situation.

Major Harold Smith Laverack (LG 1/10/17)
For conspicuous gallantry in action. He commanded the leading Company, and though wounded early in the day, remained with his company all day, greatly encouraging his men by his coolness and courage.

Captain J.P. Hogan
2/Lieutenant G.W. Silk
13/1085 CSM Douglas Sandilands, DCM (LG 1/1/17)
Captain W.L. Smith (USR)
2/Lieutenant Herbert Storch (LG 16/9/18)
Major L. Thorns
Captain C.A. Watts
2/Lieutenant Bertram James Wilkins (attached 92 TMB)
(LG 11/5/17)
13/297 CSM John Bennett Wilson, DCM
(LG 11/5/17)
For conspicuous gallantry in action. He with his Company

Commander and eight men consolidated two shell holes, and though unsupported held this post against repeated counter-attacks for seven hours. He set a splendid example throughout.

Captain Harold Ernest Pierpoint Yorke (RAMC. att. 13th East Yorks) (LG 10/1/17)
For conspicuous gallantry and devotion to duty. He displayed great courage and determination in tending the wounded under very heavy fire. Later, although himself wounded, he continued to carry out his work.

Distinguished Conduct Medal

10th BATTALION

220016 CSM C E Allen of Bridlington (LG 3/9/19)
From 25th February to 16th September 1918. He has done excellent work throughout the last six months as CSM. He has always performed his duties in a cheerful and capable manner, and has shown a fine sense of leadership. His organisation both in and out of the line gave proof of energy and keenness. In particular on the 12th April 1918, near Merris, he rallied his men under heavy machine-gun and rifle fire, and caused heavy fire to be brought on the advancing enemy. He showed complete disregard of his own personal safety.

10/251 Corporal C Collinson of Beverley (LG 3/9/18)
For conspicuous gallantry and devotion to duty. When the Platoon Commander was badly wounded and the Platoon was completely cut off by the enemy this NCO sent out patrols to find a way out, and in broad daylight safely evacuated the whole of the men and the wounded officer. It was entirely due to his efforts that all were not captured.

10/721 Corporal S Edlington of Hull (LG 10/1/17)
For conspicuous gallantry in action. He displayed great courage and determination when in charge of two machine guns, repelled several bombing attacks, and accounted for many of the enemy. He set a splendid example throughout.

7127 CSM J Graham of Huddersfield (LG 3/9/18)
For conspicuous gallantry and devotion to duty. Throughout a night of street fighting, when one officer and ten other ranks of the enemy were captured, this warrant officer showed fine qualities as a leader.

21924 Private T Green (LG 18/7/17)
For conspicuous gallantry and devotion to duty. During an attack upon the enemy line he located and bombed a hostile machine gun, bayonetted the gunner, and captured nine prisoners. His courage and initiative saved his comrades from heavy casualties.

10/868 Private L Nowell (LG 20/10/16)
For conspicuous gallantry during operations. He jumped into a bay in the enemy's trenches, shot two of the enemy and captured another.

10/14 Corporal T E Saunderson of Hull (LG 17/4/17)
For conspicuous gallantry and devotion to duty. Although very severely wounded, he continued to encourage his

men, and refused help until the company had taken up its new position. He was exposed to heavy fire throughout, and in great pain.

10/317 Sergeant H E Sendall (LG 18/7/17)

For conspicuous gallantry and initiative. During an attack, in which his Section Commander was killed, he assumed command and led his men into the enemy trench, where he bombed and successfully kept back the enemy bombing party, thereby keeping their machine gun from coming into action. He showed most marked resource at very short notice.

10/1134 Private W Singleton, MM of Hull (LG 30/10/18)

For conspicuous gallantry and devotion to duty. During our attack a gap was formed between the battalion and the unit on its flank. Pte. Singleton, on his own initiative, took up a position with his Lewis Gun and kept the gap covered with his fire until the final objective was reached and the gap was made good. He materially assisted in the capture of a farm that was held by the enemy by engaging with great effort a machine gun that was holding up the movement of our troops. On both occasions his ready action and skilful management of his gun, which he used with most resolute courage, prevented much delay and saved many casualties.

10/47 Sergeant (A/CSM) C Street of Hessle (LG 11/3/20)

As a stretcher-bearer at Ploegsteert Wood, on the 28th September 1918, he did excellently. He controlled a large squad of stretcher-bearers and worked with them under heavy fire for twenty-four hours, evacuating quickly a large number of wounded.

3/5555 Private E Thynne of Felling-on-Tyne (LG 30/10/18)

For conspicuous gallantry and devotion to duly. During an advance this soldier was ever in the forefront of the attack. When the advance was delayed at a farm that was determindly held by the enemy, he rushed forward through heavy machine gun fire and forced his way into the buildings. Pte. Thynne captured three prisoners; the remainder of the garrison retired precipatately. The final objective having been reached he volunteered to take back the information to battalion headquarters. After making his way through a heavy hostile barrage, he safely delivered his message, together with a most useful account of the precise situation and the requirements of the frontline. His behaviour throughout was distinguished by brilliant gallantry.

10/742 Private C H Vollans (LG 22/9/16)

For conspicuous bravery and devotion to duty. Though wounded he stuck to his sentry post until his tour of duty was ended. He then insisted on waiting till more seriously wounded men had been attended to before going to a dressing station.

10/765 Sergeant F Willis (LG 11/12/16)

For conspicuous gallantry in action. He led a patrol under heavy fire with great courage and determination. Later, he rescued a wounded man from "No Man's Land", and carried in a man who had been killed.

11th BATTALION

22510 Corporal J W Atkin - claimed by the battalion but not recorded by the regiment.

11/293 Sergeant J W Clayton, B Company (LG 18/8/17)

For conspicuous gallantry and devotion to duty. He displayed the greatest coolness and resource in rallying and in the dark reorganising two platoons which were leaderless and under an intense fire. He then led them to the attack, which was repulsed, and having withdrawn to their assembling trench he again rallied them and consolidated and organised the defence with very great skill and determination. Throughout the day his example was one of complete fearlessness and contempt of danger.

11/989 CSM T Farey, C Company (LG 3/9/19)

He has served almost continually with the unit since it proceeded overseas on December 11th 1915. Throughout this period he has been thorough and conscientious in his work, and his devotion to duty has been a splendid example to all ranks. During the enemy offensive in March and April, 1918, he repeatedly displayed great courage and determination in assisting to rally and reorganise his company.

7651 Private W Fortes, D Company (LG 3/9/18)

For conspicuous gallantry and devotion to duty in March, 1918. When taken prisoner, this man seized a rifle from one of the escort, killed three of them, and brought the fourth one back to the lines. After handing over his prisoner, he returned to his Company and fought splendidly throughout the battle.

11/1456 Lance Corporal J Hackitt, MM of Doncaster (LG 28/3/18)

For conspicuous gallantry and devotion to duty when in charge of his company stretcher-bearers. He went forward with the first wave of a daylight raid. Throughout the raid, and after, he went backwards and forwards to the enemy frontline carrying back wounded men on his shoulders, though snipers were most active and there was a hostile barrage on our trench.

Second Award (LG 3/9/18)

For conspicuous gallantry and devotion to duty. He repeatedly went forward in charge of parties to collect wounded. Under heavy fire he was responsible for removing twenty men to a place of safety who would otherwise have been made prisoners. London Gazette 3/9/18.

203811 Private R Harris, A Company (LG 3/9/18)

For conspicuous gallantry and devotion to duty. He was in charge of a Lewis gun post, which had to be held at all costs. When the gun teams were all casualties this man held on till the gun was destroyed by gun fire. He then used his rifle in the moonlight with such accuracy that the enemy was held in check until he was relieved.

41761 Private E J Heller, D Company (LG 6/2/18)

For conspicuous gallantry and devotion to duty. He reorganised and led forward a wavering line composed of men of various units, and single-handed, rushed an enemy post, killing and capturing twelve of the enemy. His magnificent courage and disregard of danger were conspicuous throughout the operations.

11/785 Sergeant E Marritt, A Company, of Hull (LG 1/1/18)

For conspicuous gallantry and devotion to duty in an attack. He was in command of his Lewis gun section, and by his courage and resource he was mainly responsible for the capture of two enemy strong points and a machine gun.

11/497 Lance-Corporal J Morrod, B Company, Hull (LG 28/3/18)

For conspicuous gallantry and devotion to duty when in charge of his Company stretcher-bearers during a daylight raid. After the enemy second line had been rushed he brought back a wounded man from there to our line, afterwards returning to the enemy front line and remaining there after his Company had withdrawn until all the wounded had been sent back. He then worked for eight hours in our line, sending the wounded back to the advance dressing station.

11/225 Sergeant H Often, A Company of Hull (LG 30/10/18)

For conspicuous gallantry and devotion to duty. This NCO was acting as Company Sergeant Major during our attack. Single-handed, he captured five of the enemy who were delaying our advance with machine gun fire, and, on reaching the final objective, he was of the greatest assistance to the Company and Platoon commanders in reorganising the men and consolidating the captured position. Throughout the attack and during the very intense hostile bombardment that followed he set a very fine example of steadfast determination and cheerful fortitude to all his company.

204301 Private B P Porter, A Company of Weston-super-Mare (LG 30/10/18)

For conspicuous gallantry and devotion to duty while in charge of a Lewis gun team. Realising the right flank of his Company was in danger, he skilfully manoeuvred his team, under heavy fire, to the exposed flank, and brought his gun into action at a critical moment, with the result that he gained superiority of fire and enabled his Company to advance.

18332 Sergeant T Radcliffe, A Company of Nuneaton (LG 3/9/19)

From 25th February to 16th September 1918. He has on many occasions during the last six months distinguished himself in action. He has constantly shown extraordinary coolness under fire, and has always set an example of pluck and endurance to his men. He is a splendid leader and has rendered excellent service to the battalion.

11/1207 Corporal T Sawyers, D Company (LG 30/10/18)

For conspicuous gallantry in leading his section against an enemy post which was holding up the general advance. The situation called for immediate action, and realising this, he skilfully pushed his section forward and eventually rushed the position. When the line was established he organised parties to carry ammunition to the posts under very trying circumstances. His courage and determination were a fine example to his men.

11/812 Sergeant E M Thompson, HQ Company (LG 3/9/18)

At Ervillers on the 24th/25th March, 1918, this NCO, who was the Orderly Room Sergeant, when men from Headquarters were asked for, left his desk and proceeded with other men of Headquarters to the firing line. On the way up an enemy patrol of one officer, twelve men and a machine gun were encountered. Owing to the courage, determination and skill with which this NCO handled his men, the whole patrol was captured with only one casualty to his party. After this encounter this NCO and his men again started for the line, but another enemy patrol was met, and close fighting ensued, during which one enemy prisoner was taken and the patrol dispersed with casualties. In the line this NCO showed great coolness in organising his command under heavy shell and machine gun fire. He remained here until all was quiet, and then returned to his clerical duties. This NCO's work was beyond all praise, and throughout he set a splendid example under heavy shell fire and trying circumstances.

36489 Lance-Corporal J E Wilson, A Company (LG 28/3/18)

For good work during a raid on the German trenches in front of Fresnoy (Arras-Lens sector) on the 8th November, 1917. The work consisted of getting his men into line after they had made a mistake in getting into our own barrage. He also did good destructive work, since he had two R.E 's attached to his section.

11/707 CSM W Woodall, D Company (LG 18/7/17)

For conspicuous gallantry and devotion to duty in twice reorganising his Company under very heavy hostile barrage and leading them to the attack. All his company officers were out of action and the Company suffered very heavy losses, so he decided to consolidate and hold on. The leadership he displayed under such adverse circumstances was magnificent.

15383 Lance-Corporal F Wright, B Company (LG 30/10/18)

For conspicuous gallantry and devotion to duty. During our attack this NCO was in the first wave of his company when the advance was being delayed by the fire of an enemy machine gun in a concealed position. He dashed through a hedge, and, discovering the emplacement of the gun, shot and killed the gunner; the remainder of the detachment surrendered. The captured gun was then turned on the enemy. He displayed great coolness and gallantry, and his prompt action overcame what might undoubtedly have proved a very serious obstacle to the advance.

12th BATTALION
12/510 Acting Sergeant G A Aket (LG 10/1/17)
For conspicuous gallantry in action. He assumed command of and handled his Company with great courage and skill, reorganising his men and sent parties forward to the second line.

12/1071 Sergeant A V Bell of Hull (LG 10/1/20)
During the fighting in the Foret de Mormal, 4th and 5th November 1918, he displayed great gallantry and ability throughout. After his officer was killed he carried out his duties during the day until relieved by an officer. He made a reconnaissance under heavy fire and succeeded in getting in touch with the division on the left, and guided them to form a liaison post between the Corps.

12/888 Sergeant W A Bone of Hull (LG 10/1/20)
During an attack at Neuvilly on 10th October 1918, he was in command of a Platoon guiding the right flank of the attack. His leadership and utter disregard of personal danger materially assisted towards the success of the operation, getting his men by his determined example across the River Selle. He then led them against an enemy machine-gun post, capturing two guns and killing the teams.

12/288 Acting Sergeant H Dewson (LG 10/1/17)
For conspicuous gallantry in action. He led his Platoon with great courage and determination, and held a post. Later, he went back and brought up a supply of bombs under heavy fire.

12/28 Sergeant P Freeman (10/1/17)
For conspicuous gallantry in action. He took several bombing parties over the open and drove back some enemy bombers who were attacking the right flank. Later, he continued to carry on his work alone.

8773 Sergeant E H Jenkins (LG 20/9/16)
For conspicuous gallantry during a raid on the enemy's trenches. He showed great coolness, and set a fine example, bringing back the wounded to our line, and later returning to the enemy wire and helping to bring in a wounded enemy.

12/299 Private E Spafford (LG 10/1/17)
For conspicuous gallantry in action. He carried a message while under very heavy fire. Later, with some other men, he held a communication trench for five hours against several enemy attacks.

12/257 Sergeant A Walters (LG 10/1/17)
For conspicuous gallantry in action. With five men he cleared part of the enemy trench and captured one officer and the crew of a trench mortar gun. Later he consolidated

a post and held it for nine and a quarter hours against several enemy attacks.

13th BATTALION
13/310 Corporal W. Aspinall of Hull (LG 20/10/16)
For conspicuous gallantry during a raid on the enemy's trenches. Though wounded in two places the day before he insisted on taking part in the raid, and displayed great dash in the enemy's trenches, inflicting loss on the occupants.

13/15 Private W Bailey of Hull (LG 3/9/18)
For conspicuous gallantry and devotion to duty during a strong enemy attack. He was sent to a spot with two signallers to establish communication with battalion headquarters. The spot indicated was occupied by the enemy, but he managed to signal successfully with his towel from a secondary position. He subsequently crept back to his secondary post under machine gun and shell fire and from an exposed position successfully maintained communication for two days.

13/690 Corporal G Cotton of Hull (LG 28/3/18)
For conspicuous gallantry and devotion to duty. On hearing sounds of movement in front of his post at night he went forward alone and succeeded in capturing four of the enemy, who were in a shell hole in front of the wire. By his prompt action he secured a valuable identification.

13/1408 Lance-Corporal B Fairfield of Hull (LG 22/9/16)
For conspicuous gallantry under fire. He pursued four enemy down a trench, wounding one. Subsequently, under heavy fire, he brought in a wounded officer.

13/997 Lance-Corporal W Fletcher (LG 10/1/17)
For conspicuous gallantry in action. He displayed great courage and determination while his Company was consolidating the position won. He held a communication trench with two men against repeated enemy bombing attacks.

13/562 Private H Foster (LG 22/9/16)
For conspicuous gallantry and dash. He was alone when he reached an enemy dug-out containing an officer and five men. He threw two bombs, killing four, and taking two prisoners.

13/380 Sergeant S Russell of Elloughton (LG 17/4/18)
For conspicuous gallantry and devotion to duty. He showed great resource in patrol work, often obtaining most valuable information, in spite of adverse conditions. His courage and determination have always been most inspiring to all with him.

13/1085 CSM D Sandilands MC (LG 10/1/17)
For conspicuous gallantry in action. He assumed command of and handled his Company with great courage and determination. He set a splendid example throughout.

13/297 Sergeant (A/CSM) J B Wilson (LG 25/11/16)
For conspicuous gallantry and initiative during a raid. It was in a large measure due to this NCO's successful

patrolling that the raid was practicable. On two occasions he went well into the enemy wire and tested its strength, and during the raid took control of the party, after his officer had been wounded. After returning to our lines he called for volunteers and returned to the wire to search for wounded.

MILITARY MEDAL
10th Battalion
MM and Bar
10/1191	Private L. Jarvis, MM
10/603	Sergeant G. Page, MM
11/493	Corporal W.H. Noble, MM

MM
10/697	Sergeant A.C. Abba
10/102	Corporal F. Baker
10/656	Sergeant A. Baldwin
31498	Private B. Bell
10/986	Sergeant E. Best
10/735	Sergeant W.R. Boag
10/913	Sergeant F. Bold
10/736	Sergeant J.W. Brown
10/691	Lance-Corporal B. Brumby
10/1201	Sergeant A. Charles Worth
10/188	Corporal C. Clarke
10/464	Lance-Corporal F. Clipson
10/992	Corporal J.H. Crooks
10/296	Corporal F. Davie
10/1014	Private W. Dawson
10/246	Corporal J. Dixon
10/507	Private J.A. Dobbs
10/290	Private H. Dover
10/243	Sergeant J. Ellis
10/445	Sergeant H. Fisher
10/437	Corporal J. Godman
10/663	Private H. Graystone
10/847	Sergeant W. Hall
10/439	Corporal C. Hermann
10/1029	Sergeant F.E. Hermann
10/1191	Lance-Corporal L. Jarvis
10/7	Private G.E. Ledraw
10/1000	Sergeant R. Lee
10/1306	Private J. Lewis
10/495	Private E. Marsden
10/1185	Lance-Corporal E. Mowforth
10/115	Corporal E.A. Nunns
10/603	Corporal F.G. Page
10/1099	Lance-Corporal J.D. Petty
10/768	Corporal J.G. Pippett
10/1362	Lance-Corporal H. Rawling
10/668	Private C.C. Reynolds
10/586	Lance-Corporal W. Robinson
225198	Sergeant J.W. Roo
10/1372	Private L. Shapero
10/664	Lance-Corporal S. Schottlander
10/583	Private C. Simpkins

10/361	Private J.E. Simpson
10/1134	Private W. Singleton, OCM
10/663	Lance-Corporal G.A. Smith
10/205	Corporal J.N. Stather
10/138	Private T. Stringer
10/135	Corporal R. Terry
10/342	Sergeant W.A. Thompson
13/267	Lance-Corporal C. Verity
10/1308	Private A. Walsh
10/1335	Lance-Corproal J. Ward
10/1038	Private J.H. Wilkinson
10/1262	Sergeant W.H.V. Winter
10/589	Sergeant H. Youngson

11th BATTALION
MM and Bar
33399	Private A. Arskey, C Company
11/1289	Sergeant G.W. Bonas, B Company
11/48	Sergeant Broadhead, C Company
11/105	Sergeant C.H. Chapman, B Company
11/1191	Lance-Corporal L. Jarvis, C Company
11/720	Private T.F. Lamb, B Company
11/422	G.P. Rust, C Company
11/730	Corporal G.W. Willerton, A Company

MM
11/832	Sergeant J. Aarons, D Company
11/802	Private J.E. Allison, 92nd TMB
11/562	Lance-Corporal J.W. Anson, A Company
9448	Sergeant E. Atkin, D Company
11/538	Private L. Bailey, HQ
11/26	Private H. Bates, B Company
37647	Private F. Bentley, B Company
11/1129	Private A. Blakey, HQ
13276	Private A. Bowman
41301	Private S. Brook
———	Private S. Browne, A Company
205554	Private C. Bryers, C Company
11/402	Corporal H. Bury
11/245	Lance-Corporal F. Caborn, A Company
11/402	Private J. Clarkson, C Company
11/357	Sergeant R. Cressey, B Company
19639	Lance-Sergeant A. Davis
11/129	Corporal G. Dawson, B Company
11/805	Corporal C.L. Dearing, B Company
11/947	Lance-Corporal J.A. Deary, C Company
11/491	Lance Corporal E. Dobbs, B Company
11/792	Sergeant J.W. Downie, B Company
11/715	Private G. Downs, A Company
18905	Private J. Driver, C Company
11/891	Sergeant J. Dunn, Transport
11/923	Private W.A. Edwards, B Company
11/146	Private J.L. Elston, B Company

11/368	Corporal A. England, A Company
41725	Private F.W. Flatlow, A Company
41888	Private A. Fletcher ———
6921	Private J. Fowler ———
11/994	Sergeant L. Fussey, attached 92 TMB
20572	Private G. Gorman, D Company
11/1144	Private E. Gould, B Company
11/1456	Private J. Hackitt DCM, C Company
23691	Private W.H. Hall, B Company
11/463	Corporal F. Harrison, C Company
11/1299	Private A. Harrison, C Company
36478	Corporal F. Haynes, A Company
11/375	Private J. Hill, 92nd TMB
11/1325	Private J. Humphrey, HQ
13928	Private A.P. Jefferson, A Company
11/136	Lance-Corporal G.A. Jeffery, B Company
41769	Private F.A. Kenyon ———
11/650	Private C.H. Kitching, HQ
6773	Corporal E.C. Kitching, B Company
28067	Corporal M. Lawrence, A Company
32914	Private W. Lazenby, A Company
11/928	Private W. Marsh, C Company
11/1244	Private G.E. Lowen, C Company
6974	Lance-Corporal J. McIndoe, C Company
11/879	Private A.J. McKay, HQ
11/497	Corporal J. Morrod, B Company
11/673	Lance Corporal C.J. Nix, B Company
11/874	Private G. Oakes, B Company
11/1292	Lance-Corporal R.W. Peck, D Company
11/597	Corporal W. Pool, D Company
30522	Private G.E. Bryers, C, Company
28591	Private A. Proctor, HQ
11/9	Corporal J.H. Pyne, C Company
11/1361	Lance-Corporal H. Rawling, A Company
11/251	Private E.M. Robson, HQ
11/380	Sergeant J.E. Rudd, D Company
11/1358	Private W. Rutledge, B Company
11/772	Sergeant H. Sellers, HQ
11/393	Corporal F.L. Sharpe, C Company
11/1327	Private J.C. Shepard, D Company
40912	Private A. Skeavington, attached 92 TMB
11/234	Private J.A. Smith, C Company
3091	Corporal W.H. Smith, C Company
11/1428	Sergeant G. Sonley, D Company
11/803	Private A. Stamford, HQ
29617	Corporal P. Stokoe, D Company
11/56	Private C.W. Toogood, A Company
11/784	Corporal C.H. Thacker, C Company
28328	Private W. Tilletson, D Company
9007	Corporal H.O. Tindall, D Company

11/743	Lance-Corporal B. Trowill, D Company
11/1375	Corporal R.G. Usher, A Company
11/698	Lance-Corporal H. Whisker, A Company
36309	Private T. White
25089	Corporal T.A. Wilde, C Company
11/154	Sergeant C.W. Wilkinson, A Company
51054	Private J.W. Wilkinson, D Company
11/1221	Private D.S. Willerton, HQ
11/730	Lance-Corporal G.W. Willerton, A Company
25063	Private A.W. Windus, C Company
11/127	Private C.W. Windus, B Company
17419	Private H. Wordley, A Company
31573	Private A. Wright, A Company

12th BATTALION
MM

12/1024	Private A. Bacon
12/1485	Corporal J. Banks
12/888	Sergeant W.A. Bone, DCM
12/453	Sergeant A. Chester
12/830	Private E. Collinson
12/1264	Private A.A. Cotton
12/721	Sergeant T.F. Guest
12/608	Corporal J. Haran
12/284	Private E.B. Harrison
12/305	Private J.W. Kerry
12/650	Private C.H. Kitching
12/643	Corporal E. Robinson
12/1327	Private J.C. Shephard
12/959	Private J.W. Shields
12/1375	Corporal R.G. Usher
12/1526	Private G.H. Wollas

13th BATTALION
MM

13/306	Corporal J. Annable
13/988	Private J.E. Barkworth
13/276	Lance-Corporal J.A. Bassett
13/1308	Private W. Beacock
13/498	Private C. Benstead
13/48	Sergeant T.H. Broadhead
13/1063	Sergeant J.R. Brown
13/50	Private F.B. Challons
13/950	Private H. Chatterton
13/1016	Sergeant B. Dalton
13/772	Corporal E.H. English
13/1269	Lance-Corporal A. Fisher
13/956	Private J.W. Fisher
13/957	Private G. Foster
13/1092	Sergeant J. Hallam
13/1164	Sergeant C. Highton
13/815	Sergeant G. Hodge

13/298	Lance-Corporal J. Howlett
13/1275	Private H.G. Hutchings
13/157	Lance-Corporal W. Levitt
13/714	Private M. Lydon
13/723	Private D. Mumby
13/355	Private B. Neylon
13/790	Sergeant T.E. Norman
13/727	Sergeant H. Petrie
13/579	Lance-Corporal I. Singleton
13/887	Lance-Corporal C. Smith
13/246	Lance-Corporal H.W. Smith
13/1307	Lance-Corporal H. Tripp
13/665	Private G.R. Wilson
13/1416	Sergeant J.W. Wilson

MERITORIOUS SERVICE MEDAL
10th BATTALION
10/644	Private W. Davis
10/637	Sergeant J.M. Fenwick
10/530	CQMS A.H. Grindelle
10/553	Corporal D.A. Pudsey
10/660	Sergeant H. Swift (from Hull)
10/143	Sergeant L.M. Wrigglesworth (from Hull)

11th BATTALION
203099	Corporal G. Atkinson (from Filey)
11/299	CQMS & A/CSM H. Armstrong, D Company
220262	CQMS A.J. Dennis, B Company
11/61	Sergeant W. Pickersgill (from Hull)
11/1197	Corporal G.F. Nicholson
28149	Sergeant J. Richmond, D, Company
25213	Private C. Waudby (from Hull)

12th BATTALION
| 12/222 | RQMS W.J. Rodway |

13th BATTALION
| 13/461 | Corporal W.J. Orvis |
| 13/296 | Sergeant R.H.Yates |

MENTIONED IN DISPATCHES
10th Battalion
Lieutenant-Colonel T.A. Headlam
Major R.C. Hewson
Captain S.E. Le Blancq
Second Lieutenant J.D. Petty
Lieutenant L.D. Pierson
10/830	Private W.G. Andrew
10/286	Private W. Bailey
10/294	Private H. Clark
10/1086	CQMSS. Cressy
10/992	Corporal J.H. Crooks, D Company.
10/539	Lance-Corporal G.E. Gibson

10/437	Lance-Corporal J. Goodman
10/1430	Private W. Middleton
10/607	RQMS J.P. Milns
10/159	Corporal E. Mooton
10/927	Sergeant S.H. Moses
10/419	CSM R. Pinchon
10/140	Private H. Reveler
10/379	Private J.T. Rodham
10/1402	Lance-Corporal H. Tindale
10/915	Private F.C. Wilson
10/143	Sergeant L.M. Wrigglesworth

11th BATTALION
Second-Lieutenant G.W. Bladen, MC, MM
Lieutenant G. Bradley
Second-Lieutenant R.D. Caley
Lieutenant-Colonel S.H. Ferrand, OSO
Lieutenant-Colonel C.H. Gurney, DSO
Lieutenant G.F. Hall
Second-Lieutenant W.H. Hall
Lieutenant H. Smith, DSO (twice)
Major J. Shaw
Captain H.F. Williams, MC
22614	Lance-Sergeant W.S. Bates, B Company
11/607	CSM J. Camplin, A Company
11/868	Sergeant J.H. Gosling, C Company
11/12	RQMS H.H. Grainger, HQ
11/249	Sergeant F. Kelly, B Company
11/781	Corporal D.S. Mcintosh, B Company
7335	Lance-Corporal F.J. Mellor, C Company
11/926	CQMS C.W. Miller, A Company
30441	Private F. Smith, B Company
11/589	RQMS H. Smith, HO

12th BATTALION
12/453	Sergeant A. Chester
12/318	Sergeant A.E. Coman
12/17	CSM F. Crabtree
12/868	Sergeant J.H. Gosling
12/754	Corporal E. Kershaw
12/139	Sergeant E. Lovell
12/483	Sergeant G.W. Spence
12/40	Sergeant J.W. Wilkinson

13th BATTALION
13/1375	Private T. Flanagan
13/1115	Sergeant G. Harrison
13/727	Corporal H. Petrie, MM

FOREIGN DECORATIONS
10th BATTALION
Lieutenant-Colonel R.C. Hewson, MC, Croix de Guerre (French)

Captain C.L. Penn, Croix de Guerre (Belgian)

10/478 Lance-Sergeant J.W. Allen, Croix de Guerre (Belgian)

10/88 CQMS T. Davison, Medaille D'Honneur avec glaves en argent (France)

10/996 Private J.W. Fisher, Bronze Medal for Military Valour (Italy)

10/847 RSM W. Hall, MM, Croix de Guerre (Belgian)

10/761 Lance-Sergeant A. Jackson, Croix de Guerre (Belgian)

10/1306 Sergeant J. Lewis, MM, Croix de Guerre (Belgian)

10/586 Corporal W. Robinson, MM, Croix de Guerre (French)

10/1134 Corporal W. Singleton, DCM, MM, Croix de Guerre (French)

10/1308 Sergeant A. Walsh, Medaille Militaire (French)

10/1262 Sergeant W.H. Winter, MM, Croix de Guerre (Belgian)

11th BATTALION

Lieutenant Colonel S.H. Ferrand, DSO, MC, L'Ordre de Leopold & Croix de Guerre (French)

Lieutenant V.H. Jenkin, MC, Croix de Guerre (French)

Lieutenant J. Sever, Croix de Guerre (Belgian)

Major J. Shaw, Croix de Guerre (French)

Lieutenant P.P. Whittington-Ince, MC, Croix de Guerre (French)

11/562 Sergeant J.W. Anson, A Company, MM, Croix de Guerre (Belgian)

28091 Private S. Browne, A Company, MM, Croix de Guerre (French)

11/947 Sergeant J.A. Deary, C Company, MM, Croix de Guerre (French)

11/805 Corporal C.L. Dearing, B Company, MM, Croix de Guerre (Belgian)

11/441 Private J. Dixon, D Company, Croix de Guerre (French)

23691 Lance-Sergeant W.H. Hall, B Company, MM, Croix de Guerre (French)

11/1164 Sergeant S. Highton, 92 TMB, MM, Croix de Guerre (Belgian)

11/41 Private R.H. Landen, HQ, Medaille d'Honneur (French)

9007 Corporal H. Tindall, D Company, MM, Croix de Guerre (French)

12th BATTALION

None have been traced to this battalion

13th BATTALION

13/464 Sergeant C. Highton, Croix de Guerre (Belgian)

13/380 Private S. Russell, Croix de Guerre (Belgian)

Awards to 14th Battalion Soldiers serving with other Active Service Battalions of the East Yorkshire Regiment

14/202 Corporal F Cartledge, Mentioned in Dispatches

14/194 Corporal C S Thompson, Meritorious Service Medal 8/9/14

Plaque to Private John Cunningham VC in Chiltern Street Primary School. *The Hull Daily Mail*

Plaque to Lieutenant John Harrison, VC MC in the City Hall.

Appendix 4

10th Battalion Soldiers' deaths in date order

18/9/14	10/40	PTE	THOMAS	ADAMS	DIED AT HOME
2/4/15	14133	PTE.	JAMES LAWRENCE	SIMMONS	DIED AT HOME
29/3/16	10/716	PTE.	STANLEY	HORSFIELD	KIA
30/3/16	10738	PTE.	GEORGE ARTHUR	WELLS	KIA
17/4/16	10/1028	PTE.	EDGAR	HYDE	KIA
30/5/16	10/25	PTE.	HERBERT	GALE	KIA
31/5/16	10/180	PTE.	JOHN	GALT	DOW
4/6/16	10/267	PTE.	JOHN HENRY	MONDAY	KIA
4/6/16	10/845	PTE.	GEORGE HENRY	JOHNSON	KIA
4/6/16	10/527	PTE.	ALBERT	BLAKEMORE	KIA
4/6/16	10/855	PTE.	GEORGE WILLIAM	BRAY	KIA
4/6/16	10/121	PTE.	FRANK	JOHNSON	KIA
4/6/16	10/1392	PTE.	GEORGE	ARCHER	KIA
4/6/16	10/560	PTE.	WALTER RICHARD	RANEY	KIA
4/6/16	10/890	PTE.	HARRY	STORR	KIA
4/6/16	10/277	PTE.	WILLIAM BERNARD	ASCOUGH	KIA
4/6/16	10/734	PTE.	PERCY	BROWN	KIA
4/6/16	10/1247	PTE.	GEORGE KILBY	DEIGHTON	KIA
4/6/16	10/1155	L/CPL.	LEWIS EDWARD	PEEK	KIA
4/6/16	10/813	PTE.	JOHN RICHARD	FARNILL	KIA
4/6/16	10/1413	PTE.	HAROLD HERBERT	PAWSON	KIA
4/6/16	10/557	PTE.	WILLIAM VINCENT	MILLER	KIA
4/6/16	10/819	PTE.	CHARLES SAMSON	JOYS	KIA
4/6/16	10/1144	PTE.	ARTHUR ERNEST	WEST	KIA
4/6/16	10/128	PTE.	OSCAR ROUNDING	LEIGHTON	KIA
4/6/16	10/787	PTE.	SAMUEL	CONYERS	KIA
4/6/16	10/346	PTE.	LEONARD	WEBSTER	KIA
5/6/16	10/261	PTE.	BENJAMIN	IRELAND	DOW
5/6/16	10/827	L/CPL.	WILLIAM ARTHUR	MacPHERSON	DOW
7/6/16	10/774	PTE.	FRANK KELLETT	WOODCOCK	DOW
7/6/16	10/123	PTE.	JOHN BELL	ATKINSON	DOW
11/6/16	10/717	SGT.	THOMAS	HUNTINGTON	DOW
15/6/16	10/520	PTE.	CYRIL WINTERTON	RILEY	DOW
21/6/16	10/867	PTE.	REGINALD CONRAD	NEILL	DOW
25/6/16	10/1131	PTE.	SAMUEL	CALEY	KIA
25/6/16	10/366	PTE.	ARTUR HAROLD	NORTH	DOW
26/6/16	10/1285	PTE.	ALFRED BARRETT	NORTH	KIA
26/6/16	10/73	PTE.	GEORGE	BLENKIN	KIA
27/6/16	10/1297	PTE.	GEORGE WALTER	BUCK	KIA
28/5/16	10/466	PTE.	JOHN	BRUNYEE	KIA
28/6/16	10/1221	PTE.	JOSEPH	CHENEY	KIA
28/6/16	10/39	PTE.	JAMES STANLEY	WATSON	KIA
1/7/16	10/621	SGT.	REGINALD PERCIVAL	JONES	KIA
1/7/16	10/341	PTE.	WILLIAM HENRY	DALTON	KIA
2/7/16	10/525	PTE.	WILLIAM EDWIN	ADAMSON	DOW
2/7/16	10/561	PTE.	STANLEY	COOP	DOW
22/7/16	10/998	PTE.	CHARLES HERBERT	KINGDOM	KIA
23/7/16	10/793	PTE.	MARK	WILSON	KIA

23/7/16	2367	PTE.	DAVID	DOUGLAS	DOW
30/7/16	22122	PTE.	STANLEY HOBSON	HARSLEY	KIA
2/8/16	10/507	PTE.	JAMES APPLEYARD	DOBBS, MM	KIA
3/8/16	10/797	L/CPL.	LEONARD	JEYNES	KIA
6/8/16	21762	PTE.	FRANCIS	SMITH	KIA
6/8/16	10/100	PTE.	ALFRED	BARKER	DOW
6/8/16	10/17	L/CPL.	ALBERT WARE	TAYLOR	DOW AT HOME
11/8/16	10/136	PTE.	PERCY	LOCKEY	KIA
13/8/16	10/1123	PTE.	HERBERT	DEMPSEY	DOW
16/8/16	10/232	PTE.	ROGER LESLIE	KIDO	DOW
19/8/16	10604	PTE.	FRANCIS KENNETH	PAGE	DOW
26/8/16	10639	PTE.	ARCHIE VERNON	EMERY	DOW
11/9/16	10/1140	PTE.	FRANCIS	STONE	DOW AT HOME
16/9/16	10605	PTE.	HERBERT	GARTON	KIA
18/9/16	10/160	PTE.	EDMUND	KEENE	KIA
18/9/16	10/407	PTE.	ALFRED	WEBSTER	KIA
19/9/16	10/45	SGT.	ARTHUR	TINDALE	KIA
22/9/16	10690	CPL.	ERIC CLAUDE	DUNN	KIA
22/9/16	21718	PTE.	WILLIAM RICHARD	SKELTON	KIA
22/9/16	21053	PTE.	ROBERT HAROLD	WOFFINDEN	KIA
22/9/16	10641	PTE.	WALTER	DENNISON	DOW
22/9/16	21720	PTE.	GEORGE ALBERT	WARD	DOW
20/10/16	10/1101	PTE.	WALTER	ROBINSON	KIA
29/10/16	10684	PTE.	THOMAS PERCIVAL	MILLARD	KIA
29/10/16	10/422	PTE.	LAWRENCE FREDERICK	JEFFREY	KIA
12/11/16	26096	PTE.	WILLIAM	PARKINSON	KIA
13/11/16	10651	PTE.	GEORGE WILLIAM	TETHER	KIA
13/11/16	10653	PTE.	JAMES FRANCIS	BROCKLEHURST	KIA
13/11/16	23656	PTE.	ALBERT WILLIAM	PREGDEN	DOW
13/11/16	10672	PTE.	THOMAS ARTHUR	NASBY	KIA
13/11/16	28037	PTE.	TOM SCOTT	BRUMBY	KIA
13/11/16	19007	PTE.	NOAH	GALLEAR	KIA
13/11/16	28240	PTE.	EDWARD	MUTTER	DOW
14/11/16	10675	PTE.	WALTER STANLEY	EVERINGHAM	KIA
17/11/16	10/1029	SGT.	EDGAR	HERMANN, MM	DOW
22/11/16	10626	PTE.	WILLIAM JAMES	JACKSON	KIA
26/11/16	14/172	PTE.	GEORGE FREDERICK	WILLIAMSON	DIED AT HOME
28/11/16	10694	PTE.	REGINALD	FITTON	DOW
3/12/16	25379	PTE.	JOSEPH	DOHERTY	KIA
5/12/16	10696	PTE.	ARTHUR	SYKES	KIA
14/1/17	10659	PTE.	HARRY	ODD	DOW AT HOME
28/1/17	19000	PTE.	JOHN	MUNDAY	DIED
26/2/17	9844	PTE.	JAMES WILLIAM	JACKMAN	KIA
28/2/17	10/430	SGT.	WILLIAM ERNEST	HARRISON	KIA
26/2/17	10/401	PTE.	WILLIAM HENRY	WARN	KIA
27/2/17	19003	PTE.	JOHN	BRADLEY	KIA
27/2/17	21257	PTE.	JAMES ARTHUR	BATCHELOR	KIA
27/2/17	36313	CPL.	WILLIAM	OXFORD	KIA
27/2/17	33445	PTE.	HERBERT WILLIAM	BROWN	KIA
27/2/17	36321	PTE.	EDWARD WILUAM	SMART	KIA
28/2/17	25412	PTE.	FRANCIS ERNEST	TRAVIS	DOW
28/2/17	10/1059	PTE.	ARTHUR HENRY	DIXON	DOW
1/3/17	10/14	CPL.	THOMAS ERNEST	SAUNDERSON, DCM	DOW
4/3/17	28034	PTE.	ALBERT EDWARD	BELL	DOW
6/3/17	10/676	PTE.	ROBERT	KEAL	DOW

8/3/17	10/103	PTE.	FREDERICK	WALTON	KIA
12/3/17	10/1133	PTE.	WILLIAM SYKES	LANGDALE	KIA
12/3/17	25394	PTE.	THOMAS CYRIL	MORRELL	DOW
28/3/17	19733	PTE.	JOSEPH	CLARK	DOW
3/5/17	35028	PTE.	EDWARD JACOB	COATES	KIA
3/5/17	10/806	CPL.	THOMAS	BUCK	KIA
3/5/17	33213	PTE.	ALFRED	CHAPMAN	KIA
3/5/17	26099	PTE.	ARTHUR	SCRUBBS	KIA
3/5/17	10/958	PTE.	WALTER JAMES	CLEARY	KIA
3/5/17	21806	PTE.	HERBERT SYDNEY	SIMON	KIA
3/5/17	10/723	SGT.	BERTRAM ARTHUR	CLUBLEY	KIA
3/5/17	10/138	PTE.	JOSEPH HENRY	MORLEY	KIA
3/5/17	10/12860	PTE.	JOHN WILLIAM	CLARK	KIA
3/5/17	18745	PTE.	FRANK	OLDFIELD	KIA
3/5/17	36314	PTE.	BENJAMIN CHARLES	NICHOLAS	KIA
3/5/17	25353	PTE.	LEONARD	SEEKERSON	KIA
3/5/17	220003	CPL.	JOHN	McNALLY	KIA
3/5/17	26583	PTE.	EDGAR	MILLER	KIA
3/5/17	18919	PTE.	FRED	SCHOFIELD	KIA
3/5/17	18998	PTE.	RICHARD EDWIN	WILKES	KIA
3/5/17	28234	PTE.	CHARLES	RUNKEE	KIA
3/5/17	10/931	PTE.	JAMES	McBRIDE	KIA
3/5/17	220035	PTE.	JOHN	BAXTER	KIA
3/5/17	33105	PTE.	HORACE	BATEMAN	KIA
3/5/17	10/1186	PTE.	GEORGE WILUAM	WINTER	KIA
3/5/17	18994	PTE.	WILLIAM JOSEPH	CRESSWELL	KIA
3/5/17	36356	CPL.	SYDNEY	BLACKSHAW	KIA
3/5/17	10/609	PTE.	GEORGE	MATTHEWS	KIA
3/5/17	23939	PTE.	DAVID	BANCROFT	KIA
3/5/17	10/574	PTE.	THOMAS ALBERT	POWELL	KIA
3/5/17	35013	PTE.	CHRISTIAN	BALMFORTH	KIA
3/5/17	220043	PTE.	ERNEST	MARRITT	KIA
3/5/17	18902	PTE.	JOHN	PICKLES	KIA
3/5/17	10/286	CPL.	WILLIAM	BAILEY	KIA
3/5/17	10/92	SGT.	ERNEST WOOD	DAWSON	KIA
3/5/17	33354	PTE.	ROBERT ERNEST	ANNIS	KIA
3/5/17	10/483	PTE.	HAROLD	ABBA	KIA
3/5/17	10/266	PTE.	ALFRED	MOSS	KIA
3/5/17	20354	PTE.	EDWARD	DEIGHTON	KIA
3/5/17	25365	PTE.	BERTRAM WILLIAM	HAWKINS	KIA
3/5/17	12033	PTE.	EDWARD	GUEST	KIA
3/5/17	21671	PTE.	ROBERT	HOTSON	KIA
3/5/17	25371	L/CPL.	BERTIE	KEENAN	KIA
3/5/17	35084	PTE.	ERNEST SYLVESTER	HAIGH	KIA
3/5/17	3/6594	PTE.	SAMUEL DAVID	FRITH	KIA
3/5/17	226038	PTE.	DAVID PAGE	FOX	KIA
3/5/17	33115	PTE.	FREDERICK WILUAM	KIRKBY	KIA
3/5/17	26084	PTE.	STANLEY CRESWICK	SOUTHCOTT	KIA
3/5/17	33095	PTE.	WILLIAM EDWARD	HEESON	KIA
3/5/17	36319	PTE.	HAROLD	EASTWOOD	KIA
3/6/17	10636	L/CPL.	GEORGE LEWIS	SPRING	KIA
3/5/17	35073	PTE.	GEORGE	SPENCER	KIA
3/6/17	22914	PTE.	WILLIAM	STEWART	KIA
3/5/17	10/65	PTE.	ROBERT	UNSLEY	KIA
3/5/17	36332	PTE.	ALBERT	HOLMES	KIA

3/5/17	10/118	PTE.	HORACE		KIRKMAN	KIA
3/5/17	10/770	PTE.	WILUAM		LAZENBY	KIA
3/5/17	18965	PTE.	JOHN		JAMES	KIA
3/5/17	18906	PTE.	ZEPHANIAH		FLETCHER	KIA
3/5/17	18978	PTE.	CHARLES HARRY		WALTERS	KIA
3/5/17	28046	PTE.	JOHN THOMAS		COOK	KIA
3/5/17	220041	PTE.	ROBERT		JUBB	KIA
3/5/17	10/1054	PTE.	ERNEST WALTER		SELLERS	KIA
3/5/17	22121	PTE.	WILLIAM		LEE	KIA
3/5/17	28054	PTE.	HENRY DALTON		GOLDSPINK	KIA
3/5/17	10/1231	L/CPL.	RICHARD HENRY		SMITH	KIA
3/5/17	37902	PTE.	JOHN HENRY		DUNN	KIA
3/5/17	10/532	PTE.	HARRY		JOHNSON	MA
3/5/17	22126	PTE.	GEORGE FENBY		FISHER	KIA
3/5/17	10/677	PTE.	HERBERT		SUMMERS	KIA
3/5/17	33129	PTE.	HENRY		FUSSEY	KIA
3/5/17	10/627	L/CPL.	FREDERICK		JACKSON	KIA
4/5/17	36350	PTE.	GEORGE		EDEN	DOW
6/5/17	23964	PTE.	ERNEST WILUAM		CLARK	KIA
7/5/17	27783	PTE.	GEORGE		TURNER	KIA
7/5/17	36371	PTE.	JOHN		COOPER	DOW
7/5/17	10/1233	PTE.	ALFRED ERNEST		MESSENGER	KIA
7/5/17	33228	PTE.	BETHEL		HAYTON	KIA
7/5/17	10/932	SGT.	ALBERT HENRY		NASH	KIA
9/5/17	28042	PTE.	GEORGE FREDERICK		COCKERUNE	DOW
9/5/17	13/1134	SGT.	FRANK		MENNELL	DOW
23/5/17	21587	PTE.	LEONARD HODGSON		BROWN	KIA
26/5/17	10/67	PTE.	PERCY		RUSSELL	DOW
29/5/17	33117	PTE.	FREDERICK WILLIAM		WOODIFIELD	DOW
29/5/17	33141	PTE.	FREDERICK STUART		ROBSON	DOW
2/6/17	10/1038	SGT.	JOHN HENRY		WILKINSON. MM	DOW
13/6/17	10/1355	PTE.	JOSEPH HENRY		COBBY	DIED
20/6/17	37898	PTE.	FRANK		GUTHERLESS	KIA
22/6/17	10/672	PTE.	PERCY		MARTWOALE	KIA
22/6/17	10/968	PTE.	WALTER RAYMOND		HOMAN	KIA
25/6/17	21098	PTE.	ERNEST		DIXON	DOW
25/6/17	10/350	PTE.	LEONARD		YOUNG	DOW
25/6/17	36420	PTE.	VINCENT		WALLACE	KIA
29/6/17	10/493	SGT.	RICHARD		MILLER	KIA
6/7/17	10/1072	SGT.	FRANK		CHALMERS	DIED AT HOME
7/7/17	10/838	PTE.	JOHN		SMITH	DOW
11/7/17	10/764	PTE.	GEORGE WILLIAM		GILL	KIA
19/7/17	37886	PTE.	ROBERT NELSON		ADAMS	KIA
9/8/17	27399	PTE.	SAM		RAWSON	KIA
10/8/17	10/1207	L/CPL.	GEORGE ERNEST		BOWEN	DOW
11/8/17	28236	PTE.	ALFRED EARDSLEY		WILMOT	DOW
10/9/17	25352	PTE.	SAMUEL		BALLARD	KIA
10/9/17	36397	PTE.	ALFRED		EDMUNDS	KIA
14/9/17	25942	CPL.	MITCHELL		BALMFORTH	DIED AT HOME
18/9/17	10/318	L/CPL.	JOSEPH RONALD HERBER		TMAYOR	DOW
25/10/17	16843	PTE.	HENRY		FOSTER	DOW
28/10/17	36661	L/CPL.	EDWIN STANLEY		DUFFIELD	KIA
4/11/17	10/1008	PTE.	SIDNEY		TAYLOR	KIA
5/11/17	22603	PTE.	ROBERT GASCOIGNE		HUTTON	KIA
6/11/17	27339	PTE.	ROBERT		JACKSON	KIA

30/11/17	19285	PTE.	JOHN WILLIAM	WATSON	DOW
21/2/18	37093	PTE.	ROBERT ISAAC	DIXON	DOW
24/3/18	28057	PTE.	JAMES ALFRED	HARRIS	KIA
24/3/18	3/5568	PTE.	WALTER	PARKER	KIA
24/3/18	203649	PTE.	WILFRED	PRICE	KIA
24/3/18	225720	PTE	HARRY	SILL	KIA
24/3/18	37049	PTE.	GEORGE THOMAS	BARRS	KIA
24/3/18	36344	PTE.	JOSEPH	TUMBLETY	KIA
24/3/18	10/751	PTE.	DONALD ALFRED	ROBERTS	KIA
24/3/18	27921	PTE.	WILLIAM GEORGE	BREALEY	KIA
24/3/18	36605	SGT.	WILLIAM JOHN	PIGGOTT	KIA
24/3/18	36306	PTE.	WILLIAM	ARBON	KIA
24/3/18	27094	PTE.	ROBERT HENRY	HOLROYD	KIA
24/3/18	37945	PTE.	CUFORD	DICKINSON	KIA
24/3/18	37923	PTE.	FREDERICK THOMAS	HICKS	KIA
25/3/18	10/431	CPL.	CYRIL GEORGE	HALL	KIA
25/3/18	14147	PTE.	SAMUEL	ARMES	KIA
25/3/18	32958	PTE.	WILLIAM WARD	HAYTON	KIA
25/3/18	37904	PTE.	JOHN FOORD	HUTCHINSON	DOW
25/3/18	220017	L/CPL.	ALBERT	ARSKEY	KIA
25/3/18	36705	PTE.	PETER VEITCH	JOHNSON	KIA
25/3/18	18926	PTE.	FRANK	JAGGER	KIA
25/3/18	225291	PTE.	ALBERT EDWARD	SISSONS	KIA
25/3/18	12/1366	CPL.	WILLIAM	JACKSON	KIA
25/3/18	33021	PTE.	WILLIAM	NICHOLSON	KIA
25/3/18	3/6754	PTE.	JOHN WILLIAM	DOOSWORTH	KIA
26/3/18	37099	PTE.	JOHN THOMAS	SIMPSON	KIA
26/3/18	28679	PTE.	WILLIAM	WILSON	DOW
27/3/18	10/856	PTE.	ARTHUR HAYWARD	WRIGHT	KIA
27/3/18	26092	PTE.	WALTER	FLINTON	KIA
27/3/18	12/42	PTE.	HUNTER	HALL	KIA
27/3/18	202954	PTE.	EDWARD RICHARD	ALLCOCK	KIA
27/3/18	3/6868	PTE.	JOHN WILLIAM	BELLAMY	KIA
27/3/18	19592	PTE.	PHILIP CHEW	ANDREW	KIA
27/3/18	34257	PTE.	HENRY RICHARD	FORD	KIA
27/3/18	36711	PTE.	HARRY	HOWARTH	DOW
28/3/18	26066	PTE.	GEORGE	GILYEAD	KIA
28/3/18	27347	PTE.	ALFRED	SHAW	KIA
28/3/18	203211	PTE.	JOHN	GOLDSMITH	KIA
28/3/18	36976	PTE.	JAMES	DINSDALE	KIA
29/3/18	37065	PTE.	WILFRED	WATSON	KIA
29/3/18	17462	PTE.	JOHN WILLIAM	LAKE	KIA
29/3/18	28205	PTE.	CHARLES	NICHOLS	KIA
29/3/18	21921	PTE.	HUGH	LOFTUS	KIA
29/3/18	10/1248	PTE.	FRANK ERNEST	HARDING	DOW
30/3/18	11/1407	PTE.	WALTER	LONG	DOW
30/3/18	23878	PTE.	RICHARD	BLACKER	DOW
30/3/18	10/31	PTE.	JOHN	COMINS	DOW
2/4/18	37068	PTE.	NIXON	SMITH	DOW
2/4/18	28179	L/CPL.	HORACE ALFRED	DANIELS	DOW
4/4/18	37048	PTE.	ALBERT	MITCHELL	KIA
9/4/18	33030	PTE.	JOHN WILLIAM	KIRKBY	DOW
12/4/18	28939	PTE.	FRANK	HILL	KIA
12/4/18	30204	PTE.	WILLIAM	REID	KIA
12/4/18	10/1106	CPL.	ERNEST BENNETT	STEVENS	KIA

12/4/18	29192	PTE.	STEPHEN		HOAD	KIA
12/4/18	30337	PTE.	FRANKLIN GEORGE		BEVEN	KIA
12/4/18	30149	CPL.	JOHN		GRACE	KIA
12/4/18	10/681	L/CPL.	HENRY		HICKS	KIA
12/4/18	30288	PTE.	FREDERICK		HILL	KIA
12/4/18	36333	PTE.	ERNEST		HAYTER	KIA
12/4/18	29956	PTE	SAM		HUTTON	KIA
12/4/18	12/1445	PTE.	CHARLES		SMITH	KIA
12/4/18	10/478	PTE.	JOSEPH WILLIAM		ALLEN	DOW
12/4/18	14/208	PTE.	HARRY		HOODS	KIA
12/4/18	10/305	PTE.	FRANK		HOLMES	KIA
12/4/18	30268	PTE.	WILLIAM HENRY		RICHARDS	KIA
12/4/18	10/205	SGT.	JOHN NORRISON		STATHER. MM	KIA
12/4/18	10716	PTE.	EDWARD MILBURN		THOMPSON	KIA
12/4/18	30202	PTE.	HERBER		ROBINSON	KIA
12/5/18	14260	PTE.	HENRY		BARRASS	KIA
12/4/18	30109	PTE.	JAMES FREDERICK		ARMSTRONG	KIA
12/4/18	10/708	PTE.	GEORGE HERBERT		JESSUP	KIA
12/4/18	27244	L/CPL.	JAMES		JOHNSON	MA
12/4/18	36640	PTE.	HENRY EDWARD		ASHWORTH	KIA
12/4/18	38586	PTE.	JOHN EDWARD		WRIGHT	KIA
12/4/18	30245	PTE	JOHN		BOARDMAN	KIA
12/4/18	36642	PTE.	EDMUND		GLADWELL	KIA
12/4/18	37901	PTE.	HENRY		WLLYARD	KIA
12/4/18	10/519	PTE.	FRANK HERBERT		JOHNSON	KIA
12/4/18	17629	PTE.	MATTHEW		NICHOLSON	KIA
12/4/18	12/934	L/CPL.	JAMES		JORDAN	KIA
12/4/18	29959	PT.	JOHN		PARKER	KIA
12/4/18	21812	PTE.	GEORGE WILSON		BOOTY	KIA
12/4/18	33066	PTE.	NORMAN		RICHARDSON	KIA
12/4/18	30306	PTE.	NORMAN JOHN		McILVRIDE	KIA
12/4/18	30233	PTE.	CHARLES FREDERICK		WARNE	KIA
12/4/18	10/78	SGT.	FREDERICK ELUS		NEWBERT	KIA
12/4/18	11/1395	PTE.	JOHN		MADDRA	DOW
12/4/18	28362	CPL.	WILLIAM		CULLUM	KIA
12/4/18	24897	PTE.	TOM CAMPEY		MARSHALL	KIA
12/4/18	30176	PTE.	WILLIAM		MADDEN	KIA
12/4/18	30216	PTE.	HENRY		SHENTON	KIA
12/4/18	12/61	SGT.	CHARLES		WHITELEY	KIA
12/4/18	30104	L/CPL.	PERCY		LAWTON	KIA
12/4/18	30234	PTE.	CECIL		WILLIAMS	KIA
12/4/18	18979	PTE.	CHARLES		KNIGHT	KIA
12/4/18	10/1223	L/CPL.	GEORGE FREDERICK		LANGTHORPE	KIA
12/4/18	30145	PTE.	JOEL		FLAVELL	KIA
12/4/18	10/218	PTE.	WILLIAM HIRST		BRIGGS	KIA
12/4/18	30303	PTE.	JOSEPH		WILKINSON	KIA
12/4/18	29197	L/CPL.	BERTIE		LING	KIA
12/4/18	9767	PTE.	EDWIN GRAHAM		HEAVEN	KIA
12/4/18	28077	PTE.	ARTHUR EDWARD		SINGLETON	KIA
12/4/18	23967	PTE.	GEORGE		SLEIGHT	KIA
12/4/18	30273	PTE.	WILLIAM		SORBY	KIA
12/4/18	225794	PTE.	RICHARD JOHN THOMAS		CADOGAN RYDE SMITH	KIA
12/4/18	226045	PTE.	CHARLES EDWARD		ALLCOCK	KIA
12/4/18	13/814	PTE.	JOHN WILLIAM		HESTER	KIA
12/4/18	27960	PTE.	GEORGE		LEESON	KIA

12/4/18	29944	PTE.	FRANK	CANHAM	KIA
12/4/18	40937	PTE.	JOHN	McCABE	KIA
12/4/18	1079	PTE.	STANLEY	MARR	KIA
12/4/18	10/774	PTE.	WILSON	WEBB	KIA
12/4/18	220435	PTE.	GEORGE	SEAMAN	KIA
12/4/18	12/578	PTE.	ALFRED	BROWN	KIA
12/4/18	30315	PTE.	ARTHUR THOMAS	WHITE	KIA
13/4/18	10/314	PTE.	BERNARD	TETHER	KIA
13/4/18	30208	PTE.	ALFRED	SIMPSON	DOW
13/4/18	10/1251	PTE.	HAROLD	SMITH	DOW
13/4/18	30174	PTE.	JOHN	MAHER	KIA
13/4/18	19725	PTE.	JOHN HENRY	HARGREAVES	KIA
13/4/18	37206	PTE.	JAMES SIDNEY	HEWITT	KIA
13/4/18	29950	PTE.	THOMAS	ELLIOTT	KIA
13/4/18	10/1356	CPL.	WILLIAM	DIXON	KIA
13/4/18	33463	PTE.	ROBERT	WOOD	KIA
13/4/18	9609	SGT.	ERNEST JOHN	WALKER	KIA
13/4/16	30345	PTE.	ALFRED AUGUSTUS	BRADBROOK	KIA
13/4/18	30322	PTE.	RAYMOND CARL	ALLEN	KIA
13/4/18	10/295	PTE.	SYDNEY	LATUS	KIA
13/4/18	16890	PTE.	GEORGE	MILTON	KIA
13/4/18	28044	PTE.	RICHARD	CLAXTON	KIA
14/4/18	10/686	PTE.	PERCY CAMERON	HALL	DOW
14/4/18	15748	PTE.	JAMES	COSGRAVE	KIA
14/4/18	121035	PTE.	ERNEST WILLIAM	TAYLOR	DOW
16/4/18	13/469	PTE.	ALBERT	RUSUNG	DOW
17/4/18	30292	PTE.	THOMAS	MILLER	DOW
17/4/18	27990	PTE.	WALTER	NICHOLS	KIA
16/4/16	30219	PTE.	JOSEPH	TAYLOR	DOW
18/4/18	10/459	PTE.	HERBERT STENNETT	CORDEN	KIA
27/4/18	29963	PTE.	THOMAS LISLE	SMURTHWAITE	KIA
27/4/18	29966	PTE.	TOM	WADE	KIA
27/4/18	23959	PTE.	HENRY	BROWN	DOW
27/4/18	10/702	L/CPL.	JAMES	METCALFE	KIA
27/4/18	33051	PTE.	JOHN BROWN	CROMBIE	KIA
27/4/18	10/1206	CPL.	WALTER	THOMAS	KIA
27/4/18	10044	PTE.	ERNEST	FORD	KIA
12/5/18	28058	CPL.	ARTHUR WILLIAM	HALL	DOW
16/5/18	28038	PTE.	EDMUND WILLIAM	BAKER	DOW
19/5/18	30226	PTE.	ERNEST	WHITE	KIA
20/5/18	30238	PTE.	HENRY BAILEY	CRUMP	DOW
7/6/18	30300	PTE.	CHARLES	VERITY	KIA
15/6/18	225176	L/CPL.	JAMES	JACKSON	KIA
18/6/18	30170	L/CPL.	HARVEY INGHAM	LORD	KIA
18/6/18	30261	PTE.	DANIEL	HUTCHINSON	KIA
28/6/18	10/959	PTE.	HAROLD	DOUGHERTY	DOW
28/6/18	225889	PTE.	JOHN GILBERT	CORDON	KIA
28/6/18	30177	PTE.	JAMES	MAITLAND	KIA
28/6/18	12/971	PTE.	FREDERICK	MOTHERBY	KIA
28/6/18	11/464	PTE.	ALBERT BROWN	NAYLOR	KIA
28/6/18	12/35	PTE.	JAMES ANDREW	COOK	KIA
28/6/18	28765	PTE.	PERCY	CARRICK	KIA
28/6/18	201258	PTE.	ROBERT	FISHER	KIA
28/6/18	37047	PTE.	JOSEPH HENRY	LEDGER	KIA
28/6/18	36338	PTE.	CHARLES EDWARD	MASTERS	KIA

Date	Number	Rank	First Name	Surname	Status
28/6/18	17867	PTE.	ALBERT JOHNSON	WALKER	KIA
28/6/18	220189	PTE.	GEORGE	TWEDOLE	KIA
28/6/18	30101	PTE.	JOHN THOMAS	COWLEY	KIA
28/6/18	8775	CPL.	ERNEST	MURPHY	KIA
28/6/18	30105	PTE.	WILLIAM	POWELL	KIA
28/6/18	30274	PTE.	JOHN REVILL	SHAW	KIA
28/6/18	10/939	CPL.	ALFRED	POTTS	KIA
28/6/18	10/1045	PTE.	ISAAC	REUBEN	KIA
28/6/18	25965	CPL.	CHARLES	WILLIAMS	KIA
28/6/18	30121	PTE.	ARTHUR GEORGE	BOULTON	KIA
28/6/18	36758	PTE.	FRANK	THURLOE	KIA
28/6/18	10/693	SGT.	WILFRED	BONE	KIA
28/6/18	37899	PTE.	GEORGE	HARRISON	DOW
28/6/18	31065	PTE.	ERNEST	HAXBY	KIA
28/6/18	220019	PTE.	ALFRED	HARRISON	KIA
28/6/18	16595	SGT.	JAMES COXON	GRAHAM. MM	KIA
28/6/18	30317	PTE.	FREDERICK	ABEL	KIA
28/6/18	52800	PTE.	ERNEST EDWARD	HOLMES	KIA
28/6/18	30156	PTE.	GEORGE	HALLIWELL	KIA
29/6/18	29042	PTE.	GEORGE WILLIAM	DAWSON	KIA
29/6/18	36733	PTE.	HERBERT	RHODES	DOW
30/6/18	36799	PTE.	GEORGE SHIPLEY	TUCKER	DOW
30/6/18	41447	L/CPL.	DAVID CHARLES	COULSON	DOW
30/6/18	200854	PTE.	ALFRED	WALTON	DOW
6/7/18	10/41	L/CPL.	EDWARD RANDOLPH	PERKINS	DOW
11/7/18	10/336	PTE.	JOSEPH WILLIAM	COLLINGWOOD	DOW AT HOME
12/7/18	21563	PTE.	FRED	CAWKWELL	KIA
13/7/18	22598	PTE.	JOHN FRANCIS	MANN	KIA
14/7/18	30284	PTE.	HORACE	RUDKIN	DOW AT HOME
23/7/18	36611	PTE.	JOSEPH	PEARS	DOW
29/7/18	30213	PTE.	CHARLES EDGAR	SUTTON	KIA
29/7/18	3/6334	PTE.	ERNEST	SMETHURST	DIED
29/7/18	12/587	PTE.	ROBERT PERCY	FRANKS	DOW
1/8/18	10543	PTE.	EDWARD	PATTERN	KIA
1/8/18	30142	PTE.	CLARENCE	DAWSON	KIA
1/8/18	28504	PTE.	WILLIAM	CHRISPEN	KIA
2/8/18	30168	PTE.	CYRIL NORMAN	KELLY	KIA
2/8/18	29957	PTE.	JOHN JAMES	LUMSDON	KIA
2/8/18	29769	PTE.	EDWARD	GASH	KIA
8/8/18	51141	PTE.	HENRY	GRAHAM	DOW
11/8/18	41034	PTE.	ALBERT EDWIN	AKERS	DOW
14/8/18	30327	PTE.	WILLIAM RICHARD	ASKEM	KIA
14/8/18	41450	L/CPL.	GEORGE WILFRED	JONES	DOW
14/8/18	51213	PTE.	ROBERT HOPPER	MILLER	KIA
14/8/18	36408	PTE.	JOSEPH	COOPER	KIA
14/8/18	37914	PTE.	HERBERT WILLIAM	COX	KIA
14/8/18	202878	PTE.	ARTHUR	CROCKFORD	KIA
14/8/18	41867	PTE.	JOHN	THOMAS	KIA
14/8/18	10/528	CPL.	RALPH EDWIN	BROWNE	KIA
14/8/18	11947	PTE.	BERNARD	MURPHY	KIA
15/8/18	30280	PTE.	LAWRENCE	WILSTROP	KIA
16/8/18	27888	PTE.	ARTHUR	HILL	KIA
16/8/18	10/95	CPL.	ARTHUR	TURNER	KIA
16/8/18	22418	PTE.	GEORGE EDWARD	LILLEY	KIA
15/8/18	10/1291	PTE.	WILLIAM ERNEST	FOWLER	DOW

15/8/18	6148	PTE.	BARTHOLEMEW	SIZER	KIA
16/8/18	225198	SGT.	JAMES WILLIAM	ROO. MM	KIA
16/8/18	9461	L/CPL.	ALFRED	SMITH	DOW
18/8/18	51167	CPL.	ROBERT NEWTON	VASEY	KIA
19/8/18	30229	PTE.	JAMES	WHITTINGHAM	DOW
20/8/18	51112	PTE.	JOSEPH	LONGSTAFF	KIA
25/8/18	29467	PTE.	JOHN	HUNT	DOW
25/8/18	10/148	PTE.	GEORGE WILLIAM	WEST	KIA
2/9/18	17737	PTE.	SAMUEL CAVE	MAY	DOW
2/9/18	41449	CPL.	FRANK LOCKWOOD	GREENWOOD	KIA
3/9/18	26316	PTE.	CHRISTOPHER MAURICE	CLAYTON	KIA
3/9/18	51179	PTE.	FRANCIS	HINDMARSH	KIA
3/9/18	37890	PTE.	DOUGLAS	CLAYFORD	DIED
3/9/18	30295	PTE.	THOMAS	PICKUP	KIA
3/9/18	51133	PTE.	GEORGE WILLIAM	RAINBOW	KIA
3/9/18	21684	PTE.	JOHN WILLIAM	HALL	KIA
3/9/18	41249	PTE.	JOSEPH HAROLD	ETTRIDGE	KIA
3/9/18	51776	PTE.	ALBERT EDWARD	JOINER	KIA
3/9/18	12136	PTE.	ALBERT	MARSHALL	KIA
3/9/18	37260	PTE.	HORACE	ALLSTON	KIA
3/9/18	36403	CPL.	GILBERT HENRY	ESCOTT	KIA
3/9/18	39675	PTE.	ERNEST	GOSLING	KIA
3/9/18	5193	PTE.	ERNEST ALBERT	GOODEY	KIA
4/9/18	31473	PTE.	FREDERICK CHARLES	WARREN	KIA
4/9/18	28227	PTE.	FRANK	HINCHSLIFF	KIA
4/9/18	41442	SGT.	WILLIAM	WARD. MM	KIA
4/9/18	30318	PTE.	RICHARD FREDERICK	ADAMS	KIA
4/9/18	38897	PTE.	ALBERT	EVERITT	KIA
4/9/18	51118	PTE.	JOSEPH	HARRIS	KIA
4/9/18	12.574	SGT.	GEORGE	ARNELL	KIA
4/9/18	21970	PTE.	PHILIP GEOFFREY	JONES	KIA
4/9/18	39204	PTE.	ALFRED	HAWKSWORTH	KIA
4/9/18	25597	PTE.	FRED	BARRETT	KIA
5/9/18	27871	PTE.	JOSEPH	BRITTON	DOW
6/9/18	220642	SGT.	ALBERT WILLIAM	DRASOO	DOW
6/9/18	201350	PTE.	JAMES	BOWER	DOW
6/9/18	33451	PTE.	FREDERICK	GRINDELL	KIA
7/9/18	51194	PTE.	ALBERT HENRY	WALUNGTON	KIA
7/9/18	7883	CPL.	HERBERT	BLANCHARD	KIA
7/9/18	41072	L/CPL.	ALBERT WILLIAM	HEWITT	KIA
7/9/18	39073	PTE.	WALTER	POTER	KIA
7/9/18	25391	PTE.	GEORGE	COX	KIA
7/9/18	17067	SGT.	THOMAS	CAM	KIA
7/9/18	14/125	PTE.	CHARLES	CANTY	KIA
7/9/18	51209	PTE.	JAMES ALEXANDER	HENDERSON	KIA
7/9/18	41749	PTE.	ALFRED HURREN	HAMENWAY	KIA
7/9/18	51120	L/CPL.	GEORGE THOMAS	MORTON	KIA
7/9/18	52811	PTE.	JOHN WILLIAM	WOOD	KIA
7/9/18	38151	PTE.	HENRY LEWIS	HOYLE	KIA
7/9/18	51201	PTE.	THOMAS FREDERICK	SPIVEY	KIA
7/9/18	30483	PTE.	ARTHUR	WOMAR	DOW
7/9/18	30332	PTE.	WALTER EDWARD	BAILEY	KIA
7/9/18	51148	PTE.	JOSEPH	POLLARD	KIA
7/9/18	36981	PTE.	WILLIAM BLACK	PROUDFOOT	KIA
7/9/18	39681	PTE.	JOHN	HAGESTADT	KIA

7/9/18	30313	PTE.	ARTHUR EDWARD	PRIOR	KIA
7/9/18	51207	PTE.	WILLIAM	BRAMLEY	KIA
7/9/18	41344	PTE.	JOHN JAMES WALKER	THOMPSON	KIA
7/9/18	13022	PTE.	ERNEST	WRIGHT	KIA
7/9/18	41168	PTE.	FREDERICK	NASH	KIA
7/9/18	201869	PTE.	WILLIAM	McGUIRE	DOW
7/9/18	7723	PTE.	JOSEPH HENRY	ADAMS	KIA
7/9/18	39055	PTE.	THOMAS	PRESCOTT	KIA
7/9/18	220431	L/CPL.	BEN	CLOUGH	KIA
7/9/18	21796	PTE.	FREDERICK WILIAM	PEARCE	KIA
7/9/18	10/1249	PTE.	JOHN EDWARD	NEWTON	KIA
7/9/18	39655	PTE.	CHARLES EDWARD	WARD	KIA
8/9/18	51171	PTE.	ARTHUR JAMES	GARNHAM	DOW
10/9/18	41223	PTE.	HERBERT HACKNEY	GILLIVER	KIA
10/9/18	51177	PTE.	FREDERICK	BIGGS	KIA
10/9/18	23963	L/CPL.	ALBERT	MALLORY	KIA
11/9/18	27046	PTE.	JAMES TADMAN	MERCER	DOW
11/9/18	31445	PTE.	BENJAMIN	KAY	DOW
22/9/18	10898	PTE.	JOHN	LINFORD	KIA
22/9/18	38921	PTE.	ERNEST	GILL	DOW
22/9/18	10013	PTE.	CYRIL FRAZER	TENNISON	DIED AT HOME
26/9/18	11561	PTE.	WILLIAM	GRAYBURN	DOW
28/9/18	39492	PTE.	THOMAS VICKERSON	PLACE	KIA
28/9/18	30351	PTE.	ALBERT EDWARD	MIDDLETON	KIA
28/9/18	51168	PTE.	FRED	JACKSON	KIA
28/9/18	30235	PTE.	WILLIAM LACE	WILLIAMS	KIA
28/9/18	39561	PTE.	GEORGE HARDY	COOPER	KIA
28/9/18	36797	PTE.	ROBERT	WILSON	KIA
28/9/18	51724	PTE.	THOMAS EDWARD	CLAPTON	KIA
28/9/18	41445	CPL.	CLIFFORD	PRICE	KIA
29/9/18	51215	PTE.	STANLEY	BLAGG	KIA
29/9/18	14324	L/CPL.	RICHARD	McNALLY	KIA
29/9/18	51150	PTE.	ISAAC	LAWS	KIA
29/9/18	28220	PTE.	REGINALD	HUNT	KIA
29/9/18	12/65	PTE.	ALBERT EDWARD	HUNT	KIA
29/9/18	51312	PTE.	HORACE	PICKERSGILL	KIA
29/9/18	51734	PTE.	JOHN WILLIAM	TINDELL	DOW
29/9/18	39473	PTE.	ERNEST	SHACKLER	KIA
29/9/18	51773	PTE.	EDWARD JOSEPH	GASCOYNE	KIA
29/9/18	31048	PTE.	JOHN BERNARD	CLARK	KIA
29/9/18	39407	PTE.	ERNEST	SHOULER	KIA
29/9/18	41119	PTE.	PERCY	DOWTEN	KIA
29/9/18	12/1389	PTE.	CHARLES SYDNEY	EDWARDS	KIA
29/9/18	30241	PTE.	CHARLES ERNEST	VICKERS, MM	KIA
29/9/18	51725	PTE.	NOEL JOSEPH PICKHARD	JOHNSON	KIA
29/9/18	39412	PTE.	JAMES HERBERT	WADDINGHAM	KIA
29/9/18	39188	PTE.	AMOS	WRIGHT	KIA
29/9/18	36562	SGT.	JOSEPH BROOKS	WOOLFENDEN	KIA
29/9/18	16632	CPL.	JOHN	REDPATH, MM & BAR	DOW
29/9/18	51330	PTE.	LAWENCE	WILLIAMSON	KIA
29/9/18	51742	PTE.	HARRY	WATTS	KIA
29/9/18	51753	PTE.	JOHN	WINDER	KIA
29/9/18	28047	PTE.	GEORGE HERBERT	CHAMBERS	KIA
29/9/18	42187	PTE.	GEORGE LUTHER	BALDWIN	KIA
29/9/18	36336	PTE.	WILLIAM	BROOK	DOW

29/9/18	39189	PTE.	WALTER	MOORE	KIA
29/9/18	220653	PTE.	FRANK LOUIS	MARRIOTT	KIA
29/9/18	39190	PTE.	JOHN	RICHARDS	KIA
29/9/18	39429	PTE.	ALBERT	SEAGRAVE	KIA
29/9/18	39426	PTE.	WILLIAM HENRY	PROCTOR	KIA
29/9/18	12/236	PTE.	JOHN WILLIAM	BURDON	KIA
29/9/18	39389	PTE.	ISRAEL	WESTMORELAND	KIA
29/9/18	3.6493	PTE.	FRANK	BROTHERTON	KIA
30/9/18	36626	SGT.	FELIX	POLLON	KIA
1/10/18	220490	PTE.	THOMAS	LITTLE	DIED
1/10/18	51777	PTE.	CLIFFORD	MANNERS	DOW
2/10/18	51326	PTE.	HERBERT	TALFORD	DOW
5/10/18	39448	L/CPL.	NATHAN	MARTIN	DOW
14/10/18	26168	CPL.	RICHARD ELLIOTT	CRYER	KIA
15/10/18	10/20	PTE.	WILLIAM	HORSFALL	KIA
15/10/18	51682	PTE.	LESLIE CONRAD	SHEARIN	KIA
15/10/18	36344	PTE.	GEORGE THOMAS YELLAND	BOXALL	DOW
26/10/18	51175	PTE.	JOSEPH HENRY	LITTLE	DOW AT HOME
27/10/18	10655	PTE.	PERCY	BOYD	KIA
28/10/18	55019	PTE.	GEORGE	WADDINGHAM	KIA
28/10/18	30136	L/CPL.	JOHN ALBER	CLARKE	KIA
29/10/18	10/225	PTE.	MAURICE WILLIAM	MORACK	DOW
6/11/18	40933	PTE.	JOSEPH	BRAMWELL	DOW
11/11/18	29972	PTE.	FRANK	MOMENT	DOW
11/11/18	10/1172	PTE.	ROBERT BERNARD	STEAD	DIED
13/11/18	51686	PTE.	THOMAS	PINK	DOW
15/11/18	10/923	PTE.	CLARENCE	BILBE	DIED
19/11/18	39345	PTE.	WILLIAM RAYMOND	BOTHAM	DIED
22/2/19	51197	PTE.	NORMAN POOLE	BROWN	DOW AT HOME
21/1/20	12/433	PTE.	CLAUD	RICHARDSON	DOW AT HOME

Appendix 5

11th Battalion Soldiers' deaths in date order

7/11/14	11/528	PTE.	EDWARD ALBERT	HOLMES	DIED AT HOME
15/6/15	11/428	PTE.	FRANK	WARD	DIED AT HOME
23/9/15	11/373	PTE.	JAMES JOSEPH	MURRAY	DIED AT HOME
6/3/16	11/282	PTE.	WALTER	EDWARDS	DIED AT SEA
29/3/16	11/1078	PTE.	CHARLES WELTON	STUART	KIA
29/3/16	11/135	PTE.	GEORGE	BROWN	KIA
1/4/16	11/1045	PTE.	MARTIN	MARONEY	DIED
1/4/16	11/883	SGT.	JOHN LEONARD	HESELTINE	DOW
14/4/16	11/1255	PTE.	FREDERICK CHARLES	HAMILTON	DIED
17/4/16	11/822	PTE.	ALFRED	TENNISON	KIA
25/4/16	30368	PTE.	HERBERT	NORTH	KIA
4/5/16	11/742	PTE.	ARTHUR BARTON	COOK	DOW
10/5/16	11/541	PTE.	FREDERICK GEORGE	GREASLEY	DOW
13/5/16	11/139	CPL.	CHARLES	COLLINGWOOO	DOW

30/5/16	11/172	SGT.	HARRY	HALL	KIA
30/5/16	11/149	SGT.	ALBERT	SIMPSON	KIA
2/6/16	11/1200	PTE.	WALTER dePRESTON	PARKER	DOW
3/6/16	11/1176	PTE.	EDWARD WILLS	JOHNSON	KIA
8/6/16	11/1125	PTE.	SYDNEY	PICK	DOW
16/6/16	11/1188	PTE.	ALBERT THOMAS	MARSHALL	KIA
16/6/16	11/1216	PTE.	MICHAEL HENRY	WARD	KIA
16/6/16	11/1256	PTE.	HAROLD	JOHNSON	DOW
17/6/16	11/948	SGT.	WALTER	TOWNSEND	DIED
26/6/16	11/1393	PTE.	WILLIAM	WELLS	KIA
26/6/16	14/209	PTE.	JOHN JOSEPH	DRISCOLL	KIA
27/6/16	11/448	PTE.	WILLIAM	SAWDEN	KIA
27/6/16	11/49	SGT.	FRANK	COX	KIA
1/7/16	11/709	L/CPL.	JOSEPH WILLIAM	MASON	DOW
1/7/16	11/1186	PTE.	JOHN	MARCHANT	KIA
1/7/16	11/1432	PTE.	THOMAS	DIXON	KIA
2/7/16	11/1345	PTE.	EDWARD	HARRISON	DOW
20/7/16	11/392	PTE.	GEORGE ERNEST	GRANTHAM	KIA
20/7/16	11/105	PTE.	HAROLD	CHAPMAN. MM	KIA
21/7/16	14/133	PTE.	JAMES WILFRED	ROBSON	KIA
21/7/16	13.143	PTE.	CHARLES BERNARD	CURTIS	DOW
22/7/16	12/1267	PTE.	JOHN	WALSH	KIA
22/7/16	11/451	PTE.	JOSEPH BELL	MEGAHY	KIA
22/7/16	11/398	PTE.	WALTER	PEEPS	DOW
22/7/16	11575	PTE.	SAMUEL	CARRINGTON	DOW
23/7/16	11/902	PTE.	FREDERICK WILLIAM	HERBERT	KIA
30/7/16	11/992	PTE.	JAMES WILLIAM	MATTHEWS	DOW
31/7/16	11/263	PTE.	ALFRED CHARLES	BUTLER	DOW AT HOME
31/7/16	11/1203	PTE.	FRED	RABY	DOW
31/7/16	12/100	PTE.	GILBERT	SPINK	KIA
1/8/16	11/826	CPL.	FRANK	FEATHERSTONE	DOW
1/8/16	11/852	PTE.	ERNEST	IZOD	KIA
2/8/16	11/1279	PTE.	HERBERT	THEAKSTON	KIA
3/8/16	11/681	PTE.	HERBERT	HODGSON	KIA
3/8/16	11/314	PTE.	SYDNEY	GIBSON	KIA
4/8/16	11/429	PTE.	GEORGE	WEMYSS	DOW
9/8/16	11/395	PTE.	JOHN	McNALLY	DOW
17/8/16	11/596	PTE.	FRED	PROCTOR	KIA
19/8/16	11/746	PTE.	PERCY	BREWSTER	DIED
20/8/16	21709	PTE.	JAMES	WRIGHT	KIA
27/8/16	11/369	PTE.	BENJAMIN RHODES	ARNOLD	DIED
27/8/16	11/651	L/CPL.	CAREY	GREEN	DOW
27/8/16	11/244	PTE.	HARRY	ALLEN	DIED
2/9/16	11/1001	PTE.	JOHN	BOYES	KIA
7/9/16	11/923	PTE.	WILLIAM ALBERT	EDWARDS. MM	DOW
12/9/16	22513	PTE.	CYRIL BERTRAND	FRANKISH	KIA
17/9/16	11/777	PTE.	RICHARD JAMES GEORGE	GRIMMER	DOW
13/10/16	11/63	L/CPL.	GEORGE EDWARD	HOGG	KIA
20/10/16	11/512	CPL.	CHRISTOPHER	BARKER	KIA
20/10/16	11/893	PTE.	ARTHUR LOUIS	HAYHURST	KIA
29/10/16	11477	CPL.	THOMAS	IVESON	KIA
29/10/16	19224	PTE.	EDWARD	NELSON	KIA
29/10/16	11/781	CPL.	DOUGLAS STEWART	McINTOSH	KIA
13/11/16	11/690	CPL.	JAMES HENRY	KAY	KIA
13/11/16	11/1319	PTE.	ARTHUR BEAL	TASKER	DOW

13/11/16	1388	PTE.	JOSEPH WILLIAM	JACKSON	KIA
13/11/16	11/283	PTE.	BRIAN	VAREY	KIA
13/11/16	10/137	PTE.	SAMUEL EDWARD	WRIGHT	KIA
13/11/16	28098	PTE.	EDMUND	WALKER	DOW
13/11/16	28112	PTE.	MONTAGUE WILLIAM	CHRISTOPHER	KIA
13/11/16	10/1365	PTE.	EDWIN FRANCIS	FIELD	KIA
13/11/16	11/1180	PTE.	RICHARD	KIRBY	KIA
13/11/16	11/1015	SGT.	JOHN FRANCIS	WALTON	KIA
13/11/16	28094	PTE.	FREDERICK HENRY	THOPSON	KIA
13/11/16	11/831	PTE.	MYER	BLACK	KIA
14/11/16	28140	PTE.	GEORGE	BLANCHARD	KIA
21/11/16	14/28	PTE.	PATRICK	GALLAGHER	DOW
22/11/16	11/737	PTE.	JAMES WILLIAM	LANGHORN	DOW AT HOME
30/11/16	11/787	L/CPL.	THOMAS	OVERTON	KIA
13/12/16	11/1031	PTE.	CHARLES ALBERT	HERRING	DOW
21/12/16	36436	PTE.	FREDERICK GEORGE	WALKER	KIA
21/12/16	28133	PTE.	FREDERICK	POTS	KIA
22/12/16	36431	PTE.	CHARLES ELVEY	FISHER	DOW
23/12/16	11/489	PTE.	EDWARD	GOHL	KIA
26/12/16	11/872	PTE.	JAMES ANDREW	PATERSON	DOW
4/1/17	28135	PTE.	WILLIAM HENRY	RHODES	DOW
10/1/17	11/349	PTE.	AMOS	POLLARD	DOW AT HOME
25/2/17	11/554	PTE.	PERCY ERNEST	ROBSON	KIA
25/2/17	23699	PTE.	ALFRED ROBERT	CRUDOAS	KIA
25/2/17	11/403	PTE.	JOHN THOMAS	CLARE	KIA
8/3/17	11/1154	PTE.	JAMES	EDDISON	DOW
10/3/17	11/754	PTE.	THOMAS ARTHUR	BEADLE	DOW
2/5/17	11/473	L/CPL.	FREDERICK	SCOTTOW	KIA
3/5/17	25866	L/CPL.	CHARLES HERBERT	CAST	KIA
3/5/17	11/103	PTE.	HAROLD	RICHARDSON	KIA
3/5/17	11/704	SGT.	RICHARD ERNEST	HART	KIA
3/5/17	36521	PTE.	ROBERT	RUSSELL	KIA
3/5/17	36424	PTE.	ALBERT EDWARD	CLEMINSON	KIA
3/5/17	11/474	L/CPL.	FRANK	RASPIN	KIA
3/5/17	14/83	PTE.	SIDNEY	ROGERS	DOW
3/5/17	36539	PTE.	EDWARD GEORGE	HEMMING	KIA
3/5/17	11/1268	PTE.	HARRY	THOMPSON	KIA
3/5/17	36433	PTE.	DeLACEY CAMPWELL	EVANS	KIA
3/5/17	11/934	PTE.	RICHARD	FIELD	KIA
3/5/17	28150	PTE.	HAROLD	HILL	NA
3/5/17	28153	PTE.	ARTHUR HENRY	LEONARD	KIA
3/5/17	11/1344	PTE.	JAMES	FOSTON	KIA
3/5/17	11/1429	PTE.	JAMES HAROLD	TURNER	KIA
3/5/17	37930	PTE.	JOHN SULLIVAN	STEVENS	KIA
3/5/17	36357	PTE.	WILLIAM ERNEST COLYER	BELL	NA
3/5/17	37338	PTE.	HORACE	SILLS	KIA
3/5/17	36516	PTE.	HERBERT	CROSSLEY	KIA
3/5/17	28107	PTE.	WILLIAM KIRK	BOCOCK	DOW
3/5/17	36482	CPL.	WILLIAM	BISHOP	KIA
3/5/17	25536	L/CPL.	HERBERT	RANBY	KIA
3/5/17	9867	PTE.	JAMES EDWARD	CLARE	KIA
3/5/17	14/36	PTE.	JOSEPH	COOPER	KIA
3/5/17	11/1089	PTE.	FRANK	SHAW	KIA
3/5/17	11/1137	PTE.	THOMAS	BEELS	DOW
3/5/17	28090	PTE.	JOHN HENRY	BETHWAY	KIA

3/5/17	36507	L/CPL.	JAMES		BENNETT	KIA
3/5/17	3/7260	PTE.	JAMES		DUFFY	KIA
3/5/17	11/1053	PTE.	GEORGE THOMAS		BARKER	KIA
3/5/17	11/1351	PTE.	ALFRED		MALLENDER	KIA
3/5/17	14/187	PTE.	CHARLES ROWLAND		INGHAM	KIA
3/5/17	36462	PTE.	HARRY GEORGE		EVANS	KIA
3/5/17	11/1270	PTE.	ALBERT ROBERT		THURNELL	KIA
3/5/17	28151	PTE.	EDWARD		INGRAM	KIA
3/5/17	11/69	L/CPL.	ERNEST ARTHUR		LOCKWOOD	KIA
3/5/17	11/712	PTE.	JAMES		NEWLOVE	KIA
3/5/17	11/271	PTE.	GEORGE HENRY		HESLOP	KIA
3/5/17	11/936	PTE.	ALLEN		WARD	KIA
3/5/17	27289	PTE.	GEORGE LYAU		THOMPSON	KIA
3/5/17	11/1222	PTE.	GEORGE WILLIAM		WILLEY	KIA
3/5/17	36465	PTE	HARRY		WESTCOTT	KIA
3/5/17	28142	PTE.	JOHN WILLIAM		ANCUFF	KIA
3/5/17	11/344	CPL.	WILLIAM RICHARD		GARDNER	KIA
3/5/17	26963	PTE.	JOHN HENRY		GELDER	KIA
3/5/17	11/1234	PTE.	WILLIAM		HOLDSTOCK	DOW
3/5/17	11/50	L/CPL.	WILLIAM REGINALD		LING	KIA
3/5/17	11/1219	PTE.	ALBERT		WILCOX	KIA
3/5/17	19371	PTE.	JOHN		MORRIS	KIA
3/5/17	17596	CPL.	FRANK LESLIE		LOFTUS	KIA
3/5/17	11/30	CPL.	PERCY		KIRK	KIA
3/5/17	28127	PTE.	SEPTIMUS GRUNDY		LITTLE	KIA
3/5/17	22500	L/CPL.	RICHARD FREDERICK		THURLOE	KIA
3/5/17	28147	PTE.	ALBERT EDWARD		GOULD	KIA
3/5/17	37918	PTE.	FEDERICK THOMAS		FULKER	KIA
3/5/17	11/1183	PTE.	THOMAS		LOFT	KIA
4/5/17	36536	PTE.	BERT EMERY		GIBBS	DOW
4/5/17	32852	PTE.	THOMAS ARTHUR		JOHNSON	DOW
4/5/17	11/1063	PTE.	WILLIAM		POOL	DOW
4/5/17	36437	PTE.	HENRY ERNEST		SMITH	DOW
4/5/17	28114	PTE.	JAMES EDWARD		COLE	DOW
4/5/17	11/544	PTE.	WALTER JAMES		CAUTLEY	DOW
6/5/17	14/203	L/CPL.	EDWARD WILSON		JOHNSON	KIA
6/5/17	36501	PTE.	PETER HENRY		FIEHNEN	KIA
8/5/17	10/113	PTE.	FRED		KENDREW	DOW
12/5/17	33062	PTE.	CHARLES FREDERICK		CLARK	KIA
12/5/17	11/389	PTE.	JOSEPH		THIRSK	DOW
14/5/17	36494	PTE.	GEORGE		HIGGINBOTTOM	KIA
14/5/17	36490	PTE.	WALTER		TITFORD	KIA
16/5/17	11/1342	PTE.	ARTHUR ERNEST		ELSTON	KIA
16/5/17	11/517	PTE.	GEORGE		KIRBY	KIA
30/5/17	14/211	PTE.	JOHN WILLIAM		ANDREW	DOW
22/5/17	11/1397	PTE.	ALBERT		COOK	KIA
23/5/17	27087	PTE.	HARRY		FOSTER	KIA
26/5/17	11/14	SGT.	HENRY		BAXTER	KIA
28/5/17	11/1309	PTE.	WALTER PERCY		BUSBY	KIA
28/5/17	11/500	PTE.	THOMAS GEORGE		WOOLLONS	KIA
28/5/17	11/863	PTE.	OSCAR		JOHNSON	KIA
28/5/17	23981	PTE.	FREDERICK JAMES		BUSSELL	KIA
28/5/17	11/207	PTE.	JOHN WILLIAM		MORLEY	KIA
28/5/17	11/363	PTE.	JOHN WILLIAM		BROUGH	KIA
1/7/17	11/372	PTE.	GEORGE		ROBINSON	DOW

2/7/17	26637	PTE.	FRED	BROWN	KIA
2/7/17	11/169	PTE.	THOMAS	GLENTON	KIA
3/7/17	11/339	PTE.	THOMAS EDGAR	TEECE	KIA
5/7/17	11/532	PTE.	ERNEST	COUPLANO	KIA
5/7/17	11/545	PTE.	FREDERICK	CUDBERTSON	DOW
15/7/17	12/186	PTE.	EDWIN	PEARSON	DOW
16/7/17	30987	PTE.	GEORGE	FORTH	DOW
16/7/17	23987	PTE.	JOSEPH	McFADDEN	DOW
19/7/17	36509	L/CPL.	THOMAS	WHITE	KIA
19/7/17	12696	L/CPL.	HARRY	WHISKER. MM	KIA
26/7/17	11/691	L/CPL.	ROBERT	OLLETT	KIA
28/7/17	50938	PTE.	JOHN WILLIAM	WELTON	KIA
9/8/17	11/612	PTE.	THOMAS	SWINDEN	KIA
21/8/17	11/228	PTE.	WILLIAM	SMITH	KIA
24/8/17	36458	PTE.	FREDERICK	DOWNS	KIA
8/9/17	11/1128	PTE.	FREDERICK	CARRINGTON	KIA
10/9/17	21247	PTE.	JAMES MONTGOMERY	BARBER	DOW
26/10/17	31184	PTE.	FERGUS	PORTE	KIA
8/11/17	31513	PTE.	ALBERT	BARNES	KIA
8/11/17	11/1112	PTE.	GEORGE ERNEST	GOOOSON	KIA
8/11/17	17581	PTE.	CHRISTOPHER	MACNAMARA	KIA
8/11/17	24610	PTE.	HERBERT	MALLALIEU	DOW
8/11/17	11/785	SGT.	ERNEST	MARRITT. DCM	KIA
8/11/17	11/550	CPL.	THOMAS	COULSON	KIA
8/11/17	11/843	PTE.	FRANK	WOODS	KIA
8/11/17	28136	PTE.	CHARLES WILLIAM	SPENCER	KIA
8/11/17	11/18	PTE.	ERNEST	BEARFIELD	KIA
8/11/17	22356	PTE.	GEORGE	WHITELEY	KIA
8/11/17	36533	L/CPL.	RICHARD	HERBERT	KIA
8/11/17	12/684	PTE.	HARRY	LEAKE	KIA
8/11/17	22832	PTE.	CHARLES JAMES	PEARSON	DOW
9/11/17	8487	PTE.	GEORGE	ARNOTT	DOW
9/11/17	11/958	PTE.	FRANK	DOOK	DOW
10/11/17	11/405	SGT.	FRANK	CLARK	DOW
14/11/17	19410	PTE.	HARRY	MEDFORTH	DOW
20/11/17	225283	PTE.	GEORGE	RICHARDSON	KIA
23/11/17	3/8142	PTE.	GEORGE FREEMAN	ROBERTS	KIA
23/11/17	22482	SGT.	LEONARD JESSE LIVESEY	JAQUES	KIA
1/12/17	11/248	CPL.	CHRISTIAN FREDERICK	STOUT	DOW
3/12/17	11/226	CPL.	JOSEPH	LUMLEY	KIA
10/2/18	13/1212	L/CPL.	HERBERT	BOWS	DOW
19/2/18	22617	PTE.	ALBERT EDWARD	BURTON	KIA
19/2/18	40785	PTE.	ALBERT	BARKER	KIA
20/2/18	14/60	PTE.	GEORGE	CHARLTON	KIA
20/2/18	37303	PTE.	FRED	HANDLEY	DOW
21/2/18	28753	PTE.	MATTHEW MATTHIAS	LAVILL	KIA
12/3/18	28369	CPL.	JOHN LEONARD	HILL	DOW
24/3/18	35306	PTE.	WILLIAM	FENWICK. MM	KIA
24/3/18	225899	PTE.	WILLIAM CHARLES	ABBEY	KIA
24/3/18	24901	PTE.	STANLEY JULES	WEBB	KIA
24/3/18	36765	PTE.	ERNEST MEAL	PEARSON	KIA
24/3/18	13/414	PTE.	CHARLES	BRIDGES	KIA
24/3/18	11/622	L/CPL.	GEORGE HERBERT	BROWN	KIA
24/3/18	11/1244	PTE.	GEORGE EDWARD	LOWEN. MM	DOW
24/3/18	11/116	PTE.	JAMES WEIGHTON	MARSHALL	KIA

25/3/18	21056	PTE.	FRED	RAPER	KIA
25/3/18	13/1407	PTE.	JOHN	BLACKMORE	KIA
25/3/18	38135	PTE.	FREDERICK	TOMUNSON	KIA
25/3/18	11/896	PTE.	SIDNEY WILLIAM	LOWE	KIA
25/3/18	225852	PTE.	JACK	HUNTER	DOW
25/3/18	11/760	PTE.	PERCY	COOPER	DOW
25/3/18	11/623	PTE.	HERBERT	TEMPLE	KIA
25/3/18	18020	PTE.	WILLIAM	SWEETING	KIA
25/3/18	29782	PTE.	GEORGE WILLIAM	KYLE	KIA
26/3/18	11/1127	PTE.	THOMAS	SMART	KIA
26/3/18	28666	PTE.	RICHARD	WILLIAMS	KIA
26/3/18	17360	PTE.	HARRY	FISH	KIA
26/3/18	23870	CPL.	HARRY STANLEY	GRAY	DOW
26/3/18	22108	PTE.	GEORGE	TAYLOR	DOW
26/3/18	11/136	PTE.	GEORGE ALFRED	JEFFERY, MM	KIA
27/3/18	26462	PTE.	WILLIAM	BEAUMONT	KIA
27/3/18	225486	PTE.	THOMAS	BAILEY	KIA
27/3/18	36427	PTE.	PHILIP	GALE	KIA
27/3/18	11/1016	PTE.	GEORGE HUNTER	BELL	KIA
27/3/18	28139	PTE.	JOHN ROBERT	BRINKLEY	KIA
27/3/18	31176	PTE.	HIRBIN	HUDSON	KIA
27/3/18	225326	PTE.	DONALD	BRITTON	KIA
27/3/18	12/334	L/CPL.	CHARLES	DIXON	KIA
27/3/18	29616	L/CPL.	THOMAS	HARRISON	KIA
27/3/18	13765	PTE.	ALFRED	CHILTON	KIA
27/3/18	11/49	PTE.	JOSEPH HENRY	CHANCE	KIA
27/3/18	29773	PTE.	ERNEST	CROSS	KIA
27/3/18	30463	PTE.	GEORGE WILKINSON	DAVISON	KIA
27/3/18	22348	PTE.	ERNEST JAMES	WILSON	KIA
27/3/18	11/272	PTE.	WILLIAM BARNETT	WILSON	KIA
27/3/18	26353	PTE.	ERNEST	ABBEY	KIA
27/3/18	29770	PTE.	JOHN WILLIAM HERBERT	BRYAN	KIA
27/3/18	12/1094	PTE.	EDWARD FRANCIS	LANE	KIA
27/3/18	220021	PTE.	CLARENCE	ROBINSON	KIA
27/3/18	10204	PTE.	GEORGE EDWIN	THOMPSON	KIA
27/3/18	8502	PTE.	MATTHEW	WHARTON	KIA
27/3/18	11/1075	PTE.	THOMAS COOK	PLASKITT	DOW
27/3/18	6728	PTE.	THOMAS HENRY	TAYLOR	KIA
27/3/18	11/264	PTE.	HARRY	TAYLOR	KIA
27/3/18	28614	PTE.	ALBERT	McPHERSON	KIA
27/3/18	11/874	PTE.	GEORGE	OAKES. MM	KIA
27/3/18	13.1492	PTE.	ROBERT	KIRBY	KIA
27/3/18	11/986	SGT.	WILLIAM WILSON	NEEDLER	KIA
27/3/18	36921	PTE.	JOHN	FOWLER, MM	KIA
27/3/18	11/33	L/CPL.	HAROLD MAYNARD	McLANE	KIA
27/3/18	11/51	PTE.	JOHN WILLIAM	KIRK	KIA
27/3/18	28602	PTE.	JOHN	McGINTY	KIA
27/3/18	220264	CPL.	CYRIL	PIPPIE	KIA
27/3/18	11/87	PTE.	ROBERT	RUTLEDGE	KIA
28/3/18	11/895	PTE.	MAURICE	EVERSON	KIA
28/3/18	11/1136	PTE.	JOHN WILLIAM	BOLDER	KIA
28/3/18	11/305	L/CPL.	JAMES	TODD	DOW
28/3/18	27010	PTE.	JOHN CHADWICK	BRACE	KIA
28/3/18	24881	PTE.	THOMAS EDWARD	WILMOT	DOW
28/3/18	34962	PTE.	GEORGE	ROWLING	KIA

Date	Number	Rank	Forename	Surname	Fate
28/3/18	11/659	PTE.	MATTHEW	EMMERSON	KIA
29/3/18	13/1481	SGT.	LLEWELLYN	SCOTT	DOW
30/3/18	25069	CPL.	THOMAS ABBOTT	WILDE. MM	DOW
30/3/18	12227	PTE.	WILLIAM	JINKS	DOW
30/3/18	13.1418	PTE.	DANIEL	PARTIS	DOW
31/3/18	11/71	PTE.	HARRY	BAINES	DOW
31/3/18	220033	SGT.	FREDERICK GEORGE	FOX	DOW
8/4/18	12/1252	PTE.	FRED	GILUATT	DOW
10/4/18	9792	L/CPL.	ARTHUR	NYE	KIA
12/4/18	30535	PTE.	FREDERICK GEORGE	GROVES	KIA
12/4/18	41939	PTE.	ALEXANDER SAMUEL	MACKAY	KIA
12/4/18	11/802	PTE.	JOHN EDWARD	ALLISON. MM	KIA
12/4/18	30392	PTE.	PETER	RICHARDSON	KIA
12/4/18	36542	PTE.	ARTHUR	HOPKINSON	KIA
12/4/18	41903	PTE.	WILFRED	HALE	KIA
12/4/18	29760	PTE.	CHARLES	LEAVEY	KIA
12/4/18	35061	PTE.	FRANK	PAGDEN	KIA
12/4/18	30541	PTE.	JAMES	WOOD	KIA
12/4/18	30521	PTE.	FRED	WARD	KIA
12/4/18	25401	PTE.	FREDERICK	BARROWCLIFFE	KIA
12/4/18	30519	PTE.	CHARLES HENRY	WALLIS	KIA
12/4/18	30378	PTE.	JOSEPH	PINCHES	KIA
12/4/18	36425	PTE.	ALBERT GEORGE	COOK	KIA
12/4/18	25058	PTE.	THOMAS ALFRED	GRASSAM	KIA
12/4/18	11/1164	PTE.	EDWARD	GOULD. MM	KIA
12/4/18	41895	PTE.	CHARLES FREDERICK	GOODEY	KIA
12/4/18	29766	PTE.	LEONARD	BLANCHARD	KIA
12/4/18	11/571	PTE.	JAMES EDWARD	SPETCH	KIA
12/4/18	41899	PTE.	HORACE ALBERT	GREAVES	KIA
12/4/18	41918	PTE.	THOMAS	HODSON	KIA
12/4/18	11/519	PTE.	WILLIAM	LEWIS	KIA
12/4/18	29785	PTE.	LEONARD	RILEY	KIA
12/4/18	28595	CPL.	WILLIAM	TOWERS	KIA
12/4/18	29780	PTE.	LEO	HOGG	KIA
12/4/18	30353	PTE.	CHARLES EDWARD BONTOFT	MANN	KIA
12/4/18	28067	CPL.	MOSES	LAWRENCE	KIA
12/4/18	27907	PTE.	FRANK	ARNOLD	KIA
12/4/18	17514	PTE.	ISAAC	ATKINSON	KIA
12/4/18	11/602	PTE.	WALTER	BLANSHARD	KIA
12/4/18	11/132	PTE.	GEOGE EDWARD	WARNES	KIA
12/4/18	41922	PTE.	ERNEST KELSHAM	HOURNE	KIA
12/4/18	30413	PTE.	JOHN	SMITH	KIA
12/4/18	30396	PTE.	LEONARD	ROBINSON	KIA
12/4/18	36589	PTE.	HERBERT	FENWICK	KIA
12/4/18	30407	PTE.	ANGUS	ROBINSON	KIA
12/4/18	12/1272	PTE.	THOMAS EDWARD	WALKER	KIA
12/4/18	41946	PTE.	BENJAMIN ALLAN	MEES	KIA
12/4/18	30475	PTE.	JAMES ARCHER	TIMPSON	KIA
12/4/18	41949	PTE.	LAWRENCE	MOLDEN	KIA
12/4/18	23683	PTE.	FRANCIS SIDNEY	SHAPCOTT	KIA
12/4/18	11/393	CPL.	FRED LESLIE	SHARPE. MM	KIA
12/4/18	41872	PTE.	JOSEPH	DARLEY	KIA
12/4/18	30455	PTE.	HENRY ROLLEN	THORPE	KIA
12/4/18	30391	PTE.	ALBERT	ROSTER	KIA
12/4/18	13247	PTE.	HENRY	HUNTER	KIA

12/4/18	11/241	CPL.	WILLIAM ERNEST	USHER	KIA
12/4/18	19965	PTE.	ARTHUR	JARVIS	KIA
12/4/18	30394	PTE.	WALTER SHAW	RODGERS	KIA
12/4/18	30518	PTE.	LOUIS	WINTER	KIA
12/4/18	30459	PTE.	WILLIAM HENRY	TURPIN	KIA
12/4/18	30365	PTE.	CHARLES	MAYES	KIA
12/4/18	11/956	PTE.	WILLIAM	PALMER	KIA
12/4/18	30510	PTE.	GEORGE WILLIAM	YARROW	KIA
12/4/18	11/419	PTE.	JOHN WILLIAM	JACKSON	KIA
13/4/18	14/79	L/CPL.	FREDERICK	BARRETT	KIA
14/4/18	220059	PTE.	KENNETH HERNE	CHILD	KIA
14/4/18	131419	CPL.	ERNEST	BIGLIN	DOW
18/4/18	41897	PTE.	LAWRENCE BERTRAM	GRAY	KIA
19/4/18	205371	PTE.	CHARLES HENRY	WILLS	DOW
19/4/18	41925	PTE.	THOMAS COLIN	HUGHES	DOW
23/4/18	225242	PTE.	JOHN WILLIAM	DENNIS	DOW
23/4/18	19354	PTE.	HENRY	DAMRELL	KIA
23/4/18	11/715	PTE.	GEORGE	DOWNS. MM	KIA
25/4/18	30437	PTE.	EDWARD ELDRED	SEARING	DOW
25/4/18	30482	PTE.	LEONARD	WEBB	KIA
25/4/18	19431	PTE.	ALBERT	HIGGINSON	KIA
25/4/18	30410	PTE.	WILLIAM	ROYALL	DOW
28/4/18	19154	PTE.	ARTHUR	BRYAN	KIA
28/4/18	11/1141	PTE.	HAROLD	BENTLEY	DOW AT HOME
28/4/18	30506	PTE.	GEORGE EDWARD	WILLMER	KIA
28/4/18	30511	PTE.	STANLEY	WENTWORTH	KIA
5/5/18	28157	PTE.	CORNELIUS	MUGGLESTONE	DIED
10/5/18	27085	PTE.	ERNEST	YOUNG	KIA
12/5/18	41873	PTE.	GEORGE	DAVIES	DOW
17/5/18	30495	PTE.	JOHN ROBERT	WOOTTON	DOW
17/5/18	30534	PTE.	HORACE	FEARN	KIA
18/5/18	19191	PTE.	EDGAR	HORNSHAW	KIA
18/5/18	52677	PTE.	WILLIAM GEORGE	WILSON	KIA
18/5/18	52616	PTE.	MAURICE	LUMB	KIA
18/5/18	41937	PTE.	JOHN EDWARD	LISTER	KIA
18/5/18	52616	PTE.	MAURICE	LAMB	KIA
18/5/18	29357	PTE.	JOSEPH WILSON	HUDSON	KIA
18/5/18	41768	PTE.	HERBERT HORACE	KEITGHLEY	DOW
18/5/18	29075	PTE.	PETER HENRY	RIMMER	DOW
18/5/18	52605	PTE.	HENRY JAMES	LATIMER	KIA
21/5/18	41712	PTE.	STEPHEN HECTOR	CULL	DIED
25/5/18	11/913	SGT.	KENNETH	HODGSON	KIA
28/5/18	41916	PTE.	ARTHUR	HIGGINSON	DOW
1/6/18	22472	PTE.	SYDNEY WILLIAM	WEBB	KIA
18/6/18	11/262	PTE.	TOM	HARMAN	KIA
25/6/18	42306	CPL.	FREDERICK HERBERT	SKINNER	KIA
27/6/18	29751	PTE.	WALTER	SHADE	KIA
28/6/18	30533	PTE.	ARTHUR	CROOK	KIA
28/6/18	30364	PTE.	PERCIVAL VICTOR	MIDDLETON	KIA
28/6/18	12/64	PTE.	HENRY	HIGGINSON	DOW
28/6/18	41764	PTE.	EBENEZER	JAMES	KIA
28/6/18	22839	PTE.	FRANK	DANSON	KIA
28/6/18	41758	PTE.	JOSEPH EDWARD	HORSFIELD	KIA
28/6/18	11/978	PTE.	HAROLD FOSTER	HOUGHTON	KIA
28/6/18	52607	PTE.	THOMAS JOICEY	QUINCE	KIA

28/6/18	52791	PTE.	HUGH LANCELOT	COOPER	KIA
28/6/18	52665	PTE.	JOHN ALBERT	WALSH	KIA
28/6/18	41710	PTE.	LESLIE	COPPER	KIA
28/6/18	40868	PTE.	ROBERT	LEE	KIA
28/6/18	41756	PTE.	ALFRED	HOLLAND	KIA
28/6/18	38281	PTE.	RICHARD	DOBSON	DOW
28/6/16	220586	PTE.	HARRY GEORGE	BARTON	KIA
28/6/18	42051	PTE.	CARYL	BAKER	KIA
28/6/18	13/201	PTE.	ELIJAH	RICHARDSON	KIA
28/6/18	30477	PTE.	ROBERT	TELFORD	KIA
28/6/18	38049	PTE.	WILLIAM	BATES	KIA
28/6/18	52644	PTE.	EDWARD GLADSTONE	TARN	KIA
28/6/18	9826	PTE.	CHARLES FREDERICK	SUTTON	KIA
28/6/18	30429	PTE.	ALLEN	STEEL	KIA
28/6/18	40771	PTE.	FREDERICK	ASPINALL	KIA
28/6/18	52618	PTE.	JASPER ROBSON	RICHARDSON	KIA
28/6/18	12/90	SGT.	JOSEPH WILLIAM	BIBBY	KIA
28/6/16	30403	PTE.	LEWIS	RINGER	KIA
28/6/18	12664	PTE.	GEORGE THOMAS	SADLER	KIA
28/6/18	52610	PTE.	GEORGE	THURLOE	KIA
29/6/18	29618	CPL.	ALEXANDER SMPSON	CURRYTULLY	KIA
29/6/18	41902	PTE.	REGINALD	GREY	DOW
29/6/18	41773	PTE.	HAROLD	LINCOLN	DOW
29/6/18	41770	PTE.	ARTHUR WILLIAM	LEE	DOW
30/6/18	11/772	SGT.	HARRY	SELLERS	KIA
30/6/18	41919	PTE.	HARRY	HOLMES	KIA
30/6/18	27346	PTE.	JAMES WILLIAM	PARKER	KIA
1/7/18	30911	CPL.	WILLIAM HENRY	SMITH. MM	DOW
1/7/18	11/967	PTE.	JOHN	BRAND	DIED
2/7/18	30484	PTE.	JOHN SIDNEY	WHITEHOUSE	DOW
2/7/18	13/1347	PTE.	ALFRED	SWALES	DOW
4/7/18	28126	PTE.	JOSEPH GOODE	LEE	DOW
4/7/18	41765	PTE.	SAM	JENNINGS	DOW
5/7/18	11/980	SGT.	HAROLD	ANDREWS	KIA
11/7/18	12/1535	PTE.	HERBERT	FARROW	DOW
12/7/18	30525	PTE.	HERBERT CHARLES	BENNETT	KIA
12/7/18	28934	PTE.	HENRY EWART	CRABTREE	KIA
12/7/18	36526	PTE.	WILLIAM	JACKSON	KIA
12/7/18	28288	PTE.	FRED	TURNER	KIA
12/7/18	11038	CPL.	HAROLD	TOWSE. MM	KIA
13/7/18	10/1191	L/CPL.	LEONARD	JARVIS. MM	DOW
13/7/18	32914	PTE.	WILLIAM ARTHUR	LAZENBY. MM	DOW
28/7/18	35128	PTE.	SYDNEY JAMES	DOBSON	KIA
28/7/18	11/994	SGT.	LEONARD	FUSSEY. MM	KIA
28/7/18	19114	PTE.	WILLIAM	KEELEY	KIA
3/8/18	52612	PTE.	EDGAR WILLIAM	BOYD	KIA
3/8/18	11/954	PTE.	WILLIAM MEREDITH	GAUNT	KIA
3/8/18	11/150	PTE.	WILLIAM HENRY	CARTER	KIA
8/8/18	13/295	CPL.	WILLIAM HENRY	WOODALL	DIED
8/8/18	11/375	SGT.	HENRY	HILL. MM	KIA
8/8/18	35016	PTE.	HARRY	BOOTH	DIED
9/8/18	51096	PTE.	THOMAS	WHITTY	KIA
11/8/18	11/1389	PTE.	THOMAS FREDERICK	TURNER	KIA
11/8/18	51055	PTE.	DAVID	WILLETT	KIA
11/8/18	11/727	PTE.	CHARLES	BALDWIN	KIA

12/8/18	50936	PTE.	JOSEPH		TAYNE	KIA
12/8/18	220497	PTE.	CHARLES		RAMSDEN	KIA
12/8/18	50914	PTE.	AMOS		DAWSON	KIA
12/8/18	50904	PTE.	JAMES		VAUGHAN	DOW
13/8/18	51068	PTE.	JOHN JOSEPH GRAHAM		CROSS	KIA
13/8/18	203199	PTE.	JOHN		FRANKLAND	DOW
13/8/18	50965	PTE.	RICHARD		GALLOWAY	KIA
13/8/18	50939	PTE.	LAWRENCE EDWIN		WALTON	DOW
13/8/18	30416	PTE.	SAMUEL		SHARPE	DOW
13/8/18	41753	PTE.	LESLIE STRAY		HICKMAN	KIA
13/8/18	26045	PTE.	JOSEPH		LISTER	KIA
14/8/18	50963	PTE.	WILFRED		COCKERILL	DOW
15/8/18	30446	PTE.	ALBERT		STOCKS	KIA
15/8/18	50973	PTE.	CHARLES WILLIAM		JOHNSON	KIA
15/8/18	15794	PTE.	RICHARD WILSON		BOUSFIELD	KIA
15/8/18	8414	SGT.	GEORGE HENRY		TIPPING	KIA
15/8/18	41729	PTE.	REGINALD		FREEMAN	KIA
15/8/18	50975	PTE.	RALPH		SNAITH.MM	KIA
15/8/18	41941	PTE.	ERNEST		MANLEY	KIA
16/8/18	42327	PTE.	WILLIAM		HOLMES	DOW
16/8/18	41730	PTE.	PERCY		FRENCH	KIA
16/8/18	41888	PTE.	BERNARD		FLETCHER, MM	KIA
17/8/18	50940	PTE.	JOSEPH RICHARD		WAKEFIELD	KIA
21/8/18	41934	PTE.	ARTHUR RAYMOND		LAWSON	DOW
21/8/18	11/463	CPL.	FRED		HARRISON. MM	DOW
21/8/18	41696	PTE.	JOSEPH GEORGE		BROADHEAD	KIA
24/8/18	52658	PTE.	SEBASTIAN MOORCROFT		FLETCHER	DOW
5/9/18	11/1111	PTE.	JOHN WILLIAMS		JOHNSON	DOW
5/9/18	41713	PTE.	STANLEY		CULLINGWORTH	KIA
6/9/18	42310	PTE	ALBERT FRANCIS		BROWN	KIA
6/9/18	33399	SGT.	ALBERT		ARSKEY. MM & BAR	KIA
6/9/18	24878	CPL.	ARTHUR PEARSON		ELLIS	KIA
6/9/18	50981	PTE.	DAVID ADAMS		JOHNSON	KIA
6/9/18	50984	PTE.	GEORGE ROBERT		LAIDLOW	KIA
5/9/18	50895	PTE.	JAMES		DOLAN	KIA
6/9/18	225675	PTE.	FEDERICK		POTS	KIA
6/9/18	27076	PTE.	CARTON		LEE	KIA
6/9/18	30382	PTE.	WILLIAM HENRY		PRESTON	DOW
6/9/18	225330	L/CPL.	RUPERT		VARLEY	KIA
6/9/18	9106	PTE.	GEORGE		HARRIS	KIA
6/9/18	12/234	CPL	JOHN ARTHUR		SMITH. MM	KIA
8/9/18	11/1207	CPL.	THOMAS		SAWYER. DCM	KIA
8/9/18	51024	PTE.	JAMES		SANKEY	KIA
8/9/18	51042	PTE.	EDMUND WILLIAM		SWINDON	KIA
8/9/18	30432	PTE.	RICHARD DENIS		SKIDMORE	KIA
8/9/18	29457	PTE.	HAROLD		POWELL	KIA
8/9/18	11/600	SGT.	JOHN ALBERT		CALLAGHAN	KIA
8/9/18	51031	PTE.	THOMAS WILLIAM		SISSON	KIA
8/9/18	35009	PTE.	JAMES		APPLEYARD	KIA
8/9/18	40904	PTE.	SAMUEL LEONARD		POXON	KIA
8/9/18	35409	PTE.	JAMES		RUTHERFORD	KIA
8/9/18	41733	PTE.	ERNEST		GARRATT	KIA
8/9/18	22007	PTE.	FRANK GILBERT		LITTLEHALES	KIA
8/9/18	11/364	SGT.	JOHN HESELTINE		SMITH	KIA
8/9/18	51043	PTE.	NORMAN		SYMON	KIA

8/9/18	51021	PTE.	ALLEN	ROWLEY	KIA
8/9/18	11/1379	CPL.	PERCY	STOTHARD	KIA
8/9/18	41714	PTE.	CEDRIC PERCY	DARNELL	KIA
8/9/18	51080	PTE.	JOHN	MITCHEL	KIA
8/9/18	28091	CPL.	SIDNEY	BROWN	KIA
8/9/18	52637	PTE.	PERCIVAL EDWARD	POTTER	KIA
8/9/18	14/87	PTE.	HAROLD	POTTER	DOW
8/9/18	51054	PTE.	JOHN WILLIAM	WILKINSON. MM	KIA
8/9/18	50941	PTE.	WILFRED REGINALD	WHITTAKER	KIA
8/9/18	37168	PTE.	WILLIAM	PARKER	KIA
8/9/18	225415	PTE.	FRANK	BRAITHWAITE	KIA
8/9/18	203086	CPL.	HUBERT FREDERICK WILLIAM	JARRATT	KIA
8/9/18	41722	PTE.	OWEN WILSON	EXLEY	KIA
8/9/18	51001	PTE.	ARTHUR FREDERICK	MARKIN	KIA
8/9/18	41699	PTE.	WALTER	BROWN	KIA
8/9/18	51013	PTE.	HARRY	PHILLIPS	KIA
8/9/18	30522	PTE.	GEORGE ERNEST	POTTAGE	KIA
8/9/18	37227	PTE.	CHARLES	LANE	KIA
8/9/18	11/627	PTE.	ERNEST	KENNEBY	KIA
9/9/18	50901	PTE.	JOHN WILLIAM	STANSFIELD	DOW
8/9/18	42137	PTE.	FREDERICK GRAIGER	HOOPER	DOW
14/9/18	11/952	PTE.	ERNEST CARTER	PICKERING	DOW
21/9/18	30409	PTE.	HARRY	ROBERTS	DOW
24/9/18	51967	PTE.	WILLIAM	BARKER	KIA
25/9/18	50993	PTE.	JOHN	LYTH	KIA
25/9/18	19447	PTE.	JOHN	DEAKIN	KIA
25/9/18	15029	SGT.	LEWIS	NORMAN	KIA
27/9/18	51800	PTE.	HARRY	DOWNING	KIA
28/9/18	51959	PTE.	CHARLES	SMITH	KIA
28/9/18	29198	PTE.	AUSTIN	BRENCHLEY	KIA
28/9/18	51792	PTE.	ALBERT	BEECHER	KIA
28/9/18	42180	PTE.	HARRY	MAYOR	DOW
29/9/18	27902	PTE.	EDWARD BARBER	MITCHELL	KIA
29/9/18	51049	PTE.	HARRY	WARD	DOW
29/9/18	11/673	SGT.	CHARLES JOHN	NIX. MM	KIA
29/9/18	16404	PTE.	FRANCIS	BRADLEY	DOW
29/9/18	51984	PTE.	THOMAS	BAKER	DOW
29/9/18	29609	CPL.	JOHN GEORGE	FAWKES	DOW
29/9/18	11/435	PTE.	ALBERT WILLIAM	MARSHALL	DOW
29/9/18	33420	PTE.	JOHN	MILLER	DOW
30/9/18	51805	PTE.	JOSEPH CALADINE	GREEN	DOW
1/10/18	11522	PTE.	CHARLES STEEL	NEWBY	DOW
3/10/18	50956	PTE.	THOMAS	TYSON	KIA
6/10/18	41715	PTE.	ARTHUR	DEAKIN	DOW
25/10/18	30479	PTE.	FRANK WILLIAM	VARLEY	DIED
26/10/18	11/529	PTE.	JOHN WILLIAM	JUDGE	DIED
30/10/18	13/1227	L/CPL.	JOHN HENRY	PEARCY	DIED
30/10/18	11/229	PTE.	RICHARD	LOWTHER	DOW
2/11/18	11/1327	PTE.	THOMAS WILLIAM	EASTWOOD	DIED
2/11/18	24868	PTE.	HARRY	DOWNES	DIED
3/11/18	28649	PTE.	FRED	CAMPS	DOW
9/11/18	12/1186	PTE.	JOHN WARD	ARNOLD	DIED
14/11/18	11/670	PTE.	CHARLES FREDERICK	CLAYTON	DIED
26/11/18	13/500	L/CPL.	SIDNEY ROBERT	BROCKLESBY	DIED

Appendix 6

12th Battalion Soldiers' deaths in date order

3/11/14	12/862	PTE.	THOMAS	GILL	DIED AT HOME
1/2/15	12604	PTE.	JOHN	BEASY	DIED AT HOME
5/2/15	12/747	PTE.	ARTHUR	HALL	DIED AT HOME
27/1/16	12/96	CSM.	THOMAS	CHAPMAN	DIED AT HOME
12/4/16	12/991	L/CPL.	GEORGE	McKEE	KIA
13/4/16	117861	PTE.	WILLIAM ASHTON	HALL	KIA
14/4/16	12850	L/CPL.	GEORGE HENRY	LUN	KIA
16/4/16	12606	SGT.	ALBERT	BAYSTON	DOW
16/4/16	12/838	PTE.	HAROLD	JOHNSON	KIA
16/4/16	12/1456	PTE.	BENJAMIN WOOD	HUTCHINSON	KIA
17/4/16	12896	PTE.	EDWARD ALDRIDGE	HADLOW	DOW
16/4/16	12/1215	PTE.	THOMAS McMORRAN	WRIGHT	DOW
19/4/16	12677	L/CPL.	ALBERT	COLUNSON	DOW
20/4/16	1266	PTE.	ALFRED WILLIAM	DAVIES	DIED
3/5/16	12/1203	CPL.	ARTHUR ALFRED	CALVERT	DOW
6/5/16	14833	PTE.	JAMES WILLIAM	WOLSTENCROFT	KIA
7/5/16	12/761	PTE.	FREDERICK	RUDD	KIA
11/5/16	12/169	PTE.	EDWARD	CUFF	DOW
13/5/16	12838	PTE.	AMBROSE NEWTON	WOODALL	DOW
20/5/16	12/406	PTE.	EDWIN	WHITFIELD	DOW
25/5/16	12/1152	PTE.	HARRY	HORBERRY	KIA
25/5/16	12816	L/CPL.	GEORGE FREDERICK	BURNHAM	KIA
26/5/16	12/184	PTE.	WILLIAM	IRVING	KIA
26/5/16	12/1494	PTE.	WILLIAM	BRETT	KIA
26/5/16	12/763	PTE.	ROBERT	STOKER	DOW
26/5/16	12685	CPL.	FRANCIS	FENTON	KIA
26/5/16	12/1331	PTE.	HENRY CHARLES	BOXHALL	KIA
26/5/16	12897	SGT.	ERNEST WILLIAM	WOODS	KIA
26/5/16	12/1191	PTE.	ALFRED GARLAND	HOUGHTON	KIA
26/5/16	12641	PTE.	HARRY	SPENCER	KIA
26/5/16	12/14	PTE.	FRED	BECKETT	KIA
27/5/16	12/179	PTE.	JOHN	HALL	KIA
27/5/16	12/1501	PTE.	HAROLD WILLIAM	TOCK	KIA
27/5/16	12/1328	PTE.	RICHARD ALFRED	SMITH	KIA
27/5/16	12/481	PTE.	WILLIAM	RICHES	KIA
27/5/16	12/711	PTE.	GEORGE WILLIAM	MARTIN	KIA
27/5/16	12/129	PTE.	LEONARD	WHITE	KIA
27/5/16	10431	PTE.	WILUAM GEORGE	SMITH	KIA
27/5/16	12/49	PTE.	PERCIVAL	JONES	KIA
28/5/16	12/1468	PTE.	JAMES WILLIAM LANCELOT	FENWICK	DOW
28/5/16	12/1103	PTE.	ALBERT DALE	WOOMBLE	DOW
1/6/16	12689	PTE.	WILLIAM	HARRISON	DOW
12/6/16	14/58	L/CPL.	JOHN WILLIAM	HILL	KIA
12/6/16	12/1212	PTE.	NORRIS ALEXANDER	HUDSON	KIA
27/6/16	12/172	PTE.	ALFRED	HOLLAND	KIA
30/6/16	12669	PTE.	ARTHUR	ROO	DOW
30/6/16	10/1441	PTE.	JOHN HENRY	ARCHBUTT	DOW
5/7/16	12/171	PTE.	WILLIAM	GREEN	DOW

12/7/16	12/475	PTE.	WILLIAM	KING	DOW AT HOME
19/7/16	12/1003	PTE.	GEORGE	DEARLOVE	KIA
19/7/16	12/1241	PTE.	HAROLD	BOURNER	KIA
20/7/16	12/1384	PTE.	JAMES SIDNEY	NORTH	DOW
21/7/16	12/1360	PTE.	HARRY	FELL	KIA
23/7/16	11796	PTE.	FREDERICK	McCLOUD	DIED
24/7/16	12/1514	PTE.	ARTHUR THOMAS	BOOTHMAN	KIA
25/7/16	12/1487	L/CPL.	FRANCIS KISH GUY	VOWLES	DIED
31/7/16	12/1113	PTE.	FRANK	FULCHER	DOW
1/8/16	22437	PTE.	LEONARD	HEMINGWAY	DOW
5/8/16	12/1012	PTE.	ALFRED	HAWKINS	KIA
6/8/16	1422	PTE.	RANDOLPH CHURCHILL	COOPER	KIA
6/8/16	22506	PTE.	FRED JOHN	CHAPMAN	KIA
6/8/16	12/1522	PTE.	FREDERICK	PAGET	KIA
6/8/16	101097	PTE.	DONALD	MCKENZIE	DIED
6/8/16	12/1058	PTE.	WILLIAM	LEWIS	KIA
9/8/16	21555	PTE.	JAMES	BUGG	DOW
11/8/16	12604	PTE.	JAMES	BLAIN	DOW
15/8/16	10.1331	PTE.	SAMUEL	SUGARMAN	KIA
16/8/16	12/780	PTE.	WILLIAM JACKSON	CLARK	KIA
16/8/16	12/1275	PTE.	FRANK	COCKERILL	KIA
16/8/16	12/722	PTE.	CASTLE	BLACKBURN	KIA
16/8/16	12638	PTE.	EDWARD	GREEN	KIA
16/8/16	12/1146	PTE.	THOMAS	NEWSON	KIA
17/8/16	12/11	PTE.	RICHARD	JARVIS	DOW
18/8/16	12687	PTE.	DANIEL	BOOTHBY	DOW
18/8/16	12640	PTE.	ARTHUR	JACKSON	KIA
19/8/16	12/1518	PTE.	HARRY	SKELTON	KIA
19/8/16	12663	PTE.	JOHN WALTER	MILLS	KIA
24/8/16	10.1351	PTE.	HARRY	JIPSON	KIA
26/8/16	36684	PTE.	PERCY	WUEMAN	KIA
26/8/16	12/1155	PTE.	GEORGE	ANDERSON	KIA
30/8/16	12/1372	PTE.	WALTER REGINALD	RIDER	DOW
1/9/16	12639	PTE.	JOHN WILLIAM	FLETCHER	KIA
25/9/16	12/724	PTE.	CHRISTIAN REUBEN	WOYEN	KIA
6/10/16	22246	PTE.	KEVIN	COLUNS	DOW
24/10/16	12691	CPL.	FREDERICK RICHARDSON	MARLOW	KIA
12/11/16	28207	PTE.	FRED	ROOKYARD	DOW
12/11/16	12692	PTE.	FREDERICK ALBERT	ANDERSON	KIA
13/11/16	12/148	PTE.	ERNEST VICTOR	ROBINSON	KIA
13/11/16	12/1323	PTE.	WALTER	HARRIS	KIA
13/11/16	12/1341	PTE.	HERBERT FREDERICK	GOODFELLOW	KIA
13/11/16	12/1300	PTE.	BENJAMIN	ELLIS	KIA
13/11/16	12/1835	PTE.	GEORGE FREDERICK	SELLE	KIA
13/11/16	10.359	L/CPL.	MAURICE	SPIKINS	KIA
13/11/16	12/1451	PTE.	JOHN SEYMOUR	LEE	KIA
13/11/16	12/1295	PTE.	FREEMAN	WRIGHT	KIA
13/11/16	12/1519	PTE.	PERCY WALTER	HUNTLEY	KIA
13/11/16	12/161	PTE.	FREDERICK HAROLD	DOBBS	KIA
13/11/16	12/1526	PTE.	GEORGE HERBERT	WOLLAS. MM	KIA
13/11/16	12/1406	PTE.	EDWARD	HEENAN	KIA
13/11/16	12/1333	PTE.	WILLIAM HENRY	HODGSON	KIA
13/11/16	12/1497	PTE.	HERBERT SEPT EASTWOOD	SHORES	KIA
13/11/16	12/1196	PTE.	THOMAS CHRISTIAN	HOLMES	KIA
13/11/16	12/22	PTE.	CLARENCE	HICKS	KIA

13/11/16	12/127	PTE.	FRED		NESS	KIA
13/11/16	12/189	L/CPL.	WALTER		WILSON	KIA
13/11/16	12/1225	PTE.	ERNEST		HOTCHKIN	KIA
13/11/16	12/516	PTE.	THOMAS PARKER		EDMUNDS	KIA
13/11/16	12/1258	PTE.	WILFRED WALDERMAN		FARMERY	KIA
13/11/16	12/1226	PTE.	FRED		HOTCHKIN	KIA
13/11/16	12011	SGT.	WILFRED WAKEUN		NEAL	KIA
13/11/16	12/267	CPL.	WILLIAM ARTHUR		RUSHTON	KIA
13/11/16	12/25	PTE.	RICHARD		BROWN	KIA
13/11/16	11/387	PTE.	GEORGE		WRIDE	KIA
13/11/16	12/1259	PTE.	JAMES ALBERT		JACKSON	KIA
13/11/16	12/241	PTE.	LEONARD FRANK		BURNS	KIA
13/11/16	111088	PTE.	SAMUEL		LAUGHTON	KIA
13/11/16	12/1512	PTE.	ROBERT		SERGEANT	KIA
13/11/16	12/330	PTE.	WILLIAM ERNEST		COX	KIA
13/11/16	12035	PTE.	WALTER GEORGE		JESSOP	KIA
13/11/16	12037	L/CPL.	FRED		SAVAGE	KIA
13/11/16	12/1141	PTE.	JAMES WILLIAM		ANDREWS	KIA
13/11/16	12/1139	PTE.	HAROLD		CRAWFORD	KIA
13/11/16	12/1128	PTE.	GEORGE THOMAS		BURNETT	KIA
13/11/16	12/112	PTE.	HENRY		WOGDEN	KIA
13/11/16	12092	PTE.	ALBERT		BENN	KIA
13/11/16	12/1148	PTE.	ROBERT		HART	KIA
13/11/16	12082	PTE.	JOHN ALBERT		BARBER	KIA
13/11/16	11/971	PTE.	JOHN		GOULDING	KIA
13/11/16	12023	PTE.	THOMAS		PULLINGER	KIA
13/11/16	12/1158	PTE.	JOSEPH		BOYD	KIA
13/11/16	12029	PTE.	CHARLES WILLIAM		CRAGGY	KIA
13/11/16	12/1112	PTE.	CHARLES HENRY		BELL	KIA
13/11/16	12/110	PTE.	CHARLES OLIVER		ROBINSON	KIA
13/11/16	12/456	PTE.	HERBERT		OXENDALE	KIA
13/11/16	12/426	PTE.	WILLIAM		EMBLEY	KIA
13/11/16	12/43	PTE.	LAWRENCE		KNOWLES	KIA
13/11/16	12/1513	PTE.	JOSHUA		HARRISON	KIA
13/11/16	12/1297	L/CPL.	GEORGE WILLIAM		BARRATT	KIA
13/11/16	12/1167	PTE.	JOSEPH		CROFT	KIA
13/11/16	12/51	PTE.	CHARLES		CHALLANS	KIA
13/11/16	12/511	SGT.	CLAUDE		SCOTT	KIA
13/11/16	12/1104	PTE.	WILLIAM BERTRAM		SMITH	KIA
13/11/16	12/457	PTE.	THOMAS		EGAN	KIA
13/11/16	12/1027	CPL.	SAMUEL		BOLTON	KIA
13/11/16	12/1085	PTE.	THOMAS WILLIAM		CHARLTON	KIA
13/11/16	12/410	PTE.	THOMAS EDWARD		PEARSON	KIA
13/11/16	12/77	CPL.	THOMAS EDWARD		SMITH	KIA
13/11/16	21659	PTE.	FRANK LAMBERT		THORPE	KIA
13/11/16	21569	PTE.	GEORGE STANLEY		JACKSON	KIA
13/11/16	12/783	PTE.	THOMAS HENRY		LARVIN	KIA
13/11/16	12/800	PTE.	JAMES		McDONALD	KIA
13/11/16	12/765	PTE.	JAMES HERBERT		BRIGHAM	KIA
13/11/16	12/760	PTE.	SIDNEY		BLACKBURN	KIA
13/11/16	14483	PTE.	ERNEST		WOODGER	KIA
13/11/16	21089	PTE.	JOHN		BATTY	KIA
13/11/16	17408	PTE.	EDWARD		ARMITAGE	KIA
13/11/16	16580	PTE.	FRANK		WARBURTON	KIA
13/11/16	22506	PTE.	WILLIAM		GREEN	KIA

13/11/16	22376	PTE.	HAROLD		ALTOFT	KIA
13/11/16	21530	PTE.	ROBERT WILLIAM		SHARPE	KIA
13/11/16	12/70	L/CPL.	STANLEY		CHAPMAN	KIA
13/11/16	12/687	PTE.	JOHN ROBERT		ALCOCK	KIA
13/11/16	12/543	PTE.	FREDERICK		SEARBY	KIA
13/11/16	12/635	CPL.	STANLEY		BARKER	KIA
13/11/16	12/828	PTE.	DANIEL		McGOWAN	KIA
13/11/16	12/809	PTE.	GEORGE AUGUSTUS		SHEA	KIA
13/11/16	12/668	PTE.	DAVID		BOOTH	KIA
13/11/16	12/792	PTE.	ALFRED HENRY		COCKING	KIA
13/11/16	12/791	PTE.	HAROLD		HEBDEN	KIA
13/11/16	12/802	PTE.	HARRY		HENDERSON	KIA
13/11/16	12/72	PTE.	WILLIAM HENRY		STATHERS	KIA
13/11/16	12/53	SGT.	CHARLES FEDERICK		MORLEY	KIA
13/11/16	12/605	PTE.	SAMUEL		BLAKESTON	KIA
13/11/16	12/568	PTE.	WILLIAM STOTE		WALES	KIA
13/11/16	28160	PTE.	WALLACE		LEACH	KIA
13/11/16	14/171	PTE.	GEORGE EDWARD		BETTS	KIA
13/11/16	7656	PTE.	HARRY		WESTON	K1A
13/11/16	14/84	PTE.	WILLIAM HERBERT		HARPER	KIA
13/11/16	12/903	PTE.	GEORGE WILLIAM		TARUNG	KIA
13/11/16	12/881	PTE.	HERBERT SPENCE		LOWTHER	KIA
13/11/16	12/865	SGT.	ALBERT		BRAITHWAITE	KIA
13/11/16	12/930	PTE.	EDWARD		McMANUS	KIA
13/11/16	14/199	PTE.	WILSON		TURNBULL	KIA
13/11/16	14/244	PTE.	FRANK		MATHER	KIA
13/11/16	14/217	PTE.	STANLEY		PINDER	KIA
13/11/16	14/216	PTE.	GEORGE WILLIAM		BUTLER	KIA
13/11/16	13986	L/CPL.	WILLIAM		SCOTT	KIA
13/11/16	13476	PTE.	NICHOLAS		ROWE	KIA
13/11/16	14/66	PTE.	HENRY		MOWER	KIA
13/11/16	28211	PTE.	WILLIAM		GOODSON	KIA
13/11/16	28185	PTE.	RALPH STANLEY		HARWIN	KIA
13/11/16	28174	PTE.	FREDERICK WILLIAM		WATSON	KIA
13/11/16	34781	PTE.	THOMAS ERNEST		FRETWELL	KIA
13/11/16	31250	PTE.	HARRY		TAYLOR	KIA
13/11/16	28213	PTE.	HERBERT CHARLES		WATERTON	KIA
13/11/16	34786	PTE.	WALTER		KALE	KIA
13/11/16	14/170	PTE.	RICHARD OLIVER		FREEAR	KIA
13/11/16	14/148	PTE.	CHARLES		BOOTH	KIA
13/11/16	12/946	PTE.	WILLIAM HENRY		SPENCER	KIA
13/11/16	12/999	PTE.	JAMES		HOBSON	KIA
13/11/16	28210	PTE.	ARTHUR EDWARD		CARPENTER	KIA
13/11/16	28186	PTE.	JOHN WILLIAM		NICHOLS	KIA
13/11/16	14/1300	PTE.	OSWIN ARTHUR		JARRETT	KIA
14/11/16	28187	PTE.	JOHN		NUDD	DOW
15/11/16	12/336	SGT.	SYDNEY		JOHNSON	DOW
15/11/16	12/1189	PTE.	WILFRED		FOSTER	DOW
15/11/16	21836	PTE.	JIM		BOTTERILL	DOW
15/11/16	12/412	PTE.	WALTER		CAMPION	DOW
15/11/16	21619	PTE.	WILLIAM HENRY		BLACKBOURN	DOW AT HOME
15/11/16	28206	PTE.	SAMUEL MARK		PEPPER	DOW
17/11/16	13/13	CPL.	HARRY		SMITH	DOW
20/11/16	13/366	PTE.	WILLIAM LEONARD		MORRISON	DOW
22/11/16	12/818	PTE.	ARTHUR		BRODERICK	DOW

23/11/16	12/133	PTE.	HAROLD LESLIE	BOND	DOW
23/11/16	34776	PTE.	LOUIS JOHN	BARWELL	DOW AT HOME
24/11/16	12/1516	PTE.	WILLIAM	WOOLLER	DOW
25/11/16	12/1044	PTE.	FREDERICK	SOWERBY	DOW AT HOME
29/11/16	9/1421	PTE.	THOMAS	TAYLOR	DOW AT HOME
4/12/16	13/1467	PTE.	WILLIAM	TOLCHARD	DOW
8/12/16	28195	PTE.	HAROLD NORMAN	THIRTLE	DOW
9/12/16	28209	PTE.	SIDNEY	ARMIGER	DOW
28/12/16	28208	PTE.	EDWARD	SMITH	DOW
12/1/17	14/153	PTE.	FRANCIS REEVE	HICKS	DIED AT HOME
23/2/17	18661	PTE.	WILLIAM EDWARD	TOMLINSON	KIA
25/2/17	36724	PTE.	MARTIN	DUGGAN	KIA
25/2/17	12/302	L/CPL.	WILLIAM	MILNER	KIA
2/3/17	12/889	L/CPL.	WILLIAM ROBERT	CHAPMAN	KIA
14/3/17	15321	PTE.	THOMAS	HIGGINS	DIED
18/4/17	36564	PTE.	WILLIAM HERBERT	BARRETT	DIED
3/5/17	13.313	PTE.	JOHN BENSON	BARON	KIA
3/5/17	9912	PTE.	JAMES WILLIAM	JAMESON	KIA
3/5/17	12/879	PTE.	ERNEST	ELEY	KIA
3/5/17	12/147	PTE.	ARTHUR	BLAGG	KIA
3/5/17	12/211	SGT.	ANGUS	MCDONALD	KIA
3/5/17	6628	SGT.	FREDERICK	WOOD	KIA
3/5/17	12/396	PTE.	STANLEY	WHITEHEAD	KIA
3/5/17	12/1353	L/SGT.	JAMES WATSON	WALLACE	KIA
3/5/17	13483	PTE.	ALBERT EDWARD	BEXFIELD	KIA
3/5/17	8791	PTE.	FREDERICK	NORTHFIELD	KIA
3/5/17	33140	PTE.	THOMAS	THORNTON	KIA
3/5/17	33092	PTE.	DAVID	POTTER	KIA
3/5/17	36702	PTE.	ARTHUR PERCY	WAKEFIELD	KIA
3/5/17	35067	PTE.	FREDERICK	TURNER	DOW
3/5/17	28214	PTE.	HENRY	LOCKWOOD	KIA
3/5/17	13/1381	CPL.	HARRY	BULMAN	KIA
3/5/17	13/1414	PTE.	HAROLD	TASKER	KIA
3/5/17	24887	PTE.	WALTER ERNEST	STAMP	KIA
3/5/17	10/1446	PTE.	FRANK	ELUS	KIA
3/5/17	33024	PTE.	ARTHUR	SMITH	KIA
3/5/17	12/717	PTE.	HARRY	HEATH	KIA
3/5/17	19461	PTE.	THOMAS	KEMP	KIA
3/5/17	12/1156	PTE.	THOMAS	ANDERSON	KIA
3/5/17	22064	PTE.	CHARLES	GILL	KIA
3/5/17	19417	PTE.	SAMUEL CHARLES	LARKIN	KIA
3/5/17	18897	PTE	NOAH	KINSEY	KIA
3/5/17	23606	PTE.	WALTER	SCARBOROUGH	KIA
3/5/17	16742	CPL.	FREDERICK ARTHUR	WEBB	KIA
3/5/17	17925	PTE.	ROBERT McCALUM	NEEDHAM	KIA
3/5/17	21768	PTE.	WILLIAM	PASHBY	KIA
3/5/17	19640	PTE.	WILFRED	DEAKIN	KIA
3/5/17	12/733	PTE.	ERNEST	KIRKWOOO	KIA
3/5/17	12/851	PTE.	JOHN EDWARD	FENTON	KIA
3/5/17	12/551	L/CPL.	JOHN	BUSBY	KIA
3/5/17	12/57	PTE.	FREDERICK	BROWN	KIA
3/5/17	12/518	PTE.	GEORGE	HALL	KIA
3/5/17	12/316	SGT.	REGINALD	EASINGWOLD	KIA
3/5/17	12/1177	CPL.	EDWARD	PARK	KIA
3/5/17	12/772	PTE.	ALEXANDER PRESTON	WATERS	KIA

3/5/17	12/231	PTE.	ALFRED		MOULDS	KIA
3/5/17	12/842	PTE.	GEORGE		NEALL	KIA
3/5/17	38061	PTE.	WILLIAM FARRAR		WINTERBURN	KIA
3/5/17	25372	PTE.	ERNEST GEORGE		COOPER	KIA
3/5/17	36482	PTE	JOHN		GALLAGHER	KIA
3/5/17	36549	PTE.	JOSEPH JAMES		COX	KIA
3/5/17	220013	SGT.	HENRY WALTER		UTTON	KIA
3/5/17	37350	L/CPL.	FRANK		BRADSHAW	KIA
3/5/17	36755	PTE.	JOHN		BULCOCK	KIA
3/5/17	37871	PTE.	WALTER		ARMITT	KIA
3/5/17	26004	PTE.	JOHN THOMAS		SMITH	KIA
3/5/17	388055	PTE.	LEWIS		WHITE	KIA
3/5/17	36748	PTE.	EDGAR		CRABTREE	KIA
3/5/17	12/1006	L/CPL.	CLAUDE		JOHNSTON	KIA
3/5/17	36751	PTE.	JOHN		McCONVILLE	KIA
3/5/17	36737	PTE.	JOHN		NORFOLK	KIA
3/5/17	36734	PTE.	ALFRED		HILL	KIA
3/5/17	36726	PTE.	THOMAS HUGH		CULLEN	KIA
3/5/17	36559	PTE.	ERNEST		FRANCIS	KIA
3/5/17	36503	L/CPL.	THOMAS FREDERICK		DOUGHTY	KIA
3/5/17	28196	PTE.	SYDNEY CLAUDE		TURNER	KIA
3/5/17	36721	PTE.	ERNEST		TRIPCONY	KIA
3/5/17	36608	PTE.	HARRY		WALLER	KIA
3/5/17	34775	PTE.	FEDERICK CECIL		BAILEY	KIA
3/5/17	36603	PTE.	WILLIAM PERCY		CRIPPS	KIA
3/5/17	36568	PTE.	HAROLD WILFRED		JOHNSON	KIA
3/5/17	36576	PTE.	FRED		ROGERSON	KIA
3/5/17	11.25	L/CPL.	WILLIAM HENRY		EDSON	KIA
3/5/17	35083	PTE.	JOHN WILLIAM		WRIGHT	KIA
3/5/17	36560	PTE.	ROBERT		SWAIN	KIA
3/5/17	33221	PTE.	ERNEST		PECK	KIA
3/5/17	36719	PTE.	JOSEPH		TURNER	KIA
3/5/17	35199	PTE.	ALBERT		BOTHAMLEY	KIA
3/5/17	36621	PTE.	WILLIAM		SUTTON	KIA
3/5/17	37872	PTE.	JAMES THOMAS		BALMFORD	KIA
3/5/17	38045	PTE.	LEONARD GEORGE		SHARP	KIA
3/5/17	38039	PTE.	JAMES HAROLD		BRUMBY	KIA
3/5/17	36655	PTE.	WILLIAM ALFRED		NORRISS	KIA
3/5/17	34774	PTE.	HARRY		BAGGALEY	KIA
3/5/17	36693	PTE.	JOHN BOTTOMLEY		WARREN	KIA
3/5/17	34749	PTE.	JOHN HAROLD		JEBSON	KIA
3/5/17	33470	L/CPL.	HARRY JACKSON		BOWRON	KIA
5/5/17	12/442	PTE.	GEORGE ERNEST		BINNING	DOW
5/5/17	220027	PTE.	JOHN THOMAS		IBBETSON	DOW
7/5/17	38058	PTE.	HAROLD		CLAPHAM	KIA
9/5/17	12/1421	SGT.	HAROLD		FAULKNER	KIA
13/5/17	35219	PTE.	JAMES		RICHARDS	KIA
14/5/17	12/1386	PTE.	CHARLES WILLIAM		TACEY	DOW
14/5/17	12/384	PTE.	HAROLD		EDMOND	KIA
15/5/17	36644	PTE.	HAROLD WILLIAM		WELCH	KIA
15/5/17	12/1172	PTE.	JAMES		HARLAND	KIA
15/5/17	12/126	PTE.	GEORGE		HARRISON	KIA
15/5/17	36572	PTE.	GEORGE FRANCIS		SHENTON	KIA
16/5/17	17797	PTE.	LEONARD		WARDELL	DOW
17/5/17	12/1437	PTE.	JOSEPH WILLIAM		HIGGINS	DOW

18/5/17	38050	PTE.	JOHN THOMAS	ARNULL	DIED
23/5/17	21548	PTE	CHARLES WILLIAM	MOORE	KIA
23/5/17	12/1196	PTE.	THOMAS HARGREAVE	WILKINSON	DOW
25/5/17	33084	PTE.	CHRISTOPHER	REGAN	DOW
12/5/17	36589	PTE.	HENRY	CUTHBERT	DIED
21/6/17	10/1443	PTE.	HENRY	BUSH	DIED
22/6/17	28198	PTE.	ALFRED HENRY	BULL	KIA
23/6/17	36591	PTE.	WILLIAM	BUTLER	KIA
25/6/17	36558	PTE.	EDWIN ALBERT VIDTOR	HARRIS	KIA
25/6/17	12282	PTE.	ARTHUR	BARNES	KIA
26/6/17	3/7164	PTE.	JOHN WILLIAM	BARLOW	KIA
3/7/17	37347	L/CPL.	TOM	HINSLEY	KIA
3/7/17	37348	L/CPL.	JOHN THOMAS	BIRD	KIA
3/7/17	28175	PTE.	GEORGE	WILBY	KIA
3/7/17	220020	PTE.	FREDERICK	MOUER	KIA
4/7/17	220011	SGT.	PERCY	NICHOLSON	KIA
6/7/17	38062	PTE.	ARTHUR JAMES	MALES	DOW
6/7/17	27793	PTE.	FRED	EARNSHAW	DOW
10/7/17	24829	PTE.	JOSEPH HENRY	SCOTT	DOW
23/7/17	18137	PTE.	ARCHIBALD	CLACKER	DOW
30/7/17	12530	PTE.	EDGAR	COLLINSON	DOW
31/7/17	21539	PTE.	LAWRENCE	SMITH	KIA
14/8/17	21162	PTE.	HENRY IRVING	CATTLE	KIA
14/9/17	204121	PTE.	HAROLD	BIELBY	DOW
16/9/17	27080	PTE.	THOMAS	EVANS	KIA
16/9/17	11424	PTE.	WALTER	BENTLEY	KIA
13/10/17	12/1181	PTE.	ROBERT HOPE	WARNES	KIA
5/11/17	12/482	SGT.	HARRY	SHEPHERDSON	DOW
8/11/17	12/417	PTE.	SAMUEL	ROWBOTTOM	KIA
8/11/17	36714	L/CPL.	GEORGE HARRY	DYSON	KIA
9/11/17	14/215	CPL.	LEONARD	WHITELAM	KIA
27/11/17	36643	PTE.	JOSEPH WILLIAM	MALCOLM	DOW
29/11/17	18595	PTE.	FRANK	THOMPSON	DOW
2/1/18	12706	PTE.	THOMAS	WILES	KIA
4/1/18	36723	PTE.	ROBERT	MARSHALL	DIED
5/1/18	21829	PTE.	EDWARD	WELLS	KIA
6/1/18	12/735	PTE.	JOSEPH WILLIAM	STEELE	KIA
25/1/18	14/109	PTE.	THOMAS	PARR	DOW
31/1/18	225391	PTE.	ROBERT	EDMOND	KIA
27/2/18	12/378	PTE.	JOHN AKESTER	HODGSON	DIED
18/4/18	12/493	PTE.	HAROLD	WILSON	DOW
10/7/18	12259	PTE.	CHARLES WILLIAM	HENSON	DIED
19/10/18	12/493	PTE.	JOSEPH	DIMMACK	KIA
21/11/18	36694	PTE.	HERBERT	HAROCASTLE	DIED

Appendix 7

13th Battalion Soldiers' deaths in date order

1/10/16	13/880	PTE.	GEORGE	JOHNSON	DOW
13/11/16	13/451	PTE.	WILLIAM VINCENT	KERSHAW	KIA
13/11/16	13/183	PTE.	GEORGE	MILNER	KIA
13/11/16	13/1301	PTE.	JOHN EDWIN	WALMSLEY	KIA
13/11/16	12/978	PTE.	WILLIAM	STAINFORTH	KIA
13/11/16	13/182	PTE.	FREDERICK WILLIAM	MIDFORTH	KIA
13/11/16	14/213	PTE.	CHARLES	BELL	KIA
13/11/16	13/187	PTE.	JOHN	NELSON	KIA
13/11/16	13/1226	PTE.	JAMES	MILES	KIA
13/11/16	13/1127	L/CPL.	GEORGE HENRY	MESSENGER	KIA
13/11/16	13/38	CPL.	HENRY	BEANLAND	KIA
13/11/16	13/642	PTE.	JOHN WILLIAM	PLATTS	KIA
13/11/16	13/34	PTE.	HARRY STANLEY	BARRETT	KIA
13/11/16	25462	PTE	PERCY	MARSHALL	KIA
13/11/16	13/1379	L/CPL.	HAROLD	BARNBY	KIA
13/11/16	13/1099	PTE.	ARCHIBALD	MORRELL	KIA
13/11/16	13/35	PTE	MATTHEW	BARNABY	KIA
13/11/16	13/455	PTE.	THOMAS JOHN	McNALLY	KIA
13/11/16	13/576	PTE.	EDWARD	RICHARDSON	KIA
13/11/16	13/726	L/CPL.	WALTER	PARKER	KIA
13/11/16	13/1400	PTE.	WILLIAM HARRY	NEWLOVE	KIA
13/11/16	25923	PTE.	JOSHUA	RIDEHALGH	KIA
13/11/16	25925	PTE.	GEORGE HAROLD	PIKE	KIA
13/11/16	13/14	SGT.	FRED	ATKIN	KIA
13/11/16	28086	L/CPL.	CYRIL ALBERT	LINTON	KIA
13/11/16	13/1289	PTE.	JOHN WILLIAM	PALLISTER	KIA
13/11/16	13/1288	PTE.	JAMES SYDNEY	NEWMAN	KIA
13/11/16	13/1157	PTE.	ERNEST	JENNISON	KIA
13/11/16	13/856	PTE.	THOMAS	HULL	KIA
13/11/16	13/19	PTE.	JOHN HENRY	BETTINSON	KIA
13/11/16	13/598	PTE.	WILLIAM	BETTS	KIA
13/11/16	25864	PTE.	JESSE	HILL	KIA
13/11/16	13/705	PTE.	ALBERT BUTLER	JANNEY	KIA
13/11/16	26182	PTE	FRANK	JACKSON	KIA
13/11/16	13/94	PTE.	ROBERT JAMES	HILL	KIA
13/11/16	13/518	SGT.	CHARLES DESMOND	MCCARTHY	KIA
13/11/16	13/352	PTE	RICHARD	HUZZARD	KIA
13/11/16	25897	PTE.	TOM	LEA	KIA
13/11/16	28065	PTE.	JAMES BAGGOTT	LAWSON	KIA
13/11/16	28204	PTE.	ERNEST	LEON	KIA
13/11/16	13/571	PTE.	SYDNEY	LILLEY	KIA
13/11/16	13/155	PTE.	SYDNEY	LEWIS	KIA
13/11/16	13/1110	PTE.	FRED	KAY	KIA
13/11/16	28062	PTE.	WILLIAM HENRY	JOLLANDS	KIA
13/11/16	13/1167	PTE.	MATTHIAS	KAY	KIA
13/11/16	26910	PTE.	ARTHUR	BEANLAND	KIA
13/11/16	28068	PTE.	HENRY	LANE	KIA
13/11/16	13/210	L/CPL.	JOHN ALEXANDER	ROBBIE	KIA

13/11/16	28079	PTE.	ARTHUR		THOMPSON	KIA
13/11/16	13/740	PTE.	GEORGE ROBERT		TAYLOR	KIA
13/11/16	13/1081	PTE.	WILLIAM LEONARD		THORPE	KIA
13/11/16	17913	PTE.	CHARLES EDWARD		TINSLEY	KIA
13/11/16	23811	PTE.	CHARLES EDWARD		THURSTON	KIA
13/11/16	13/889	PTE.	THOMAS		STORK	KIA
13/11/16	13/235	CPL.	HERBERT EDWARD CHARLES		STIRK	KIA
13/11/16	13/1217	PTE.	ARTHUR		STORR	KIA
13/11/16	13/796	PTE.	JOSEPH		SYPH	KIA
13/11/16	13/1312	PTE.	JAMES HENRY		SWIFT	KIA
13/11/16	13/280	PTE.	GEORGE WILLIAM		WILLIAMS	KIA
13/11/16	13/271	PTE.	FREDERICK		WAUD	KIA
13/11/16	13/753	PTE.	MARK ADAMSON		WILSON	KIA
13/11/16	13/487	PTE.	JAMES WILLIAM		WRIGHT	KIA
13/11/16	28081	PTE.	GEORGE FREDERICK		WILSON	KIA
13/11/16	13/2	PTE.	GEORGE		ALLMAN	KIA
13/11/16	13/936	L/CPL.	THOMAS		TOALSTER	KIA
13/11/16	13/745	CPL.	FRANCIS		TURLEY	KIA
13/11/16	13/942	PTE.	WILFRED		ALLEN	KIA
13/11/16	13/1397	PTE.	ROBERT		WALKER	KIA
13/11/16	26185	PTE.	CHARLES HENRY		STANSFIELD	KIA
13/11/16	25934	PTE.	WILLIAM		RUSSELL	KIA
13/11/16	13/1439	PTE.	JOSEPH		COUPLAND	KIA
13/11/16	13/377	CPL.	ARTHUR		ROBINSON	KIA
13/11/16	13/17	CPL.	PERCY		BAILEY	KIA
13/11/16	13/310	CPL.	WILLIAM		ASPINALL, DCM	KIA
13/11/16	13/1235	L/CPL.	JOHN		SAMPLE	KIA
13/11/16	13/379	L/CPL.	ALFRED		RUTLEDGE	KIA
13/11/16	13/644	SGT.	ARTHUR		ROBINSON	KIA
13/11/16	28075	PTE.	HERBERT		ROSE	KIA
13/11/16	13/1043	PTE.	GEORGE HENRY		AUSTIN	KIA
13/11/16	14/46	PTE.	JOHN		SHORES	KIA
13/11/16	13/1484	L/CPL.	HAROLD		SHEPERDSON	KIA
13/11/16	13/474	PTE.	GEORGE ALFRED		SMITH	KIA
13/11/16	13/1273	PTE.	WILLIAM		ALLON	KIA
13/11/16	23821	PTE.	FRED		SNOWDEN	KIA
13/11/16	28216	PTE.	ALBERT		SCOTT	KIA
13/11/16	13/9	PTE.	MARK		ARMSTRONG	KIA
13/11/16	13/216	L/CPL.	SAMUEL		SHAKESPEARE	KIA
13/11/16	13/5	CQMS	HAROLD		ANDREWS	KIA
13/11/16	13/1228	PTE.	FRED		SHARP	KIA
13/11/16	13/877	PTE.	JOHN ROBERT		FARRAH	KIA
13/11/16	13/60	PTE.	ARTHUR THEODORE		COOK	KIA
13/11/16	13/325	PTE.	ROBERT JOHN		COOPER	KIA
13/11/16	13/1383	PTE.	GEORGE		COOPER	KIA
13/11/16	26123	PTE.	WALTER TOM		BOOTH	KIA
13/11/16	23829	PTE.	ERNEST		HILL	KIA
13/11/16	13/1294	PTE.	ROBERT		COOPER	KIA
13/11/16	13/62	PTE.	GEORGE ALFRED		CORNTHWAITE	KIA
13/11/16	13/94	PTE	HARRY		FALK	KIA
13/11/16	13/947	PTE.	FRANCIS HENRY		BOSTOCK	KIA
13/11/16	13/111	PTE.	FREDERICK THOMAS		GILKES	KIA
13/11/16	13/324	CPL.	ARTHUR		COLLINS	KIA
13/11/16	13/1193	PTE.	ERNEST WILLIAM		BOOTH	KIA
13/11/16	13/57	SGT.	REGINALD JAMES		CHESTER	KIA

13/11/16	25909	PTE.	BENJAMIN	GALLAGHER	KIA
13/11/16	13/993	PTE.	FRED	CONWAY	KIA
13/11/16	13/1279	PTE.	WILLIAM	COLLINSON	KIA
13/11/16	13/1386	PTE.	JOHN	DODDS	KIA
13/11/16	13/75	CPL.	ARTHUR	DONNELLY	KIA
13/11/16	13/343	PTE.	BENJAMIN	GALBRAITH	KIA
13/11/16	13/954	CPL.	JOHN WILLIAM	DADDY	KIA
13/11/16	28177	PTE.	EDGAR	BURTON	KIA
13/11/16	13/1333	PTE.	JOHN	BROWN	KIA
13/11/16	13/1197	PTE	MATTHEW HENRY	DRIVER	KIA
13/11/16	13/1017	L/CPL.	STANLEY	DOSSOR	KIA
13/11/16	13/1274	PTE.	JOHN WILLIAM	DARBY	KIA
13/11/16	13/66	PTE.	MARTIN	COWTON	KIA
13/11/16	13/876	PTE	EBENEZER	ELLINGTON	KIA
13/11/16	13/505	PTE.	GEORGE	DIGLIN	KIA
13/11/16	13/91	SGT.	JAMES HERBERT	ELSTON	KIA
13/11/16	13/826	CPL.	ALFRED	DEAN	KIA
13/11/16	23547	PTE.	LAWRENCE	CULLAM	KIA
13/11/16	13/696	PTE.	CHARLES THOMAS	ESPIN	KIA
13/11/16	13/1353	PTE.	HERBERT	EDWARDS	KIA
13/11/16	14/155	PTE.	HARRY	CATTERALL	KIA
13/11/16	13/1140	SGT.	JOHN ROBERT	HALDENBY	KIA
13/11/16	13/333	L/CPL.	DONALD	DUNCAN	KIA
13/11/16	13/1018	PTE.	GEORGE BRUNNING	HARDY	KIA
13/11/16	13/1344	PTE.	GEORGE BINKS	FENWICK	KIA
13/11/16	13/904	PTE.	ARTHUR	CARRICK	KIA
13/11/16	13/1092	SGT.	JOHN	HALLAM, MM	KIA
13/11/16	13/1503	PTE.	WILLIAM NICHOLAS	BRADY	KIA
13/11/16	13/1204	PTE.	FRED	HEBBLEWHITE	KIA
13/11/16	13/1115	SGT.	GEORGE	HARRISON	KIA
13/11/16	13/1380	L/CPL.	ALBERT EDWARD	BUFFEY	KIA
13/11/16	25480	PTE.	THOMAS HENRY	HARDY	KIA
13/11/16	24451	PTE.	HENRY WALTER	HARPER	KIA
13/11/16	13/776	PTE.	CORNELIUS PEARSON	GREENWOOD	KIA
13/11/16	26181	PTE.	JAMES HENRY	GLEDHILL	KIA
13/11/16	13/348	PTE.	GEORGE HERBERT	HARGRAVE	KIA
14/11/16	34260	PTE	JAMES EVERETT	HIGHAM	DOW
14/11/16	13/154	SGT.	LEONARD STANLEY	LANGRICH	DOW
15/11/16	13/229	PTE.	JOSEPH LAWSON	SMITH	DOW
16/11/16	13/564	PTE.	CLARENCE	HARRISON	KIA
16/11/16	13/664	CPL	ARTHUR	WILLIAMS	KIA
16/11/16	13/781	PTE.	ARTHUR	HARRISON	KIA
18/11/16	28085	PTE.	LEONARD	SHIELDS	KIA
19/11/16	13/591	PTE.	JOHN ESAU	AKRILL	DOW
19/11/16	28078	PTE.	GEORGE	THRUSSELL	KIA
19/11/16	13/147	PTE.	CHARLES WILLIAM	KAY	DOW
20/11/16	13/1405	PTE.	ARTHUR	THURLOW	DOW
26/11/16	13/386	PTE.	HENRY	STEPHENS	DOW
30/11/16	13/602	SGT.	JOHN WILLIAM	BROWN	KIA
1/12/16	25430	PTE.	JOHN WALLACE	BATTYE	DOW
2/12/16	13/804	PTE.	COLIN EDWARD	BARKER	DOW
3/12/16	13/209	PTE.	EDWARD	ROBERTS	DOW
2/1/17	13/399	PTE.	JOSEPH EDWARD	WALSH	DOW
16/1/17	13/246	PTE.	THOMAS	SUGDEN	DOW
19/1/17	14/197	PTE.	THOMAS	WOODMANSEY	DIED

28/1/17	13/218	PTE.	CHARLES EDWARD	SNOWLEY	DIED
28/1/17	23845	PTE.	HORNBY	KAY	KIA
31/1/17	13/784	PTE	WILLIAM NELSON	HOWELL	DIED
4/2/17	13/643	PTE.	HARRY	POUGHER	DOW AT HOME
8/2/17	18025	PTE.	JOHN	HOURIGAN	KIA
12/2/17	23795	PTE.	WALTER JAMES RICHARD	BRUCE	DIED
1/3/17	37220	PTE.	WILLIAM	DENT	KIA
1/3/17	16860	PTE.	THOMAS	WARD	KIA
8/3/17	28367	PTE.	GEORGE	CROPPER	KIA
8/3/17	28742	PTE.	RALPH	LIVESEY	KIA
8/3/17	28726	PTE	WILLIAM	McNULTY	KIA
8/3/17	32863	PTE.	JAMES HENRY	GOWANS	KIA
8/3/17	28732	PTE.	JOSEPH	TAYLOR	DOW
8/3/17	25020	PTE.	HORACE SAMUEL	KIRMAN	KIA
8/3/17	28734	PTE.	FRED	WATSON	KIA
8/3/17	37277	PTE.	JOSEPH	OWEN	KIA
8/3/17	25675	PTE.	ARTHUR	BARRETT	KIA
11/3/17	28637	PTE.	WALTER	LINGARD	DOW
21/3/17	25450	PTE.	FRED	TIDSWELL	DOW
23/3/17	25306	PTE.	RICHARD	MOODY	DOW
19/4/17	13/693	PTE.	ROBERT	DRIVER	KIA
29/4/17	13/344	PTE.	CHARLES	GAMBLE	KIA
29/4/17	13/46	PTE.	JOSEPH HENRY	BROCK	KIA
29/4/17	24847	PTE.	FREDERICK	MURPHY	KIA
29/4/17	28619	PTE.	HOWARTH RATCLIFFE	GREEN	KIA
29/4/17	37234	PTE.	GEORGE	BELL	DOW
1/5/17	28681	PTE.	JOSEPH MICHAEL	McGLYNN	KIA
1/5/17	26579	PTE.	JOHN WILLIAM EDWIN	DAVISON	KIA
1/5/17	23882	PTE.	JOSEPH	BEBBINGTON	KIA
1/5/17	28643	PTE.	ROBERT JOHN	WHALEY	KIA
1/5/17	25367	PTE.	LEONARD	BURGESS	KIA
1/5/17	13/1256	PTE.	JAMES FRANCIS	FORTMAN	KIA
2/5/17	13/541	SGT.	ROBERT STANLEY	TEMPLE, MM	KIA
2/5/17	24858	PTE.	CHARLES ALBERT	SHARP	KIA
2/5/17	37221	PTE.	WILLIAM	ELLERBY	KIA
2/5/17	28652	PTE.	ASHTON	GREENWOOD	DOW
2/5/17	28635	PTE.	GEORGE	SAVAGE	KIA
2/5/17	25600	PTE	WALTER RICHMOND	BAKER	KIA
2/5/17	28594	PTE.	ALBERT	SCHOFIELD	KIA
3/5/17	28359	PTE.	PERCY	NOBBS	KIA
3/5/17	13/1174	PTE.	JOHN WILLIAM	O'NEAL	KIA
3/5/17	34990	PTE.	ARTHUR	SMITH	KIA
4/5/17	28653	PTE.	WALTER JAMES	BARNES	KIA
4/5/17	26018	PTE.	SYDNEY	ARSKEY	KIA
5/5/17	26575	PTE.	SLOMON	SOLE	DIED
6/5/17	26009	PTE.	SYDNEY HAROLD	FRYER	KIA
6/5/17	13/1150	SGT.	REGINALD COOPER	MAUGHAM	DOW
6/5/17	26633	PTE.	JAMES HENRY	TAYLOR	DOW
6/5/17	28171	PTE.	ROBERT SAMUEL	SPORLE	DIED
7/5/17	26064	PTE.	HENRY	ROBINSON	DOW
8/5/17	220133	PTE.	WALTER	PALMER	DOW
13/5/17	26001	PTE.	PERCY WILLIAM	DENT	DOW
14/5/17	12/1115	PTE.	WALTER	GARFITT	KIA
14/5/17	28710	PTE.	PERCY	BULL	KIA
14/5/17	37278	CPL.	JOSEPH ALBERT	WILLEY	KIA

16/5/17	37223	PTE.	HARRY	HOWELL	DOW
20/5/17	28691	PTE.	FRED	HOBSON	DOW
22/5/17	15335	PTE.	RICHARD THOMAS	WILLIAMS	DOW
16/6/17	25092	PTE.	ERNEST	TOMKINS	DOW AT HOME
23/6/17	26547	L/CPL	CHARLES	METCALF	KIA
23/6/17	13/657	CPL.	ALFRED	TAYLOR	KIA
28/6/17	14501	CPL.	GEORGE SMITH	HUDDART	KIA
29/6/17	28567	PTE.	ERNEST WILLIAM	GELDER	DOW
20/7/17	13/775	PTE.	JOHN	GRAYBURN	KIA
21/7/17	37282	PTE.	FRANK	TAYLOR	DOW
24/7/17	28683	PTE	HENRY	WILKINSON	KIA
30/7/17	13/1357	PTE.	GEORGE ERNEST	REED	KIA
30/7/17	25669	PTE	WILLIAM ALBERT	LOWE	DOW
30/7/17	26095	PTE	FRANK WILIAM	JACKSON	DOW
30/7/17	9627	PTE.	ALBERT	CAPES	DOW
30/7/17	28737	PTE.	WILLIAM MALBON	BROWN	KIA
30/7/17	28356	PTE.	WILFRED	ROBINS	DOW
30/7/17	23847	PTE.	WILLIAM	STELLINGS	KIA
30/7/17	28368	PTE.	GEORGE HOWARD	DRINKWATER	KIA
2/8/17	26421	PTE.	JAMES WILLIAM	MOORE	DOW
2/8/17	10/372	PTE.	EDWIN THOMAS	JACKSON	KIA
10/8/17	19227	PTE.	WILLIAM STEWART	FEATHERBY	DOW
10/9/17	13/446	PTE.	ARTHUR	JOHNSON	DOW
18/9/17	13/40	PTE.	ALBERT	BLENKINSOP	KIA
31/10/17	26745	PTE.	THOMAS ARTHUR	LANGTHORPE	KIA
4/11/17	13/1494	PTE.	ERNEST	WINTER	KIA
4/11/17	28717	PTE.	FRED	ELSEY	KIA
4/11/17	28360	PTE.	JAMES	PEPPER	KIA
4/11/17	28954	PTE.	WALLACE	SPARK	KIA
5/11/17	13/1292	CPL.	HARRY	GREEN	DOW
7/11/17	13/754	PTE.	GEORGE	WRIGHT	DOW
8/11/17	28163	PTE.	DANIEL EDMUND	OAKES	KIA
8/11/17	13/146	SGT.	GEORGE STANLEY	JOHNSON	KIA
8/11/17	26139	PTE.	TOM ROBERT	MILLER	KIA
29/11/17	28158	PTE.	ALFRED JAMES	PHILLIPS	KIA
29/11/17	13/1233	CPL.	GEORGE FRANK	WALLER	KIA
7/1/18	28578	PTE.	WILLIAM THOMAS	BINNS	KIA
22/1/18	28579	PTE.	SAMUEL	CAMM	DOW
27/1/18	8376	SGT.	WILLIAM	REDFERN.MM	KIA
27/1/18	13/1195	PTE.	JAMES THOMAS	CLATER	KIA
3/2/18	27293	L/CPL.	JOSEPH	WOMACK	DOW
31/3/18	34981	PTE.	HENRY	ROBINSON	DIED AT HOME
15/5/18	13/1305	PTE.	GIBSON	WHITE	KIA

Appendix 8

10th Battalion Officers' deaths in date order

4/6/16	SPINK	CECIL COOPER	2/LT.	KIA
4/6/16	PALMER	DEREK WILLIAM ONSLOW	LT.	KIA
25/6/16	FLINTOFF	RANDOLPH ALEX	LT.	KIA
27/6/16	DAVIS	OWEN MAZZINGHI	2/LT.	KIA
30/10/16	PIERSON	LESLIE D. MID	LT.	KIA
27/2/17	FRICKER	ALBERT CHARLES	2/LT.	KIA
13/4/17	SANGER	HENRY KEITH	2/LT.	KIA
3/5/17	ADDY	JAMES CARLTON MC	CAPT.	KIA
3/5/17	WEBSTER	ARTHUR CECIL	2/LT.	KIA FROM 4thBN
3/5/17	CARLISLE	REGINALD	CAPT.	KIA
3/5/17	STRINGER	DUDLEY	2/LT.	KIA
10/5/17	LEECH	NORMAN BLACK	CAPT.	DOW
14/5/17	JACKSON	HAROLD WILLOWS	L.T	DOW
1/7/17	JONES	ARTHUR GODMAN	2/LT.	DOW
9/7/17	RICE	BERNARD NEVILLE	CAPT.	DIED
10/7/17	CLARK	WILLIAM SOWERBY MC	CAPT.	KILLED
12/9/17	SOUTHERN	MATHEW	2/LT.	KIA
23/3/18	ANDREW	ERNEST JOHN	LT.	KIA SERVING WITH 1st BN
25/3/18	JOHNSTON	ALEXANDER	2/LT	KIA
31/3/18	HOUGHTON	ALBERT WILLIAM	2/LT.	DOW
12/4/18	McDERMOTT	EDWARD MC & BAR	2/LT.	
19/4/18	RUTHERFORD	WILLIAM McCONNELL	2/LT.	DOW
28/6/18	TRAILL	COLIN BLAFOUR MC	MAJOR	KIA
20/8/18	BUTTERY	WALTER	2/LT.	KIA FROM 5TH BN
4/9/18	RAYNER	HAROLD	2/LT.	KIA FROM 4TH BN
4/9/18	EARLE	CEDRIC	2/LT.	KIA FROM 4TH BN
7/9/18	KROG	EUSTACE JOHN MC	LT.	KIA
7/9/18	BRADBURY	WILLIAM ROWLAND	2/LT.	KIA
10/9/18	HUTCHINSON	LESLIE GWYNNE	LT.	KIA
24/9/18	CHEESBROUGH	HAROLD	2/LT.	KIA FROM 2nd W/YORKS
26/9/18	MARSHALL	ANDREW FAIRLIE WILSON	2/LT.	DIED AS POW
28/9/18	DOBSON	FRANK RAYNER	2/LT.	FROM 3rdYORKS & LANCS
28/9/18	DUGDALE	DANIEL	CAPT.	KIA
28/9/18	PIGGOTT	FREDERICK	2/LT.	KIA FROMY & LANCS
1/10/18	RENDLE	GEORGE	2/LT.	KIA FROM 4TH BN
29/5/21	BROMBY	WILLIAM GIRDESTONE	LT.	DIED

Appendix 9

11th Battalion Officers' deaths in date order

18/4/16	MUIR	HARRY	2/LT.	KILLED
30/7/16	WIGGINTON	ARTHUR	2/LT.	KIA
9/9/16	SISSONS	NORMAN LEA	LT.	KIA
8/10/16	HOPKINS	WILLIAM JONES	2/LT.	DOW
12/11/16	McREYNOLDS	JOHN BERNARD	HON. LT/ QMLT.	KIA
3/5/17	HALL	ALLAN BERNARD	LT.	FROM ARMY CYCLIST CORPS
3/5/17	EKINS	WILLINGHAM RICHARD	2/LT.	KIA FROM 3rd BN
3/5/17	HIGNETT	WILLIAM ROWLAND	2/LT.	KIA FROM 4th BN.
3/5/17	HARRISON	JOHN VC, MC	2/LT.	FROM 12th BN
3/5/17	REEVE	ERNEST WILLIAM	CAPT.	KIA
3/5/17	HUTCHINSON	BENJAMIN MC	2/LT.	KIA
3/5/17	PURLL	WILLIAM ALBERT GEORGE	2/LT.	KIA
3/5/17	STAVELEY	HUGH SHEARDOWN	LT.	KIA
2/6/17	DAVIE	FRANK MM	2/LT.	DOW
8/11/17	SAVILLE	CLIFFORD ALLEN	CAPT.	KIA
8/11/17	CLIFT	MARCUS HENRY	2/LT.	KIA
8/11/17	WRIGHT	HAROLD IVAN	LT.	KIA FROM 4th BN
8/11/17	OLIVER	ARTHUR HAROLD	2/LT.	KIA
25/3/18	TOMEY	DONALD STUART	LT.	KIA
27/3/18	JAMES	RUPERT FREDERICK	LT.	KIA
27/3/18	PHILLIP	KENNETH	CAPT.	FROM 4th BN
3/4/18	MITCHELL	HENRY	2/LT.	DOW
25/4/18	RICHARDSON	FRANK ARNOLD	2/LT.	ATTACHED TO 11th BN
17/5/18	WALLIS	FRANCIS HERBERT GUY	CAPT.	DOW
25/7/18	McINTYRE	ROBERT WILLIAM	2/LT.	KIA MBE
8/8/18	OAKE	DOUGLAS MC	CAPT.	KILLED ATHD 92 TMB
9/8/18	COWLEY	FRANK WHEATLEY MC & BAR	LT.	DOW ATHD 92 TMB
15/8/18	WRIGHT	HAROLD IVAN	2/LT.	KIA FROM 4th BN
15/8/18	COATES	JOHN	2/LT.	KIA FROM E R YEOMANRY
21/8/18	BOCKING	BERNARD MC	2/LT.	FROM 12th YORKSHIRE REGT
8/9/18	SKEVINGTON	WILLIAM PERCY	2/LT.	KIA
29/9/18	SOUTHERN	THOMAS WILLIAM MC	CAPT.	FROM 4th BN
1/10/18	WATTS	CYRIL GEORGE	CAPT.	DOWATHD 93 BRIGADE
1/11/18	BERRY	HARRY	2/LT.	FROM 8th WEST YORKS
9/11/18	GOUGH	CYRIL	LT.	POW FROM 4th BN
11/11/18	WHITTINGTON-INCE	RALPH PIGGOTT MC	LT.	DOW
6/12/18	THORPE	ALBERT EDWARD	2/LT.	DIED
31/1/19	WAITE	CLEMENT WILLIAM	MAJOR	DIED DSO, MID
26/5/16	TAYLOR	RICHARD NEVILLE	2/LT	KIA
28/6/16	CRABTREE	STEPHEN MARK	LT.	KIA

Appendix 10

12th Battalion Officers' deaths in date order

29/6/16	DREWETT	CHARLES	2/LT.	DOW
19/7/16	WALKER	SYDNEY STRATTON	CAPT.	KIA
15/8/16	BECKH	ROBERT HAROLD	2/LT.	DOW
13/11/16	LIVSEY	ERNEST CLAUDE	2/LT.	KIA
13/11/16	HABERSHON	LEONARD OSBORNE	CAPT.	KIA
13/11/16	MORGAN	RICHARD GODFREY	2/LT.	KIA
13/11/16	MARRIOTT	HERBERT NORMAN	CAPT.	KIA
13/11/16	FRIZONI	OSCAR LORENZO	LT.	KIA
13/11/16	ESTRIDGE	EDWARD WILFRED	2/LT.	KIA ATT. FROM CAN ARMY
13/11/16	ELFORD	ARTHUR DOUGLAS	LT.	KIA
13/11/16	FAKER	FRANK LEONARD	2/LT.	KIA
17/11/16	HEATHCOTE	RALPH NOEL	2/LT.	DOW
17/11/16	HOULT	ARTHUR	2/LT.	DIED
24/11/16	MONTCRIEFF	CHARLES GORDON CONRAD	2/LT.	DOW
3/5/17	CARROLL	WILLIAM	CAPT.	MC
3/5/17	CARRALL	JOHN EDWIN	2/LT.	KIA
3/5/17	CATTLEY	WILLIAM	CAPT.	MC
3/5/17	DUGUID	ALEXANDER RITCHIE	2/LT.	KIA FROM 4thBN.
3/5/17	JENNING	HUGH COTTON	2/LT.	DIED ATT. FROM ASC
5/5/17	HALL	JOSEPH STANLEY	2/LT.	KIA
5/5/17	MOORE	PERCY	2/LT.	DOW
10/5/17	OFFICER	ARNOLD VINCENT	2/LT.	DIED

Appendix 11

13th Battalion Officers' deaths in date order

21/7/16	RANSOM	RICHARD EDWARD CROFT	CAPT.	DOW
24/7/16	PUDDICOMBE	DONALD RAMSEY	2/LT.	DOW
13/9/16	BURBIDGE	HOWARD CHURCHILL	2/LT.	DOW
13/11/16	DORMAN	ANTHONY GODFREY MC	LT.	KIA
13/11/16	BINNING	ALBERT HUTESON	2/LT.	KIA
13/11/16	BELL	HAROLD	2/LT.	KIA
13/11/16	PETERS	ASHLEY	2/LT.	KIA
13/11/16	HUTCHINSON	TOM MACINTOSH	2/LT.	KIA
13/11/16	LEWIS	NORMAN VICTOR	LT.	KIA
13/11/16	WOOD	JOHN	2/LT.	KIA
14/11/16	BEECHEY	FRANK COLLETT REEVES	2/LT.	DOW
20/11/16	WATTS	ROBERT STAPLETON	2/LT.	DOW
20/12/16	KERR	NORMAN JAMES	2/LT	DOW Attached 92 MGC
8/3/17	BROWN	FREDERICK DAVID	2/LT.	KIA
29/4/17	HORN	JOHN CYRIL	2/LT.	KIA
2/5/17	MACAULAY	GEORGE CECIL GORDON	2/LT.	FROM 3rd Bn
2/5/17	HAMM	WILLIAM GEORGE	2/LT.	KIA MC
28/6/17	SAWDON	ARTHUR TINDALE	2/LT.	KIA
31/3/18	BROOKE	CLARENCE	2/LT.	KIA WITH 10th or11th BN
16/4/18	JOHNSTON-STUART	CYRIL GEORGE	LT.	KIA
24/8/18	STORCH	HERBERT MC	2/LT.	SERVING WITH 1st BN

Appendix 12
Original Hull Pals Casualty Details

10TH BATTALION

ABBA, PRIVATE HAROLD. 10/483. Killed in action on 3/5/17. Born in Hull. Commemorated on the Arras Memorial.

ADAMS, PRIVATE THOMAS. 10/1040. Died in Hull on September 18th 1914 aged 30 from Brain Fever. Buried in Western Cemetery, Hull, with a full military funeral procession. Born in Derby but resident in Hull. Son of Thomas and Louise Adams. He was single.

ADAMSON, PRIVATE WILLIAM EDWARD (TEDDY), of V Company. 10/525. Died of wounds on July 2nd 1916, aged 21. Born in Hull, Buried in Euston Road Cemetery. Only son of Edward and Emily Adamson of 45, Leonard Street, Beverley Road, Hull.

ALLEN, PRIVATE JOSEPH WILLIAM, Croix de Geurre (Belgium). 10/478. Died of wounds on April 12th 1918, aged 24. Born in Hull. Son of Mr and Mrs. J.T. Allen, of 13, Williams Terrace, Woodhouse Street, Hull. Husband of Eleanor Ann Allen of 11. Florence Terrace, Waterloo Street, Hull. Commemorated on the Ploegsteert Memorial.

ARCHER, PRIVATE GEORGE, of 'C' Company. 10/392. Killed in action June 4th 1916, aged 26. Born in Hull. Buried in Sucrerie Military Cemetery. Colincamps. Son of George and Louisa Archer, of 42 Field Street, Holderness Road, Hull.

ARNELL, SERGEANT GEORGE. 12/574. Killed in action on September 4th 1916, aged 18. Born in Driffield. Commemorated on the Ploegsteert memorial. Son of John and Mary Ann Amell of 2 Selinas Crescent, Rosemead Street, New Bridge Road, Hull.

ASCOUGH, PRIVATE WILLIAM BERNARD (BERT), of 'C' Company. 10/277. Killed in action June 4th 1916, aged 25. Buried in Sucrerie Military Cemetery, Colincamps. Son of Robert Boulton Ascough and Caroline Elizabeth Ascough of 3. Malvern Avenue, Ella Street, Hull.

ATKINSON, PRIVATE JOHN BELL. 10/1230. Died of wounds on June 7th 1916. Born in Thorsenfield, enlisted in Hornsea whilst resident in Hull. Buried in Abbeville Communal Cemetery. Son of John Clifford and Mary Atkinson of Newland Avenue, Hull.

BAILEY, CORPORAL WILLIAM GILBERT. 10/286. Killed in action on May 3rd 1917 aged 21. Born in Hull. Son of George and Sarah Elizabeth Bailey of 29 St. Paul Street, Hull. Buried in Orchard Dump Cemetery.

BARKER, PRIVATE ALFRED ERNEST. 10/100. Died of wounds August 6th 1916. aged 19. Born in Beverley. Attached to MGC. Son of John and Annie Barker of 35 Cornwall Street. Cottingham. Buried in Longuenesse Souvenir Cemetery (St Omer).

BIDDLECOMBE, PRIVATE J. 10/694. Died of sickness on June 22nd 1916 aged 23. Son of Stephen and Kate Elizabeth Biddlecombe of 109 St. Augustine Road, Southsea, Hampshire. Born at Eastney. Buried in Patrington (St Patrick) Churchyard.

BILBE, PRIVATE CLARENCE. 10/923. Died on November 15th 1918 in France of pneumonia, aged 21. Buried in Terlincthum British Cemetery. Born in Hull. Son of William and Mary Bilbe of 131 Fountain Road, Hull. He served in Egypt and on The Western Front.

BLAKEMORE, PRIVATE ALBERT. 10/527. Killed in action on June 4th 1916 aged 19. Buried in Sucrerie Military Cemetery, Colincamps. Born in Leeds but resident in Hull. Lived at 9 King's Cross Avenue, Bean Street, Hull. His name appears on the Bean Street Roll of Honour.

BLENKIN, PRIVATE GEORGE. 10/73. Signaller. Killed in action on June 26th 1916 aged 20. Buried in Sucrerie Military Cemetery, Colincamps. Born in Hull. Son of Harry and the late Maria Blenkin of 47 Seaton Street. Hull.

BONE, SERGEANT WILFRED, of 'C' Company. 10/693. Killed in action on June 28th 1918 aged 26. Buried in Aval Wood Military Cemetery. Born in Hull. Son of John William and Mary Elizabeth Bone. Husband of Rosie Bone of 12 Park Lane West, Anlaby Park, Hull. His brother served in France.

BOWEN, LANCE-CORPORAL GEORGE ERNEST (known as Sonny). 10/1207. Died at 42nd Casualty Clearing Station, of wounds to the head, on August 10th 1917. Buried in Aubigny Communal Cemetery extension. Born in Hull. He returned from the USA at the start of the war to enlist.

BOYD, PRIVATE PERCY. 10/655. Killed in action on October 27th 1918 aged 23. Born in Hull. Son of Thomas and Claygna Margaret Boyd. Buried in Harlebeke New British Cemetery.

BRAY, PRIVATE GEORGE WILLIAM, of 'C' Company. 10/855. Killed in action on June 4th 1916 aged 21. Buried in Sucrerie Military Cemetery, Colincamps. Born in Hull. Enlisted during September 1914. Son of Charles and Alice Bray of 81 Garnet Terrace, Oakley Grove, Dewsbury Road, Leeds, late of Hull.

BRIGGS, PRIVATE WILLIAM HURST. 10/218. Killed in action on April 12th 1918 aged 21. Commemorated on the Ploegsteert Memorial. Born in Beverley. Son of W.H. Briggs of Newbegin House, Beverley. His name appears on St. Mary's Church Roll of Honour, Beverley and on the Beverley Grammar School Memorial in The Minster. Beverley.

BROCKLEHURST, PRIVATE JAMES FRANCIS. 10/653. Served in the Battalion Machine Gun Section. Killed in action on November 13th 1916 aged 21. Born in Victoria, near Vancouver BC, but resident in Hull. Son of James Clark and Margaret Brocklehurst of 56 Plane Street, Hull. Commemorated on the Thiepval Memorial.

BROWN, PRIVATE ALFRED. 12.578. Killed in action on April 12th 1918 aged 26. Commemorated on the Ploegsteert Memorial. Born in Hull. Son of Alfred and Ann Brown of 23 Wyndham Street, Hull. He lived at 3 Rowland Terrace, St. Paul Street, Hull.

BROWN, PRIVATE PERCY. 10/734. Killed in action on June 4th 1916 aged 25. Son of Robert Thomas and Elizabeth Brown of 39 High Street, Bridlington, East Yorkshire. Born in Bridlington but resident in Hull. Buried in Sucrerie Military Cemetery. Colincamps.

BROWNE, CORPORAL RALPH EDWIN. 10/528. Killed in action on August 14th 1918 aged 24. Born in Goole, enlisted in Hull but resident in Goole. Son of George Leonard and the late Emily Browne of Goole. Buried in Le Grand Hasard Military Cemetery.

BRUNYEE, PRIVATE JOHN. 10/1297. Killed in action on June 28th 1916. Born in Goole, enlisted in Hull but resident in Goole. Buried in Sucrerie Military Cemetery, Colincamps.

BUCK, PRIVATE GEORGE WALTER. 10/1297. Killed in action on June 27th 1916 aged 35. Son of Michael Buck of Pierpoint Hotel. Cheltenham and the late Maria Buck of Buchanan Street, Corn Mill, Blackpool. Lancashire. Buried in Sucrerie Military Cemetery. Colincamps.

BUCK, CORPORAL THOMAS. 10/805. Killed in action on May 3rd 1917 aged 25. Commemorated on the Arras Memorial. Born in Hull. Husband of May Buck (nee Kitchen) and father of one child, resident at 4A Brunswick Avenue, Beverley Road, Hull. Son-in-law of John Kitchen of St. George's Road, Hull.

BURDON, PRIVATE JOHN WILLIAM. 12/236. Killed in action on September 29th 1918 aged 25. Commemorated on the Tyne Cot memorial. Born in Hull. Son of John James and Ellen Burdon of 55 Abbey Sreet, Hull.

CALEY, PRIVATE SAMUEL. 10/1131. Killed in action on June 25th 1916 aged 35. Born in Hull. Son of George and Eliza Caley of 8 East Park Avenue, Holderness Road, Hull. Buried in Bertrancourt Military Cemetery. His name appears on the Hull Stevedores Society Roll of Honour in the Oddfellows Hall, Hull.

CANTY, PRIVATE CHARLES, of 3rd Platoon, 'A' Company. 14/125. Killed in action on September 7th 1918 aged 26. Son of Henry and Annie Canty of 110a Porter Street, Hull. Born in Hull. Commemorated on the Ploegsteert Memorial.

CHALMERS, SERGEANT FRANK. 10/1072. Died in the UK on July 6th 1917. Born in Perth but resident in Hull. Buried in Hooton Pagnell (All Saints) Churchyard.

CHENEY, PRIVATE JOSEPH, of 'A' Company. 10/1221. Killed in action on June 28th 1916 aged 22 (struck by the base of a shell during a bombardment). Born in Norwich but resident at 80 Sherburn Street, Hull at the time of enlistment. Son of Joseph and Minnie Cheney of Norwich. His brother Fred also served in France. His fiancee Fanny died on June 17th 1918. He was a riveter at Earles Shipyard in Hull. Buried in Sucrerie Military Cemetery. Colincamps.

CLARK, PRIVATE JOHN WILLIAM. 10/1286. Killed in action on May 3rd 1917. Born in Hull. Son of Charles M and E Clark. Commemorated on the Arras Memorial.

CLEARY, PRIVATE WALTER JAMES. 10/958. Killed in action on May 3rd 1917 aged 24. Born in Hull. Son of Emma E and the late Walter H Geary of 42 Edgecombe Street, Newland Avenue, Hull. Commemorated on the Arras Memorial.

CLUBLEY, SERGEANT BERTRAM ARTHUR. 10/723. Killed in action on May 3rd 1917 aged 28. Born in Sutton near Hull. Son of Thomas Cross Clubley and Emma Jane Clubley. Commemorated on the Arras Memorial.

COBBY, PRIVATE JOSEPH HENRY. 10/1355. Died of fever in Hospital in France. Born in Hull. Son of F H and R Cobby of 74 Sandringham St. Hull. Buried in Wimereux Communal Cemetery.

COLLINGWOOD, PRIVATE JOSEPH WILLIAM. 10/338. Died of wounds in a hospital in the UK on July 11th 1918 aged 21. Born in Hull. Son of Joseph and Margaret Collingwood of 536 Holderness Road, Hull. Buried in Hedon Road Cemetery, Hull. COMINS, PRIVATE JOHN L G. 10/31. Died of wounds on March 30th 1918 aged 22. Born in Hull. Son of George and Elizabeth Comins of 73 Goddard Avenue, Hull. Buried in St. Hilaire Cemetery Extension.

CONYERS, PRIVATE SAMUEL. 10/787. Killed in action on June 4th 1916 aged 26 during a German barrage on the front line trenches. Born in Hull. Son of Samuel and Phoebe A Conyers of 40 Richmond Terrace, Liddell Street, Hull. Buried in Sucrerie Military Cemetery. Colincamps.

COOK, PRIVATE JAMES ANDREW 12/350. Killed in action on June 28th 1918. Born in Battersea. Enlisted in Hull but resident in Acton. London. Buried in Aval Wood Military Cemetery.

COOP, PRIVATE STANLEY. 10/561. Died of wounds on July 2nd 1916, aged 21. Born in Clapham Common but resident in Hull. Enlisted September 4th 1914. Son of Edith Coop of 26 Chaucer Street, Westcott Street, Hull. Buried in St Sever Cemetery, Rouen.

CORDEN, PRIVATE HERBERT STENNETT. 10/459. Killed in action on April 13th 1918 aged 20. Son of Stennett W and Florence Corden of 4 Chapman Street, Hull. Commemorated on the Ploegsteert Memorial.

CRAYTON, PRIVATE TOM HAROLD, of 'D' Company. 10/1124. Died on March 11th 1918 aged 33. Son of the late Richard and Elizabeth Crayton of Nottingham. Buried in Northern Cemetery, Cottingham Road, Hull.

DALTON, PRIVATE WILLIAM HENRY. 10/341. Killed in action on July 1st 1916. Born in Hull.

DAWSON, SERGEANT ERNEST WOOD. 10/92. Killed in action on May 3rd 1917. Commemorated on the Arras Memorial.

DEIGHTON, PRIVATE GEORGE KILBY. 10/1247. Killed in action on June 4th 1916. Born in Hull. Buried in Sucrerie Military Cemetery, Colincamps.

DEMPSEY, PRIVATE HERBERT. 10/1123. Died of wounds on April 13th 1916. Born in Hull. Buried in Merville Communal Cemetery.

DENNISON, PRIVATE WALTER. 10/641. Died of wounds on September 22nd 1916. Born in Hull. Buried in Merville Communal Cemetery Extension.

DIXON, PRIVATE ARTHUR HENRY, of 'A' Company. 10/1059. Killed in action on February 28th 1917 aged 21. Born in Hull. Son of Harry and Louise Dixon of 18 Norman Terrace, Roundhay, Leeds. Buried in Couin New British Cemetery.

DIXON, CORPORAL WILLIAM, of 'A' Company. 10/1356. Killed in action on April 10th 1918 aged 25. Son of Mrs. Davinia D Commemorated on the Ploegsteert Memorial.

DOBBS, PRIVATE JAMES APPLEYARD, MM. 10/507. Killed in action on August 2nd 1916 aged 21. Born in Hull. Son of Albert Edward and Charlotte Ann Dobbs of 23 Southcoates Avenue, Holderness Road, Hull. Buried in Le Touret Military Cemetery.

DOUGHERTY, PRIVATE HAROLD. 10/959. Died of wounds on June 28th 1918 aged 22. Born in Goole but resident in Hull. Son of John F and Annie Dougherty of Goole.

DUNN, CORPORAL ERIC CLAUDE. 10/990. Killed in action on September 22nd 1916 aged 21. Son of Mr and Mrs Fred C C Dunn of 9 Pembroke Terrace, Bridlington, East Yorkshire. Born in Brixton but resident in Hull. Buried in St. Vaast Post Military Cemetery Richebourg L'Avouée.

EDWARDS, PRIVATE CHARLES SIDNEY. 12/1389. Killed in action September 29th 1918 aged 27. Born in Hull. Buried in Bedford House Cemetery Enclosure No. 4.

EMERY, PRIVATE ARCHIE VERNON. 10/639. Died of wounds August 26th 1916. Born in Hull. Buried in Le Touret Military Cemetery.

EVERINGHAM, PRIVATE WALTER STANLEY. 10/875. Killed in action on November 13th 1916. Born in Hull. Buried in Euston Road Cemetery.

FANTHORPE, HARRY. 10/1061. Discharged from the army. Died of wounds in hospital in Newcastle on October 9th 1916 aged 34. Husband of Madeline Fanthorpe of 61 Mowpeth Street, Hull. Buried in Gateshead (Saltwell) Cemetery.

FARNILL, PRIVATE JOHN RICHARD. 10/813. Killed in action on June 4th 1916 aged 22. Born in North Newington. Resident at 82 Glencoe Street, Hull. Buried in Sucrerie Military Cemetery, Colincamps.

FITTON, PRIVATE REGINALD, of 'D' Company. 10/894. Died of wounds on November 26th 1916 aged 30. Born in Ashton-under-Lyne but resident in Hull at the time of enlistment. Son of Simeon and Ann Fitton of Hull. Buried in Couin British Cemetery.

FOWLER, PRIVATE WILLIAM ERNEST SKELTON, of 'C' Company 10/1291. Died of wounds on August 15th 1918 aged 34. Born in Hull. Youngest son of Mary and the late Skelton Fowler of 112 Plane Street, Anlaby Road, Hull. Buried in Longuenesse Souvenir Cemetery, St. Omer.

FRANKS, PRIVATE ROBERT PERCY. 12/587. Died of wounds on July 29th 1918 aged 20. Born in Bewholme. Yorkshire but resident in Hull. Son of George Robert and Emma Franks. Buried in Longuenesse Souvenir Cemetery, St. Omer.

GALE, PRIVATE HERBERT. 10/25. Killed in action on May 30th 1916 aged 21. Son of Mr IJ and Mrs E Gale of 9 Daltry Street, Hull. Born in Hull. Buried in Sucrerie Military Cemetery, Colincamps.

GALT, PRIVATE JOHN THORNTON. 10/180. Died of wounds May 31st 1916. Born in Hull. Buried in Gezaincourt Communal Cemetery Extension.

GARTON, PRIVATE HERBERT. 10/505. Killed in action on September 16th 1916 aged 24. Son of Edward Carton of 11 Denmark Street, Bright Street, Holderness Road, Hull. Born in Hull. Buried in St. Vaast Post Military Cemetery. Richebourg L'Avouée.

GILL, PRIVATE GEORGE WILLIAM. 10/764. Killed in action on July 11th 1917 aged 23. Son of George Gledhill and Glenda Gill of Hull. Born in Hull. Buried in Coxyde Military Cemetery.

GUEST, SERGEANT J. 10/632. Died on February 17th 1919 30. Husband of Florence Guest of 25 Falmouth Street, Hull. Buried in Northern Cemetery, Hull.

HALL, CORPORAL CYRIL GEORGE, of 'A' Company. 10/431. Killed in action on March 25th 1918 aged 24. Son of Albert Henry and Eva Mary Hall of 124 St. Paul's Street, Hull. Commemorated on the Arras Memorial.

HALL PRIVATE HUNTER. 12/42. Killed in action on March 27th 1918. Born in Durham but resident in Hull. Commemorated on the Arras Memorial.

HALL, PRIVATE PERCY CAMERON. 10/886. Died of wounds on April 14th 1918. Born in Hull. Husband of Mrs C C Hall of Endyke Lane, Newlands, Hull. Buried in Longuenesse Souvenir Cemetery, St. Omer.

HARDING, PRIVATE FRANK ERNEST. 10/1248. Died of wounds on March 29th 1918 aged 25. Born in Hull. Son of Henry Bell and Jane Ann Harding of 24 Grey Street, Hull. Buried in Bac-Du-Sud British Cemetery.

HARRISON, SERGEANT WILLIAM ERNEST. 10/430. Killed in action on February 26th 1917 aged 27. Born in Hull. Son of Frederick Walter and Emma Francis Harrison of 8 Summergangs, Southcoates Station, Hull. Buried in Euston Road Cemetery.

HERMANN, SERGEANT EDGAR, MM.10/1029. Died of wounds on November 17th 1916 aged 26. Born in Hull. Son of Niels Christian Hermann of Hull. Husband of Elizabeth Mary Hermann of 79 Westboume Avenue, Hull. Buried in Corbie Communal Cemetery Extension.

HESTER, PRIVATE JOHN WILLIAM, OF 'B' Company. 13/814. Killed in action on April 12th 1918 aged 27. Husband of Maud Hester of 3 Cottingham Avenue, Osborne Street, Hull.

HICKS, LANCE-CORPORAL HENRY. 10/681. Killed in action on April 12th 1918. Son of Thomas William and Susan Hicks of 41 Arthur Street, Newington, Hull. Born in Hull. Commemorated on the Ploegsteert Memorial.

HODDS, PRIVATE HARRY. 14/208. Killed in action on April 12th 1918 aged 20. Born in Goole but resident in Hull. Son of Arthur J and Alice E Hodds of 8 Kelvin Street, Hull. Buried in Croix-du-Bac British Cemetery, Steenwerck.

HOLMES, PRIVATE FRANK. 10/305. Killed in action on April 12th 1918. Born in Hull. Commemorated on the Ploegsteert Memorial.

HOMAN, PRIVATE WALTER RAYMOND. 10/968. Killed in action on June 2nd 1917. Born in South Newington. Yorkshire but resident in Hull. Commemorated on the Arras Memorial.

HORSFALL, PRIVATE WILLIAM of 'A' Company. 10/20. Killed in action on October 15th 1918 aged 22. Son of James R and Annie Horsfall of 68 Marshall Street, Hull. Born in Hull. Buried in Berlin South-Western Cemetery.

HORSFIELD, PRIVATE STANLEY. 10/716. Killed in action on March 29th 1916 aged 24 by the explosion of a Minnie (Minenwerfer) in the trenches where he was positioned. Buried in Auchonvillers Military Cemetery. Born in Anlaby Common, near Hull but resident in Hull at the time of enlistment. Son of Geoffrey William and Kate Horsfield of 12 Curzon Street, Hull.

BUNT, PRIVATE ALBERT EDWARD. 12/65. Killed in action on September 29th 1918. Born in Hull. Buried in Underhill Farm Cemetery.

HUNTINGTON, SERGEANT THOMAS. 10/717. Died of wounds on June 11th 1916 aged 24. Son of John and Emily Huntington of Ousedene, Goole. Born in Goole, enlisted in Hull but resident in Goole. Buried in St. Sever Cemetery, Rouen.

HYDE, PRIVATE EDGAR. 10/1028. Killed in action on April 17th 1916 aged 25. Son of Mr J.F. and Mrs M.R. Hyde of West Garth. The Leys. Hornsea, East Yorkshire. Born in Hull. Buried in Sucrerie Military Cemetery, Colincamps.

IRELAND, PRIVATE BENJAMIN. 10/261. Died of wounds on June 5th 1916 aged 21. Son of Charles Doughty and Ellen Margaret Ireland of Ellesmere. North Ferriby, Yorkshire. Buried in Abbeville Communal Cemetery.

JACKSON, LANCE-CORPORAL FREDERICK. 10/627. Killed in action on May 3rd 1917 aged 33. Born in Hull. Son of Walter and Frances M Jackson of 1 Belgrave Mansions, Marine Drive, Bridlington, Yorkshire. Before the war he was a cashier at the Halifax Commercial Bank in Hull. Commemorated on the Arras Memorial.

JACKSON, CORPORAL WILLIAM. 12/1366. Killed in action on March 25th 1918. Born in Hull.

JACKSON, PRIVATE WILLIAM JAMES. 10/626. Killed in action on November 22nd 1916 aged 29. Son of William J and Ada Jackson of Hull. Husband of Alice Jackson of 27 Newstead Street, Hull. Buried in Sailry-au-Bois Cemetery. Born in Hull.

JEFFREY, PRIVATE LAWRENCE FREDERICK. 10/422. Killed in action on October 29th 1916. Born in Hull. Commemorated on the Thiepval Memorial.

JESSUP, PRIVATE GEORGE HERBERT, of 'C' Company. 10/708. Killed in action on April 12th 1918 aged 21. Son of Walter George and Julia Jessup. Born in Hessle. Commemorated on the Ploegsteert Memorial.

JEYNES, LANCE-CORPORAL LEONARD. 10/797. Killed in action on August 3rd 1916. Born in Hull. Buried in St. Vaast Post Military Cemetery, Riehebourg L'Avouée.

JOHNSON, PRIVATE FRANK. 10/1210. Killed in action on June 4th 1916 aged 31. Son of William Burn Johnson and Mary Ann Johnson of 20 Brindley Street, Hull. Born in Hull. Buried in Sucrerie Military Cemetery, Colincamps.

JOHNSON, PRIVATE FRANK HERBERT, of 'C' Company. 10/519. Killed in action on April 12th 1918 aged 25. Son of Walter Herbert and Bella Johnson of 156 Alliance Avenue, Hull. Born in Hull. Commemorated on the Ploegsteert Memorial.

JOHNSON, PRIVATE GEORGE HENRY. 10/845. Killed in action on June 4th 1916 aged 23. Son of William A and Ellen Johnson of 46 Morrill Street, Hull. Born in Hull. Buried in Sucrerie Military Cemetery, Colincamps.

JOHNSON, PRIVATE HARRY, of 'C' Company. 10/532. Killed in action on May 3rd 1917 aged 24. Son of William and E.J. Johnson of 35 Raglan Street. Hull. Commemorated on the Arras Memorial.

JONES, SERGEANT REGINALD PERCIVAL. Killed in action on July 1st 1916. Born in Birmingham but resident in Hull. Commemorated on the Thiepval Memorial.

JORDAN, LANCE-CORPORAL JAMES. 12/934. Killed in action on April 12th 1918 aged 25. Son of Walter James and Jane Ann Jordan of 1 Thomas Square, Drypool, Hull. Born in Hull. Commemorated on the Ploegsteert Memorial.

JOYS, PRIVATE CHARLES SAMSON. 10/819. Killed in action on June 4th 1916 aged 19. Son of James H and A Joys of 12 Wellstead Street, Hessle Road, Hull. Born in Hull. Buried in Sucrerie Military Cemetery, Colincamps.

KEAL, PRIVATE ROBERT. 10/676. Died of wounds on March 6th 1917 aged 26. Born in Hull. Son of the late Richard and Mary Keal of Hull. Husband of Bessie Keal of 128 Summergangs Road, Hull. Buried in Couin New British Cemetery.

KEENE, PRIVATE EDMUND of X Company. 10/160. Killed in action on September 18th 1916 aged 24. Son of John and Mary Ann Elizabeth Keene of 52 Earle's Road, Nuneaton. Born in Hinckley, Leicestershire, but resident in Hull. Buried in St. Vaast Post Military Cemetery, Riehebourg L'Avouée.

KIDD, PRIVATE ROGER LESLIE. 10/232. Died of wounds on August 16th 1916. Born in Hull. Son of Mrs M.E. Kidd of 39 Blenheim Street, Hull. Buried in Merville Communal Cemetery.

KINGDON, PRIVATE CHARLES HERBERT. 10/998. Killed in action on July 22nd 1916. Born in Hull. Buried in Rue-Du-Bacquerot No 1 Military Cemetery, Laventie.

KIRKMAN, PRIVATE HORACE, of 'D' Company. 10/118. Killed in action on May 3rd 1917 aged 24. Born in Hull. Son of Matthew James and Louisa Ellen Kirkman of 46 Folkestone Street, Hull. Commemorated on the Arras Memorial.

LANGDALE, PRIVATE WIILIAM SYKES. 10/1133. Killed in action on March 12th 1917 aged 22. Born in Hull. Son of William and Kate Langdale of 34 Cannon Street, Hull. Buried in Euston Road Cemetery.

LANGTHORNE, LANCE-CORPORAL GEORGE FREDERICK. 10/1223. Killed in action on April 12th 1918 aged 31. Son of William Edwin and Mary Ann Langthorne of 630 Holderness Road, Hull. Husband of Edith Langthorne of 65 Park Street, Spring Bank, Hull. Born in Hull. Commemorated on the Ploegsteert Memorial.

LATUS, PRIVATE SYDNEY. 10/295. Killed in action on April 12th 1918 aged 21. Son of William S and Edith Latus of 52 Pelham Street, Hedon Road. Hull. Born in Hull. Commemorated on the Ploegsteert Memorial.

LAZENBY, PRIVATE WILLIAM. 10/770. Killed in action on May 3rd 1917. Commemorated on the Arras Memorial. Born in Beverley but resident in Hull. Brother of Elsie Shearer of 33 New Garden Street, Hull.

LEIGHTON, PRIVATE OSCAR ROUNDING. 10/128. Killed in action on June 4th 1916 aged 25. Son of Robert Watson Leighton and Hannah Leighton of 19 Thoresby Street, Princes Avenue, Hull. Born in Hull. Buried in Sucrerie Military Cemetery, Colincamps.

LINSLEY, PRIVATE ROBERT. 10/65. Killed in action on May 3rd 1917. Born in Hull. Commemorated on the Arras Memorial.

LOCKEY, PRIVATE PERCY. 10/136. Killed in action on August 11th 1916. Born in Hull. Buried in St. Vaast Post Military Cemetery, Richebourg L'Avouée.

LONG, PRIVATE WALTER. 11/1407. Died of wounds on March 30th 1918. Born in Everton, Nottinghamshire, enlisted in Hull but was resident in Bawtry. Commemorated on the special memorial at Rumacourt Communal Cemetery.

MacBRIDE, PRIVATE JAMES TAYLOR, of 'D' Company. 10/931. Killed in action on May 3rd 1917, aged 21. Born in Beverley. Commemorated on the Arras memorial. Nephew of Mrs. Margaret Jane Taylor of 65 Woods Lane, Cottingham.

MacPHERSON, LANCE-CORPORAL WILLIAM ARTHUR. 10/827. Died of wounds on June 5th 1916 aged 26. Son of James Coppock and Fanny Jane MacPherson of Hull. Buried in Abbevile Communal Cemetery.

MADDRA, PRIVATE JOHN. 11/1395. Died of wounds on April 12th 1918 aged 21. Son of Sarah and the late Joseph Madra of 8 Marsh Street, Scott Street, Hull. Born in Hull. Commemorated on the Ploegsteert Memorial.

MARR, PRIVATE STANLEY, of 'C' Company. 10/79. Killed in action on April 12th 1918 aged 25. Son of Philip and Kate Marr of 13 Colenson Street, St. George's Road, Hull. Born in Newington, Hull. Commemorated on the Ploegsteert Memorial.

MARTINDALE, PRIVATE PERCY. 10/672. Killed in action on June 22nd 1917 aged 27. Born in Newington, Yorkshire, enlisted in Hull but resident in Bridlington. Son of the late Thomas Vessey and Fanny Martindale of Wycar, Haslemere Avenue, Bridlington, Yorkshire. Commemorated on the Arras Memorial.

MATTHEWS, PRIVATE GEORGE, of 'B' Company. 10/609. Killed in action on May 3rd 1917 aged 25. Born in Hull. Son of H.W. and Kate Matthews of 38 Victoria Avenue, Hull. Commemorated on the Arras Memorial.

MAYOR, LANCE-CORPORAL JOSEPH RONALD HERBERT. 10/318. Died of wounds on September 18th 1917 aged 22. Son of Joseph F and Ethel L Mayor of 26 Cave Street, Beverley Road, Hull. Born in Louth but resident in Hull. Buried in St. Sever Cemetery Extension, Rouen.

MENNELL, SERGEANT FRANK. 13/1134. Died of wounds on May 9th 1917 aged 23. Born in Hull. Son of Harry and Frances B A Mennell of 71 Derrigham Street, Hull. Buried in Aubigny Communal Cemetery Extension.

MESSENGER, PRIVATE ALFRED ERNEST of 'A' Company. 10/1233. Killed in action on May 7th 1917 aged 22. Born in Hull. Son of Robert and Elizabeth Messenger of 11 Brazil Street, Hull. Born in Douai Communal Cemetery.

METCALFE, LANCE-CORPORAL JAMES. 10/702. Killed in action on April 27th 1918 aged 25. Born in Cottingham, enlisted in Hull but resident in Cottingham at the time of enlistment. Son of William and Edith Metcalf (Stepmother) of 59 Oakland Cottages, Waterworks Lane, Cottingham. Buried in Chocques Military Cemetery.

MILLARD, PRIVATE THOMAS PERCIVAL. 10/384. Killed in action on October 29th 1916 aged 26. Son of Mr and Mrs James Millard of 72 Holland Street, Hull. Husband of Edith Millard of 71 King's Bench Street, Hull. Born in Pembroke, South Wales but resident in Hull. Commemorated on the Thiepval Memorial.

MILLER, SERGEANT RICHARD. 10/493. Killed in action on June 29th 1917. Born in Kronstadt, Cape Colony but resident in Hull. Buried in Album Cemetery.

MILLER, PRIVATE WILLIAM VINCENT 10/557. Killed in action on June 4th 1916 aged 24. Son of Charles Richard and Elizabeth Miller of Council Cottages, Stokham, Retford, Nottinghamshire. Born in Willerby, East Yorkshire, enlisted in Hull but resident in Willerby. Buried in Sucrerie Military Cemetery, Colincamps.

MONDAY, PRIVATE JOHN HENRY. 10/267. Killed in action on June 4th 1916. Born in Lincoln but resident in Hull. Buried in Sucrerie Military Cemetery, Colincamps.

MORACK, PRIVATE MAURICE WILLIAM. 10/225. Died of wounds on October 29th 1918 aged 24. Son of Mrs. Matilda Morack of 32 Pryme Street, Hull. Born in Leeds. Buried in Kezelberg Military Cemetery.

MORLEY, PRIVATE JOSEPH HENRY, of 'B' Company. 10/1380. Killed in action on May 3rd 1917. Born in Beverley. Commemorated on the Arras Memorial. Husband of Ann Morley of 37 The Woodlands, Beverley. Only son of Frederick Matthew and Ann Morley. His name appears on the Hengate War Memorial, St. Mary's Church Roll of Honour and the Beverley Grammar School Memorial in Beverley Minster.

MOSS, PRIVATE ALFRED, of 'A' Company. 10/266. Killed in action on May 3rd 1917 aged 21. Born in Hull. Son of Thomas and Amy Moss of 9 Beech Grove, Wellstead Street, Hull. Buried in Orchard Dump Cemetery.

MOTHERBY, PRIVATE FREDERICK. 12/971. Killed in action on June 26th 1918. Born in Hull. Commemorated on the Ploegsteert Memorial.

NASBY, PRIVATE THOMAS ARTHUR. 10/572. Killed in action on November 13th 1916. Born in Hull. Commemorated on the Thiepval Memorial.

NASH, SERGEANT ALBERT HENRY. 10/932. Killed in action on May 7th 1917. Born in Northampton, enlisted in Hull but resident in Scarborough. Commemorated on the special memorial in Orchard Dump Cemetery.

NAYLOR, PRIVATE ALBERT BROWN. 11/464. Killed in action on June 28th 1918. Born in Hull. Buried in Aval Wood Military Cemetery.

NEILL, PRIVATE REGINALD CONRAD. 10/867. Died of wounds on June 21st 1916 aged 28. Born in Hull, enlisted in Hull but resident in London. Son of the late Captain R R and Alice Neill of Hull. Husband of Alice Neill of 11 Stanmore Road, West Green, London. Buried in Abbeville Communal Cemetery.

NEWBERT, SERGEANT FREDERICK ELLIS. 10/78. Killed in action on April 12th 1918. Born in Hull. Commemorated on the Ploegsteert Memorial.

NEWTON, PRIVATE JOHN EDWARD. 10/1249. Killed in action on September 7th 1918, aged 33. Born in Hull. Son of I Newton husband of Dorothy Alexandra Newton of 50 Rustenbury Street, New Bridge Road, Hull. Buried in Pont d'Achelles Military Cemetery, Nieppe.

NORTH, PRIVATE ALFRED BARRETT. 10/1285. Killed in action on June 26th 1916. Born in Bradford but resident in Hull. Commemorated on the Thiepval Memorial.

NORTH, PRIVATE ARTHUR HAROLD. 10/365. Died of wounds due to gas on June 25th 1916 aged 26. Born in Hull. Son of Richard and Charlotte T North of Hull. Buried in Bertrancourt Military Cemetery.

PAGE, PRIVATE FRANCIS KENNETH of 'A' Company. 10/694. Died of wounds on August 19th 1916 aged 22. Born in Hull. Son of Frederick Walter and Florence Page of 95 Alliance Avenue, Hull. Buried in Merville Communal Cemetery.

PATTERN, PRIVATE EDWARD. 10/543. Killed in action on August 1st 1918 aged 22. Son of Joseph William and Charity Pattern of 105 Regent Street, Hull. Born in Hull. Buried in St. Vaast Post Military Cemetery, Riehebourg L'Avouée.

PAWSON, PRIVATE HAROLD HERBERT. 10/1413. Killed in action on June 4th 1916 aged 20. Son of William and Edith Annie Pawson of Skipsea. Hull. Born in Catfoss, East Yorkshire, enlisted in Hull but resident in Skipsea. Buried in Sucrerie Military Cemetery, Colincamps.

PEEK, LANCE-CORPORAL LEWIS EDWARD. 10/1155. Killed in action on June 4th 1916 aged 23. Son of Mrs E R Peek of 84 Summergangs Road, Holderness Road, Hull and the late Captain Peek. Born in Hull. Buried in Sucrerie Military Cemetery. Colincamps.

PERKINS, LANCE-CORPORAL EDWARD RANDOLPH. 10/841. Died of wounds on July 6th 1918 aged 29. Son of John T and Ada E Perkins of 11 Victoria Promenade. Northampton. Born in Northampton but resident in Hull. Buried in Berlin South-Western Cemetery.

POTTS, CORPORAL ALFRED. 10/939. Killed in action on June 28th 1918 aged 27. Born in West Bridgeford, Nottinghamshire but resident in Hull. Son of the Reverend Edmund and Mrs Potts. Buried in Aval Wood Military Cemetery.

POWELL, PRIVATE THOMAS ALBERT. 10/574. Killed in action on May 3rd 1917 aged 26. Born in Hull. Son of Jonathan and Frances Powell of 15 May Street, Hull. Commemorated on the Arras Memorial.

RANEY, PRIVATE WALTER RICHARD. 10/569. Killed in action on June 4th 1916 aged 20. Son of Mrs A Raney of 46 Manuel Street, Goole. Born in Selby, enlisted in Hull but resident in Goole. Buried in Sucrerie Military Cemetery, Colincamps.

REUBEN, PRIVATE ISAAC. 10/1045. Killed in action on June 28th 1918. Born in Hull. Buried in Aval Wood Military Cemetery.

RICHARDSON, PRIVATE CLAUD. 12/433. Died of wounds on January 21st 1920. Born in Goole, enlisted in Hull but was resident in Goole at the time of enlistment. Buried in Rawcliffe (St. James) Churchyard.

RILEY, PRIVATE CYRIL WINTERTON. 10/520. Died of wounds on June 15th 1916 aged 21. Son of Sara and the late John Riley. Born in Hull. Buried in St. Sever Cemetery, Rouen.

ROBERTS, PRIVATE DONALD ALFRED. 10/751. Killed in action on March 24th 1918. Born in Hull. Son of Mr C F Roberts of 14 Cavendish Street, Margaret Street, Hull. Buried in Gomiecourt South Cemetery.

ROBINSON, PRIVATE WALTER. 10/1101. Killed in action on October 20th 1916 aged 24. Born in Hull. Son of Maria Robinson of 25 Pryme Street, Hull and the late Samuel Robinson. Buried in Hebuterne Military Cemetery.

RUSSELL, PRIVATE PERCY. 10/67. Died of wounds on May 20th 1917 aged 22. Son of William Percy and Laura Russell of 74 Queen's Street, Withernsea, East Yorkshire. Born in Hull, enlisted in Hull but resident in Withernsea at the time of enlistment. Buried in Hamburg Cemetery. Germany.

RUSLING, PRIVATE ALBERT. 13/469. Died of wounds on April 16th 1918. Born in Hull aged 23. Buried in Longuenesse Souvenir Cemetery, St. Omer. Son of George Edward and Hannah Rebecca Rusling of 93 Walcott Street, Hessle Road, Hull.

SAUNDERSON, CORPORAL THOMAS ERNEST, of 'A' Company. DCM. 10/14. Died of wounds on March 1st 1917 aged 24. Born in Hull. Son of Harry and Sarah Ann Saunderson. Buried in Couin New British Cemetery.

SELLERS, PRIVATE ERNEST WALTER. 10/1054. Killed in action on May 3rd 1917 aged 21. Born in Hull. Son of Walter James and Minnie Sellers of 7 Cynthia Grove, Division Road, Hull. Commemorated on the Arras Memorial.

SMITH, PRIVATE CHARLES. 12/1445. Killed in action on April 12th 1918 aged 27. Husband of Baetrice Smith of 183 Woodcock Street, Hull. Born in Hull. Commemorated on the Ploegsteert Memorial.

SMITH, PRIVATE HAROLD. 10/1251. Reported to have died of wounds whilst in German hands on April 13th 1918 aged 24. Buried in Outtersteene Communal Cemetery Extension, Ballieul. Born in Beverley, the 4th son of William Smith of 20 Cherry Tree Lane, Beverley.

SMITH, PRIVATE JOHN. 10/838. Died of wounds on July 7th 1917 aged 22. Born in Hull. Nephew of Mary J Smith of Brookleigh, St. John's Avenue, Bridlington. Buried in Duisans British Cemetery.

SMITH, LANCE-CORPORAL RICHARD HENRY. 10/1231. Killed in action on May 3rd 1917 aged 23. Born in Hull. Son of Robert Smith of Stone Creek, Sunk Island, Hull. Commemorated on the Arras Memorial.

SPRING, LANCE-CORPORAL GEORGE LEWIS, of 'C' Company. 10/836. Killed in action on May 3rd 1917 aged 22. Born in Hull. Son of James and Kate Ellen Spring of 401 Anlaby Road, Hull. Commemorated on the Arras Memorial.

STATHER, SERGEANT JOHN NORRISON, MM. 10/205. Killed in action on April 12th 1918. Commemorated on the Ploegsteert Memorial.

STEAD, PRIVATE ROBERT BERNARD, of 'A' Company. 10/1172. Died in hospital on November 11th 1918 aged 21. Buried in Terlincthun British Cemetery. Born in Driffield but resident in Hull. Son of Richard and Julia Stead of 46 Clarendon Street, Spring Bank, Hull.

STEVENS, CORPORAL ERNEST BENNETT. 10/1106. Killed in action on April 12th 1918. Born in Hull. Commemorated on the Ploegsteert Memorial.

STONE, PRIVATE FRANCIS CARL GERRARD. 10/1140. Died of wounds on September 11th 1916 aged 20. Born in Goole, enlisted in Goole. Buried in Grimsby (Scartho Road) Cemetery.

STORR, SERGEANT GEORGE. 10/1454. Died on December 17th 1918 after being transferred to the reserve. Buried in Bridlington Cemetery.

STORK, PRIVATE HARRY. 10/890. Killed in action on June 4th 1916 aged 19. Son of Mr S Storr of 30 Elmsdale Avenue, Foleshill Road, Little Heath, Coventry. Born in Goole, enlisted in Hull but resident in Goole. Buried in Sucrerie Military Cemetery, Colincamps.

SUMMERS, PRIVATE HERBERT, of 'B' Company. 10/677. Killed in action on May 3rd 1917 aged 21. Born in Cottingham but resident in Hull. Son of Samuel and Sarah Summers of 78 King Street, Cottingham. Buried in Orchard Dump Cemetery.

SYKES, PRIVATE ARTHUR. 10/396. Killed in action on December 5th 1916. Born in Goole, enlisted in Hull but resident in Goole. Buried in Sailly-au-Bois Military Cemetery.

TAYLOR, LANCE-CORPORAL ALBERT WARE. 10/17. Died of wounds on August 6th 1916. Born in Bromyard, Herefordshire but resident in Hull. Husband of Mrs B A Taylor of 112 Regent Street, Anlaby Road, Hull. Buried in Western Cemetery, Spring Bank, Hull.

TAYLOR, PRIVATE ERNEST WILLIAM. 12/1035. Died of wounds on April 14th 1918. Born in Preston, near Hull but resident in Hull. Son of Mr G Taylor of 47 Arundle Street, Holderness Road, Hull. Buried in Ebblinghem Military Cemetery.

TAYLOR, PRIVATE SYDNEY. 10/1008. Killed in action on November 4th 1917 aged 23. Son of Mrs J W Taylor of Wood Grange, Holderness Road, Hull. Born in York but resident in Hull. Buried in Roclincourt Military Cemetery.

TENNISON, PRIVATE CYRIL FRAZER. 10/313. Died in the UK on September 25th 1918 aged 23. Born in Hull, enlisted in Hull but resident in Hessle. Buried in Haltemprice (Hessle) Cemetery.

TETHER, PRIVATE BERNARD. 10/314. Killed in action on April 13th 1918 aged 27. Son of Sarah Jane Tether of 7 West View. Sculcoates, Hull and the late Robert Tether. Born in Hull. Buried in Outtersteene Communal Cemetery Extension, Bailleul.

TETHER, PRIVATE GEORGE WILLIAM. 10/951. Killed in action on November 13th 1916 aged 20. Son of George Walter Tether of "Roseway", Hull Road, Cottingham, East Yorkshire and the late Elizabeth Tether. Born in Hull, enlisted in Hull but resident in Hessle at the time. Commemorated on the Thiepval Memorial.

THOMAS, CORPORAL WALTER. 10/1268. Killed in action on April 27th 1918 aged 25. Born in Hull.

Husband of Grace Thomas of 101 Day Street, Anlaby Road, Hull. Buried in Chocques Military Cemetery.

TINDALE, SERGEANT ARTHUR JAMES. 10/45. Killed in action on September 19th 1916 aged. Born in Hull. Son of Caroline Tindale of 18 Suffolk Street, Hull and the late James Tindale. Commemorated on the Loos Memorial.

TODD, PRIVATE HARRY RUPERT. 10/859. Died of wounds on January 14th 1917 aged 25. Born in Barton-on-Humber but resident in Hull. Son of the late William Henry and Mary Ann Todd of Barton-on-Humber. Buried in Western Cemetery. Spring Bank, Hull.

TURNER CORPORAL ARTHUR. 10/950. Killed in action on August 15th 1918 aged 24. Son of Robert and the late Emily Turner of 11 Lambert Street, Hull. Born in Hull. Commemorated on the Ploegsteert Memorial.

WALTON, PRIVATE FREDERICK, of 'D' Company. 10/103. Killed in action on March 8th 1917 aged 25. Born in Hull. Buried in Faubourg D'Amiens Cemetery, Arras. Son of Susan Walton and the late John Henry Walton of 7, Cornwall Gardens, Brunswick Avenue, Hull.

WARN, PRIVATE WILLIAM HENRY, of 'A' Company. 10/401. Killed in action on February 26th 1917 aged 25. Born in Hedon. East Yorkshire, enlisted in Hull but was resident in Hedon at the time of enlistment. Son of Mr W H L and Mrs M A Warn. Buried in Euston Road Cemetery.

WATSON, PRIVATE JAMES STANLEY, of 'B' Company. 10/39. Killed in action on June 28th 1916 aged 26. Son of Arthur and Edith Mary Watson of Cottingham, East Yorkshire. Born in Cottingham, enlisted in Hull but was resident in Cottingham. Buried in Sucrerie Military Cemetery, Colincamps.

WEBB, PRIVATE WILSON. 10/774. Killed in action April 12th 1918 aged 35. Commemorated on the Ploegsteert Memorial. Born in Hull. Son of William Webb of 4 Barnsley Street, Hull.

WEBSTER, PRIVATE ALFRED of 'A' Company. 10/407. Killed in action on September 18th 1916 aged 22. Buried in St. Vaast Post Military Cemetery, Richebourg L'Avouée. Born in Hull. Son of Richard and Florence Eleanor Webster of 36 Haworth Street, Hull. His name appears on the Haworth Street Roll of Honour.

WEBSTER PRIVATE LEONARD. 10/346. Killed in action on June 6th 1916. Born in Sutton, Yorkshire but resident in Cottingham. Commemorated on the special memorial at Sucrerie Military Cemetery, Colincamps.

WELLS, PRIVATE GEORGE ARTHUR. 10/738. Killed in action on March 30th 1916 aged 24. Buried in Auchonvillers Military Cemetery. Born in Newington.

Only son of George William (Fruit Merchant) and Asenath Burn Wells of 31 Marlborough Avenue, Hornsea and 13 Lowther Streeet, Albert Avenue, Hull. George Wells had been a pupil of St. George's Road Council School and won a Scholarship at The Boulevard Secondary School. After leaving School he went to work for Messrs. Dumoulin and Gosschalk. He was an enthusiastic sportsman, playing cricket for Newington Parish Church Team.

WEST, PRIVATE ARTHUR ERNEST. 10/1114. Killed in action on June 4th 1916 aged 21. Buried in Sucrerie Military Cemetery, Colincamps. Born in Hull. Son of Mrs. Sarah West of 6 King's Cross Terrace, Bean Street, Hull.

WEST, PRIVATE GEORGE WILLIAM. 10/148. Killed in action on August 25th 1918 aged 25. Buried in Lille Southern Cemetery. Born in Hull. Son of John and Louisa West. The family grave inscription states that he died as a Prisoner of War.

WHTTELEY, SERGEANT CHARLES. 12/61. Killed in action on April 12th 1918. Son of the late Henry and Sarah Ann Whiteley. Husband of Mary Whiteley of Gretna, Carlisle. Born in Hull. Commemorated on the Ploegsteert Memorial.

WILKINSON, SERGEANT JOHN HENRY, MM. 10/1038. Died of wounds on June 2nd 1917 aged 25. Buried in Etaples Military Cemetery. Born in Hull. Son of J.W and Jessie Wilkinson of Hull.

WILLIAMSON, PRIVATE GEORGE FREDERICK. 14/172. Died on November 26th 1916 from mushroom poisoning while at home on leave. He was aged 20. Buried in Western Cemetery, Hull. Born in Hull. Son of Mrs. Emma J. Williamson of 31 St. Andrew's Street. Hessle Road. Hull

WILSON, PRIVATE MARK. 10/793. Killed in action on July 23rd 1917. Born in Grimsby but resident in Hull.

WINTER, PRIVATE GEORGE WILLIAM. 10/1186. Killed in action on May 3rd 1917. Commemorated on the Arras Memorial. Born in Hull.

WOODCOCK, CORPORAL CHARLES, of 'A' Company. 10/147. Died of sickness following gas wounds on February 2nd 1921 aged 32. Son of Henry and Emily Woodcock of "Sunbury", Hunmanby, East Yorkshire. Buried in Western Cemetery, Hull.

WOODCOCK, PRIVATE FRANK KELLETT. 10/744. Died of wounds on June 7th 1916 aged 21. Born in Hook (Goole) and resident in Goole at the time of enlistment. Son of Samuel Francis and Ada Woodcock of 15 Bournville, Goole, Yorkshire. Buried jn Abbeville Communal Cemetery.

WRIGHT, PRIVATE ARTHUR HAYWARD. 10/856. Killed in action on March 27th 1918, aged 23. Born in Hull. Son of John and Ada Margaret Wright of 96 Legsby Avenue, Grimsby. Commemorated on the Arras Memorial.

YOUNG, PRIVATE LEONARD. 10/350. Died of wounds on June 25th 1917 aged 19. Commemorated on the Arras Memorial. Born in Hull. Son of W Young of 1 Derwent Avenue, Alphonse Street, Boulevard, Hull.

11TH BATTALION

ALLEN, PRIVATE HARRY. 11/244. Killed in an accident on 27th August 1916. Born in Hull. Buried in Vielle-Chapelle New Military Cemetery.

ALLISON, PRIVATE JOHN EDWARD, MM. 11/802. Killed in action on October 27th 1918. Born in Barton-on-Humber but resident in Grimsby when he enlisted. Commemorated on the Ploegsteert Memorial. Son of Mrs Florence Brannen (formerly Allison) of 7, Lockes Place. Chapel Lane. Hull. His name appears on the Roll of Honour at St. Mary's Church, Lowgate, Hull.

ANDERTON, CORPORAL F 11/654. Died on November 23rd 1915 aged 40. Buried in Howden (St. Peter's) Churchyard.

ANDREWS, SERGEANT HAROLD. 11/980. Killed in action on July 5th 1918, aged 26. Buried in Le Grand Hasard Military Cemetery. Morbeque. Born in Hull. Son of Mrs. Edith E. and the late Mr. Andrews. One of seven children. Husband of Mrs. Andrews of 2, Victoria Avenue, Scarborough Street, Hull.

ANDREWS, PRIVATE JOHN WILLIAM. 14/211. Died of wounds on May 30th 1916 aged 26. Born in Brisbane, Australia but resident in Hull. His real name was Andrew William James Reid. Son of Andrew and Annie Reid of Gibbotson, South Island, New Zealand. Buried in Bertrancourt Military Cemetery.

ARNOLD, PRIVATE BENJAMIN RHODES. 11/369. Died in France on August 27th 1916 aged 23. Son of Joseph Rhodes Arnold and Ada E Arnold of 3 Dunhill Road, Goole, Yorkshire. Born in Goole. He was living in Goole when he enlisted. Buried in Vielle-Chapelle New Military Cemetery.

ARNOLD, PRIVATE JOHN WARD. 12/1186. Died of pneumonia on November 9th 1918, aged 22. Born in Hull. Buried in Longuenesse Souvenir Cemetery, St. Omer. Only son of Lilian Arnold and the late Robert Arnold of 14 Worship Street, Hull. He was married and had one son.

BAINES, PRIVATE HARRY. 11/71. Died of wounds on March 31st 1918. Born in Harewood, Yorkshire, enlisted in Hull but was resident in Leeds at the time of enlistment.

BALDWIN, PRIVATE CHARLES. 11/727. Killed in action on August 11th 1918 aged 22. Born in Willerby, East Yorkshire but resident in Hull. Son of Joseph James and Phoebe Baldwin of 1 South View, Willerby, Hull. Buried in Outtersteene Communal Cemetery Extension. Bailleul.

BARKER, CORPORAL CHRISTOPHER. 11/512. Killed in action on October 20th 1916 aged 25. Commemorated on the special memorial in Hebuterne Military Cemetery. Born in Hull. Son of Mary Ann Barker of 64 Seaton Street, Hull. One of a family of seven children (five sons, three of whom served in France, and two daughters).

BARKER, PRIVATE GEORGE THOMAS. 11/1053. Killed in action on May 3rd 1917 aged 31. Buried in Orchard Dump Cemetery. Born in France. Son of John Charles Barker. His name appears on the Wilmington Roll of Honour, Hull.

BARRETT, LANCE-CORPORAL FREDERICK. 14/79. Killed in Action on April 13th 1918. Born in Leeds, enlisted in Hull while resident in Leeds. Commemorated on the Ploegsteert Memorial.

BAXTER, SERGEANT HENRY. 11/14. Killed in action on June 26th 1917. Buried in Albuera Cemetery North. Born in Hull.

BEADLE, PRIVATE THOMAS ARTHUR. 11/754. Died of wounds on March 10th 1917 aged 26. Buried in Varennes Military Cemetery. Born in Hull. Son of Thomas and the late Emma Beadle of Southcoates Lane, Hull. He was married with children.

BEARFIELD, PRIVATE ERNEST. 11/18. Killed in action on November 8th 1917. Born in Hull.

BEELS, PRIVATE THOMAS. 11/1137. Died of wounds on May 3rd 1917 aged 23. Buried in St. Catherine British Cemetery. Born in Hull. Son of John Maddison and Sarah Beels of 6 Newtown Terrace. Hedon Road, Hull. Employed by the Hull and Barnsley Railway Dock Department. His name appears on the Hull and Barnsley Roll of Honour kept by Hull Museum.

BELL, PRIVATE GEORGE HUNTER, of 'B' Company. 11/1016. Killed in action on March 27th 1918 aged 25. Commemorated on the Arras Memorial. Born in Hull. Enlisted in September 1914 and went with the battalion to Egypt in 1915. Son of Raimes Morton and Mary Ann Bell of 2 Lincoln Street, Hull.

BENTLEY, PRIVATE HAROLD. 11/1141. Lewis gunner. Died of wounds on April 28th 1918 aged 23. Buried in Western Cemetery. Hull. Born in Hull. Son of Robert and Amanda Bentley of 50 Sharp Street, Newland Avenue, Hull.

BENTLEY, PRIVATE R. 11/1435. Died of pneumonia on December 5th 1918, aged 27. Buried in Hull Western Cemetery in the same grave as his brother (see above entry). Son of Robert and Amanda Bentley of 50 Sharp Street, Hull.

BIBBY, SERGEANT JOSEPH WILLIAM. Croix de Guerre (Belgium). 12/90. Killed in action on June 28th 1918 aged 28. Commemorated on the Ploegsteert Memorial. Born in Hull. Son of William Bibby of 23 Seaton Street, Hull.

BIGLIN, CORPORAL ERNEST. 13/1419. Died of wounds on April 14th 1918 aged 21. Born in Easington, East Yorkshire but resident in Hull. Son of Mrs W Biglin of Winsette House, Skeffling, Hull. Buried in Borre Churchyard.

BLACK, PRIVATE MYER. 11/831. Killed in action on November 13th 1916 aged 23. Buried in Euston Road Cemetery. Born in Hull. He is commemorated on the family grave in the Hebrew Cemetery, Marfleet, Hull.

BLACKMORE, PRIVATE JOHN. 13/1407. Killed in action on March 25th 1918 aged 23. Commemorated on the Arras Memorial. Born in Hull. Son of John and Ada Blackmore of 28 Naburn Street, Hull. He was engaged to Annie Williamson at the time of his death.

BLANCHARD, PRIVATE WALTER. 11/602. Killed in action on April 12th 1918. Commemorated on the Ploegsteert Memorial. Born in Hull. His parents resided at 6 Ash Grove, Dalton Street. Hull.

BOLDER, PRIVATE JOHN WILLIAM, of X Company. 11/1136. Killed in action on March 28th 1918 aged 29. Buried in Benvillers Military Cemetery. Born in Hull. Son of Joseph and Annie Bolder of 86 Subway Street, Hessle Road, Hull.

BOWS, LANCE-CORPORAL HERBERT. 13/1212. Died of wounds in the UK on February 10th 1918 aged 35. Son of Mrs Emma Pearson of Laxton, Howden. Born in Weaverthorpe. Yorkshire, enlisted in Hull but resident in Laxton. Buried in Laxton (St. Peter) Churchyard.

BOYES, PRIVATE JOHN. 11/1001. Killed in action on September 3rd 1916 aged 20. Buried in Le Touret Military Cemetery. Born in Scarborough. Lived at 10 Devon Grove, Sculcoates Lane, Hull.

BRAND, PRIVATE JOHN. 11/967. Died as a Prisoner of War on July 1st 1918 aged 35. Buried in Niederzwehren Cemetery, Germany. Born in Preston. Lancashire but resident in Hull. Son of Mr and Mrs Richard Brand of 38 Lorne Street, Hull.

BREWSTER, PRIVATE PERCY. 11/746. Died on August 10th 1916 aged 19. Buried in Le Touret Military Cemetery. Born in Hull. Son of Charles and Charlotte Brewster of 5 Beualah Place, Leonard Street. Hull. His name appears on the Clifton Street School Roll of Honour.

BRIDGES, PRIVATE CHARLES (known as Charlie). 13/414. Killed in action on March 24th 1918 aged 22. Commemorated on the Arras Memorial. Born in Hull. Son of M.E. Bridges of 64 Sharp Street, Hull.

BROCKLESBY, LANCE-CORPORAL SIDNEY ROBERT (known as Bob). 13/500. Missing in action on April 10th 1918. Died on November 26th 1918, while a Prisoner of war at Munster, aged 22. Buried in Hamburg Cemetery, Germany. Son of Aaron and Mary Brocklesby of 1 Romany Terrace, Ferries Street, Hedon Road, Hull. His brother who was stationed in India survived the war. Before enlisting, he lived with his sister, Mrs. Cunningham, at 4 Clyde Avenue, Balfour Street, Hull.

BOUGH, PRIVATE JOHN WILLIAM (known as Willie). 11/363. Killed in action on June 28th 1917 aged 18. Commemorated on the Arras Memorial. Born in Hull.

BROWN, PRIVATE GEORGE. 11/135. Killed in action on March 20th 1916 aged 29. Buried in Mesnil Communal Cemetery. Born in Hull. Son of William and Elizabeth Brown of 94 St. Paul's Street, Hull. Husband of Rebecca Brown and children, residing at 3 Providence Street, Myton Street. Hull.

BROWN, LANCE-CORPORAL GEORGE HERBERT. 11/622. Killed in action on March 29th 1918 aged 24. Commemorated on the Arras Memorial. Born in Hull. Son of George and Alice Brown of 164 Somerset Street, Hull.

BUSBY, PRIVATE WALTER PERCY. 11/1309. Killed in action on June 28th 1917. Commemorated on the Arras Memorial. Born in Hull. Married with three children.

BUTLER, PRIVATE ALFRED CHARLES. 11/263. Originally with the Depot Company. Died in the United Kingdom on July 31st 1916, aged 34, of wounds received in France. Buried in Hedon Road Cemetery, Hull. Born in St. Pancras but resident in Hull. Husband of A. E. Butler and children of 59 Woodhouse Street, Hedon Road, Hull.

CALLAGHAN, SERGEANT JOHN ALBERT, of 'D' Company. 11/600. Killed in action on September 8th 1918 aged 21. Born in Hull. Son of William and Mary Callaghan of 2 Sarah Ann's Terrace, Spyvee Street, Hull. Buried in Trois Arbres Cemetery. Steenwerck.

CARRINGTON, PRIVATE FREDERICK. 11/1128. Killed in action on September 8th 1917. Born in Hull. Commemorated on the Arras Memorial.

CARRINGTON, PRIVATE SAMUEL. 11/575. Died of wounds on July 22nd 1916 aged 24. Born in Hull. Son of Mrs M A Carrington of 4 Richmond Terrace, West Parade, Hull. Formerly lived at Nafferton, Yorkshire. His name appears on the West Parade Shrine/Roll of Honour. Buried in Merville Communal Cemetery.

CARTER, PRIVATE WILLIAM HENRY. 11/150. Killed in action on August 3rd 1918. Born Hertford. Buried in Le Grand Hasard Military Cemetery.

CAUTLEY, PRIVATE WALTER JAMES. 11/544. Died of wounds on May 3rd 1917 aged 20. Son of William and Margaret Holmes Cautley of George Street, Hedon. Hull. Born in Hedon. Buried in Duisans British Cemetery.

CHANCE, PRIVATE JOSEPH HENRY, of 'B' Company. 11/190. Killed in action on March 27th 1918 aged 22. Born in Hull, enlisted in Beverley but resident in Hull. Son of Mr & Mrs W Chance of 7 Gladstone Avenue, Beecroft Street, Hull. Commemorated on the Arras Memorial.

CHAPMAN, PRIVATE HAROLD, MM. 11/105. Died on July 20th 1916 of wounds received during a trench raid on the same night. Born in Huddersfield but resident at 109 St. George's Road, Hull with his wife, Beatrice May to whom he had been married for a year at the time of his death. Buried in Rue Du Bacquerot No 1 Military Cemetery. His parents lived at 6 Willow Grove, Somerset Street, Hull. Before enlisting he was an employee of Messrs H Wilson of Saville Street, Hull. His name appears on the Somerset Street Shrine/Roll of Honour. In his letter of condolence Private Chapman's Captain wrote "I had your boy with me when he first joined, and it was always a pleasure to see his bright fresh face. Last evening in the march down a country lane I had a little chat with him. He seemed so bright, but thought that he would not come back, so he said. But he did not seem to mind. I can assure you it is a great sorrow to me to lose him. He was full of pluck, and always such a steady boy. His end is most deeply regretted by his comrades and officers."

CHARLTON, PRIVATE GEORGE. 14/60. Killed in action on February 20th 1918 aged 32. Born in Hull. Son of Joseph P M Charlton of 20 Waterloo Street, Hull. He was an employee of Reckitt's of Hull, at their Morley Street works. Buried in Roclincourt Military Cemetery.

CHILTON, PRIVATE ALFRED. 13/765. Killed in action on March 27th 1918 aged 24. Born in Burstwick but enlisted in Hull while resident in Burstwick. Son of Anthony and Sarah Chilton. Commemorated on the Arras Memorial.

CLARE, PRIVATE JOHN THOMAS. 11/403. Killed in action on February 25th 1917. Born in Middlesborough but resident in Hull. Buried in Sailly-au-Bois Military Cemetery.

CLARK, SERGEANT FRANK, of 'B' Company. 11/405. Born in Sherbrooke, Canada. Enlisted in Hull but resident in Canada. Died of wounds on November 10th 1917. Buried in Douai Communal Cemetery.

CLAYTON, PRIVATE WILLIAM. 11/670. Died on November 14th 1918. Born in Grimsby but resident in Hull. Buried in Terlincthun British Cemetery.

COLLINGWOOD, CORPORAL CHARLES. 11/139. He was a member of the marine gun section. Shot by a sniper and died of his wounds on May 13th 1916 aged 29. Born in Hull. Son of Charles and Jemima Collingwood of Hull. Husband of Harriet J Collingwood and father of three children. He resided at 9 Spyvee Street, Hull and was a painter and paperhanger by trade. His name appears on the Courtney Street Shrine/Roll of Honour. Buried in Sucrerie Military Cemetery, Colincamps.

COOK, PRIVATE ALBERT. 11/1397. Killed in action on June 22nd 1917 aged 19. Born in Hull. Son of George Albert and Lily Cook of 106 Rosamund Street, Hull. Commemorated on the Arras Memorial.

COOK, PRIVATE ALBERT BARTON. 11/472. Died of wounds on May 4th 1916 aged 22. Born in Hull. He enlisted in Hull but was a resident of Hornsea, Yorkshire. Son of Arthur William and Mary Cook of 4 Hessle View, Barton-on-Humber, Lincolnshire. Buried in Gezaincourt Cemetery Extension.

COOPER, PRIVATE JOSEPH. 14/36. Killed in action on May 3rd 1917 aged 24. Born in Hull. Resident at 23 Naylor Row, Hull. Commemorated on the Arras Memorial.

COOPER, PRIVATE PERCY VICTOR. 11/760. Died of wounds on March 25th 1918 aged 29. Born in Hull. Son of George and Christiana Cooper of 20 Bean Street, Anlaby Road, Hull. Buried in Ayette British Cemetery.

COULSON, CORPORAL THOMAS. 11/550. Killed in action on November 8th 1917. Born in Boston, Lincolnshire but resident in Hull. Commemorated on the Arras Memorial.

COUPLAND, PRIVATE ERNEST. 11/532. Died of wounds on July 5th 1917 aged 25. Born in Hull. Son of George and Annie Cooper of Avenue House, Northumberland Avenue, Hull. Buried in Cologne Southern Cemetery.

COX, SERGEANT FRANK. 11/49. Killed in action on June 27th 1916 aged 25. He was married and had two sons. Son of Alfred and Mary-Jane Cox of Roseville, East Acridge, Barton-on-Humber. Lincolnshire. Buried in Knightsbridge Cemetery, Mesnil-Martinsart.

CRACROFT, PRIVATE THOMAS RICHARD. 11/1374. Died on August 26th 1921 aged 40. Buried in Northern Cemetery, Cottinham Road, Hull. Son of John James and Catherine Cracroft of 68 Symonds Street. Fountain Road, Hull.

CUDBERTSON, PRIVATE FREDERICK. 11/545. Died of wounds on July 5th 1917 aged 24. Born in Hull. Son of Frederick and the late Annie Cudbertson of 7 Fern Grove. Folkestone Street, Beverley Road, Hull. Buried in Duisans British Cemetery.

CURTIS, PRIVATE CHARLES BERNARD. 13/1430. Died of wounds on July 21st 1916 aged 21. Born in Hull. Son of Thomas and Catherine Curtis of 12 Ada's Terrace, Seaton Street, Hull. Buried in Merville Communal Cemetery.

DIXON, LANCE-CORPORAL CHARLES. 12/334. Killed in action on March 27th 1918 aged 27. Born in Hull. Son of George and Margaret Dixon. Husband of Lillian Dixon. Commemorated on the Arras memorial.

DIXON, PRIVATE THOMAS. 11/1432. Killed in action on July 1st 1916. Born in Hull. Commemorated on the Thiepval Memorial.

DOOK, PRIVATE FRANK. 11/958. Died of wounds on November 9th 1917 aged 22. Born in Hull. Son of Charles Edward and Lizzie Dook of 51 Campbell Street, Hull. Buried in Duisans British Cemetery.

DOWNS, PRIVATE GEORGE, MM. 11/715. Killed in action on April 23rd 1918. Born in Hull. Commemorated on the Ploegsteert Memorial.

DRISCOLL, PRIVATE JOHN JOSEPH. 14/209. Killed in action on June 26th 1916. Born in Manchester but resident in Hull. Commemorated on the Thiepval Memorial.

EASTWOOD, PRIVATE THOMAS WILLIAM. 11/1327. Died of disease on November 2nd 1918 aged 42. Husband of Isabella Eastwood of 2 Jane Terrace, Jane Street, Hull. Born in Hull. Buried in Terlincthun British Cemetery.

EDDISON, PRIVATE JAMES. 11/1154. Died of wounds on March 8th 1917 aged 39. Born in Leeds but resident in Hull. Son of Eli and Hannah Eddison of Armley. Leeds. Buried in Boulogne Eastern Cemetery.

EDMOND, PRIVATE S. 11/1328. Died on August 4th 1919. Buried in Western Cemetery, Spring Bank, Hull.

EDWARDS, PRIVATE WALTER. 11/282. Died on March 6th 1916 aged 18. Buried at sea and commemorated on the Chatby Memorial. Born in Hull. Son of Walter and Mary Edwards of 7 Henry's Terrace, Rodney Street, Hull.

EDWARDS, PRIVATE WILLIAM ALBERT. 11/923. Died of wounds on September 7th 1916 aged 34. Born in Hull. Son of William Albert and H A Edwards. Buried in Bethune Town Cemetery.

ELLINGTON, PRIVATE GEORGE. Died on November 13th 1918.

ELSTON, PRIVATE ARTHUR ERNEST. 11/1342. Killed in action on May 16th 1917. Born in Hull. Commemorated on the Arras Memorial.

EMMERSON, PRIVATE MATTHEW 11/659. Killed in action on March 28th 1918. Born in Hull. Commemorated on the Arras Memorial.

EVERSON, PRIVATE MAURICE. 11/895. Killed in action on March 28th 1918 aged 23. Born in Hull. Son of Andrew and Martha Everson of Bon Accord, New North Road, Withernsea, Yorkshire. Commemorated on the Arras Memorial.

FARROW, PRIVATE HERBERT. 12/1535. Died on September 11th 1918, aged 34 from wounds received on June 28th 1918. Born in Goxhill, Lincolnshire but resident in Hull at the time of enlistment. Husband of Rosa Farrow of 18 Wesley square, Boothferry Road, Hull. Buried in Longuenesse Souvenir Cemetery, St. Omer.

FEATHERSTONE, CORPORAL FRANK. 11/826. Died of wounds on August 1st 1916 aged 23. Born in Hull. Son of William John and the late Lavinia

Featherstone of 61 King's Bench Street, Hull. Buried in Bethune Town Cemetery.

FIELD, PRIVATE EDWIN. 10/1365. Killed in action on November 13th 1916 aged 19. Born in Hull. Son of Edwin James and Susanah Field of 4 Marmaduke Street, Hull. Born in Hull. His name appears in the St. Barnabus Book of Rememberance. Commemorated on the Thiepval Memorial.

FIELD, PRIVATE RICHARD. 11/934. Killed in action on May 3rd 1917 aged 23. Born in Hull. Resident at 15 Cornwall Street, Wilmington, Hull. Commemorated on the Arras Memorial.

FOSTON, PRIVATE JAMES. 11/1344. Killed in action on May 3rd 1917. Born in Hull but resident in Beverley at the time of enlistment. Commemorated on the Arras Memorial.

FUSSEY, SERGEANT LEONARD. MM. 11/991. Killed in action on July 28th 1918 aged 22. He was attached to the 92nd Light Trench Mortar Battery. Born in Hull. Son of Henry and Frances Fussey of 135 Adelaide Street, Hull. Buried in Le Grand Hasard Military Cemetery.

GALLAGHER, PRIVATE PATRICK. 14/28. Died of wounds on November 21st 1916, aged 39. Born in York but resident in Hull. Son of William and Mary Gallagher of Sharp Street, Hull. Buried in Monthuon Military Cemetery. Le Treport.

GARDNER, CORPORAL WILLIAM RICHARD. 11/344. Killed in action on May 3rd 1917. Born in Hull. Commemorated on the Arras Memorial.

GAUNT, PRIVATE WILLIAM MEREDITH. 11/954. Killed in action on August 3rd 1918 aged 25. Born in Louth, Lincolnshire but resident in Hull. Son of William and Helen L Gaunt of 163 New Lane, Greengates, Bradford, Yorkshire. Buried in Le Grand Hasard Military-Cemetery.

GIBSON, PRIVATE SYDNEY. 11/314. Killed in action on August 3rd 1916. Born in Dunswell, East Yorkshire, enlisted in Hull but resident in Dunswell. Son of Mrs W Gibson of Dunswell, Hull. Buried in LeTouret Military Cemetery.

GILLIATT, PRIVATE FRED. 12/1252. Died of wounds on April 8th 1918 aged 29. Son of George Henry and Mary Elizabeth Gilliatt of Hull. Husband of Clarissa Gilliatt of 83 Trinity Street. Hull. Buried in Mons (Bergen) Communal Cemetery.

GLENTON, PRIVATE THOMAS. 11/169. Killed in action on July 2nd 1917. Born in Hull. Commemorated on the Arras Memorial.

GOHL, PRIVATE EDWARD. 11/489. Killed in action on December 23rd 1916 aged 25. Born in Hull. Son of Julius and Susanah Gohl. Commemorated on the Thiepval Memorial.

GOODSON, PRIVATE GEORGE ERNEST. 11/1112. Killed in action on November 8th 1917. Born in Barton-on-Humber, Lincolnshire. Commemorated on the Arras Memorial.

GOULD, PRIVATE EDWARD. MM. 11/1164. Killed in action on April 12th 1918. Born in Hull. Commemorated on the Ploegsteert Memorial.

GRANTHAM, PRIVATE GEORGE ERNEST. 11/392. Killed in action on July 20th 1916. Born in Cottingham, East Yorkshire, enlisted in Hull but resident in Cottingham. Buried in Rue-Du-Bacquerot No 1 Military Cemetery. Laventie.

GREASLEY, PRIVATE FREDERICK GEORGE. 11/541. Died on May 3rd 1917 aged 20. Son of William and Margaret Holmes Cautley of George Street, Hedon, Hull. Born in Hedon. Buried in Duisans British Cemetery.

GREEN, LANCE-CORPORAL CAREY. 11/651. Died of wounds on August 27th 1916 aged 25. Son of George Green of 24 Earlsgate, Winterton. Lincolnshire and the late Sarah Green. Born in Winterton, Lincolnshire, enlisted in Hull but was resident in Winterton. Buried in Vielle-Chapelle New Military Cemetery.

GRIMMER, PRIVATE RICHARD JAMES GEORGE. 11/777. Died of wounds on September 17th 1916 aged 38. Born in Caistor, Lincolnshire but resident in Hull. Son of James Walter and Teresa Adline Martha Grimmer of 95 Rosamund Street, Hessle Road, Hull. Buried in Holy Trinity Cemetery, Hessle Road, Hull.

HALL, SERGEANT HARRY 11/172. Killed in action on May 30th 1916. Born in Howden, East Yorkshire, enlisted in Hull but was resident in Howden. Buried in Sucrerie Military Cemetery, Colincamps.

HAMILTON, PRIVATE FREDERICK CHARLES. 11/1255. Died on April 14th 1916 aged 37. Son of F C and Emma Hamilton of Hull. Born in Hull. Husband of Sarah Mary Ann Hamilton of 16 Barnston Street, Borough Road, Birkenhead. Buried in Abbeville Communal Cemetery.

BARMAN, PRIVATE TOM. 11/262. Killed in action on June 28th 1918. Born in Hull. Buried in Aval Wood Military Cemetery.

HARRISON, PRIVATE EDWARD. 11/1345. Died of wounds on July 2nd 1916 aged 22. Born in Bradford but resident in Hull. Son of Mr and Mrs Emma Harrison of 86 Goulton Street, Eton Street, Hessle Road, Hull. Buried in Couin British Cemetery.

HARRISON, CORPORAL FRED. MM, of 'C' Company. 11/463. Died of wounds on August 21st 1918 aged 21. Born in Hull. Son of Charles and Ellen Harrison of 7 Gertrude's Terrace, Northumberland Avenue, Fountain Road, Hull. Buried in Longuenesse Souvenir Cemetery, St. Omer.

HART, SERGEANT RICHARD ERNEST. 11/794. Killed in action on May 3rd 1917 aged 23. Born in Brough, enlisted in Hull but resident in Hessle. Son of William and Annie Hart of 3 Park Row, Hessle,

Yorkshire. Commemorated on the Arras Memorial.

HAYHURST, PRIVATE ARTHUR LOUIS. 11/893. Killed in action on October 20th 1916. Born in Cottingham, East Yorkshire but was resident in Hull. Commemorated on the special memorial in Hebuterne Military Cemetery.

HERBERT, PRIVATE FREDERICK WILLIAM. 11/902. Killed in action on July 23rd 1916. Born in Hull. Buried in Rue-Du-Bacquerot No 1 Military Cemetery, Laventie.

HERRING, PRIVATE CHARLES ALBERT. 11/1031. Died of wounds on December 13th 1916 aged 27. Born in Hull. Son of the late John and Sophia Herring. Husband of of the late C A Herring. Buried in Etaples Military Cemetery.

HESELTINE, SERGEANT JOHN LEONARD. 11/883. Died of wounds on April 17th 1916. Born in Hull. Buried in Beauval Communal Cemetery.

HESLOP, PRIVATE GEORGE HENRY. 11/271. Killed in action on May 3rd 1917. Born in Hull. Commemorated on the Arras Memorial.

HIGGINSON, PRIVATE HENRY. 12/64. Died of wounds on June 28th 1918 aged 29. Born in Hull. Husband of Mrs H Higginson of 20 Pennington Street, Holdemess Road, Hull. Buried in Chocques Military Cemetery.

HILL, SERGEANT HENRY, MM. 11/375. Killed in action (died of accidental injuries) on August 8th 1918 aged 21. Born in Hull. Son of John and Maria Hill of Hull. Buried in Le Grand Hasard Military Cemetery.

HODGSON, PRIVATE HERBERT. 11/681. Killed in action on August 3rd 1916. Born in Newcastle-on-Tyne but resident in Hull. Buried in Le Touret Military Cemetery.

HODGSON, SERGEANT KENNETH. 11/913. Killed in action on May 25th 1918. Born in Hull. Buried in Lille Southern Cemetery.

HOGG, LANCE-CORPORAL GEORGE EDWARD. 11/63. Killed in action on October 13th 1916 aged 23. Born in Hull. Son of Samuel and Sophia Hogg of 5 Prison Bungalows, Hedon Road, Hull. Buried in Euston Road Cemetery.

HOLDSTOCK, PRIVATE WILLIAM. 11/1234. Died of wounds on May 3rd 1917 aged 31. Born in Hull. Husband of Jane Hoidstock of 5 Villa Terrace, Swann Street, Hull. Buried in Duisans British Cemetery.

HOLMES, PRIVATE EDWARD ALBERT. 11/528. Died at home on November 7th 1914 aged 22. Born in Beverley. Buried in St. Martin's Cemetery, Beverley. Son of Horatio Thomas and Sarah Holmes of the Dog and Duck Inn, Ladygate. Beverley.

HOUGHTON, PRIVATE HAROLD FOSTER. 11/978. Killed in action on June 28th 1918. Born in Sutton-on-Sea but resident in Hull. Buried in Aval Wood Military Cemetery.

INGHAM, PRIVATE CHARLES ROWLAND. 14/187. Killed in action on May 3rd 1917. Born in Leeds but resident in Hull. Commemorated on the Arras Memorial.

IVESON, CORPORAL THOMAS. 11/477. Killed in action on October 29th 1916. Born in Hull. Commemorated on the Thiepval Memorial.

IZOD, PRIVATE ERNEST. 11/852. Killed in action on August 1st 1916. Born in Bethnal Green but resident in Hull. Buried in Le Touret Military Cemetery.

JACKSON, PRIVATE JOHN WILLIAM. 11/419. Killed in action on April 12th 1918. Born in Hull. Commemorated on the Ploegsteert memorial.

JACKSON, PRIVATE JOSEPH WILLIAM, of 'D' Company. 11/1388. Killed in action on November 13th 1916 aged 31. Born in Hull. Son of James Thicken Jackson of Hull. Husband of Elizabeth Cole Jackson of 5 Pettingell Terrace, Daltry Street, Hull. He enlisted on January 8th 1915. Buried in Euston Road Cemetery.

JARVIS, LANCE-CORPORAL LEONARD, MM. 10/1191. Died of wounds on July 13th 1918 aged 26. Born in Hull. Son of Thomas and Sarah Jarvis of The Gables, Dunnington, York. Buried in Longuenesse Souvenir Cemetery, St. Omer.

JEFFREY, PRIVATE GEORGE ALFRED. MM. 11/136. Killed in action on March 26th 1918. Born in Hull. Commemorated on the Arras Memorial.

JOHNSON, PRIVATE EDWARD WILLS. 11/1176. Killed in action on June 3rd 1916 aged 36. Son of Elizabeth Bennett (formerly Johnson) of 61 Tudor Road, Cardiff and the late Mr C Johnson. Born in Warter, East Yorkshire but resident in Hull. Buried in Sucrerie Military Cemetery, Colincamps.

JOHNSON, LANCE-CORPORAL EDWARD WILSON, of 'B' Company. 14/203. Killed in action on May 6th 1917 aged 21. Born in Warter, East Yorkshire, but resident in Hull. Son of Anthony Bannister and Sarah Ellen Johnson of 18 Pendrill Street, Hull. He was a student before the war. Buried in Albuera Cemetery.

JOHNSON, PRIVATE HAROLD. 11/1256. Died of wounds on June 16th 1916 aged 25. Son of Mary Jane Johnson of 35 Albermarle Street, Boulevard, Hull. Born in Hull. Buried in St. Sever Cemetery, Rouen.

JOHNSON, PRIVATE JOHN WILLIAM. 11/1111. Died of wounds on September 5th 1918. Born in Hull. Buried in New Irish Farm Cemetery.

JOHNSON, PRIVATE OSCAR. 11/863. Killed in action on June 28th 1917. Born in Hull. Commemorated on the Arras Memorial.

JUDGE, PRIVATE JOHN WILLIAM. 11/529. Died on October 28th 1918 of influenza aged 22. Son of Eliza Fairbank (formerly Judge) and Tom Fairbank (Stepbrother), of 5 Nicholson Street. Hull. Born in Hempholme, Yorkshire but resident in Hull. Buried in Pont-De-Nieppe Communal Cemetery.

KAY, CORPORAL JAMES HENRY. 11/690. Killed in action on November 13th 1916. Born in Hull. Buried in Euston Road Cemetery.

KENDREW, PRIVATE FRED. 10/1130. Died of wounds on May 8th 1917. Born in Sutton, near Hull but resident in Hull. Son of M A Kendrew of 14 Russell Street, Hull. Buried in Duisans British Cemetery, Hull.

KENNEBY, PRIVATE ERNEST. 11/627. Killed in action on September 8th 1918. Born in Hull. Buried in Trois Arbres Cemetery, Steenwerck.

KING, PRIVATE GEORGE EDWARD. 11/965. Died on March 10th 1916 aged 35. Husband of Florence King of 11 Clipwin Terrace, Hull. Buried in Western Cemetery, Hull.

KING, PRIVATE STANLEY. 12/1334. Died on March 27th 1919 aged 22. Son of Charles and Sarah King of Sunnyside, New Holland, Barrow-on-Humber. He died after being officially discharged to the reserve. Buried in Barrow-upon-Humber Cemetery.

KIRBY, PRIVATE GEORGE CECIL. 11/517. Killed in action on May 16th 1917 aged 21. Born in Coniston, enlisted in Hull but resident in Coniston. Son of George and Mary Isabell Kirby of Coniston. Hull. Commemorated on the Arras Memorial.

KIRBY, PRIVATE RICHARD. 11/1180. Killed in action on November 13th 1916 aged 21. Son of the late William and Margaret Kirby. Born in Hull. Commemorated on the Thiepval Memorial.

KIRBY, PRIVATE ROBERT. 13/1492. Killed in action on March 27th 1918 aged 25. Born in Roos, East Yorkshire, enlisted in Hull but resident in Roos at the time of enlistment. Son of Mrs. Elizabeth Kirby of Pilmoor Lane, Roos, Hull. Commemorated on the Arras Memorial.

KIRK, PRIVATE JOHN WILLIAM. 11/51. Killed in action on March 27th 1918 aged 24. Born in Barton-on-Humber, Lincolnshire, enlisted in Hull but resident in Barton-on-Humber. Son of Ira and Polly Kirk of 197 King Street, Barton-on-Humber. Commemorated on the Arras Memorial.

KIRK, CORPORAL PERCY, of 'B' Company. 11/30. Killed in action on May 3rd 1917 aged 30. Born in Hull. Son of the late Mr and Mrs H Kirk of Newstead Street, Hull. Husband of Hannah Kirk of 5 Mayo Terrace, Stanley Street, Hull. Commemorated on the Arras Memorial.

LANE, PRIVATE EDWARD FRANCIS. 12/1094. Killed in action on March 27th 1918 aged 35. Born in Marylebone, Middlesex but resident in Hull. Son of the late Francis and Adeline Lane of London. Husband of Phoebe Lane of 7 Beech Grove, Ringrose Street, Hawthorn Avenue, Hull. Commemorated on the Arras Memorial.

LANGHORNE, PRIVATE JAMES WILLIAM. 11/737.

Died in the UK, of wounds on November 22nd 1916 aged 23. Son of William and J Langhorne of 50 Rosemead Street, New Bridge Street, Hull. Born in Fort William, Inverness but resident in Hull. Buried in Howden (St. Peter) Churchyard.

LEAKE, PRIVATE HARRY. 12/684. Killed in action on November 8th 1917. Born in Stoneferry, Hull. Commemorated on the Arras Memorial.

LEWIS, PRIVATE WILLIAM. 11/519. Killed in action on April 12th 1918. Born in Hull. Buried in Outtersteene Communal Cemetery Extension, Bailleul.

LING, LANCE-CORPORAL WILLAM REGINALD. 11/50. Killed in action on May 3rd 1917 aged 22. Born in Barton-on-Humber, Lincolnshire, enlisted in Hull but resident in Barton-on-Humber. Son of the late Thomas Enderby and Kate Emily Ling. Commemorated on the Arras Memorial.

LOCKWOOD, LANCE-CORPORAL ERNEST ARTHUR. 11/69. Killed in action on May 3rd 1917 aged 31. Born in Hull. Son of John and Ellen Lockwood of 18 Goodrich Terrace, Cave Street, Beverley Road, Hull. Buried in Orchard Dump Cemetery.

LOFT, PRIVATE THOMAS. 11/1183. Killed in action on May 3rd 1917. Born in Hull. Commemorated on the Arras Memorial.

LOWE, PRIVATE SIDNEY WILLIAM. 11/896. Killed in action on March 25th 1918 aged 25. Born in Hull. Son of Mrs Emily Lowe of 7 Vine Terrace, Alexandra Street, Hull. Commemorated on the Arras Memorial.

LOWEN, PRIVATE GEORGE EDWARD, MM. 11/1244. Died of wounds on March 24th 1918. Born Newcastle-upon-Tyne but resident in Hull. Buried in Bac-Du-Sud British Cemetery.

LOWTHER, PRIVATE RICHARD. 11/229. Died of wounds on October 30th 1918 aged 19. Husband of P Lowther of 12 Outran Street, Outran Terrace, Rodney Street, Hull. Buried in Kezelberg Military Cemetery.

LUMLEY, CORPORAL JOSEPH. 11/226. Killed in action on December 3rd 1917 aged 23. Born in Houghton-le-Spring, enlisted in Hull but resident in Houghton-le-Spring. Son of Joseph Alfred and Mary Ann Lumley of 17 Pit Row, Houghton-le-Spring, County Durham. Buried in Roclincourt Military Cemetery.

MALLENDER, PRIVATE ALFRED. 11/1351. Killed in action on May 3rd 1917 aged 18. Born in Everton, Nottinghamshire, enlisted in Hull but resident in Everton. Son of John and Annie Mallender. Commemorated on the Arras Memorial.

MARCHANT, PRIVATE JOHN. 11/1186. Killed in action on July 1st 1916. Born in Leeds enlisted in Hull. Commemorated on the Thiepval Memorial.

MARONEY, PRIVATE MARTIN. 11/1045. Died on April 1st 1916. Born in Stockton-on-Tees, enlisted in Hull but resident in Stockton-on-Tees. Buried in Aubigny Communal Cemetery Extension.

MARRITT, SERGEANT ERNEST, DCM. 11/785. Killed in action on November 8th 1917 aged 19. Born in Hull. Son of Arthur and Annie Marritt, of 24, Montrose Street, Hull. Commemorated on the Arras Memorial.

MARSHALL, PRIVATE ALBERT THOMAS. 11/1188. Killed in action on June 16th 1916. Born in Hull. Buried in Sucrerie Military Cemetery, Colincamps.

MARSHALL, PRIVATE ALBERT WILLIAM. 11/435. Died of wounds on September 29th 1918. Born in Hull. Buried in La Kreule Military Cemetery.

MARSHALL, PRIVATE JAMES WILLIAM. 11/116. Killed in action on March 28th 1918 aged 34. Born in Hull. Son of Horatio and Mary Marshall of Hull. Husband of Ruth Heathcote Marshall of 8 Portland Street, Hull. Commemorated on the Arras Memorial.

MASON, LANCE-CORPORAL JOSEPH WILLIAM. 11/799. Died of wounds on July 1st 1916 aged 24. Only son of Joseph and Esther Mason of Northend, Kneadby, Doncaster. Born in Keadby. Doncaster. enlisted in Hull but resident in Doncaster. Buried in St. Sever Cemetery, Rouen.

MATTHEWS, PRIVATE JAMES WILLIAM. 11/992. Died of wounds on August 1st 1916 aged 36. Born in Hull. Son of Mr and Mrs John Matthews of 12 Redcar Street, St. Mark's Street, Hull. Buried in Bethune Town Cemetery.

McNALLY, PRIVATE JOHN. 11/395. Died of wounds on August 9th 1916. Born in Hull. Buried in Boulogne Eastern Cemetery.

McINTOSH, CORPORAL DOUGLAS STEWART. 11/781. Killed in action on October 29th 1916. Born in Hull. Commemorated on the Thiepval Memorial.

McLANE, LANCE-CORPORAL HAROLD MAYNARD. 11/33. Killed in action on March 27th 1918. Born in Hull. Commemorated on the Arras Memorial.

MEE, PRIVATE G. 12/573. Died on April 13th 1921 aged 32. Brother-in-law of Mrs Kate Grundy of 60 Rugby Street, Hessle Road, Hull. Buried in Western Cemetery, Spring Bank, Hull.

MEGAHY, PRIVATE JOSEPH BELL. 11/451. Killed in action on July 22nd 1916 aged 32. Born in Carluke, Lanarkshire but resident in Hull. Buried in Rue-Du-Bacquerot No 1 Military Cemetery. Laventie.

MORLEY, PRIVATE JOHN WILLIAM. 11/207. Killed in action on June 28th 1917. Born in Hull. Commemorated on the Arras Memorial.

MURRAY, PRIVATE JAMES JOSEPH. 11/373. Died in the UK on September 23rd 1915. Born in Kilrush, County Clare, enlisted in Hull but resident in Kilrush. Buried in Ripon Cemetery.

NEEDLER, SERGEANT WILLIAM WILSON. 11/986. Killed in action on March 27th 1918 aged 25. Born in Hull. Son of John William and Annie E Needler of 163 Woodcock Street, Hessle Road. Hull. Commemorated on the Arras Memorial.

NEWBY, PRIVATE CHARLES STEEL. 13/522. Died of wounds on October 1st 1918 aged 24. Born in Hull. Buried in La Kreule Military Cemetery.

NEWLOVE, PRIVATE JAMES WILLIAM. 11/712. Killed in action on May 3rd 1917 aged 22. Born in Scarborough but resident in Hull. Son of Robert and Elizabeth Newlove of 4 Omdurmere Avenue, Rosamond Street, Hull. Commemorated on the Arras Memorial.

NIX, SERGEANT CHARLES JOHN, MM. 11/673. Killed in action on September 29th 1918 aged 29. Husband of Elsie May Nix of 2 Story Street, Hull. Born in Hull. Buried in Strand Military Cemetery.

OAKES, PRIVATE GEORGE, MM. 11/874. Killed in action on March 27th 1918 aged 25. Born in Grimsby but resident in Hull. Son of Ellen Elizabeth and the late George Oakes of 123 Porter Street, Hull.

OLLETT, LANCE-CORPORAL ROBERT. 11/691. Killed in action on July 26th 1917 aged 27. Born in Hull. Son of Edward James and Clara Ollett of 1 Cammidge Street, Withernsea, East Yorkshire. Buried in Bumble Trench Cemetery, Vuny Memorial.

OVERTON, LANCE-CORPORAL THOMAS, of 'C' Company. 11/787. Killed in action on November 30th 1916 aged 20. Son of Mrs H L Overton of 22 Withernsea Street, Wilmington, Hull. Born in Hull. Buried in Sailly-au-Bois Military Cemetery.

PALMER, PRIVATE WILLIAM. 11/956. Killed in action on April 12th 1916, aged 26. Son of Mrs Rachel Palmer of 96 North Street, Scarborough. Born in Scarborough. Commemorated on the Ploegsteert Memorial.

PARKER, PRIVATE WALTER de PRESTON. 11/1200. Killed in action on June 2nd 1916 aged 22. Born in Hessle. Yorkshire, enlisted in Hull but was resident in Hessle at the time of enlistment. Son of Amandus Francis Charles and Henrietta Parker of Hessle Railway Sorting Office. Buried in Bertrancourt Military Cemetery.

PARTIS, PRIVATE DANIEL 13/1418. Died of wounds on March 30th 1918 aged 20. Born in Hull. Son of Daniel and Margaret Partis of 13 Garden Terrace, Courtney Street, Holderness Road, Hull.

PATERSON, PRIVATE JAMES ANDREW. 11/872. Died of wounds on December 26th 1916 aged 29. Born in Leeds, enlisted in Hull but resident in Leeds. Son of Robert and Maggie Paterson of 8 Archery Street, Blackman Lane, Leeds. Buried in Mont Huon Military Cemetery.

PEARCY, LANCE-CORPORAL JOHN HENRY. 13/1227. Died in France on October 30th 1918. Born in Hollym near Hull. Buried in Duhallow ADS Cemetery.

PEARSON, PRIVATE EDWIN. 12/186. Died of wounds on Jury 15th 1917. Born in Hull. Buried in Aubigny Communal Cemetery Extension.

PEEPS, PRIVATE WALTER. 11/398. Died of wounds on July 22nd 1916 aged 32. Born in Hull. Son of Charles and Emily Peeps of 9 Charlotte's Terrace, Clarendon Street, Hull. Buried in Merville Communal Cemetery.

PICK, PRIVATE SYDNEY. 11/1125. Died of wounds on June 8th 1916. aged 21. Born in Hull. Buried in Gezaincourt Communal Cemetery Extension.

PICKERING, PRIVATE ERNEST CARTER. 11/952. Died of wounds, caused by gas, on September 14th 1918 aged 23. Son of Edward and Jenny Pickering of 6 Ethels Villas, Blake Street, Brunswick Avenue, Hull. Born in Hull. Buried in Terlincthun British Cemetery.

PLASKITT, PRIVATE THOMAS COOK. 11/1075. Died of wounds on March 27th 1918. Born in Hull. Buried in St. Pol Communal Cemetery Extension.

POLLARD, PRIVATE AMOS of 'A' Company. 11/349. Died of wounds on January 10th 1917. Son of Oliver and Mary Dewry Pollard of 3 Scaife Street, York. Born in Walkden but resident in Hull. Buried in York Cemetery.

POOLE, PRIVATE WILLIAM. 11/1063. Died of wounds on May 4th 1917. Born in Hull, enlisted in Hull but resident in Cottingham at the time. Son of Mrs E Poole of 221 Hallgate, Cottingham. Buried in Duisans British Cemetery.

POTTER, PRIVATE HAROLD. 14/87. Died of wounds on September 8th 1918. Born in Withernsea. Commemorated on the Ploegsteert Memorial.

PROCTOR, PRIVATE FRED. 11/596. Killed in action on August 17th 1916. Born in Hull. Buried in Le Touret Military Cemetery.

RABY, PRIVATE FRED. 11/1203. Died of wounds on July 31st 1916. Born in Hull. Buried in Bethune Town Cemetery.

RASPIN, LANCE-CORPORAL FRANK. 11/474. Killed in action on May 3rd 1917. Born in Hull. Buried in Orchard Dump Cemetery.

RICHARDSON, PRIVATE ELIJAH. 13/201. Killed in action on June 28th 1918. Born in Hull. Buried in Aval Wood Military Cemetery.

RICHARDSON, PRIVATE HAROLD. 11/103. Killed in action on May 3rd 1917. Born in Hull. Buried in Orchard Dump Cemetery.

ROBINSON, PRIVATE GEORGE. 11/372. Died of wounds on July 1st 1917 aged 21. Born in Goole, enlisted in Hull but resident in Goole. Only son of Arthur and the late Ada Robinson of 31 Henry Street.

Goole, Yorkshire. He enlisted on September 8th 1914. Buried in Duisans British Cemetery.

ROBSON, PRIVATE JAMES WILLIAM. 14/133. Killed in action on July 21st 1916. Born in Beverley. Buried in Rue-Du-Bacquerot No. 1 Military Cemetery. Brother of Mr. H.S. Robson (a hairdresser) of Wednesday Market, Beverley. His name appears on the Hengate War Memorial.

ROBSON, PRIVATE PERCY EDWARD. 11/554. Killed in action on February 25th 1917. Born in Hull. Buried in Euston Road Cemetery.

ROGERS, PRIVATE SIDNEY. 14/83. Died of wounds on May 3rd 1917. Born in Hull. Buried in Lievin Communal Cemetery Extension.

RUTLEDGE, PRIVATE ROBERT. 11/87. Killed in action on March 27th 1918. Born in Hull. Commemorated on the Arras Memorial.

SAWDON, PRIVATE WILLIAM. 11/448. Killed in action on June 27th 1916 aged 22. Son of Mr and Mrs Kirk of Hull. Born in Driffield but resident in Hull. Buried in Sucrerie Military Cemetery, Colincamps.

SAWYER, CORPORAL THOMAS, DCM. 11/1207. Killed in action on September 8th 1918. Born in Hull. Commemorated on the Ploegsteert Memorial.

SCOTT, SERGEANT LLEWELLYN. 13/1481. Died of wounds on March 29th 1918 aged 33. Born in Ossett but resident in Hull. Son of Abraham Scott. Husband of Emily Andrews (formerly Scott) of 3 Hessle Avenue, Dansom Lane, Hull. Buried in Bac-du-Sud British Cemetery.

SCOTTOW, LANCE-CORPORAL FREDERICK. 11/473. Killed in action on May 2nd 1917. Born in Hull. Husband of Endymion Scottow of Harriets Square, Scott Street, Hull. Commemorated on the Arras Memorial.

SELLERS, SERGEANT HARRY, MM, of 'D' Company. 11/772. Killed in action on June 30th 1918 aged 25. Born in Hull. Son of William Joshua and Amelia Mary Sellers of 140 Severn Street, Holderness Road, Hull. Buried in Aval Wood Military Cemetery.

SHARPE, CORPORAL FRED LESLIE, MM. 11/393. Killed in action on April 12th 1918. Born in Hull. Commemorated on the Ploegsteert Memorial.

SHAW, PRIVATE FRANK. 11/1089. Killed in action on May 3rd 1917 aged 24. Son of John and Eliza Shaw of 15 Carlton Street, Hessle Road, Hull. Born in Hull. Buried in Orchard Dump Cemetery.

SIMPSON, SERGEANT ALBERT. 11/149. Killed in action on May 30th 1916 aged 23. Son of William and Hannah Simpson of 4 Butcher Row, Seaton, Hull. Born in Hull. Buried in Sucrerie Military Cemetery, Colincamps.

SMART, PRIVATE THOMAS. 11/1127. Killed in action on March 26th 1918. Born in Caistor, Lincolnshire but resident in Hull. Commemorated on the Arras Memorial.

SMITH, COPORAL, JOHN ARTHUR, MM. 12/234. Killed in action on September 6th 1918. Born in Rochester, Kent but resident in Hull. Son of Mr E Smith of 4 Nomabell Street, Holderness Road, Hull. Buried in Pont d'Achelles Military Cemetery, Nieppe.

SMITH, SERGEANT JOHN HESELTLNE. 11/364. Killed in action on September 8th 1918. Husband of Mrs A Warcup (formerly Smith) of 16 Granville Terrace, West Dock Street, Hull. Buried in Pont d'Achelles Military Cemetery, Nieppe. Born in Hull.

SMITH, PRIVATE WILLIAM. 11/228. Killed in action on August 21st 1917. Buried in New Irish Farm Cemetery. Born in Hull.

SPETCH, PRIVATE JOHN EDWARD. 11/571. Killed in action on April 12th 1918. Born in Selby and resident in Selby at the time of enlistment. Commemorated on the Ploegsteert Memorial.

SPINK, PRIVATE GILBERT. 12/100. Killed in action on July 31st 1916 aged 29. Born in Hull. Son of Mr and Mrs W O Spink of 8 Brunswick Avenue, Franklin Street, Holderness Road, Hull. Buried in Le Touret Military Cemetery.

STOTHARD, CORPORAL PERCY. 11/1379. Killed in action on September 8th 1918 aged 29. Commemorated on the Ploegsteert Memorial. Born in Beverley. Husband of Emily Florence Stothard of 20 Sisters Terrace, Tadman Street, Hull.

STOUT, CORPORAL CHRISTIAN FREDERICK JOHN. 11/248. Died of wounds on December 1st 1917 aged 25. Born in Liverpool but resident in Hull. Son of William and Ellen Stout of Hull. Buried in Boisguillaume Communal Cemetery Extension.

STUART, PRIVATE CHARLES WELTON, of 'C' Company. 11/1078. Killed in action on March 29th 1916 aged 32. Buried in Mesnil Ridge Cemetery. Born in Hull. Son of Daniel and Catherine Stuart of 6 May Villas, May Street, late of Rutland Terrace, Norfolk Street, Hull.

SWALES, PRIVATE ALFRED. 13/1347. Died of wounds on July 2nd 1918. Born in Hull. Buried in Longuenesse Souvenir Cemetery, St. Omer.

SWEETING, PRIVATE GEORGE WILLIAM. 11/1296. Died on June 15th 1921 aged 33. Son of Mrs A Sweeting of Low Street, Laxton, Howden and the late Mr T W Sweeting. Husband of the late J A Sweeting. Buried in Laxton (St Peter) Churchyard.

SWINDEN, PRIVATE THOMAS. 11/612. Killed in action on August 9th 1917. Born in Hull. Buried in Berlin South-Westem Cemetery.

TASKER, PRIVATE ARTHUR BEAL. 11/319. Died of wounds on November 13th 1916. Born in Hull. Husband of Mrs M Tasker of 43 New George Street, Hull. Buried in Corbie Communal Cemetery Extension.

TAYLOR, PRIVATE HARRY, of 'D' Company. 11/264. Killed in action on March 27th 1918 aged 21. Born in Norton, Yorkshire, enlisted in Hull but was resident in Norton at the time of enlistment. Son of Richard and Isabel Taylor of 54 Mill Street, Norton, Malton. Yorkshire. Commemorated on the Arras Memorial.

TEECE, PRIVATE THOMAS EDGAR. 11/339. Killed in action on July 3rd 1917. Born in Hoyland, enlisted in Hull but was resident in Belper (Derbyshire) at the time of enlistment. Buried in Albuera Cemetery.

TEMPLE, PRIVATE HERBERT. 11/623. Killed in action on March 25th 1918 aged 46. Born in Hull. Husband of Mary Helen Temple of 9 Coral Grove, Grange Street, Hull. Commemorated on the Arras Memorial.

TENNISON, PRIVATE ALFRED. 11/822. Killed in action on April 17th 1916 aged 19. Son of Edward and Laura Tennison of 109 Great Thornton Street, Hull. Born in Hull. Buried in Sucrerie Military Cemetery, Colincamps.

THEAKSTON, PRIVATE HERBERT. 11/1279. Killed in action on August 2nd 1916 aged 28. Born in Hull. Son of William and Ann Theakstone of Hull. Husband of Mary Elizabeth Theakstone of Mentone Avenue, Arundle Street, Hull. Buried in Le Touret Military Cemetery.

THIRSK, PRIVATE JOSEPH. 11/389. Died of wounds on May 13th 1917 aged 28. Born in Hull. Son of Joseph and Jane Thirsk. Buried in Etaples Military Cemetery.

THOMPSON, PRIVATE HARRY. 11/1268. Killed in action on May 3rd 1917. Born in Hull. Commemorated on the Arras Memorial.

THURNELL, PRIVATE ALBERT ROBERT. 11/1270. Killed in action on May 3rd 1917. Born in Hull. Commemorated on the Arras Memorial.

TODD, LANCE-CORPORAL JAMES. 11/305. Died of wounds on March 28th 1918 aged 24. Born in Hull. Son of John William and Sarah Todd of Hull. Buried in Doullens Communal Cemetery Extension No. 1.

TOWNSEND, SERGEANT WALTER. 11/948. Died of sickness on June 17th 1916 aged 32. Born in Nottingham, enlisted in Hull but resident in Southwell, Nottinghamshire. Husband of Lottie Townsend of 3 Brecon Avenue, Brecon Street, Holderness Road. Hull. Buried in Beauval Communal Cemetery.

TURNER, PRIVATE JAMES HENRY, of 'C' Company. 11/1429. Killed in action on May 3rd 1917 aged 19. Born in Hull. Son of Margaret and the late G W Turner of 65 Edinburgh Street, Hessle Road, Hull. Commemorated on the Arras Memorial.

TURNER, PRIVATE THOMAS FREDERICK. 11/1389. Killed in action on August 11th 1918 aged 22. Born in Hull. Son of Mr and Mrs Turner of Hull. Buried in Le Grand Hasard Military Cemetery.

USHER, CORPORAL WILLIAM ERNEST. 11/241. Killed in action on April 12th 1918 aged 35. Son of

Thomas and Elizabeth Usher. Husband of Florence Jane Usher of 60 Folkestone Street, Beverley Road, Hull. Born in Hull. Commemorated on the Ploegsteert Memorial.

VAREY, PRIVATE BRIAN. 11/823. Killed in action on November 13th 1916. Born in Hull. Buried in Euston Road Cemetery.

WALKER, PRIVATE THOMAS EDWARD. 12/1272. Killed in action on April 12th 1918 aged 21. Husband of M. Hagar (formerly Walker) of Green Lane, Barrow-on-Humber, Lincolnshire. Born in Barrow-on-Humber. Commemorated on the Ploegsteert Memorial.

WALSH, PRIVATE JOHN. 12/1267. Killed in action on July 22nd 1916. Born in Hull. Buried in Rue-du-Bacqueret No.l Military Cemetery, Laventie.

WALTON, SERGEANT JOHN FRANCIS. 11/1015. Killed in action on November 13th 1916 aged 35. Buried in Euston Road Cemetery. Born in Cairo, Egypt. Husband of Clara Walton of 3 Princess Terrace, Alexander Street, Hull.

WARD, PRIVATE ALLEN. 11/936. Killed in action on May 3rd 1917. Born in Canning Town, Middlesex, enlisted in Hull but resident in Canning Town. Commemorated on the Arras Memorial.

WARD, PRIVATE FRANK. 11/428. Died of pneumonia on June 16th 1915 aged 32. Born in Hull. Buried in Hedon Road Cemetery, Hull. Lived at 50 Wassand Street, Hull. His brother Fred served in France. His name appears in the St. Barnabas Book of Rememberance (now kept at St. Matthew's Church, Anlaby Road, Hull).

WARD, PRIVATE MICHAEL HENRY. 11/1216. Killed in action on June 16th 1916. Buried in Sucrerie Military Cemetery, Colincamps. Born in Hull.

WARNES, PRIVATE GEORGE EDWARD. 11/1320. Killed in action on April 12th 1918. Born in Fort William, Inverness but resident in Hull at the time of enlistment. Commemorated on the Ploegsteert Memorial.

WELLS, PRIVATE WILLIE. 11/1393. Killed in action aged 42. Commemorated on the Thiepval Memorial. Born in Colne, Lancashire. Son of Mr. and Mrs. Robert Wells of Colne. Husband of Ada Wells (nee Ranch) of 5 Henry's Terrace, Wassand Street, Hessle Road, Hull.

WEMYSS, PRIVATE GEORGE. 11/429. Died of wounds on August 4th 1916 aged 22. Buried in Bethune Town Cemetery. Born in Hull. Son of William and Fanny M. Wemyss of 78 English Street, Hull. One of his brothers, Corporal Leonard Wemyss (2nd Yorkshire Regiment) was killed in action on April 9th 1917 aged 21.

WHISKER, LANCE-CORPORAL HARRY, MM. 12/698. Served with 'A' Company Machine Gun Section. Killed in action on March 26th 1918 aged 26. Commemorated on the Arras Memorial. Born in Hull.

Enlisted in Hull on September 28th 1914. Son of John and Ann Whisker of 21 Prospect Place, Church Street, Drypool, Hull. One of five children (three sons). He was engaged to be married at the time of his death.

WILLCOX, PRIVATE ALBERT. 11/1219. Killed in action on May 3rd 1917 aged 30. Commemorated on the Arras Memorial. Born in Hull. Fourth son of Edward Thomas and the late Elizabeth Willcox. One of four children (three sons). Husband of Catherine Willcox of 4 Matlock Villas, Estcourt Street, Hull. Before the war he was employed as a Stevedore. One of his brothers, George William Willcox (11/1220), was killed in action on March 27th 1918 aged 24, serving with the 4th East Yorkshire, even though he had joined the 11th battalion at the same time as his brother. He also has no known grave.

WILLEY, PRIVATE GEORGE WILLIAM. 11/1222. Killed in action at Oppy Wood on May 3rd 1917 aged 23. Buried in Orchard Dump Cemetery, Arleux-en-Gohelle. Born in Hull. Son of the Late William Richard Willey of 2 Busby Terrace, Durham Street, Hull.

WILSON, PRIVATE WILLIAM BARNETT. 11/272. Killed in action on March 27th 1918. Commemorated on the Arras Memorial. Born in Hull.

WOODALL, CORPORAL WILLIAM HENRY. 13/295. Attached to the 92nd Trench Mortar Battery. Died on August 8th 1918. Buried in Le Grand Hasard Military Cemetery, Hazebrouck. Born in Wressle, near Hull. Son of George Robert and Sarah Martha Woodall of Hull.

WOODS, PRIVATE FRANK. 11/843. Killed in action on November 8th 1917 aged 22. Born in Cambridge, enlisted in Hull but resident in Cambridge. Son of Henry William and Harriet Woods of Coventry Cottage, Six Mile Bottom, Cambridgeshire. Commemorated on the Arras Memorial.

WOOLLONS, PRIVATE THOMAS GEORGE. 11/500. Killed in action on June 28th 1917 aged 29. Commemorated on the Arras Memorial. Born in Hull. Son of Mrs. Theresa Woollons and the late Thomas George Woollons of 71 Bean Street, Hull.

WRIGHT, PRIVATE SAMUEL EDWARD. 10/1370. Killed in action on November 13th 1916. Commemorated on the Thiepval Memorial. Born in Hull.

12TH BATTALION

ALCOCK, PRIVATE JOHN ROBERT. 12/687. Killed in action on November 13th 1916, aged 32. Buried in Euston Road Cemetery. Born in Hull. Son of Robert and Alice Alcock of 2, Breamer Terrace, Walcott Street, Hull. Commemorated in the St. Barnabas Book of Rememberance (now kept at St. Matthew's Church, Anlaby Road, Hull).

ANDERSON, PRIVATE FREDERICK ALBERT. 12/892. Killed in action on September 12th 1916, aged

29. Commemorated on the Thiepval Memorial. Born in Hull. Son of Mrs. Matilda Anderson of 26, Beech Avenue, Garden Village, Hull. Husband of Greta Anderson of 9, Brunswick Terrace, Durham Street, Hull.

ANDERSON, PRIVATE GEORGE. 12/1155. Killed in action on August 28th 1916. Buried in St. Vaast Post Military Cemetery, Richebourg L'Avouée. Born in Hull.

ANDERSON, PRIVATE THOMAS. 12/1156. Killed in action on May 3rd 1917, aged 20. Commemorated on the Arras Memorial. Born in Hull.

ANDREWS, PRIVATE JAMES WILLIAM. 12/1141. Killed in action on November 13th 1916. Buried in Euston Road Cemetery. Born in Hull. He lived at 19, Balfour Street, Hull at the start of the war.

ARCHBUTT, PRIVATE JOHN HENRY. 10/441. Died of wounds on June 30th 1916, aged 21. Buried in Doullens Communal Cemetery Extension No. 1. Son of Abel and Eliza Archbutt of Cottingham. Born in Cottingham but resident in Hull.

BARBER, PRIVATE JOHN ALBERT. 12/382. Killed in action on November 13th 1916. Born in Hull. Commemorated on the Thiepval Memorial.

BARKER, CORPORAL STANLEY. 12/635. Killed in action on November 13th 1916. Commemorated on the Thiepval Memorial. Born in Hull.

BARNES, PRIVATE ARTHUR. 12/282. Killed in action in France by a sniper on June 25th 1917 aged 30. Buried in Orchard Dump Cemetery. Arleux-en-Gohelle. Born in Hull. Husband of Edith Barnes (nee Shaw) of 2 Rose View, Courtney Street, Hull. Two of his three brothers, John and George were also killed in the war. Son of Robert and Ann Barnes.

BARON, PRIVATE JOHN BENSON. 13/313. Killed in action on May 3rd 1917 aged 33. Buried in Orchard Dump Cemetery. Born in Hull. Son of Joseph and Sarah Ann Baron. Husband of Mary Baron of 16 York Terrace, Barnsley Street, Hull.

BARRATT, LANCE-CORPORAL GEORGE WILLIAM. 12/1297. Killed in action on November 13th 1916 aged 39. Born in Welton, East Yorkshire, enlisted in Hull but resident in South Cave, East Yorkshire. Son of the late George William and Elizabeth Barrett. Commemorated on the Thiepval Memorial.

BAYSTON, SERGEANT ALBERT. 12/508. Died of wounds on April 16th 1916 aged 36. Buried in Gezaincourt Communal Cemetery Extension. Born in Middlesborough but resident in Hull. Son of Robert and Elizabeth Bayston of Sutton, Hull. Husband of Edith C. Bayston (nee Houghton) and father of Jack, both residing at 4 Haworth Street, Newland Avenue, Hull.

BEASY, PRIVATE JOHN. 12/604. Died in the UK on February 1st 1915 aged 46. Son of Charles and Ann Beasy. Husband of Harriet A Beasy of 53 Walliker Street, Anlaby Road, Hull. Born in Cromer, Norfolk, enlisted in Hull but resident in Withernsea. Buried in Withernsea Cemetery.

BECKETT, PRIVATE FREDERICK. 12/14. Killed in action on May 26th 1916 aged 26. Buried in Sucrerie Military Cemetery, Colincamps. Born in Hull. He was married but had no children.

BELL, PRIVATE CHARLES HENRY, of 'C' Company. 12/1112. Killed in action on November 13th 1916 aged 27. Commemorated on the Thiepval Memorial. Born in Lowestoft but resident in Hull. Son of George William and Jemima Bell of 1 Somerset Terrace, Gillett Street, Hessle Road, Hull.

BENN, PRIVATE ALBERT. 12/392. Killed in action on November 13th 1916. Born in Scarborough but resident in Hull. He was a married man with children. Commemorated on the Thiepval Memorial.

BETTS, PRIVATE GEORGE EDWARD. 14/171. Killed in action on November 13th 1916 aged 20. Buried in Euston Road Cemetery. Born in Hull. Son of Joshua and Harriet Betts of 6 Lucas Square, Sykes Street, Hull.

BINNING, PRIVATE GEORGE ERNEST. 12/412. Died of wounds on May 5th 1917 aged 25. Born in Atwick, East Yorkshire, enlisted in Hull but resident in Hornsea. Son of Mr and Mrs George Binning of 37 Southgate, Hornsea. Buried in Aubigny Communal Cemetery Extension.

BLACKBURN, PRIVATE CASTLE. 12/722. Killed in action on August 16th 1916. Buried in Le Touret Military Cemetery. Born in Hull.

BLACKBURN, PRIVATE SIDNEY. 12/760. Killed in action on November 13th 1916 aged 21. Commemorated on the Thiepval Memorial. Born in Hull. Son of Mrs Sarah Blackburn of 12 Ellis's Terrace, Wassand Street, Hessle Road, Hull. His name appears in the St Barnabas Church Book of Rememberance.

BLAGG, PRIVATE ARTHUR. 12/1470. Killed in action on May 3rd 1917. Born in Hessle but resident in Hull. Commemorated on the Arras Memorial.

BLAIN, PRIVATE JAMES. 12/904. Died of wounds on August 11th 1916 aged 41. Buried in St. Vaast Post Military Cemetery. Born in Hull. He enlisted at the City Hall in September 1914 and went with the battalion to Egypt and then to France. Son of Mrs. Emily Home. Husband of the late Gertrude Blain and father of five children residing at 6 Holborn Mount, Holborn Street, Hull. His name appears on the Damson Lane Roll of Honour, Hull.

BLAKESTONE, PRIVATE SAMUEL 12/605. Killed in action on November 13th 1916 aged 45. Commemorated on the Thiepval Memorial. Born in Hull. Son of Samuel and Sarah Ann Blakestone. Husband of May Ann Blakestone of Hull.

BOLTON, CORPORAL SAMUEL (known as Sam). 12/1027. Killed in action on November 13th 1916. Buried in Euston Road Cemetery. Born in Hull. A married man. His daughter Margaret, died of pneumonia on November 3rd 1918.

BOND, PRIVATE HAROLD LESLIE. 12/1330. Died of wounds on November 23rd 1916 aged 21. Born in London, enlisted in Hull but resident in New Eltham. Son of Herbert George Frederick and Sarah Ann Bond of 4 Victoria Cottages, Green Lane, New Eltham, London. Buried in Boulogne Eastern Cemetery.

BOOTH, PRIVATE CHARLES. 14/148. Killed in action on November 13th 1916. Buried in Serre Road Cemetery No. 1. Born in Goole but resident in Hull. His mother and brothers lived at 11 Lockwood Street, Hull.

BOOTH, PRIVATE DAVID. 12/668. Killed in action on November 13th 1916 aged 20. Commemorated on the Thiepval Memorial. Born in Hull. Son of Mr and Mrs Booth of 132 Chiltern Street, Hessle Road, Hull.

BOOTHBY, PRIVATE DANIEL 12/887. Died of wounds on August 18th 1916. Buried in Chocques Military Cemetery.

BOOTHMAN, PRIVATE ARTHUR THOMAS. 12/514. Killed in action on Jury 24th 1916 aged 28. Son of Thomas and Ada H Boothman of Mill Road, Crowle. Born in Crowle, Lincolnshire but resident in Hull. Buried in St Vaast Post Military Cemetery, Richebourg L'Avouée.

BOURNER, PRIVATE HAROLD. 12/1241. Killed in action on July 19th 1916 aged 28. Born in Driffield but resident in Hull. Husband of Mrs. Boumer of 9 Albert Terrace, Terry Street, Hull. Son of Mary and the late David Edward Boumer of 20 Chestnut Grove, Park Road, Hull. His four brothers all served in the army, two were killed - Sergeant George Bourner of the Cheshire Regiment and Officer Cadet Percy Boumer. (See 3rd Battalion) Buried in Rue-du-Bacquerot No 1 Military Cemetery, Laventie.

BOXHALL, PRIVATE HENRY CHARLES. 12/1331. Killed in action on May 26th 1916. Buried in Sucrerie Military Cemetery, Colincamps. Born in Hull. Married with five children. An ex-seaman who resided at 10 Granville Terrace, Strickland Street, Hull. His name appears in the St Barnabas Book of Rememberance.

BOYD, PRIVATE JOSEPH. 12/1158. Killed in action on November 13th 1916. Born in Goxhill, Lincolnshire but resident in Hull. Buried in Euston Road Cemetery.

BRAITHWAITE, SERGEANT ALBERT. 12/865. Killed in action on November 13th 1916. Commemorated on the Thiepval Memorial. Born in Nafferton but resident in Rolston near Hornsea.

BRETT, PRIVATE WILLIAM. 12/1494. Killed in action trying to save injured men during an attack on enemy lines on May 26th 1916 aged 20. Buried in Sucrerie Military Cemetery, Colincamps. Born in Hull. His brother Albert was killed on the first day of the Somme.

BRIGHAM, PRIVATE JAMES HERBERT (known as Jim). 12/765. Killed in action on November 13th 1916 aged 22. Commemorated on the Thiepval Memorial. Born in Hull. Son of James and Mary Brigham of 12 Richard's Terrace, Barnsley Street, Hull. Husband of Mary Brigham and father of one daughter, resident at 9 Rose Terrace, Barnsley Street, Hull.

BRODERICK, PRIVATE ARTHUR. 12/818. Died of wounds on November 22nd 1916 aged 32. Buried in Warlincourt Halte British Cemetery, Saulty. Born in Hull. Son of Peter and Harriet Broderick. His brother Thomas lived at 6 Frederick's Terrace, Nornabell Street, Hull.

BROWN, PRIVATE FREDERICK. 12/57. Killed in action on May 3rd 1917. Born in Goole but resident in Newington, Hull. Commemorated on the Arras Memorial.

BROWN, PRIVATE RICHARD. 12/25. Killed in action on November 13th 1916. Buried in Euston Road Cemetery. Born in Leeds but resident in Hull.

BULMAN, CORPORAL HARRY. 13/1381. Killed in action on May 3rd 1917. Commemorated on the Arras Memorial. Born in Newark but resident in Hull.

BURNETT, PRIVATE GEORGE THOMAS. 12/1128. Killed in action on November 13th 1916 aged 19. Commemorated on the Thiepval Memorial. Born in Hull. Son of John Richard and Emilie Burnett of 22 Bluebell Entry, High Street, Hull.

BURNHAM, LANCE-CORPORAL GEORGE FREDERICK. 12/216. Killed in action on May 25th 1916. Buried in Sucrerie Military Cemetery, Colincamps. Born in Hull.

BURNS, PRIVATE LEONARD FRANK. 12/241. Killed in Action on November 13th 1916. Commemorated on the Thiepval Memorial. Born in Harwich, Essex but resident in Bradford at the time of enlistment. His brother Jack was killed in action on July 31st 1917.

BUSBY, LANCE-CORPORAL JOHN, of 'D' Company. 12/551. Killed in action on May 3rd 1917 aged 28. Commemorated on the Arras Memorial. Born in Hull. Son of Thomas and Elizabeth Busby of 22 New Parade, Damson Lane, Hull. Husband of Annie Elizabeth Busby of 12 Balfour Crescent, Nornabell Street, Holderness Road, Hull. He was father of four children.

BUSH, PRIVATE HENRY. 10/1443. Reported missing but Prisoner of War. Died on June 21st 1917 aged 19. Buried in Niederzwehren Cemetery, Germany. Born in Hull. Son of Frederick and Amy C. Bush of 3 Woodland Villas, Rustensburg Street, New Bridge Road, Hull. Before the war he was employed at the De La Pole Cafe. His brother Horace served with the New Zealand Forces.

BUTLER, PRIVATE GEORGE WILLIAM. 14/216. Killed in action on November 13th 1916. Buried in Euston Road Cemetery. Born in Skegness but resident in Hull. Only son of Mr and Mrs Butler.

CALVERT, CORPORAL ALFRED ARTHUR. 12/1203. Died of wounds on May 3rd 1917 aged 27. Born in Hull. Son of Arthur and Sarah Fowler of 33 Sutton Street, Spring Bank, Hull. Buried in Ste. Marie Cemetery.

CAMPION, PRIVATE WALTER. 12/412. Died of wounds on November 15th 1916. Born in Hull. Buried in Porte-de-Paris Cemetery.

CHALLONS, PRIVATE CHARLES SAMUEL 12/51. Killed in action on November 13th 1916 aged 30. Born in Portsmouth but resident in Hull. Husband of Mrs Charlotte Elizabeth Challans (nee Hull) of 68 Charles Street, Hull. Father of three children. Commemorated on the Thiepval Memorial.

CHAPMAN, COMPANY SERGEANT-MAJOR THOMAS. 12/96. Died in the UK on January 27th 1916. Born in St John's, New Brunswick, North America but resident in Hull. Husband of Maud May Chapman. Buried in Western Cemetery, Hull.

CHAPMAN, LANCE-CORPORAL STANLEY. 12/70. Killed in action on November 13th 1916. Born in Hull. Resident at 6 Spring Terrace, Spring Street, Hull. Husband and father of two children. Employed before the war by the NER as a Dredgerman at Hull. His name appears on the NER Roll of Honour. Buried in Euston Road Cemetery.

CHAPMAN, LANCE-CORPORAL WILLIAM ROBERT. 12/889. Killed in action on March 8th 1917. Born in Chapeltown, Yorkshire but resident in Hull at the time of enlistment. Buried in Euston Road Cemetery.

CHARLTON, PRIVATE THOMAS WILLIAM. 12/1085. Killed in action on November 13th 1916 aged 19. Born in Skidby, near Hull but resident in Hull. Son of Elizabeth Spesk (formerly Chariton) of 38 Witham, Hull and the late John William Chariton. Commemorated on the Thiepval Memorial.

CLARK, PRIVATE WILLIAM JACKSON, of 'C' Company. 12/780. Killed in action on August 16th 1916 aged 26 by shell fire. Born in Hull. Son of Thomas and Catherine Clark. Husband of Eliza Clark and father of one daughter. Resided at 1 Union Court, Great Union Street, Hull. Buried in Le Touret Military Cemetery.

CUFF, PRIVATE EDWARD. 12/169. Died of wounds on May 11th 1916. Born in Hull. Buried in Beauval Communal Cemetery.

COCKERILL, PRIVATE FRANK. 12/1275. Killed in action on August 16th 1916 aged 25. Born in Hull. Son of Mr. A Cockerill of 5 Oak Terrace, Swann Street, Hull. Buried in Le Touret Military Cemetery.

COCKING, PRIVATE ALFRED HENRY. 12/792. Killed in action on November 13th 1916. Born in Barrow-on-Haven, Lancashire but resident in Hull. Buried in Euston Road Cemetery, Colincamps. Husband of Ellen Cocking.

COLLINSON, LANCE-CORPORAL ALBERT. 12/877. Died of wounds on April 19th 1916. Born in Ledgate, County Durham but resident in Hull. Husband of Annie Maria Lacey (formerly Collinson) of 16 Eliza's Terrace, West Parade, Hull. Buried in Beauval Communal Cemetery.

COLLINSON, PRIVATE EDGAR, MM. 12/830. Died of wounds on July 30th 1917 aged 24. Born in Aldborough, Yorkshire. Enlisted in Hull but resident in Coniston, Yorkshire. Son of W J and K A Collinson. Buried in Etaples Military Cemetery.

COOPER, PRIVATE RANDOLPH CHURCHILL. 14/22. Killed in action on August 6th 1918 aged 25. Born in Hull. Husband of Ida Cooper (nee Turner) of 14 Damson Lane, Hull. His brother Ernest of the 13th battalion was reported missing on November 13th 1916 aged 32 (survived the war); father of two children aged eight and ten. Buried in St. Vaast Post Military Cemetery, Richebourg L'Avouée.

COX, PRIVATE WILLIAM ERNEST. 12/330. Killed in action on November 13th 1916 aged 36. Born in Hainton, Lincolnshire but resident in Hull. Son of John and Sarah Cox of Louth, Lincolnshire. Husband of Emelia Henrietta Cox of 47 St. Luke's Street, Hull. Served in the South African War. Buried in Euston Road Cemetery.

CRAGGY, PRIVATE CHARLES WILLIAM. 12/329. Killed in action on November 13th 1916. Commemorated on the Thiepval Memorial. Born in Beverley but resident in Hull.

CRAWFORD, PRIVATE HAROLD. 12/1139. Killed in action on November 13th 1916. Born in Scarborough but resident in Hull. Commemorated on the Thiepval Memorial.

CROFT, PRIVATE JOSEPH. 12/1167. Killed in action on November 13th 1916. Born in Hull. Commemorated on the Thiepval Memorial.

DAVIES, PRIVATE ALFRED WILLIAM. 12/56. Died in France on April 20th 1916 aged 32. Son of the late George William and Ann Esther Davies of Hull. Born in Hull. Buried in Ste. Marie Cemetery.

DEARLOVE, PRIVATE GEORGE. 12/1003. Killed in action on July 19th 1916 aged 20. Son of Mr and Mrs George Dearlove of 9 Alexandra Avenue, Bridlington Street, Hull. Born in Hull. Buried in Rue-Du-Bacquerot No 1 Military Cemetery, Laventie.

DIMMACK, PRIVATE JOSEPH. 12/303. Killed in action on October 19th 1918. Born in Hull. Buried in Berlin South-Western Cemetery.

DOBBS, PRIVATE FREDERICK HAROLD. 12/161. Killed in action on November 13th 1916. Born in Hull. Buried in Euston Road Cemetery.

EASINGWOOD, SERGEANT REGINALD. 12/316. Killed in action on May 3rd 1917 aged 24. Born in Hull. Husband of Ada Easingwood of 16 Granville Avenue, Reynoldson Street, Newland Avenue, Hull. Commemorated on the Arras Memorial.

EDMOND, PRIVATE HAROLD. 12/384. Killed in action on May 14th 1917 aged 22. Commemorated on the Arras Memorial. Born in Beverley. Son of John Bryan and Sarah Edmond of 9 Earles Row, Withernsea Street, Wilmington, Hull. Commemorated on the Arras Memorial.

EDMUNDS, PRIVATE THOMAS PARKER. 12/516. Killed in action on November 13th 1916. Born in Willoughby, Nottinghamshire, enlisted in Hull but resident in Leeds at the time of enlistment. Husband of Lily Adamson (formerly Edmunds) of 4 Caladonia Avenue, Brighton Street, Hull. Commemorated on the Thiepval Memorial.

EDSON, LANCE-CORPORAL WILLIAM HENRY. 11/25. Killed in action on May 3rd 1917. Born in Dewsbury but resident in Hull at the time of enlistment.

EGAN, PRIVATE THOMAS. 12/457. Killed in action on November 13th 1916. Born in Stranton, County Durham, enlisted in Hull but resident in Middlesborough at the time of enlistment. Son of the late John and Bridget Egan. Commemorated on the Thiepval Memorial.

ELEY, PRIVATE ERNEST. 12/879. Killed in action on May 3rd 1917. Born in Hull. Commemorated on the Arras Memorial.

ELLIS, PRIVATE BENJAMIN. 12/1300. Killed in action on November 13th 1916. Born in Hull. Commemorated on the Thiepval Memorial.

ELLIS, PRIVATE FRANK. 10/1446. Killed in action on May 3rd 1917 aged 20. Born in Hull. Son of Francis and Emma Ellis of 42 Glasgow Street, Hull. Commemorated on the Arras Memorial.

EMBLEY, PRIVATE WILLIAM. 12/426. Killed in action on November 13th 1916. Born in Cottingham, East Yorkshire but resident in Hull. Buried in Euston Road Cemetery.

FAULKNER, SERGEANT HAROLD. 12/1421. Died of wounds on May 9th 1917 aged 25. Taken prisoner May 3rd at Oppy Wood and died at Aachen. Born in Hull. Son of Thomas William and the late Edith Faulkner of Glenhoune, 92 Cottingham Road, Hull. Buried in Cologne Southern Cemetery, Germany.

FARMERY, PRIVATE WILFRED WALDERMAR. 12/1258. Killed in action on November 13th 1916 aged 33. Born in Hull. Son of Thomas Colbridge and Sarah Farmery. Husband of Alice Eleanor Farmery of 86 Clifton Terrace, Courtney Street, Hull. Commemorated on the Thiepval Memorial.

FELL, PRIVATE HARRY. 12/1360. Killed in action on July 21st 1916. Born in Hull. Buried in Rue Du Bacquerot No.1 Military Cemetery, Laventie.

FENTON, LANCE-CORPORAL FRANK. 12/585. Killed in action aged 24, by a shell burst while talking to 2/Lt Taylor who was also killed. Born in Hull. Son of Florence and William Francis Fenton of 105 Severn Street, Hull. Married and father of a two year old boy. Buried in Sucrerie Military Cemetery, Colincamps.

FENTON, PRIVATE JOHN EDWARD. 12/851. Killed in action on May 3rd 1917. Born in Hull. Commemorated on the Arras Memorial.

FENWICK, PRIVATE JAMES WILLIAM LANCELOT. 12/1468. Died of wounds on May 28th 1916 aged 19. Born in Hull. Resident in Bay House, Courtney Street, Hull. Son of Moses and Annie Fenwick. Buried in Gezaincourt Communal Cemetery Extension.

FLETCHER, PRIVATE JOHN WILLIAM. 12/939. Killed in action on September 1st 1916. Born in Hull. Buried in St. Vaast Military Cemetery, Richebourg L'Avouée.

FOSTER, PRIVATE WILFRED. 12/1189. Died of wounds on November 15th 1916 aged 30. Born in Hull. Husband of H A Foster of 7 Florence Avenue, Grange Street, Hull. Buried in Couin British Cemetery.

FREEAR, PRIVATE RICHARD OLIVER. 14/170. Killed in action on November 13th 1916, aged 19. Commemorated on the Thiepval Memorial. Born in Beverley. Son of Charles Freear of Cherry Burton, near Beverley.

FULCHER, PRIVATE FRANK, of 'A' Company. 12/1113. Died of wounds at Merville on July 31st 1916 aged 25. Born in Hull. Son of Emma and the late Joseph Fulcher of 3 Alexandra Avenue, Bridlington Street, Hull. He was engaged to be married to Florrie Sutton. Buried in Merville Communal Cemetery.

GILL, PRIVATE THOMAS, of 'C' Company. 12/862. Died in the UK on November 3rd 1914 aged 24. Buried in Western Cemetery, Hull. Born in Hull. Son of Annie Gill and the late Thomas Gill. Husband of Mabel Rapson (formerly Gill) of 2 Lillian's Terrace, Woodhouse Street Hedon Road. Hull.

GOODFELLOW, PRIVATE HERBERT FREDERICK, of 'D' Company. 12/1341. Killed in action on November 13th 1916 aged 30. Born in Hull. Husband of Theana Goodfellow (nee Palmer) of 18 Wassand Terrace, Strickland Street, Hessie Road, Hull. Buried in Euston Road Cemetery.

GOULDING, PRIVATE JOHN, of 'D' Company. 11/971. Killed in action on November 13th 1916 aged 20. Born in Hull. Son of William Goulding. Buried in Euston Road Cemetery.

GREEN, PRIVATE EDWARD. 12/938. Killed in action on August 16th 1916. Born in Hull. Buried in Le Touret Military Cemetery.

GREEN, PRIVATE WILLIAM. 12/171. Died of wounds on July 5th 1916 aged 21. Adopted son of Mr and Mrs Skinner of 26 Haddon Street, Hawthorn Avenue, Hull. Born in Hull. Buried in St Sever Cemetery. Rouen.

HADLOW, PRIVATE EDWARD ALDRIDGE. of 'A' Company. 12/296. Died of wounds on April 17th 1916 aged 26. Born in Mexborough but resident in Hull. Husband of Jane Fugal Hadlow of 6 Goods Avenue, Buckingham Street, Holderaess Road, Hull. Buried in Beauval Communal Cemetery.

HALL, PRIVATE ARTHUR 12/747. Died on February 5th 1915. Buried in Hull Western Cemetery. Born in Aldershot but resident in Hull.

HALL, PRIVATE GEORGE. 12/518. Killed in action on May 3rd 1917, aged 26. Born in Idle, Yorkshire, enlisted in Hull but resident in Bradford at the time of enlistment. Son of Mary Hamet Voss (formerly Hall) and Fred J Voss (stepfather) of 6 Nelson's Villas. Egton Street Hull. Commemorated on the Arras Memorial.

HALL, PRIVATE JOHN. 12/179. Killed in action on May 27th 1916. Born in Hull. Buried in Sucrerie Military Cemetery, Colincamps.

HARDING, PRIVATE WILLIAM WALTER. 12/2. Died on June 10th 1916 aged 28. Son of the late W Harding and M Neale (formerly Harding). Buried in Western Cemetery, Hull.

HARLAND, PRIVATE JAMES. 12/1172. Killed in action on May 15th 1917. Born in Hull. Commemorated on the Arras Memorial.

HARPER, PRIVATE WILLIAM HERBERT. 14/84. Killed in action on November 13th 1916. Born in Hull. Buried in Euston Road Cemetery.

HARRIS, PRIVATE WALTER. 12/1323. Killed in action on November 13th 1916 aged 33. Son of Mrs Sarah Harris of 41 Pentland Street, North East Valley, Dunedin, New Zealand. Husband of Florence Harris of 11 Mappleton Grove, Preston Road, Hull. Born in Hull. Commemorated on the Thiepval Memorial.

HARRISON, PRIVATE GEORGE. 12/126. Killed in action on May 15th 1917. Born in Hull. Commemorated on the Arras Memorial.

HARRISON, PRIVATE JOSHUA 12/1513. Killed in action on November 13th 1916. Son of Hardisty and Emma Harrison of 86 Goutton Street, Hessie Road, Hull. Born in Bradford but resident in Hull. Commemorated on the Thiepval Memorial.

HARRISON, PRIVATE WILLIAM. 12/589. Died of wounds on June 1st 1916 aged 29. Born in Hartlepool but resident in Hull. Son of George and Emily Harrison. Husband of Gertrude Harrison of 5 Florence Avenue, Grange Street, Hull. Buried in Etaples Military Cemetery.

HART, PRIVATE ROBERT. 12/1148. Killed in action on November 13th 1916 aged 40. Born in Hull. Son of William and Sarah Hart of Hull. Buried in Euston Road Cemetery.

HAWCROFT, PRIVATE HARRY. 12/377. Died on December 18th 1916 aged 33. Buried in Western Cemetery, Spring Bank, Hull.

HAWKINS, PRIVATE ALFRED. 12/1012. Killed in action on August 5th 1916. Born in Hull. Buried in St. Vaast Post Military Cemetery, Richebourg L'Avouée.

HEATH, PRIVATE HARRY. 12/717. Killed in action on May 3rd 1917 aged 32. Born in Hull. Husband of the late Maud Heath. Commemorated on the Arras Memorial.

HEBDEN, PRIVATE HAROLD, of 'C' Company. 12/791. Killed in action on November 13th 1916 aged 20. Husband of Bertha Ward (formerly Hebden) of 39 Exeter Grove, Southcoates Lane, Hull. Born in Welton, East Yorkshire but resident in Hull. Commemorated on the Thiepval Memorial.

HEENAN, PRIVATE EDWARD. 12/1406. Killed in action on November 13th 1916. Born in Goole but resident in Hull. Commemorated on the Thiepval Memorial.

HENDERSON, PRIVATE HARRY. 12/802. Killed in action on November 13th 1916. Born in Leeds but resident in Hull. Commemorated on the Thiepval Memorial.

HENSON, CORPORAL CHARLES WILLIAM. 12/259. Died in France on July 10th 1918. Born in Newington, Yorkshire but resident in Hull.

HICKS, PRIVATE CLARENCE. 12/22. Killed in action on November 13th 1916. Born in New Holland, Lincolnshire but resident in Hull. Commemorated on the Thiepval Memorial.

HICKS, PRIVATE FRANCIS REEVE. 14/153. Died in the UK on January 12th 1917. Born in Hull. Commemorated on the Thiepval Memorial.

HILL, LANCE-CORPORAL JOHN WILLIAM. 14/58. Killed in action on June 12th 1916. Born in Hull. Buried in Sucrerie Military Cemetery, Colincamps.

HIGGINS, PRIVATE JOSEPH WILLIAM. 12/1437. Died of wounds on May 17th 1917 aged 19. Born in Hull. Son of James and Caroline Higgins of 3 Wares Buildings, Stamford Place, Hessle Road, Hull. Buried in Boulogne Eastern Cemetery.

HOBSON, PRIVATE JAMES. 12/999. Killed in action on November 13th 1916. Born in Hull. Commemorated on the Thiepval Memorial.

HODGSON, PRIVATE JOHN AKESTER. 12/378. Died on February 27th 1918. Born in Hull. Buried in Berlin South-Western Cemetery.

HODGSON, PRIVATE WILLIAM HENRY. 12/1333. Killed in action on November 13th 1916 aged 22. Son of Mrs Margaret Hodgson of 6 Hodgson Street, Hull. Born in Hull. Commemorated on the Thiepval Memorial.

HOLLAND, PRIVATE ALFRED. 12/172. Killed in action on June 27th 1916. Born in Willmington but resident in Hull. Commemorated on the Thiepval Memorial.

HOLMES, PRIVATE FRANK HAROLD. 12/1364. Died on March 6th 1919 aged 33. Son of Henry and Annie Elizabeth Holmes. Husband of Beatrice Gertrude Holmes of 9 Malvern Terrace, Gillet Street, Hessie Road, Hull. Buried in Western Cemetery, Spring Bank, Hull.

HOLMES, PRIVATE THOMAS CHRISTIAN. 12/1198. Killed in action on November 13th 1916. Born in Hull. Buried in Euston Road Cemetery.

HORBERRY, PRIVATE HARRY. 12/1152. Killed in action on May 25th 1916. Born in Hull. Buried in Sucrerie Military Cemetery, Colincamps.

HOTCHKIN, PRIVATE ERNEST. 12/1225. Killed in action on November 13th 1916 aged 28. Son of Mark and Minnie Hotchkin of 7 Sophia's Terrace, Spyvee Street, Hull. Born in Hull. Husband of Evelyn Marsden (formerly Hotchkin) of 2 Crofton Avenue, Egton Street, Cleveland Street, Hull. Born in Hull. Commemorated on the Thiepval Memorial.

HOTCHKIN, PRIVATE FRED. 12/1226. Killed in action on November 13th 1916 aged 22. Son of Mark and Minnie Hotchkin of 7 Sophia's Terrace, Spyvee Street, Hull. Born in Hull. Commemorated on the Thiepval Memorial.

HOUGHTON, PRIVATE ALFRED GARLAND. 12/1191. Killed in action on May 25th 1916. Born in Hull. Buried in Sucrerie Military Cemetery. Colincamps. Married with two children. He lived at 2 Lorne Terrace, Lorne Street, Hull. He served in Egypt.

HUDSON, PRIVATE NORRIS ALEXANDER. 12/1212. Killed in action on June 12th 1916. Born in Middlesbrough but resident in Hull. Buried in Sucrerie Military Cemetery, Colincamps.

HUNTLEY, PRIVATE PERCY WALTER. 12/1519. Killed in action on November 13th 1916. Born in Islington, enlisted in Hull but resident in Islington. Commemorated on the Thiepval Memorial.

HUTCHINSON, PRIVATE BENJAMIN WOOD. 12/1456. Killed in action on April 16th 1916. Born in Keighley, Yorkshire, enlisted in Hull but resident in Keighley. Buried in Sucrerie Military Cemetery, Colincamps.

IRVING, PRIVATE WILLIAM. 12/184. Killed in action on May 26th 1916. Born in Thirsk, Yorkshire, enlisted in Hull but resident in Knaresborough. Buried in Sucrerie Military Cemetery, Colincamps.

JACKSON, PRIVATE ARTHUR. 12/940. Killed in action on August 18th 1916 aged 36. Born in North Dalton, East Yorkshire, enlisted in Hull but resident in Driffield. Son of Mrs B Jackson of 10 Queen Street, Driffield, Yorkshire. Buried in Le Touret Military Cemetery.

JACKSON, PRIVATE JAMES ALBERT. 12/1259. Killed in action on November 13th 1916. Born in Hull. Commemorated on the Thiepval Memorial.

JARRETT, PRIVATE OSWIN ARTHUR. 14/13. Killed in action on November 13th 1916. Born in Hull. Commemorated on the Thiepval Memorial.

JARVIS, PRIVATE RICHARD, of 'B' Company. 12/11. Died of wounds on August 17th 1916 aged 36. Born in Hull. Son of Benjamin and Eliza Jarvis of Hull. Husband of Ada Jarvis of 2 Selkirk Street, Newstead Street, Hull. Buried in Chocques Military Cemetery.

JESSOP, PRIVATE WALTER GEORGE. 12/335. Killed in action on November 13th 1916. Born in Hull. Commemorated on the Thiepval Memorial.

JIPSON, PRIVATE HARRY. 10/1351. Killed in action on August 24th 1916 aged 16. Born in Eastrington, East Yorkshire but resident in Hull. Son of Arthur and Emily Jipson of 73 Regent Street, Anlaby Road, Hull. Commemorated on the Loos Memorial.

JOHNSON, PRIVATE ARTHUR. 12/1124. Died on July 19th 1918 aged 29. Husband of Violet Gertrude Johnson of 12 Victoria Terrace, Beeton Street, Holderness Road, Hull. Buried in Western Cemetery, Spring Bank, Hull.

JOHNSON, PRIVATE HAROLD. 12/838. Killed in action on April 16th 1916. Born in Hull. Buried in Sucrerie Military Cemetery. Colincamps.

JOHNSON, SERGEANT SYDNEY WILLIAM HENRY. 12/336. Died of wounds on November 16th 1916 aged 27. Born in Boston, Lincolnshire, enlisted in Hull but resident in Grimsby. Son of James and Emily Johnson of Boston, Lincolnshire. Buried in Corbie Communal Cemetery Extension.

JOHNSTON, LANCE-CORPORAL CLAUDE. 12/1006. Killed in action on May 3rd 1917 aged 25. Born in Hull but resident in Goole at the time of enlistment. Son of Sam Johnston of 53 Clifton Gardens, Goole, Yorkshire. Commemorated on the Arras Memorial.

JONES, PRIVATE PERCIVAL 12/49. Killed in action on May 27th 1916 aged 40. Father of Mr. P T Jones of 4 Moylan Road, Hammersmith, London. Born in Egremont, Cumberland but resident in Hull. Buried in Sucrerie Military Cemetery, Colincamps.

KING, PRIVATE WILLIAM. 12/745. Died on July 12th 1916. Stepbrother of Mrs A Watson of 2 Adelaide Street, Scott Street, Hull. Buried in Western Cemetery, Spring Bank, Hull.

KIRKWOOD, PRIVATE ERNEST WILLIAM. 12/733. Killed in action on May 3rd 1917 aged 20. Born in Hull. Son of Annie Hardman (formerly Kirkwood) and Joseph Hardman (Stepfather) of 9 Caroline Place, Charles Street, Hull. Commemorated on the Arras Memorial.

KNOWLES, PRIVATE LAWRENCE. 12/43. Killed in action on November 13th 1916. Born in Hull. Buried in Euston Road Cemetery.

LARVIN, PRIVATE THOMAS HENRY. 12/783. Killed in action on November 13th 1916 aged 29. Son of Mrs Ann Larvin of 1 Ann's Place, Marlborough Crescent, Norfolk Street, Hull. Born in Hull. Commemorated on the Thiepval Memorial.

LAUGHTON, PRIVATE SAMUEL 11/1088. Killed in action on November 13th 1916. Born in Hull. Buried in Euston Road Cemetery.

LEE, PRIVATE JOHN SEYMOUR. 12/1451. Killed in action on November 13th 1916 aged 19. Born in Hull. Son of John and Mary Alice Lee of Hull. Buried in Euston Road Cemetery.

LEWIS, PRIVATE WILLIAM. 12/1058. Killed in action on August 6th 1916. Born in Hull. Buried in St. Vaast Post Military Cemetery, Richebourg L'Avouée.

LOWTHER, PRIVATE HERBERT SPENCE. 12/881. Killed in action on November 13th 1916 aged 29. Born in Hull. Son of Joseph Lowther. Husband of Elizabeth Ellen Jackson (formerly Lowther) of 43 Eastbourne Street, Hessle Road, Hull. Buried in Euston Road Cemetery.

LUN, LANCE-CORPORAL GEORGE HENRY. 12/250. Killed in action on April 14th 1916. Born in Usworth, County Durham but resident in Hull. Buried in Sucrerie Military Cemetery, Colincamps.

MARLOW, CORPORAL FREDERICK RICHARDSON. 12/391. Killed in action on October 24th 1916 aged 34. Born in Hull. Husband of Beatrice White (formerly Marlow) of 6 Goulton Street, Hessle Road, Hull. Buried in Hebuterae Military Cemetery.

MARTIN, PRIVATE GEORGE WILLIAM. 12/711. Killed in action on May 27th 1916. Born in Hull. Buried in Sucrerie Military Cemetery, Colincamps.

MATHER, PRIVATE FRANK. 14/244. Killed in action on November 13th 1916 aged 21. Born in Hull. Son of Robert John and Elizabeth Mather of 23 Ripon Grove, Brunswick Avenue, Beverley Road, Hull. Buried in Euston Road Cemetery.

McDONALD, SERGEANT ANGUS. 12/211. Killed in action on May 3rd 1917 aged 24. Born in Hull. Son of Angus and Harriet McDonald of Hull. Husband of Florence Kate McDonald of 8 Herbert's Terrace.

McDONALD, PRIVATE JAMES. 12/800. Killed in action on November 13th 1916. Born in York, enlisted in Hull but resident in York at the time of enlistment. Commemorated on the Thiepval Memorial.

McGOWAN, PRIVATE DANIEL. 12/828. Killed in action on November 13th 1916 aged 30. Husband of Ellen McGowan of 88 Westminster Avenue, Holderness Road, Hull. Born in Hull. Commemorated on the Thiepval Memorial.

McKEE, LANCE-CORPORAL GEORGE of 'B' Company. 12/991. Killed in action on April 12th 1916 near Colincamps aged 25. Born in Hull. Son of G.W. and Clara McKee. Lived with his wife Nellie McKee (nee Rutter) at 7 Perth Street, Hull. He was a bus conductor on the Anlaby Road route. His wife went to live at 21 Arthur Street, Withernsea, East Yorkshire after his death. His name is on the Withernsea War Memorial. Buried in Sucrerie Military Cemetery, Colincamps.

McKENZIE, PRIVATE DONALD. 10/1097. Died in France on August 6th 1916. Born in Hull but was resident in Harrogate. Buried in St. Vaast Post Military Cemetery, Richebourg L'Avouée.

McMANUS, PRIVATE EDWARD, of 'C' Company. 12/930. Killed in action on November 13th 1916 aged 21. Son of Cornelius and Rose McManus. Born in Hull. Commemorated on the Thiepval Memorial.

MEE, PRIVATE GEORGE. Died on April 13th 1921 aged 32. Brother-in-law of Mrs Kate Grundy of 60 Rugby Street, Hessle Road, Hull. Buried in Western Cemetery, Spring Bank, Hull.

MILLS, PRIVATE JOHN WALTER. 12/963. Killed in action on August 19th 1916. Born in St. Pancras but resident in Hull. Buried in Le Touret Military Cemetery.

MILNER, LANCE-CORPORAL WILLIAM. 12/302. Killed in action on February 25th 1917 aged 19. Son of Edward and Hannah E Milner of 4 Granville Terrace. Studland Street, Hull. Born in Hull. Buried in Sailly-au-Bois Military Cemetery.

MOWER, PRIVATE HENRY. 14/66. Killed in action on November 13th 1916. Born in Hull. Buried in Euston Road Cemetery.

MORLEY, SERGEANT CHARLES FREDERICK. 12/53. Killed in action on November 13th 1916. Born in Hull. Commemorated on the Thiepval Memorial.

MORRISON, PRIVATE WILLIAM LEONARD. 13/366. Died of wounds on November 20th 1916. Born in Hull. Buried in Ontario Cemetery. Sains-les-Marquion.

MOULDS, PRIVATE ALFRED, of 'B' Company. 12/231. Killed in action on May 3rd 1917 aged 29. Born in Hull. Son of Charles and Hilda Moulds of 67 Brunswick Avenue, Hull. Husband of Alice Moulds of 1 Alexandra Avenue, Bridlington Street, Hull. Commemorated on the Arras Memorial.

NEAL, SERGEANT WILFRED WAKELIN. 12/311. Killed in action on November 13th 1916 aged 23. Born in Hull. Son of Oswald and Alice Neal of 28 Redbourne Street, Hull. Buried in Euston Road Cemetery.

NEALL, PRIVATE GEORGE, of 'A' Company. 12/842. Killed in action on May 3rd 1917 aged 32. Born in Killingholme, Yorkshire but resident in Hull. Son of Vincent and Emma Neall of Frederick's Terrace, Nornabell Street, Hull. Husband of Mary Neall of 13

Victoria Road, Driffield, East Yorkshire. Commemorated on the Arras Memorial.

NESS, PRIVATE FRED. 12/127. Killed in action on November 13th 1916. Born in Hull. Buried in Euston Road Cemetery.

NEWSON, PRIVATE THOMAS. 12/1146. Killed in action on August 16th 1916. Born in Hull. Buried in Le Touret Military Cemetery.

NORTH, PRIVATE JAMES SIDNEY, of 'B' Company. 12/1384. Died of wounds on July 20th 1916 aged 22. Born in Hull. Son of James and Alice North of Hull. Husband of Elizabeth Mallory (formerly North) of 42, Garden Village, Holderness Road, Hull. Buried in Merville Communal Cemetery.

OXENDALE, PRIVATE HERBERT. 12/456. Killed in action on November 13th 1916. Born in Beverley and resident at 3, Spencer Street. Commemorated on the Thiepval Memorial.

PAGET, PRIVATE FREDERICK. 12/1522. Killed in action on August 6th 1916 aged 28. Son of John and Rebecca Pagett of 11 Oriental Street, Wesley Road, Armley, Leeds. Born in Armley, Yorkshire but resident in Hull. Buried in St. Vaast Post Military Cemetery, Richebourg L'Avouée.

PARK, CORPORAL EDWARD. 12/1177. Killed in action on May 3rd 1917 aged 20. Born in Hull. Son of Mrs Mary W Park of 70 Nornabell Street, Holderness Road, Hull. Commemorated on the Arras Memorial.

PARR, PRIVATE THOMAS. 14/109. Died of wounds on January 25th 1918. Born in Newport but resident in Hull. Son of Mr. F W Parr of 3 North Street, Wetherby, Yorkshire. Buried in Anzin-St. Aubin British Cemetery.

PEARSON, PRIVATE THOMAS EDWARD. 12/410. Killed in action on November 13th 1916. Born in Goole, enlisted in Hull but resident in Goole.

PINDER, PRIVATE STANLEY. 14/217. Killed in action on November 13th 1916. Born in Hull. Commemorated on the Thiepval Memorial.

PULLINGER, PRIVATE THOMAS. 12/323. Killed in action on November 13th 1916. Born in St. George's, Middlesex but resident in Hull. Commemorated on the Thiepval Memorial.

RICHARDSON, PRIVATE C. 12/433. Died on January 21st 1920. Buried in Rawcliffe (St. James) Churchyard, Yorkshire.

RICHES, PRIVATE WILLIAM. 12/481. Killed in action on May 27th 1916. Born in Neatishead, Norwich, enlisted in Hull but resident in Neatishead.

RIDER, PRIVATE WALTER REGINALD. 12/1372. Died of wounds on August 30th 1916 aged 22. Born in Hull. Son of Alice and Charles Aubrey Penny (Stepfather) of 3 Park Avenue, Haddon Street, Hull. Buried in Chocques Military Cemetery.

ROBINSON, PRIVATE CHARLES OLIVER. 12/110. Killed in action on November 13th 1916 aged 22. Born in Hessle but resident in Hull. Son of Mr and Mrs. J A Robinson of 18 Salisbury Street, Hessle, Yorkshire. Buried in Euston Road Cemetery.

ROBINSON, PRIVATE ERNEST VICTOR. 12/148. Killed in action on November 13th 1916 aged 24. Born in Hessle but resident in Hull. Husband of Hannah Robinson of 4 Rosehill Road, Rawmarsh, Rotherham. Buried in Euston Road Cemetery.

ROGERS, PRIVATE JOSEPH WILLIAM. 12/1429. Died of heart failure on October 23rd 1918 aged 37. Husband of the late Helen Ryan (formerly Rogers). Buried in Western Cemetery, Spring Bank, Hull.

ROO, PRIVATE ARTHUR, MM. 12/869. Died of wounds on June 30th 1916, aged 30. Born in Bradford, enlisted in Hull but resident in Bradford. Son of George Edwin and Eva Roo of Bradford. Buried in Doullens Communal Cemetery Extension.

ROWBOTTOM, PRIVATE SAMUEL. 12/417. Killed in action on November 8th 1917. Born in Goole but resident in Hull. Commemorated on the Arras Memorial.

RUDD, PRIVATE FREDERICK. 12/761. Killed in action on May 7th 1916. Born in Hull. Buried in Sucrerie Military Cemetery, Colincamps.

RUSHTON, CORPORAL WILLIAM ARTHUR. 12/267. Killed in action on November 13th 1916 aged 24. Born in Hull. Son of William and the late Annie Rushton of Hull. Husband of Daisy May Rushton of 6 Colenso Avenue, Edinburgh Street, Hull. Buried in Euston Road Cemetery.

SAVAGE, LANCE-CORPORAL FRED. 12/337. Killed in action on November 13th 1916. Born in Hull. Commemorated on the Thiepval Memorial.

SCOTT, SERGEANT CLAUDE. 12/511. Killed in action on November 13th 1916. Born in Wakefield, enlisted in Hull but resident in Barnsley. Buried in Euston Road Cemetery.

SEARBY, PRIVATE FREDERICK. 12/543. Killed in action on November 13th 1916 aged 30. Born in Hull. Son of Mr and Mrs F K Searby of Hull. Husband of L G Carr (formerly Searby) of 5 Ivy Villas, Franklin Street, Hull. Buried in Euston Road Cemetery.

SELLE, PRIVATE GEORGE FREDERICK. 12/1835. Killed in action on November 13th 1916. Born in Hull. Buried in Euston Road Cemetery.

SERGEANT, PRIVATE ROBERT. 12/1512. Killed in action on November 13th 1916 aged 27. Son of Mrs R Sergeant of Cliffe Fields Cottages, Selby, Yorkshire. Born in Hull. Commemorated on the Thiepval Memorial.

SHEA, PRIVATE GEORGE AUGUSTUS. 12/809. Killed in action on November 13th 1916 aged 19. Born in Hull. Son of Alfred Thomas and Louisa Ellis Shea of 2 Bond Street, Hull. Buried in Euston Road Cemetery.

SHEPERDSON, SERGEANT HARRY. 12/482. Died of wounds on November 5th 1917 aged 27. Born in Hull. Husband of Ethel Sheperdson of 9 Amys Terrace, Ferries Street, Hedon Road, Hull. Buried in Duisans British Cemetery.

SHORES, PRIVATE HERBERT SEPTIMUS EASTWOOD. 12/1497. Killed in action on November 13th 1916 aged 21. Born in Hull. Brother of Mrs. Alice Marion Blain of 187 Somerset Street, Hull. Buried in Euston Road Cemetery.

SKELTON, PRIVATE HARRY. 12/1518. Killed in action on August 19th 1916. Born in Hull. Buried in Le Touret Military Cemetery.

SMITH, CORPORAL HARRY. 13/1300. Died of wounds on November 17th 1916. Born in Ovington, Essex but resident in Hull. Buried in Ontario Cemetery, Sains-Les-Marquion.

SMITH, PRIVATE RICHARD ALFRED. 12/1328. Killed in action on May 27th 1916. Born in Hull. Buried in Sucrerie Military Cemetery, Colincamps.

SMITH, CORPORAL THOMAS EDWARD. 12/77. Killed in action on November 13th 1916. Born in Chelsea but resident in Hull. Commemorated on the Thiepval Memorial.

SMITH, PRIVATE WILLIAM BERTRAM. 12/1104. Killed in action on November 13th 1916. Born in Leeds but resident in Hull. Buried in Euston Road Cemetery.

SOWERBY, PRIVATE FREDERICK. 12/1044. Died of wounds on November 25th 1916 aged 39. Son of Alison Sowerby. Husband of Mary Ann Sowerby of 3 Sarah Ann's Terrace, Spyvee Street, Hull. Buried in Hedon Road Cemetery, Hull.

SPENCER, PRIVATE HARRY. 12/841. Killed in action on May 26th 1916. Born in Buckhurst Hill, Essex, enlisted in Hull but resident in Forest Gate, Essex. Buried in Sucrerie Military Cemetery, Colincamps.

SPENCER, PRIVATE WILLIAM HENRY. 12/946. Killed in action on November 13th 1916, aged 41. Born in Hull. Buried in Euston Road Cemetery, Colincamps.

SPOONS, LANCE-CORPORAL MAURICE KNOWLES. 10/359. Killed in action on November 13th 1916 aged 19. Son of Ernest Ashton and Mary Elizabeth Spikins of 7 Gladstone Street, Hull. Born in Hull. Commemorated on the Thiepval Memorial.

STATHERS, PRIVATE WILLIAM HENRY. 12/72. Killed in action on November 13th 1916 aged 28. Husband of Gertrude Stathers of 50 St. Mark Street, Hull. Born in Hull. Commemorated on the Thiepval Memorial.

STEELE, PRIVATE JOSEPH WILLIAM. 12/735. Killed in action on January 6th 1918. Born in Goole but resident in Hull. Buried in Roclincourt Military Cemetery.

STOKER, PRIVATE ROBERT, 12/763. Died of wounds on May 26th 1916. Born in Jarrow-on-Tyne, enlisted in Hull but resident in Jarrow-on-Tyne. Buried in Sucrerie Military Cemetery, Colincamps.

SUGARMAN, PRIVATE SOLOMON. 10/1331. Killed in action on August 15th 1916 aged 21. Born in Hull. Son of M Sugarman of Hull. Buried in Cabaret-Rouge British Cemetery.

TACEY, PRIVATE CHARLES WILLIAM. 12/1386. Died of wounds on May 14th 1917. Born in Hull. Buried in Aubigny Communal Cemetery-Extension.

TARUNG, PRIVATE GEORGE WILLIAM. 12/903. Killed in action on November 13th 1916 aged 40. Born in Gloucester but resident in Hull. Son of Edwin and Emma Tarung. Buried in Euston Road Cemetery, Colincamps.

TASKER, PRIVATE HAROLD. 13/1414. Killed in action on May 3rd 1917 aged 19. Born in Malton but resident in Driffield. Son of John and Jane Elizabeth Tasker of 35 Washington Street, Driffield, East Yorkshire. Commemorated on the Arras Memorial.

TAYLOR, PRIVATE HENRY WRIGHT. 12/894. Died on March 25th 1919 aged 37 after being discharged from the army. Son of William and Mary Taylor of 14 Lime Terrace, Crowle Street, Hedon Road, Hull. Born in Walkington, near Beverley, East Yorkshire. Buried in Hedon Road Cemetery, Hull.

TOCK, PRIVATE HAROLD WILLIAM. 12/1501. Killed in action on May 27th 1916. Born in Brough, East Yorkshire but resident in Hull. Buried in Sucrerie Military Cemetery, Colincamps.

TOLCHARD, PRIVATE WILLIAM DANIEL. 13/1467. Died of wounds on December 4th 1916 aged 37. Born in Hull. Son of Henry Ponsonby and Louise Tolchard. Husband of Lilian Tolchard of 4 Park Road, Beverley Road, Hull. Buried in Etaples Military Cemetery.

TURNBULL, PRIVATE WILSON. 14/199. Killed in action on November 13th 1916. Son of Mr T Turnbull of the Laurels, Hedon, East Yorkshire. Born in Hedon. East Yorkshire but resident in Hull. Commemorated on the Thiepval Memorial.

VOWLES, LANCE-CORPORAL FRANCIS KISH GUY. 12/1487. Died in France on July 25th 1916. Born in Barrow Guemey. Somerset, enlisted in Hull but resident in Barrow Guerney. Buried in St. Vaast Post Military Cemetery, Richebourg L'Avouée.

WALES, PRIVATE WILLIAM STOTE, of 'D' Company. 12/568. Killed in action on November 13th 1916 aged 25. Buried in Euston Road Cemetery. Born in Hull. Son of Richardson Stole and Sarah Ann Wales of 7, Georges Avenue, Lake Street, Hull.

WALLACE, SERGEANT JAMES WATSON, of 'D' Company. 12/1353. Killed in action on May 3rd 1917 aged 24. Commemorated on the Arras Memorial.

Born in Hull. Son of J.W Wallace of 40, Newbridge Road, Hull.

WARNES, PRIVATE ROBERT HOPE. 12/1181. Killed in action on October 13th 1917 aged 21. Son of Robert and Annie Warnes of Earle's Cottages, East Halton, Lincolnshire. Born in Helensburgh. Fifeshire, enlisted in Hull but resident in Killingholme, Grimsby. Buried in Roclincourt Military Cemetery.

WATERS, PRIVATE ALEXANDER PRESTON. 12/772. Killed in action on May 3rd 1917 aged 22. Commemorated on the Arras Memorial. Born in Hull. Son of Mrs. Kate Kingston of 51 Hedon Road, Hull.

WHITE, PRIVATE LEONARD. 12/129. Killed in action on May 27th 1916. Buried in Sucrerie Military Cemetery, Colincamps. Born in Hull.

WHITEHEAD, PRIVATE STANLEY. 12/396. Killed in action on May 3rd 1917. Commemorated on the Arras Memorial. Born in Hull.

WHITFIELD, PRIVATE EDWIN. 12/406. Died of wounds at Le Treport Hospital on May 20th 1916 aged 35. Buried in Le Treport Military Cemetery. Born in Hull. Son of Edwin and Rebecca Whitfield. He was married and had one child. Before the war he worked for the NER as a Rulleyman in Hull. His name appears on the NER Roll of Honour.

WILES, PRIVATE THOMAS. 12/706. Killed in action on January 2nd 1918. Son of Matthew Wiles of Water End, Holme-on-Spalding Moor. Born in Holme-on-Spalding Moor, enlisted in Hull but resident in Holme-on-Spalding Moor. Buried in Berlin South-Western Cemetery.

WILKINSON, THOMAS HARGREAVE. 12/1196. Died of wounds on May 23rd 1917 aged 37. Buried in Duisans Cemetery. Born in Goole but resident in Hull. Husband of Sarah Ellen (Nellie) Smith (formerly Wilkinson) of 19, Chestnut Avenue, Buckingham Street, Holderness Road, Hull.

WILSON, PRIVATE HAROLD. 12/493. Died of wounds on April 18th 1918 aged 23, while attached to the 31st Battalion Machine Gun Corps. Buried in Etaples Cemetery. Born in Hull. Son of Albert and Elizabeth Wilson of 48 Raywell Street, Hull.

WILSON, LANCE-CORPORAL WALTER. 12/189. Killed in action on November 13th 1916. Born in Hull. Commemorated on the Thiepval Memorial.

WOGDEN, PRIVATE HENRY. 12/112. Killed in action on November 13th 1916 aged 37. Commemorated on the Thiepval Memorial. Born in Hull. Husband of Alice Wogden and Children.

WOLLAS, PRIVATE GEORGE HERBERT. MM. 12/1526. Killed in action on November 13th 1916. Born in Cottingham, East Yorkshire. Enlisted in Hull but resident in Cottingham. Commemorated on the Thiepval Memorial.

WOODALL, PRIVATE AMBROSE NEWTON. 12/238. Died of wounds on May 13th 1916 aged 29.

Born in Chorlton-cum-Hardy, Lancashire. Son of Emily Ann Petler (formerly Woodall) of 51 Richmond Street, Hull and the late Ambrose Parker Woodall. Buried in Baeuval Communal Cemetery.

WOODS, SERGEANT ERNEST WILLIAM, of 'A' Company. 12/297. Killed in action on May 26th 1916 aged 36. Buried in Sucrerie Military Cemetery, Colincamps. Born in Hull but resident in North Ferriby at the time of his enlistment. Son of Thomas and Matilda Woods of Hull. Husband of Annie Jeanette Woods of 1 Humber Road, North Ferriby near Hull.

WOOLLER, PRIVATE WILLIAM. 12/1516. Died of wounds November 24th 1916 aged 39. Buried in Boulogne Eastern Cemetery. Born in Hull. Husband of Katie Annie Wooller of 4 Holderness Avenue, Hyde Park, Leeds.

WOOMBLE, PRIVATE ALBERT DALE, of 'D' Company. 12/1103. Died on May 28th 1916, aged 20, of wounds caused by a shell burst. He was a member of the Lewis Gun detachment. Buried in Beauval Communal Cemetery. Born in Hull. Son of James and Meady Woomble of 11 Lockwood Street, Hull. His father also served in the East Yorkshire Regiment stationed at High Horton. "You will have no doubt already heard of the death of your son, Pte A. D. Woomble, of this battalion. Please accept my deepest sympathy with you and yours at this time. I was deeply shocked when I heard that he had died in hospital. His wounds were caused by the bursting of an enemy shell in the part of the trench where he was standing. He was conveyed to the dressing station as quickly as possible, during which passage he showed wonderful courage and pluck, never once complaining. I can assure you that, with your son's death, my Lewis Machine Gun Detachment has lost one of its best and most cheerful members. From the first he has tried hard, and taken keen interest in his work, and I have always considered him one of the most reliable men in my command". (From a letter by his officer printed in the *Hull Times*)

WOYEN, PRIVATE CHRISTOPHER REUBEN. 12/724. Killed in action on September 25th 1916. Buried in St. Vaast Post Military Cemetery, Richebourg L'Avouée. Born in Hull.

WRIDE, PRIVATE GEORGE. 11/387. Killed in action on November 13th 1916. Born in Bermondsey but resident in Hull at the time of enlistment. He had been a tram conductor for five years. Married to Marion Wride. He had two sons. Commemorated on the Thiepval Memorial.

WRIGHT, PRIVATE FREEMAN. 12/1295. Killed in action on November 13th 1916, aged 40. Born in East Halton, Lincolnshire, but resident in Hull. Son of George and Maria Wright. Buried in Euston Road Cemetery.

WRIGHT, PRIVATE THOMAS McMORRAN. 12/1215. Died of wounds on April 18th 1916. Buried in Beauval Communal Cemetery. Born in Hull. Married with one child. He lived in Durham Street, Hull.

13TH BATTALION

AKRILL, PRIVATE JOHN ESAU, of 'D' Company. 13/591. Died of wounds on November 19th 1916, aged 35. Buried in Boulogne Eastern Cemetery. Born in Beverley. Husband of Violet M. Hewson (formerly Akrill) of 69, Walcott Street, Hull. He was a father.

ALLATT, PRIVATE CYRIL JOHN PEASEGOOD. 13/546. Died of wounds on May 26th 1916, aged 23. Buried in Beauval Communal Cemetery. Born in Adelaide, Australia. Husband of Ellen Allatt of 8, Holborn Street. Witham, Hull.

ALLEN, PRIVATE WILFRED. 13/942. Killed in action on November 13th 1916, aged 27. Buried in Euston Road Cemetery. Born in Hull. Son of Mrs C. Allen of 95 St. Paul's Street, Hull.

ALLMAN, PRIVATE GEORGE. 13/2. Killed in action on November 13th. 1916, aged 29. Commemorated on the Thiepval Memorial. Born in Hull. One of four children.

ALLON, PRIVATE WILLIAM GEORGE. 13/1273. Killed in action on November 13th 1916. Commemorated on the Thiepval Memorial. Born in Hull. Son of Mr and Mrs Allon of 115 Waterloo Street, Hull. He was a married man, residing at 29 North Street, Hull.

ANDREWS, COMPANY QUARTERMASTER SERGEANT HAROLD. 13/5. Killed in action on August 26th 1916, aged 22. Born in Hull. Buried in Le Touret Military Cemetery. Son of John and Kate Andrews of 3. Holmes Street, Beech Street, Hull. His name appears on the Clifton Street School Roll of Honour.

ARMSTRONG, PRIVATE MARK. 13/9. Killed in action on November 13th 1916. Commemorated on the Thiepval Memorial. Born in Hutton Ambro.

ASHLEY, ACTING LANCE-CORPORAL EDWARD ALBERT. 13/589. Died of wounds on May 8th 1916, aged 39. Buried in Gezaincourt Communal Cemetery Extension. Born in Hull. Husband of Ada Ashley and children of 18, Southcoates Lane, Holderness Road, Hull. His name appears on the Holy Trinity Church Roll of Honour for the Free Gardeners Friendly Society, Hull District.

ASPINALL, CORPORAL WILLIAM, DCM. 13/310. Killed in action on November 13th 1916. Buried in Euston Road Cemetery. Born in Bolton but resident in Hull at the time of enlistment

ATKIN, SERGEANT FRED. 13/14. Killed in action on November 13th 1916, aged 24. Born in Hull. Son of James and Ada Atkin of 4 Hutt Street, Hull. He was employed as a clerk for the passenger section of the North Eastern Railway in Hull. His name appears on the North Eastern Railway Roll of Honour. Buried in Euston Road Cemetery.

ATTWOOD, SERGEANT ROBERT. 13/896. Killed in action on July 16th 1916. Born in Motherwell, Lanarkshire but resident in Hull. Buried in Rue-du-Bacquerot No 1 Military Cemetery, Laventie.

AUSTIN, GEORGE HENRY. 13/1043. Killed in action on November 13th 1916, aged 29. Buried in Luke Copse British Cemetery. Born in Barton in Lincolnshire. Son of R. Austin of 15 Tennyson Avenue, Ferries Street, Hull. One of four brothers who served in the Great War. Husband of Alice M. Austin of 6, Clarence Avenue, St. Mark's Street, Hull. His only child, Margaret, died on February 9th 1918 aged 4 years and 5 months.

BAILEY, CORPORAL PERCY. 13/17. Signaller in 'A' Company. Killed in action on November 13th 1916 aged 20. Commemorated on the Thiepval Memorial. Born in Hull. Son of George and Sarah Elizabeth Bailey of 29 St. Paul Street, Hull.

BAKER, PRIVATE CHARLES WILFORD, OF 'C' Company. 13/897. Died of sickness on March 6th 1915 aged 24. Son of Charles Baker of Hull. Husband of Ruth Esther Miller (formerly Baker) of 49 Eton Road, Stockton-on-Tees. Buried in Holy Trinity Cemetery, Hessle Road, Hull.

BANKS, PRIVATE CHARLES EDWIN (known as Ted). 13/780. Killed in action on August 6th 1916 aged 19. Buried in St. Vaast Post Military Cemetery, Richebourg L'Avouée. Born in Hull. Son of Zachariah Dawson and Eleanor Banks of 1 Floral Avenue, Edinburgh Street, Hessle Road, Hull. His brother Harold was in the 4th East Yorkshires and was taken prisoner on May 27th 1918, dying on November 18th 1918 in Germany.

BARKER, PRIVATE COLIN EDWARD. 13/804. Died of wounds on December 2nd 1916 while a POW. Born in Hull. Buried in Berlin South-Western Cemetery.

BARNABY, PRIVATE MATTHEW. 13/15. Killed in action on November 13th 1916 aged 21. Son of Benjamin and Emily J Barnaby of Barton-on-Humber. Born in Barrow-on Humber but resident in Hull. Buried in Queens Cemetery, Puiseux.

BARNBY, LANCE-CORPORAL HAROLD, of 'A' Company. 13/1379. Killed in action on November 13th 1916 aged 21. Commemorated on the Thiepval Memorial. Born in Hull. Son of Thomas and Sophia Annie Barnby of 28 Sharp Street, Newland Avenue, Hull. Before the war he had been a GPO employee for seven years.

BARRETT, PRIVATE HARRY STANLEY. 13/34. Killed in action on November 13th 1916. Buried in Euston Road Cemetery. Born in Hull. He lived at 89 Thoresby Street, Hull.

BEANLAND, CORPORAL HENRY. 13/38. Killed in action on November 13th 1916 aged 23. Commemorated on the Thiepval Memorial. Born in Bradford but resident in Hull. Husband of Ellen Beanland of 5 Grove Terrace, Courtney Street, Hull.

BELL, PRIVATE CHARLES. 14/213. Killed in action on November 13th 1916. Buried in Euston Road Cemetery. Born in Louth, Lincolnshire but resident in Hull. Before the attack a few men were required to stay behind to form a cadre for the new drafts coming in should the battalion be destroyed. A coin was tossed to decide whether Pte. Bell or Pte. Surfleet stayed. Pte. Surfleet won and Pte. Bell went into action on the 13th.

BETTINSON, PRIVATE JOHN HENRY (known as Jack). 13/19. Killed in action on November 13th 1916. Buried in Euston Road Cemetery. Born in Hull. Son of William Bettinson of 1 Goodwin Terrace, Goodwin Street, Hull. His brother William died of wounds on May 12th 1917.

BETTS, PRIVATE JOSEPH WILLIAM (known as Joel). 13/1047. Killed in action on July 20th 1916 aged 27. Buried in Rue-Du-Bacquerot No. 1 Military Cemetery, Laventie. Born in Hull. Husband of Lily Betts and father of one son, both resident at 1 Hannah's Terrace, Spyvee Street, Hull.

BETTS, PRIVATE WILLIAM. 13/598. Killed in action on November 13th 1916. Buried in Euston Road Cemetery. Born in Hull. He was a porter/operator for the NER at Sculcoates, Hull. His name is on the NER Roll of Honour. Buried in Rue-Du-Bacquerot No 1 Military Cemetery, Laventie.

BLENKINSOP, PRIVATE ALBERT. 13/40. Killed in action on September 18th 1917 aged 22. Buried in Roclincourt Military Cemetery. Born in Hull. Son of Mr. B and Mrs A. Blenkinsop of 78 Nicholson Street, Hull.

BODFIELD, PRIVATE ALBERT EDWARD. 13/677. Died in the UK on February 25th 1916 aged 36. Buried in Western Cemetery, Hull. Born in Hull. Son of the late William and Mary Bodfield of Hull. Husband of Susannah Bodfield of 24 Oxford Street, Scarborough. He was a father.

BOOTH, PRIVATE ERNEST WILLIAM. 13/1193. Killed in action on November 13th 1916 aged 23. Buried in Euston Road Cemetery. Born in Hull. He was married to Marie Booth and was a father. His brother served in France and survived the war.

BOSTOCK, PRIVATE FRANCES HENRY. 13/947. Killed in action on November 13th 1916 aged 20. Buried in Euston Road Cemetery. Born in Doncaster but resident in Hull. He lived at 40 Field Street, Hull.

BRADY, PRIVATE WILLIAM NICHOLAS. 13/503. He was a signaller. Killed in action on November 13th 1916 aged 20. Commemorated on the Thiepval Memorial. Born in Hull. Son of George Edward and Hannah Brady of 33 Scott Street, Hull. Employed before the war by the NER as an assistant signaller in Hull. His name appears on the NER Roll of Honour.

BROCK, PRIVATE JOSEPH HENRY. 13/46. Killed in action on April 29th 1917 aged 26. Buried in Albuera Cemetery. Born in Hull. Son of Joseph Thomas and Mary Elizabeth Brock of 277 Wincolmlee, Hull. Husband of Ethel Brock (nee Townend) and father of two children all resident at 10 Albert's Terrace, Green Lane, Hull.

BROOKS, PRIVATE CHARLES HENRY of A Company. 13/949. Died of wounds, caused by gassing, on May 6th 1918 aged 36. Son of Thomas and Ellen Brooks of Grimsby. Husband of the late Selina Brooks. Buried in Hedon Road Cemetery, Hull.

BROWN, PRIVATE ADRIAN. 13/44. Died on March 5th 1919 aged 30. Buried in Hedon Road Cemetery, Hull. Husband of Emma Brown of 2 Scarborough Terrace, Barnsley Street, Holderness Road, Hull.

BROWN, SERGEANT JOHN. 13/602. Killed in action on November 13th 1916. Buried in Porte-de-Paris Cemetery. Born in Hull.

BROWN, PRIVATE JOHN WILLIAM. 13/1333. Killed in action on November 13th 1916 aged 20. Commemorated on the Thiepval Memorial. Born in Hull. Enlisted January 1915. Son of John Horton and Mary Ellen Brown of 31 Barnsley Street, Hull. Employed before the war by Hull Skin and Hide Market of Finkle Street, Hull.

BUFFET, LANCE-CORPORAL ALBERT EDWARD, of A Company. 13/1380. Killed in action on November 13th 1916 aged 23. Commemorated on the Thiepval Memorial. Born in Hull. Son of William H. and Elizabeth Buffet of 99 De Grey Street, Hull.

CARRICK, PRIVATE ARTHUR, of 'A' Company. 13/904. Killed in action on November 13th 1916 aged 22. Born in Upper Holloway. Middlesex but resident in Hull. Son of Henry Kilvington and Alice Carrick of Easington, East Yorkshire. Buried in Euston Road Cemetery.

CATTERALL, PRIVATE HARRY. 14/155. Killed in action on November 13th 1916 aged 21. Born in Preston, Lancashire but resident in Hull. Son of Anne Chapman (formerly Catterall) and the late James Catterall of 6 Newport Street, Nelson, Lancashire. Commemorated on the Thiepval Memorial.

CAWKWELL, PRIVATE WALTER THOMAS. 13/55. Killed in action on August 23rd 1916 by a piece of shrapnel aged 23. Born in Hull. Son of Thomas Cawkwell of 6 Fern Avenue, Fern Street. Hull. Buried in St. Vaast Post Military Cemetery, Richebourg L'Avouée.

CHESTER, SERGEANT REGINALD JAMES. 13/57. Killed in action on November 13th 1916 aged 28. Born in Hull. Son of James and Annie Chester of Hull.

Husband of Gladys Enid Chester of 63 Bannister Street, Withernsea. Buried in Queens Cemetery, Puiseux. He had three children.

CLATER, PRIVATE JAMES THOMAS. 13/1195. Killed in action on January 27th 1918. Born in Hull. Husband of Annie Clater and father of seven children. Resided at 6 Crossland Avenue, Holland Street, Hull. Buried in Roclincourt Military Cemetery.

CLINTON, PRIVATE GEORGE WILLIAM. 13/766. Signaller in 'D' Company. Died of sickness in Garforth War Hospital on December 12th 1918 aged 33. Enlisted on November 5th 1914. Born in Hull. Son of Charles Edward and Elizabeth Clinton. Husband of Fanny Chilton and father of one son. He resided at 15 Florence Avenue, Cave Street, Hull. Buried in Western Cemetery, Hull.

COLLINS, CORPORAL ARTHUR. 13/324. Killed in action on November 13th 1916. Born in Doncaster but resident in Hull. Buried in Euston Road Cemetery. Husband of Sarah C Collins of 3 Edna Grove, Haddon Street, Hawthorne Avenue. Hull. Before the war he worked for the NER as a Brush Hand in the Engineers Dept. in Hull. His name appears on the NER Roll of Honour.

COLUNSON, PRIVATE WILLIAM, of C Company. 13/1279. Killed in action on November 13th 1916 aged 40. Born in Hull. Commemorated on the Thiepval Memorial. Husband of Margaret Ann Collinson of 5 Walter's Terrace, Walton Street, Hull. Commemorated on the Thiepval Memorial.

CONWAY, PRIVATE FRED. 13/993. Killed in action on November 13th 1916 aged 33. Born in Driffield but resident in Hull. Son of Mrs Mary Conway of 4 Anvil's Terrace, Spring Street. Hull. Husband of Eliza Mary Conway of 7 Story's Buildings, Spring Street, Hull. Commemorated on the Thiepval Memorial.

COOK, PRIVATE ARTHUR THEODORE. 13/60. Killed in action on November 11th 1916 aged 18. Son of William Clifton Cook and Sarah Ann Cook of 31 Middleburg Street, Hull. Commemorated on the Thiepval Memorial.

COOPER, PRIVATE GEORGE. 13/1381. Killed in action on November 13th 1916. Born in Hull. Buried in Euston Road Cemetery.

COOPER, PRIVATE ROBERT. 13/1294. Killed in action on November 13th 1916 aged 20. Born in Boston, Lincolnshire. Resident at 99 Craven Street, Hull. Buried in Luke Copse British Cemetery.

COOPER, PRIVATE ROBERT JOHN. 13/325. Killed in action on November 13th 1916 aged 20. Born in Wotton-under-Edge. Gloucestershire but resident in Hull. Resident at 3 Cobden Place, Fountain Road, Hull. Buried in Euston Road Cemetery. Colincamps.

CORNER, PRIVATE ERNEST. 13/59. Killed in action on August 6th 1916 aged 21. Born in Hull. Son of Ada Comer of 10 Alfred's Terrace, Daltry Street, Hull.

Before the war he was employed by C Butters on Hull Fish Dock. Buried in St. Vaast Post Military Cemetery. Richebourg L'Avouée.

CORNTHWATTE, PRIVATE GEORGE ALFRED. 13/62. Killed in action on November 13th 1916. His body was found between the lines and later buried at Euston Road Cemetery. He was a battalion signaller. Son of Frances and the late G Cornthwaite of 4 Gladstone Terrace, Courtney Street, Hull. His father died on February 27th 1917 after an illness.

COUPLAND, PRIVATE JOSEPH. 13/1439. Killed in action on November 13th 1916. Born in Hull. He was engaged to be married at the time of his death. Buried in Euston Road Cemetery.

COWTON, PRIVATE MARTIN. 13/66. Killed in action on November 13th 1916 aged 19. Born in Nafferton, Yorkshire. Resident in Hull. Son of Mr J Y and Mrs M A Cowton of 3 Arch Avenue, Holmes Street, Hull. Buried in Queens Cemetery, Puisieux.

DADDY, CORPORAL JOHN WILLIAM. 13/954. Killed in action on November 13th 1916 aged 31. Born in Hull. Husband of Alice Daddy of 38 Alaska Street, Buckingham Street, Holderness Road. Hull. Buried in Euston Road Cemetery.

DARBY, PRIVATE JOHN WILLIAM. 13/1274. Killed in action on November 13th 1916. Born in Hull. Son of late Robert and Margaret Darby. Husband of Mary Tremble (formerly Darby) of 3 Bickerton Buildings, William Street, Hull. Commemorated on the Thiepval Memorial.

DAWSON, PRIVATE GEORGE. 13/611. Killed in action on August 9th 1916 aged 22. Born in Hull. Son of the late Alfred and Harrie Dawson. Buried in Le Touret Military Cemetery.

DEAN, CORPORAL ALFRED. 13/826. Killed in action on November 13th 1916. Born in Hull.

DENT, CORPORAL GEORGE. 13/427. Killed in action on August 21st 1916. Born in Hull. Buried in St Vaast Post Military Cemetery. Richebourg L'Avouée.

DIGLIN, PRIVATE GEORGE. 13/505. Killed in action on November 13th 1916. Born in Hull. Commemorated on the Thiepval Memorial.

DIXON, PRIVATE ALONSA. 13/556. Died in the UK on July 11th 1916 aged 29. Son of Alonsa and Caroline Dixon of 3 Argyle Street, Anlaby Road, Hull. Born in Hull. Buried in Wincanton Cemetery.

DODDS, PRIVATE JOHN. 13/1386. Killed in action on November 13th 1916. Born in Hull. Commemorated on the Thiepval Memorial.

DONNELLY, CORPORAL ARTHUR. 13/75. Killed in action on November 13th 1916. Born in Goole but resident in Hull. Buried in Euston Road Cemetery.

DOSSOR, LANCE-CORPORAL STANLEY. 13/1017. Killed in action on November 13th 1916. Born in Hull. Commemorated on the Thiepval Memorial.

DRIVER, PRIVATE MATTHEW HENRY. 13/1197. Killed in action on November 13th 1916. Born in Hull. Commemorated on the Thiepval Memorial.

DRIVER, PRIVATE ROBERT. 13/693. Killed in action on April 19th 1917. Born in Hull. Buried in Mons (Bergen) Communal Cemetery.

DUNCAN, LANCE-CORPORAL DONALD. 13/333. Killed in action on November 13th 1916, aged 21. Born in Hull. Son of late Thomas Daniels Duncan and Louisa Elizabeth Ann King (formerly Duncan). Commemorated on the Thiepval Memorial.

EDDON, PRIVATE JOHN WILLIAM. 13/337. Killed in action on July 20th 1916 aged 26. Son of John Charles and Annie Elizabeth Eddon of Hull. Husband of Florence Eddon of 68 Great Thornton Street, Hull. Born in Hull. Buried in Rue-du-Bacquerot No 1 Military Cemetery. Laventie.

EDWARDS, PRIVATE HERBERT. 13/1353. Killed in action on November 13th 1916 aged 19. Born in Hull. Son of Charles Edwards of 2 Harrow Terrace, Harrow Street, Hessle Road, Hull. Buried in Luke Copse British Cemetery.

ELLINGTON, PRIVATE EBENEZER. 13/879. Killed in action on November 13th 1916 aged 39. Husband of M Ellington of 8 Norfolk Terrace, Russell Place, Norfolk Street, Hull. Born in Isleham, Cambridgeshire but resident in Hull. Buried in Queens Cemetery, Puiseux.

ELSTON, SERGEANT JAMES HERBERT. 13/91. Killed in action on November 13th 1916. Born in Hull. Commemorated on the Thiepval Memorial.

ESPIN, PRIVATE CHARLES THOMAS. 13/696. Killed in action on November 13th 1916. Born in Hull. Commemorated on the Thiepval Memorial.

ESPINER, PRIVATE ARTHUR CHARLES. 13/336. Died in France on August 14th 1916. Born in North Ferriby, East Yorkshire but resident in Hull. Commemorated on the Loos Memorial.

FALK, PRIVATE HARRY. 13/94. Killed in action on November 13th 1916 aged 21. Born in Hull. Son of John and Annie Falk of 89 Day Street, Hull. Commemorated on the Thiepval Memorial.

FARNILL, PRIVATE DAVID WILLIAM, of 'C' Company. 13/431. Died of wounds on September 9th 1916 aged 19. Born in Hull. Son of Walter and Nancy Farnill of 3 Fosters Buildings, North Street, Hull. Buried in Chocques Military Cemetery.

FARRAH, PRIVATE JOHN ROBERT. 13/877. Killed in action on November 13th 1916. Born in Hull. Son of Alfred and Maria Farrah. His brother Richard was killed in action on April 23rd 1917 serving with the 5th Border regiment. Commemorated on the Thiepval Memorial.

FENWICK, PRIVATE GEORGE BINKS. 13/1344. Killed in action on November 13th 1916 aged 42. Born in Hull. Husband of Ellinor Fenwick of 3 Ann's Place, Neapur Terrace, Norfolk Street, Hull. Commemorated on the Thiepval Memorial.

FISHER, PRIVATE FRED. 13/1249. Discharged from the army and died of his wounds (gas) on January 25th 1921 aged 25. Buried in Western Cemetery. Spring Bank, Hull. Son of the late Thomas and Elizabeth Fisher.

FORTMAN, PRIVATE JAMES FRANCIS HOLMANS of 'C' Company. 13/1256. Killed in action on May 1st 1917 aged 26. Born in Hull. Son of Mr. W F and the late Mary Fortman of 127 Gillett Street, Hull. Commemorated on the Arras Memorial.

GALBRAITH, PRIVATE BENJAMIN. 13/343. Killed in action on November 13th 1916. Born in Hull. Buried in Euston Road Cemetery.

GAMBLE, PRIVATE CHARLES EDWARD. 13/344. Killed in action on April 29th 1917 aged 23. Born in Hull. Son of Thomas and Annie Gamble of 134 Glasgow Street, Hull. Buried in Albuera Cemetery, Bailleul-sire-Bertholt.

GARFITT, PRIVATE WALTER. 12/1115. Killed in action on May 3rd 1917 aged 35. Born in Hull. Son of William and Harriet Garfitt of 31 Cleveland Street, Hull. Commemorated on the Arras Memorial.

GILL, PRIVATE VINCENT VICTOR. 13/914. Killed in action on August 10th 1916. Born in Bradford but resident in Hull. Buried in Le Touret Military Cemetery.

GILKES, PRIVATE FREDERICK THOMAS. 13/111. Killed in action on November 13th 1916 aged 30. Born in Lichfield, Staffordshire but resident in Hull. Huband of Mabel Gilkes of 10 Sabina Avenue, Balfour Street, Holderness Street, Holderness Road, Hull. Buried in Euston Road Cemetery.

GRAYBURN, PRIVATE JOHN. 13/775. Killed in action on July 20th 1917. Born in Hull. Buried in Bumble Trench Cemetery, Vimy Memorial.

GREEN, CORPORAL HARRY. 13/1292. Died of wounds on November 5th 1917 aged 34. Born in Pinchbeck, Yorkshire but resident in Hull. Husband of Catherine K Green of 17 Fredericks Terrace, Nornabell Street, Holderness Road, Hull. Buried in Duisans British Cemetery.

GREENWOOD, PRIVATE CORNELIUS PEARSON. 13/776. Killed in action on November 13th 1916. Born in Hull. Commemorated on the Thiepval Memorial.

HACKETT, PRIVATE JAMES RICHARD. 13/122. Killed in action on July 20th 1916 aged 27. Husband of Sarah Ann Hackett of 11 Eugenie Terrace, Kent Street, Holderness Road, Hull. Born in Hull. Buried in Rue-Du-Bacquerot No 1 Military Cemetery, Laventie.

HALDENBY, SERGEANT JOHN ROBERT, of 'C' Company. 13/1140. Killed in action on November 13th 1916 aged 30. Born in Cottingham, East

Yorkshire, enlisted in Hull but resident in Cottingham. Son of David and Hannah Haldenby of Scruton Cottage. George Street, Cottingham. He was the eldest of six children and was unmarried. Before he enlisted he was a gardener at Sewerby Hall, near Bridlington. He enjoyed racing pigeons with his only brother, Alfred, who served in the Northumberland Fusiliers (and survived the war). The family attended the Wesleyan Church in Cottingham. Buried in Luke Copse Cemetery.

HALLAM, SERGEANT JOHN, MM. 13/1092. Killed in action on November 13th 1916 aged 28. Son of Frederick and Fanny Hallam of Martson, Grantham, Lincolnshire. Born in Brandon, enlisted in Hull but resident in Grantham. Commemorated on the Thiepval Memorial.

HARDY, PRIVATE GEORGE BRUNNING. 13/1018. Killed in action on November 13th 1916. Born in Little Weighton, East Yorkshire but resident in Hull. Commemorated on the Thiepval Memorial.

HARGRAVE, PRIVATE GEORGE HERBERT. 13/348. Killed in action on November 13th 1916. Born in Goole but resident in Hull. Commemorated on the Thiepval Memorial.

HARRISON, PRIVATE ARTHUR. 13/781. Killed in action on November 13th 1916 aged 33. Born in Hull. Husband of Ada Harrison of 7 Minerva Terrace, Gibson Street, Hull. Buried in Euston Road Cemetery.

HARRISON, PRIVATE ERNEST CLARENCE. 13/564. Killed in action on November 16th 1916 aged 22. Born in Hull. Son of William Henry and Emily Gertrude Harrison of 10 York Avenue, Liverpool Street, Hessle Road, Hull. Buried in Douchy Les Ayette British Cemetery.

HARRISON, SERGEANT GEORGE, MID. 13/1115. Killed in action on November 13th 1916 aged 23. Born in Epworth, Lincolnshire but resident in Sheffield. Son of John Holt Harrison of Rose Cottage, Belton Road, Epworth, Lincolnshire. He was a Schoolmaster before the war. Buried in Euston Road Cemetery.

HASNIP, SERGEANT CLIFFORD CHAWNER. Discharged and died of wounds on February 12th 1919 aged 39. Buried in Hull Western Cemetery. Son of James Edward and Ann Sophia Hasnip of Hull. Husband of Florence Hasnip of 13 Wyndham Street, Hull.

HEBBLEWHITE, PRIVATE FRED. 13/1201. Killed in action on November 13th 1916. Born in Brandesburton, East Yorkshire but resident in Hull. Buried in Euston Road Cemetery.

HESELTINE, PRIVATE FRANK RICHARDSON. 13/782. Killed in action on September 3rd 1916 aged 31. Born in Hull. Son of Alfred and Harriet Heseltine. Husband of Beatrice E Marshall (formerly Heseltine) of 15 Ockley Terrace, West Parade, Hull. Buried in Le Touret Military Cemetery.

HILL, PRIVATE ROBERT JAMES. 11/94. Killed in action on November 13th 1916. Commemorated on the Thiepval Memorial. Born in Atwick. Son of Mrs. Hill of 3 Papes Yard, Keldgate, Beverley.

HOWELL, PRIVATE WILLIAM NELSON. 13/784. Died in France on January 31st 1917. Born in Bardney, Lincolnshire, enlisted in Hull but resident in Hessle. Commemorated at Tincourt New British Cemetery.

HULL, PRIVATE THOMAS. 13/856. Killed in action on November 13th 1916 aged 22. Son of Francis John and Ada Hull of 33 Chiltem Street, Anlaby Road, Hull. Born in Hull. Commemorated on the Thiepval Memorial.

HUZZARD, PRIVATE RICHARD. 13/352. Killed in action on November 13th 1916 aged 23. Son of Richard and Mary Huzzard of 41 Queen's Gate Street, Hull. Husband of Elsie Huzzard of 6 Blanche Grove, Brighton Street, Hessle Road, Hull. Born in Hull. Commemorated on the Thiepval Memorial.

JACKSON, PRIVATE ARTHUR EDWARD. 13/139. Killed in action on August 9th 1916. Born in Burstwick but resident in Hull. Buried in Merville Communal Cemetery.

JACKSON, PRIVATE EDWIN THOMAS. 10/372. Killed in action on August 2nd 1917. Aged 22. Son of Thomas and Priscilla E Jackson of 455 Hessle Road, Hull. Born in Battersea. Buried in New Irish Farm Cemetery.

JANNEY, PRIVATE ALBERT BUTLER. 13/705. Killed in action on November 13th 1916. Born in Thornton Curtis, Lincolnshire but resident in Hull. Commemorated on the Thiepval Memorial.

JENNISON, PRIVATE ERNEST. 13/1157. Killed in action on November 13th 1916 aged 21. Husband of Ada M Jennison of 2 Crystal Avenue, Subway Street, Hull. Born in Hull. Commemorated on the Thiepval Memorial.

JOHNSON. PRIVATE ARTHUR. 13/446. Died of wounds on September 10th 1917 aged 24. Born in Hull. Son of John Wilford Johnson. Husband of Florence Mander (formerly Johnson) of Indiana, Pennsylvania, USA. Buried in Duisans British Cemetery.

JOHNSON, PRIVATE GEORGE. 13/880. Died of wounds on October 1st 1916. Born in Stocksmith-on-Trent. Buried in Longuenesse Souvenir Cemetery, St. Omer.

JOHNSON, PRIVATE GEORGE FARTHING. 13/919. Killed in action on May 25th 1916 aged 30. Husband of Edith Susannah Johnson of 3 Churchill Street, Hedon Road, Hull. Born in Hull. Buried in Sucrerie Military Cemetery, Colincamps.

JOHNSON, SERGEANT GEORGE STANLEY. 13/146. Killed in action on November 8th 1917. Born in Hull. Commemorated on the Arras Memorial.

KAY, PRIVATE CHARLES WILLIAM, of 'D' Company. 13/147. Died of wounds on November 19th 1916 aged 23. Son John Robert and Dinah Kay of 19 Northumberland Avenue, Hull. Born in Hull. Buried in Ontario Cemetery, Sains-Les-Marquion.

KAY, PRIVATE FRED, of C Company. 13/1110. Killed in action on November 13th 1916 aged 22. Born in Hull. Son of Sarah Ann Kay of 7 Lucas Square. New George Street, Hull. Buried in Euston Road Cemetery.

KAY, PRIVATE MATTHIAS. 13/1167. Killed in action on November 13th 1916 aged 26. Born in Goole, enlisted in Hull but resident in Goole. Son of John Alma and Sarah Elizabeth Kay of 18, Henry Street, Goole, Yorkshire. Buried in Ontario Cemetery. Sains-Les-Marquion. Commemorated on the Thiepval Memorial.

KERSHAW, PRIVATE WILLIAM VINCENT. 13/451. Killed in action on November 13th 1916 aged 22. Son of Sarah Kershaw of 8 Burleigh Grove, Courtney Street, Holderness Road, Hull and the late Joseph Kershaw. Born in Hull. Commemorated on the Thiepval Memorial.

LANGFORD, PRIVATE LEONARD. 13/153. Killed in action on May 25th 1916 aged 20. Son of Mrs Mary Langford of 7 Queen's Terrace, Gillett Street, Hessle Road, Hull. Born in Hessle, East Yorkshire but resident in Hull. Buried in Sucrerie Military Cemetery, Colincamps.

LANGRICH, SERGEANT LEONARD STANLEY. 13/154. Died of wounds on November 14th 1916. Born in Hull. Buried in Euston Road Cemetery.

LAUGHTON, PRIVATE F. 13/1211. Died on July 2nd 1918. Husband of A Laughton of 5 Norfolk Place, Norfolk Street, Hull. Buried in Western Cemetery, Spring Bank, Hull.

LEWIS, PRIVATE SYDNEY. 13/155. Killed in action on November 13th 1916 aged 21. Son of Louisa Lewis of 17 Great Thornton Street, Hull. Born in Hull. Commemorated on the Thiepval Memorial.

LILLEY, PRIVATE SYDNEY. 13/571. Killed in action on November 13th 1916. Born in Hull. Buried in Luke Copse British Cemetery.

MAJOR, PRIVATE GEORGE. 13/722. Killed in action on April 14th 1916. Born in Hull. Buried in Sucrerie Military Cemetery. Colincamps.

MAUGHAN, SERGEANT REGINALD COOPER. 13/1150. Died of wounds on May 6th 1917. Born in Sheffield but resident in Hull. Buried in Bois-Carre British Cemetery.

McCARTHY, SERGEANT CHARLES DESMOND. 13/518. Killed in action on November 13th 1916 aged 22. Born in Grimsby but living in Beverley at the time. Buried in Queens Cemetery, Puisieux. Son of Emma McCarthy of 19 Walkergate, Beverley. His name appears on the War Memorial, Hengate, Beverley.

McKERNAN, PRIVATE WALTER. 13/181. Died of wounds on June 2nd 1916 aged 20. Born in Hull. Son of Mrs A A and the late Mr H McKernan of Hull. Buried in Bertrancourt Military Cemetery.

McNALLY, PRIVATE THOMAS JOHN. 13/455. Killed in action on November 13th 1916 aged 22. Born in Armagh, enlisted in Hull but resident in Belfast. Son of Martina Long of 4 Parkend Street, Belfast. Buried in Euston Road Cemetery.

MERRYLEES, PRIVATE ARTHUR. 13/1486. Died of wounds on June 29th 1916. Born in Hull. Buried in Ste Marie Cemetery. Le Harve.

MESSENGER, LANCE-CORPORAL GEORGE HENRY. 13/1127. Killed in action on November 13th 1916 aged 32. Son of Thomas and Mary Ann Messenger of 37 Southcoates Lane, Holderness Road, Hull. Born in Hull. Commemorated on the Thiepval Memorial.

MIDFORTH, PRIVATE FREDERICK WILLIAM. 13/182. Killed in action on November 13th 1916, aged 23. Son of Alfred and Ada Midforth of 1 Richmond Terrace, Durham Street, Hull. Born in Hull. Buried in Luke Copse British Cemetery.

MILES, PRIVATE JAMES. 13/1226. Killed in action on November 13th 1916. Born in Bridlington, enlisted in Hull but resident in Dundee. Commemorated on the Thiepval Memorial.

MILNER, PRIVATE GEORGE. 13/183. Killed in action on November 13th 1915 aged 26. Son of Mrs Hannah Milner of 3 Gladys Grove, Courtney Street, Hull. Born in Hull. Commemorated on the Thiepval Memorial.

MORRELL, PRIVATE ARCHIBALD. 13/1099. Killed in action on November 13th 1916 aged 21. Son of Mrs Sarah Jane Morrell of 11 Charlotte's Terrace, Clarendon Street, Hull. Born in Hull. Commemorated on the Thiepval Memorial.

NELSON, PRIVATE JOHN. 13/187. Killed in action on November 13th 1916. Born in Hull. Commemorated on the Thiepval Memorial.

NEWLOVE, PRIVATE WILLIAM HENRY. 13/1400. Killed in action on November 13th 1916. Born in Weaverthorpe but resident in Hull. Buried in Euston Road Cemetery.

NEWMAN, PRIVATE JAMES SIDNEY. 13/1288. Killed in action on November 13th 1916 aged 20. Son of George Sidney and Ann Newman of Laxton, Howden, East Yorkshire. Born in Hull. Commemorated on the Thiepval Memorial.

O'NEAL, PRIVATE JOHN WILLIAM. 13/1174. Killed in action on May 3rd 1917 aged 19. Born in Hull. Son of James and Emma O'Neal of 17 East Cheapside, Hull. Commemorated on the Arras Memorial.

PALLISTER, PRIVATE JOHN WILLIAM. 13/1289. Killed in action on November 13th 1916. Born in Hull. Buried in Euston Road Cemetery.

PARKER, LANCE-CORPORAL WALTER. 13/726. Killed in action on November 13th 1916. Born in Caistor, Lincolnshire, enlisted in Hull but resident in Barton-on Humber. Commemorated on the Thiepval Memorial.

PLATTS, PRIVATE JOHN WILLIAM. 13/642. Killed in action on November 13th 1916 aged 23. Son of Mrs Elizabeth Platts of 5 Ingrams Place, Porter Street, Hull. Born in Hull. Buried in Serre Road Cemetery No 2.

PLOUGHER, PRIVATE HARRY, of C Company. 13/643. Died, aged 32, on February 4th 1917, of wounds received on November 13th 1916. Born in Beverley but resident in Hessle. He is buried in St. Martin's Cemetery, Beverley. Husband of Mabel Jeanette Plougher of 14 Well Gardens, Well Lane, Beverley. His mother lived at 1 St. Martin's Place, Butcher Row, Beverley.

PRESTON, PRIVATE JAMES ROUTLEDGE. 13/923. Killed in action on May 25th 1916. Born in Hornsea but resident in Hull. Buried in Sucrerie Military Cemetery, Colincamps.

PULLEN, PRIVATE ROBERT EVISSON. 13/198. Died of wounds on July 20th 1916 aged 24. Son of Mr and Mrs Pullen of 23 Gillett Street, Hessle Road, Hull. Born in Hull. Buried in Vielle-Chapelle New Military Cemetery.

RALPH, PRIVATE TOM. 13/925. Died of wounds on August 15th 1916. Born in Hull. Buried in Aire Communal Cemetery.

REED, PRIVATE GEORGE ERNEST. 13/1357. Killed in action on July 30th 1917 aged 26. Born in Hull. Son of Clara Reed of 8 Nelson Square, New George Street, Hull. Buried in La Targette British Cemetery.

RICHARDSON, PRIVATE EDWARD. 13/576. Killed in action on November 13th 1916. Born in Sutton but resident in Hull. Buried in Euston Road Cemetery.

ROBBIE, LANCE-CORPORAL JOHN ALEXANDER. 13/210. Killed in action on November 13th 1916. Born in Consett but resident in Hull. Buried in Euston Road Cemetery.

ROBERTS, PRIVATE EDWARD. 13/209. Died of wounds on December 3rd 1916. Born in Hull. Buried in Porte-de-Paris Cemetery.

ROBERTS, PRIVATE GEORGE. 13/895. Died of wounds on July 18th 1916. Born in Hull. Buried in Merville Communal Cemetery.

ROBINSON, CORPORAL ARTHUR. 13/377. Killed in action on November 13th 1916. Born in Hull. Commemorated on the Thiepval Memorial.

ROBINSON, SERGEANT ARTHUR. 13/644. Killed in action on November 13th 1916. Born in Scarborough but resident in Hull. Buried in Serre Road Cemetery No 2.

ROBINSON, PRIVATE RICHARD WILLIAM. 13/375. Killed in action on November 13th 1916 aged 23. Born in Hull. Son of Mr T K Robinson of 3 Alfrede Terrace, Daltry Street, Hull. Buried in Euston Road Cemetery.

ROGERS, PRIVATE JAMES WILLIAM. 13/212. Killed in action on August 7th 1916. Born in Hull. Buried in Le Touret Military Cemetery.

ROSE, PRIVATE CHARLES. 13/1005. Killed in action on May 25th 1916. Born in Hull. Buried in Sucrerie Military Cemetery, Colincamps.

RUTLEDGE, LANCE-CORPORAL ALFRED. 13/379. Killed in action on November 13th 1916. Born in Hull. Commemorated on the Thiepval Memorial.

RYAN, PRIVATE JOHN. 13/373. Killed in action on August 14th 1916. Born in Hull. Buried in Le Touret Military Cemetery.

SAMPLE, LANCE-CORPORAL JOHN. 13/1235. Killed in action on November 13th 1916 aged 30. Born in Little Cressingham, Norfolk but was resident in Hull at the time of his enlistment. His name appears on the Hengate War Memorial, Beverley.

SANDS, PRIVATE JOHN EDWARD. 14/210. Killed in action on August 10th 1916. Born in Hull. Buried in Le Touret Military Cemetery.

SCOTT, PRIVATE GEORGE THOMAS. 13/1059. Died of wounds on July 16th 1916 aged 40. Husband of E M Scott of 14 Seymour Street, Hawthorne Avenue, Hull. Born in Hull. Buried in Vielle-Chapelle New Military Cemetery.

SHAKESPEARE, LANCE-CORPORAL SAMUEL. 13/216. Killed in action on November 13th 1916 aged 22. Born in Hull. Son of Thomas and Sarah Shakespeare of 83 Barmston Street, Hull. Buried in Euston Road Cemetery.

SHARP, PRIVATE FRED. 13/1228. Killed in action on November 13th 1916 aged 19. Born in Hull. Youngest son of Edwin and Mary Ann Sharp of 44 Buckingham Street, Holderness Road, Hull. Buried in Euston Road Cemetery.

SHEARSMITH, PRIVATE THOMAS. 13/1318. Killed in action on August 4th 1916. Born in Pocklington, Yorkshire but resident in Hull. Commemorated on the Loos Memorial.

SHEPERDSON, LANCE-CORPORAL HAROLD. 13/1484. Killed in action on November 13th 1916. Born in Hull. Buried in Euston Road Cemetery.

SHORES, PRIVATE JOHN. 14/46. Killed in action on November 13th 1916 aged 20. Son of John William and Annie Shores of 845 Coltman Street, Hull. Born in Hull. Commemorated on the Thiepval Memorial.

SMITH, PRIVATE GEORGE ALFRED. 13/474. Killed in action on November 13th 1916 aged 24. Born in Hull. Son of Mrs. M Smith of 3 Cobden Street, Albert Avenue, Anlaby Road, Hull. Buried in Euston Road Cemetery Extension.

SMITH, PRIVATE JOSEPH LAWSON. 13/229. Died of wounds on November 15th 1916 aged 31. Born in Hull. Son of the late Martha and the late J A Smith of

Hull. Buried in Corbie Communal Cemetery Extension.

SNOWLEY, PRIVATE CHARLES ALFRED. 13/218. Died in France on January 28th 1917. Born in Great Yarmouth but resident in Hull.

STAINFORTH, PRIVATE WILLIAM. 12/978. Killed in action on November 13th 1916. Born in Hull. Buried in Euston Road Cemetery.

STEVENS, PRIVATE HENRY, of 'B' Company. 13/386. Died of wounds on November 26th 1916 aged 30. Son of the late Robert and Rose Ann Stevens of Hull. Born in Hull. Buried in Porte-de-Paris Cemetery.

STIRK, CORPORAL HERBERT EDWARD CHARLES. 13/235. Killed in action on November 13th 1916. Born in Hull. Buried in Euston Road Cemetery.

STORK, PRIVATE THOMAS. 13/889. Killed in action on November 13th 1916 aged 21. Son of Mrs Annie Johnson of 10 Porter Place, Porter Street, Hull. Born in Hull. Commemorated on the Thiepval Memorial.

STORR, PRIVATE ARTHUR. 13/1217. Killed in action on November 13th 1916 aged 20. Son of Arthur and Minnie Storr of 2 Percy's Avenue, Rugby Street, Hessle Road, Hull. Husband of Minnie Bilton (formerly Storr) of 7 Paull Terrace. Wassand Street. Hessle Road. Hull. Born in Hull. Commemorated on the Thiepval Memorial.

SUGDEN, PRIVATE THOMAS. 13/246. Died of wounds on January 16th 1917 aged 33. Son of Richard and Elizabeth Sugden of Hull. Born in Hull. Buried in Port-de-Paris Cemetery.

SWIFT, PRIVATE JAMES HENRY. 13/1312. Killed in action on November 13th 1916, aged 19. Born in Hull. Son of Victor and Ellen Swift of 6 Midgley Terrace, Bean Street, Hull. Buried in Queens Cemetery, Puisieux.

SYPH, PRIVATE JOSEPH. 13/796. Killed in action on November 13th 1916 aged 32. Son of Mr and Mrs Syph of 1 Marsh Street, Hull. Born in Hull. Commemorated on the Thiepval Memorial.

TAYLOR, CORPORAL ALFRED. 13/657. Killed in action on June 23rd 1917 aged 26. Son of Alfred and Alice Taylor. Husband of Olive Simpson (formerly Taylor) of 144 Porter Street, Hull. Born in Hull. Buried in Orchard Dump Cemetery.

TAYLOR, PRIVATE GEORGE ROBERT. 13/740. Killed in action on November 13th 1916. Born in Hull. Buried in Euston Road Cemetery.

TEMPLE, SERGEANT ROBERT STANLEY, MM, of 'C' Company. 13/541. Killed in action on May 2nd 1917 aged 23. Born in Stockton-on-Forest, Yorkshire but resident in Hull. Son of Robert and Clara Temple of 30 Wassand Street, Hull. Buried in Orchard Dump Cemetery.

THORPE, PRIVATE WILLIAM LEONARD. 13/1081. Killed in action on November 13th 1916 aged 35. Husband of Polly Thorpe of 8 Ansley Terrace, Spyvee Street, Hull. Born in Hull. Commemorated on the Thiepval Memorial.

THURLOW, PRIVATE ARTHUR. 13/405. Died of wounds on November 20th 1916 aged 30. Born in Driffield and enlisted in Driffield. Son of Robert and Mary Thurlow of 5 Providence Place, Driffield, East Yorkshire. Buried in Corbie Communal Cemetery Extension.

TOALSTER, LANCE-CORPORAL THOMAS. 13/936. Killed in action on November 13th 1916. Born in Hull. Commemorated on the Thiepval Memorial.

TOMLINSON, PRIVATE HERBERT. 13/356. Killed in action on July 20th 1916 aged 24. Husband of Mrs Tomlinson of 15 Clarendon Terrace, Clarendon Street, Hull. Born in Hull. Buried in Rue-Du-Bacquerot No. 1 Military Cemetery, Laventie.

TURLEY, CORPORAL FRANCIS of 'B' Company. 13/745. Killed in action on November 13th 1916 aged 34. Son of Robert and Eliza Turley of Belfast. Husband of Florence May Turley of 11 Pelham Terrace, Beaumont Street, Hull. Born in Belfast but resident in Hull. Buried in Queens Cemetery, Puisieux.

WALKER, PRIVATE ROBERT. 13/1397. Killed in action on November 13th 1916 aged 20. Buried in Puisieux Cemetery. Born in Barton-on-Humber but resident in Hull at the time of enlistment. Son of Wallis and Kate Walker of 6 Lee Street, Holderness Road, Hull.

WALLER, CORPORAL GEORGE FRANK. 13/1233. Killed in action on November 29th 1917. Buried in Roclincourt Military Cemetery. Born in Hull.

WALMSLEY, PRIVATE JOHN EDWARD. 13/1301. Killed in action on November 13th 1916. Born in Todmorden but resident in Hull. Buried in Euston Road Cemetery.

WALSH, PRIVATE JOSEPH EDWARD. 13/399. Wounded and taken prisoner on the Somme on November 13th 1916. Died of wounds as a Prisoner of War at Elberfeld, Germany on January 2nd 1917. Buried in Cologne Southern Cemetery. Married with one child.

WATTS, PRIVATE CHARLES. 13/1396. Killed in action on April 1st 1916 aged 28. Buried in Mesnil Ridge Cemetery, Mesnil, Somme. Born in Hull. Son of Mrs. Sarah Ann Watts of 13 Blenheim Terrace, Norfolk Street, Hull.

WAUD, PRIVATE FREDERICK (known as Little Freddie). 13/271. Killed in action on May 1st 1916. Buried in Euston Road Cemetery. Born in Hull. Former Ship's Steward.

WHITE, PRIVATE GIBSON. 13/1305. Killed in action on May 15th 1918 aged 22. Born in Hollym, enlisted in Hull but resident in Hollym. Son of W H and Mary Ellen White of Hollym. Hull. Buried in Abbeville Communal Cemetery.

WILLIAMS, CORPORAL ARTHUR. 13/664. Killed in action on November 16th 1916 aged 19. Buried in Douchy Les Ayette British Cemetery. Born in Hull. Son of Thomas Richard and Rachel Williams of 17 Granville Gardens, Jesmond, Newcastle-upon-Tyne.

WILLIAMS, PRIVATE GEORGE WILLIAM, of 'B' Company. 13/280. Killed in action on November 13th 1916 aged 22. Buried in Euston Road Cemetery. Born in Hull. Enlisted in November 1914. Son of Annie M. Williams and the late William Williams of 4 Burleigh Street, Hull.

WILSON, PRIVATE MARK ADAMSON. 13/753. Killed in action on November 13th 1916. Buried in Queens Cemetery, Puisieux. Born in Hull.

WINTER, PRIVATE ERNEST. 13/1494. Killed in action on November 4th 1917. Buried in Roclincourt Military Cemetery. Born in Hull.

WOODMANSEY, PRIVATE THOMAS. 14/197. Believed to have been one of four soldiers who died of mistreatment at Ven Dhuile. Officially listed as died on January 1st 1917. Buried in Porte-de-Paris Cemetery. Born in Beverley and resident in Beverly at the time of enlistment. Son of Mr. T. Woodmansey of 35 Day Street, Hull.

WRIGHT, PRIVATE GEORGE, of 'D' Company. 13/754. Died of wounds on November 7th 1917 aged 20. Born in Cottingham. enlisted in Hull but was resident in Cottingham at the time. Son of Mr and Mrs W Wright of 143 King Street, Cottingham, East Yorkshire. Buried in Duisans British Cemetery.

WRIGHT, PRIVATE JAMES WILLIAM. 13/487. Killed in action on November 13th 1916 aged 21. Buried in Serre Road Cemetery No. 1. Born in Hull. Husband of Alice Wright and father of Florence (d.2/11/18) of 22 Grosvenor Terrace, Grosvenor Street, Hull.

14TH BATTALION

REDMORE, LANCE-CORPORAL HAROLD. 10/544. Died in the UK on September 13th 1916 aged 25. Buried in Western Cemetery, Hull. Born in Hull. Son of Edward King and Catherine Redmore of Hull. Husband of Minnie Ida Redmore of 7 Glencoe Avenue, Flinton Street, Hull.

STEPHENSON, PRIVATE NEVILLE ARTHUR. 14/123. Died in the UK on February 11th 1916 aged 23. Born in Willerby. East Yorkshire but resident in Hull. Son of Mr. N Stephenson of Willerby. Buried in Kirk Ella Church Cemetery.

HULL PALS SERVING WITH OTHER BATTALIONS OF THE EAST YORKSHIRE REGIMENT

1ST BATTALION

ALEXANDER, PRIVATE WILLIAM HENRY. 10/479. Died of wounds on April 22nd 1918 near Poperinghe, aged 29. Born in Hull. Buried in Haringhe (Bandaghem) Military Cemetery. Son of George and Anne Alexander, one of 7 children. At the time of his death all the family were resident at 92 Grafton Street, Hull. He was married to Clara May Alexander. His wife and two children lived at 121 Belvoir Street, Hull.

ATKINSON, SERGEANT GEORGE ERNEST. 13/1181 of 14th Platoon. 'B' Company. Killed in action on April 25th 1918, aged 41. Commemorated on the Tyne Cot Memorial. Born in Whitby but resident in Hull at the time of enlistment. Son of Mr. J and Mrs. M.F Atkinson of 32 Colonial Street, Hull. He was engaged to be married at the time of his death.

BAINES, PRIVATE JOSEPH. 12/1216. Died of wounds on August 26th 1918 aged 26. Buried in Warlencourt British Cemetery. Born in Rutland but resident in Hull. Son of Samuel and Eliza Baines of 14 Alpha Avenue, Nornabell Street, Hull.

BANKS, PRIVATE GEORGE THOMAS. 13/1033. Killed in action on October 7th 1918 aged 23. Son of George and Eliza Banks of 29 Gilliatt Street, Scunthorpe. Lincolnshire. Born in Butterwick. Lincolnshire but resident in Hull. Commemorated on the Vis-en-Artois Memorial, Haucourt.

BOAST, PRIVATE GARFORTH. 13/1061. Killed in action on October 7th 1918. Commemorated on the Vis-en-Artois Memorial, Haucourt. Son of Herbert Boast of 365 Hawthorne Avenue, Hessle Road, Hull. Husband of Rebecca Boast of 5 Harrow Street, Hessle Road, Hull. His name appears in the St. Barnabas Church Roll of Honour.

BOLSOVER, PRIVATE GEORGE HERBERT. 13/551. Killed in action on April 9th 1917 aged 29. Buried in Cojuel British Cemetery, St. Martin-sur-Cojuel. Born in Hull. He was a widower. Son of Annie Elizabeth Coleman (formerly Bolsover) of 47 Havelock Street, Hessle Road, Hull.

BOWES, PRIVATE WILLIAM (known as Willie). 10/1260. Killed in action on March 22nd 1918 aged 20. Commemorated on the Pozieres Memorial. Born in Hull. Son of William and Eleanor Bowles of Hull.

BRADLEY, PRIVATE JOSEPH PARKINSON. 13/1495. Died on February 18th 1917 aged 30. Buried in Mont-Bemanchon Churchyard. Born in Hull. Son of John and Ann Bradley. Husband of Margaret M. Bradley of 2 Mason's Terrace, Wellington Lane, Hull.

BROWNRIGG, LANCE-CORPORAL PERCY JAMES, of 'HQ' Company. 10/280. Died of wounds in Hospital in Rouen on March 28th 1918 aged 26. Buried in Boisguillaume Communal Cemetery Extension. Born in Hull. Son of James and Lizzie S. Brownrigg of 150 Alliance Avenue, Hull. Husband of Eveline Annie Brownrigg (nee Cattley) of 46 Lister Street, Hull.

CANNELL, SERGEANT WALTER CECIL, 11TH PLATOON. 'B' Company. 13/54. Killed in action on September 10th 1918 aged 27. Born in Hull. Enlisted in Hull but resident in Hornsea. Son of Mrs E and the late R H Cannell of 9 Clifford Street, Hornsea. Commemorated on the Vis-en-Artois Memorial. Haucourt.

COLLINGWOOD, PRIVATE JOSEPH JESSIE. 13/1184. Killed in action on October 4th 1917. Born in Scunthorpe. Enlisted in Hull but resident in Scunthorpe. Commemorated on the Tyne Cot Memorial.

COOPER, PRIVATE ALBERT EDWARD, of 'D' Company. 12/91. Killed in action on April 9th 1917 aged 26. Born in Hull. Son of William Henry and Charlotte Cooper of 7 Edward's Place, Commercial Road, Hull. Commemorated on the Arras Memorial.

DAKIN, PRIVATE MICHAEL JAMES. 10/1173. Killed in action on April 9th 1917. Born in Leicester but resident in Hull. Buried in Cojuel British Cemetery, St. Martin-sur-Cojuel.

DEYES, SERGEANT EDWARD. 11/1038. Killed in action on April 29th 1917 aged 34. Born in Hull. Son of Edward and Alice Ann Deyes of Hull. Husband of Edith Jackson Mitchell (formerly Deyes) of 39 Massey Street, St. George's Road, Hull. Buried in Cojuel British Cemetery.

DORAN, SERGEANT JAMES WILLIAM. 13/77. Died of wounds as a POW on July 5th 1918 aged 24. Son of the late Mr and Mrs J A Doran of Hull. Born in Hull. Buried in Niederzwehren Cemetery, Germany.

DYMOCK, CORPORAL WILLIAM DUNCAN. 10/1288. Killed in action on October 4th 1917 aged 26. Son of William Dymock of Welbeck Street, Hull. Husband of Emily Dymock of 205 Alliance Avenue, Hull. Born in Hull. Commemorated on the Tyne Cot Memorial.

GOODILL, PRIVATE GEORGE. 10/1267. Died of wounds on October 23rd 1918 aged 23. Son of Mr and Mrs E Goodill of 2 Jubilee Avenue, Harrow Street, Hull. Born in Hull. Buried in St. Souplet British Cemetery.

GOULDING, PRIVATE HARRY. 13/114. Killed in action on August 26th 1918. Born in Kirkella, East Yorkshire, enlisted in Hull but resident in Kirkella.

GOUNDRILL, PRIVATE DAVID. 13/1126. Killed in action on October 7th 1918 aged 37. Born in Keyingham, East Yorkshire but resident in Hull. Son of Mr and Mrs Goundrill of Keyingham, East Yorkshire. Buried in Naves Communal Cemetery Extension.

GRAY, PRIVATE GEORGE WILLIAM. 13/774. Killed in action on April 25th 1918. Born in North Ferriby. Resident in Hull at the time of enlistment. Commemorated on the Tyne Cot Memorial.

HAMSHAW, PRIVATE JAMES ALBERT. 13/347. Killed in action on April 9th 1917. Born in Hull. Commemorated on the Arras Memorial.

HARTLEY, PRIVATE GEORGE. 13/1257. Killed in action on September 16th 1916. Born in Hull. Commemorated on the Thiepval Memorial.

HESLEWOOD, PRIVATE RONALD EDWARD. 13/1105. Died of wounds on September 5th 1918. Born in Hull. Buried in Terlincthun British Cemetery.

JACKSON, PRIVATE WALTER CHARLES. 12/347. 'A' Company. Killed in action on April 9th 1917, aged 22. Born in Hull. Son of Mrs Elizabeth Ann Jackson of 111 Spyvee Street, Hull. Buried in Cojeul British Cemetery, St Martin-sur-Cojeul.

KILLEEN, PRIVATE ALBERT EDWARD. 13/452. Killed in action on August 15th 1918 aged 21. Son of Mrs Alice Killeen of 10 St. Mary's Walk, Redbourne Street, Hull. Born in Hull. Commemorated on the Vis-en-Artois Memorial, Haucourt.

LACEY, PRIVATE GEORGE FALKINGHAM. 10/120. Killed in action on October 18th 1918 aged 22. Son of George William and Frances Ellen Lacey of 14 Stirling Street, Anlaby Road, Hull. Buried in Erquelinnes Communal Cemetery.

MANN, PRIVATE JOHN. 13/1148. Died of pneumonia, on November 16th 1918 following wounds received in France, aged 26. Son of James and Sarah Mann of 97 Arundel Street, Holderness Road, Hull. Enlisted in December 1914, served in Egypt and in France. Buried in Hedon Road Cemetery, Hull.

MORFITT, PRIVATE GEORGE. 12/929. Killed in action on March 22nd 1918 aged 32. Son of William and Emily Morfitt of 37 Shaw Street, Hull. Born in Hull. Buried in Ste. Emilie Valley Cemetery, Villers-Faucon.

O'DELL, LANCE-CORPORAL FRANK. 10/1229. Killed in action on March 22nd 1918. Born in Hull.

PAYNE, PRIVATE JOHN HOWARD, of 'A' Company. 13/1475. Killed in action on March 22nd 1918 aged 19. Son of Ernest Dodson Payne and Alice Emily Payne of 15 Trinity Square, Southwark, London. His eldest brother was also killed in action. Born in Margate, Kent, enlisted in Hull but resident in Brixton. Commemorated on the Pozieres Memorial.

SAUNDBY, PRIVATE REGINALD EDWARD, of 'C' Company. 10/860. Killed in action on February 8th 1918 aged 24. Born in Hull. Son of Edward S and Emily Saunby of 29 Sandringham Street, Hull. Buried in Epehy Wood Farm Cemetery, Epehy.

SHIELDS, LANCE-CORPORAL JOHN WILLIAM, MM. 12/959. Died of wounds on October 22nd 1917. Born in Hull. Buried in Lyssenthouek Military Cemetery.

SMELT, PRIVATE JACK. 10/748. Died of wounds on June 5th 1916 aged 21. Son of William Henry and Eliza Smelt of 126 College Grove, Southcoates Lane, Hull.

Buried in Gezaincourt Communal Cemetery Extension.

STARK, PRIVATE LEWIS HENRY. 11/1281. Killed in action on April 25th 1918. Born in Hull. Commemorated on the Tyne Cot Memorial.

STEAD, PRIVATE GEORGE MARTIN. 13/820. Killed in action on September 16th 1916 aged 19. Son of George M and Louisa Stead of 54 Arthur Street, St. George's Road, Hull. Born in Hull. Commemorated on the Thiepval Memorial.

THOMPSON, PRIVATE WALTER. 13/1278. Died on October 13th 1918 aged 24. Born in South Ferriby, Lincolnshire, enlisted in Hull but resident in South Ferriby. Son of William and Harriet Thompson of Hill Foot, South Ferriby, Barton-on-Humber, Lincolnshire. Buried in Hautmont Communal Cemetery.

TURNER, PRIVATE FREDERICK. 13/395. Killed in action on September 10th 1918. Born in Hull. Commemorated on the Vis-en-Artois Memorial, Haucourt.

VASEY, SERGEANT HERBERT HENRY. 12/129. Killed in action on December 6th 1917 aged 26. Born in Hull. Son of Mrs Mildred Vasey of 6 Shaftesbury Avenue, Sutton Ings, Hull. Commemorated on the Cambrai Memorial.

WAUDBY, SERGEANT ARTHUR. 14/164. Killed in action on January 15th 1918. Commemorated in Ephy Wood Cemetery. Husband of Emma Alice Waudby of 4 Emerald Terrace, Campbell Street, Hull. Born in Hull.

WILCOCKSON, PRIVATE GEOFFREY. 10/773. Killed in action at Mont Kemmel on April 25th 1918 aged 24. Commemorated on the Tyne Cot Memorial. Born in Hull. Only son of John and Ada Wilcockson.

WILKINSON, CORPORAL JAMES WILLIAM. 13/1446. Killed in action on October 4th 1917. Commemorated on the Tyne Cot Memorial. Born in Hull.

WINTER, PRIVATE HARRY. 10/955. Killed in action on April 25th 1918. Commemorated on the Tyne Cot Memorial. Born in Hull. Son of F Winter of 24 Cadogan Street, Hull.

WOODCOOK, PRIVATE JOSEPH HERBERT. 14/127. Died of wounds on May 17th 1918 aged 24. Buried in Tournai Communal Cemetery Allied Extension. Born in High Town, Yorkshire but resident in Hull at the time of his enlistment. Son of Percy Brooke and Mary Ann Woodcock of 99 Newcomen Street, Hull.

2ND BATTALION

HUTESON, PRIVATE JOHN. 11/791. Killed in action on December 3rd 1917. Born in Hull. Buried in Roclincourt Military Cemetery.

RUSSELL, PRIVATE ERNEST. 10/18. Died in Salonika on October 1st 1918. Born in Hull. Buried in Kirechkoi-Hortakoi Military Cemetery, Greece.

SKINNER, PRIVATE FRANK. 14/225. Died of dysentery in Alexandria, Egypt on December 13th 1916 aged 20. He had been wounded in the arm and chest while serving in Salonika resulting in 12 weeks hospitalisation. Born in Beverley. Buried in Alexandria War Memorial Cemetery. Son of Mr and Mrs C. Skinner of Lairgate, Beverley. He had played rugby for Hull Kingston Rovers Rugby Club. His name appears on the St. Mary's Church Roll of Honour and on the Hengate War Memorial. His brother was a Sergeant in the Royal Garrison Artillery.

3RD BATTALION

BARLEY, PRIVATE DAVID. 13/1044. Died in the UK on April 23rd 1918. Born in South Cave, East Yorkshire, enlisted in Hull but resident in South Cave. Buried in South Cave Church Cemetery.

BOURNER, PRIVATE PERCY. 10/35. Officer Cadet with the 3rd battalion East Yorkshire Regiment. Died in the UK on May 16th 1918 aged 24. Buried in Holy Trinity Cemetery, Hessle Road, Hull. His name appears on a memorial in Northern Cemetery, Hull. His two brothers, Harold and George both died in France (see H. Bourner 12th battalion). Son of Mary Bourner of 20 Chestnut Grove, Park Road, Hull and the late David Edward Bourner.

BROWN, PRIVATE JOHN HENRY. 12/328. Died of tuberculosis on January 19th 1920 aged 20. Son of William James and Mary Elizabeth Brown of 2 Railway Cottages, Sutton Bank, Dansom Lane, Hull. Buried in Hedon Road Cemetery, Hull.

GUEST, SERGEANT J. 10/632. Died on February 17th 1919 aged 30. Husband of Florence Guest of 25 Falmouth Street, Hull. Buried in Northern Cemetery, Cottingham Road, Hull.

HICKS, PRIVATE FRANCIS REEVE. 14/153. Died of wounds on January 12th 1917 aged 26. Son of John Reeve and Fanny Hicks of Hull. Husband of Daisy Stone (formerly Hicks) of 67 Walmsley Street, Hull. Buried in Northern Cemetery, Cottingham Road, Hull.

JOHNSON, SERGEANT FREDERICK WALTER. 13/962. Killed in action on February 19th 1919. Buried in Soroka Zavode Cemetery. Commemorated on the Archangel Memorial. Son of F Johnson of 242 Newland Avenue, Hull. Sergeant Johnson was married.

JUDE, LANCE-CORPORAL MARTIN V. 10/1448. Died on December 15th 1916 after being discharged from the army. Buried in Northern Cemetery, Cottingham Road, Hull.

SMITH, PRIVATE G. 12/1235. Died on December 7th 1918. Husband of Mrs. B B W Smith of Nelson Terrace, Bean Street, Hessle Road, Hull. Buried in Western Cemetery, Spring Bank, Hull.

SMITH, REGIMENTAL QUARTER MASTER SERGEANT R. 11/589. Died on April 3rd 1918.

Husband of Mrs M E Smith of Hull. Buried in Western Cemetery, Hull.

SMITH, PRIVATE THOMAS ARTHUR. 13/231. Died of cerebral haemorrhage on October 31st 1918 aged 35. Husband of Fanny Elizabeth Smith of 5 William's Terrace, Walcott Street, Hull. Buried in Western Cemetery, Spring Bank, Hull.

TAYLOR, HENRY WRIGHT. 12/894. Died on March 25th 1919 aged 37. Son of William and Mary Taylor of 14 Lime Terrace, Crowle Street, Hedon Road, Hull. Resident in Walkington, East Yorkshire. Buried in Hedon Road Cemetery, Hull.

1ST/4TH & 4TH (RESERVE) BATTALION

BOGG, PRIVATE CHARLES. 11/636. Killed in action on April 23rd 1917. Born in Hull. Buried in Heninel Communal Cemetery Extension.

BROWN, PRIVATE ERNEST, of 'D' Company. 11/483. Killed in action on May 27th 1918. Commemorated on the Soissons Memorial. Born in Hull. Son of the late G.H. Brown of Kent Street, Hull. His wife lived at 3 Brighton Terrace, Kent Street, Hull.

CROSS, CORPORAL JOHN HENRY of 'C' Company. 13/65. Died on September 23rd 1918 aged 27. Born in Hull. Son of George Henry and Elizabeth Cross of 88 Brunswick Avenue, Beverley Road, Hull. Commemorated on the Soissons Memorial.

CRUDDAS, PRIVATE ARTHUR.10/1447. Killed in action on March 23rd 1918 aged 32. Born in Bridlington enlisted in Hull but resident in Bridlington. Son of Thomas and Annie Elizabeth Cruddas of 30 South Bank Lane, Bridlington, Yorkshire. Buried in Hancourt British Cemetery.

DALE, CORPORAL JOHN. 13/72. Died on September 15th 1918. Born in Hull. Commemorated on the Soissons Memorial.

DREWERY, PRIVATE HARRY. 13/1363. Killed in action on September 12th 1917. Born in Hull. Buried in Heninel Communal Cemetery Extension.

DONNELLY, JAMES CORNELIUS. 13/76. Killed in action on April 10th 1918 aged 27. Son of William and Jane Ann Donnelly. Born in Goole but resident in Hull at the time of enlistment. Commemorated on the Ploegsteert Memorial.

FINCH, SERGEANT JOSEPH WILLIAM. 10/455. Wounded in action on April 23rd 1917 and died the next day (24th) aged 24. Born in Thirkleby, Yorkshire but resident in Hull. Eldest son of A and E Finch of Durham Street, Hull.

FISHER, SERGEANT HORACE, MM. 10/445. Killed in action on May 27th 1918 aged 23. Born in Hull. Enlisted on September 4th 1914. Son of Amy and the late W S C Fisher of 34 Washington Street, Beverley Road, Hull. Commemorated on the Soissons Memorial.

HODGSON, PRIVATE JOHN. 10/166. Died of sickness in the UK on September 9th 1916 aged 22. Born in Hull. Son of John Henry and Clara Fanny Hodgson of 139 De Grey Street, Hull. Buried in Northern Cemetery, Hull.

JOHNSON, PRIVATE JOHN. 14/52. Died on October 1st 1918, of dysentery whilst a POW. Born in Hull. Husband of Edith Davidson (formerly Johnson) of 6 Waterloo Place, John Street, Hull. Buried in Worms (Hocheim Hill) Cemetery.

JOHNSON, CORPORAL REGINALD WILLIAM. 10/971. Killed in action on June 19th 1918. Born in Goole, enlisted in Hull but resident in Goole. Buried in Marfaux British Cemetery.

LEONARD, PRIVATE GEORGE LAWRENCE. 13/1002. Killed in action on March 23rd 1918 aged 22. Son of Mr and Mrs Leonard of 5 Shaw Street, Holderness Road, Hull. Born in Hull. Commemorated on the Pozieres Memorial.

McCOLL, PRIVATE CHARLES FRANCIS. 11/81. Shot for desertion on December 28th 1917. Born in Hull. Buried in Ypres reservoir Cemetery. (See Appendices)

MILLER, CQMS CHARLES WILLIAM MID. 11/926. Died on August 26th 1918 aged 40. Husband of G E Miller of 91 Chanterlands Avenue, Hull. Buried in Northern Cemetery, Cottingham Road. Hull.

MILNER, PRIVATE LOUIS WILLIAM. 11/406. Died of wounds on March 2nd 1918 aged 22. Son of Louis and Elizabeth Annie Milner of 47 James Street, East Hull. Born Eastney Barracks. Portsmouth. Buried in Nine Elms British Cemetery.

MOOR, PRIVATE HERBERT. 11/120. Killed in action on March 31st 1918. Born in Hull. Commemorated on the Pozieres Memorial.

PORTER, PRIVATE WALTER. 14/7. Killed in action on May 27th 1918. Born in Hull. Commemorated on the Soissons Memorial.

ROBINSON, CORPORAL ALFRED. 13/468. Killed in action on May 27th 1918. Born in Hessle. Enlisted in Hull but resident in Hessle. Commemorated on the Soissons Memorial.

SMITH, PRIVATE HARRY. 13/652. Died of wounds on March 31st 1918 aged 20. Son of Harry and Louisa Smith of 10 Clifton Avenue. Victor Street. Holderness Road, Hull. Commemorated on the Pozieres Memorial. Born in Hull.

WILKINSON, SERGEANT HARRY MANLEY. 13/286. Killed in action on March 25th 1918 aged 25. Commemorated on the Pozieres Memorial. Born in Hull. Son of Mrs. W Wilkinson of 9 South View, St. George's Road, Hull. Husband of Ivy Wilkinson (nee Osbourne) and father of Marjorie (died 25/12/1930 aged 15) of 94 Plane Street, Hull. He was a Hull Corporation employee. His brother Raymond served in the Royal Garrison Artillery and survived the War.

WILLCOX, PRIVATE GEORGE WILLIAM. 11/1220. Killed in action on March 27th 1918 aged 24. Commemorated on the Pozieres Memorial. Born in Hull. Son of Edward Thomas and Elizabeth Willcox of Hull. His brother Private Albert Willcox 11/1219 was also killed in action (see 11th battalion).

6TH BATTALION
DADDY, PRIVATE HARRY. 12/1059. Died of wounds on March 14th 1918 aged 26. Buried in Lapugnoy Military Cemetery. Born in Hull. Son of William Daddy of 28 Cheapside, Cleveland Street, Hull.

HATCH, PRIVATE WALTER. 12/952. Died of wounds on July 26th 1917 aged 34. Buried in Etaples Military Cemetery. Born in Hull. Son of Thomas William Hatch. Husband of Gertrude Hatch of 6 Edwards Terrace, Hessle Road, Hull.

LYDON, SERGEANT MICHAEL, MM. 13/714. Killed in action on March 13th 1918. Buried in Philosphe Military Cemetery, Mazingarbe. Born in Hull. Husband of C. Lydon of 27 Christopher Street, Hull.

PRITCHETT, PRIVATE WILLIAM JOHN. 11/141. Died of wounds on November 4th 1918. Buried in Ourgies Communal Cemetery. Born in Hull.

7TH BATTALION
ARSKEY, PRIVATE JOSEPH WILLIAM. 13/308. Died of wounds on August 25th 1918 aged 39. Born in Long Riston but resident in Hull. Husband of A Cressy (formerly Arskey) of Collingwood Brickyard, Barrow Haven, Lincolnshire. Buried in Fienvillers British Cemetery.

ATKINSON, PRIVATE MOSS. 14/17. Killed in action on March 31st 1918, aged 21. Commemorated on the Arras Memorial. Born in Hull. Son of Mrs Sarah Atkinson of 77 Greek Street, Hawthorne Avenue, Hull. He was engaged to be married at the time of his death. According to my grandmother (his cousin) he was the kindest man that she knew in her 93 years!!

BINGE, PRIVATE HARMAN. 12/132. Died of wounds on January 3rd 1917 aged 23. Buried in Grove Town Cemetery. Born in Hull. Son of Walter and Henrietta Binge of 1 Humber Place, Humber Dock, Hull.

BINNINGTON, PRIVATE SAMUEL. 12/866. Killed in action on October 12th 1918. Buried in Montay-Neuvilly Road Cemetery. Born in Hull. Husband of Lucy May Binnington of 91 Craven Street, Hull. Buried in Montay-Neuvilly Road Cemetery.

BLANCHARD, LANCE-CORPORAL ERNEST EDWARD of 'B' Company. 11/1187. Died of wounds on April 20th 1917 aged 26. Buried in Feuchy British Cemetery. Born in Hull. Son of John William and Margaret Hannah Blanchard of 5 City Grove, Harrow Street, Hessle Road, Hull. Husband of Ellen Cook (formerly Blanchard) of 3 Olive Grove, Harrow Street.

His name appears in the St. Barnabas Roll of Honour. His brother Percy died of wounds (gassed) received at Kemmel Hill.

BREALEY, PRIVATE ARTHUR. 10/467. Killed in action on May 12th 1917 aged 23. Commemorated on the Arras Memorial. Born in Hull. Enlisted in September 1914. Son of Arthur and Jane Eleanor Brealey of 53 Blake Street, Brunswick Avenue, Hull. His two brothers Lieutenant A. Brealey and Bombadier H. Brealey, both served in France and survived the war. He was an employee of Thomas Wilson and Son Ltd. of Hull.

BROWN, PRIVATE JOHN FREDERICK. 12/1218. Killed in action on June 28th 1916. Commemorated on the Thiepval Memorial. Born in Hull. Only son of Mary and the late Robert Brown.

BUXTON, PRIVATE JOSEPH. 13/1064. Killed in action on February 9th 1917 aged 34. Commemorated on the Thiepval Memorial. Born in Hull. Husband of Ada Buxton of 7 Welton Terrace, Courteney Street, Hull.

CAIN, PRIVATE HARRY. 11/1249. Died of wounds on November 4th 1918. Born in Hull. Buried in Forest Communal Cemetery.

CASS, PRIVATE ALEX. 13/1442. Killed in action on May 22nd 1917 aged 28. Born in Hull, enlisted in Beverley but resident in Hull. Husband of Fanny Mover (formerly Cass) of 3 Cyprus Walk, Alexandra Street, Hull. Commemorated on the Arras Memorial.

CLARKE, PRIVATE CHARLES. 11/1336. Killed in action on October 27th 1918. Born in Garton, Yorkshire but resident in Hull. He was married with children. Buried in Poix-du-Nord Communal Cemetery Extension.

CORDOCK, LANCE-CORPORAL JOHN WILLIAM. 12/1220. Killed in action on June 28th 1916 aged 29. Born in Hull. Buried in Serre Road Cemetery No. 3. Husband of Florence Lucy Webster (formerly Cordock) of 8 Middleton Villas, Clyde Street, Hawthorne Avenue, Hull. He was a father of an eight year old child. Before the war he worked for the NER as a Loader at Hull. His name appears on the NER Roll of Honour.

COULSON, PRIVATE CHARLES HENRY. 12/1484. Killed in action on March 21st 1918 aged 30. Born in Bridlington. Yorkshire but resident in Hull. Husband of Eveline Coulson of 9 Campbell Terrace, Rodney Street, Hull. Commemorated on the Arras Memorial.

COWLAM, PRIVATE EDWIN. 12/873. Killed in action on July 29th 1917. Born in Sheffield but resident in Hull. Buried in Brown's Copse Cemetery, Roeux.

COX, CORPORAL JOHN. 11/458. Killed in action on October 15th 1917. Born in Hull. Commemorated on the Tyne Cot Memorial.

CROOKS, REGIMENTAL SERGEANT MAJOR

HERBERT CLIFFORD, of "D' Company, MID. 13/32. Transferred to the Reserve upon demobilisation but died on March 30th 1919 aged 35 as a result of being gassed during the war. Son of Joseph and Elizabeth Crooks of Hull. Husband of Ada Crooks of 12 Kimberley Street, Argyle Street, Hull. Buried in Western Cemetery, Hull.

DALTON, PRIVATE CHARLES EDWIN. 12/554. Killed in action on March 31st 1918. Born in Hull. Husband of the late Gertrude Annie Dalton. Commemorated on the Arras Memorial.

DAVIS, PRIVATE THOMAS. 13/1421. Killed in action on November 5th 1916. Born in Sunderland but resident in Hull. Buried in the AIF Burial Ground.

DUKES, PRIVATE CHARLES WILLIAM. 12/200. Killed in action on August 28th 1918 aged 27. Commemorated on the Vis-en-Artois Memorial, Haucourt. Son of Mrs. Dukes of 2 Laburnum Avenue, Hardy Street, Hull. Born in Beverley.

EDSON, PRIVATE JAMES FREDERICK. 10/1095. Killed in action on November 5th 1916 aged 25. Born in Hull. Son of Charles H and Louisa A Edson of 4 Heaton Street, Brampton, Chesterfield. Husband of Gertrude A Edson. Commemorated on the Thiepval Memorial.

GREEN, PRIVATE CHARLES ALFRED, of 'D' Company. 11/613. Killed in action on February 8th 1917 aged 19. Son of George Alfred and Alice Mary Green, of 88 Summergangs Road, Holderness Road, Hull. Born in Goole but resident in Hull. Commemorated on the Thiepval Memorial.

HERRON, PRIVATE JAMES. 14/156. Killed in action on March 31st 1918. Born in Gateshead but resident in Hull. Commemorated on the Arras Memorial.

HOBSON, PRIVATE WALTER. 12/642. Died of wounds on September 12th 1918 aged 24. Son of Mr and Mrs W Hobson of 1 Hastings Street, Hull. Born in Hull. Buried in Niederzwehren Cemetery, Germany.

HOLMES, SERGEANT JOHN THOMAS. 12/407. Killed in action on March 31st 1918 aged 21. Born in Hull. Son of Thomas and Ann Holmes of 84 New Bridge Road, Hull. Commemorated on the Arras Memorial.

INGLIS, PRIVATE JOHN. 13/1052. Killed in action on May 12th 1917. Born in Scarborough but resident in Hull. Commemorated on the Arras Memorial.

JAMESON, PRIVATE WILLIAM. 12/451. Killed in action on August 25th 1917 aged 29. Born in Hull. Husband of Martha Annie Shann (formerly Jameson) of 8 Pine Grove, Bellamy Street, Hull. Buried in Brown's Copse Cemetery.

JEFFERSON, PRIVATE THOMAS WILLIAM CHRISTOPHER. 13/1491. Killed in action on August 24th 1918 aged 23. Son of Fred and Edith Jefferson of Winestead, Hull. Born in Hull. Commemorated on the Vis-en-Artois Memorial, Haucourt.

KEABLE, CORPORAL JAMES WILLIAM, MM. 11/1348. Died of wounds on November 5th 1918 aged 25. Born in Hull. Son of J W and Lydia Keable of 112 York Street, Hull. Buried in Caudry British Cemetery.

LAURIE, PRIVATE JOHN. 10/1138. Died in the UK on June 13th 1918 of paralysis. Born in Kiermill, Dumfries but resident in Hull. Buried in Epsom Cemetery.

LAWSON, PRIVATE JOHN WILLIAM. 12/1325. Killed in action on March 31st 1918 aged 39. Born in Hull. Husband of Mary Elizabeth Lawson of 1 Courtney Street, Holderness Road, Hull. Buried in Bouzincourt Ridge Cemetery.

LEEMING, PRIVATE ARTHUR. 10/388. Killed in action on January 31st 1917 aged 29. Son of Samuel and Elizabeth Leeming. Husband of Margaret Ann Leeming of 15 Westmoreland Street, Hull. Born in Hull. Commemorated on the Thiepval Memorial.

MARTIN, PRIVATE THOMAS JAMES. 13/177. Killed in action on July 19th 1917. Born in Southampton but resident in Hull. Buried in Brown's Copse Cemetery.

NELSON, PRIVATE CHARLES VICTOR. 13/859. Served in Egypt with the 13th battalion. Wounded in France during 1916. Killed in action on May 12th 1917 aged 19. Born in Hull, enlisted in Hull but resident in Etton, East Yorkshire. Commemorated on the Arras Memorial. Son of Charlotte and the late Richard Nelson of 55 Westwood Road, Beverley. His name appears on the Hengate War Memorial, Beverley.

PICKERING, PRIVATE FRED. 12/1390. Killed in action on March 31st 1918. Born in Scarborough but resident in Hull. Buried in Bouzincourt Ridge Cemetery.

PLEWS, LANCE-CORPORAL SPENCER MARKHAM. 12/1499. Killed in action on October 11th 1918 aged 35. Husband of Frances L Plews of 2 Marlborough Place, Marlborough Terrace, Beverley Road, Hull. Born in Hull. Commemorated on the Vis-en-Artois Memorial, Haucourt.

POWER, LANCE-CORPORAL MATTHEW 11/378. Killed in action on May 12th 1917. Born in South Shields but resident in Hull. Commemorated on the Arras Memorial.

PRATLEY, PRIVATE EDEN. 12/709. Died of wounds received in an enemy air raid on August 13th 1918 aged 25. Born in Ascott-under-Wychwood, Oxfordshire, enlisted in Hull but resident in Ascott. Son of James and Jane Pratley of Fairspeir, Ascott-under-Wychwood. Buried in Daours Communal Cemetery Extension.

ROBINSON, LANCE-CORPORAL EDWARD. 10/1010. Killed in action on April 24th 1917 aged 24. Born in Todmorden, Yorkshire but resident in Hull.

Son of Mrs. E M Robinson of 158 Clarendon Street, Spring Bank, Hull. Commemorated on the Arras Memorial.

SHEPPERSON, ERNEST. 11/780. Killed in action on March 25th 1918 aged 19. Born in Hull. Son of Mr and Mrs A Shepperson of 330 Holderness Road, Hull. Commemorated on the Arras Memorial.

SIMPSON, PRIVATE WILLIAM.13/534. Killed in action on July 29th 1917. Born in South Shields but resident in Hull. Buried in Brown's Copse Cemetery.

SUMMERLAND, PRIVATE RALPH WALTER. 13/795. Killed in action on March 22nd 1918 aged 32. Born in Kirton Lindsey, Lincolnshire but resident in Hull. Son of the late James and Harriet Summerland. Husband of Kate Eva Summerland of 2 Cornwall Gardens, Raglan Street, Hull. Commemorated on the Arras Memorial.

TAYLOR, SERGEANT DAWSON. 12/420. Died in Belgium on November 15th 1918. Born in Preston near Hull. Buried in Heverle War Cemetery.

TOMLINSON, PRIVATE CHARLES. 10/1325. Killed in action on February 9th 1917 aged 19. Son of John Henry and Jane Tomlinson of Top End Cottage, Cliffe, Selby, Yorkshire. Born in Castleford, Yorkshire but resident in Hull. Commemorated on the Thiepval Memorial.

TOMLINSON, PRIVATE JOSEPH HENRY. 12/665. Killed in action on March 25th 1918. Born in Hull. Commemorated on the Arras Memorial.

TONNECLIFFE, CORPORAL JOSEPH. 12/142. Killed in action on January 12th 1918 aged 24. Born in Derby, enlisted in Hull but resident in Hull. Son of Mrs E Chapman of 41 William Street, Derby.

TOWNEND, PRIVATE CYRIL PYBUS. 10/1068. Killed in action near Ypres on October 15th 1917 aged 34. Son of George and Mary Jane Townend, of 365, Holderness Road, Hull. Born in Hull. Buried in Cement House Cemetery.

WATKIN, LANCE-CORPORAL FREDERICK AMOS. 13/398. Died of wounds on April 12th 1918 aged 22. Buried in Pemes British Cemetery. Born in Hull. Son of Charles Robert and Rachel Watkin of 37, Walcott Street, Hessle Road, Hull. His name appears in the St. Barnabas Church Book of Rememberance. Buried in Pernes British Cemetery.

WATSON, PRIVATE ALEXANDER. 11/583. Killed in action on March 31st 1918. Born in Anderston, Glasgow. An employee of East Hull Gas Works. Commemorated on the Arras Memorial.

WAUDBY, SERGEANT ARTHUR CLEMENT. 11/641. Killed in action on September 8th 1917. Buried in Brown's Copse Cemetery. A prewar Fireman with the NER. Listed on the NER Roll of Honour.

WELLS, PRIVATE WILLIAM. 11/125. Killed in action on August 6th 1918 aged 18. Buried in Dantzig Alley British Cemetery. Born in Hull. Son of Alfred and Lavinia Sophia Wells of 15 Albert Avenue, Wellstead Street, Hull.

WEST, CORPORAL HAROLD FREDERICK. 10/272. Killed in action on October 10th 1918. Buried in Neuvilly Communal Cemetery and Extension. Born in Hull.

WOOD, PRIVATE FREDERICK. 14/61. Killed in action on May 12th 1917 aged 23. Commemorated on the Arras Memorial. Born in Hull. Son of William Pashby and Phoebe Wood of 1 the Avenue, Linnaeus Street, Hull.

YOUNG, PRIVATE ALLEN. 12/494. Killed in action on March 25th 1918. Commemorated on the Arras Memorial. Born in Hull. One of four children (three brothers).

8TH BATTALION

ALDERTON, PRIVATE ROBERT GEORGE. 14/5. Killed in action on July 21st 1916. Born in Bradfield, Suffolk, enlisted in Hull but resident in Bradfield. Commemorated on the Thiepval Memorial.

ALLEN, PRIVATE THOMAS. 12/401. Died on January 19th 1917, aged 39, from wounds received on the January 4th. Buried in Etaples Military cemetery. Born in Hull. Son of Elizabeth Allen of Cartwright's Place, Spring Bank, Hull. Husband of Elsie Hilda Allen of Wetwang, near Malton, Yorkshire. Father of two children.

BARTRAM, PRIVATE JOHN HENRY. 10/1397. Killed in action on July 14th 1916 aged 28. Son of the late Alfred and Emily S Bartram of the Manor House, Little Weighton, East Yorkshire. Born in Little Weighton, enlisted in Hornsea. Commemorated on the Thiepval Memorial.

BIRKS, PRIVATE GEORGE. 10/472. Killed in action on May 3rd 1917. Buried in Windmill British Cemetery. Born in Hull.

BOAST, PRIVATE FRANCIS DANIEL. 10/1255. Killed in action on July 14th 1916 aged 32. Commemorated on the Thiepval Memorial. Born in Kingham, Norfolk but resident in Hull. Son of Fred and Helen Boast. Husband of Patience Waugh (formerly Boast) of 13 Harcourt Terrace, Buckingham Street, Holderness Road, Hull. The Chaplain wrote to his wife, "I have just buried your husband where he fell on the Field of Battle. Although I am a stranger, I hope you will allow me to express my deep sympathy. It is terrible out here to see our gallant lads die, yet you at home have the hardest part to carry a brave heart and be worthy of the men who die for you. I pray God to help you do this, and be with your children."

BROWN, PRIVATE ABRAHAM. 13/1448. Killed in action on July 14th 1916 aged 19 years and 8 months. Commemorated on the Thiepval Memorial. Born in Hull. His name is inscribed on his mother's grave stone in Hull Western Synagogue Cemetery: she died, at the age of 48, just over three months after his death.

BROWN, PRIVATE SPENCELEY. 12/1251. Died of wounds on April 25th 1917 aged 23. Born in Burton Pisdsea. East Yorkshire but resident in Hull. Son of Mr and Mrs H Brown of Roos, Ottringham. Hull. Husband of Nellie Brown of Marton, Skirlaugh, East Yorkshire. Buried in Faubourg 'D'Amiens Cemetery, Arras.

CALLAGHAN, FRANCIS. 14/140. Killed in action on July 14th 1916. Born in Glasgow but resident in Hull. Buried in Quarry Cemetery (Montauban).

CAMPBELL, PRIVATE ALBERT. 10/1375. Died of wounds on September 30th 1917, aged 23. Born in Thealby, Lincolnshire, enlisted in Hull but was resident in Doncaster. Son of George and Mary Elizabeth Campbell of 4 Chapel Lane, Winterton, Scunthorpe. Buried in Mendinghem Military Cemetery, Poperinghe.

CAPES, PRIVATE HERBERT. 11/274. Killed in action on July 14th 1916. Born in Hull. Commemorated on the Thiepval Memorial.

COLLETT, PRIVATE CLARENCE HENRY. 14/165. Killed in action on June 14th 1916 aged 27. Born in Hull. Son of Thomas and Rosa Collett of Malksham. East Ella Drive, Anlaby Road, Hull. Commemorated on the Thiepval Memorial.

CORLYON, PRIVATE VICTOR WILLIAM. 10/1287. Killed in action on July 14th 1916 aged 18. Born in Hull. Son of William and Jane Corylon of the Tally Ho Hotel, 26 Bond Street, Hull. He was an ex-employee of the Micklefield Colliery Company. Commemorated on the Thiepval Memorial. His name appears on the Roll of Honour of St Mary's Church, Lowgate, Hull.

CROSS, PRIVATE HERBERT. 10/1270. Killed in action on July 14th 1916 aged 22. Born in Hull. Eldest son of Mr and Mrs Cross of 10 Dorset Street, Gypsyville, Hull. Worked before the war for the NER as a telephone attendant. Commemorated on the Thiepval Memorial.

DAWSON, PRIVATE ADRIAN. 14/182. Killed in action on May 4th 1917, aged 21. Born in Hull. Son of Edward and Ellen Adelaide Dawson of 129 Anlaby Road, Hull. Husband of late Clarice Dawson. Buried in Faubourg d'Amiens Cemetery, Arras.

DELL, PRIVATE SYDNEY HERBERT. 11/353. Killed in action on March 17th 1917. Born in Padbury but resident in Hull. Buried in Faubourg d'Amiens Cemetery, Arras.

DIMMOCK, SERGEANT GEORGE HENRY. 10/1329. Killed in action on August 18th 1916 aged 22. Born in Headingley but resident in Hull. Son of George Dimmock of Knaresborough. Husband of Frances Dimmock of Dodsworth House, Wakefield Road, Normanton, Yorkshire. Buried in Guillemont Road Cemetery.

DOBBS, PRIVATE JOSEPH WELLINGTON. 11/1405. Killed in action on September 26th 1917 aged 23. Son of Joseph Mundy and Alice Wellington Dobbs. Husband of Rose Tong (formerly Dobbs) of 68 Woodhouse Street, Hedon Road, Hull. Born in Hull. Commemorated on the Tyne Cot Memorial.

EARLE, PRIVATE ALBERT HENRY. 13/1449. Died of wounds on June 27th 1917 aged 19. Son of Henry and Mary Frances Earle of 32 Farringdon Street, Stepney Lane, Hull. Buried in Northern Cemetery, Nottingham Road. Hull.

FOSTER, LANCE-CORPORAL HARRY NETTLETON. 14/81. Went to France in November 1915. Killed in action on July 14th 1916 aged 19. Born in Hull. Son of Joseph Henry and Mary Jane Foster of 53 Louis Street, Spring Bank, Hull. Attended Craven Street School where he won a scholarship. Commemorated on the Thiepval Memorial.

FRANKS, PRIVATE CHARLES HERBERT. 14/128. Killed in action on April 13th 1917 aged 22. Born in Hull but resident in Manchester at the time of enlistment. His parents lived at 5 Park Avenue, Perth Street, Hull. Commemorated on the Arras Memorial.

GIBSON, LANCE-CORPORAL ARTHUR. 13/1431. Killed in action on May 5th 1917. Born in Hull. Commemorated on the Arras Memorial.

GUISE, LANCE-CORPORAL CHARLES. 10/1377. Killed in action on July 14th 1916 aged 21. Born in Droitwich (Worcestershire), enlisted in Hull but resident in Droitwich. Son of William Seymour and Henrietta Guise of Droitwich. Buried in Cerisy-Gailly Military Cemetery.

HARWOOD, PRIVATE SAMUEL EDGAR. 10/501. Killed in action on July 19th 1916. Born in Hull. Buried in London Cemetery Extension.

HIGH, PRIVATE WILLIAM. 10/1215. Killed in action on June 15th 1916. Born in Middlesborough but resident in Hull.

HILL, PRIVATE JOHN HOWARD. 14/173. Killed in action on July 24th 1916. Born in Hull, enlisted in Hull but resident in Hedon. Commemorated on the Thiepval Memorial.

HOLMES, PRIVATE WILLIAM. 10/1395. Killed in action on July 14th 1916. Born in Burton Agnes, East Yorkshire but resident in Bridlington. Commemorated on the Thiepval Memorial.

HOLMES, PRIVATE MARK HORACE. 10/1403. Died on June 25th 1916, aged 21. Died of wounds received at St. Eloi. Born in Hull. Son of John and Anne Holmes of Hull. Buried in Etaples Military Cemetery.

HUMPHREY, PRIVATE GEORGE HENRY. 12/5. Killed in action on April 13th 1917. Born in Hull. Commemorated on the Arras Memorial.

ILLINGWORTH, PRIVATE HARRY OAKDEN, of 'C' Company. 10/879. Killed in action on September 26th

1917 aged 21. Son of Mary Annie Illingworth of 6 Lily's Terrace, Finsbury Street, Hull. Born in Hull. Commemorated on the Tyne Cot Memorial.

JACKSON, PRIVATE REGINALD. 14/42. Died of wounds on July 15th 1916 aged 21. Born in Goole, enlisted in Hull but resident in Goole at the time. Son of John Thomas and Matilda Jackson of 37 Hook Road, Goole, Yorkshire. Buried in Corbie Communal Cemetery Extension.

JORDAN, PRIVATE HAROLD HOOPER. 10/1432. Killed in action on July 25th 1916 aged 27. Son of Mrs Susan Jordan. Born in Hull. Commemorated on the Thiepval Memorial.

JOYCE, PRIVATE ALFRED. 13/1208. Killed in action on July 24th 1916. Born in Hull. Commemorated on the Thiepval Memorial.

KINGSTON, PRIVATE ERNEST EDWARD. 11/237. Died of wounds on October 4th 1917. Born in Hull. Buried in Mont Huon Military Cemetery.

LINSLEY, PRIVATE FREDERICK. 10/1328. Killed in action July 14th 1916 aged 20. Son of Thomas and Sarah Jane Linsley of 14 Sutton Street, Goole, Yorkshire. Born in Goole, enlisted in Hull but resident in Goole. Commemorated on the Thiepval Memorial.

MASTERS, LANCE-CORPORAL JOHN. 10/1364. Killed in action on June 15th 1916, aged 24. Born in Market Drayton enlisted in Hornsea but was resident in Longford, son of the late William Henry Masters and Emma Masters of the Limes Lodge, Longford, Gloucester. Buried in Elzenwalle Brasserie Cemetery, Voormezelle, Ypres.

NORMAN, PRIVATE JOHN WILLIAM, of 'B' Company. 12/1495. Died of wounds on November 3rd 1917 aged 31. Born in Hornsea, enlisted in Hull but was resident in Hornsea at the time of enlistment. Son of John and Ada Norman of Hornsea. Husband of Florence Norman of 10 Belle Vue Terrace, Alexandra Street, Hull. Buried in Favreuil British Cemetery.

PEARSON, PRIVATE ALFRED. 11/78. Killed in action on November 26th 1916. Born in Rochester, Kent but resident in Hull. Buried in Sailly-au-Bois Military Cemetery.

PENNOCK, PRIVATE THOMAS PROUD. 13/861. Killed in action on April 13th 1917. Born in Cropton, Yorkshire but resident in Hull. Commemorated on the Ronville Military Cemetery Memorial.

REDFEARN, PRIVATE CHRISTOPHER WILLIAM. 11/1442. Killed in action on June 4th 1917 aged 39. Born in Hull. Son of George Henry and Mary Ann Redfearn of Hull. Husband of Hannah Redfearn of 1 Devon Grove, Sculcoates Lane, Beverley Road. Hull. Buried in Monchy British Cemetery.

ROCKINGHAM, PRIVATE WILLIAM BEECROFT. 10/1336. Killed in action on July 14th 1916. Born in Hull. Commemorated on the Thiepval Memorial.

SANDERS, PRIVATE GEORGE HENRY, of A Company. 14/105. Killed in action on November 13th 1916 aged 19. Born in Beverley. Buried in Caterpillar Valley Cemetery. Son of George and Julia Sanders of 6. Minster Street, Moorgate, Beverley. His name appears on the Hengate War Memorial.

SISSONS, SERGEANT SAMUEL. 13/1232. Killed in action on July 14th 1916. Born in Hull. Commemorated on the Thiepval Memorial.

SMITH, PRIVATE ALBERT HENRY. 14/39. Killed in action on July 14th 1916 aged 25. Brother of Mrs A J Spence of 9 Claremont Terrace, Day Street. Hull. Born in Hull. Commemorated on the Thiepval Memorial.

SMITH, PRIVATE GEORGE COLLEY WHELDALE. 11/1459. Died of wounds on May 3rd 1917 aged 21. Son of John William and Eliza Jane Smith of 64 Church Street. Hull. Born in Hull. Buried in St. Hilaire Cemetery.

SPILMAN, PRIVATE HENRY. 14/86. Died of wounds on May 2nd 1917 aged 21. Born in Whitton, enlisted in Hull but was resident in Doncaster at the time. Son of Thomas and Helena Blanche Spilman of Cliffhouse. Whitton, Scunthorpe. Buried in Duisans British Cemetery.

STONEHOUSE, PRIVATE HAROLD. 10/1347. Killed in action on July 14th 1916 aged 22. Son of Henry and A Stonehouse of 35 Woodhouse Road, Mansfield, Nottinghamshire. Born in Withernsea, East Yorkshire but resident in Hull. Commemorated on the Thiepval Memorial.

SUTTON, PRIVATE ARTHUR JOSEPH. 10/1451. Killed in action on July 14th 1916 aged 20. Son of John Albert and Bertha E Sutton of Aireville School, Hessle, East Yorkshire. Born in Manchester, enlisted in Hull but resident in Hessle. Commemorated on the Thiepval Memorial.

TAYLOR, PRIVATE GEORGE WILLIAM. 10/1349. Killed in action on July 19th 1916. Born in Hull. Commemorated on the Thiepval Memorial.

TINDALE, PRIVATE FRANK. 10/1324. Killed in action on July 14th 1916 aged 19. Son of James and Caroline Tindale of 18 Suffolk Street, Hull. Born in Hull. Commemorated on the Thiepval Memorial.

TONKINSON, PRIVATE STANLEY. 10/1426. Killed in action on July 14th 1916. Commemorated on the Thiepval Memorial. Born in Kidderminster but resident in Beverley at the time of enlistment. Youngest son of Mr. E.L. Tonkinson, the Beverley Postmaster. His name appears on the Norwood Roll of Honour, the Hengate Roll of Honour and St. Mary's Church Roll of Honour, Beverley.

UNDERWOOD, PRIVATE JOHN WILLIAM. 13/1102. Killed in action on September 26th 1917 aged 30. Son of John and Emily Elizabeth Underwood. Husband of Margaret Mabel Weldon (formerly Underwood) of 16 Cotton Terrace, Barnsley

Street, Holderness Road, Hull. Born in Hull. Commemorated on the Tyne Cot Memorial.

VOAKES, PRIVATE ARTHUR CYRIL. 13/81. Died of wounds on September 7th 1916 aged 19. Born in Hull. Son of John George and Jane Elizabeth Voakes of Hull. Buried in Barlin Communal Cemetery.

VOSE, PRIVATE WILLIAM. 13/660. Died of wounds on August 1st 1916 aged 41. Son of John and Elizabeth Vose of St. Helens, Lancashire. Husband of Eleanor Vose of 69A Parker Street, Byker, Newcastle-upon-Tyne. Born in St. Helens but resident in Hull. Buried in St. Sever Cemetery, Rouen.

WARDLE, PRIVATE JOHN GEORGE. 10/1299. Killed in action on July 14th 1916. Commemorated on the Thiepval Memorial. Born in Hull but resident in Hessle. Married to Gertie Wardle of Marlborough Avenue, Hessle.

WASS, PRIVATE JOHN EDWARD. 11/639. Killed in action on May 4th 1917. Commemorated on the Arras Memorial. Born in Hull. Son of Mr. L & Mrs. Wass of 4, Robinson's Place, Princess Street, Hull. His brother George was killed in action by a shell exploding in his dugout in March 1917. Brother James was killed in action with the 6th battalion on September 17th 1917. A third brother was discharged from the army with Consumption and died on May 26th 1917.

WEST, PRIVATE WALTER HICKS. 12/513. Killed in action on July 14th 1916 aged 22. Commemorated on the Thiepval Memorial. Born in Skirlaugh but resident in Hull. Son of Mrs. M. Bowman of 38 Crowle Street, Hull.

WHYTE, PRIVATE WILLIAM JAMES. 10/1344. Killed in action on July 25th 1916 aged 18. Commemorated on the Thiepval Memorial. Born in Hull. His name appears on the Brunswick Avenue Roll of Honour.

WILKINSON, PRIVATE WILLIAM HENRY. 13/1261. Died of wounds on July 25th 1916 aged 35. Buried in Corbie Communal Cemetery Extension. Born in Hull. Son of Mrs. Wilkinson of 115 Walton Street, Hull. Husband of Agnes Jane Wilkinson and Children of 66 Wheeler Street, Hull.

WILSON, PRIVATE PERCY. 10/1444. Killed in action on July 14th 1916 aged 21. Son of Thomas and Susannah Wilson of 22 Lansdowne Road, Bridlington, Yorkshire. Born in Bridlington, enlisted in Beverley but resident in Bridlington. Commemorated on the Thiepval Memorial.

WRIGHT, PRIVATE JAMES. 13/486. Killed in action on November 13th 1916 aged 21. Husband of Alice May Wright of 22 Grosvenor Terrace, Grosvenor Street, Hull. Born in Hull. Buried in Serre Road Cemetery No 1.

14TH BATTALION

FREEMAN, PRIVATE REGINALD CHARLES, of 'A' Company. 10/330. Died in the UK on January 1st 1916

aged 30. Son of George and Mary Ann Freeman of Highfield, 11 Heene Road, West Worthing. Born in Guernsey, Channel Islands, enlisted in Hull but was resident in Ramsgate. Buried in Durrington Cemetery.

HARDING, PRIVATE WILLIAM WALTER. 12/2. Died on June 10th 1916 aged 28. Buried in Hull Western Cemetery.

HODGSON, PRIVATE JOHN. 10/166. Died of sickness on September 9th 1916 aged 22. Son of John Henry and Clara Fanny Hodgson of 139 De Grey Street, Hull. Buried in Northern Cemetery, Hull.

LING, PRIVATE GEORGE EDWARD KING. 11/965. Died on March 10th 1916 aged 35. Buried in Hull Western Cemetery.

REDMORE, LANCE-CORPORAL HAROLD. 10/544. Died in the UK on September 13th 1916 aged 25. Son of Edward King and Catherine Redmore of Hull. Husband of Minnie Ida Redmore of Glencoe Avenue, Flinton Street, Hull. Born in Hull. Buried in Western Cemetery, Hull.

STEPHENSON, PRIVATE NEVILLE ARTHUR. 14/123. Died on February 11th 1916 aged 23. Born in Willerby, East Yorkshire but resident in Hull. Son of Mr N Stephenson of Willerby. Buried in Kirkella Church Cemetery.

1ST GARRISON BATTALION

OSBORNE, LANCE-CORPORAL ALFRED. 13/524. Died in India on June 22nd 1917. Born in Hull. Buried in Lucknow Cantonment Military Cemetery.

HULL PALS WHO DIED SERVING WITH OTHER REGIMENTS

BARTON, PRIVATE THOMAS WILLIAM. 42546. 8th Yorkshire Regiment. Formerly 13/671 East Yorkshire regiment. Died of wounds on June 10th 1917, aged 37. Born in London but resident in Hull. Husband of Sarah Barton of 31 Fleet Street, Hull. Buried in Lyssenthoek Military Cemetery. Poperinghe.

BASLINGTON, PRIVATE JAMES. 203050 l/5th West Yorkshire Regiment. Formerly 12/1420 East Yorkshire Regiment. Killed in action on April 25th 1918. Born in Horkstow Bridge, Lincolnshire, but resident in Hull.

BULLEYMENT, WO II GEORGE. 51999. 2nd King's Own Yorkshire Light Infantry. Formerly 13/1221 East Yorkshire Regiment. Shot by a sniper, on August 23rd 1917 (aged 27), while he was rounding up prisoners. Born in Keyingham, East Yorkshire. He was a married man with one son. Buried in Heath Cemetery. Harbonnieres. Nephew of Mr G Cooper of 16 Pryme Street, Anlaby.

BURNHAM, CORPORAL HAROLD. TR5/80278 of the 53rd Young Soldiers Battalion of the KOYLI. Died in the UK on October 24th 1917. Formerly 14/185 of the East Yorkshire Regiment.

BURR, PRIVATE JAMES. 605926 42nd Prisoner of War Company. Labour Corps. Formerly 13/847 of the East Yorkshire Regiment. Buried in Hedon Road Cemetery, Hull. Died on May 7th 1919. Husband of Mrs Booth (formerly Burr) of 15 George's Terrace, Hull.

CADE, PRIVATE A. 372182 Died of wounds on March 22nd 1918 serving with the Labour Corps. Formerly 11/1312 of the East Yorkshire Regiment. Buried in Grevillers, British Cemetery.

CLARK, PRIVATE HENRY. 27227 l/5th West Yorkshire Regiment. Formerly 13/1361 East Yorkshire Regiment. Killed in action July 15th 1916. Born in Hull.

DOUGHTY, PRIVATE A. Died on January 26th 1919 serving with the Labour Corps. Formerly 12/1054 of the East Yorkshire Regiment. Buried in Terlincthun British Cemetery.

FISHER, PRIVATE CHARLES HERBERT. 416904. Transferred to the Labour Corps. Died on August 29th 1919 aged 38. Husband of Harriet Fisher of 2 Sophia's Place, Percy Street, Hull. Buried in Hedon Road Cemetery. Previously 11/1157 of the East Yorkshire Regiment.

HADWIN, WARRANT OFFICER II JOHN. 134041. Transferred to the Labour Corps. Died on July 28th 1920 aged 55. Previously CQMS of the 11th battalion. Buried in Everigham Roman Catholic Cemetery. Previously 11/809 of the East Yorkshire Regiment

HUDDLESTONE, CORPORAL C. 79243 Transferred to 2nd DLI. Died of wounds on April 20th 1918. Born in Beverley. Formerly 13/785 of the East Yorkshire Regiment.

LEE, PRIVATE CLIFFORD. 27315. 11th East Lancashire regiment. Killed in action on July 1st 1916, aged 28. Born in Hull. Formerly ??/111 East Yorkshire Regiment. Son of Harry and Ada Faith Lee of 88 Londesborough Street, Hull. Buried in Queens Cemetery. Puisieux.

McNALLY, PRIVATE A. Killed in action - date or regiment not traced. Previously 13/456 East Yorkshire Regiment. Brother of Private T J McNally 13/455 East Yorkshire Regiment.

MILLS, PRIVATE THOMAS. 28791. Transferred to 2nd Royal Dublin Fusiliers. Killed in action on October 18th 1918. Formerly 14/59 of the East Yorkshire Regiment. Buried in Highland Cemetery, Le Cateau.

MOORE, LANCE-CORPORAL ARTHUR. 27277. 11th East Lancashire Regiment. Killed in action on July 1st 1916. aged 21. Formerly ??/122 East Yorkshire Regiment. Born in Hull. Son of Arthur and Norah Ann Moore, of 62 Freehold Street, Hull. Buried in Serre Road Cemetery No. 2.

PADGET, PRIVATE CHARLES of 'D' Company. 13/368. Died of Phthisis on August 23rd 1921 aged 26. Son of Hannah Mary of 31 Brook Street, Hull and the late John Padget. Buried in Hedon Road Cemetery, Hull.

SANDERS, PRIVATE GEORGE. 27254. 11th East Lancashire Regiment. Killed in action on July 1st 1916. Born in Hull. Formerly ??/106 East Yorkshire Regiment. Son of the late Mr and Mrs George Sanders. Commemorated on the Thiepval Memorial.

TUTON, PRIVATE JOHN HENRY. 11th East Lancashire Regiment. Killed in action on July 2nd 1916. Formerly 12/489 East Yorkshire Regiment and 31st Division ACC. Commemorated on the Thiepval Memorial.

Appendix 13
Officers Died – Details

10TH BATTALION

ADDY, CAPTAIN JAMES CARLTON, MC, of A Company. Served in Egypt and France. Killed in action May 3rd 1917, aged 26. Commemorated on the Arras Memorial. Son of Mr & Mrs J.J. Addy of "Carlton", Holbeck Hill, Scarborough.

ANDREW, LIEUTENANT ERNEST JOHN. Killed in action on March 23rd, 1918, near St. Quentin, serving with the 1st battalion, aged 30. Commemorated on the Pozieres Memorial. Son of M.J. Andrew and John Mann Andrew. Husband of Ethel Florence Andrew of Grafton House, Grafton Street, Hull.

BRADBURY, SECOND LIEUTENANT WILLIAM ROWLAND. Killed in action on September 7th 1918 during the attack from Prompt Farm to the River Lys. Aged 29. Buried in Trois Arbres Cemetery, Steenwerck. Son of Azubah and the late Henry Bradbury of South Elmsall. He was married to Martha Bradbury of 155 High Street, Heckmondyke.

BROMBY, LIEUTENANT WILLIAM GIRDESTONE. Died on May 29th 1921, aged 26, as a result of sickness caused by being gassed during the war. Buried in St. Nicholas' Churchyard, Withernsea. Son of Laura Bromby of "Maridene", Princes Avenue, Withernsea and the late Alfred Bromby.

BUTTERY, SECOND LIEUTENANT WALTER. Killed in action August 20th 1918 aged 32. Buried in Outersteerne Communal Cemetery, Bailleul. Son of Walter and Jane Buttery of "Ingleside", Cottingham Road, Hull. He was originally commissioned into the 5th (Cyclist) Battalion.

CARLISLE, CAPTAIN REGINALD. Killed in action on May 3rd 1917 aged 22. Commemorated on the Arras Memorial. Son of Percy and Ellen Carlisle of 34, Riverdale, Sheffield.

CHEESBOROUGH, SECOND LIEUTENANT HAROLD. Killed in action on September 4th 1918 aged 26, near Steenwerck. Enlisted in December 1914 into the 15th West Yorks. Served in Egypt and France. Before the war he was a Bank Clerk. He was married in July 1917 to Nellie Mitchell in Morley, near Dewsbury. Educated at Batley Grammar School. He lived at 5 Ellard Road, Churwell, near Leeds before the war. His wife lived at 6 Hughendon View, Springfield Road, Morley. Originally commissioned into the 52nd battalion of the West Yorkshire Regiment he was later transferred to the East Yorkshire regiment. Buried in Pont D'Achelles Military Cemetery, Nieppe.

CLARK, CAPTAIN WILLIAM SOWERBY. Accidentally killed in bombing practice on July 10th 1917, aged 23 and buried in Ecoivres Military Cemetery, Mont St. Eloy on the 11th. Son John Munro and Martha Minnie Clark of Hull. His name appears on the Methodist Church War Memorial, Princes Avenue, Hull.

DAVIS, SECOND LIEUTENANT OWEN MAZZINGHI. Killed in action on June 26th 1916 aged 33. Buried in Sucrerie Military Cemetery. Colincamps. He was a civil servant before the war. His mother (his next of kin) lived at 89 Shepherds Bush Road, London. He attested on August 5th 1914 in the 15th (Civil Service Rifles) London Regiment serving with them in France from March 1915 to December 1915 when he returned to England for a commission.

DOBSON, SECOND LIEUTENANT FRANK RAYNER. Commissioned into the 3rd Battalion of the Yorks and Lancs but served with the 10th East Yorkshires. Killed in action on September 28th 1918 aged 30. Buried in Pont D'Achelles Military Cemetery, Nieppe. Son of John and Sarah Jane Dobson of Green End Farm. Carlton. Wakefield.

DUGDALE, CAPTAIN DANIEL. Killed in action September 28th 1918 in Ploegsteert Wood during the battle of Ypres while attacking under a creeping barrage. Buried at Pont D'Achelles Military Cemetery, Nieppe. He was an original member of the battalion. Son of Fred and Alice Ann Dugdale of "Beverley", Lambs Road.Thornton-Le-Fylde. He was educated at Rossal School. A pre-war member of the Hull Philharmonic Society.

EARLE, SECOND LIEUTENANT CEDRIC. Killed in action September 4th 1918, aged 20. Buried in Le Grand Beaumart British Cemetery, Steenwerck. Son of Ernest Haworth and Mary Earle of 168 Victoria Avenue, Hull.

FLINTOFF, LIEUTENANT RANDOLPH ALEX. Killed in action on June 25th 1916 by German gas, at the front line near Bess Street and Warley Avenue, north of John Copse, aged 33. Buried in Bertrancourt Military Cemetery. Son of Churchill and Susan Hephzibah Flintoff of Alnwick. Before the war he had been Manager of Russell & Sons, Coal Merchants Exporters, 2 Marlborough Street, for six years. He was highly respected in Hull Commercial circles and a popular member of the Hull Exchange.

FRICKER, SECOND LIEUTENANT ALBERT CHARLES, BSc (LONDON), of 'B' Company. Killed during an attack on the Hindenburg Line on February 27th 1917, aged 23. Buried in Euston Road Cemetery,

Colincamps. Son of Albert Edwin and Mary Ann Fricker of Close Cottage, Rodbourne Cheny, Swindon.

HOUGHTON, SECOND LIEUTENANT ALBERT WILLIAM. He joined the army in London at the start of the war (26/9/1914) serving in the Queen's Regiment, going overseas in December 1916. He was commissioned into the East Yorkshire Regiment and joined the 10th Battalion May 30th 1917. Before the war he was a clerk. He was born on February 1st, 1889. Died of wounds on March 31st 1918 aged 29. Buried at Etaples Military Cemetery. Son of Herbert and Elizabeth Houghton of 6, Duesbury Street, Princess Avenue, Hull.

HUTCHINSON, LIEUTENANT LESLIE GWYNNE. Killed in action by a sniper on September 10th, 1918, near Steenwerck, aged 24. Buried at Trois Arbres Cemetery, Steernwerck. He attended Sedbergh School and was an undergraduate at Clare College, Cambridge when the war started. Originally commissioned into the 8th battalion. He lived at Heatherleigh. Burley in Wharfedale, Yorkshire. His brother served in the RFA and was also killed in action. Lt. Hutchinson left a will of £5582 12 shillings and 3 pence.

JACKSON, LIEUTENANT HAROLD WILLOWS. Enlisted as a Private at the start of the war. Commissioned into the 4th Battalion. Died of wounds on April 15th 1917 aged 20. Buried in Duisans Cemetery, Etrun. Son of Caroline Maud Jackson and the late John Henry Jackson. He was a native of Hornsea. One of three children; an only son.

JOHNSTON, SECOND LIEUTENANT ALEXANDER, of 'A' Company. Killed in action March 25th 1918. Commemorated on the Arras Memorial. Before the war he lived at 168 Bishopthorpe Road, York.

JONES, LIEUTENANT ARTHUR GODMAN, of 'B' Company. Died of wounds on July 1st 1917, aged 36. Buried at Duisans British Cemetery, Etrun. Son of Robert Thomas and Mary A. Jones of Hull.

KROG, LIEUTENANT EUSTACE JOHN, MC. Wounded in the battle of Flers-Courcelette, September 1916. Killed in action on September 7th 1918, aged 25, near Steernwerck. Buried in Pont d'Achelles Military Cemetery, Nieppe. Son of Eustace Krog. Married to Ada Krog of 76, Middle Street, Brighton.

LEECH, CAPTAIN NORMAN BLACK. Died of wounds on May 10th 1917 aged 22. Admitted to the 1st Red Cross Hospital at Le Touquet on May 4th dangerously ill with a gunshot wound in the left thigh. His mother was given permission to visit him while he was in hospital. Buried in Etaples Military Cemetery. His parents lived at Lindenhurst, Bourne

End, Buckinghamshire. Educated at Rugby where he was a member of the OTC. Emigrated to Canada and at the start of the war joined the 1st British Columbia Regiment in the 2nd Canadian Brigade. Applied for a commission when the battalion arrived in England.

MARSHALL, SECOND LIEUTENANT ANDREW FAIRLIE WILSON. Died as a Prisoner-of-War in Germany on September 26th 1918, aged 33. Buried in Niederzwechren Cemetery, Cassel. Son of William Marshall of 7, Broompark Drive, Dennistoun, Glasgow.

McDERMOTT, SECOND LIEUTENANT EDWARD, MC & BAR. Wounded in a raid on enemy trenches, west of Fresnou Wood on September 12th 1917. Killed in action on April 12th 1918 during the German attack on Doulieu. Buried in Ousteerne Communal Cemetery, Bailleul.

PALMER, LIEUTENANT DEREK WILLIAM ONSLOW. Commissioned Lieutenant in January 1915. Killed in action on June 4th 1916, aged 22. Killed alongside Lt. Spink during enemy shelling of the front line trenches east of Engelbelmer. Buried in Bertrancourt Military Cemetery, only son of Edith Fiennes and T.W Palmer of Brough. He was educated at Aysgarth and Winchester. His name appears on the Elloughton War Memorial and on the Elloughton Parish Church brass commemorative tablet.

PIERSON, LIEUTENANT LESLIE DILWORTH, MID. Killed in action October 30th 1916, aged 20, while on a patrol, prior to a raid to be carried out on the night of the 31st. Commemorated on the Thiepval Memorial. Son of Sarah M Pierson of 12 Stanhope Gardens, South Kensington, London and the late Reverend W B Pierson, of Rothwell Vicarage, Leeds.

PIGGOTT, SECOND LIEUTENANT FREDERICK. Killed in action on September 28th 1918 during the attack along the North-Eastern edge of Ploegsteert Wood. Buried in Pont d'Achelles Military Cemetery, Nieppe.

RAYNER, SECOND LIEUTENANT HAROLD, of 'C' Company. Originally commissioned into the 1st/4th Battalion. Killed in action at Verligham, in the advance to occupy Hill 63, on September 4th 1918, aged 25. Buried in New Irish Farm Cemetery, St. Jean Les Ypres. Son of Joe and Kate Rayner of 30, Sholebroke Avenue, Leeds. He lived at 56, Westbourne Avenue, Hull before the war.

RENDLE, SECOND LIEUTENANT GEORGE. Originally commissioned into the 1st/4th Battalion. Killed in action on October 1st 1918, aged 26. Commemorated on the Tyne Cot Memorial. Husband of Nellie Rendle of 2, Rock House, Victoria Square, Portishead, Bristol.

RICE, CAPTAIN BERNARD NEVILLE. Died of wounds, in Britain on July 7th 1917 aged 22. Buried in

Leamington (Milverton) Cemetery. Son of Bernard Rice, MD, JP and Lillian Rice of Cloister Cottage, Leamington Spa.

RUTHERFORD, SECOND LIEUTENANT WILLIAM McCONNELL. Enlisted as a private in the RAMC in October 1914. Served in Egypt. Commissioned into the East Yorkshire Regiment in June 1917. Died of wounds on April 19th 1918, aged 37. Buried in Wimereux Communal Cemetery. Son of William and Lily Rutherford of College Green, Belfast.

SANGER, SECOND LIEUTENANT HENRY KEITH. Killed in action April 13th 1918, aged 19. Buried in Outersteerne Communal Cemetery extension, Ballieul. Son of Henry and Leila Somers Sanger of 258 Euston Road, London.

SOUTHERN, SECOND LIEUTENANT MATTHEW of 'B' Company. Killed in action during a very successful raid on the enemy trenches on September 12th 1917 aged 31. Buried in Roelincourt Military Cemetery. A pre-war schoolmaster who attested in Newcastle, on August 27th 1914. He joined the 6th East Yorkshire Regiment and served in Gallipoli and Egypt. After serving in France from July 1916 to January 1917 he transferred to the UK for officer training. He was resident at 3 Ord Street, Gateshead. His father resided at 11 Alexander Terrace, Haydon Bridge.

SPINK, SECOND LIEUTENANT CECIL COOPER. Commissioned in 1914. Killed in action on June 4th 1916, aged 24. Killed alongside Lt. Palmer, during the German bombardment of the front line trenches east of Engelbelmer. Buried in Bertrancourt Military Cemetery. Eldest son of Frederick W. Spink, of "Inglehurst". Bridlington. Before the war he was an articled solicitor to his father's Law practice. Attended Bridlington Grammar School. Studied at Cambridge achieving a B.A. and LL.B. His name appears on the Bridlington War Memorial and the Priory Church War Memorial.

STRINGER, SECOND LIEUTENANT DUDLEY. Killed in action on May 3rd 1917. Commemorated on the Arras Memorial. Husband of Bertha Stringer of 8, Auckland Avenue, Hull.

TRAILL, MAJOR COLIN BALFOUR, MC, O/C 'C' Company. He joined the battalion at Hornsea in late 1914 after being commissioned into the 24th London on September 14th 1914. Killed in action on June 26th 1918 aged 23. He is believed to have died of shock/concussion from a British shell falling short and bursting close to him - no wound was found on his body. Buried in Le Grand Hassard Military Cemetery. Morbecque. Son of Gilbert Francis and Edith Elizabeth Traill of "Broadlands", Tunbridge Wells. Left a will of £5087-15-9d to his brother and sister. Born in Ceylon. On May 2nd 1917 he was blown out of a trench and into a shell hole by a high explosive shell and during the attack on the 3rd he suffered shell concussion caused by a shell explosion during the attack and a gun shot wound to the chin caused by a shell splinter. Commemorated by a brass plaque in St. James' Church in Tunbridge Wells.

WEBSTER, SECOND LIEUTENANT ARTHUR CECIL. Originally commissioned into the 1st Battalion. Killed in action on May 3rd 1917 aged 23. Commemorated on the Arras Memorial. Fourth son of George William and the late Eveline Rose Webster of 113 Westbourne Avenue, Hull. There is a memorial tablet inside Holy Church. Hull where he was a chorister. His brother Second Lieutenant George Alan Webster was killed in action on September 18th 1918 aged 29.

11TH BATTALION

BERRY, SECOND LIEUTENANT HARRY. Originally enlisted on September 7th 1914 and commissioned into the 8th West Yorkshire Regiment. Killed in action on November 1st 1918 by a shell which landed near him while he was on his way to hospital to have his wounds treated. Buried in Sailly-sur-La-Lys Canadian Cemetery. He left a wife and children living at 13, Shakespear Street. Hull.

BOCKING, SECOND LIEUTENANT BERNARD, MC. Commissioned into the 12th Yorkshire regiment but attached to the 12th East Yorks at the time of his death in action on August 21st 1918, aged 20. Buried in Outtersteene Communal Cemetery Extension, Bailleul. Son of Reverend J C Bocking of Gnossall Vicarage, Stafford. Before the war he was a student. Educated at Newport Grammar School, Salop. Joined the 28th Royal Fusiliers in Edinburgh on May 23rd 1916. Transferred to 18 OCB and was commissioned on September 28th 1917 into the 12th Yorkshire Regiment.

COATES, SECOND LIEUTENANT. Commissioned into the East Riding Yeomanry. Killed in action on August 15th 1918 aged 29. Son of Thomas and Anne Coates of Harrogate. Husband of Margery Coates of West Field, Fimber, Malton. Yorkshire.

CLIFT, SECOND LIEUTENANT MARCUS HENRY. Killed in action on November 8th 1917 during a trench raid, aged 30. Commemorated on the Arras Memorial. Son of Henry C. Clift and M.S. Clift of 24, Redlington Road, Hampstead, London. He was one of three brothers who served in the war, two of whom were killed.

COWLEY, LIEUTENANT FRANK WHEATLEY, MC & BAR. Enlisted and discharged to a commission. Died of wounds, aged 21, while attached to 92 TMB. Buried in Longuenesse Cemetery, St. Omer. Eldest son of Mr. and Mrs. A.H. Cowley of 55 St. John's Avenue, Bridlington. He was educated at Hymers College, Hull.

DAVIE, SECOND LIEUTENANT FRANK, MM. Commissioned into the 4th battalion but transferred to the 11th Battalion. Died of wounds on June 2nd 1917, aged 27. Buried in Western Cemetery, Hull. Son of John and Louisa Davie of 62, Sunnybank, Hull.

EKINS, SECOND LIEUTENANT WILLINGHAM RICHARD. Commissioned into the 3rd battalion but serving with the 11th at the time of his death in action on May 3rd 1917 aged 20. He is commemorated on the Arras Memorial. Son of the Reverend George Richard Ekins and Beatrice Emma Ekins of St. Timothy's Vicarage, Crookes, Sheffield.

GOUGH, LIEUTENANT CYRIL. Commissioned into the 4th battalion but transferred to the 11th. He was wounded in the chest on September 8th 1918 during fighting around Soyers Farm, near Steernwercke and taken prisoner, dying as a prisoner of war on October 11th, aged 45.

HALL, LIEUTENANT ALLAN BERNARD. Commissioned into the Army Cyclists Corps but attached to the 11th Battalion. Killed in action during the attack on Oppy Wood, May 3rd 1917, aged 23. Commemorated on the Arras Memorial. Son of Allan T. Hall, J.R, and Cordelia B. Hall of Kirk Ella.

HARRISON, SECOND LIEUTENANT JOHN, VC, MC. Killed in action on May 3rd 1917. Born on 12/11/90 in Hull, he attended Craven Street School, Hull Secondary School and St. John's College, York where he trained to be a teacher. Before the war he was an Assistant School master in Estcourt and Lime Street Schools. He was also a rugby league player for Hull. In 1915 he scored a record total of 52 tries - unbroken to this day. His four year league career resulted in 116 appearances for Hull and 106 tries. His father was a master plater. He was married and had a son called Jack. Lime Street School unveiled a plaque in his honour in 1921. His wife resided at 75 Wharncliffe Street, Spring Bank West, Hull. He enlisted in the Inns of Court, OTC on November 4th 1915 with the service number 7203. On August 4th he gained his commission and the next day was gazetted to the East Yorkshire Regiment, joining the 14th (Hull) Reserve Battalion. Considerable efforts were made to trace him and one report by a Private Blake who was in the Oppy attack stated, "He was our platoon officer. I saw him hit by a shell at Ypres on May 3rd out in the open. He was killed outright. I saw him brought in but don't know where they buried him. He had not been with us long. He had a thin face and a dark moustache". He has no known grave and is commemorated on the Arras Memorial.

HIGNETT, SECOND LIEUTENANT WILLIAM ROWLAND. Killed in action on May 3rd 1917 aged 37. Son of William Rowland Hignett of Nottingham. Husband of Millicent Florence Hignett of "Hazelmere", Barrow-on-Soar, Loughborough, Leicestershire. Commemorated on the Arras Memorial.

HOPKINS, SECOND LIEUTENANT WILLIAM JONES. Died of wounds on October 8th 1916 aged 26. Buried in St. Venant Communal Cemetery. Son of Daniel N. and Catherine Hopkins of Bryffynone, Criag-Cefn-Parc, Clydach-on-Tawe, Glamorganshire.

HUTCHINSON, SECOND LIEUTENANT BENJAMIN, M.C. Killed in action on May 3rd 1917. Commemorated on the Arras Memorial. Son of Frank and Betsey Hutchinson of 72 Cannon Hall Road. Sheffield.

JAMES, SECOND LIEUTENANT RUPERT FREDERICK. Wounded during the battle of Arras on April 9th 1917. Killed in action on March 27th 1918 aged 35. Buried in Douchuy Les Ayette Cemetery. Son of Frederick John Augustine James of Seaview, Isle of Wight.

McINTYRE, SECOND LIEUTENANT ROBERT WILLIAM, MBE. Killed in action on July 25th 1918, aged 22, by enemy machine gun fire during an attack on Tool and Infantry trenches during the third battle of the Scarpe. Buried in Le Grand Hasard Military Cemetery. Marbeque. Born in Hollywood, County Down, he was educated at the Royal Academical Institution in Belfast. Before the war he was a Linen Merchant apprentice. He attested in Belfast on September 17th 1914 into the 20th Royal Fusiliers and served overseas from November 1915 until July 1916 when he suffered gun shot wounds to the face, back and right arm, at the same time he fractured his right shoulder blade. He joined 8 OCB and was commissioned on March 27th 1917. Son of Mrs Jeanie Isabel McIntyre and the late John McIntyre of 2 Whittinghome Villas, 7 Knock Road. Knock, Belfast.

McREYNOLDS, HONORARY LIEUTENANT AND QUARTERMASTER. Joined the East Yorkshire Regiment on June 13th 1887, at the age of 18, and joined the 2nd battalion on December 12th 1888, serving until November 5th 1907. During his time in the army he became Sergeant in charge of gymnastics and physical training. He left the colours in 1894, joining the Army Reserve. After a brief period in civilian life he returned to the 2nd battalion and became a Colour Sergeant. During this second period of service with the 2nd battalion he spent some time in South Africa fighting the Boers but was invalided home in 1901 to serve on the permanent staff of the 3rd Battalion. He served briefly as the Sergeant-Major of the 2nd Volunteer battalion and upon its disbanding in 1908 he became Sergeant Major of the 5th (Territorial) battalion of the Yorkshire Regiment at its headquarters in Scarborough. On April 1st 1912 he was discharged to pension but remained on the active list for a further three possible years during which time he played professional football for Sheffield Wednesday, Paisley Abercorn and Greenock Morton, playing with the latter until the semi-final of the Scottish Cup. He was also gymnastic and athletic tutor to Greenock Academy and twice gave evidence before a Royal Commission on Physical Training. While playing football he also was the Landlord of the "Durham Hotel", on North Marine Drive. On the outbreak of war he joined the 11th battalion as Regimental Sergeant-Major becoming Quartermaster in October 1915 and was subsequently promoted Lieutenant and Quartermaster. He was killed in action by a stray shell, on November 12th 1916, aged 45, whilst taking supplies to his Battalion. Buried in Couin Cemetery. He was survived by his wife, Ella, and five children who lived on North Marine Road, Scarborough. Lieutenant McReynolds was well known as an all round athlete and was very popular with all ranks.

MITCHELL, SECOND LIEUTENANT HENRY. Died of wounds on April 3rd 1918, aged 23 at Number 8 General Hospital. Son of John Mitchell. Buried in Boulogne Eastern Cemetery. Attested, at Guildford, to the 11th Hampshire Regiment on September 4th 1914. Born in Johannesburg, South Africa. Before the war he was a labourer. He served in France from December 1915 to December 1916. Wounded July 1916. Commissioned from 6 OCB on September 25th 1917. Address before the war was Mareside, Dunmow Hill, Fleet, Hampshire.

MUIR, SECOND LIEUTENANT HARRY. Killed on April 18th 1916 aged 32. Buried in Sucrerie Military Cemetery, Colincamps. Son of Charles William and Sarah Muir of Hull. Resident at 30 Thornleigh Road, Jesmond. Served for five years in the 1st Newcastle RE Volunteers from 1900 to 1905. Enlisted in the 9th Northumberland Fusiliers in September 1914. After attaining the rank of Sergeant was promoted to commissioned rank. (See chapter 3 for further details of his death)

OAKE, CAPTAIN DOUGLAS, MC. Commissioned as a Regular Army Officer on October 19th 1914 he had previously trained with the Public School Special Corps OTC at Epsom. His address was Ferndale, Lewisham High Street, Catford. Attached to 92 Trench Mortar Battery. Returned to the UK for six months rest in March 1918 and became an APM at Southend-on-Sea and later became an instructor to the American Army. Except for a period of six months from July to December 1916, which he spent in England recovering from wounds received in June 1916, he had been with the battalion throughout. He was accidentally killed at a Trench Mortar demonstration by the premature detonation of a Stokes bomb on

August 8th 1918 aged 26. He had previously been wounded on June 28th 1918. Since 1916 he had been a member of the battalion and later the brigade Concert Party, "The Tonics". His next of kin was his uncle, C V Bisley, Redriff, Avondale Road, Hove, Sussex.

OLIVER, SECOND LIEUTENANT ARTHUR HAROLD. Killed in action on November 8th 1917 during a raid on the enemy trenches. Buried in Roclincourt Military Cemetery. He was born in Hull and attended The Boulevard Secondary School. Enlisted in 'C' Company of the 7th Hull Battalion on September 7th 1914. Before the war he was a clerk. He served in Egypt and France before being commissioned on June 26th 1917. His next of kin, his sister, lived at 21 Desmond Avenue, Newland, Hull.

PHILIP, CAPTAIN KENNETH. Attached to the 11th battalion from the 1st/4th. He was killed in action on March 27th 1918 aged 30. Commemorated on the Pozieres Memorial. He was the fourth son of R.H. Philip of 7, Bank Terrace, Hornsea.

PURLL, SECOND LIEUTENANT WILLIAM ALBERT GEORGE. Killed in action on May 3rd 1917 at Oppy Wood, aged 24. Commemorated on the Arras Memorial. Son of Henry Charles and Janet Purll (stepmother) of 52, Belleville Road, Wandsworth Common, London.

REEVE, CAPTAIN ERNEST WILLIAM, MC. Killed in action on May 3rd 1917, aged 39. Commemorated on the Arras Memorial. Brother of Charles T. Reeve of 18, Eton Road, West Worthing, Sussex.

RICHARDSON, SECOND LIEUTENANT FRANK ARNOLD. Died in an accident on April 25th 1918 while attached to the 11th Battalion. While attached to the 3rd battalion in Withernsea in April 1918 2/Lt Richardson appeared to have vanished but had received orders to move to Perham Down Camp, Andover. He was killed in an aircraft accident a few days after his arrival at the camp. 2/Lt Richardson had joined the army in June 1910 as a drummer and in August 1914 was a corporal. He was posted to France in June 1915. In November he was wounded with a gun shot wound to the abdomen. He went to 4 OCB in March 1917 and was commissioned into the 1st battalion of the East Yorkshire Regiment. In October 1916 he was married to Sarah Louise Richardson, at St. Mark's Church, Hull. They had one son and the family resided at White Cottage, Sutton-on-Hull. He was wounded again in September 1917 and he was sent home to convalesce. Buried in Tidworth Military Cemetery, North Tidworth, Wiltshire.

SAVILLE, CAPTAIN CLIFFORD ALLEN. One of the original officers of the battalion and C/O of number 6 Platoon, Bombing Officer and O/C 'A' Company from May to November 1917. He was responsible for organising every kind of sport within the Battalion. Killed in action during a daylight raid on the enemy's trenches on November 8th 1917. He endeared himself to all who served with him by his gift of apologetic satire when times were bad and his unfailing readiness to help on each and every occasion. He is commemorated on the Arras Memorial. Son of Walter and Emma Saville of 17, Wadham Gardens, Hampstead, London and husband of Melville Saville of 5, Derby Road, Southport.

SISSONS, LIEUTENANT NORMAN LEA. He joined the East Riding Yeomanry the day following the declaration of war. Three months later he was granted a commission and joined the East Yorkshire regiment. Killed in action on September 9th 1916, aged 21. Buried in Le Touret Cemetery, Richebourg L'Avouee. Eldest son of Harold and Ethel Sissons of North Ferriby. Educated at Rugby and spent six months before the war with Sissons Brothers of which firm his father was a director.

SKEVINGTON, SECOND LIEUTENANT WILLIAM PERCY of 'B' Company. At the outbreak of the war he joined the 10th battalion as a Private and saw service in Egypt and in France being wounded three times. In July 1917, after attaining the rank of Sergeant he was recommended for a commission. He joined the OTC at Rhyl, gaining his commission on January 29th 1918 and joining his battalion in April 1918. Killed in action on September 8th 1918, aged 27. He was shot through the head charging, with his men, the enemy trenches near Soyer Farm. His body was found on October 11th by Lieutenant Colonel Ferrand who pronounced that death had been instantaneous. Buried in Trois Arbres Cemetery, Steenwerck. Third son of Charles and Annie Skevington of "The Hawthorns", Brough, East Yorkshire. His brother George Skevington, a pre-war golf professional, had been killed in action in June 1917 while his remaining three brothers, all of whom served in the army, survived the war. His name is commemorated on the Elloughton War Memorial and on a tablet erected inside St. Mary's Church, Elloughton. Prior to enlistment he had been employed at the Hull & Barnsley Railway in Hull.

SOUTHERN, CAPTAIN THOMAS WILLIAM, MC. Originally commissioned into the 4th battalion as Officer Commanding 'B' Company. He was killed in action on September 29th 1918 during a raid on the enemy trenches west of Fresnou Wood. Buried in Ballieul Communal Cemetery extension. Son of Frank Southern of 18, Wright Street, Hull.

STAVELEY, LIEUTENANT HUGH SHEARDOWN. Commissioned from the ranks on November 13th 1914. He lived at 46 Coltman Street, Hull. Commanded 'C' Company temporarily from January to February 1917. Killed in action on May 3rd 1917, aged 29 at around 5am in Oppy village. Commemorated on the Arras Memorial. Son of Colonel John Alfred Staveley of the 5th battalion, East Yorkshire Regiment. Enlisted on September 8th 1914 when he was an articled law student. Educated at Cambridge where he was in the OTC. Originally reported as missing he was later reported killed. Corporal Farnill, a POW in Soltau and Sergeant Mill both reported that he was seen in a shell hole dead, Private Lee reported that he had been shot in the head. Private Nurse reported that he had been shot by a sniper. The final proof of his death for the War Department came from Pte. Robertson who wrote: "After being captured I and a batch of others were escorted through the village of Oppy. I saw Lt. Staveley lying dead in the road. He was examined by some of my party in my presence and found to be dead".

THORPE, SECOND LIEUTENANT ALBERT EDWARD. Died of paralysis on December 6th 1918 aged 26. Son of George and Ellen Thorpe of Wisbech. Husband of Dora Thorpe of 30 Milner Road, Wisbech. Cambridgeshire. Buried in Longuenesse Souvenir Cemetery, St. Omer.

TOMEY, LIEUTENANT DONALD STUART. Killed in action on March 25th 1918 aged 21. Commemorated on the Arras Memorial. Before the war he was a student at Birmingham University where he was a member of the OTC. He lived at Shirley Lodge, Trinity Road, Birchfields, Birmingham.

WATTE, MAJOR CLEMENT WILLIAM, DSO, MID. Died accidentally, aged 27, on January 31st 1919. His body was found in the river near Norwich. Buried in Bridlington Cemetery. He was born in Bridlington, the son of George H. and Belle Waite. Husband of Vera Kingsley (formerly Waite) of "Red Tiles", The Avenue, Potters Bar, Middlesex.

WALLIS, CAPTAIN FRANCIS HERBERT GUY. Company commander from September 1916 to October 1916, during November 1916 and from January 1917 to June 1917. Died of wounds at 95 Field Ambulance on May 17th 1918 aged 28 and was buried at Caestre Military Cemetery. His father, Francis Ashby Wallis, lived at Sherbourne House, Basingstoke. He had originally applied for a commission in the Army Service Corps. Before the war he had served in the OTC. Upon his death his father received his son's effects: a silk tie, a cheque book, a silver cigarette case, a note book, a pencil case, a pocket wallet, a wristlet watch, a whistle & lanyard, a pocket knife, three collar studs, a handkerchief, a small key, an identification disc and various papers and letters.

WATTS, CAPTAIN CYRIL GEORGE. Attached to the 93rd Infantry brigade when he was mortally wounded in action near Messines Ridge on October 1st 1918, aged 27. Buried at Underhill Farm. Son of John Watts of "Devonia", Cardigan Road. Bridlington.

WHITTINGTON-INCE, LIEUTENANT RALPH PIGGOTT. MC & CROIX-de-GUERRE (BELGIUM). Died of wounds on November 11th 1918 in 36 CCS, aged 20. Buried in Vichte Military Cemetery, Belgium. Son of Mrs Whittington-lnce of 74 Princes Street, Bayswater. Born in Milan. His father was a clerk in Holy orders. Educated at Cranleigh School, Surrey. Graduated from the Royal Military College as a Regular Army Officer.

WIGGINTON, SECOND LIEUTENANT ARTHUR. Wounded at the battle of Loos on October 4th 1915. Killed in action on July 30th 1916, aged 25 during heavy fighting west of Serre. Buried in Le Touret Cemetery, Richebourg L'Avouee. Husband of Glenora Wigginton of 27, Guildford Road, Brighton.

WRIGHT, LIEUTENANT HAROLD IVAN. Attached to the 11th battalion from the lst/4th EastYorks. Killed in action on November 8th 1917, aged 30, during a raid on enemy trenches. Commemorated on the Arras Memorial. Son of Henry Wright of Welton Manor. Brough. Husband of the late Charlotte Hester Wright. He is commemorated on the War Memorial inside St. Helen's Church, Welton.

12TH BATTALION

BECKH, SECOND LIEUTENANT ROBERT HAROLD. On the outbreak of the war he enlisted in the University and Public Schools Brigade and was gazetted to the East Yorkshire Regiment in June 1915. Died on the German wire while on patrol near Boar's Head. Richebourg L'Avouee on August 15th 1916, aged 22. Buried in Caberet-Rouge Cemetery. Younger son of Victor and Edith M. Beckh of "Thele", Great Amwell, Hertfordshire. Educated at Haileybury and on leaving in 1913, gained the Evers Exhibition and also an open exhibition at Jesus College which was increased to a scholarship in 1914. He was a member of the OTC at Haileybury for five years, attaining the rank of Colour Sergeant.

CARRALL, SECOND LIEUTENANT JOHN EDWIN. Killed in action on May 3rd 1917 aged 19. Commemorated on the Arras Memorial. Educated at Archbishop Holgates Grammar School. York. He classed himself as a student of science. Enlisted in the 28th Royal Fusiliers in July 1915, transferring to the 18th in November. He went overseas in November and joined the 19th brigade Cyclist Company in January 1916. He returned to the UK and was commissioned in September 1916. He was the youngest son of John William and Isabella Lucy Carrall of 5, Cygnet Street, York. His father was a printer who at the time of his death was serving in the RAMC. His two other brothers served in France.

CARROLL, CAPTAIN WILLIAM, MC. Killed in action on May 3rd 1917 aged 38. He originally enlisted in November 1898 at the age of 19 and a half in the 5th Volunteer Liverpool Regiment. He was a painter by trade. After serving in the South African War for which he received The Queen's South Africa Medal with clasps for Cape Colony, Orange free State and the Transvaal he transferred to the regular army. He achieved his 2nd class certificate of education in 1903 and his 1st class certificate in 1910. Before the war he had served in South Africa, Burma and India. He was a mounted Infantry instructor and was qualified in Musketry and the Maxim Gun. Before the war he had re-enlisted to complete 21 years of service. Prior to being commissioned he had achieved the rank of RSM in the 1st Royal Irish Rifles on December 16th 1915. He went to France in November 1914 and was wounded in the right thigh by a rifle bullet on September 25th 1915. He was mentioned in dispatches on April 4th 1915, on October 2nd was awarded the Russian Medal of St. George, 1st Class and was gazetted the MC on June 23rd 1916. On November 22nd 1916 he was granted a permanent commission in the East Yorkshire Regiment. His brother served in the 2nd Garrison battalion of the Cheshire Regiment. His father was Thomas Carroll of 5 Garibaldi Street, Liverpool. Buried in Albuera Cemetery, Bailleul-Sire-Bertholt.

CATTLEY, CAPTAIN WILLIAM, MC. Killed in action May 3rd 1917. (No papers traced.)

CRABTREE, LIEUTENANT STEPHEN MARK. Killed in action on June 28th/29th 1916, during a raid on enemy trenches near Engelbelmer aged 21. Buried in the AIF Burial Ground. He was single and lived in India at the start of the war. Educated at Hymers College in Hull where he spent two years in the OTC and on enlistment in the 1st Hull Battalion became a platoon sergeant. He became a 2/Lt. in the 3rd Hull Battalion on September 11th 1914. His parents, John and Sarah Crabtree, lived at Woodside, North Ferriby.

DUGUID, SECOND LIEUTENANT ALEXANDER RITCHIE. Killed in action on May 3rd 1917 aged 19. Commissioned into the 4th East Yorkshire Regiment but attached to the 12th Battalion. Son of Robert and Elizabeth C Duguid of Priory Close, Bridlington, Yorkshire. Buried in Orchard Dump Cemetery.

DREWETT, SECOND LIEUTENANT CHARLES. Died of wounds received during an abortive trench raid on June 29th 1916 aged 25. Commemorated on the Thiepval Memorial. Son of Benjamin B and Jane Ann Drewett of "Charnley", Coalville, Leicester.

ELFORD, LIEUTENANT ARTHUR DOUGLAS. Killed in action during the Battle of the Ancre on November 13th 1916 aged 19. Commemorated on the Thiepval Memorial. Son of Mr W.H. Elford of Treven,

South Hill, Callington, Cornwall. Educated at Lipson School, Plymouth. Before the war he was a student at Dublin University where he was a member of the OTC. His brother was a surgeon on HMS Raven II. He took a regular army commission in the 9th battalion of the East Yorkshire Regiment before attending the School of Instruction in Dublin on December 18th 1915. He was wounded on August 6th 1916.

ESTRIDGE, SECOND LIEUTENANT EDWARD WILFRED. Enlisted in the 88th Canadian Fusiliers (British Columbia). Commissioned into the 3rd battalion but attached to the 12th battalion when he was killed in action on November 13th 1916, aged 31. Commemorated on the Thiepval Memorial. Son of Edward and Elizabeth Estridge of "The Square House", Abingdon, Berkshire.

FAKER, SECOND LIEUTENANT FRANK LEONARD. Killed in action on November 13th 1916 aged 24. Commemorated on the Thiepval Memorial. Son of Henry Walter and Alice Faker of 22, Hegworth Road, Clapton, London.

FRIZONI, LIEUTENANT OSCAR LORENZO. Killed in action on November 13th 1916, aged 25. Commemorated on the Thiepval Memorial. Son of Julius Lorenzo and Marianne Hester Frizoni of "The Moorings", Lindisfarne, Tasmania.

HABERSOHN, CAPTAIN LEONARD OSBORN. Killed in action on November 13th 1916, aged 23. Commemorated on the Thiepval Memorial. Youngest son of Catherine Habersohn of 7, Westbourne Crescent, Hyde Park and the late Dr. S.H. Habersohn. Brother of Captain Kenneth Rees Habersohn of the Rifle Brigade who was killed in action in February 1916.

HALL, SECOND LIEUTENANT JOSEPH STANLEY. Killed in action on May 5th 1917. Commemorated on the Arras Memorial. Attended Alderman Newton's School in Leicester. His father Joseph Hall, of 27 Mansell Road, Acton was a hosiery expert. Before the war he was employed as a confidential Clerk (Civil Servant) on the General Staff at the War Office; he resided at 31 Arnold Road. Tottenham. Originally enlisted into the 2nd/28th London Regiment. Commissioned into the Territorial Force he transferred to the 3rd EYR in October 1916. Originally listed as missing he appears to have died while a POW Private Temple of 'B' Company, stated that: "Mr Hall was an officer in my Company 'B' in the attack at Oppy Wood. The Germans surprised us, coming round our flank. I could see Mr. Hall and a party of about 12 men being marched off by the Germans as prisoners. Then we had to retire".

HEATHCOTE, SECOND LIEUTENANT RALPH NOEL. Died on November 17th 1916, aged 30, of wounds received on the 13th. Buried in Couin British Cemetery. Son of Dr. Ralph George and Emily VJ. Heathcote of 143, Barlow Moor Road West, Didsbury, Manchester. Husband of Eve Mary Heathcote, eldest daughter of Mr. R. Reynolds, Principal of St. Bede's School, Hornsea. He was married on December 18th 1915 in St. Nicholas Church, Hornsea.

HOULT, SECOND LIEUTENANT ARTHUR. Died in 44 CCS on November 17th 1916 aged 22 of acute Nephritis and Bronchitis. Buried in Puchevillers British Cemetery. Enlisted as a private, aged 19 and 350 days old, on September 10th 1914 in the 12th KOYLI and by September 1915 was orderly room Sergeant. He was commissioned into the 9th East Yorkshire Regiment on September 15th 1915. He was born in Long Eaton, Derbyshire and lived at 111 Burcot Road, Meeresbrook, Sheffield. Before the war he was a clerk.

JENINGS, SECOND LIEUTENANT HUGH COTTON. Commissioned into the Army Service Corps but attached to the 12th East Yorkshire at the time of his capture. He died, on May 3rd 1917 at the age of 19, while a Prisoner of War. Son of the late Richard and Ann Hannah Jenings of "Southbank", 97, Station Road, Redhill, Surrey.

LIVSEY, LIEUTENANT ERNEST CLAUDE. Killed in action on November 13th 1916. Commemorated on the Thiepval Memorial. Husband of Mrs F Bentley (formerly Livsey) of 1, Richmond Mansions, East Twickenham, Middlesex.

MARRIOTT, CAPTAIN HERBERT NORMAN. In December 1914 he obtained a commission in the East Yorkshire Regiment. He was gazetted to Captain on July 2nd 1916 and commanded a company. In August 1916 he organised and carried out a company raid for which he received congratulations from the Brigade Commander. Killed in action on November 13th 1916 during an advance on Serre, aged 35. Buried in Serre Road Cemetery No. 2, Beaumont-Hamel and Hebuterne. Eldest son of Herbert Mayo and Florence Emily Marriott of St. George's, Hinton Street, St. George, Somerset and Torcross, Devon. He was educated at Park House, Reading, Charterhouse and Brasenose College, Oxford, where he took Second Class Honours. When the war broke out he was engaged in journalism in the Malay States and at once came home to join the army.

MONTCRIEFF, SECOND LIEUTENANT CHARLES GEORGE CONRAD. He enlisted in the RAMC at the start of the war and at the end of 1915 received a commision in the 9th battalion of the East Yorkshire Regiment. On November 13th 1916 he was wounded and on his return to the front was fatally wounded, dying on November 24th, aged 20. Buried in Abbeville Communal Cemetery. Younger son of Annie

Thompson, formerly Montcrieff, of Craven Terrace, Halifax, and the late Reverend James Montcrieff of The Parsonage, Warley, Halifax formerly Minister of Warley Congregational Church, Halifax. He was educated at Silcoates School, Wakefield and was on the staff of the Halifax Borough Treasurer when he enlisted in the RAMC. Second Lieutenant Montcrieff was well known in Driffield, Yorkshire.

MOORE, SECOND LIEUTENANT PERCY. Died of wounds on May 3rd 1917 aged 22. Buried in Aubigny Communal Cemetery extension. Son of Abraham and Amelia Moore of "Rockville", Stepney Road, Scarborough.

MORGAN, SECOND LIEUTENANT RICHARD GODFREY. Killed in action on November 13th 1916 aged 26. Buried in Euston Road Cemetery, Colincamps. Son of Reverend David Richard and Agnes Morgan of 33, Sunny Gardens, Hendon. He was a native of Chalford in Gloucestershire.

OFFICER, SECOND LIEUTENANT ARNOLD VINCENT. Died of wounds after an operation on May 10th 1917, aged 28. Buried in Etaples Military Cemetery. Son of Harry Smith and Mary Officer of Hull and Withernsea. His name appears on the War memorial in Withernsea and in St. Nicholas' Church War Memorial in Withernsea.

TAYLOR, SECOND LIEUTENANT RICHARD NEVILLE. Killed in action on May 26th 1916 aged 24. Buried in Sucrerie Military Cemetery, Colincamps. Before the war he was a teacher. He enlisted in the RAMC in September 1914 and was a sergeant by January 1915. He was commissioned in April 1915. He was resident at 26 Stanfield Road, Winton, Bournemouth.

WALKER, CAPTAIN SYDNEY STRATTON. Killed in action on July 19th 1916, aged 38. Buried in Rue-Du-Bacquerot No. 1 Military Cemetery, Laventie. Son of Thomas and Sophie Walker of 295 Woodstock Road. Oxford. He was a native of Lechlade in Gloucestershire.

13TH BATTALION

BEECHEY, SECOND LIEUTENANT FRANK COLLETT REEVES. Died on November 14th 1916, aged 30, of wounds received on November 13th. Buried in Warlincourt Halte British Cemetery, Saulty. Son of Reverend RWT and Amy Beechey of 197 Wragby Road, Lincoln.

BELL, SECOND LIEUTENANT HAROLD. Killed in action on November 13th 1916, aged 22. Buried in Serre Road Cemetery. Son of William John and Martha Cummins Bell of 11, Egerton Road, Tyne Dock, South Shields. He was a Theological student.

BINNING, SECOND LIEUTENANT ALBERT HUTESON. Pre-war he had served with the Territorials. He was promoted from the ranks in July 1916 and served in 'A' Company until his death in action, while leading his platoon and successfully taking the enemy trench, on November 13th 1916 at the age of 26. Commemorated on the Thiepval Memorial. Son of John Alfred and Sarah Hanning Binning of 2, Bachelor Street, Hull. He was a single man. At the outbreak of the war he was employed by Messrs. A. Brown and Sons, publishers and printers of Hull.

BROOKE, SECOND LIEUTENANT CLARENCE. Killed in action on March 31st 1918, aged 33. Commemorated on the Arras Memorial. Son of Frederick and Ada Brooke of 24 Ruthven View, Harehills, Leeds. Husband of Annie Brooke of Ferndale, Roundhay, Leeds.

BROWN, SECOND LIEUTENANT FREDERICK DAVID. Killed in action on March 8th 1917 aged 33. Born in Hull. Before the war he was a leather merchant. Enlisted on September 2nd 1914 in the 1st Hull battalion and served in Egypt. His father lived at 86 Porter Street, Hull. Commissioned into the 13th battalion in February 1917. Posted as missing, attempts were made to trace him. Pte. Naylor a POW in Soltau Camp, Hanover reported "Lt. Brown was lying close to me when I received my bit of iron. I saw him, and he was killed by a wound in the head. Both I and Pte. Naylor knew Lt. Brown well, he had been promoted from the ranks and was very popular". He is commemorated on the Thiepval Memorial.

BURBIDGE, SECOND LIEUTENANT HOWARD CHURCHILL. Died of a shrapnel wound to the head on September 13th 1916 while in 1st CCS, aged 26. Buried in Chocques Military Cemetery. Born in Brought. Enlisted in the 1st Hull battalion on September 1st 1914. Commissioned on November 10th 1914 into the 4th Hull Battalion. He was a flour miller by trade.

DORMAN, LIEUTENANT ANTHONY GODFREY, MC. Killed in action on November 13th 1916, aged 30. Commemorated on the Thiepval Memorial. Son of John Joseph and Emily Keziah Dorman of Brooklands, Horeham Road. Sussex.

HAMM, SECOND LIEUTENANT WILLIAM GEORGE, MC. Killed in action on May 2nd 1917, aged 20. Buried in Orchard Dump Cemetery, Arleux-en-Gohelle. Son of William and Pauline Hamm of "Crofton", 5, Marine Parade, Hoylake, Cheshire.

HORN, SECOND LIEUTENANT JOHN CYRIL. Killed in action on April 29th 1917, aged 20. Buried in Orchard Dump Cemetery, Arleux-en-Gohelle. Born in Liverpool. Son of John and Helen Horn of "Glencaple", 12, Sunnyside, Princes Park, Liverpool.

HUTCHINSON, SECOND LIEUTENANT TOM MACINTOSH. Commissioned into the 4th battalion but attached to the 13th. Killed in action on November 13th 1916, aged 19. Buried in Queens Cemetery, Puisieux. Son of William Edward and Isabel Hutciason of 2, Havelock Terrace, Sunderland. He was a native of Middlesbrough.

JOHNSTON-STUART, LIEUTENANT CYRIL GEORGE. Killed in action on April 16th 1918, aged 24. Killed during a German attack on the British Lines near St. Eloi. Commemorated on the Tyne Cot Memorial. Son of Mrs. Mary M. Taylor of 87. Leander Road. Thornton Heath, Surrey. He was a native of Aberdeen.

KERR, SECOND LIEUTENANT NORMAN JAMES. Died of wounds December 20th 1916, aged 21. He was wounded on November 18th while attached to the MGC. Found wounded in the head in No Man's Land. Engaged to the daughter of Alderman Hargreaves (ex-Hull Mayor), she was at his bedside when he died. He lived at 6 Sunnybank, Spring Bank, Hull. Buried in Etaples Military Cemetery.

LEWIS, LIEUTENANT NORMAN VICTOR. Killed in action on November 13th 1916 aged 21. Commemorated on the Thiepval Memorial. Son of VE and Edith Lewis of 90 Charing Cross Road, London. His father was a theatrical manager. Educated at Westminster School where he served in the Junior OTC from September 1909 until he left school in July 1912, attaining the rank of Corporal. Originally reported missing, Lance-Corporal Ainsworth, POW in Duisburg Camp, reported: "I am certain of the body (sic) was that of 2nd Lt. N.V. Lewis since I went up to it and took away his revolver".

MACAULEY, SECOND LIEUTENANT GEORGE CECIL GORDON. Killed on May 2nd 1917 aged 22. Son of Margaret Macauley of "Cardros", Oak Villas, Bradford and the late A Macauley. Buried in Orchard Dump Cemetery.

PETERS, SECOND LIEUTENANT ASHLEY. Killed in action on November 13th 1916 aged 19. Commemorated on the Thiepval Memorial. Attended Loretto School before the war, where he was a member of the OTC. Son of James Frank and Annie Gertrude Peters of 5 College Road, Windemere. Commissioned into the Regular Army on a Temporary commission on November 18th 1915. Joined the 9th East Yorkshire Regiment before being attached to the

School of Instruction in Dublin on December 18th 1915. Initially listed as missing but later reported killed by Private Jefferson (POW). This was confirmed by Captain Wooley (POW) who reported that he had been killed near the German Second Line trenches near Serre.

PUDDICOMBE, SECOND LIEUTENANT DONALD RAMSEY. Died of wounds on July 24th 1916, aged 21. Buried in Merville Communal Cemetery. Only son of Robert Westacott and Isabella Reid Puddicumbe of Regent House, Leytonstone, London.

RANSOM, CAPTAIN RICHARD EDWARD CROFT. Died of wounds on July 21st 1916, aged 24. Served in Egypt and in France with the Battalion. Buried in Merville Communal Cemetery. Only son of Edward and Eleanor Ransom of "Maisonette", 8, Harbour Road, Thorpe Hamlet, Norwich. He was the nephew of Colonel Ransom and Miss Ransom of 88. Spring Bank. Hull.

SAWDON, SECOND LIEUTENANT ARTHUR TINDALE. Killed in action on June 28th 1917, aged 32. Buried in Orchard Dump Cemetery, Arleux-en-Gohelle. Son of Robert Sawdon. Husband of the late Ann T Sawdon of Chubb Hill, Whitby.

STORCH, SECOND LIEUTENANT HERBERT, MC. Died of wounds on August 24th 1918 while serving with the 1st Battalion, aged 31. Buried in Serre Road Cemetery No. 1. Born in Hartlepool. Son of John and Annie Sword of 8, Millbank Terrace. Station Town, Wingate, Co. Durham.

WATTS, SECOND LIEUTENANT ROBERT STAPLETON of 'B' Company. Died on November 20th 1916, aged 21 from wounds received on November 13th. Buried in Etaples Military Cemetery. Son of Robert and Kate Watts of "Inchthrone", The Park, Hull. He was a native of Blundell Sands, Liverpool and attended Merchant Taylor's School in Crosby and Mostyn House School. Parkgate. Cheshire.

WOOD, SECOND LIEUTENANT JOHN. Killed in action on 22 November 13th 1916, aged 30. Buried in Queens Cemetery, Puisieux. Son of the late Andrew Samuel Hunter and Mary Grace Wood of 7, Colville Square, Notting Hill, London.

Appendix 14
Officer and Other Ranks Deaths

10th (Service) Battalion (1st Hull)
BATTLES

1916

Albert	July 1st to 13th
Ancre	November 13th to 18th

1917

Operations on the Ancre	February 22nd to March 12th
The Third Battle of the Scarpe	May 3rd to 5th
Capture Of Oppy Wood	June 28th

1918

The First Battle of Bapaume	March 24th to 25th
Arras	March 28th
Lys	April 9th to 29th
Estaires	April 11th
Hazebrouck	April 12th to 15th
Scherpenberg	April 29th
La Becque	June 28th
Capture of Vieux Berquin	August 13th
Ypres	September 28th to October 2nd

OFFICER DEATHS

Year	Total	Rank at death	Total
1914	0	Lieutenant-Colonel	0
1915	0	Major	1
1916	5	Captain	6
1917	12	Lieutenant	8
1918	18	Second-Lieutenant	21
1921	1		
Total	36	*Total*	36

SOLDIER DEATHS

Year	Total	Rank at death	Total
1914	1	Warrant Officers & Colour	
1915	1	Sergeant-Majors	0
1916	86	Sergeants & Lance-Sergeants	26
1917	127	Corporals & Lance-Corporals	61
1918	357	Privates	487
1919	1	*Total*	574
1920	1		
Total	574	15% of deaths were NCOs.	

SOLDIERS DEATHS BY MONTH AND YEAR							
	1914	1915	1916	1917	1918	1919	1920
January		0	0	2	0	0	1
February		0	0	10	1	1	
March		0	2	7	45	0	
April		1	1	0	99	0	
May		0	2	82	4	0	
June		0	35	9	40	0	
July		0	8	4	9	0	
August		0	10	3	30	0	
September	1	0	10	4	110	0	
October	0	0	3	2	13	0	
November	0	0	13	4	6	0	
December	0	0	2	0	0	0	
Total	1	1	86	127	357	1	1

The greatest number of deaths in one day was 69, on May 3rd 1917 during the Third Battle of the Scarpe.

11th (Service) Battalion (2nd Hull)

BATTLES

1916

Albert	July 1st to 13th
Ancre	November 13th to 18th

1917

Operations on the Ancre	February 22nd to March 12th
Arleux	April 18th to 29th
The Third Battle of the Scarpe	May 3rd to 5th
Capture of Oppy Wood	June 28th

1918

The First Battle of Bapaume	March 24th to 25th
Arras	March 28th
Lys	April 9th to 29th
Estaires	April 11th
Hazebrouck	April 12th to 15th
Scherpenberg	April 29th
La Becque	June 28th
Capture of Vieux Becquin	August 13th
Ypres	September 28th to October 2nd
Tieghem	October 31st

OFFICER DEATHS

Year	Total	Rank at death	Total
1914	0	Lieutenant-Colonel	0
1915	0	Major	1
1916	5	Captain	7
1917	13	Lieutenant	10
1918	17	Second-Lieutenant	18
1919	1	*Total*	36
Total	36		

	SOLDIERS DEATHS		
Year	*Total*	*Rank at death*	*Total*
1914	1	Warrant Officers & Colour	
1915	3	Sergeant-Majors	0
1916	85	Sergeants & Lance-Sergeants	26
1917	127	Corporals & Lance-Corporals	64
1918	347	Privates	473
Total	563	*Total*	563

SOLDIER DEATHS BY MONTH AND YEAR					
	1914	1915	1916	1917	1918
January		0	0	2	0
February		0	0	3	6
March		0	3	2	72
April		1	4	0	74
May		0	5	72	18
June		1	11	12	39
July		0	17	8	19
August	0	0	13	3	37
September	0	1	4	2	69
October	0	0	6	1	7
November	1	0	16	20	6
December	0	0	6	2	0
Total	1	5	85	127	347

The greatest number of deaths in one day was 56, on May 3rd 1917 during the Third Battle of the Scarpe.

12th (Service) Battalion (3rd Hull)	
BATTLES	
1916	
Albert	July 1st to 13th
Ancre	November 13th to 18th
1917	
The Third Battle of the Scarpe	May 3rd to 5th
Capture of Oppy Wood	June 28th

	OFFICER DEATHS		
Year	*Total*	*Rank at death*	*Total*
1914	0	Lieutenant-Colonel	0
1915	0	Major	0
1916	16	Captain	5
1917	8	Lieutenant	3
1918	0	Second Lieutenant	16
Total	24	*Total*	24

SOLDIER DEATHS

Year	Total	Rank at death	Total
1914	1	Warrant Officers & Colour	
1915	2	Sergeant-Majors	1
1916	218	Sergeants & L/Sergeants	15
1917	134	Corporals & L/Corporals	36
1918	11	Privates	314
Total	*366*	*Total*	*366*

14% of deaths were NCOs

SOLDIER DEATHS BY MONTH AND YEAR

	1914	1915	1916	1917	1918
January		0	1	1	6
February		2	0	3	1
March		0	0	2	0
April		0	10	1	1
May		0	27	99	0
June		0	6	7	0
July		0	9	10	1
August	0	0	24	1	0
September	0	0	2	3	0
October	0	0	2	1	1
November	1	0	133	6	1
December	0	0	4	0	0
Total	1	2	218	134	11

The greatest number of deaths in one day was 138, on November 13th 1916 during The Battle of the Ancre.

13th (Service) Battalion (4th Hull)

BATTLES

1916

Albert	July 1st to 13th
Ancre	November 13th to 18th

1917

Arleux	April 28th to 29th
The Third Battle of the Scarpe	May 3rd to 5th
Capture of Oppy Wood	June 28th

OFFICER DEATHS

Year	Total	Rank at death	Total
1914	0	Lieutenant-Colonel	0
1915	0	Major	0
1916	13	Captain	1
1917	5	Lieutenant	3
1918	3	Second-Lieutenant	17
Total	21	*Total*	21

SOLDIER DEATHS			
Year	Total	Rank at death	Total
1914	0	Warrant Officers & Colour	
1915	2	Sergeant-Majors	1
1916	190	Sergeants & L/Sergeants	15
1917	95	Corporals & L/Corporals	33
1918	6	Privates	244
Total	293	Total	293

17% of deaths were NCOs.

SOLDIER DEATHS BY MONTH AND YEAR

	1914	1915	1916	1917	1918
January		0	0	7	3
February		1	0	3	1
March		1	0	12	1
April		0	2	8	0
May		0	6	28	1
June		0	2	5	0
July		0	9	13	0
August	0	0	14	5	0
September	0	0	2	2	0
October	0	0	1	1	0
November	0	0	151	11	0
December	0	0	3	0	0
Total	0	2	190	95	6

The greatest number of deaths in one day was 140, on November 13th 1916 during The Battle of the Ancre.

Euston Road Cemetery. Mrs Donnelly kneeling at the grave of her son, Arthur, who was killed in action on November 13th 1916 with the 13th Battalion.

Appendix 15
Relative Fatal Casualty Rates

BATTLE	10TH	11TH	12TH	13TH	TOTAL
The Ancre (13/11/16)	7	12	106	138	263
Oppy Wood (3/5/17)	69	56	81	3	209
Ervillers (24&25/3/18)	24	17	0	0	41
Hamelincourt/Bucquoy Line (27/3/18)	0	34	0	0	34
Ablainzeville/Moyenville Rd. (27/3/18)[1]	8	0	0	0	8
Estaires (12/4/18)	65	55	0	0	120
Hazebrouck (13/4/18)	15	0	0	0	15
Vieux Berquin (13&14&15/8/18)	16	15	0	0	31
La Becque/Le Cornet Perdu (28/6/18)	29	30	0	0	59
Trois Pipes/Nieppe (4/9/18)	10	0	0	0	10
River Lys (7/9/18)	30	43	0	0	73
Ploegsteert Wood (29/9/18)	41	12	0	0	53
TOTAL	306	274	187	141	909

[1] *Mentioned in Haig's Dispatches*

Appendix 16
Hull Pals Court-martialled for Desertion

10th Battalion

10/1408	Pte. Alfred Conman	Deserted on 12/8/18	Medals forfeit

11th Battalion

11/81	Pte. Charles F McCol	Deserted on 28/10/17	Medals forfeit[1]
11/141	Pte. William J Pritchett	Deserted on 20/1/17	Medals forfeit[2]
11/567	Pte. Arthur Welsh	Deserted on 1/10/16	Medals forfeit
11/842	Pte. Richard Read	Deserted on 23/10/18	Medals forfeit
11/1026	Pte. Alfred Barker	Deserted on 3/10/18	Medals forfeit
11/1054	Pte. Alfred Watson MM	Deserted on 5/11/17	Medals forfeit
11/1227	Pte. Robert Wise	Deserted on 6/9/18	Medals forfeit
11/1240	Pte. John E Stephenson	Deserted on 8/5/18	Medals forfeit

11/1285	Pte. Arthur Lister	Deserted on 14/12/18	Medals forfeit
11/1360	Pte. Walter T Wales	Deserted on 21/9/18	Medals forfeit
11/1365	Pte. George Hawkins	Deserted on 10/8/18	Medals forfeit[3]

12th Battalion

12/237	Pte. Joseph C Godson	Deserted	Medals forfeit[4]
12/678	Pte. Francis R Wilson	Deserted on 5/2/19	Medals forfeit
12/729	Pte. Harry Easton	Deserted on 23/10/18	Medals forfeit
12/808	Pte. James E Kemp	Deserted on 10/10/17	Medals forfeit
12/853	Pte. Christopher Turpin	Deserted on 1/10/16	Medals allowed
12/1023	Pte. Charles Ward	Deserted on 10/3/20	Medals forfeit

13th Battalion

13/48	Pte. John Burns	Deserted on 26/4/18	Medals forfeit
13/84	Pte. Alfred Dunn	Deserted on 3/12/18	Medals allowed
13/86	Pte. William Edwards	Deserted on 19/7/17	Medals forfeit
13/819	Pte. Alfred Rushforth	Deserted on 13/11/18	Medals forfeit
13/1359	Pte. Robert S Peak	Deserted on 15/12/16	Medals forfeit
13/1387	Pte. Robert Edward	Deserted on 3/3/20	Medals forfeit
14/154	Pte. Ralph Hess	Deserted on 5/3/17	Medals forfeit
14/162	Pte. Thomas A Hay	Deserted on 29/10/17	Medals forfeit

14th Battalion

14/154	Pte. R Hess	Deserted on 5/3/17	Medals forfeit[5]
14/162	Pte. T A Hay	Deserted on 29/10/17	Medals forfeit[6]

Non-Wound Discharges (reason unknown)

12/237	Pte. Joseph C Godson	Discharged para 392(XII)KR	Medals forfeit[7]
12/653	Pte. Albert Dixon	Discharged para 392(XI)KR	Medals forfeit
13/1159	Pte. Harry Smith	Discharged para 392(X)KR	Medals forfeit

Other 10th & 11th Battalion Soldiers Court-martialled

Pte. S E Bell	11th EYR	Desertion on 22/7/18[8]
Pte. H J Donovan	11th EYR	Quitting his post & Insubordination on 27/6/16[9]
Pte. G Hawkins	10th EYR	Mutiny on 24/3/19[10]
Pte. E Stovin	14th EYR	Desertion on 24/11/16[11]
Pte. E Stovin	10th EYR	Desertion on 12/8/18[12]

1 *Sentenced to death and executed on 28/12/17; PRO WO71/628*

2 *Died of wounds November 4th 1918 while serving with 6th Battalion. The battalion was shelled while repairing roads in the Presau area.*

3 *Sentenced to death but sentence commuted to 10 years Penal servitude; PRO WO213/26*

4 *Sentenced to death but sentence commuted to 10 years Penal servitude; PRO WO213/10; also convicted by Civil Powers and discharged under para 392 (XII) KR.*

5 *Served with 8th EYR.*

6 *Served with 12th and 7th EYR; battalion at time of offence unknown. Demobilised to the reserve at the end of the war.*

7 *See footnote 4.*

8 *Sentenced to death but sentence commuted to 10 years Penal servitude; PRO WO213/24*

9 *Sentenced to death but sentence commuted to 5 years Penal servitude; PRO WO213/10*

10 *Sentenced to 18 years Penal servitude.*

11 *Sentenced to death but sentence commuted to 5 years Penal servitude; PRO WO213/12; battalion at the time of the offence is unknown.*

12 *Sentenced to death but sentence commuted to 15 years Penal servitude; PRO WO213/25.*

Appendix 17
Commanding Officers

10th Battalion

Lieutenant-Colonel Arthur Johnstone Richardson, DSO, MID (LG 20/10/16 & 4/1/17), passed Staff College course, was a retired pre-war officer, born on July 19th 1862 to Charles Richardson of Springfield, County Down and Mary Richardson. His mother was the daughter of William Reeves, Bishop of Down. He married Emily Armitage (daughter of Reverend Armitage of Breckenborough, Cheltenham) and had three sons and one daughter. He was educated at Haileybury College and the Royal Military Academy at Sandhurst from where he was gazetted on September 9th 1882 to the East Yorkshire Regiment.

He had served with the Mounted Infantry, commanding a company, during the Burmese Expedition of 1885 to 1887 for which he was awarded the India General Service Medal with two bars. In 1892 he graduated from the Staff College. He later served with the West African Frontier Force during 1897 and 1898, helping to raise its 1st battalion. With this force he took part in Operations on the Niger receiving the East and West Africa Medal with the clasp NIGER 1897. During the South African War, in which he served from 1900 to 1902, he saw action in the Transvaal and Orange River Colony receiving the Queen's South Africa Medal with two clasps and the King's South Africa medal also with two clasps. He went on to command the 1st battalion of the East Yorkshire Regiment, retiring from the army on August 15th 1911 on completing his command.

Recalled for service at the start of the war, while he was working at Rugby School, he commanded the 10th Battalion during their training but did not go overseas with them. He later went to France where he commanded the 8th battalion of the South Lancashire Regiment until 1917 when he left the army to return to the retired list. His removal from command was a direct consequence of his views on execution for cowardice.

In 1933, at the age of 65, he obtained his Pilot's Licence and in retirement he wrote and privately published a book called Skeletons of World History BC 1010 to 1928. He lived in Uttoxeter, Staffordshire until his death on January 1st 1940.

DSO - London Gazette October 20th 1916 (for bravery during August and September 1916).

Major William H. Carver, DL JP. Born 27th May, 1868. Fourth son of the late Benjamin Carver, JP of Polesfield, Prestwich, Lancashire. Married in 1895 to Florence Rosalie (died 1937), 2nd daughter of the late Edward Philip Maxsted JP of "The Cliff", Hessle, East Lancashire. One son, two daughters. Educated at Uppingham School. Gazetted on February 29th 1908 to the Militia Battalion of the King's Own Yorkshire Light Infantry, later serving in the 3rd Battalion. Raised the 10th Battalion in September 1914. Served in Egypt and the Western Front as a major in the battalion. Commanded the battalion

until replaced by Lieutenant-Colonel Richardson. By July 1918 he had been classified as a non-effective officer retiring from the army in March 1919. In 1926 became an MP for Howdenshire. Honorary Colonel EYR from 1939. President of the Hull Chamber of Commerce 1925 and 1926. He had been in business in Hull since 1890. Member of the E.R.C.C. since 1915. Director of the LNER and Wilson's Brewery Ltd, Manchester. He lived at "The Croft", North Cave, East Yorkshire.

Lieutenant-Colonel Daniel Burges, VC, DSO (1918), MID (LG 22/6/15 & 11/6/18), Croix de Guerre avec Palme and Greek Military Cross (second class), mentioned in French General Orders, was born on July 1st 1873 in London, the only son of D. Travers Burges, Town Clerk of Bristol. He married Katherine Blanche Foretescue in 1905, who died in 1931 (she was the second daughter of the late Captain Edmund Fortescue of the Rifle Brigade). They had no children. His second wife, who he married in 1932, was Mrs Florence Wray Taylor, daughter of the late W.G. Cox of Nutgrove, Rathfranham, Dublin. He was educated at Winchester and the Royal Military College, Camberley and was originally commissioned into the Second battalion of the Gloucestershire Regiment.

He served in South Africa from 1899 to 1902 as Acting Signalling Officer to the Mounted Company of Signallers attached to the Headquarters, moving later to a Staff appointment. He participated in the Relief of Kimberley, Operations in the Orange Free State, actions at Poplar Grove, Dreifontein, Vet river, Zand river, Operations in the Transvaal, Rhenoster Kop, Operations in the Orange River Colony and Operations in the Cape Colony. For service during the South Africa War he received the Queen's South Africa Medal with four clasps and the King's South Africa Medal with two clasps. From 1908 to 1913 he was Adjutant of the Punjab Volunteer Rifles.

At the start of the Great War he returned to Britain to serve with the Second Battalion of the Gloucestershire Regiment and was present at the Second Battle of Ypres where he was wounded and mentioned in dispatches for his services there. He took over command of the 10th Battalion on November 11th 1915, leaving on July 30th 1916 to become Instructor at the Senior Officers' School. In September 1917 he took command of the 7th South Wales Borderers in Salonika. He was awarded the Victoria Cross for leading the battalion in an attack on Jumeaux on September 18th 1918. As a result of this action he lost a leg.

In 1923 he retired from the army to become Resident Governor and Major of the Tower of London until 1933. He moved to Durdham Down, near Bristol and from 1943 to 1945 was the County Director of the Red Cross. He died on October 24th 1946.

VC Citation LG 14/12/18 - On September 18th 1918 at Jumeaux, in the Balkans, valuable reconnaissance of the enemy front line trenches enabled Lt. Colonel Burges to bring his Battalion, without casualties, to the assembly point, but later while some distance from the objective they came under severe machine-gun fire. Although he himself was wounded the Colonel continued to lead his men with skill and courage until he was hit again twice and fell unconscious. He was taken prisoner by the Bulgars, but was abandoned in a dug-out with one of his legs shattered.

Lieutenant-Colonel Walter Bagot Pearson, CMG, CBE, MID (11/12/17 & 20/12/18), Chevalier of the Legion of Honour (5th class) was born on November 19th 1872, the second son of A.G.B. Pearson of Abbots Brow, Kirby Lonsdale, Westmorland. He was educated at Dover College, Liege University, King William's College (Isle of Man) and at the Royal Military College, Sandhurst. On June 18th 1892 he was gazetted as a Second Lieutenant in the Second Battalion of the Lancashire Fusiliers, becoming a Lieutenant in 1893, Captain in 1899, Major in 1910 and Lieutenant-Colonel in 1916. He joined the East Yorkshire Regiment from the 2nd Battalion of the Lancashire Fusiliers.

He served in India from 1892 to 1898 and in 1898 went to Egypt, serving in the Nile Expedition of 1898 and was at the Battle of Khartoum. For service in this campaign he was awarded the Queen's medal and Khedive's Sudan medal with bar. He was present during the Cretan Insurrection of 1898-99. During the South African War he served with his regiment in South Africa from 1899 to 1902 and also on the staff as an Assistant Provost Marshall and Captain of Intelligence. He was present at Operations in the Transvaal, East of Pretoria from July 1899 to November 1900 and was awarded the Queen's South Africa medal with three clasps and the King's South Africa medal with two clasps. From 1907 to 1910 he served in Ireland and in 1910 he returned to India where he served until 1914. During the Delhi Durbar of 1911, to commemorate the Coronation of King George V, he was on the Staff of the 3rd Lahore Division as APM, receiving the Delhi Durbar medal.

After the outbreak of the War he served in Aden and throughout the Gallipoli campaign. In 1916 he went to France, serving with his regiment from 1917 to 1920. He became a staff officer in November 1917 with the rank of Colonel. From 1921 to 1922 he was on Special Duty at GHQ in Ireland and from 1922 to 1926 he was Officer in Charge of Infantry Records at Warwick. In retirement (from 1926) he moved to Kingsdown, near Deal where he spent his time gardening, fishing and shooting. He died on March 29th 1954.

Lieutenant-Colonel Charles Cyril Stapledon, MID (LG 25/5/17), was born on August 26th 1880. He was commissioned into the 2nd Manchester Regiment on August 11th 1900 becoming a Lieutenant on July 1901, a Captain in July 1912 and a Major in September 1915.

From May 1909 to May 1912 he was adjutant of the 2nd. During the South African War he served with the Mounted Infantry (1901 and 1902) and was involved in Operations in the

Transvaal and Cape Colony. He received the Queen's South Africa Medal with five clasps.

Prior to joining the 10th battalion he commanded the 16th battalion of the Lancashire Fusiliers from April 1916 to August 1916. He commanded the 10th battalion from August 1916 to February 1918. After relinquishing his command he continued to serve with the East Yorkshire Regiment until July 1919. He continued to serve in the army after the war becoming a substantive Lieutenant-Colonel in February 1915. He retired in 1927.

Lieutenant-Colonel Thomas Alexander Headlam, MID (23/5/18), was born on April 5th 1875. He was gazetted on May 15th 1897 into the East Yorkshire Regiment as a Second-Lieutenant, becoming a Lieutenant in February 1889, a Captain in June 1903 and a Major in October 1914. From July 1899 to July 1903 he was adjutant of the 2nd battalion. During service in India he was a General Staff Officer 3 Instructor at the School of Musketry.

Before commanding the 10th battalion he served in Mesopotamia from June 5th 1916 to November 30th 1916. On February 22nd 1918 he became acting Lieutenant-Colonel and on the 23rd temporary Lieutenant-Colonel of the battalion. He became Commanding Officer of the 4th Reserve Battalion of the Welsh Regiment after serving with the 10th East Yorkshires. At the end of the war he returned to his substantive rank of Major becoming a substantive Lieutenant-Colonel in November 1919.

Lieutenant-Colonel Edward Harrison Rigg, DSO and two bars, MID (LG 15/6/16 & 24/5/18), Medal of La Solidaridad, was born on December 8th 1880, son of Reverend W.H. Rigg. He married Clara Benita Douglas, daughter of Reverend J.H. Douglas. On December 6th 1899 he was gazetted to the Yorkshire Light Infantry. In January 1901 he became a Lieutenant and in June 1906 a Captain.

He was an Acting Major in the 6th battalion of the King's Own Light Infantry on October 29th 1914 and a substantive Major from September 1915. From May 22nd 1917 to March 18th 1918 he commanded a battalion of the Royal Inniskilling Fusiliers and from March 19th 1918 to May 18th 1918 was in command of the 5th (Territorial) battalion of the West Yorkshire Regiment. After commanding the 10th battalion he transferred, on November 23rd 1918 to the 3rd battalion of the Lancashire Fusiliers. He returned to his substantive rank of Major in the Yorkshire Light Infantry after the war. In 1920 he became an instructor in English at a French Military School.

DSO - London Gazette June 3rd 1916, June 3rd 1918 and February 1st 1919.

Lieutenant-Colonel Reginald C Hewson, MC, MID (LG 27/12/18), Croix-de-Guerre, was born on April 24th 1895. He started the war as a Temporary Second Lieutenant in the battalion and in November 1918 became its last commanding officer. He was one of four officers still serving in the battalion who had served with the battalion prior to embarkation for Egypt. He was wounded in April 1916 by a bullet in the left arm.

On January 1st 1917 he transferred to the MGC joining 48 Company with whom he was serving when in June of the same year he was again wounded by a rifle bullet. On recovery he rejoined the 10th battalion. He was demobilised on June 18th 1919 when he returned to County Kerry, Ireland to continue his civilian occupation of Engineer.

11th Battalion

Lieutenant-Colonel John L. Stanley, VD, commanded the battalion while it was being recruited. When the 13th was being formed he commanded that battalion. Before the war he had served with the 2nd Volunteer Battalion and had been made an Honorary Major on May 4th 1901. On April 1st 1908 he became a Lieutenant-Colonel.

Lieutenant-Colonel Beauchamp St. Clair - Ford, MID, was born on April 7th 1867 and gazetted on September 14th 1887. He became a Major on September 17th 1904 and retired on April 26th 1911. He was in the reserve of officers at the start of the war. During 1901 and 1902 he had served in the South African War and was involved in action during the Operations in the Cape Colony. For his services during the South African War he received the Queen's South African Medal with three clasps. He was recalled at the start of the war and commanded the 11th Battalion until July 3rd 1916 when he returned to Britain to become a Major in the 3rd battalion. Before the end of the war he had returned to the retired list.

Lieutenant-Colonel Harold Robinson Pease was in the Special Reserve and an Honorary Major before the war. He had served in South Africa during 1902 and had been involved in Operations in the Orange River Colony and in the Cape Colony, receiving the Queen's South Africa medal with three clasps. He retired from the army on February 2nd 1917 as an Honorary Colonel in the Special Reserve. His eldest son was killed in action on October 20th 1914 serving with the 1st battalion of the East Yorkshire Regiment. Colonel and Mrs. Pease lived at Westwood House in Beverley.

Lieutenant-Colonel John Brereton Owst Trimble, DSO, MC, MID (LG 12/3/17 & 18/12/17), was a pre-war regular officer. He was born on August 28th 1881 and was originally commissioned on to the Unnattached List on January 8th 1901. He was immediately attached to the East Yorkshire Regiment serving in South Africa, where he saw active service in 1901 and 1902 being involved in operations in the Orange River Colony and received the Queen's South Africa Medal with four clasps. From April 24th 1909 to April 23rd 1914 he was adjutant to the Indian volunteers.

At the start of the war he was a Captain in the 2nd Battalion. In January 1916 he was promoted to Major and from June to August 1916 he served as Second-in-command of a Service Battalion of the Yorks & Lancaster Regiment. On the 17th of August he became Commanding Officer of the 11th East Yorks. In January 1917 he commanded the 9th Battalion of the Norfolk Regiment, moving in Febuary to command the 9th Battalion of the Suffolk Regiment. From May to November of the same year he commanded the 5th (Territorial) Battalion of the Leicestershire Regiment. He returned to the 1st battalion of the East Yorkshire Regiment in November of 1917 but in May of 1918 transferred as a Temporary Lt. Colonel in the Machine Gun Corps. He was wounded during the war. At the end of the war he reverted to his substantive rank of Major. He stayed in the army after the war and was awarded an O.B.E. For his war service he qualified for the 1914-15 Star, the British War Medal and the Victory medal.

DSO - London Gazette January 1st 1918.

Major John Shaw, MC, OBE, MID (2), Croix de Guerre, was born on December 18th 1869 and originally served in the ranks for 12 years and 155 days before becoming a Warrant Officer in which capacity he served for 9 years and 257 days. He was commissioned into the East Lancashire regiment in September 1910. After briefly commanding the 11th Battalion he went on to command the 11th Battalion of the York and Lancaster Regiment.

Lieutenant-Colonel F. Hardman, MC, was a pre-war Territorial officer in the 10th Battalion of the Manchester Regiment based in Oldham. He was commissioned as a Second Lieutenant in August 1910 becoming a Lieutenant in June 1912, Captain in August 1915, Major in February 1921 and Lieutenant-Colonel in January 1928. He was awarded the Territorial Decoration (TD) in 1926. During the war, after initial service during 1914 and 1915 with the 1st/10th in Gallipoli and Egypt, he returned to England to serve with the 3rd/10th Battalion (a training battalion). In 1916 he commanded the 11th Battalion before returning to the 1st/10th Manchesters.

Lieutenant-Colonel Stafford Hubert Ferrand, DSO, MC, MID (LG 1/1/16, 21/12/17), Officer of the Belgian Order of Leopold (4th class) with War Cross, French Croix de Guerre, was born on March 1st 1898 and was gazetted on September 19th 1908 into the King's Royal Rifle Corps. In August 1911 he became a Lieutenant and in April 1915 a Captain. He commanded the battalion from January 2nd 1917 (acting Lieutenant-Colonel) to the end of the war (temporary Lieutenant-Colonel) except for a short period (12/4/18 to 24/8/18) when he commanded the 49th Training Reserve Battalion in England. In June 1919 he became a brevet Major.

DSO - London Gazette June 3rd 1919.

Lieutenant-Colonel Clement Henderson Gurney, DSO and bar, MID (LG 4/1/17, 23/5/18 & 20/12/18) was born on September 14th 1881 and was a married man with one daughter. He was a solicitor in civilian life. He had served in the Artist's Rifles for five years and had served in the South African War with the King's Liverpool Regiment being commissioned as a Second Lieutenant in the 4th battalion on January 2nd 1902. He resigned his commission in June 1904 due to pressure of work.

He was originally commissioned as a Lieutenant in the 10th Norfolk Regiment, transferring as a Captain in the 13th

York and Lancaster on April 30th 1915. In June 1915 he suffered an attack of traumatic Synovitis of the left knee. On July 2nd 1916 he was moved to the 12th Battalion as a Major, transferring to the 12th East Yorkshires as a Temporary Lieutenant-Colonel in February 1917. In May 1917 he was invalided home to recover from Trench Fever and general malaise. When the 12th was disbanded he became Commanding Officer of the 11th battalion. During the war he became an Instructor at the Senior Officers School in Aldershot.

DSO - London Gazette January 1st 1917 and July 26th 1918.

Lieutenant-Colonel David Dick Anderson, MC, was born in March 1889. Before the war he was an unmarried schoolteacher in Scotland. He was commissioned in August 1914 and first served in France in February 1915. On 16th July 1915 a spent rifle bullet entered his right thigh where it remained. A year later he was wounded again, this time by shrapnel, which once again was left in place. He commanded the battalion only briefly while Lt. Colonel Gurney was absent. At the end of the war, as a substantive Major, he volunteered for the Army of Occupation until he was invalided out of the army with sciatica in July 1919. He was not demobbed until October 1919 when he was 30 and a half years old.

12th Battalion

Lieutenant-Colonel Harold Robinson Pease (see 11th Battalion)

Lieutenant-Colonel C.G. Wellesley, OBE, MID (4/1/17), was a pre - war officer in the third battalion. He had served in the South African War during 1902 and been involved in Operations in the Cape Colony for which he received the Queen's South Africa Medal with two clasps. During the war he became a member of the East Riding Territorial Force Association.

Lieutenant-Colonel C.H. Gurney, DSO and bar, MID(2)
See 11th Battalion notes.

13th Battalion

Lieutenant-Colonel J.L. Stanley, VD, originally served with the 5th (Cyclist) Battalion of the East Yorkshire Regiment (T.F.). He joined the Militia as a Second-Lieutenant in May 1891 becoming a Captain in the 2nd VF of the East Yorkshire Regiment which became the 5th Battalion in 1908. He was qualified as an Instructor of Musketry. In April 1908 he became a Temporary Lieutenant-Colonel. After raising the Battalion he was replaced by Lieutenant-Colonel Dewing and retired from the army at the end of 1915. By October 1917 he had become a Class HH draft conducting officer.

Lieutenant-Colonel Robert Henry Dewing was born on August 6th 1863. He served with the 76th Punjabi Regiment of the Indian Army before the war although he had originally been gazetted to the 1st West India Regiment as a Lieutenant

on August 23rd 1884. He had served in the Burmese Expedition of 1887 to 1889 for which he received the India General Service medal with two clasps. He became a Captain in August 1895 and a Major in August 1902. From November 1895 to January 1896 he was adjutant to the Indian Volunteers. In October 1908 he became a substantive Lieutenant Colonel and retired four years later.

Lieutenant-Colonel Arnold Kenneth Malcolm Cecil Wordsworth Savory, DSO and bar, MID (LG 4/1/17) was born on June 24th 1882, son of the Reverend A. Wordsworth Savory, M.A. He married B K N (Kathleen) Molineux in 1912 and had three sons and one daughter. Educated at Wellington College he was commissioned into the 3rd Battalion of the Lincolnshire Regiment in 1903 from the Militia in which he served for 1 year and 290 days. He became a Lieutenant in 1905 and was battalion Adjutant between 1907 and 1910, resigning his commission in 1911 to become a tea and rubber planter in Ceylon.

In November 1914 he was granted a temporary Captaincy in the 13th Battalion, rapidly becoming a temporary Major and second-in-command by January 1915. In March 1917 he became a Temporary Lieutenant-Colonel in charge of the battalion, transferring later to a battalion of the East Lancashire regiment. After the war he went to live in West Vancouver, British Columbia. He was still alive in 1962.

DSO - London Gazette January 1st 1917.

Lieutenant-Colonel Clifford Charles Horace Twiss, DSO, MID (18/12/17) was born on January 22nd 1879 and worked in the Indian Educational Service before the war. He attended Shrewsbury School where he was Head of School and went on to study Classics at Christ Church College. While at Oxford he served for two years in the Oxford University Volunteers and in India served in the United Provinces Light Horse. In 1900 he had applied for a commission in the Infantry. At the start of the war he was a widower.

He was appointed as a Captain in the 12th Battalion on November 16th 1914 becoming its adjutant on August 16th 1915. He transferred to the 13th Battalion and was promoted to Major on June 25th 1917 and then Temporary Lieutenant-Colonel on September 17th 1917. He took over command of the battalion on January 21st 1918. When the Battalion was disbanded he was given command of the 15th West Yorkshire Regiment and was taken prisoner on March 27th 1918. He was left for dead after being knocked over by a bullet through his helmet. On recovering he moved forward to find his men surrendering because they were being fired at from behind as well as from the front flanks. Hoping to avoid detection he hid in a shell hole but unfortunately a section of German troops passing by spotted him and threw a grenade at him. Upon being attacked by two more soldiers wielding rifles and bayonets he surrendered. On repatriation he was given two months leave prior to taking up a new post with Eastern Command in the United Kingdom. He returned to civilian life at the start of 1920.

DSO - London Gazette January 1st 1918.

Appendix 18
31st Division (originally 38th Division)

Divisional and Brigade Commanders
Divisional Commanders

From July 26 1915	Major-General E A Fanshawe
From August 16 1915	Brigadier-General E H Molesworth
From August 24 1915	Major-General R Wanless O'Gowan
From March 21 1918	Major-General R J Bridgford
From May 6 1918	Major-General J Campbell

92 Brigade (originally 113 Brigade)
Brigade Commanders

From December 31 1914	Brigadier-General Sir H G Dixon
From July 2 1915	Brigadier-General A. Parker
From June 10 1916	Brigadier-General O de L Williams

Major-General Edward Arthur Fanshawe CB (1914), KCB (1917) and MID (LG 17/2/15, 22/6/15, 28/1/16, 13/7/16, 25/9/16, 4/1/17, 15/5/17, 11/12/17 and 20/5/18) was born on April 4th 1859, the second son of the Reverend H.L. Fanshawe of Chilworth, Oxfordshire. He married Rose Higgison, daughter of Sir James Higgison, KCB in 1893. They had three sons. He was educated at Winchester.

In 1878 he was commissioned into the Royal Artillery becoming a Captain in 1886, a Major in 1896, a Lieutenant-Colonel in 1903, Colonel in 1908, Major-General in 1915 and a Lieutenant-General in 1919. He served in the Afghan War of 1878 to 1880, receiving the Afghanistan Medal. He was in the Sudan Expedition of 1885 being involved in the following actions: Suakin, reconnaissance towards and advance on Hasheen, action at Hashoen, advance on 22 March in support of Tofrek Zareba, advance on Tamai and the burning of Hasheen village. For his services he was awarded the Egyptian Medal with clasp and the Khedive's Bronze Star.

He began the war as Commander, Royal Artillery of the Wessex (43rd Division) Territorial Division but was soon sent to France as Brigadier General of the 1st Division. In July 1915 he was promoted Major-General and CRA of Haigh's 1st Army and shortly afterwards was given command of the 31st Division, then training in England before moving on to the 11th (Northern) Division on Gallipoli. In July 1916 he was promoted to GOC of V Corps on the Somme, succeeding his younger brother (he had two brothers who were generals). V Corps was involved in the battles of the Ancre (capturing Beaumont Hamel and Beaucourt), Bullecourt and Third Ypres. During the German Spring Offensive he was relieved of his command and sent home for failing to evacuate the Flesquieres salient sufficiently quickly after the German attack. The Official History later exonerated him.

He retired in 1923 and became Colonel Commandant of the Royal Artillery until 1934. At the time of his death on November 13th 1952 he was living in Naas, County Kildare.

Brigadier E.H. Molesworth, CB(1907), MID, was born on May 2nd 1854 and entered the army in 1872 becoming a Captain in 1885, a Major in 1893, Lieutenant-Colonel in 1899 and Colonel in 1908. Serving in the Indian Army he was Assistant Adjutant General to the Lucknow Division in 1902.

He had served in the Afghan War with the Zaimusht Expedition receiving the Afghan Medal. During 1883 to 1884 he served with the Akha Expedition and was mentioned in Dispatches. In 1894 he was a member of the Abor Expedition and between 1900 and 1901 took part in the Mishmi expedition. From 1906 to 1909 he was a Brigade Commander (8th Brigade) in the Lucknow Division, retiring from the army in 1911. During the Great War he was mentioned in the Secretary of State's dispatches. He lived in Lambridge, near Bath at the time of his death on March 17th 1943.

Major-General Wanless Robert O'Gowan CB(1915), CMG (1919), MID (8/2/01, 10/9/01, 19/10/14, 17/2/15, 22/6/15, 4/1/17, 11/12/17 and 20/5/18), Officer of the Order of St. Vladimir (4th class with swords), Croix de Guerre with Palme (France), Commander of the Order de la Couronne (Belgium), was born on September 5th 1864. He entered the army in 1886 and the following year married Alice Phillis Bland (who died in 1940), daughter of F.C. Bland of Derryquin Castle, County Kerry. They had one son and one daughter. In 1896 he was promoted to Captain, Major in 1903, Lieutenant Colonel in 1909 and Colonel in 1913.

During the South African War he was present at the Relief of Ladysmith, including action at Colenso. He was severely wounded in action at Spion Kop. Upon recovery he fought in Operations in the Transvaal and in Cape Colony. In August 1901 he transferred to a staff appointment as a Railway Officer, with the brevet rank of Major. For his service in South Africa he received the Queen's Medal with five clasps. Returning to England he became District Inspector of Musketry, Southern District until 1903 moving on to be Deputy Assistant Adjutant General of the NE District until 1905. In 1914 he was Assistant Quarter Master General and later in the same year AAG moving in October 1914 to be AA & Acting Assistant Quarter Master General of the 6th Division after which he became Temporary Brigadier General Commanding 13 Brigade in the 5th Division from February to August 1915. In 1915 he transferred to become Major-General Commanding the 31st Division until March 1918 when he took over a Reserve Centre. At the end of the Great War he was a Substantive Colonel. On leaving the army in 1920 he moved to Tilford in Surrey. He died on December 15th 1947.

Major-General Robert James Bridgford CB (1918), CMG (1915), DSO, MID (10/9/01, 22/6/15, 15/6/16, 4/1/17, 15/5/17 and 11/12/17), JP, DL was born on March 10th 1869, son of Sir Robert Bridgford, KCB, JP, DL of Upper Newton, Kinnersley, Herefordshire. He married in 1896, Mary Constance Hamilton, daughter of The Venerable Frederic Charles Hamilton; they had one daughter. Educated at Charterhouse, he was in the Militia before being commissioned into the Manchester Regiment on February 21st 1889. In December 1891 he was promoted to Lieutenant and in January 1898 to Captain. After being promoted to Major in February 1904 he was transferred to the King's Shropshire Light Infantry. He was a substantive Lieutenant-Colonel from February 1914 to February 1918 when he become a substantive Colonel.

He served in the South African War from 1899 to 1902 with the Mounted Infantry and was involved in Operations in Natal, including Reitfontein, Lombard's Kop and the Defence of Ladysmith; Operations in Natal including Laing's Nek; Operations in the Transvaal, including action at Belfast and Lyndenburg. From December 1900 to to 1902 he was involved in Operations in the Transvaal, Orange River Colony and Cape Colony. He commanded a battalion of the Johannesburg Mounted Rifles from April 1901. For his service in South Africa he was Mentioned in Dispatches and awarded the DSO. He also received the Queen's South Africa Medal with five clasps and the King's South Africa Medal with two Clasps.

He commanded the 2nd Battalion of the Shropshire Light Infantry until the end of August 1915. From then until May 1916 he commanded the 18th Infantry Brigade moving in July 1916 to command the 141st Infantry Brigade, returning to the 18th Brigade in August 1916. After a year with the 18th he returned to England to become Commanding officer of the 2nd Reserve Infantry Brigade. In April 1918 he took command of the 31st Division for 17 days. He then commanded the 32nd Division for a month before returning to England to become Commander of the 222nd Brigade (Home Forces).

At the end of the Great War he was a Brevet Colonel. He retired in 1922 and became a JP in Herefordshire where he lived until his death in April 1954.

Major-General John Campbell DSO (1900), CB (1918), CMG (1915), MID (LG 24/5/98, 30/9/98, 10/9/01, 22/6/15, 4/1/17, 15/5/17, 11/12/17 and 20/5/18), Belgian Order of the Crown with War Cross (3d Class), Legion of Honour (3rd Class) and Order of St. Stanislas (3rd Class with swords). He was born on March 7th 1871. His father was Captain W H Campbell of the Madras Staff Corps. He attended Haileybury School and entered the army from Sandhurst on January 7th 1892. Two days later he was commissioned as a Second-Lieutenant in the Cameron Highlanders, becoming a Lieutenant in April 1893 and a Captain in May 1898. From February 1898 to April 1901 he was Battalion Adjutant. He gained his Majority in March 1905 and became substantive Lieutenant-Colonel in April 1916. From October 1915 to April 1918 he was a Temporary Brigadier-General becoming a Temporary Major-General in April 1918. At the end of the war he was a substantive Colonel in the Cameron Highlanders.

He served in the Nile Expedition of 1898 as Adjutant of the 1st battalion of the Cameron Highlanders and was present at the battles of Atbara and Khartoum. He was mentioned in dispatches for service in this campaign, became a brevet Major and received the Egyptian Medal with two clasps. Still serving as Adjutant to the 1st battalion of the Cameron Highlanders he fought in the South African War from March 1900 to December 1901. During this time he was involved in Operations in the Orange Free State, including actions at Vet and Zand river; Operations in the Transvaal, including actions near Johannesburg, Pretoria and Diamond Hill; Operations in Orange River Colony, including actions at Wittebergen and Ladybrand. For his services in the South African War he was awarded the DSO, Queen's South Africa Medal with five clasps and was mentioned in dispatches. On returning to England he was made a Staff Captain in Army Headquarters and a Brigade Major of 3 Brigade and 5 Brigade eventually becoming Chief Instructor and Staff Officer at the School of Musketry.

After active service at the start of the war he was employed at the War Office from August to October 1915. In the same month he was appointed Brigade Commander of the 121st Brigade which he commanded until April 1918 when he took over the 33rd Division. In May 1918 he transferred to the 31st Division which he commanded until March 1919. When the division was reduced to cadre in March 1919, he was appointed as Brigade Commander of the 1st Brigade of the Highland Division in the British Army of the Rhine. In October 1919 he returned to England to command the 11th Brigade, 4th Division in Eastern Command. He retired in 1921. At the time of his death on April 5th 1941 he was living in Waldron in Sussex. He was married in 1901 to Amy Leighton.

Brigadier-General Henry Grey Dixon KCB (1902), CB (1896), MID (1880, 11/1/89, 15/11/95, 5/4/98, 17/6/02), was born on August 14th 1850, third son of Colonel John Dixon (Royal Scots) of Astle Manor , Cheshire and Sophie, daughter of T. Tatton of Wythenshawe in Cheshire. His first marriage was to Helen Mary Frost (died in 1893), daughter of L.J. Frost of Copenhagen. His second marriage, in 1900, was to Constance Ethel Mitchell-Innes, daughter of Captain William Mitchell-Innes (13th Hussars) of Ayton Castle and Whitehall, Berwickshire. They had two sons. He was Educated at Bridgeman's and Woolwich.

In 1868 he joined the 25th Regiment of Foot and from 1878 to 1880 served with the Peshawar Field Force in Afghanistan as an orderly officer. During his service in Afghanistan he was with the expedition to the Bazar Valley and also with the Khyber Line Forces. For his work he was mentioned in dispatches and received the Medal for Afghanistan. During his service in the Sudan he was present at the action of Gamaizah in 1888 and Operations on the Nile in 1889; again he was mentioned in dispatches and received the Eygptian Medal, the Khedive's Bronze Star and the Tukish Order of the Medijidie (4th Class). While serving in India he served with the Relief Force in the Chitral in 1895 and the Storming of the Malakand Pass (mentioned in dispatches, CB and India medal with clasp) and the Tirah in 1897, where as ADC9 to the Queen he was mentioned in dispatches and recieved the clasp Tirah 1897-98. From 1896 to 1898 he was commandant at the School of Instruction for Auxilliary Forces at Aldershot and in 1899 commanded the 25th Regimental district. He was ADC to the Queen in 1898.

He served in the South African War during 1901 and 1902. During February and March 1901 he was a Special Service Officer (graded Colonel on the Staff). In April 1901 he became a Brigadier General on the Staff but served as commander of a Mobile Column and later as GOC of Baberton District. For his services in South Africa he was mentioned in Dispatches, awarded the KCB and received the Queen's South Africa Medal with four clasps.

In 1914 he was appointed first commander of the Hull Brigade. Upon relinquishing command of the brigade he was sent to Egypt where he served until October 1916. He was appointed Officer In Charge of all troops in Cyprus in the same month and served there until July 1918 when he returned to the retired list. His hobbies were hunting, shooting and fishing. He died on February 7th 1931.

Brigadier-General Arthur Parker CMG (1915), MID (8/1/01, 29/7/02 and 4/12/14), was born on January 14th 1867, the second son of Lieutenant-Colonel C J B Parker of Stonebridge, Grantham, Lincolnshire. In 1891 he married Eleanor Augusta Hilton, daughter of the Reverend A.D. Hilton, Vicar of Uxbridge Moor. He had one daughter. In 1887 he was commissioned into the 5th Royal Irish Lancers becoming a Captain in 1894, a Major in 1903 and a Lieutenant Colonel in 1913.

He served in the South African War from 1899 to 1902. During this time he was involved in the following: Operations in Natal, including actions at Elandslaagte, Rietsfontein and Lombard's Kop; defence of Ladysmith, including the sortie of December 7 1899 and the action of January 6th 1900; Operations in the Transvaal and Operations in Cape Colony. He was mentioned in dispatches for his services in South Africa and received the Queen's South Africa Medal with five clasps and the King's South Africa Medal with two clasps. At the end of the Great War he was a substantive Colonel. He retired in 1919. At the time of his death on January 28th 1941 he was living in Langley, Buckinghamshire.

Brigadier-General Oliver de Lancey Williams CMG (1917), DSO (1915), MID (17/2/15, 22/6/15, 15/6/16 15/5/17 20/5/18 and 20/12/18) was born on November 5th 1875, the son of Lieutenant-General Sir W G Williams, KCB. He married Mildred Lota Ramsay-Hill, of Oberland, Guernsey, in 1924; she was the daughter of A.H. Baines of Bournemouth and Rosario. Educated at Oxford Military College and the Royal Military College, Sandhurst he was commissioned in to the Second Battalion of the Royal Welsh Fusiliers on October 10th 1894, becoming a Lieutenant in September 1896 a Captain in 1903 and a Major in 1913.

During the South African War, in which he served from 1899 to late 1900, he was involved in the Relief of Ladysmith, including action at Colenso; Operations on Tugela Heights; Operations in the Transvaal, west of Pretroia; Operations in Orange River Colony; Operations in Cape Colony, north of Orange River, including action at Ruidam. For his services he received the Queen's South Africa Medal with five clasps. For his services in the Great War, during which he was wounded, he was awarded the DSO, CMG and was mentioned in dispatches. He was a Brevet Colonel in the Royal Welsh Fusliers at the end of the war. Upon retirement in 1921 he went to live in Guernsey. He died on November 27th 1959.

Appendix 19 and 20
Divisional, Brigade and Battalion Badges and Regimental Service Numbers, Memorials and Standards

Divisional Sign

This Division was composed of Yorkshire and Lancashire men. The badge was two crossed roses with green stalks, on a black circular ground. The left hand one was white, the other red. In the case of Lancastrian Units and the Divisional Artillery the red rose overlapped the white. In the case of Yorkshire Units and other Divisional Troops the white rose overlapped the red.

Brigade Sign

All members of 92 Brigade wore a red over white rectangle on their back, just below their collar.

BATTALION SIGNS
10th Battalion

Due to the lack of uniforms it was necessary to provide the members of the battalion with a cloth armlet, worn on the left arm, to distinguish them from the other three battalions of the Hull Brigade. The colour and design of the armlet is unknown.

While serving in Egypt the battalion wore the brigade sign on the pagri of the Wolseley helmet and when the battalion arrived in France the flash was transferred to the back of the tunic, directly below the collar. The brigade sign was a square divided equally horizontally with white on top of red. A separate battalion flash was worn on both arms. This consisted of a red vertical cloth bar and was worn on both arms throughout the war by all ranks.

11th Battalion

Before the issue of uniform, in November 1914, the 11th battalion wore civilian clothing and an armlet on the left upper arm. This armlet was light blue and had 2nd HULL printed on it. While serving in Egypt the battalion wore the 92nd brigade sign on the pagri of the Wolseley helmet and in France, like the 10th battalion, it wore the brigade sign on its back. As a battalion flash the 11th wore two vertical red cloth bars on both upper arms. The brigade and battalion flash were worn by all ranks.

12th Battalion

While wearing civilian clothing the battalion wore an armlet on the left upper arm; no details of its colour or wording are known. In Egypt the battalion wore the 92nd Brigade sign on the Wolseley helmet and on arrival in France the brigade sign was moved to the centre of the back just below the collar. To indicate that it was the third battalion in the brigade the 12th battalion wore three vertical red cloth bars on both upper arms. Both the brigade and battalion flashes were worn by all ranks.

13th Battalion

Before receiving a uniform members of the battalion wore an armlet on the left upper arm. The armlet was divided horizontally into three equal bands of blue over white over red with 4th Hull Battn. in black on the central band. In Egypt the battalion wore the 92 Brigade flash on the pagri of the Wolseley helmet and in France this flash was worn on the back of the tunic. Also worn in France was a specific battalion flash of IV in red cloth on a khaki square which was worn on both arms. These flashes were worn by all ranks.

Appendix 20
Regimental Service Numbers

The Hull Battalions – Each member of the four battalions carried a service number between 1 and approximately 1500 (this included those who were part of the Depot Company and not the original battalion) and a prefix (which corresponded to the battalion number) to distinguish between the battalions, for example, 13/1019 for soldier number 1019 in the 13th Battalion. Replacements for casualties came from the general East Yorkshire Regiment pool and did not use a battalion.

Memorials

Like all the regiments of the British army in the Great War, the dead of the East Yorkshire Regiment are commemorated in numerous War Memorials and churches in the towns and villages where the soldiers came from. The fallen soldiers of Kingston-upon-Hull are remembered by a Cenotaph in the City and a memorial at Oppy Wood, in France, close to where Second Lieutenant Harris won the Victoria Cross.

On June 16th 1921, Lord Nunburnholme, the Lord Lieutenant of the East Riding, and Major-General Inglefield, Colonel of the Regiment unveiled a series of six stained glass windows representing the struggle between good and evil and a shrine to the dead of the East Yorkshire Regiment which is surrounded by carved oak panels; on the shrine are recorded the names of the fallen. The shrine was dedicated by the Archbishop of York.

Regimental Standards
At the end of the Great War, with the disbanding of the war raised battalions, each battalion's King's Colours were laid-up. These are similar to those of the permanent battalions colours but with no scrolls and a gilt spear-shaped point instead of the crown and Lion. Those of the 6th, 7th, 8th, 12th, 13th Battalions and the 1st Garrison Battalion were laid-up in Beverley Minster, the Garrison church, while those of the 4th, 10th and 11th Battalions were laid-up in The Holy Trinity Church, Kingston-upon-Hull in 1921.

Upon the amalgamation of the West and East Yorkshire Regiments in 1958 the Colours of the 1st Battalion were laid-up in Beverley Minster. Those of the 2nd Battalion had been previously laid-up in the Minster in 1926.

The 5th Battalion, being a cyclist battalion of the Territorial Force had no colours.

Appendix 21
A Brief History of the 31st Division

On August 6th 1914 an increase of 500,000 all ranks to the Regular Army was sanctioned by Parliament, paving the way for the raising of five new armies, comprising the 9th to 42nd divisions. On the 10th December 1914 the formation of the Fifth New Army was authorised, comprising the 37th to 42nd Divisions.

The Hull Pals were to have been part of the 38th Division, that is the second senior division in the Fifth army. However, in April 1915 it was realised that the first three New Armies would need reinforcements so the Fourth New Army was broken up into Reserve Battalions for the Service Battalions already in the field. The Fifth New Army then became the Fourth New Army and the divisions were renumbered 30th to 35th, with the 38th Division becoming the 31st, and at the same time its three infantry brigades, 113, 114 and 115 were also renumbered 92, 93 and 94.

This division was the second of the Pals divisions and each of its battalions had two titles. In 92 Brigade the subtitles of the four battalions were 1st, 2nd, 3rd and 4th Hull, while their official designations were the 10th, 11th, 12th and 13th Battalions of the East Yorkshire Regiment. 93 Brigade consisted of the 1st Leeds (15th West Yorkshires), 1st and 2nd Bradford (16th and 18th West Yorkshire) and 1st County of Durham (18th Durham Light Infantry), while 94 Brigade comprised the Accrington Pals (11th East Lancashires), the Sheffield City Battalion (12th York and Lancaster), and the 1st and 2nd Barnsley Pals (13th and 14th York and Lancaster). The three artillery brigades also came from Yorkshire and had supplementary titles, CLV brigade (West Yorkshire), CLXI (Yorkshire) and CLXIV (Huddersfield), the divisional artillery column came from Hull. The Royal Engineer field companies were designated Leeds, and the Pioneer battalion had the sub-title Miners.

The 18th DLI was the first battalion of Kitchener's New Armies to see active service, albeit in the UK. This battalion was raised and equipped by the Earl of Durham and a committee of County Durham Gentlemen. Lord Durham placed Cockpen Hall at their disposal for their initial training. Minimum height requirement for the battalion was 5 foot 9 inches but even so the battalion was recruited up to full strength during October 1914, the men having come from Durham, South Shields, Sunderland, Hartlepool and Darlington. On November 16th the Commanding Officer was ordered to send two companies to Hartlepool to assist in coast defence duty – sending those who had already fired a course on an open range. On December 15th 1914 the officer in command of the Tyne and Tees defences was warned that on the following day there might be a raid on the East Coast by German Warships. The detachment of the 18th DLI manned its trenches and was in position on the morning of the 16th December when the warships *Derfflinger*, *Von der Tann* and *Blucher* opened fire on Hartlepool. The German ships fired around 1500 shells resulting in 119 killed and 300 wounded, including 6 killed and 10 wounded from the 18th DLI.

During November 1914 the 1st Hull Battalion was moved to huts near the East Yorkshire coast in order to strengthen the Humber Defences. Unfortunately for the men the huts were in an unfinished state, many having no windows or doors; sixty men having to be crowded into every hut instead of the normal thirty. In December the Commanding Officer of the battalion was asked to report on the efficiency of the rifles which had been issued to his men. The rifles were old and his truthful reply was 'Rifles will certainly go off, doubtful which end'.

In most units, until early in 1915, the men of the division were billeted in their own homes with all preliminary training and instruction being carried out anywhere that they could be accommodated. Individuals with any previous military training were rare, while men with experience of active service were even rarer still. The development of the battalions as efficient fighting units was delayed, in the early months, by an almost complete absence of trained instructors and the lack of equipment and modern firearms.

Local training came to an end towards the end of May 1915 and the units of the 31st Division began to assemble at South Camp in Ripon. Brigade training began and in August musketry training was undertaken. In September the division moved from Ripon to Fovant for final preparations on Salisbury Plain prior to leaving for active service.

On November 29th the division was informed that it was to leave for France on December 6th, with advance parties leaving on the 30th for Southampton and Folkestone on the 1st. However on December 2nd the division was warned that it was to go to Egypt, accompanied by the 32nd Division artillery. Owing to an injury received in France, HM the King was unable to inspect the 31st Division before it embarked. The 31st Division artillery proceeded to France in January to join the 32nd Division.

Embarkation began on December 7th at Devonport and on Christmas Eve the Divisional Headquarters reached Port Said and by January 26th 1916 the last unit of the division (CLXXI brigade, RFA) had disembarked in Egypt. The division took over number 3 Section of the Suez Canal Defences and on January 23rd Divisional Headquarters moved from Port Said to Qantara. However, due to the changing situation in the Middle East and in France the division began embarking on March 1st for France and by the 16th disembarkation in Marseille was complete. The 31st Division then concentrated south of the Somme around Hallencourt (SE of Abbeville) in the VIII Corps area.

For the remainder of the war the division served on the Western Front in France and Belgium and was engaged in the following operations:

1916
Battles of the Somme

1 July	Battle of Albert (VIII Corps, Fourth Army)
1 July	Attack on Serre (VIII Corps, Fourth Army)
13–18 November	Battle of the Ancre (XIII Corps, Fifth Army)

1917

22 Feb–12 March	Operations on the Ancre (V Corps, Fifth Army)

Battles of Arras

3 & 4 May	Third Battle of the Scarpe (XIII Corps, First Army)
28 June	Capture of Oppy Wood (XIII Corps, First Army)

1918
First Battles of the Somme

23 March	Battle of St. Quentin (VI Corps, Third Army)
24 & 25 March	Battle of Bapaume (VI Corps, Third Army)
28 March	First Battle of Arras (VI Corps, Third Army)

Battles of the Lys

11 April	Battle of Estaires (XV Corps, First Army)
12–14 April	Battle of Hazebrouck (XV Corps, First Army, until noon) 12/4 then to XV Corps, Second Army
12–14 April	Defence of Nieppe Forest (4th Guards Brigade) (XV Corps)
28 June	La Becque (under XI Corps, First Army)

The advance to Victory

18 August	Capture of Vieux Berquin (XV Corps, Second Army)

The final Advance in Flanders

28 Sept.–2 Oct.	Battle of Ypres (XV Corps, Second Army)
31 October	Tieghem (II Corps, Second Army)

The division was withdrawn into Second Army Reserve on November 3rd and billeted around Halluin (S of Menin). However, on November 5th the division was informed that it was to be transferred to XIX Corps, on the night of the 6th/7th, to take over

443

part of the line near Avelghem (W of the Schelde). On November 9th the Schelde was bridged and crossed. The division then pushed forward and by 11 am on November 11th the Brigade Headquarters had been opened at Renaix, and the leading brigade (92) had reached Everbecq. Divisional Cyclists had pushed on further, reaching the bank of the Dendre and finding them clear of the enemy.

With the cessation of hostilities the division began to move back on the 13th and by the 30th it was stationed around Arcques and Blendecques (S of St. Omer). Demobilisation, chiefly of coalminers, began on December 11th and by the end of the year five officers and 1691 other ranks had left the division for England. The demobilisation process picked up speed during January and by the end of that month 110 officers and 4931 other ranks had left the division. January also saw the start of the demobilisation of the division's un-needed animals. In February 1919 a further 113 officers and 3634 men left and during March the division was reduced to cadre. The cadres of the various units began entraining at Wizernes on May 13th to move to England through the port of Dunkirk. On May 20th 1919 the Division ceased to exist.

Appendix 22
31st Division Deaths (other ranks)

92 Brigade		**4th Guards Brigade**[5]	
10th East Yorkshire	573	4th Grenadier Guards	163
11th East Yorkshire	563	3rd Coldstream Guards (Figures not available)[6]	
12th East Yorkshire[1]*	367	2nd Irish Guards	122
13th East Yorkshire*	293		
		94 Brigade[7]	
93 Brigade		2nd North Lancashire	0
15th West Yorkshire*	582	2nd Royal Munster Fusiliers	0
16th West Yorkshire*	452	2nd Royal Dublin Fusiliers	1
18th West Yorkshire*	376		
18th DLI	525	**94th (Yeomanry) Brigade**[8]	
15th/17th West Yorkshire[2]	345	12th Norfolk	97
		12th Royal Scots Fusiliers	106
94 Brigade		24th Royal Welsh Fusiliers	80
11th East Lancashire[3]	732		
12th Yorks & Lancs*	427	*Total*	**6603**
13th Yorks & Lancs[4]	475		
14th Yorks & Lancs*	324		

1. *Battalions ceased to exist from February 1918 onwards.*
2. *Casualties from February 1918.*
3. *Total includes deaths while in 92 Brigade.*
4. *Total includes deaths while in 93 Brigade.*
5. *Brigade joined the division on February 8th 1918 and left May 20th.*
6. *'Soldiers Died in the Great War' does not differentiate between the battalions.*
7. *Brigade formed May 30th 1918 and ceased to exist by June 22nd 1918.*
8. *Brigade formed June 21st 1918.*

Appendix 23
New Army Division Casualties

Division	Total Casualties	Division	Total Casualties
21st	55581	38th Welsh	28635
9th Scottish	52055	16th Irish	28398
25th	48289	39th	27869
63rd Royal Naval[2]	47953	35th	23915
18th Eastern	46503	23rd	23574
15th Scottish	45542	40th	19179
12th Eastern	41363	13th Western[4]	12656
34th	41183	10th Irish[5]	9363
17th Northern	40258	26th[6]	8022
19th Western	39381	22nd[7]	7728
33rd	37404		
14th Light	37100		
20th Light	35470		

Comparative Rates of New Army Casualties on July 1st 1916

Division	Casualties
24th	35362
30th	35182
32nd	34226
36th Ulster	32186
11th Northern[3]	32165
41st	32158
31st	**30091**
37th	29969

Division	Casualties
34th	6380
36th (Ulster)	5104
21st	4256
32nd	3949
31st	**3599**
18th (Eastern)	3115
30th	3011

1. Casualties include dead and wounded.
2. Division fought on Gallipoli and the Western Front.
3. Division fought on Gallipoli and the Western Front.
4. Division fought on Gallipoli and then Mesopotamia.
5. Division fought on Gallipoli then Salonika and finally Mesopotamia.
6. Division fought on the Western Front before moving to Macedonia.
7. Division fought on the Western Front before moving to Macedonia.

Appendix 24
The Tonics

We're the Tonics gay, and we sing and play,
In a pierrot way every night.
And with song and jest, we all do our best
To cheer up your lives when you're out on rest.
When you've done your time, six days in the line
And you want to be merry and bright,
Come and see the Tonics, yes the good old Tonics
In their pierrot show at night.

This was the opening chorus of the 10th Battalion Concert Party and according to the battalion history was:

'a prelude to an evening's entertainment full of variety, yet having each and every item bearing the hallmark of talent.'

When the battalion went to Hornsea it was often entertained by visiting Concert Parties who would use members of the battalion to assist in the band. At Ripon a number of the battalion formed an ad hoc group and gave concerts in the local assembly rooms to both the public and the soldiers in the camp. During the journey to Egypt, when HMT Minnewaska was in Valetta harbour the group, as yet un-named, gave an impromptu concert.

In the spring of 1916 in Warnimont Wood the group performed for the brigade while it was on rest. But it was not until September 1916 that the "Tonics" were born. The battalion history described the reason for their birth:

'By this time the party had, along with the rest, realised that the war was likely to last some considerable time and had decided to do their bit on more orthodox lines. To this end white pierrot costumes with black poms and skull caps had been obtained, the appearances in service uniform becoming with this innovation a thing of the past'.

On September 23rd a performance by the "Tonics" was watched by the 92 Brigade Commander and his staff. Shortly after this the Concert Party were informed that they had been transferred to 92 Brigade HQ and that they were to be relieved of front-line duties so that they could concentrate on their rehearsals without interruptions. The battalion history recorded that:

'Captain Douglas Oake, 92nd T.M.B., was appointed officer-in-charge, a piano was purchased, and Corporal Bartindale, having been given the post of producer, was despatched on leave to purchase costumes and draperies'.

Being a member of "The Tonics" did not remove the soldier from military duty; each was given duties at Brigade HQ and many became gas guards, guides and runners or sentries in charge of ammunition dumps. According to the battalion history they all did sterling work during the March and April retirements.

On August 8th Captain Oake was accidentally killed by the premature explosion of a mortar shell during a demonstration.

"The Tonics" continued until the end of the war, setting up their theatres wherever they could. Throughout, all the performances were deliberately kept free of risque material. As a result of the talent in the Concert Party it was frequently loaned to nearby RFC squadrons, Casualty Clearing Stations and the Canadian Divisions during the time the Brigade was serving in the Vimy area. At times the party were assisted by the band of the 11th East Lancashires.

The full personnel of "The Tonics" was Captain D Oake (Light Comedian), Corporal W S Bartindale (Comedian and Producer), Lance-Corporal A A Lamb (Light Comedian), Private E E Draper (Baritone), Private A Tinn (Tenor), Private R C Hall (Female Impersonator) and Private Farnill-Clayton (Pianist). Guest artistes included Captain C Oake, Lieutenant T Brandon and Private Betting de Boer.

"The Tonics" in their pierrot outfits.

Sergeants Mess of reserve battalions at Seaton Delaval.

Appendix 25
The Reserve Battalions

14th (Local Reserve) Battalion

This battalion was formed at Whittington Barracks, Lichfield in August 1915 as a local reserve battalion from the depot companies of the 10th, 11th, 12th and 13th Battalions (The Hull Brigade) of the East Yorkshire Regiment. During its thirteen month existence it was commanded by Lt. Colonel J A Cole. Its function was to provide drafts of trained men to the four Hull battalions.

In January 1916 the battalion was moved to Clipstone and in April to Seaton Delaval[1], near Newcastle where it took on an anti-invasion role. On 1st September 1916 the battalion became the 90th Training Reserve Battalion in the 21st Reserve Brigade and ceased to be a battalion of the East Yorkshire Regiment. Upon the disbandment of the Training Reserve the battalion became the 51st Battalion of the KOYLI and eventually served overseas as part of the British Army Of the Rhine - The Hull Pals did get to go to Germany after all!

Only four casualties for the battalion are recorded:

Private Reginald Charles Freeman who was an early volunteer to the 10th battalion who had previously served with the Depot Company; Private Neville Arthur Stephenson an early member of the 14th battalion; Private Robert Wilson, and East Yorkshire Regiment Kitchener volunteer of 1915 and Acting Lance-Corporal Harold Redmore who had originally served with the 10th Battalion in the Depot Company.

15th (Reserve) Battalion

The 15th (Reserve) Battalion was formed in Seaton Delaval in February 1916 by taking two half companies from the 14th Battalion. It was commanded by Lt. Colonel A C de Trafford from its inception to its demise.

Its function was to train and despatch drafts to the 12th and 13th Battalions. Recruits for this battalion came from the 'Local Reserve Depot' at Hull and the Regimental Depot at Beverley. On formation its strength was 20 officers and 840 men. The battalion was absorbed by the 15th Battalion of the York and Lancaster Regiment on September 1st to form the 91st Training Reserve Battalion in the 21st Reserve Brigade. This severed its connection with the East Yorkshire Regiment and the 'Hull Pals'.

Two casualties for the battalion are recorded: Lt. Norman Victor Lewis killed in action on November 13th 1916 in the attack near Serre and Lt. Stephen Tucker Read who died of disease on December 11th 1918 while serving with the King's African Rifles.

Appendix 26
Private C F McColl – Shot at Dawn

Charles Frederick McColl was born in the Sculcoates[1] area of Hull in 1891. By trade he was a shipyard plater, an exempted trade which could have kept him out of the army. He joined the 2nd Hull Pals Battalion, the Tradesmen's Battalion on September 7th receiving the service number 81, later 11/81. As there was no compulsion to join the army at this time he must have joined willingly to do his bit or at least was persuaded by his friends or the propaganda that it was the right thing to do.

Nothing is known about his early life but he does still have relatives living in the Hull area. His nephew was interviewed in *The Hull Daily Mail* about his execution in an article appearing on May 14th 1996. Until contacted by *The Hull Daily Mail* the nephew had no idea of the ignominious end of his uncle.

Records in the PRO[2] show that Private McColl had committed a number of offences prior to that which resulted in his execution. Initially he was like the rest of his battalion. However, on March 25th 1915 at Millington Camp he was given six days CB[3] for irregular conduct on parade - stealing eggs. Four months later on July 18th 1915 at South Camp, Ripon he received 3 days CB for being absent from Tatoo until 10.45pm, a total of 45 minutes. While still at Ripon, on October 9th 1915 he received five days CB for drunk and irregular conduct about 9.30pm.

When the battalion sailed for Egypt Private McColl did not go with them[4]. Instead, he went to Astley Camp. While he was there he was charged with:

'while on Active Service having been warned for draft overseas breaking barracks and absenting himself from reveille 18 o'clock. (12½).' For this he received five days Field Punishment Number 2.[5]

On May 15th Private McColl was in trouble once again. He was charged with:

'when on Active Service

1) when employed on munitions absent from 6am until apprehended by GMP in Hull about 6.20 pm (12 hours 20 minutes)

447

2) defrauding the Railway Company by travelling without a ticket from Newcastle to Hull.'

He was sentenced to 7 days CB and to pay for the ticket.

There is no extant record of what Private McColl did over the next nine months. He could have been on a draft to France like he claimed at his final trail. The next record of his activities is again a criminal record. In February 1917 he was stationed at Withernsea and on the 24th he was sentenced for being absent without leave for 29 days but the sentence was expunged by Higher Authority. He was then transferred to the 3rd Battalion which was stationed at Withernsea. After staying out of trouble for three months he was charged with overstaying his pass from 10.30pm on May 30th to reporting to L/cpl. Ferguson at 6.50am on June 1st. A total of 1 day eight hours and 20 minutes absence. He was docked four days pay and given seven days CB.

Shortly after this Private McColl was sent to France where he joined not the Hull Pals with whom he had trained but the 1st/4th East Yorks, a Territorial Battalion. Not long after settling in he was convicted again, on July 27th 1917 of:

'when on Active Service - deserting his Majesty's Service, in that he, in the field, on July 22nd 1917 absented himself from the 4th Bn East Yorks Regt. and remained absent until apprehended at Etaples on 25/8/17 by the Military Camp Police.'

For this offence he was tried by Field General Court Martial (FGCM) on September 13th 1917 while the battalion was in the field. The finding was Guilty and the sentence - 10 years Penal Servitude which was commuted to two years hard labour. The sentence was confirmed but on October 2nd it was suspended by order of the III Army.

Less than two months later on September 22nd he was charged with:

'when on Active Service - deserting His Majesty's Service, in that he, in the field on 22/9/17 absented himself from his Company in the front line trenches, without permission and remained absent until apprehended by Cpl. Winterburn 4 EYR at the Bn Details Camp, about 3 miles behind the front line, on the same day.'

He was tried, in the field, by a FGCM, on October 11th 1917. This time he was found not guilty of desertion but guilty of absence without leave. The sentence was confirmed on October 11th 1917 and he received 90 days Field Punishment Number 1[6]. But before this punishment was completed Private McColl was absent again.

The final trangression occured on October 28th 1917 when he absented himself from his battalion until he was apprehended on November 1st by the Military Foot Police in Calais. Private McColl entered a plea of 'Not Guilty'.

Private McColl in 1915.

President of the court hearing the case of Private McColl, was Major Graham from the 5th Yorkshire Regiment. The three other members of the court were Captain Pollock of the 4th East Yorkshire Regiment, Lt. Morrison of the 5th DLI and Captain Baker. For its first witness the court called Sergeant Cavinder of the 4th East Yorks. After swearing his oath he stated:

'I am the accused's platoon Sergeant. On 28.10.17 at 9-0 A.M. at Marsoin Farm, near Langemarck, I paraded my platoon & issued rum to them. I gave the accused his rum. I then warned the platoon for rifle inspection at 9-30 A.M.

'At 9-30 A.M. I called the platoon roll & found the accused was absent. At this parade I gave a warning.

'I searched for accused but could not find him but found his equipment & rifle & steel helmet in the bivouac where he had been living. I recognised the accused's marks on his equipment. I did not see accused again until 7.11.17. We moved off to the front line on 30/10/17 & stayed there for 24 hours; the accused was not with us.'

When he was cross-examined by the defendant, Sergeant Cavinder added that: 'there was no mark on the steel helmet I found'.

The defendant added that:

'At Marsoin Farm we were in Bgde support & were living either in bivouacs or old concrete dugouts. There was very little shelling there & what there was did no damage to the camp or its occupants.'

The second witness called was L/Cpl. Dearing of the Military Foot Police. On oath he stated:

'At Calais on 1.11.17 at about 8p.m. I was on duty in Rue Roy ale where I saw accused. He asked me to direct him to the rest camp. I questioned him & he said "I am making my way home to Blighty". I asked for his warrant & he said "I have been drinking and lost it".

I arrested accused & took him to the guard room where he was detained. Accused was properly dressed in overcoat & puttees & with a F.S. Cap & badge. He showed no signs of having been drinking.'

When cross-examined L/Cpl. Dearing repeated that the first question the accused had asked was to be directed to the Rest Camp.

In his defence Private McColl called no witnesses. On oath he stated:

'I was brought out of the guard room before going up to the line & was in a weak condition. This was on about 26.10.17. We marched up to Marsoin Farm. I had complaints brought on by shell fire. I have heart failure & nervousness. I have been with this bn 6 months but only reported sick once.

I always shake from head to foot when we go into the trenches.

I enlisted in September 1914 & went to Egypt in November 1915 & came to France in April 1916. I was buried by a shell at Colincamps in September 1916 with 12th E.Yorks. I was on 2 or 3 raids & then my nerves went, I was invalided home in September 1916 suffering from heart failure & nervousness & was classified A-3 at the finish & sent back to France without any examination.

Since joining this bn I have tried to do my best.

When I went off they dropped shells all round me & this upset me more & more & I wandered away.

At Calais I was in a weak condition & gave myself up to the M.P.

I am not fit now.

I had a knock on the head from a shell in BUS wood.'

Private McColl was then cross-examined by the prosecutor and stated:

'I have been in front line trenches with this bn on about 6 different occasions. I have been here since July. The trenches I was in were at places I can't remember. One place was Bullfinch trench, I was there 8 days. Another was Jackdaw trench.'

The court called for medical evidence but it was not available.

Private McColl was found guilty of desertion. His final statement to the court was a weak attempt at leniency:

'I came from an exempted trade - shipyard plater - to join the army voluntarily in 1914.

I am the only support of my mother who is widow.

I have tried to do my best.'

The sentence of death was confirmed by Field Marshal Douglas Haig on December 21st 1917. He was to be executed on December 28th.

Len Cavinder, Private McColl's platoon sergeant recorded his memoirs in 1982.[7] He recalled that Private McColl was:

'subnormal actually. He was unstable. There was something wrong with him... I realised that you couldn't get him to slope arms correctly, and all that sort of thing. He wasn't simple, but he was slow - but he'd not been slow to live with this woman in St. Omer'.

Private McColl had not been told of his fate when he was taken to Ypres gaol and Sergeant Cavinder and Private Danby had the job of keeping him quiet, to which end they had been given a half bottle of scotch and some tablets. At midnight a number of Staff Officers arrived at his cell and the death sentence was read out. Cavinder recorded that, in response to this, his prisoner behaved like a raving maniac. When he had calmed down the Padre came to talk to him but instead of supporting him told him that he deserved to die. At this point Cavinder felt it necessary to take over and try to calm McColl down again. The padre left threatening to report Cavinder.

Around seven a.m. two Military Policemen came in and put a respirator over his head backwards so that he could not see what was happening and then pinned a piece of paper over his heart. Cavinder shook hands with McColl before they manacled his arms behind him. He was escorted to the execution area and sat on a chair with his hands behind the back of the chair.

The firing squad consisted of ten men[8] from Sergeant Cavinder's platoon, five kneeling and five standing. The party took aim and on the command of 'Fire!', at 7.41am, on December 28th, Private McColl died. Death was instantaneous.

After the firing party had left the RAMC were supposed to bury the body but after they had unmanacled him and put him on a stretcher they left. Cavinder and Danby dropped him into the previously dug grave and attempted to cover him with frozen clods of clay. No padre was present so Cavinder muttered a few words over the grave as they dropped the ice cold clumps on to him.

In the 1914-18 War Medal roll he is recorded as dead; medals forfeit for desertion. His company commander, Captain Slack, wrote home to Private McColl's mother to tell her that he had been killed in action. Whether or not the War Office informed her that he had been shot is not known, although it was standard practice at this point in the war.

1. *Lt J Harrison VC. MC was also born in the Sculcoates area in 1890.*

2. *WO71/628.*

3. *CB - Confined to Barracks.*

4. *There is no entry in the 1914-15 star medal roll for Private McColl.*

5. *Field Punishment Number 2 consisted of full pack-drill with a sergeant standing by shouting right turn, left turn, about turn and so on, but all at the double, generally accompanied by verbal abuse.*

6. *Field Punishment Number 1 consisted of being tied in a cross shape across a wagon wheel for a certain amount of time each day.*

7. *An account of this appears in Gunfire No 1. The journal of the WFA.*

8. *Most of these men were from the Black Hand Gang - the toughest men in the battalion who did not mix with the rest of the Company except in the line. They invariably did the trench raiding.*

Appendix 27
Four Hull Pals Stories

FARMERY, PRIVATE WILFRED WALDEMAR. 12/1258. Killed in action on November 13th 1916 aged 33. Born in Hull. Son of Thomas Colbridge and Sarah Farmery. Husband of Alice Eleanor Farmery of 86 Clifton Terrace, Courtney Street, Hull. Commemorated on the Thiepval Memorial.

Before the war Wilfred worked for the Aire and Calder Navigation Company as First Mate to his father who was the Captain of a cattle ship which worked from Hull to Gibraltar. Wilfred also had his Captain's papers but preferred to work with his father. He married Alice Hardwick at Holy Trinity Church in Hull and they had five children, Muriel (b.1905), Hilda (b.1907), Frank (b.1908), Jessie (b.1911) and Wilfred (b.1913). Upon joining the army on December 22nd 1914 he was billeted at home until the battalion went to South Dalton. He served in Egypt and on the Western Front where he was killed in action at Serre leaving behind a wife and five children who received an army pension. On July 11th 1918 Alice (the mother) died of acute bronchitis aged 32. The five children were placed in the Hull Seamans and General Orphan Asylum on Spring Bank in Hull. Two of the children, Frank and Jessie, are still alive and recall the loss of their father.

BUSBY, PRIVATE WALTER PERCY. 11/1309. Killed in action on June 27th 1917. Commemorated on the Arras Memorial. Born in Hull. Married with three children.

Walter Busby and wife Louise with their three children Hilda, Walter and George, taken in 1915.

BUSBY, LANCE-CORPORAL JOHN of 'D' Company. 12/551 Killed in action on May 3rd 1917 aged 28. Commemorated on the Arras Memorial. Born in Hull. Son of Thomas and Elizabeth Busby of 12 Balfour Crescent, Nornanbell Street, Holderness Road, Hull. Father of four children. John Busby joined the 12th Battalion in the autumn of 1914 while his elder brother Walter joined the Depot Company of the 11th Battalion in early 1915. John was 25 and Walter 29 when they enlisted. Both were family men from East Hull.

John, the youngest of eleven children, was born with a caul over his face and this, in a sea-faring town, was considered to be extremely lucky. Such 'treasures' were always preserved and sailors would pay a lot of money to own one as they were considered a protection from drowning. Unfortunately this protection did not extend to infantrymen. John's mother died while giving birth to him and he was adopted, along with his brother Walter, by a kindly neighbour, who was herself to die (also in childbirth) when he was nine years old. At the time of his enlistment John was a fireman which may account for him being made a lance-corporal. Both brothers were accomplished harmonica players and they had played in a band along with their father and four older brothers, they had won local talent contests together and Walter used to play accompaniments to the silent movies at the Grande Theatre in Hull. No doubt they played their harmonicas for their platoons in the trenches. Both of them served in Egypt and both survived November 13th 1916.

The wedding of John Busby to Annie Holdstock on August 3rd 1907.

Both brothers were killed at Oppy Wood in 1917. John on May 3rd, the first day of the battle, while Walter was killed on the first day of the second battle, June 28th. John left a widow and three young children with a fourth child on the way (born August 1917 and christened Walter Arras). Walter left a widow and three children.

Neither brother's body was recovered after the battle.

HUNTINGTON, SERGEANT THOMAS. 10/717. Died of wounds on June 11th 1916 aged 24. Son of John and Emily Huntington of Ousedene, Goole. Born in Goole, enlisted in Hull but resident in Goole. Buried in St. Sever Cemetery, Rouen.

Thomas Huntington was born in 1892, the second child of John and Emily Huntington of Goole. His grandfather Thomas Huntington had established a successful Linen and Woollen Drapers in 1849 on Boothferry Road in Goole. His father, John extended the scope of the family business to include funerals and also the Goole Carriage Company.

Thomas's father was a well known pillar of the community who had connections with the local cricket and rugby football clubs as both player and President. In 1892 he was selected as a member of the Goole Board of Guardians and in 1906 became a Justice of the Peace.

The family led comfortable lives with Thomas Jnr set to take over the business when his father retired. Coming from the affluent section of society Thomas Junior could easily have been commissioned, like his younger brother was, but instead he enlisted as a private soldier on September 4th 1914 into C Company of the 1st Hull Battalion which he served with until his death. He became a sergeant before the battalion sailed for Egypt and was a senior member of the Company. On the night of June 4th 1916 during a prolonged and very intense barrage he was wounded and taken in the morning to Casualty Clearing and then on to the Base Hospital at Rouen where he died on June 11th.